BARRON'S

AP*

ART HISTORY

3rd EDITION

John B. Nici, M.A.
Adjunct Lecturer in Art History
Queens College
Flushing, New York

Teacher, Advanced Placement Art History (retired)
Lawrence High School
Cedarhurst, New York

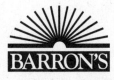

BARRON'S

for Judy, Laura, and Andrew
and all my art history students—past, present, and future

About the Author

John B. Nici has a master's degree in art history and is retired from teaching at Lawrence High School in Cedarhurst, New York. He is currently a professor of art history at Queens College in Flushing, New York. In 2004 he was the recipient of Queens College's President's Award for Excellence in Teaching by Adjunct Faculty. He has published extensively on art history pedagogy and has presented and published scholarly papers on topics that include Byzantine art, Gothic art, and Delacroix. He is the author of *Famous Works of Art—and How They Got that Way*.

All inquiries should be addressed to:
Barron's Educational Series, Inc.
250 Wireless Boulevard
Hauppauge, New York 11788
www.barronseduc.com

ISBN: 978-1-4380-0493-8
ISBN (with CD-ROM): 978-1-4380-7513-6

ISSN (print only): 2164-6597
ISSN (print w-CD-ROM): 2164-6600

PRINTED IN THE UNITED STATES OF AMERICA

9 8 7 6 5 4 3 2 1

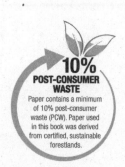
10%
POST-CONSUMER WASTE
Paper contains a minimum of 10% post-consumer waste (PCW). Paper used in this book was derived from certified, sustainable forestlands.

CONTENTS

PART FOUR: PRACTICE TESTS

As you review the content in this book and work toward earning that **5** on your AP Art History Exam, here are five things that you **MUST** know above everything else:

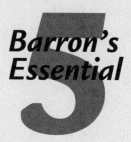

Barron's Essential

1 **Learn to fully identify each object completely.** Multiple-choice questions may ask you to know all the details about a work (for example: name of artist, if known; name of work; date; medium; location of architecture).

Examples:
- Funerary Banner of Lady Dai (Xin Zhui), 180 B.C.E., painted silk
- Ogata Korin, *White and Red Plum Blossoms*, 1710–1716, watercolor on paper
- Templo Mayor (Main Temple), 1375–1520, stone, Tenochtitlan, Mexico City, Mexico

2 **Study works of art in context.** It is important to know the names of the artists and the titles of the works, but it is *required* to know how these were meant to be seen and understood. You must know a given work's context to understand how the work can be interpreted.

3 **Study in-depth works that are important because of their location.** Many of the works that are now required have significant locations, and it is wise to study how their location influences their design. This is often asked.

Examples:
- Lanzón Stela
- Smithson, *Spiral Jetty*
- Dome of the Rock

4 **Learn vocabulary!** Most of the multiple-choice questions require you to know the basic terms art historians use to discuss great works of art. This is particularly important when discussing ancient and medieval art. Study the vocabulary sections at the end of each chapter. The most common vocabulary terms include **but are not limited to**:
- Painting techniques (including pottery)
- Parts of architectural monuments (like ancient temples and medieval churches)
- Types of printmaking (etching, woodcut, engraving, etc.)
- Methods of sculpture (lost wax process, repoussé, etc.)

5 **Select works that have cross-cultural connections.** On the newly redesigned exam, many questions focus on the interconnections between cultures.

Examples:
- Works from New Spain that show indigenous American and Spanish influence
- European works that show a Japanese influence
- Islamic works that show an influence from Chinese sources

Acknowledgments

I have a number of people to thank for their contributions, good wishes, and general support, but the most important is my editor Linda Turner, whom I suspect Barron's does not pay enough for the job she ably does. I also wish to thank Wendy Free, who offered criticism in a spirit of constructive frankness and was greatly influential in the shaping of this book.

For this third edition, I would like to thank all those students who generously contributed to the essays used in this book. From Lawrence High School in Cedarhurst, New York: Katrina Anutunyan, Ryan Bae, Brandon Behar, Jessica Beyer, Victoria DiCeglio, Emily DiNardi, Dean Fujimoto, Remy Geier, Jennifer Kendal, Andy Lochan, Justin Mahabir, Victoria Miller, Joseph Padilla, Tara Philippou, Jonathan Rutchik, Gunnveet Sandhu, Alexandra Spinelli, and Alp Uygan. Special thanks to Jonathan Rutchik for designing many of the ground plans used in this book. From Oakton High School in Vienna, Virginia: Eileen Chen, Yao Chen, Giovanni D'Ambrosio, Ellen Gurung, Sehej Johar, Mrinalini Kataria, Jasbir Kaur, Andrew Lokay, Haley Platt, Judy Nguyen, and Evelyn Wang. Special thanks to Margaret Sharkoffmadrid for facilitating the Oakton essays.

PART ONE
Getting to Know the AP Exam in Art History

Introduction

HOW TO USE THIS BOOK

Students who come to Advanced Placement Art History, unlike students who take almost any other AP exam, often approach the material afresh at the beginning of the school year, with no prior study and no prior understanding of the subject. This is an extraordinary opportunity for the teacher as well as the student to confront a new subject with no preestablished prejudices. However, because the student has little background and must learn everything from scratch, the course can seem unusually daunting. All those works of art! All those images! All those unfamiliar names! All those vocabulary words! Civilizations rise and fall in only a week's time in an art history classroom. There is definitely a need for this Barron's book.

Ideally, this book serves as a refresher to complement a complete art history survey course. It does not function to replace any of the excellent survey texts available on the subject, nor does it pretend to duplicate any of the materials available through the College Board. However, it is a good way to easily organize study patterns for students who must deal with hundreds of images and must learn to discuss them in an intelligent way. This book can also double as a ready reference for teachers, students, and devotees of the subject as an educational resource.

Unlike textbooks in math, science, or social studies, art history books do not have review questions at the end of each chapter, and do not summarize what the student has learned. To meet this need, the teacher may wish to use the practice exams as a warm-up to the actual test. The more familiar students are with the actual exam, the more likely they are to score well on it.

A Note to the Student

You should be aware that this book is not a magic bullet to solve a year's worth of lethargy. Optimally it should be used as a complement to the course, but it will also serve well as a systematic study program to prepare you for the exam. By March you should be reviewing the earliest material, slowly going over one art period after another. It is worthwhile going over every image in the book, whether or not it is familiar to you. The more breadth of experience you have, and the greater your understanding of the subject, the more likely you will be able to handle any question that comes your way.

THE ADVANCED PLACEMENT EXAMINATION
IN THE HISTORY OF ART: AN OVERVIEW

The Advanced Placement Examination in Art History is a 3-hour test composed of an hour of multiple-choice, followed by a short break, and then 2 hours of free-response. The format is as follows:

SECTION I: MULTIPLE-CHOICE QUESTIONS. 1 hour.

This section features 80 multiple choice questions. Some of the questions have images accompanying them, some do not. All of the images on the exam will be in color. You may move freely throughout this section. It is wise to answer those questions that you do know immediately and go back to ponder those that might cause a problem.

There is no penalty for guessing! Every answer should be filled in. Nothing should be left blank. If you are told by the proctor that you only have a few minutes left, bubble in all the remaining answers.

This is extremely important because the multiple-choice questions account for 50 percent of the grade!

SECTION II: FREE-RESPONSE SECTION. 2 hours.

This section is composed of six free-response questions, most associated with illustrations. There are two 30-minute essays and six shorter essays that are timed at 15 minutes apiece.

The two 30-minute essays usually allow students to choose from a wide array of options spanning much of the course. More rarely, they address one or two periods. You are free to move among the essays; they are not individually timed. You can answer them in any order, but make sure you answer all of them. Even if you draw a complete blank, do the best you can to respond.

HOW THE TEST IS GRADED

A complicated series of calculations converts the combined raw score of the multiple-choice questions and the free-response essays into a grade of 1–5. A general rule of thumb is that three-quarters of correct responses will earn the candidate a top score of a 5. Two-thirds is a 4, and a little over half is a 3. These are guidelines, of course, but useful benchmarks nonetheless.

The five-point scoring system is standard among all AP exams:

> 5. Extremely well qualified. Almost all colleges and universities accept this score.
> 4. Well qualified. Accepted by most colleges and universities.
> 3. Qualified. Accepted by many colleges and universities.
> 2. Possibly qualified. Accepted by few colleges and universities.
> 1. No recommendation. Not accepted anywhere.

There is no score of 0, although, believe it or not, there are students who submit completely blank exams.

As with every Advanced Placement exam, a percentage of students get a final score of a 1, 2, 3, 4, or 5. Care is taken to adjust scores according to the difficulty of the exam. Sometimes an examination that seems fair going into the process turns out to be difficult when students actually take it. Adjustments are made in the final scoring to balance a test that is unintentionally too easy or too difficult.

In May 2014, 23,213 students took the Advanced Placement Examination in Art History. Although that may sound like a huge number, it pales in comparison to most exams; Advanced Placement U.S. History gathered 462,766 students. However, art history, unlike most exams, has six written responses, all of which have to be individually read and scored over the course of one week of intensive grading.

A team of dedicated professionals (both college professors and high school teachers) form a leadership team, along with assessment experts, that sets the standards for the exam before marking. Art historians from all over the United States, indeed from some parts of the world, then gather in Salt Lake City in June to mark the free-response sections of the test. A hundred or so teachers use the standards set by the leadership team as guidelines for scoring. All graders are supervised, and teachers even self-check their own work. Even supervisors are monitored. Readers are encouraged to consult one another if a question comes up about an essay. Everything is done to ensure equality of grading across the spectrum. All of this checking and rechecking has made art history one of the most reliable Advanced Placement exams for consistency of scoring.

To the greatest extent possible, every paper is given just consideration. You should know that everything you write is taken very seriously and is considered fairly.

EXAM NOMENCLATURE

The efforts to find precise and inoffensive terms to describe commonly held ideas have been a labor at the College Board. Instead of B.C. and A.D., which have been used as standard abbreviations in the Western world, a substitution of B.C.E. and C.E. ("Before the Common Era" and "Common Era") has been introduced. While this removes the potentially biased word "Christian," it creates the paradox of using a Christian numbering system without recognizing it.

Also, several terms like "non-Western," "Pre-Columbian," and "primitive," once standard in discussing art history, have been replaced by terms that are less exact, such as "art beyond the European tradition," the "art of the Americas," and "Oceanic art"—terms that are occasionally problematic.

You should also note that there are several ways of spelling names and objects that come from non-Roman scripts. In cases such as Mohammed/Muhammad, there is little to fear. But Dong QiChang is Tung Chi'Chang, depending on the method of translation used by a textbook. Every effort has been made to use the standard appearing across the spectrum of textbooks likely to be used in this class.

DATES

You have to study hundreds of works of art, and are required to know myriad facts about each. Unfortunately, the dates leave the head almost immediately upon finishing the examination. The 2009 released exam has only two multiple-choice questions that ask for dates. Instead of learning a huge number of dates, concentrate on centuries: for example, the Baroque is seventeenth century, Rococo is early eighteenth, Neoclassicism is late eighteenth, and so on. Only when the artwork approaches the late nineteenth century is it likely that the exam will ask for decades rather than centuries. Here, general dates will help to serve you best: early twentieth century has movements such as Cubism and Fauvism. Mid-twentieth century has movements such as Abstract Expressionism and Social Realism. Late twentieth century has movements such as Digital Art and Computer Graphics.

Sometimes historical events can help place an art-historical period. Columbus "discovered" America in 1492—in the middle of the Renaissance, which extends one hundred years in either direction.

WHAT'S NEW ABOUT THE REDESIGNED AP EXAM?

A great deal is new about the revised Advanced Placement Art History curriculum. The emphasis is still on addressing major works of art, but which works of art and how they will be addressed has changed. Here are the key differences:

1. Your teacher must teach all the works on the AP image list. Nominally there are **250** such works, but actually there are more like **400** because many of the monuments contain multiple views or ancillary material. Each of these works is pictured in this book.

2. Your teacher can teach additional works as well. These will not be tested in the multiple-choice section, but you can use them to answer any essay that says it welcomes choices outside the list. You can choose your own works as well and use them on the test where appropriate.

3. The new curriculum says that every work must be **completely identified**. In the past it had become acceptable to state the name and the artist of a work in order for it to be a complete identification. Now a complete identification is **very** complete. It includes:

    a. Title
    b. Artist, if known
    c. Date
    d. Medium
    e. Culture or Period
    f. Location of architectural monuments

4. If you choose to use a work outside the official list, **you must be able to identify it as completely as any work on the list.**

5. Traditional discussions in art history are still in place. You still need to be able to intelligently describe what an object looks like (a formal analysis) and trace the history of artistic movements. A new emphasis, however, is placed on **why** and **how** the artistic movements change from one time and place to another.

6. **Function and context** are now stressed. Each work was created for a purpose, has a message, and was placed someplace significant. You should be able to intelligently discuss the circumstances around its creation, presentation, and reception.

7. Students will have to consider **the role of the audience** of a work of art. How can a work be interpreted one way by one group (i.e. a given culture, gender, or age) and differently by another group? How can context lead to a different interpretation?

8. The test has become more **studio art oriented**. Students are expected to have a firmer understanding of the various processes used to create works of art and of how these processes have an impact on what we see.

9. Students are expected to know the **history of each object**. You should be able to answer questions like:

    a. What has happened to this object after it was created?
    b. Does it still have the same significance it had when it was created? Why or why not?

c. How has it been altered since its creation?

d. Why or how do artistic traditions change and how is that seen in individual works?

10. There have always been attribution questions in the Advanced Placement Examination in Art History. That will not change. The attribution will shift to concentrating more on movements and periods than on individual artists. Students must be able to compare an unknown work to a work they know using stylistic analysis and contextual clues.

11. Most important: you must be able to **compare works from various cultures and time periods**. The comparisons could be of two landscapes, two still lifes, or two portraits. They could also be two works of very different functions, different contexts, and different intentions. A good exercise is to try to make the comparisons yourself to see how the works complement or challenge each other.

12. **Your writing counts.** What you say is as important as how you say it. There is no escaping this truth: in almost every test, a good writer outperforms a poor writer even when they both know the same amount of material.

THE REDESIGNED CURRICULUM

Big Idea 1: Artists creatively use various materials to create a work of art.

ESSENTIAL QUESTION: How do the materials used to make art affect what we see?

Learning Objective 1.1: Students understand what goes into making an art work:

a. The **context** in which it is created.

b. What its **function** might have been.

c. What it looks like (its **form**, or formal qualities).

d. What its **content** is about.

e. Students must be able to identify two of the ideas in Learning Objective 1.1 for every work of art discussed. These identifications have to be complete and fully developed.

f. In discussing these ideas, students must be able to draw parallels between how these objectives interact. For example, students should be able to comment on how what it looks like is determined by what it is made of, or how the context of a work of art is reflected in its content.

Learning Objective 1.2: Students should consider how an artist makes creative decisions in rendering the form of a work.

a. Students have to know what a work of art is made of; how that material affects the look of the work and its context.

b. Students are to explain how the choice of materials is determined by artistic and contextual influences. For example, it is not enough to say that a statue is made of marble. The student must be able to comment on the qualities that marble possesses that would make it a desirable medium, or on how the availability of marble affected the choice, or what marble has traditionally symbolized and what it now stands for in this work.

Learning Objective 1.3: Students must understand the context of a work of art. In other words, an understanding of how things like patronage, technology, religious traditions, cultural ideas, or geographic placement would affect how a work of art looks is required. Each work will bring up its own issues. For example, technology, religious traditions, and geographical placement figure strongly in the Easter Island sculptures.

Learning Objective 1.4: Students should be able to understand what the original form and intention of a work of art is.

    a. Students begin by examining the ideas in Learning Objective 1.1, and then they apply them to what could have been the original intention.

    b. It is sometimes difficult to determine the original intention of a work of art. More can be learned about a work by using context, content, function, and form, and by thinking about how they contributed to an original intention. For example, the Etruscan *Sarcophagus of the Spouses* from Cerveteri, Italy (Figure 5.4) can be interpreted when we know where it was found or what objects surrounded it, and by its particular form and medium.

Big Idea 2: Art changes meaning in time.

ESSENTIAL QUESTION: How does art change meaning?

Learning Objective 2.1: Students can describe how traditions in art works change over time.

    a. Students should be able to explain how images change meaning over time, even if they are the same image. For example, images of Mary and Jesus Christ are far different in various works like the Lippi, *Madonna and Child with Two Angels* (Figure 15.3) and the Byzantine icon of *Virgin (Theotokos)* and *Child between Saints Theodore and George* (Figure 8.8).

    b. Students should be able to understand how a religious or historical background determines the form of a work of art, and then express how various cultures interpret that form differently, perhaps using different materials, content, or styles.

Learning Objective 2.2: Students understand why art changes.

    a. Art could change for many reasons. Students need to be aware of the social, political, and religious transformations that occur that could affect interpretation. For example, some cultures show images of Buddha on a grand scale; others are more intimate. There may be contextual reasons for the change.

    b. Students should be able to identify a tradition seen in a work of art.

    c. Students should be able to identify changes within that tradition.

Learning Objective 2.3: Students should understand how a work of art can influence another work.

    a. Students should know how a work of art was influential. Is it the style? The patronage? The message? The content?

    b. Students should know which other works were influenced by the original work in question.

Big Idea 3: Ideas about works of art never stop changing. Interpretation is changeable.

ESSENTIAL QUESTION: How can we describe art?

Learning Objective 3.1: Students should be able to completely identify a work of art. Students need to be able to identify the following about each work of art:

    a. Title

    b. Artist (if known)

c. Date

d. Culture

e. Period

f. Materials

g. Location of larger objects, like buildings

Learning Objective 3.2: What kinds of responses do works of art elicit in the viewer?

a. Students should use their knowledge of formal analysis to show how the audience will respond. For example, repetitive patterns could cause an intellectual and emotional response.

b. Students should use their knowledge of content and context to show how an audience will respond.

c. Students need to be able to accurately describe an audience response.

Learning Objective 3.3: Students should describe how context can lead to different interpretations of works of art.

a. Students should be able to explain how a work of art was originally viewed (for example, in a chapel) and how it might be viewed today (for example, in a museum or in a private collection).

b. Students should be able to explain how the meaning of the work has changed from one context to another.

Learning Objective 3.4: Now that the student has studied many works of art, can he or she apply what is learned to an unknown object? This learning objective tests the student's ability to apply knowledge already learned to new works.

a. Students should be able to tell what culture or period, or even artist, an unknown work would come from.

b. Students must be able to justify their attribution with a level of plausibility.

Learning Objective 3.5: Students should be able to compare and contrast works of art from across time and cultural barriers. The comparisons can be simple formal analyses, or more complicated contextual issues.

ANSWERING THE MULTIPLE-CHOICE QUESTIONS

The Advanced Placement Examination in Art History requires the student to correctly answer as many of the 80 multiple-choices as possible. Each question has four possible responses, and you are asked to find the BEST answer. Often a case can be made for a second choice, but it does not fit as well as the first.

As with all multiple-choice questions, be careful to scan for terms such as:

- Except
- None of the above
- All of the above
- Always
- Never
- Sometimes, often, frequently

These terms indicate that the question has to be analyzed more carefully, since the possibilities are more complicated. In that regard, you should always do the following when approaching an AP multiple-choice question:

- Read each question twice.
- Remember that guessing is now permissible on all AP exams. Therefore, there should be no blanks on your paper!

Types of Multiple-Choice Questions

Typically, multiple-choice questions ask for the following information	Study recommendations
Name of artist	Absolutely essential
Name of work	Absolutely essential
Period or movement of a work	Absolutely essential
Medium of the work	Absolutely essential
Date of the work	Essential; however, don't overreact and spend all your time memorizing dates at the expense of other things. Century is generally good enough.
Location	Absolutely essential only for architecture; for paintings and sculpture, it is not necessary to know the names of museums they are currently in.
Identification of key figures in the work	Absolutely essential
Art history vocabulary, and how these terms can be seen in an individual work	Absolutely essential
Influences on the artist	Important, and often asked
How the work fits in/does not fit in with its times	Increasingly stressed. Works that have a political or cultural message are more apt to be used for questions like this.
Original setting of the work	Sometimes asked, especially if the setting is important to the interpretation of the work
Patron	Asked if the patron had a great influence on the outcome of the work
Symbolism/Subject matter	Sometimes asked, but increasingly this has fallen from favor. Symbols are mutable and subject to interpretation.
Key formal characteristics	A mainstay of traditional art history books

As you can see, there is much to know about each object, and each object raises individual concerns expressed independently from this chart.

Examples of Multiple-Choice Questions

Changing interpretations of works of art:

1. All of the following are valid theories about Jan van Eyck's *Arnolfini Portrait* EXCEPT

    (A) that it is a memorial to a dead wife
    (B) that it represents a betrothal or a wedding ceremony
    (C) that Arnolfini is conferring legal and business privileges on his wife during an absence
    (D) that Arnolfini is pledging support in a legal proceeding about to take place

Answer: (D)

Decision about how works of art will be designed:

2. Louis Sullivan's decision to use steel coated in ceramic was a result of

    (A) his experience working on the Eiffel Tower.
    (B) his understanding of why buildings were damaged by the Chicago Fire.
    (C) new technologies available at the beginning of the nineteenth century.
    (D) the introduction of cantilevers into early modern architecture.

Answer: (B)

Cross-cultural comparisons:

3. Works of architecture often use water as integral parts of their design. All of the following works have water as a key design component EXCEPT:

    (A) Versailles
    (B) Ryoan-ji
    (C) Alhambra
    (D) Monticello

Answer: (D)

Location and meaning:

4. The location of the Vietnam Veterans Memorial is important because

    (A) it stresses the political statement the artist was making
    (B) the artist needed an intimate space to make the message seem personal to the viewer
    (C) the monument aligns with the sun and has a cosmic interpretation
    (D) it lies between other monuments and can be interpreted in a larger context

Answer: (D)

Cross-cultural impact on a work of art:

5. Gottfried Lindauer's portrait of Tamati Waka Nene shows the impact of European art on an image of a Maori chieftain in all of the following ways EXCEPT:

    (A) it is done in oil on canvas, a European technique
    (B) the chief is wearing modern dress and is seen as if he were a European ruler
    (C) the artist has used atmospheric perspective, a technique unknown in the Pacific at the time
    (D) the forms are rendered in a careful and subtle use of shading techniques

Answer: (B)

The function of an object:

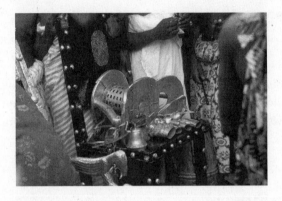

6. This object has the function of being

    (A) a crown placed over the head of a king
    (B) an object to be circumambulated as part of a ritual
    (C) a symbol of the soul of a nation
    (D) a memory device that recalls ancestors and spirits

Answer: (C)

The influence of a single work on later works:

7. Monuments like the Hagia Sophia directly influenced the construction of buildings like

    (A) Mosque of Selim II
    (B) Great Stupa
    (C) the Kaaba
    (D) Chartres Cathedral

Answer: (A)

Materials:

8. The materials used to create the Hawaiian 'ahu 'ula were meant to signify

    (A) the fleeting nature of life
    (B) the rich abundance of tropical vegetation
    (C) the sea, a main source of living things in the Pacific
    (D) protection for the wearer from harm

Answer: (D)

Attribution:

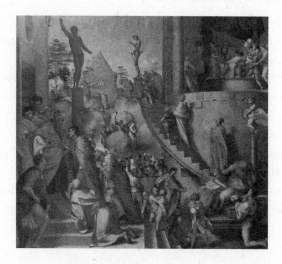

9. The painting shown can be attributed to Pontormo because of

    (A) its use of balance and symmetry
    (B) the flattening of perspective
    (C) the crowded and complex composition
    (D) the fact that it is an engraving

Answer: (C)

Influence:

10. Mary Cassatt drew inspiration from

    (A) African masks
    (B) Chinese scroll paintings
    (C) Aztec sculptures
    (D) Japanese prints

Answer: (D)

There are two types of essays on the Advanced Placement Art History Examination: the four short essays of 15 minutes each and the two longer, more comprehensive essays that take 30 minutes each to write. Each essay type has a different function. Short essays concentrate on a particular work of art or architecture, asking specific questions and demanding concise responses.

The 30-minute essays generally span great oceans of time, asking the student to call upon images that may have similarities but are expressed by different civilizations at different times.

THE TWO 30-MINUTE ESSAYS

The questions that give you the freest range of expression—and the most challenges—are the two 30-minute questions. These questions give students great latitude in choice, but correspondingly ask for a more complete understanding of a work.

Each 30-minute essay is scored on a scale of 0–7. Blank papers or essays on a summer vacation merit a 0. Scores of 6 and 7 are difficult to earn, requiring you to present a polished essay on a given topic.

The first step is to read the question carefully, being sure to note any qualifiers to the essay. Qualifiers may be words like "works from two different periods" or "works of architecture," which will limit your choices.

All exam questions will appear as though they are in a list. They will not be in a paragraph form. The hope is that students will not miss any part of the question if the parts are listed independently.

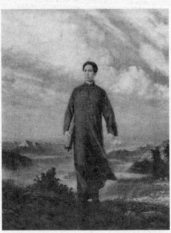

This work is *Chairman Mao en Route to Anyuan.*

Often works of art show a number of influences from many different sources.

Discuss what culture produced this work.

Discuss how this artist was influenced by other cultures in the creation of this work.

Choose another work in which the artist shows a number of influences.

Discuss what culture produced the work.

Discuss how this artist was influenced by other cultures in the creation of this work.

You may either select a work from the list below or select one of your own choosing. You are not limited to the works in the official image set.

Rodriguez, *Spaniard and Indian Produce a Mestizo*
Cassatt, *The Coiffure*
Great Mosque of Djenne

Your task is to answer these questions in the order that they appear, as logically as possible. Each one of these tasks is assigned a point or two, and the reader will score the points as he or she measures your response.

For example:

Question	Point Value
Discuss what culture produced this work.	1 point
Discuss how this artist was influenced by other cultures in the creation of this work.	0–2 points
Choose another work in which the artist shows a number of influences.	1 point
Discuss what culture produced the work.	1 point
Discuss how this artist was influenced by other cultures in the creation of this work.	0–2 points

Student Response:

This work was produced in China and is Chinese. This work shows the influence of European art in a number of ways. First, it is done as a lithograph, a European invention that had spread to the rest of the world. Then, it shows a great number of Western painting techniques. There is atmospheric perspective in the background, with soft passages that seem to diminish in the distance. Then, there is a Western painterly technique. Also, Chinese art prefers monochrome painting; this work is done in a full array of colors.

A second work is Mary Cassatt's The Coiffure from 1890. It is done in aquatint and drypoint on paper. This work was produced by an American artist living in France. It was done during the Impressionist period. This work has a number of artistic influences. Cassatt was inspired by Japanese prints in her work. You can see this by the odd angle that the figure is painted in. Also there is a figure seen from the back, as is typical with many Japanese prints.

Discuss what culture produced this work.

Student Response	Commentary	Points
This work was produced in China and is Chinese.	This earns a point.	1 point

Discuss how this artist was influenced by other cultures in the creation of this work.

Student Response	Commentary	Points
This work shows the influence of European art in a number of ways. First, it is done as a lithograph, a European invention that had spread to the rest of the world. Then, it shows a great number of Western painting techniques. There is atmospheric perspective in the background, with soft passages that seem to diminish in the distance. Then, there is a Western painterly technique. Also, Chinese art prefers monochrome painting; this work is done in a full array of colors.	This response needs two solid reasons. The essay provides more than two.	2 points

Choose another work in which the artist shows a number of influences.

Student Response	Commentary	Points
A second work is Mary Cassatt's *The Coiffure* from 1890. It is done in aquatint and drypoint on paper.	This second choice is from the list, but it is careful to add two extra identifications: date and technique.	1 point

Discuss what culture produced the work.

Student Response	Commentary	Points
This work was produced by an American artist living in France. It was done during the Impressionist period.	This is a bit of a complication because Cassatt is American by birth, but French by inclination. This response records both possibilities.	1 point

Discuss how this artist was influenced by other cultures in the creation of this work.

Student Response	Commentary	Points
This work has a number of artistic influences. Cassatt was inspired by Japanese prints in her work. You can see this by the odd angle that the figure is painted in. Also there is a figure seen from the back, as is typical with many Japanese prints.	This is a beginning, but does not fully explore the influence of Japanese art on Mary Cassatt's work, as seen in this print. Better answers could have included: No posing or acting; figures possess a natural charm; decorative charm influenced by Japanese art; Japanese hair style; Japanese point of view: figure seen from the back; pastel color scheme.	1 point

Total points earned: 6 of 7.

APPROACHING THE SHORT ESSAY

Your short essays are marked on a scale of 0–5, based on a rubric that is agreed on before the marking session by a leadership committee of teachers and experts in the various fields of art history. It may seem simplistic to say, but the key ingredient in getting a good mark on the written essays is to read the question completely and thoroughly, and to fully answer each part. Readers are looking for how well you addressed the question, not for how well you may know everything there is to know about the image. If you are including information about an object that is not called for in the question, it will be ignored by the reader. You MUST answer the question completely and directly in order to earn the highest grade possible.

All exam questions will appear as though they are in a list. They will not be in a paragraph form. The hope is that students will not miss any part of the question if the parts are listed independently.

For example:

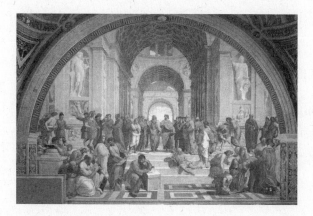

This work is the *School of Athens* by Raphael.

Where is this work located?

What is the significance of the placement of this work in this location?

What connections to the past are being made with this work?

What did this work say to its contemporary audience?

Your task is to answer these questions in the order that they appear, as logically as possible. Each one of these tasks is assigned a point or two, and the reader will score the points as he or she measures your response.

For example:

Question	Point Value
Where is this work located?	1 point
What is the significance of the placement of this work in this location?	1 point
What connections to the past are being made with this work?	1 point
What did this work say to its contemporary audience?	0–2 points

Student example:

The *School of Athens* is located in what was the Pope's library in the Vatican Palace. This work is placed in the Vatican Palace because this room was originally the Pope's library. As such, he kept his books along the walls at the base of the painting. In this case, the Pope kept his philosophy books on this wall. The painting represents the great philosophers of the ancient world, some of whom wrote those books. The Renaissance was at time of renewal. Artists were keen to look back on the classical past as a source of inspiration. The Pope, as an important figure in the Renaissance, would have treasured classical learning, and thus he places the books prominently on the wall of his library below this painting. This work says to the contemporary audience that you should study and be smart just like Renaissance men. If you study, you will succeed also.

Where is this work located?

Student Response	Commentary	Points
The *School of Athens* is located in what was the Pope's library in the Vatican Palace.	Very exact, earning a point.	1 point

What is the significance of the placement of this work in this location?

Student Response	Commentary	Points
This work is placed in the Vatican Palace because this room was originally the Pope's library. As such, he kept his books along the walls at the base of the painting. In this case, the Pope kept his philosophy books on this wall. The painting represents the great philosophers of the ancient world, some of whom wrote those books.	This answers the placement part of the question very well.	1 point

What connections to the past are being made with this work?

Student Response	Commentary	Points
The Renaissance was at time of renewal. Artists were keen to look back on the classical past as a source of inspiration. The Pope, as an important figure in the Renaissance, would have treasured classical learning, and thus he places the books prominently on the wall of his library below this painting.	This answers the connections part of the question very well.	1 point

What did this work say to its contemporary audience?

Student Response	Commentary	Points
This work says to the contemporary audience that you should study and be smart just like Renaissance men. If you study, you will succeed also.	**Be careful!** The verb "did" indicates that a contemporary Renaissance audience is implied, not a modern audience. This is not a convincing response to this question.	0 points

Total points earned: 3 of 5.

GENERAL RULES ABOUT ESSAYS

1. Never use value judgments or matters of taste or opinion in an essay. For example, never say that a work of art is "better" than another, or that the artist used perspective "better" or color "better." Instead, express differences in terms of values that few can object to, such as: "Painting A has more vivid colors than painting B, as can be seen in the figure on the left"; "sculpture A is more classically composed than sculpture B, as can be seen in the contrapposto in the figure on the left"; "building A is located in a city square, whereas building B was built in a rural area."

2. Never use the word "perfect" or say that a work of art is, for example, "the perfect expression of Christian belief."

3. Never use "able" or "unable," as in "The artist was unable to capture the feelings of sorrow in..." Also don't use "attempt," as in "The artist attempts to show foreshortening." What precisely does this mean?

4. Never express a preference. Don't tell the reader that you like one work more than another. It is irrelevant to the exam.

5. Be careful of the word "unique"—it means one of a kind. It does not mean special. If a work of art is unique, it means that there is no other work like it. Use it sparingly. Avoid redundant expressions like "very unique."

6. Avoid complimenting the artist on the work he or she has done. Do not say that "Michelangelo did a good job of showing perspective..."

7. People in works of art are "figures," not "characters." Characters are parts in plays.

8. Avoid phrases like "piece of art." Use "work of art" or "work."

9. It is permissible in questions with two illustrations to simply refer to them as right and left, rather than repeating a title. Once you have established what they are, left and right, or even L and R, are sufficient.

10. It is correct form to underline the titles of works of art, with the exception of the names of buildings. In this book, italics have been substituted for underlining.

11. Always identify a work of art clearly, not generically. For example, don't identify by simply using the word "icon." There are so many! Say, instead, "the icon of the "Virgin and Child between Saints Theodore and George." Similarly, don't use words such as "cathedral" or "pyramid" as a method of identification. Use instead "Chartres Cathedral" or "the Pyramids of Giza, Egypt."

12. Do not list your response. Do not use bullet points. Write complete sentences. Make sure that you write in full paragraphs.

PART TWO
Diagnostic Test

ANSWER SHEET
Diagnostic Test

Section 1

#					#					#					#				
1.	Ⓐ	Ⓑ	Ⓒ	Ⓓ	21.	Ⓐ	Ⓑ	Ⓒ	Ⓓ	41.	Ⓐ	Ⓑ	Ⓒ	Ⓓ	61.	Ⓐ	Ⓑ	Ⓒ	Ⓓ
2.	Ⓐ	Ⓑ	Ⓒ	Ⓓ	22.	Ⓐ	Ⓑ	Ⓒ	Ⓓ	42.	Ⓐ	Ⓑ	Ⓒ	Ⓓ	62.	Ⓐ	Ⓑ	Ⓒ	Ⓓ
3.	Ⓐ	Ⓑ	Ⓒ	Ⓓ	23.	Ⓐ	Ⓑ	Ⓒ	Ⓓ	43.	Ⓐ	Ⓑ	Ⓒ	Ⓓ	63.	Ⓐ	Ⓑ	Ⓒ	Ⓓ
4.	Ⓐ	Ⓑ	Ⓒ	Ⓓ	24.	Ⓐ	Ⓑ	Ⓒ	Ⓓ	44.	Ⓐ	Ⓑ	Ⓒ	Ⓓ	64.	Ⓐ	Ⓑ	Ⓒ	Ⓓ
5.	Ⓐ	Ⓑ	Ⓒ	Ⓓ	25.	Ⓐ	Ⓑ	Ⓒ	Ⓓ	45.	Ⓐ	Ⓑ	Ⓒ	Ⓓ	65.	Ⓐ	Ⓑ	Ⓒ	Ⓓ
6.	Ⓐ	Ⓑ	Ⓒ	Ⓓ	26.	Ⓐ	Ⓑ	Ⓒ	Ⓓ	46.	Ⓐ	Ⓑ	Ⓒ	Ⓓ	66.	Ⓐ	Ⓑ	Ⓒ	Ⓓ
7.	Ⓐ	Ⓑ	Ⓒ	Ⓓ	27.	Ⓐ	Ⓑ	Ⓒ	Ⓓ	47.	Ⓐ	Ⓑ	Ⓒ	Ⓓ	67.	Ⓐ	Ⓑ	Ⓒ	Ⓓ
8.	Ⓐ	Ⓑ	Ⓒ	Ⓓ	28.	Ⓐ	Ⓑ	Ⓒ	Ⓓ	48.	Ⓐ	Ⓑ	Ⓒ	Ⓓ	68.	Ⓐ	Ⓑ	Ⓒ	Ⓓ
9.	Ⓐ	Ⓑ	Ⓒ	Ⓓ	29.	Ⓐ	Ⓑ	Ⓒ	Ⓓ	49.	Ⓐ	Ⓑ	Ⓒ	Ⓓ	69.	Ⓐ	Ⓑ	Ⓒ	Ⓓ
10.	Ⓐ	Ⓑ	Ⓒ	Ⓓ	30.	Ⓐ	Ⓑ	Ⓒ	Ⓓ	50.	Ⓐ	Ⓑ	Ⓒ	Ⓓ	70.	Ⓐ	Ⓑ	Ⓒ	Ⓓ
11.	Ⓐ	Ⓑ	Ⓒ	Ⓓ	31.	Ⓐ	Ⓑ	Ⓒ	Ⓓ	51.	Ⓐ	Ⓑ	Ⓒ	Ⓓ	71.	Ⓐ	Ⓑ	Ⓒ	Ⓓ
12.	Ⓐ	Ⓑ	Ⓒ	Ⓓ	32.	Ⓐ	Ⓑ	Ⓒ	Ⓓ	52.	Ⓐ	Ⓑ	Ⓒ	Ⓓ	72.	Ⓐ	Ⓑ	Ⓒ	Ⓓ
13.	Ⓐ	Ⓑ	Ⓒ	Ⓓ	33.	Ⓐ	Ⓑ	Ⓒ	Ⓓ	53.	Ⓐ	Ⓑ	Ⓒ	Ⓓ	73.	Ⓐ	Ⓑ	Ⓒ	Ⓓ
14.	Ⓐ	Ⓑ	Ⓒ	Ⓓ	34.	Ⓐ	Ⓑ	Ⓒ	Ⓓ	54.	Ⓐ	Ⓑ	Ⓒ	Ⓓ	74.	Ⓐ	Ⓑ	Ⓒ	Ⓓ
15.	Ⓐ	Ⓑ	Ⓒ	Ⓓ	35.	Ⓐ	Ⓑ	Ⓒ	Ⓓ	55.	Ⓐ	Ⓑ	Ⓒ	Ⓓ	75.	Ⓐ	Ⓑ	Ⓒ	Ⓓ
16.	Ⓐ	Ⓑ	Ⓒ	Ⓓ	36.	Ⓐ	Ⓑ	Ⓒ	Ⓓ	56.	Ⓐ	Ⓑ	Ⓒ	Ⓓ	76.	Ⓐ	Ⓑ	Ⓒ	Ⓓ
17.	Ⓐ	Ⓑ	Ⓒ	Ⓓ	37.	Ⓐ	Ⓑ	Ⓒ	Ⓓ	57.	Ⓐ	Ⓑ	Ⓒ	Ⓓ	77.	Ⓐ	Ⓑ	Ⓒ	Ⓓ
18.	Ⓐ	Ⓑ	Ⓒ	Ⓓ	38.	Ⓐ	Ⓑ	Ⓒ	Ⓓ	58.	Ⓐ	Ⓑ	Ⓒ	Ⓓ	78.	Ⓐ	Ⓑ	Ⓒ	Ⓓ
19.	Ⓐ	Ⓑ	Ⓒ	Ⓓ	39.	Ⓐ	Ⓑ	Ⓒ	Ⓓ	59.	Ⓐ	Ⓑ	Ⓒ	Ⓓ	79.	Ⓐ	Ⓑ	Ⓒ	Ⓓ
20.	Ⓐ	Ⓑ	Ⓒ	Ⓓ	40.	Ⓐ	Ⓑ	Ⓒ	Ⓓ	60.	Ⓐ	Ⓑ	Ⓒ	Ⓓ	80.	Ⓐ	Ⓑ	Ⓒ	Ⓓ

Diagnostic Test

SECTION 1

TIME: 60 MINUTES
80 MULTIPLE-CHOICE QUESTIONS

DIRECTIONS: Answer the multiple-choice questions below. Some are based on images. In this book the illustrations are at the top of each set of questions. Select the multiple-choice response that best completes each statement or question, and indicate the correct response on the space provided on your answer sheet. You will have 60 minutes to answer the multiple-choice questions.

Questions 1–5 are based on Figure 1.

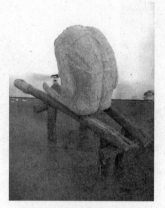

Figure 1

1. Works like Magdalene Abakanowicz's *Androgyn III* symbolize the

    (A) emptiness of modern life
    (B) horrors of World War II
    (C) advance of modern technology and its effect on the human condition
    (D) effects of pollution and global warming

2. The artist uses burlap as a material in part because it

    (A) is transparent and encourages us to see through the figures
    (B) is inexpensive and therefore symbolizes economic depression
    (C) imitates the appearance of human skin
    (D) is durable and needs no further care

3. The work is placed in the center of the room so that

    (A)   other figures can be placed around it and interact with it

    (B)   a contrast between solids and voids can be appreciated

    (C)   people can be encouraged to touch the work and experience it first hand

    (D)   it will block people from passing through the room and force them to consider it

4. An abstracted human form such as this resembles the

    (A)   *Kouros* from Anavysos

    (B)   *Ikenga* shrine figure

    (C)   Nio guardian figure

    (D)   *Portrait of Sin Sukju*

5. The figure sits on a wooden framework that resembles a

    (A)   wagon

    (B)   cot

    (C)   stretcher

    (D)   couch

Questions 6–12 are based on Figures 2 and 3.

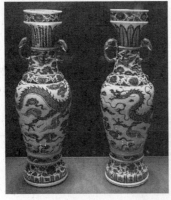 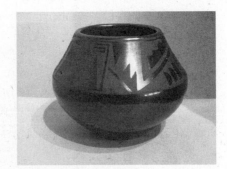

        Figure 2   **Figure 3**

6. The objects on the left, called The David Vases, were made for

    (A)   export to Europe because Asian art was greatly prized

    (B)   Sir Percival David, a collector of Chinese ceramics

    (C)   practical use in a Chinese home

    (D)   an altar in a Chinese Daoist temple

7. The works on the left are made of

   (A) porcelain that has a fine luster added by a glaze
   (B) porcelain, but unglazed and with a matte finish
   (C) clay with blue cobalt added for color
   (D) clay treated with white gypsum

8. Sources for the designs of works on the left are most likely from

   (A) Chinese bronzes
   (B) Japanese wood-block prints
   (C) Indian Buddhist sculpture
   (D) contact with Europeans

9. The work on the right represents a

   (A) revival of interest in pottery making in a culture that had seen a decline in that art
   (B) change to a more practical type of pottery rather than just aesthetically pleasing work
   (C) change from a tourist driven pottery market to a practical use market
   (D) move to reestablish pottery in European markets after a serious decline in quality

10. The work on the right was done in which of the following cultures?

    (A) Eastern Shoshone
    (B) Northwest Coast Indian
    (C) Lenape
    (D) Puebloan

11. The work on the right can be compared with the works on the left in that both

    (A) are done by unidentified artists
    (B) use a combination of polished and matte surfaces
    (C) are dominated by zigzag and geometric motifs
    (D) were probably not meant to contain anything inside

12. The work on the left has an inscription that indicates all of the following EXCEPT

    (A) that the vases are accompanied by an incense burner
    (B) how the vases should be used
    (C) who the donor is
    (D) when the vases were created

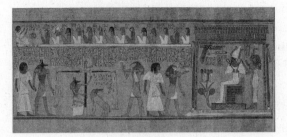

Figure 4

Figure 5

13. Both of these works are done on scrolls. The work on the top uses

    (A) paper
    (B) silk
    (C) papyrus
    (D) vellum

14. The work on the bottom uses

    (A) paper
    (B) silk
    (C) papyrus
    (D) vellum

15. Both of these works incorporate narrative, but the narrative is different in that

    (A) one tells the stories of the gods and their punishment of humans, and the other tells of the gods and how they help humans achieve enlightenment
    (B) one is in hieroglyphics and the other is in Arabic
    (C) one is read from right to left and the other from left to right
    (D) one has an uncertain ending and the other has been predetermined

16. The work on the top was meant to explain

    (A) vengeance upon a sinful man
    (B) an innocent person's journey to salvation and enlightenment
    (C) coming of age in a tumultuous era
    (D) the weighing of souls in the afterlife

17. The work on the bottom illustrates

    (A) an historical episode seen from the victor's point-of-view
    (B) a mythical event that sheds light on contemporary society*
    (C) an allegory of war and violence
    (D) a personal challenge in the face of overwhelming odds

18. The work on the bottom was meant to be

    (A) on permanent display in a palace

    (B) put away and taken out occasionally to be viewed by interested parties

    (C) housed in a religious shrine as a moral lesson

    (D) periodically studied and examined in a library

19. The work on the top is thematically linked with certain elements in

    (A) the Tympanum at Conques

    (B) *The Lindisfarne Gospels*

    (C) Justinian and Theodora at San Vitale

    (D) Lippi's *Madonna and Child*

20. The work on the bottom is thematically linked with certain elements in

    (A) Notre Dame de la Belle Verriere window

    (B) Giotto's *Lamentation*

    (C) Dürer's *Adam and Eve*

    (D) frontispiece of the Codex Mendoza

Questions 21–25 are based on Figures 6 and 7.

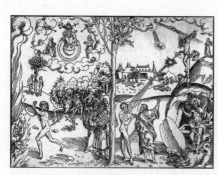

Figure 6

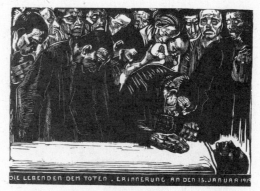

Figure 7

21. The print on the left was conceived as

    (A) an illustration of the effects of the Thirty Years War

    (B) an indictment of Catholicism and a promotion of Protestantism

    (C) propaganda for the Counter-Reformation agents in Europe

    (D) an affirmation of the Old Testament over the New Testament

22. These works are prints which

    (A) were attached to early forms of newspapers and used as illustrations

    (B) were used as ways to educate children in schools

    (C) were deemed a higher art form than more traditional paintings

    (D) could make multiple original copies and be distributed more widely

23. These prints were done in a format called a woodcut which has a style that can be characterized as

    (A) achieving precise details
    (B) using sfumato to shade figures
    (C) using stiff and angular figures
    (D) using the pointillist techniques

24. The work on the right was done in the memory of

    (A) a king of France who fell in love with an Italian princess and tragically died
    (B) a Catholic martyr who was misunderstood by native people and was killed
    (C) the artist's brother who died tragically in war
    (D) a slain member of the Communist party who led a revolt in Germany

25. The work on the right

    (A) depicts a real event
    (B) has no political overtones or references
    (C) is art for art's sake and has no purpose
    (D) depicts a mythical event using real people

Questions 26–32 are based on Figures 8 and 9.

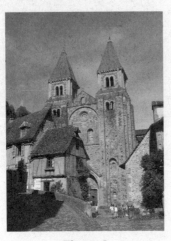

Figure 8

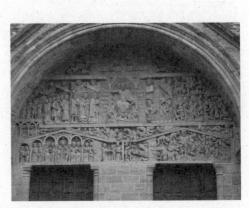

Figure 9

26. This church was built along pilgrimage roads headed to

    (A) Jerusalem
    (B) Rome
    (C) Canterbury
    (D) Santiago de Compostela

27. In order accommodate the number of pilgrims, the church has been designed with

    (A) a large pair of bell towers
    (B) sculpture on the façade
    (C) an ambulatory around the altar
    (D) a transept

28. As a pilgrimage center, it performs essentially the same role as

    (A) The Palace of Versailles
    (B) The Forbidden City
    (C) The Great Stupa at Sanchi
    (D) Monticello

29. As a pilgrimage center, this building houses reliquaries. A reliquary can be defined as

    (A) an object that holds sacred objects
    (B) a place where people were baptized into the Christian faith
    (C) a series of carvings that tell the story of Jesus' life
    (D) a woven product that is designed on a loom

30. This building was done in which of the following styles?

    (A) Gothic
    (B) Romanesque
    (C) Renaissance
    (D) Merovingian

31. The style of this building is revealed by the

    (A) asymmetrical arrangement of the forms
    (B) use of stained glass
    (C) introduction of fan vaulting
    (D) use of bays on the side walls

32. On the façade is a sculpture that depicts

    (A) The *Lamentation*
    (B) The *Pietà*
    (C) The Last Judgment
    (D) Adam and Eve

33. Which of the following works has experienced a form of iconoclasm?

    (A) Bamiyan Buddhas
    (B) Merovingian fibulae
    (C) *Lukasa Memory Board*
    (D) Velázquez, *Las Meninas*

34. Which of the following contains an imperial portrait?

    (A) White Temple and its ziggurat
    (B) Taj Mahal
    (C) San Vitale
    (D) Machu Picchu

35. The bas-reliefs on the walls of the Palace at Persepolis depict

    (A) Trajan's conquering of the Dacians
    (B) the battle between the gods and the giants
    (C) Darius' imperial guard, called the Immortals
    (D) a lamassu

Questions 36–38 refer to Figure 10.

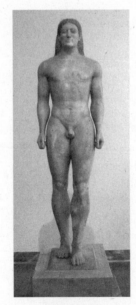

Figure 10

36. This statue is similar to other Greek kouroi in that it is inspired by

    (A) Ancient Near Eastern figures
    (B) Egyptian sculptures
    (C) Roman emperors
    (D) Polykleitos' theories

37. This sculpture was different from female sculptures of the same date in that it

   (A) was unpainted
   (B) is disproportionate to the human body
   (C) is nude
   (D) is young

38. The sculpture probably

   (A) saluted a fallen emperor or king
   (B) saluted a heroic figure from a battle
   (C) was placed in a tomb so that the spirit of the deceased could visit the earth
   (D) was designed as a symbol of a Greek city-state

Questions 39–45 refer to Figures 11, 12, and 13.

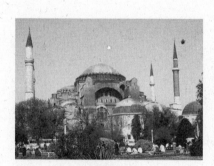

Figure 11

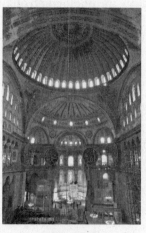

Figure 12

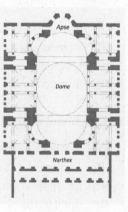

Figure 13

39. This building is located in

   (A) Ravenna
   (B) Rome
   (C) Jerusalem
   (D) Istanbul

40. Who was the patron of this building?

   (A) Constantine the Great
   (B) Justinian and Theodora
   (C) Augustus of Primaporta
   (D) Suleyman the Magnificent

41. A key architectural feature first developed in this building is the

   (A) squinch
   (B) nave
   (C) narthex
   (D) pendentive

42. Originally this building was constructed for the worship of

   (A) Christians
   (B) Protestants
   (C) Buddhists
   (D) Jews

43. Later this building was converted into a mosque, and the towers visible in the left photograph were added outside to

   (A) watch for enemies
   (B) fire down on the populace
   (C) call people to prayer
   (D) point the way to Mecca

44. The interior, as is visible in the photograph on the right, is greatly changed from its original condition. Originally, the interior was filled with

   (A) fresco
   (B) stained glass
   (C) tempera
   (D) mosaic

45. The ground plan reflects

   (A) a typical axially planned structure
   (B) a typical centrally planned structure
   (C) a combination of an axial and a centrally planned structure
   (D) none of the above

_____

46. Julie Mehretu's works have an animation and a sweeping vibrant pulse similar to the works of

   (A) Pablo Picasso
   (B) Constantin Brancusi
   (C) Vassily Kandinsky
   (D) Meret Oppenheim

47. A pyxis is a

   (A) container for aromatic spices
   (B) flattened column against a wall
   (C) type of Islamic script
   (D) memory board

48. We know that the *Basin* by Muhammad ibn al-Zain must have been a special work for the artist because

    (A) it ended up in the possession of the King of France
    (B) he signed the work six times
    (C) he decorated it with hunting scenes
    (D) it is made of pewter

Questions 49–54 refer to Figures 14 and 15.

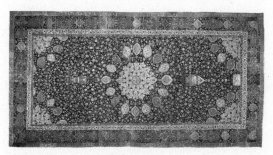

Figure 14

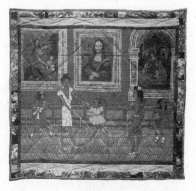

Figure 15

49. Both of these works are woven objects. The one on the left is

    (A) a wool carpet
    (B) an embroidery
    (C) a tapestry
    (D) a quilt

50. The one on the right is

    (A) a wool carpet
    (B) an embroidery
    (C) a tapestry
    (D) a quilt

51. The work on the left was used for prayer for which faith?

    (A) Buddhism
    (B) Hinduism
    (C) Judaism
    (D) Islam

52. All of the following is true about the work on the left EXCEPT it

    (A) has a known artist
    (B) was meant for prayer
    (C) is one of a pair
    (D) has calligraphy

53. The work on the right is woven because it is

    (A) the traditional artistic occupation of women
    (B) meant to be beautiful but also have a function
    (C) a commentary on the contemporary neglect of woven works of art
    (D) meant to be worn

54. The artist in the work on the right appropriates images from the works of

    (A) Michelangelo
    (B) Gustave Courbet
    (C) Leonardo DaVinci
    (D) Rembrandt

_____

55. The general Muslim and Jewish ban on religious images influenced the destruction of images in which period?

    (A) Byzantine
    (B) Romanesque
    (C) Gothic
    (D) Late Antique

56. Northern European altarpieces are different from Italian ones in that the Northern ones

    (A) have predellas
    (B) are cupboards with wings that close
    (C) have fanciful frames
    (D) are located in a church

57. The discovery of the caves at Lascaux solidified the opinion that

    (A) the Trojan epics were retellings of actual events
    (B) Pompeii was buried by volcanic ash
    (C) Stonehenge was a unique ancient monument
    (D) prehistoric cave paintings are genuine and not the work of modern forgers

58. The lost wax process, sometimes called *cire perdue* is a method of sculpture seen in which of the following works?

    (A) Greek marble sculpture
    (B) Islamic ivories
    (C) Northwest Coast Indian transformation masks
    (D) Benin brasses and bronzes

59. All of the following are characteristic of the Colosseum in Rome EXCEPT

   (A) the use of groin and barrel vaults
   (B) it was used for chariot races
   (C) it once had a retractable canvas roof
   (D) it was built of concrete and brick and faced with marble

Questions 60–63 refer to Figure 16.

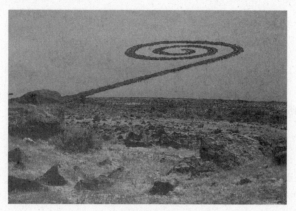

Figure 16

60. This work is *in situ* meaning it

   (A) is made of man-made products
   (B) can be seen with the use of a special device
   (C) changes color depending on the time of day
   (D) is in its original location

61. This work has been particularly designed

   (A) to be far from civilization
   (B) align with the movements of the sun and the moon
   (C) so that boats can dock alongside it
   (D) to be viewed both by day and night

62. This work draws inspiration from works like

   (A) The Great Stupa at Sanchi
   (B) The Serpent Mound in Ohio
   (C) Machu Picchu in Peru
   (D) the ruins of the city of Pompeii

63. This work has much in common with the modernist movement known as

   (A) Pop Art
   (B) Abstract Expressionism
   (C) Post-Modernism
   (D) Minimalism

64. The Harlem Renaissance refers to a period that

   (A) spurned African art and promoted the African-American experience instead
   (B) aggressively rejected modernism
   (C) promoted African-American aesthetics in all the arts
   (D) encouraged African-Americans to conform to white standards of art production

65. In which culture is calligraphy an important artistic expression?

   (A) Byzantine
   (B) Islam
   (C) Roman
   (D) Etruscan

66. Etchings are different from engraving in that etchings

   (A) require a metal plate as a ground
   (B) use a tool to cut into a surface
   (C) must be realized by passing paper over the impression
   (D) must be immersed in acid to achieve an image

67. Leonardo Da Vinci's *Last Supper* is in a ruined condition today because

   (A) Leonardo experimented with different types of paint
   (B) the patrons were angry at the outcome and had the work mutilated
   (C) tastes change, and the work was going to be replaced because it looked out of fashion
   (D) the Nazis tried to remove it in World War II and damaged it

Questions 68–70 refer to Figure 17.

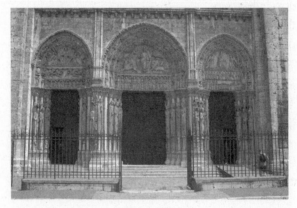

Figure 17

68. The Royal Portals at Chartres are so named because

   (A) French kings were crowned there
   (B) Old Testament kings and queens are depicted on the jambs
   (C) the kings of France are depicted on the jambs
   (D) French kings came to worship here

69. Contextually, these figures

    (A)   physically and morally support the church behind them
    (B)   act as an interpreter for those who are not Christian
    (C)   are in the spot where royalty must pray
    (D)   are symbols of the revival of the Catholic faith during the Counter-Reformation

70. This kind of grouping of sculpture and architecture can be found also at

    (A)   The Taj Mahal
    (B)   The Dome of the Rock
    (C)   The Hagia Sophia
    (D)   The Lakshmana Temple

---

71. Quoins are architectural features used primarily

    (A)   around a pediment
    (B)   for rusticating a surface
    (C)   on the edges of buildings
    (D)   along stringcourses and cornices

72. Etruscan architecture is largely known to us today through the

    (A)   writings of Vitruvius
    (B)   excavations at Pompeii
    (C)   books of Palladio
    (D)   descriptions made by Greek historians

73. The veristic sculptures of Roman art are usually images of

    (A)   emperors
    (B)   senators
    (C)   gladiators
    (D)   women

74. The art of the Amarna period is different from the art of earlier Egyptian periods in that the figures are

    (A)   more stiff and tense
    (B)   cut away from the stone
    (C)   done in relief
    (D)   more relaxed and realistic

75. Which of the following periods in art history was rejected by the public when it first debuted?

    (A) Romanticism
    (B) Impressionism
    (C) Neoclassicism
    (D) Rococo

76. A manuscript that is a Moralized Bible is one in which

    (A) only excerpts from the Bible that end with morals are represented
    (B) the Old Testament stories are juxtaposed to New Testament stories
    (C) the Bible has added pages with modern commentaries
    (D) the Bible is thoroughly footnoted and researched

77. Jan Vermeer's paintings suggest that he had knowledge of

    (A) lithography
    (B) the daguerreotype
    (C) the camera obscura
    (D) the orrery

78. The material used to make Bandolier bags relies on

    (A) trade with European settlers
    (B) manufactured goods available during the Industrial Revolution
    (C) the reuse of older material in a new context
    (D) the recycling of older bags for more modern use

79. In Claude Monet's *Saint-Lazare Station,* the artist represented the

    (A) effect of light and air on a given subject
    (B) breakdown of reality into its composite forms
    (C) rearranging of reality into different geometric shapes
    (D) sharp contrast of light and dark areas

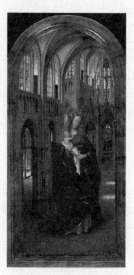

Figure 18

80. This painting can be attributed to Jan van Eyck because of the

    (A) broad open brushwork

    (B) meticulous use of detail

    (C) symmetrical composition

    (D) use of contrapposto

SECTION II

TIME: 120 MINUTES
6 QUESTIONS

Section II has two parts, each an hour. Part A contains two 30-minute questions. Part B contains four 15-minute questions. Although it is permissible to move freely among all the questions in Section II, it is advisable to stick to the time limits for each question to ensure an adequate response. During the actual exam, proctors will announce when each time period is over, and suggest that you move on to the next question.

Part A

> **DIRECTIONS:** You have 1 hour to answer the two questions in Part A. You are advised to spend 30 minutes on each question. Be sure to respond completely to all sections of every question.

1. Books have been created not only to preserve the written word but also to illustrate important concepts that the words represent. Often books have become highly decorated works of art in their own right, as much treasured for their illustrations as for their words.

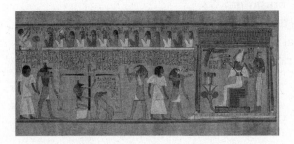

This book shows a section from *The Last Judgment of Hu-Nefer* from *The Book of the Dead*, c. 1275 B.C.E., painted papyrus scroll.

Describe the scene that is taking place in this book.

Analyze how the written content adds meaning to the illustrations of this book.

Choose and completely identify another book.

Describe the scene that is taking place in this book.

Analyze how the illustrations add meaning to the written content of this book.

You may either select a work from the list below or select one of your own choosing. You are not limited to the works in the official image set. (Suggested time: 30 minutes)

The Court of Gayumars, folio from *Shah Tahmasp's Shahnama*
Frontispiece of the Codex Mendoza
Golden Haggadah (The Plagues of Egypt, Scenes of Liberation, and Preparation for Passover)
Lindisfarne Gospels: St. Matthew, cross-carpet page; St. Luke portrait page; St. Luke incipit page

2. Artists use a variety of materials to create a work of art. Often the function of the work inspires the artist to choose materials that contribute to the meaning of the work. This is Jan van Eyck's *Arnolfini Portrait* done in oil paint on wood.

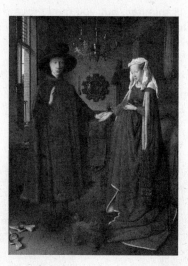

Explain HOW and WHY the materials enhance the meaning and function of the object.

Select and completely identify another work of art whose function has inspired the artist to choose materials that contribute to the meaning.

Explain HOW and WHY the materials enhance the meaning and the function of the object.

The choice may be from any medium, in any period or culture you find relevant.

You may either select a work from the list below or select one of your own choosing. You are not limited to the works in the official image set. (Suggested time: 30 minutes)

Cadzi Cody, Hide Painting of a Sun Dance
Miguel González, *Virgin of Guadalupe*
Jeff Koons, *Pink Panther*
Meret Oppenheim, *Object*
Sarcophagus of King Tutankhamun

Part B

DIRECTIONS: You have 1 hour to answer the four questions in Part B. The suggested time for each question is 15 minutes, but you may move freely among the questions. Be sure to respond completely to all sections of every question.

3. The image on the left is a Ndop, a Portrait Figure of King Mishe miShyaang maMbul. On the right is a contextual image of Kuba Nyim (ruler) Kot a Mbweeky III in state dress with royal drum in Mushenge, Congo. The sculpture and the photograph represent a continuing tradition of the Kuba people which extends to today.

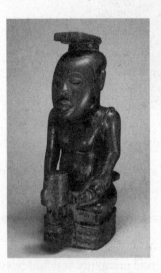 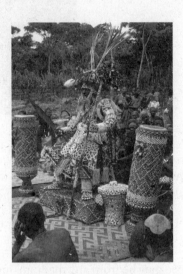

Explain the purpose of Ndop figures.

Discuss which specific elements in this work help illustrate its purpose.

Show how these elements continue to represent the Kuba king today, as seen in the contextual photograph. (Suggested time: 15 minutes)

4. This work is the Funeral Banner of Lady Dai (Xin Zhui), 180 B.C.E., painted silk.

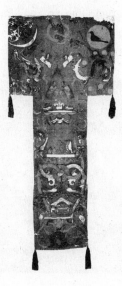

Where was this work found?

Many artists use symbolism to create a deeper meaning in a work of art. What are the symbolic elements on this work?

Analyze how the symbolic elements are used to enhance the original function of the work. (Suggested time: 15 minutes)

5. The building and the plan show the Carson, Pirie, Scott building by Louis Sullivan.

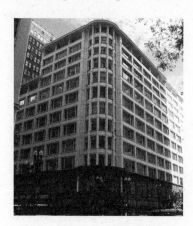 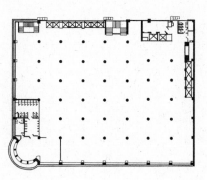

What is the purpose of this building?

Louis Sullivan used certain design elements with its purpose in mind. Using both the photograph and the plan, discuss what those design elements are.

Discuss how buildings like these left an important influence on the history of architecture. (Suggested time: 15 minutes)

6. Contemporary artist Xu Bing has stated in his letter to a young artist:

"My viewpoint is that wherever you live, you will face that place's problems. If you have problems then you have art. Your plight and your problems are actually the source of your artistic creation."

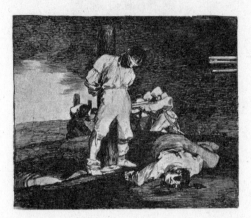

The image shown illustrates a moment of crisis occurring during the lifetime of a great artist.

Fully identify this work.

Explain what problems the artist is illustrating.

How has he taken his problem and made it into an artistic statement?

What is the artist's intention in creating this work? (Suggested time: 15 minutes)

Section 1

1. **A**	21. **B**	41. **D**	61. **A**
2. **C**	22. **D**	42. **A**	62. **B**
3. **B**	23. **C**	43. **C**	63. **D**
4. **B**	24. **D**	44. **D**	64. **C**
5. **C**	25. **A**	45. **C**	65. **E**
6. **D**	26. **D**	46. **C**	66. **D**
7. **A**	27. **C**	47. **A**	67. **A**
8. **A**	28. **C**	48. **B**	68. **B**
9. **A**	29. **A**	49. **A**	69. **A**
10. **D**	30. **B**	50. **D**	70. **D**
11. **D**	31. **D**	51. **D**	71. **C**
12. **B**	32. **C**	52. **D**	72. **A**
13. **C**	33. **A**	53. **A**	73. **B**
14. **A**	34. **C**	54. **C**	74. **D**
15. **C**	35. **C**	55. **A**	75. **B**
16. **D**	36. **B**	56. **B**	76. **B**
17. **A**	37. **C**	57. **D**	77. **C**
18. **B**	38. **B**	58. **D**	78. **A**
19. **A**	39. **D**	59. **B**	79. **A**
20. **D**	40. **B**	60. **D**	80. **B**

ANSWERS EXPLAINED

Section I

1. **(A)** Abakanowicz's hollow sculptures symbolize the emptiness of modern life, and the shallowness of people.

2. **(C)** The artist has said on occasion that the use of burlap has the texture of human skin and therefore symbolizes it.

3. **(B)** When placed in the center of the room, the emptiness of the insides of the sculpture become apparent. Many of this artist's works are placed in open spaces or in the center of rooms so they can be appreciated from all sides.

4. **(B)** The *Ikenga* (shrine figure) is an abstracted human form. The other three are very or fairly realistic in comparison.

5. **(C)** The wooden framework looks like a stretcher, which adds to the melancholy feel of the piece.

6. **(D)** The David Vases were originally meant to be placed on the altar of a Chinese Daoist temple.

7. **(A)** The David Vases are made of glazed porcelain, which accounts for the luxurious surface.

8. **(A)** The artists were inspired by the decorations on Chinese bronzes.

9. **(A)** American Indian pottery had begun to decline when Europeans, with mass produced pots, began to arrive. Martinez rescued the art of pottery and revived it as an art form.

10. **(D)** Martinez lived in the Pueblo culture of the American southwest.

11. **(D)** Neither work was done to be useful, in the sense that they may have stored or held items.

12. **(B)** The inscription of The David Vases tells us the names of the donors, when they were created, and the fact that they were part of a set that included an incense burner. It does not tell us how they were intended to be used other than indicating they should be on an altar.

13. **(C)** The Egyptian scroll is done on papyrus.

14. **(A)** The Japanese scroll is done on paper; sometimes Japanese scrolls were done on silk, but this one is on paper.

15. **(C)** Egyptian writing is read left to right; Japanese writing is read right to left.

16. **(D)** The work on the left depicts the weighing of the soul of Hu-Nefer.

17. **(A)** The work on the right is a depiction of an historical episode from Japanese history, specifically, a civil war culminating in the burning and looting of the Sanjô Palace.

18. **(B)** The work on the right, as is true with almost all Japanese scrolls, was never meant to be on permanent display. It was meant to be taken out, appreciated, and then stored away in scroll cabinets.

19. **(A)** The weighing of souls is a theme that is taken up in medieval tympana, including the one above the doors in Conques, France.

20. **(D)** The violence depicted in the *Night Attack on the Sanjô Palace* is similar to the violence shown on the frontispiece of the Codex Mendoza.

21. **(B)** The Cranach print on the left is meant to promote Protestantism at the expense of Catholicism during the early stages of the Reformation.

22. **(D)** One of the many features of prints is that multiple original images can be mass produced and marketed.

23. **(C)** Angular and stiff figures are often rendered in woodcuts because the carving tools are affected by the grain of the wood.

24. **(D)** The Kollwitz work on the right depicts the mourning over a deceased member of the Communist party.

25. **(A)** The work on the right depicts a real event in German history.

26. **(D)** The church of Sainte-Foy was built along a pilgrimage road to Santiago de Compostela in northwestern Spain.

27. **(C)** The huge number of pilgrims were accommodated by using an ambulatory around the apse. This architectural structure moved people from chapel to chapel without interfering with the main services held in the altar area.

28. **(C)** The Great Stupa at Sanchi was another point of pilgrimage.

29. **(A)** A reliquary is an object that houses sacred objects within it. Often the shape of the reliquary reflects the shape of the object it contains.

30. **(B)** Sainte-Foy is a Romanesque building started in the eleventh century.

31. **(D)** The basic unit of construction in Romanesque buildings is the bay, a vertical wall section, that was repeated around the structure.

32. **(C)** The façade of the building has a scene of the Last Judgment on it.

33. **(A)** Iconoclasm is the destruction of images. The Bamiyan Buddhas were blown up in 2001 by the Taliban in Afghanistan as an act of iconoclasm.

34. **(C)** The imperial portraits of Justinian and Theodora are housed in the church of San Vitale in Ravenna.

35. **(C)** The bas-reliefs on the walls of the Palace of Persepolis depict the imperial guard of the Persian king, Darius. Their numbers always held at 10,000, and were thus called the Immortals.

36. **(B)** The stiffness of kouros figures is similar to the erect stance of Egyptian sculptures.

37. **(C)** Both male and female Greek Archaic sculptures are painted, young, and had large human heads, but only the males are nude.

38. **(B)** The sculpture probably represents a heroic male warrior.

39. **(D)** This building is located in what is today Istanbul, but was originally called Constantinople.

40. **(B)** The patrons of the Hagia Sophia were Emperor and Empress Justinian and Theodora.

41. **(D)** This building offered the first use of pendentives, a triangular structure that transitions the space between the round dome and the flat wall.

42. **(A)** The original purpose of this building was to celebrate rites associated with the Christian faith.

43. **(C)** Mosques add tall towers, called minarets, to call people to prayer five times a day.

44. **(D)** Originally the interior of the Hagia Sophia was entirely covered in mosaic.

45. **(C)** The ground plan reveals neither an axially nor a centrally planned structure, but a combination of both.

46. **(C)** Vassily Kandinsky was noted for his sweeping animated work that initiated the world of modern abstract art.

47. **(A)** A pyxis is a small container for aromatic spices.

48. **(B)** The artist signed his name six times on this bowl, indicating a certain degree of pride in his work.

49. **(A)** The work on the left is a wool carpet.

50. **(D)** The work on the right is a quilt.

51. **(D)** The work on the left is used in Islamic prayer rituals.

52. **(D)** The work on the left has no calligraphy.

53. **(A)** Weaving traditionally has been thought of as a female art form.

54. **(C)** The works in the background are three paintings by the Renaissance artist, Leonardo DaVinci. These paintings are on display in the Louvre museum.

55. **(A)** The active Muslim and Jewish ban on images influenced the Byzantine ban on Christian images in the ninth and tenth centuries.

56. **(B)** Northern Renaissance altarpieces, like the *Isenheim Altarpiece*, are cupboards that open and close.

57. **(D)** The prehistoric cave paintings were thought to be forgeries until the caves of Lascaux were discovered.

58. **(D)** The lost wax process is a way of creating bronze or brass sculptures.

59. **(B)** The Colosseum was never used, nor intended to be used, for chariot races.

60. **(D)** *In situ* is a Latin expression that means "in its original place."

61. **(A)** This work is located in a remote section of the Utah desert on the Great Salt Lake.

62. **(B)** *Spiral Jetty* resembles the curvilinear forms found at Great Serpent Mound in Ohio.

63. **(D)** The simplicity of the lines in *Spiral Jetty* have much in common with the Minimalist movement in American art.

64. **(C)** The Harlem Renaissance was a rich period that celebrated African-American culture in all artistic avenues.

65. **(B)** Calligraphy is a high art in Islam and China, because it symbolizes an artistic form half-way between painting and writing.

66. **(D)** Etchings are dipped in acid after being covered in wax. The acid eats into the surface and produces grooves filled with ink so that images can be reproduced on paper.

67. **(A)** Leonardo DaVinci was an endless experimenter, particularly in the types of paints he used. He combined watercolor, oil, and tempera paint in the creation of the *Last Supper*.

68. **(B)** Old Testament kings and queens are depicted on the Royal Portals at Chartres.

69. **(A)** The Royal Portal figures symbolically hold up and support the church and its teachings.

70. **(D)** Like the Royal Portals, the Lakshmana Temple has sculpture carved on its façade.

71. **(C)** Quoins are architectural features that are prominently placed on the edges of buildings to emphasize their perimeter.

72. **(A)** Most architecture from the Etruscan period does not survive. We know about it through the writings of the Roman author, Vitruvius.

73. **(B)** Veristic Roman sculptures are done in the Republican period and depict Roman senators. The Emperors are depicted in the Imperial period.

74. **(D)** The Amarna period shows a more relaxed, softer approach to Egyptian art than the previous periods.

75. **(B)** Most art periods are accepted by the general population when they are introduced. However, Impressionism was ridiculed by the French public when it debuted in Paris in the 1870s.

76. **(B)** A moralized Bible compares the Old and New Testament stories, by placing them side by side.

77. **(C)** Scholars have demonstrated that Vermeer's paintings were influenced by the use of the camera obscura.

78. **(A)** The beads used in Bandolier bags were obtained by trading with the Europeans.

79. **(A)** Impressionist paintings, particularly those by Claude Monet, are especially concerned with the atmospheric effects of light and air on objects.

80. **(B)** The meticulous use of detail is a hallmark of the style of Jan van Eyck. None of the other characteristics apply to him.

MODEL RESPONSE FOR QUESTION 1

Throughout history, written works have often been accompanied by illustration to add meaning and further explain the text. This is evident in the Last Judgment of Hu-Nefer, from his tomb, which is a page from the Book of the Dead. This papyrus scroll is from the ancient Egyptian New Kingdom. It clearly utilizes text hand in hand with illustration to gets its full meaning across; it is the final judgment of the scribe, Hu-Nefer, before he can go to heaven.

Similar to pyramid and coffin texts, this scroll text was a set of instructions that Hu-Nefer would need in the afterlife. The writing would help lead Hu-Nefer through his judgment so that his soul could finally be weighed and he could go to heaven. The writing also includes prayers. These prayers were to aid the dead in getting through their final judgment. Lastly, the writing allows us to identify who Hu-Nefer is in the first place. We can follow the story of the ancient scribe using the text; however, the illustration helps us to visualize it.

The illustration helps to further explain what the text is saying. It fully shows the trip that Hu-Nefer took to be judged. The illustration also helps to clarify what Hu-Nefer may have somewhat looked like, as well as how important Hu-Nefer was. He is dressed in a white robe, white being a pure color associated with high status in art. In one scene on the top left, Hu-Nefer is kneeling in front of many figures. He is pleading with them and telling them that he is in fact a good person, worthy of heaven. On the bottom far left, the man in the white robe, the god, Anubis, leads Hu-Nefer. Hu-Nefer's heart is being weighted against a feather to find the purity of soul. Thoth stands on the other side of the scale, recording what is going on to see if Hu-Nefer has truly lived an ethical life. In one final scene on the right, Hu-Nefer is introduced to one of the supreme gods, Osiris, by Osiris' son, Horus, with the falcon head. Osiris sits in front of a lotus, a flower that represents eternal life.

Another important book is the Frontispiece of the Codex Mendoza, c. 1542, done on pigment on paper. Although named after the viceroy of New Spain, the work actually shows scenes of the founding of Tenochtitlan in Mexico City.

The work uses two different kinds of writing: Spanish, to explain the story to a European audience, and Aztec pictograms that illustrate the story in a native language.

The purpose of the book is to show life in New Spain to an audience that would probably never go there. To that end, Aztecs carry out events in daily life, as well as military conquests, both legible in their language and in the European tongue. Skulls, for example, represent sacrificial victims offered up in Aztec ceremonies. They are also words that symbolize this sacrifice. Therefore in the case of the Codex Mendoza, the words and pictures are actually one.

So powerful has this imagery become, that the current Mexican flag has some of the symbols seen on this frontispiece: an eagle, a cactus, and a rock.

Criteria	Student Response	Points Allotted for Task	Points Earned
Task: Describe the scene that is taking place in *The Book of the Dead*.			
The essay must identify the exact scene in the book.	"…this scroll text was a set of instructions that Hu-Nefer would need in the afterlife. The writing would help lead Hu-Nefer through his judgment so that his soul could finally be weighed and he could go to heaven."	1	1
Task: Analyze how the written content adds meaning to the illustrations of this book.			
The essay must analyze, so therefore must point to exact places in the text, where the written content adds meaning to the illustrations.	"The writing would help lead Hu-Nefer through his judgment so that his soul could finally be weighed and he could go to heaven. The writing also includes prayers. These prayers were to aid the dead in getting through their final judgment… We can follow the story of the ancient scribe using the text; however, the illustration helps us to visualize it."	0–2	2
Task: Choose and completely identify another book.			
If a work from the list is selected, two other identifiers are needed.	"Another important book is the *Frontispiece of the Codex Mendoza*, c. 1542, done on pigment on paper."	1	1
Task: Describe the scene that is taking place in this book.			
The essay must identify the exact scene in the book.	"…Aztecs carry out events in daily life, as well as military conquests…"	1	0 This response is too vague.
Task: Analyze how the illustrations add meaning to the written content of this book.			
The essay must analyze, so therefore must point to exact places in the text, where the illustrations add meaning to the written content of the book.	"Skulls, for example, represent sacrificial victims offered up in Aztec ceremonies. They are also words that symbolize this sacrifice. Therefore in the case of the Codex Mendoza, the words and pictures are actually one…"	0–2	2
		Total Points Possible: 7	This essay earned: 6

Arnolfini and His Bride, painted by Jan van Eyck, was completed in the fifteenth century during the Northern Renaissance. Now located in the National Gallery in London, this painting was viewed to be one of the most meticulous and extraordinarily executed works to surface during the Northern Renaissance. Flemish artist Jan van Eyck, noted as a master of art across Northern Europe, fashioned this piece of art by using the new painting medium, oil. The scene taking place in the picture is traditionally assumed to be a wedding; however, some scholars disagree. Despite the discrepancy on the ceremony portrayed, Jan van Eyck chooses to use oil for several reasons. Due to the great concentration of minute details, oil allowed van Eyck to focus on each aspect and carry out each brushstroke as precisely as possible. Van Eyck used oil in a way that had never before him been recognized. This type of paint generates enamel-like surfaces and sharp details, which stands as an impeccable quality that van Eyck clearly used to its fullest extent. He even went as far as to draw the scene in the mirror hanging in the background to give the viewer the picture he/she would see if it was observed from behind. In the previous era, tempera was the medium that was most common.

Tempera, having a base of egg yolk, sticks to just about anything and does not allow for the continuous application of thin transparent layers, which can produce a variety of effects. If van Eyck chose to use tempera or fresco, he would not have the luxury of being able to manipulate the colors because of their short drying times. In addition, the intensity of the texture would be very weak, lacking a glowing aura and exhibiting a faded appearance.

Due to the flexible properties of oil, Arnolfini and His Bride communicates rich, luminous colors that a tempera base would not be able to achieve. Because oil allows the artist to create this fruitfulness of color, the viewer becomes captured by the incandescent quality, thus being drawn into the scene. In addition, van Eyck applies multiple coatings of oil. Accordingly, a unique quality of this type of paint is the ability to layer without ruining the wood. Jan van Eyck now had the ability to create shadows on the figures as well as on the fruit on the windowsill, because oil paint has the capacity to accurately imitate natural hues and tones. These shadows really accentuate van Eyck's love of light. The shadows that he managed to create make Arnolfini and Cenami appear real. Oil greatly helped Jan van Eyck communicate this scene to its utmost potential. By using this innovative style of paint, he was able to create various visually appealing features in the picture that were unprecedented.

Because oil has all of these groundbreaking properties, Jan van Eyck was able to portray a scene that integrated shadows, color, intensity, and light. Without these imperative characteristics, he would not have been able to capture the essence of the setting and atmosphere. Thus, oil becoming a prominent painting material helped in the brilliant execution of Arnolfini and His Bride.

Another work that uses different media is Cadzi Cody's Hide Painting of a Sun Dance, c. 1890–1900. American Indians have had a tradition of using locally found materials in creating their works. It comes as no surprise that elk hide would be used to create a painting surface for American Indians. Although Cody lived at a time when western artistic materials such as oil and canvas were readily available, he chose to paint on hides to evoke the traditional training of the eastern Shoshone Indians. Because elk were in numerous quantities in Wyoming, it was natural to use their hide for painting.

After using the animals for meat, the skins were removed and dried and prepared for painting. Cody used a variety of images on his work, some incorporating motifs he felt would appeal to prospective buyers. He combined a number of motifs from traditional Sun Dance and bison hunts into a pictorial display that is enhanced by the fact that it appears on an animal hide. Thus, the hide and the content of the work are equally matched.

Criteria	Student Response	Points Allotted for Task	Points Earned
Task: Explain HOW the materials enhance the meaning and function of the *Arnolfini Portrait*.			
The essay must express how oil paint makes its effect.	"This type of paint generates enamel-like surfaces and sharp details, which stands as an impeccable quality that van Eyck clearly used to its fullest extent..."	1	1
Task: Explain WHY the materials enhance the meaning and function of the *Arnolfini Portrait*.			
The essay must express why van Eyck chose oil paint.	"Due to the great concentration of minute details, oil allowed van Eyck to focus on each aspect and carry out each brushstroke as precisely as possible..."	0–2	2
Task: Select and completely identify another work of art whose function has inspired the artist to choose materials that contribute to the meaning.			
If a work from the list is selected, two other identifiers are needed.	"Cadzi Cody's *Hide Painting of a Sun Dance*, c. 1890–1900... eastern Shoshone Indians."	1	1
Task: Explain HOW the materials enhance the meaning and the function of the object.			
The essay must address how the materials contribute to the meaning of the content of the work.	"He combined a number of motifs from traditional Sun Dance and bison hunts into a pictorial display that is enhanced by the fact that it appears on an animal hide. Thus, the hide and the content of the work are equally matched."	1	1
Task: Explain WHY the materials enhance the meaning and the function of the object.			
The essay must state why the artist chose these materials.	"Although Cody lived at a time when western artistic materials such as oil and canvas were readily available, he chose to paint on hides to evoke the traditional training of the eastern Shoshone Indians."	0–2	2
		Total Points Possible: 7	**This essay earned: 7 This is an exceptional essay.**

MODEL RESPONSE FOR QUESTION 3

This Ndop on the left is one of numerous other commemorative portraits portraying a Kuba ruler's idealized spirit that celebrates the success and achievements contributed by each respective African ruler's reign. Since these wooden figures were commissioned posthumously, they replaced deceased kings and acted as containers for their spirit. The Kuba people believed in the secular value of material possessions and the Ndop reflects this through the usage of royal regalia.

The King is shown sitting cross-legged on a base instead of directly on the surface, suggesting his high status. His facial expression appears disinterested, reflecting a detachment from worldly affairs. The peace knife in his left hand has its handle turned outward, symbolizing the peace that Kuba enjoyed under his authority.

The amount of accessories the artist included in this statue, such as the headdress or necklace, serves to communicate the economic prosperity of the rule and affluence of the King. His stiff posture evokes an aura of dignity to the audience.

The photo of Kuba King Nyim in regal dress on the right was taken during a royal event. Just as the Ndop figure, the King in the picture stands on a platform as opposed to directly on the ground with his subjects. As seen in the photograph, this ruler also wears an excessive amount of royal regalia. This method of conveying wealth, status, and power through costume and dress is a continuation within African art. Lastly, the amount of effort put into this event reveals the lasting tradition of honoring the Kuba kings with grand festivity and many celebratory objects.

Criteria	Student Response	Points Allotted for Task	Points Earned
Task: Explain the purpose of Ndop figures.			
The essay must express the purpose of a Ndop figure.	"Since these wooden figures were commissioned posthumously, they replaced deceased kings and acted as containers for their spirit."	1	1
Task: Discuss which specific elements in this work help illustrate its purpose.			
The essay needs to fully articulate at least two elements in the work that help express its purpose.	"The king is shown sitting cross-legged on a base instead of directly on the surface, suggesting his high status. His facial expression appears disinterested, reflecting a detachment from worldly affairs. The peace knife in his left hand has its handle turned outward, symbolizing the peace that Kuba enjoyed under his authority."	0–2	2
Task: Show how these elements continue to represent the Kuba king today, as seen in the contextual photograph.			
The essay must meaningfully connect the contextual photograph with the Ndop figure.	"Just as the Ndop figure, the king in the picture stands on a platform as opposed to directly on the ground with his subjects..."	0–2	2
		Total Points Possible: 5	This essay earned: 5 A superior essay.

MODEL RESPONSE FOR QUESTION 4

This work was found in a funerary tomb from ancient China. The banner is made of silk and was placed over the coffin of Lady Dai. Because of the banner's shape, with its long arms, it was probably carried as a banner in a procession, with a rod running through the arms to create a cross-shaped piece.

There are many symbols in the work, including the yin and the yang, which represent ancient Chinese philosophies.

The banner has three different sections. The top represents heaven; the middle, earth; and the bottom the underworld. Each has a different set of symbols. For example, the moon and the sun appear in heaven; Lady Dai appears on earth with a walking stick; low critters like turtles and fish appear in the underworld.

Criteria	Student Response	Points Allotted for Task	Points Earned
Task: Where was this work found?			
The essay must state that the work was found in a tomb.	"This work was found in a funerary tomb from ancient China."	1	1
Task: Many artists use symbolism to create a deeper meaning in a work of art. What are the symbolic elements on this work?			
The essay must state where some of the symbolic elements would be, and what they refer to.	"The banner has three different sections. The top represents heaven; the middle, earth; and the bottom, the underworld. Each has a different set of symbols..."	0–2	2
Task: Analyze how the symbolic elements are used to enhance the original function of the work.			
The essay must address how the symbolic elements are tied to the unified artistic vision of the work.	—	0–2	0 This part of the question is not addressed.
		Total Points Possible: 5	This essay earned: 3

MODEL RESPONSE FOR QUESTION 5

The Carson, Pirie, Scott building, by Louis Sullivan, was very innovative for its time and those innovative characteristics led to greater future possibilities, such as the building of skyscrapers, such as the Woolworth Building. The building functioned as a department store.

A key characteristic of the building is its use of steel and concrete. The steel made the building stronger and more stable, allowing for it to be built taller. Likewise, the use of concrete permitted the building to be thinner, lessening the amount of land needed for the construction of the building.

Another characteristic were large windows and large window areas (made possible by the steel-framed structure, as seen in the floor plan) because they provided the rooms with abundant light, which solved any problems created by darkness. The windows also allowed for display of goods to people passing on the street.

The building also included elevators. They were vital as they provided people easy transportation to any floor of the building. Now, as people didn't have to worry about climbing up dozens of staircases in order to reach their destination, taller and bigger buildings seemed attractive to architects.

Criteria	Student Response	Points Allotted for Task	Points Earned
Task: What is the purpose of this building?			
The building is a department store.	"The building functioned as a department store."	1	1
Task: Louis Sullivan used certain design elements with its purpose in mind. Using both the photograph and the plan, discuss what those design elements are.			
The essay should indicate at least two design elements and explain them.	"A key characteristic of the building is its use of steel and concrete…" "Another characteristic were large windows and large window areas…"	0–2	2
Task: Discuss how buildings like these left an important influence on the history of architecture.			
The essay should express how future buildings were dependent on the design of this building.	"…taller and bigger buildings seemed attractive to architects."	0–2	1 This part of the question is not directly addressed. Only a passing reference is made.
		Total Points Possible: 5	**This essay earned: 4**

Contemporary artist Xu Bing once wrote, "My viewpoint is that wherever you live, you will face that place's problems. If you have problems then you have art. Your plight and your problems are actually the source of your artistic creation."

The work that illustrates this best is Francisco de Goya's, And There's Nothing to Be Done (from the Disasters of War) from about 1820.

The work was conceived during the Napoleonic wars when France had occupied Spain, which is reflected in the original title of the work which calls the time period "Spain's Bloody War with Bonaparte."

The work is bitterly ironic, because the French guns are pointed at the Spanish citizens, and the title is "And There's Nothing to be Done." Goya was famous for exploring the themes of individuals caught in a whirlwind of events beyond their control. Goya intents on showing the viewer the helplessness of people during turbulent times.

Goya also emphasizes the bloodiness of the situation, concentrating on one figure, and the nameless attackers who appear only in the margins of the work. He makes you feel the crisis very personally. This is how Goya lives up to Xu Bing's quotation, "Your plight and your problems are actually the source of your artistic creation."

Criteria	Student Response	Points Allotted for Task	Points Earned
Task: Fully identify this work.			
At least two identifiers are needed to answer this question.	"Francisco de Goya's, *And There's Nothing to Be Done* (from the *Disasters of War*) from about 1820."	1	1
Task: Explain what problems the artist is illustrating.			
The essay must describe the context of the work.	"The work was conceived during the Napoleonic wars when France had occupied Spain, which is reflected in the original title of the work which calls the time period 'Spain's Bloody War with Bonaparte.'"	1	1
Task: How has he taken his problem and made it into an artistic statement?			
The essay needs to point out examples of artistic expression.	"Goya also emphasizes the bloodiness of the situation, concentrating on one figure, and the nameless attackers who appear only in the margins of the work."	1	1
Task: What is the artist's intention in creating this work?			
The essay needs to explain why Goya created this work.	"Goya intents on showing the viewer the helplessness of people during turbulent times."	0–2	1 (The essay needs a fuller response to this question.)
		Total Points Possible: 5	**This essay earned: 4**

EVALUATION OF DIAGNOSTIC TEST

NOTE: Because the AP Art History exam will be new in 2016, there is no way of knowing exactly how the raw scores on the exams will translate into a 1, 2, 3, 4, or 5. The formula provided below is based on past commonly accepted standards for grading the AP Art History exam. Additionally, the score range corresponding to each grade varies from exam to exam, and thus the ranges provided below are approximate.

Section I: Multiple-Choice (50% of grade)

Your diagnostic test score can now be computed. The multiple-choice section of the actual test is scored by computer, but it uses the same method you will use to compute your score manually. Each correct answer earns one point. Each incorrect answer has no value, and cannot earn or lose points. Omitted questions or questions that the computer cannot read because of smudges or double entries are not scored at all. Go over your answers and mark the ones correct with a "C" and the ones incorrect with an "X."

Enter the total number of correct answers: _____

Conversion of Raw Score to Scaled Score

Your raw score is computed from a total of 80 questions. In order to coordinate the raw score of the multiple-choice section with the free-response section, the multiple-choice section is multiplied by a factor of 1.25. For example, if the raw score is 6, the weighted score is 81.25. Enter your weighted score in the box on the right.

> **Enter your weighted multiple-choice score:**
> _____

Section II: Essay (50% of grade)

When grading your essay section, be careful to follow the rubric so that you accurately assess your achievement. Grade each long essay on a scale of 0–7 and each short essay on a score of 0–5. Total the scores for this section. The highest point total for this section is 34.

Essay 1: (Total score: 7 points) _____

Essay 2: (Total score: 7 points) _____

Essay 3: (Total score: 5 points) _____

Essay 4: (Total score: 5 points) _____

Essay 5: (Total score: 5 points) _____

Essay 6: (Total score: 5 points) _____

Total Raw Score on Essay Section: _____

In order to weight this section appropriately, the raw score is multiplied by 2.942, so that the highest weighted score is 100.

> **Enter your weighted essay score:**
> _____

Final Scoring

Add your weighted scores. A perfect score is 200. Although the weighting changes from year to year, a general rule of thumb is that 75% correct is a 5, 66% is a 4, and 55% is a 3. Use the following table as an estimate of your achievement.

Enter your total weighted score:

_____

5	150–200 points
4	132–149 points
3	110–131 points
2	75–109 points
1	0–74 points

Enter your AP score:

_____

EXAMPLE

Section I: Multiple-Choice:

Number correct: ___60___ (out of 80)

Number correct × 1.25: ___75___ (out of 100)

Section II: Scores on the six essays could be:

Essay 1:	4
Essay 2:	5
Essay 3:	4
Essay 4:	3
Essay 5:	4
Essay 6:	2
Total:	$22 \times 2.942 = 64.7$

Section I score: 75
Section II score: 64.7

Total score: 139.7
This test would likely score a 4.

PART THREE
Content Review

Prehistoric Art

1

TIME PERIOD

Paleolithic Art 30,000 B.C.E.–8000 B.C.E. in the Near East; later in the rest of the world
Neolithic Art 8,000 B.C.E.–3000 B.C.E. in the Near East; later in the rest of the world

ENDURING UNDERSTANDING: Prehistoric art existed before writing.

Essential Knowledge:

- Prehistoric art has been affected by climate change.
- Prehistoric art can be seen in practical and ritual objects.

ENDURING UNDERSTANDING: The oldest objects are African or Asian.

Essential Knowledge:

- Prehistoric art is concerned with cosmic phenomena as well as down-to-earth concerns.
- Human behavior is charted in the earliest art works.
- Ceramics are first produced in Asia.
- The people of the Pacific are migrants from Asia, who bring ceramic making techniques with them.
- European cave paintings indicate a strong tradition of rituals.
- Early American objects use natural materials, like bone or clay, to create ritual objects.

ENDURING UNDERSTANDING: Prehistoric art is best understood as an interdisciplinary activity.

Essential Knowledge:

- Scientific dating of objects has shed light on the use of prehistoric objects.
- Archaeology increases our understanding of prehistoric art.
- Basic art historical methods can be used to understand prehistoric art, but our knowledge increases with findings made in other fields.

PREHISTORIC BACKGROUND

Although prehistoric people did not read and write, it is a mistake to think of them as primitive, ignorant, or even nontechnological. Some of their accomplishments, like Stonehenge, continue to amaze us forty centuries later.

Archaeologists divide the prehistoric era into periods, of which the two most relevant to the study of art history are Paleolithic (the Old Stone Age) and Neolithic (the New Stone Age). These categories roughly correspond to methods of gathering food: In the Paleolithic period people were hunter-gatherers; those in the Neolithic period cultivated the earth and raised livestock. Neolithic people lived in organized settlements, divided labor into occupations, and constructed the first homes.

People created before they had the ability to write, cipher math, raise crops, domesticate animals, invent the wheel, or use metal. They painted before they had anything that could be called clothes or lived in anything that resembled a house. The need to create is among the strongest of human impulses.

Unfortunately, it is not known why these early people painted or sculpted. Since no written records survive, all attempts to explain prehistoric motivations are founded on speculation. From the first, however, art seems to have a function. These works do not merely decorate or amuse, they are designed with a purpose in mind.

Prehistoric Sculpture

Most prehistoric sculpture is portable; indeed, some are very small. Images of humans, particularly female, have enlarged sexual organs and diminutive feet and arms. Carvings on cave walls make use of the natural modulations in the wall surface to enhance the image. More rarely, sculptures are built from clay and lean upon slanted surfaces. Some sculptures are made from found objects such as bones, some from natural material such as sandstone, and some carved with other stones. Early forms of human-made materials, such as ceramics, are also common.

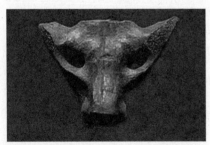

Figure 1.1: Camelid sacrum in the shape of a canine, c.14,000-7,000 B.C.E., bone, National Museum of Anthropology, Mexico

Camelid sacrum in the shape of a canine, 14,000–7,000 B.C.E., bone, National Museum of Anthropology, Mexico (Figure 1.1)

- From Tequixquiac, Mexico
- Bone sculpture from a camel-like animal
- Sacrum is the triangular bone at the base of a spine
- Bone has been worked to create the image of a dog or wolf
- One natural form used to take the shape of another
- Carved to represent a mammal's skull
- Mesoamerican idea that a sacrum is a "second skull"
- Found in 1870
- **Cross-Cultural Comparisons: The Depiction of Animals**
  - Tuffery, *Pisupo Lua Afe (Corned Beef 2000)* (Figure 26.15)
  - Muybridge, *The Horse in Motion* (Figure 21.5)
  - Cotsiogo (also known as Cadzi Cody), Hide Painting of a Sun Dance (Figure 26.13)

Anthropomorphic stele, fourth millennium B.C.E., sandstone, Pergamon Museum, Berlin (Figure 1.2)

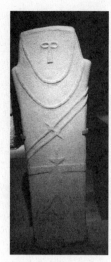

Figure 1.2: Anthropomorphic stele, 4th millennium B.C.E., sandstone, Pergamon Museum, Berlin

- One of the earliest known works of art from Arabia
- Found in an area that had extensive ancient trade routes
- Religious or burial purpose
- Belted robe from which hangs a double bladed knife or sword
- Anthropomorphic: resembling human form, but not in itself human
- **Cross-Cultural Comparisons: Anthropomorphic Images**
  - Mutu, *Preying Mantra* (Figure 29.25)
  - Female Deity from Nukuoro (Figure 28.2)
  - Braque, *Portuguese* (Figure 22.6)

Jade *cong* from Liangzhu, China, c. 3,300-2,200 B.C.E., jade, Zhejiang Institute of Archaeology, Hangzhou (Figure 1.3)

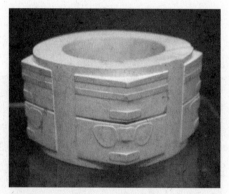

Figure 1.3: Jade *cong* from Liangzhu, China, c. 3,300-2,200 B.C.E., jade, Zhejiang Institute of Archaeology, Hangzhou

- Circular hole placed within a square
- Abstract designs; main decoration is a face pattern, perhaps of spirits or deities
- Four corners of the cong usually carry mask-like images with pronounced eyes and fanged mouth
- Jades appear in burials of people of high rank
- Jade religious objects found in tombs; interred with the dead in elaborate rituals
- Chinese linked jade with virtues: durability, subtlety, beauty
- Placed in a burial around bodies, some broken, some show signs of intentional burning
- Made in the Neolithic era in China
- **Cross-Cultural Comparisons: Geometric Designs**
  - Mondrian, *Composition with Red, Blue and Yellow* (Figure 22.14)
  - Relief Sculpture from Chavín de Huántar (Figure 26.1c)
  - Martínez, Black-on-black ceramic vessel (Figure 26.14)

The Ambum Stone from Papua New Guinea, c. 1500 B.C.E., greywacke, National Gallery of Australia, Canberra (Figure 1.4)

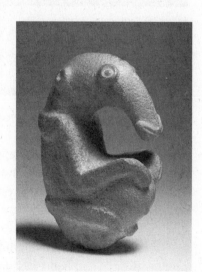

Figure 1.4: The Ambum Stone from Papua New Guinea, c. 1500 B.C.E., greywacke, National Gallery of Australia—Canberra

- Stone Age work, artists used stone to carve stone
- Found in Ambum Valley in Papua New Guinea
- Composite human/animal figure; perhaps an anteater head and a human body
- Theories:
  - Masked human
  - Anteater embryo in a fetal position
  - Anteaters thought of as significant because of their fat deposits
  - May have been a pestle
  - Perhaps a ritual purpose; considered sacred
- **Cross-Cultural Comparisons: Animal Forms**
  - Detail from the Lakshamana Temple (Figure 23.7c)
  - Tuffery, *Pisupo Lua Afe (Corned Beef 2000)* (Figure 26.15)
  - Buk Mask (Figure 28.9)

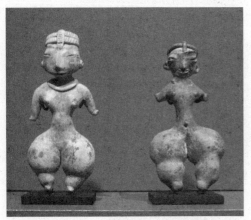

Figure 1.5: Tlatilco Female Figures, c. 1200–900 B.C.E., ceramic, Princeton University Art Museum, Princeton, New Jersey

Tlatilco Female Figures, c. 1200-900 B.C.E., ceramic, Princeton University Art Museum, Princeton, New Jersey (Figure 1.5)

- Tlatilco, Mexico, noted for pottery
- Many shapes and forms: male, female, couples, genre scenes, ball playing games, animals, imaginary creatures, etc.
- Female figures show elaborate details of hair styles, clothing, and body ornaments
- Many show deformities including the two-headed females: perhaps signifying a cluster of conjoined or Siamese twins; stillborn
- Theories that they show bifacial images, and therefore would show the first evidence of congenital defects
- May have had shamanistic function
- Style: flipper-like arms, huge thighs, pronounced hips, narrow waists, unclothed except for jewelry; arms extend from body
- **Cross-Cultural Comparisons: Human Figure**
  - Veranda post (Figure 27.14)
  - Power figure (Figure 27.6)
  - *Reliquary of Sainte-Foy* (Figure 11.6c)

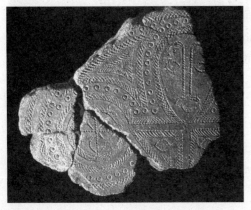

Figure 1.6: Terra-cotta fragment from the Solomon Islands, 1000 B.C.E., terra-cotta, University of Aukland, New Zealand

Terra-cotta fragment. Lapita, from the Solomon Islands, 1000 B.C.E., terra cotta, University of Aukland, New Zealand (Figure 1.6)

- Lapita culture of the Solomon Islands, known for their pottery
- Characteristic use of curved stamped patterns: dots, circles, hatching
- Outlined forms: used a comb-like tool to stamp designs onto the clay
- One of the oldest human faces in Oceanic Art
- **Cross-Cultural Comparisons: Motifs in Pacific Art**
  - Hiapo (Figure 28.6)
  - Malagan mask (Figure 28.8)
  - Lindauer, *Tamati Waka Nene* (Figure 28.7)

Prehistoric Painting

Most prehistoric paintings that survive exist in caves, sometimes deeply recessed from their openings. Images of animals dominate with black outlines emphasizing their contours. Paintings appear to be placed about the cave surface with no relationship to one another. Indeed, cave paintings may have been executed over the centuries by various groups who wanted to establish a presence in a given location.

Although animals are realistically represented with a palpable three-dimensionality, humans are depicted as stick figures with little anatomical detail.

Handprints abound in cave paintings, most of them as negative prints, meaning that a hand was placed on the wall and paint blown or splattered over it, leaving a silhouette. Since most people are right-handed, the handprints are of left hands, the right being used to apply the paint. Handprints occasionally show missing joints or fingers, perhaps indicating that prehistoric people practiced voluntary mutilation. However, the thumb, the most essential finger, is never harmed.

Apollo 11 stones, c. 25,500–25,300 B.C.E., charcoal on stone, State Museum of Namibia, Windhoek, Namibia (Figure 1.7)

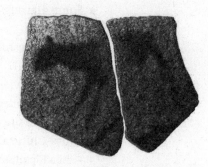

Figure 1.7: Apollo 11 stones, c. 25,500–25,300 B.C.E., charcoal on stone, State Museum of Namibia, Windhoek, Namibia

- Some of the world's oldest works of art, found in Wonderwerk Cave in Namibia
- Profile of an animal seen in profile, done in charcoal
- Several stone fragments found
- Named after the Apollo 11 moon landing; cave was discovered at the time of the moon landing

Lascaux Caves, 15,000–13,000 B.C.E., pigment on rock, Dordogne, France (Figure 1.8)

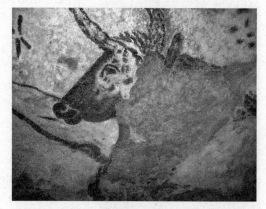

Figure 1.8: Great Hall of the Bulls, 15,000–13,000 B.C.E., pigment on rock, Dordogne, France

- Natural products used to make paint: charcoal, iron ore, plants
- 650 paintings: most common are cows, bulls, horses, and deer
- Animals placed deep inside cave, some hundreds of feet from the entrance
- Bodies seen in profile; frontal or diagonal view of horns, eyes, and hooves; some animals appear pregnant
- Many overlapping figures
- Evidence still visible of scaffolding erected to get to higher areas of the caves
- Caves were not dwellings because prehistoric people led migratory lives following herds of animals; some evidence exists that people sought shelter at the mouths of caves
- Walls were scraped to an even surface; paint colors were bound with animal fat; lamps light the interior of caves; flat stones served as palettes
- Many theories about reasons for the paintings:
  - Traditional view that they were used to ensure a successful hunt
  - Ancestral animal worship
  - Shamanism: a religion based on the idea that the forces of nature can be contacted by intermediaries, called shamans, who go into a trancelike state to reach another state of consciousness
- **Cross-Cultural Comparisons: Mural Paintings**
  - Tomb of the Triclinium (Figure 5.3)
  - Leonardo DaVinci, *Last Supper* (Figure 16.1)
  - Walker, *Darkytown Rebellion* (Figure 29.21)

Running Horned Woman, 6,000–4,000 B.C.E., rock painting, Tassili n'Ajjer, Algeria (Figure 1.9)

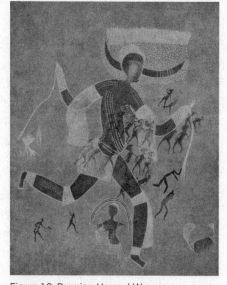

Figure 1.9: Running Horned Woman, 6,000–4,000 B.C.E., rock painting, Tassili n'Ajjer, Algeria

- More than 15,000 drawings and engravings found at this site
- At one time the area was grasslands; climate changes have turned it into desert

- Some drawings are naturalistic, some abstract; some Negroid features, some Caucasian features
- Depicts livestock (cows, sheep, etc.); wildlife (giraffes, lions, etc.); humans (hunting, harvesting, etc.)
- Composite view of the body
- Dots may reflect body paint applied for ritual
- The entire site was probably painted by many different groups over a large expanse of time
- **Cross-Cultural Comparisons: Masks and Headdresses**
  - Aka Elelphant Mask (Figure 27.12)
  - Ikenga (Figure 27.10)
  - Malagan mask (Figure 28.8)

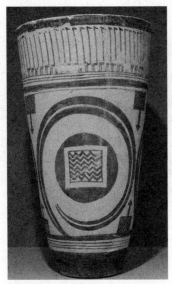

Figure 1.10: Beaker with ibex motifs, 4,200–3,500 B.C.E., terra-cotta, Louvre, Paris

Beaker with ibex motifs, 4,200–3,500 B.C.E., terra-cotta, Louvre, Paris (Figure 1.10)

- Found near a burial site, but not with human remains
- Found with hundreds of baskets, bowls, and metallic items
- Use of potter's wheel, a technological advance
- Thin walls of pot
- Frieze of stylized aquatic birds on top; below stylized running dogs with long narrow bodies
- Oversized horns, abstract stylized motif
- In the middle of the horns is a clan symbol of family ownership
- Perhaps the image identifies the deceased as belonging to a particular group or family
- Made in Susa, in Southwestern Iran
- **Cross-Cultural Comparisons: Ceramics**
  - Martínez, Black-on-black ceramic vessel (Figure 26.14)
  - The David Vases (Figure 24.11)
  - Koons, *Pink Panther* (Figure 29.9)

Prehistoric Architecture

Prehistoric people were known to build shelters out of large animal bones heaped in the shape of a semicircular hut. However, the most famous structures were not for habitation but almost certainly for worship. Sometimes **menhirs**, or large individual stones, were erected singularly or in long rows stretching into the distance. Menhirs cut into rectangular shapes and used in the construction of a prehistoric complex are called **megaliths**. A circle of megaliths, usually with lintels placed on top, is called a **henge**. These were no small accomplishments, since these Neolithic structures were built to align with the important dates in the calendar. Prehistoric people built structures in which two uprights were used to support a horizontal beam, thereby establishing **post-and-lintel** (Figure 1.11) architecture, the most fundamental type of architecture in history.

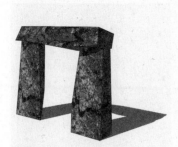

Figure 1.11: Post-and-lintel construction

Stonehenge, c. 2500–1600 B.C.E., Sandstone, Wiltshire, England (Figures 1.12a and 1.12b)

- Perhaps took a thousand years to build, gradually redeveloped by each succeeding generation
- Post-and-lintel building; lintels grooved in place by the mortise-and-tenon system of construction
- Large megaliths in center are over 20 feet tall and form a horseshoe surrounding a central flat stone
- Ring of megaliths, originally all united by lintels, surrounds central horseshoe
- Some stones over 50 tons
- Hundreds of smaller stones of unknown purpose placed around monument
- Some stones imported from over 200 miles away
- Generally thought to be oriented toward sunrise on the longest day of the year; may also predict eclipses
- New theory posits that Stonehenge was the center of ceremonies concerning death and burial
- One of many henges in southern England; the most recently discovered in July 2009 is called Bluehenge
- **Cross-Cultural Comparisons: Ritual Centers**
  - Chavín de Huántar (Figure 26.1a, 26.1b)
  - Pantheon (Figures 6.11a, 6.11b)
  - Great Mosque of Djenne (Figure 27.2)

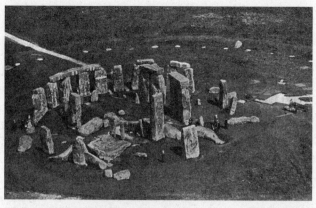

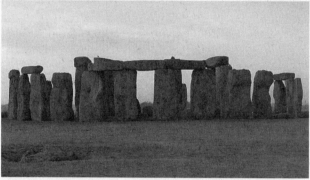

Figures 1.12a and 1.12b: Stonehenge, c. 2500–1600 B.C.E., sandstone, Wiltshire, England

VOCABULARY

Anthropomorphic: having characteristics of the human form, although the form itself is not human (Figure 1.2)

Archaeology: the scientific study of ancient people and cultures principally revealed through excavation

Cong: a tubular object with a circular hole cut into a square-like cross section (Figure 1.3)

Henge: a Neolithic monument, characterized by a circular ground plan. Used for rituals and marking astronomical events (Figure 1.12b)

Lintel: a horizontal beam over an opening (Figure 1.12)

Megalith: a stone of great size used in the construction of a prehistoric structure

Menhir: a large uncut stone erected as a monument in the prehistoric era; a standing stone

Mortise-and-tenon: a groove cut into stone or wood, called a mortise, that is shaped to receive a tenon, or projection, of the same dimensions

Post-and-lintel: a method of construction in which two posts support a horizontal beam, called a lintel (Figure 1.11)

Shamanism: a religion in which good and evil are brought about by spirits which can be influenced by shamans, who have access to these spirits

Stele (plural: **stelae**): an upright stone slab used to mark a grave or a site (Figure 1.2)

Stylized: a schematic, nonrealistic manner of representing the visible world and its contents, abstracted from the way that they appear in nature (Figure 1.2)

SUMMARY

Prehistoric works of art have the power to amaze and intrigue viewers in the modern world, even though so little is known about their original intention, creation, or meaning. The creative impulse exists with the earliest of human endeavors, as is evidenced by the cave paintings from Lascaux and sculptures such as the anthropomorphic stele. The first type of construction, the post-and-lintel method, was developed during the Neolithic period to build monumental structures like Stonehenge.

PRACTICE EXERCISES

Multiple-Choice

1. Artists working on prehistoric caves used all of the following tools to create their images EXCEPT

    (A) scaffolds to reach high areas in a cave
    (B) paints made from ocher and natural materials
    (C) brushes made from human hair
    (D) flat stones used as palettes

2. Stylized animal forms appear in all of the following EXCEPT

    (A) terra-cotta fragment, Lapita, Solomon Islands
    (B) Apollo 11 Stones
    (C) The Ambum Stone
    (D) camelid sacrum in the shape of a canine

3. Prehistoric images of people wearing masks, such as the "Running Horned Woman," indicate an ancient interest in

    (A) coronation of royalty and a sophisticated power structure
    (B) a formal hierarchy of religious leaders, including women
    (C) ceremonial centers and designated performers
    (D) ritual presentations in which the participants paint their bodies and dance

4. The "beaker with ibex motifs" was found at a site in the city of Susa, indicating that it was used

    (A) as part of a burial tradition
    (B) in business transactions
    (C) in a domestic setting
    (D) for governmental correspondence

5. Many prehistoric works were layered by successive generations of artists over the course of centuries. This is true of all of the following works EXCEPT

(A) Stonehenge
(B) Lascaux
(C) Running Horned Woman
(D) camelid sacrem in the shape of a canine

Short Essay

This jade cong was made in Neolithic China. It has a function that can be surmised from the site it is associated with.

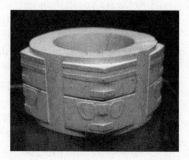

Where were jade congs found?

What can be understood about jade congs given their find spot?

Describe the images done in relief on the cong, *and* interpret their possible meanings.

ANSWER KEY

1. **C**   2. **A**   3. **D**   4. **A**   5. **D**

ANSWERS EXPLAINED

Multiple-Choice

1. **(C)** A prehistoric artist's toolkit included scaffolds, palettes, brushes, and paints. Human hair, however, is too supple to be used as brushes. Animal bristles were preferred.

2. **(A)** All of these have animal designs, except for the terra-cotta fragment, which has an anamorphic face.

3. **(D)** Rituals were important aspects of prehistoric culture; hence, they are depicted fairly regularly in the prehistoric art that survives in Africa.

4. **(A)** The beaker was found at a burial site and was used for mortuary purposes, although no trace of human remains were found inside.

5. **(D)** It took hundreds, in fact sometimes thousands, of years to complete monuments like Stonehenge or Lascaux. "Running Horned Woman" is layered atop many elements of preexisting paintings and was later painted over by other artists. This is not true of the camelid sacrum, which is a lone object.

Short-Essay Rubric

Question	Points	Key Points in a Good Response
Where were jade congs found?	1	Jades appear in burials of people of high rank. Jade religious objects are found in tombs; they're interred with the dead in elaborate rituals.
What can be understood about jade congs given their findspot?	2	Answers could include: ■ Placed in burials around bodies, some are broken and some show signs of intentional burning. ■ Jade is treasured by Chinese for its durability and its color. ■ Jade buried along with dead indicates a special reverence for the dead. ■ Jade must have possessed a special spiritual quality since it was found in so many burials.
Describe the images done in relief on the cong, and interpret their possible meanings.	2	Answers could include: ■ Abstract designs; main decoration is a face pattern, perhaps of spirits or deities ■ Four corners of the cong usually carry mask-like images with pronounced eyes and fanged mouth. ■ Chinese linked jade with virtues: durability, subtlety, beauty.

Content Area: Ancient Mediterranean

Ancient Near Eastern Art

2

TIME PERIOD: 3500 B.C.E.–641 C.E.

Sumerian Art	c. 3500–2340 B.C.E.	Iraq
Babylonian Art	1792–1750 B.C.E.	Iraq
Assyrian Art	883–612 B.C.E.	Iraq
Persian Art	c. 559–331 B.C.E.	Iran

ENDURING UNDERSTANDING: Ancient Near Eastern art concentrates on royal figures and gods.

Essential Knowledge:

- Ancient Near Eastern art takes place mostly in city-states of Mesopotamia.
- Art from this region is one of the foundations of art history.

ENDURING UNDERSTANDING: Ancient Near Eastern art is inspired by religion; kings often assume divine attributes.

Essential Knowledge:

- Figures are constructed within stylistic conventions of the time, including hierarchy of scale, registers, and stylized human forms.
- Ancient Near Eastern architecture is characterized by ziggurats and palaces.

HISTORICAL BACKGROUND

The Ancient Near East is where almost everything began first: writing, cities, organized religion, organized government, laws, agriculture, bronze casting, even the wheel. It is hard to think of any other civilization that gave the world as much as the ancient Mesopotamians.

Large populations emerged in the fertile river valleys that lie between the Tigris and Euphrates Rivers. City centers boomed as urbanization began to take hold. Each group of people vied to control the central valleys, taking turns occupying the land and eventually relinquishing it to others. This layering of civilizations has made for a rich archaeological repository of successive cultures whose entire history has yet to be uncovered.

Patronage and Artistic Life

Kings sensed from the beginning that artists could help glorify their careers. Artists could aggrandize images, bring the gods to life, and sculpt narrative tales that would outlast a king's lifetime. They could also write in cuneiform and imprint royal names on everything from cylinder seals to grand relief sculptures. This was the start of one of the most symbiotic relationships in art history between patron and artist.

ANCIENT NEAR EASTERN ART

One of the most fundamental differences between the prehistoric world and the civilizations of the Ancient Near East is the latter's need to urbanize; buildings were constructed to live, govern, and worship in. However, in the Near East, stone was at a premium and wood was scarce but earth was in abundant supply. The first great buildings of the ancient world, **ziggurats**, were made of baked mud, and they were tall, solid structures that dominated the flat landscape. Although mud needed care to protect it from erosion, it was a cheap material that could be resupplied easily.

Human beings did not play a central role in prehistoric art. Lascaux has precisely one male figure but six hundred cave paintings of animals. A few human figures like the Anthromorphic Stele populated a sculptural world full of animals and spirals. However, in the Near East artists were more likely to depict clothed humans with anatomical precision. Near Eastern figures are actively engaged in doing something: Hunting, praying, performing a ritual.

One of the characteristics of civilizations that settle down rather than nomadically wander is the size of the sculpture they produce. Nomadic people cannot carry large objects on their migrations, but cities retain monumental objects as a sign of their permanence. Near Eastern sculptures could be very large—the **lamassus**, man-headed winged bulls, at Persepolis are gigantic. The interiors of palaces were filled with large-scale relief sculptures gently carved into stone surfaces.

The invention of writing enabled people to permanently record business transactions in a wedge-shaped script called **cuneiform**. Laws were written down, taxes were accounted for and collected, and the first written epic, *Gilgamesh*, was copied onto a series of tablets. Stories needed to be illustrated, making narrative painting a necessity. Walls of ancient palaces not only had sculptures of rulers and gods but also had narratives of their exploits.

Near Eastern art begins a popular ancient tradition of representing animals with human characteristics and emotions; some Sumerian animals have human heads. The personification of animals was continued by the Egyptians (the Sphinx) and the Greeks (the Minotaur), sometimes producing dreadful and harmful creations. There was also a trend to combine animal parts, as in the *Lamassu* (c. 700 B.C.E.) (Figure 2.5), with the human head at the top of a hoofed winged animal.

SUMERIAN ART

Sumerian art, as contrasted with prehistoric art, has realistic looking figures acting out identifiable narratives. Figures are cut from stone, with **negative space** hollowed out under their arms and between their legs. Eyes are always wide open; men are bare-chested and wear a kilt. Women have their left shoulder covered; their right is exposed. Nudity is a sign of debasement; only slaves and prisoners are nude. Sculptures were placed on stands to hold them upright. There was a free intermixing of animal and human forms, so it is common to see human heads on animal bodies, and vice versa. Humans are virtually emotionless.

Important figures are the largest and most centrally placed in a given composition. Such an arrangement is called **hierarchy of scale** and can be seen in the **Standard of Ur** (c. 2600 B.C.E.) (Figures 2.3a, 2.3b), in which the king is the tallest figure, located in the middle of the top register.

In the Sumerian world the gods symbolized powers that were manifest in nature. The local god was an advocate for a given city in the assembly of gods. Thus, it was incumbent upon the city to preserve the god and his representative, the king, as well as possible. The temple, therefore, became the center point of both civic and religious pride.

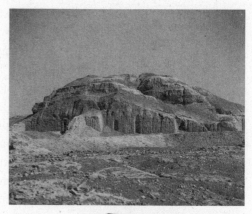
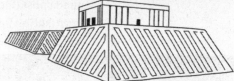

Figures 2.1a and 2.1b: White Temple and its ziggurat with reconstruction, c. 3500–3000 B.C.E., mud brick, Uruk, Iraq

White Temple and its ziggurat, c. 3500–3000 B.C.E., mud brick, Uruk, Iraq (Figure 2.1)

- Large settlement at Uruk of 40,000 based on agriculture and specialized labor
- Deity was Anu, the god of the sky, the most important Sumerian deity
- Mud-brick building on a colossal scale
- Buttresses spaced across the surface to create a light and shadow pattern
- Whitewash used to disguise the mud appearance
- Tapers down so that rainwater washes off
- Temple on the top was small, set back, and removed from the populace; accessed reserved for royalty and clergy, only base of temple remains
- Temple interior contains a cella, and smaller rooms
- On top of the ziggurat is a terrace for outdoor rituals; temple for indoor rituals
- Entire form resembles a mountain; contrast of vast flat terrain and man-made mountain
- Gods descend from the heavens to a high place on earth, hence the Sumerians built ziggurats as high places
- Four corners oriented to the compass
- **Cross-Cultural Comparisons: Religious Centers on Hilltops**
  - Yaxchilán Structure 40 (Figure 26.2a)
  - Templo Mayor, Tenochtitlan (Figure 26.5a)
  - Acropolis (Figure 4.16a)

Statues of votive figures, from the Square Temple at Eshnunna (modern Tell Asmar, Iraq), c. 2700 B.C.E., gypsum inlaid with shell and black limestone, Iraq Museum, Baghdad and the University of Chicago, Chicago (Figure 2.2)

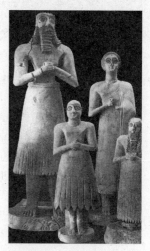

Figure 2.2: Statues of votive figures, from the Square Temple at Eshnunna (modern Tell Asmar, Iraq), c. 2700 B.C.E., gypsum inlaid with shell and black limestone, Iraq Museum, Baghdad and the University of Chicago, Chicago

- Figures are of different heights, denoting hierarchy of scale
- Hands are folded in gesture of prayer
- Huge eyes in awe, spellbound, perhaps staring at the deity
- Men: bare upper chest; skirt from waist down; beard flows in ripple patterns; wear a belt

- Women: dress draped over one shoulder
- Arms and feet cut away
- Pinkie in a spiral; chin a wedge shape; ear a double volute
- Inscribed on back: "It offers prayers"
- Figures represent mortals, placed in a temple and praying—perhaps to the god Abu
- Figures sometimes hold either cups or branches in their hands
- Gods and humans physically present in their statues
- None have been found *in situ* but buried in groups under the temple floor
- Hundreds of statuettes survive
- **Cross-Cultural Comparisons: Shrine Figures**
  - Female Deity from Nukuoro (Figure 28.2)
  - Veranda post (Figure 27.14)
  - *Ikenga* (shrine figure) (Figure 27.10)

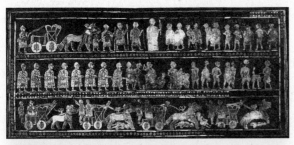

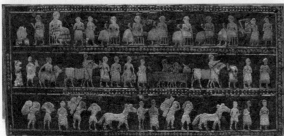

Figures 2.3a and 2.3b: *Peace* (left) and *War* (right) from the Standard of Ur, c. 2600–2400 B.C.E., wood inlaid with shell, lapis lazuli, and red limestone, British Museum, London

Standard of Ur, c. 2600–2400 B.C.E., wood inlayed with shell, lapis lazuli, and limestone, British Museum, London (Figures 2.3a and 2.3b)

- Two sides: war side and peace side; may have been two halves of a narrative; early example of a historical narrative
- Perhaps used as part of soundbox for a musical instrument
- War side: Sumerian king half a head taller, has descended from his chariot to inspect captives brought before him, some debased by their nakedness; chariots advance over the dead in lowest register
- Peace Side: food brought in a procession to the banquet; musician playing a lyre; ruler wears a kilt made of tufts of wool; larger than others
- Reflects extensive trading network: lapis lazuli from Afghanistan; shells from Persian Gulf; red limestone from India

- Figures have broad frontal shoulders, body in profile
- Emphasized eyes, eyebrows, ears
- Organized in registers; figures stand on ground lines; reads from bottom to top
- **Cross-Cultural Comparisons: Narrative in Art**
  - *Bayeux Tapestry* (Figures 11.7a, 11.7b)
  - Column of Trajan (Figure 6.16)
  - *Night Attack on the Sanjô Palace* (Figures 25.3a, 25.3b)

BABYLONIAN ART

Because of the survival of the famous **Stele of Hammurabi** (c. 1792–1750 B.C.E.) (Figure 2.4), Babylon comes down to us as a seemingly well-ordered state with a set of strict laws handed down from the god, Shamash, himself. Nothing was spared in the decoration of the capital, Babylon, covered with its legendary hanging gardens and walls of glazed tile.

Stele of Hammurabi, c. 1792–1750 B.C.E., basalt, Louvre, Paris (Figures 2.4a and 2.4b)

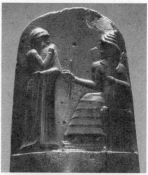

- Hammurabi 1792–1750 B.C.E. united Mesopotamia in his lifetime
- Took Babylon from a small power to a dominant kingdom, but at his death the empire dwindled
- Text in Akkadian language, read right to left and top to bottom in fifty-one columns
- Contains one of the earliest law codes ever written below the main scene and on the reverse
- Sun god, Shamash, enthroned on a ziggurat and handing Hammurabi a rope, a ring, and a rod of kingship
- Shamash: frontal and profile at the same time, headdress in profile; rays (wings?) from behind his shoulder
- Shamash, judge of the sky and the earth, with tiara of four rows of horns, presents signs of royal power, the scepter and the ring, to Hammurabi
- Shamash's beard is fuller than Hammurabi's
- Hammurabi with a speaking/greeting gesture
- They stare at one another directly, even though their shoulders are frontal; composite views
- 300 law entries placed below the grouping, symbolically given from Shamash himself to Hammurabi
- Bas-relief
- **Cross-Cultural Comparisons: Humans and the Divine**
  - Jayavarman VII as Buddha (Figure 23.8d)
  - Bichitr, *Jahangir Preferring a Sufi Shaikh to Kings* (Figure 23.9)
  - Bernini, *Ecstasy of Saint Teresa* (Figures 17.4a, 17.4b)

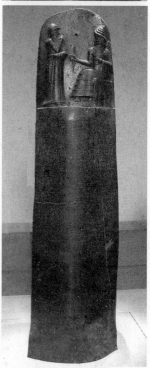

Figure 2.4a and 2.4b: Stele of Hammurabi, c. 1792–1750 B.C.E., basalt, Louvre, Paris

ASSYRIAN ART

Assyrian artists praised the greatness of their king, his ability to kill his enemies, his valor at hunting, and his masculinity. Figures are stoic, even while hunting lions or defeating an enemy. Animals, however, possess considerable emotion. Lions are in anguish and cry out for help. This domination over a mighty wild beast expressed the authority of the king over his people and the powerful forces of nature.

Cuneiform appears everywhere in Assyrian art; it is common to see words written across a scene, even over the bodies of figures. Shallow **relief sculpture** is an Assyrian specialty, although the lamassus are virtually three-dimensional as they project noticeably from the walls they are attached to.

Lamassu, c. 720–705 B.C.E., alabaster, Louvre, Paris (Figure 2.5)

- Human-headed animal guardian figures
- Winged
- Five legs: when seen from front seems to be standing at attention; when seen from side, seems to be walking by you as you walk by it
- Meant to ward off enemies both visible and invisible, apotropaic
- Has a feeling of harmony and stability

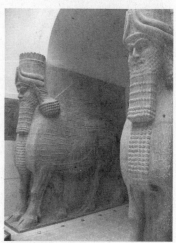

Figure 2.5: Lamassu, c. 720–705 B.C.E., alabaster, Louvre, Paris

- Sargon II founded a capital at Khorsabad, surrounded by a city wall with seven gates
- Protective spirits placed at either side of each gate as guardians; also bore the weight of the arches above the gates
- **Cross-Cultural Comparisons: Hybrid Figures**
  - Sphinx (Figure 3.6a)
  - Buk Mask (Figure 28.9)
  - Mutu, *Preying Mantra* (Figure 29.25)

PERSIAN ART

Persia was the largest empire the world had seen up to this time. As the first great empire in history, it needed an appropriate capital as a grand stage to impress people at home and dignitaries from abroad. The Persians erected monumental architecture, huge audience halls, and massive subsidiary buildings for grand ceremonies that glorified their country and their rulers (Figure 2.6). Persian architecture is characterized by columns topped by two bull-shaped **capitals** holding up a wooden roof.

Persepolis, c. 520–465 B.C.E., limestone, Iran (Figures 2.6a and 2.6b)

- Built by Darius I and Xerxes I; destroyed by Alexander the Great
- Built not so much as a complex of palaces but rather as a seat for spectacular receptions and festivals
- Built on artificial terraces, as is most Mesopotamian architecture
- Mud-brick with stone facing

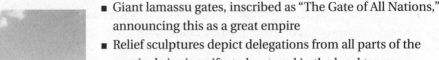

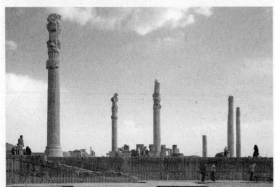

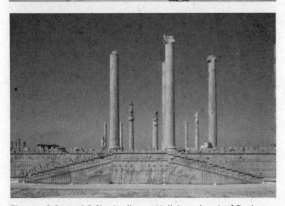

- Giant lamassu gates, inscribed as "The Gate of All Nations," announcing this as a great empire
- Relief sculptures depict delegations from all parts of the empire bringing gifts to be stored in the local treasury; Darius selected this central location in Persia to ensure protection of the treasury
- Audience hall: apadana, had 36 columns covered by a wooden roof; held thousands of people; used for the king's receptions; stairways adorned with reliefs of the New Year's festival and a procession of representatives of 23 subject nations
- Columns had a bell-shaped base that is an inverted lotus blossom, capitals are bulls or lions
- Carved onto the stairs are the Immortals, the King's Guard, who were so-called because they always numbered 10,000
- Many cultures (i.e., Greeks, Egyptians, Babylonians) contributed to the building of the site
- Everything seems to have been built to dwarf the viewer
- Stairs have a central relief of the king enthroned with attendants; crown prince behind him with dignitaries bowing before him
- Orderly and harmonious world symbolized by static processions

Figures 2.6a and 2.6b: Audience Hall (apadana) of Darius and Xerxes, c. 520–465 B.C.E., limestone, Persepolis, Iran

■ **Cross-Cultural Comparisons: Ceremonial Spaces**
  - Forum of Trajan (Figure 6.10a)
  - Forbidden City (Figure 24.2a)
  - Great Zimbabwe (Figures 27.1a, 27.1b)

VOCABULARY

Apadana: an audience hall in a Persian palace (Figure 2.6a)

Apotropaic: having the power to ward off evil or bad luck

Capital: the top element of a column

Cella: the main room of a temple where the god is housed

Cuneiform: a system of writing in which the strokes are formed in a wedge or arrowhead shape

Façade: the front of a building. Sometimes, more poetically, a speaker can refer to a "side façade" or a "rear façade"

Ground line: a base line upon which figures stand (Figure 2.3)

Ground plan: the map of a floor of a building

Hierarchy of scale: a system of representation that expresses a person's importance by the size of his or her representation in a work of art (Figure 2.3)

Lamassu: a colossal winged human-headed bull in Assyrian art (Figure 2.5)

Negative space: empty space around an object or a person, such as the cut-out areas between a figure's legs or arms of a sculpture

Register: a horizontal band, often on top of another, that tells a narrative story (Figure 2.3)

Relief sculpture: sculpture that projects from a flat background. A very shallow relief sculpture is called a **bas-relief** (pronounced: bah-relief) (Figure 2.4)

Stele (plural: **stelae):** a stone slab used to mark a grave or a site (Figure 2.4)

Votive: offered in fulfillment of a vow or a pledge (Figure 2.2)

Ziggurat: a pyramid-like building made of several stories that indent as the building gets taller; thus, ziggurats have terraces at each level (Figure 2.1)

SUMMARY

The Ancient Near East saw the birth of world civilizations, symbolized by the first works of art that were used in the service of religion and the state. Rulers were quick to see that their image could be permanently emblazoned on stelae that celebrated their achievements for posterity to admire. The new invention of writing created a systematic historical and artistic record of human achievement.

Common characteristics of Ancient Near Eastern art include the union of human and animal elements in a single figure, the use of hierarchy of scale, and the deification of rulers.

Because the Mesopotamian river valleys were poor in stone, most buildings in this region were made of mud-brick and were either painted or faced with tile or stone. Entranceways to cities and palaces were important; fantastic animals acted as guardian figures to protect the occupants and ward off the evil intentions of outsiders.

Multiple-Choice

1. The Standard of Ur, an ancient Sumerian work, shows that at an early date there was extensive trading between peoples. All of the following elements on this work were imported through trade EXCEPT

    (A) lapis lazuli from Afghanistan
    (B) shells from the Persian Gulf coast
    (C) red limestone from India
    (D) marble from Greece

Questions 2–4 refer to the images below.

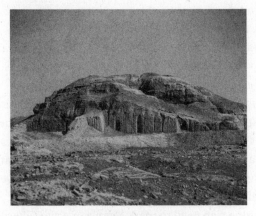

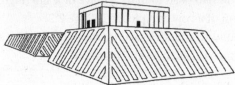

2. The White Temple is constructed on a large platform base that raises it above the ground and gives the structure considerable height. This technique was highly influential for hundreds of years and can be seen in

    (A) the Great Stupa from Sanchi, India
    (B) the Great Pyramids of Gizeh, Egypt
    (C) the Palace of Darius, at Persepolis, Iran
    (D) Stonehenge in Wiltshire, England

3. The White Temple and its ziggurat symbolize all of the following EXCEPT

    (A) the gods required their buildings to be of mud-brick to represent the impermanence of life
    (B) the gods live in a place high above the mortals
    (C) the gods live in relative seclusion at the top of a ziggurat, approachable by a select few
    (D) the gods have a central role in daily life

4. The White Temple and its ziggurat has all of the following design elements EXCEPT

   (A) it has tapered sides for the purpose of washing off rain water
   (B) it was originally painted to relieve the oppressiveness of the color of mud
   (C) the entire structure was meant to physically and symbolically represent a mountain
   (D) it has a small interior chamber that held the tomb of the King

---

5. The laws expressed on the Code of Hammurabi can be summarized as

   (A) forgiveness is the highest form of justice
   (B) the only way to deter crime is to muse the death penalty
   (C) justice depends on your ability to pay
   (D) the punishment reflects the crime

Short Essay

This is the Code of Hammurabi. A common feature in ancient art is the depiction of a human interacting with a god.

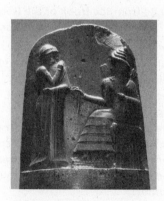
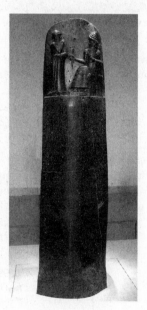

Who is the god in this sculpture?

Identify another work in which the gods interact with humans.

Analyze how the artist has represented the interaction of humans and gods in both works.

ANSWER KEY

1. **D**   2. **C**   3. **D**   4. **A**   5. **D**

Multiple-Choice

1. **(D)** This work has no marble in it.

2. **(C)** The Palace of Darius is also raised on a high platform to give it a more formidable presence.

3. **(D)** The ziggurat is not built of impermanent materials because it represents the passing of life; it was built of mud-brick because that was the only building material available to the Sumerians.

4. **(D)** There is no indication that there were any burials associated with the White Temple or its ziggurat.

5. **(A)** The laws on the Hammurabi code can be summarized as the punishment fits the crime. What you have done will be done unto you.

Short-Essay Rubric

Question	Points	Key Points in a Good Response
Who is the god in this sculpture?	1	The Babylonian god Shamash
Identify another work in which the gods interact with humans.	2	Answers could include: ■ *Palette of King Narmer*, Predynastic Egypt, c. 3000–2920 B.C.E. Greywacke ■ *Last Judgment of Hu-Nefer*, from his tomb (page from the Book of the Dead), Egyptian, c. 1275 B.C.E., painted papyrus scroll
Analyze how the artist has represented the interaction of humans and gods in both works.	2	Answers could include: ■ Humans are secondary, subservient, and stand before the gods. ■ The gods appear as enthroned, seated, and larger than the humans. ■ The gods are elaborately adorned and highlighted against an empty space; they generally have fanciful headdresses. ■ The humans wear respectful, but plainer, clothes. ■ The gods carry emblems of their power and their faith. ■ Humans listen attentively to the gods.

Egyptian Art

3

TIME PERIOD: 3000–30 B.C.E.

The most relevant artistic periods in Egyptian art are the following:

Old Kingdom	2575–2134 B.C.E.
New Kingdom	1550–1070 B.C.E.

ENDURING UNDERSTANDING: Egyptian art was created around ideas concerning eternity, the afterlife, and rebirth.

Essential Knowledge:

- Funerary objects dominate, including large-scale sculptures, stone architecture, and tomb artifacts—all in the service of the god-like pharaoh.
- Strict Egyptian stylistic formulas are applied to the gods and pharaohs; they clearly show others to be subordinate and lacking in idealization.

HISTORICAL BACKGROUND

Egypt gives the appearance of being a monolithic civilization whose history stretches steadily into the past with little change or fluctuation. However, Egyptian history is a constant ebb and flow of dynastic fortunes, at times at the height of its powers, other times invaded by jealous neighbors or wracked by internal feuds.

Historical Egypt begins with the unification of the country under King Narmer in predynastic times, an event celebrated on the **Narmer Palette** (3000–2920 B.C.E.) (Figure 3.4). The subsequent early dynasties, known as the Old Kingdom, featured massively built monuments to the dead, called **pyramids**, which are emblematic of Egypt today.

After a period of anarchy, Mentihotep II unified Egypt for a second time in a period called the Middle Kingdom. Pyramid building was abandoned in favor of smaller and certainly less expensive rock-cut tombs.

More anarchy followed the breakdown of the Middle Kingdom. Invaders from Asia swept through, bringing technological advances along with their domination. Soon enough, Egyptians righted their political ship, removed the foreigners, and embarked upon the New Kingdom, a period of unparalleled splendor.

One New Kingdom pharaoh, Akhenaton, markedly altered Egyptian society by abandoning the worship of the many gods and substituting one god, Aton, with himself portrayed as his representative on Earth. Aton was different from prior Egyptian gods because he was represented as a sun disk emanating rays, instead of gods that were human and/or animal symbols. This new religion ushered in a dramatic change in artistic style called the **Amarna Period**. Although Akhenaton's religious innovations did not survive him, the artistic changes he promoted were long lasting.

After the demise of the New Kingdom, Egypt felt prey to the ambitions of Persia, Assyria, and Greece, ultimately undoing itself at the hands of Rome in 30 B.C.E.

Modern Egyptology began with the 1799 discovery of the Rosetta Stone, from which hieroglyphics could, for the first time, be translated into modern languages. Egyptian paintings and sculpture, often laden with text, can now be read and understood.

The feverish scramble to uncover Egyptian artifacts culminated in 1922 with the discovery of King Tutankhamun's tomb by Howard Carter. This is one of the most spectacular archaeological finds in history because it is the only royal Egyptian tomb that has come down to us undisturbed.

Patronage and Artistic Life

Egyptian architecture was designed and executed by highly skilled craftsmen and artisans, not by slaves, as tradition often alleges. The process of mummification, which became a national industry, was handled by embalming experts who were paid handsomely for their exacting and laborious work.

Most artists like Imhotep, history's first recorded artist, should more properly be called artistic overseers, who supervised all work under their direction. They were likely ordained high priests of Ptah, the god who created the world in Egyptian mythology.

As the royal builder for King Djoser, Imhotep erected the first and largest pyramid ever built, the Stepped Pyramid. Indeed, Imhotep's reputation as a master builder so fascinated later Egyptians that he was deified and worshipped as the god of wisdom, astronomy, architecture, and medicine. Few other Egyptian artists' names come down to us.

EGYPTIAN ARCHITECTURE

The iconic image of Egyptian art is the **pyramid**, sitting as it does adrift in the sands of the Sahara. Pyramids were never built alone but as part of great complexes, called **necropolises**, dedicated to the worship of the spirits of the dead and the preservation of an individual's **ka**, or soul.

At first, Egyptians buried their dead in more unassuming places called **mastabas** (Figure 3.1). A mastaba is a simple tomb that has four sloping sides and an entrance for mourners to bring offerings to the deceased. The body was buried beneath the mastaba in an inaccessible area that only the spirit could enter.

Later rulers with grander ambitions began to build larger monuments, heaping the mastaba form one atop the other in smaller dimensions until a pyramid was achieved. The first such example of this is the Stepped Pyramid of King Djoser. Imhotep's complex included temples with **engaged columns** (Figure 3.2).

After several experiments with the pyramid form, the archetypal pyramids such as the ones at Giza (Figure 3.6) evolved with sleek prismatic surfaces. Interiors included false doors so that the ka could come and go when summoned by the faithful.

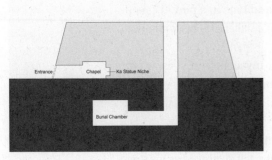

Figure 3.1: Diagram of a mastaba

An Egyptian specialty is carving from living rock. Huge monuments such as the **Great Sphinx** (c. 2500 B.C.E.) (Figure 3.6a) were hewn out of a single great rock; tombs like those at Beni Hasan were carved into hillsides, hollowing out chambers filled with **reserve columns**.

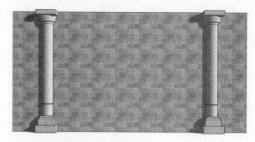

Figure 3.2: Engaged columns

In the New Kingdom, temples continued to be built into the sides of rock formations, as at **Hatshepsut's Mortuary Temple** (1473–1458 B.C.E.) (Figure 3.9a). However, this period also produced free-standing monuments as at **Amen-Re** (Figure 3.8a), which had massive **pylons** on the outside protecting the sanctuary. Behind the pylons lay a central courtyard that greeted the worshipper. The god was housed in a sacred area just beyond, which was surrounded by a forest of columns, called a **hypostyle** hall. Some of the columns were higher than others, allowing limited light and air to enter the complex. This upper area is called a **clerestory**. In a sanctuary submerged in the half-light of the closely placed columns, the god was sheltered so completely that only the high priest could enter.

Egyptian pyramids are known for their sleek solid surfaces and their monumental scale. They are made from stone blocks and built without mortar. Once the dead were interred, no one was permitted entry into these sealed structures. The sides of the pyramids are oriented to the four cardinal points of the compass. The benben (coming from a root meaning to "swell up") was a pyramid-like stone at Heliopolis, Egypt, which formed the prototype for the capstone of the pyramids and/or the pyramids themselves. Pyramid Texts, the oldest religious texts in existence, confirm that the pharaoh's body could be reenergized after death and ascend to the heavens using ramps, stairs, or ladders. He could even become airborne.

The pyramids do not exist in isolation, but are part of a vast temple complex that was strictly organized. The complexes are on the west side of the Nile, so that the pharaoh was interred in the direction of the setting sun. The temples are on the east side of the pyramids, facing the rising sun. Like the pyramids, most Egyptian temples have an astronomical orientation.

Columns used in New Kingdom temples were based on plant shapes: the lotus, the palm, and the papyrus. These column types reflected early construction methods done at a time when Egyptian buildings were supported by perishable materials (Figure 3.3).

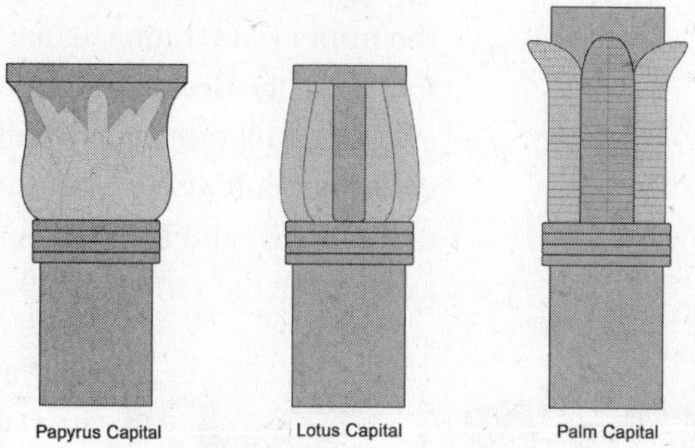

Papyrus Capital   Lotus Capital   Palm Capital

Figure 3.3: Papyrus, lotus, and palm capitals

EGYPTIAN PAINTING AND SCULPTURE

The monumentality of stone sculpture, unseen in ancient Sumeria, is new to art history. Even Egyptian **sarcophagi** were hewn from enormous stones and placed in tombs to protect the dead from vandals.

Hieroglyphics describe the deceased and his or her accomplishments in great detail, without which the dead would have incomplete afterlives. Writing appears both on relief sculpture and on sculpture in the round, as well as on a paper surface called **papyrus**. Hieroglyphics help modern Egyptologists rediscover some of the original intentions of works of art.

Egyptians believed superhuman forces were constantly at work and needed continuous worship. Egyptian funerary art was dedicated to the premise that things that were buried were to last forever and that this life must continue uninterrupted into the next world. To that end, artists affirmed this belief by representing the human figure as completely as possible.

The Egyptian canon of proportions allows for little individuality. Shoulders are seen frontally, while the rest of the body, except the eye, is turned in profile. Often, heads face one direction while the legs face another. Men are taller than women and are painted a ruddy brown or red. Women are shorter—children shorter still—and are painted with a yellowish tinge. Shading is rare.

The ideal is to represent successful men and women acting in a calm, rational manner. Episodes of violence and disorder are limited only to scenes of slaughtering animals for sacrifices or overthrowing the forces of evil; otherwise, Egyptian art is a picture of contentment and stability.

Figures rest on a **ground line** often at the front of the picture plane. When figures are placed on a line above in a **register**, they are thought to be receding into the distance.

Because Egyptians believed in a canon of proportions, artists placed a grid over the areas to be painted and outlined the figures accordingly. Unfinished figures rendered the subject's existence incomplete in the afterlife. Even animals had to be drawn as completely as possible.

In the **Amarna Period** there is a general relaxation of canon rules. Figures are depicted as softer, with slack jaws and protruding stomachs over low-lying belts. Arms become thinner and limbs more flexible, as in the sculpture of **Akhenaton and His Family** (Figure 3.10) in the fourteenth century B.C.E.

Egyptian sculpture ranges in size from the most intimate pieces of jewelry to some of the largest stone sculptures ever created. Huge portraits of the pharaohs are meant to impress and overwhelm; individualization and sophistication are sacrificed for monumentality and grandeur. The stone of choice is limestone from Memphis. Other stones, like gypsum and sandstone, are also used, but hard stones like granite are avoided when possible because of the difficulty in carving with soft metal tools. Wooden sculpture is painted unless made of exceptionally fine material. Metal sculptures of copper and iron also exist.

Large-scale sculptures are rarely entirely cut free of the rock they were carved from. For example, **Menkaura and His Queen** (c. 2490–2472 B.C.E.) (Figure 3.7) has the legs attached to the front of the throne, making the figures seem more permanent and solid. Colossal sculptures, like the **Great Sphinx**, are carved on the site, or **in situ**, from the local available rock.

Relief sculptures follow the same figural formula as paintings. When relief sculptures are carved for outdoor display, they are often cut into the rock so that shadows showed up more dramatically, and the figures thereby become more visible. When carved indoors, reliefs are raised from the surface for visibility in a dark interior.

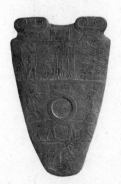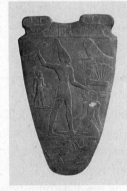

Narmer Palette, 3000–2920 B.C.E., slate, Egyptian Museum, Cairo (Figures 3.4a and 3.4b)

- Relief sculpture depicting King Narmer uniting Upper and Lower Egypt
- Hathor, a god as a cow with a woman's face, depicted four times in the top register
- Figures stand on a ground line
- Hierarchy of scale

Figures 3.4a and 3.4b: Narmer Palette, 3000–2920 B.C.E., greywacke, Egyptian Museum, Cairo

- On front:
  - Narmer, who is the largest figure, wears the cobra crown of lower Egypt and is reviewing the beheaded bodies of the enemy, bodies that are seen from above, with heads carefully placed between their legs
  - Narmer is preceded by four standard bearers and a priest and followed by his foot washer or sandal bearer
  - In the center are harnessed lionesses with elongated necks, possibly symbolizing unification; at the bottom is a symbol of a bull knocking down a city fortress—Narmer knocking over his enemies
- On back:
  - Hawk is Horus, god of Egypt; triumphs over Narmer's foes; Horus holds a rope around a man's head and a papyrus plant, symbols of Lower Egypt
  - Narmer has a symbol of strength, the bull's tail, at his waist; wears a bowling pin-shaped crown as king of united Egypt, beating down an enemy
  - Servant holds Narmer's sandals because he stands on the sacred ground as a divine king
  - Defeated Egyptians lie beneath his feet
- Schematic lines delineate Narmer's muscle structure: forearm veins and thigh muscles are represented by straight lines; half circles for the kneecaps
- Palette used to prepare eye make-up for the blinding sun, although this palette was probably commemorative, or ceremonial
- Hieroglyphics explain and add to the meaning
- Scholars believe the palette conflates actions taking place over many years into one event
- Narrative
- **Cross-Cultural Comparisons: Symbolism**
  - Delacroix, *Liberty Leading the People* (Figure 20.4)
  - Cotsiogo, Hide Painting of a Sun Dance (Figure 26.13)
  - Ruler's Feathered Headdress (Figure 26.6)

Seated scribe, c. 2620–2500 B.C.E., painted limestone, Louvre, Paris (Figure 3.5)

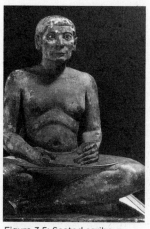

- Created for a tomb at Saqqara as a provision for the ka
- Not a pharaoh: sagging chest and realistic rather than idealistic features
- Color still remains on the sculpture
- Amazingly lifelike, but not a portrait—rather, a conventional image of a scribe
- Attentive expression; thin, angular face
- Contrasts with the ideally portrayed pharaoh
- Holds papyrus in his lap; his writing instrument (now gone) was in his hand ready to write
- **Cross-Cultural Comparisons: Human Figure**
  - Shiva as Nataraja (Figure 23.6)
  - Great Buddha from Todai-ji (Figure 25.10b)
  - Abakanowicz, *Androgyn III* (Figure 29.7)

Figure 3.5: Seated scribe, c. 2620-2500 B.C.E., limestone, Louvre, Paris

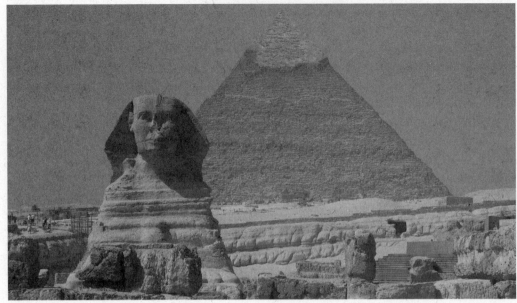

Figure 3.6a: Great Pyramids and the Great Sphinx, c. 2550–2490 B.C.E., limestone, Giza, Egypt

Great Pyramids, c. 2550–2490 B.C.E., limestone, Giza, Egypt (Figures 3.6a and 3.6b)

- Giant monuments to dead pharaohs
- Each pyramid has an enjoining mortuary temple
- Huge pile of limestone with minimal interior for the deceased; pharaoh buried within the pyramid, unlike at the Stepped Pyramid, in which the pharaoh is buried under the building
- Each side of the pyramid oriented toward a point on the compass
- Great Pyramids were faced with stone, most of which has been lost
- Each pyramid has a funerary complex adjacent connected by a formal pathway used for carrying the dead pharaoh's body to the pyramid to be interred
- Shape may have been influenced by a sacred stone relic, called a benben, shaped like a sacred stone found at Heliopolis. Heliopolis was the center of the sun god cult
- Tombs of pharaohs Menkaura, Khufu, and Khafre
- **Cross-Cultural Comparisons: Commemoration of Ruler and Country**
  - Taj Mahal (Figures 9.17a, 9.17b)
  - Houdon, *George Washington* (Figure 19.7)
  - Terra-Cotta Warriors (Figures 24.8a, 24.8b)

Great Sphinx, c. 2500 B.C.E., limestone, Giza, Egypt (Figure 3.6a)

- Very generalized features, although some say it may be a portrait of Khafre, whose pyramid stands behind the Sphinx
- Carved *in situ* from a huge rock, symbol of the sun god
- Body of a lion, head of a pharaoh and/or god
- Sphinx seems to protect the pyramids behind it

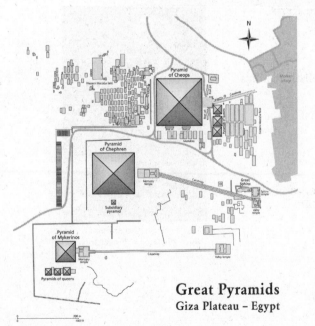

Great Pyramids
Giza Plateau – Egypt

Figure 3.6b: Plan of the Pyramid field

- Originally brightly painted to stand out in the desert
- Cats are royal animals in ancient Egypt, probably because they saved the grain supply from mice
- Head of the Sphinx badly mauled in the Middle Ages
- Fragment of the Sphinx's beard in the British Museum

Menkaura and His Queen, 2490–2472 B.C.E., greywacke, Museum of Fine Arts, Boston (Figure 3.7)

- Figures attached to the block of stone; arms and legs not cut free
- Figures stare out into space
- Wife's simple and affectionate gesture, and/or presenting him to the gods
- Menkaura's powerful physique and stride symbolize his kingship
- Society's view of women expressed in the ankle length and tightly draped gown revealing her form covering her body; men and women the same height, indicating equality
- Original location in the temple of Menkaura's pyramid complex at Gizeh
- **Cross-Cultural Comparisons: Royalty**
  - Lindauer, *Tamati Waka Nene* (Figure 28.7)
  - Wall Plaque from Oba's Palace (Figure 27.3)
  - *Augustus of Prima Porta* (Figure 6.15)

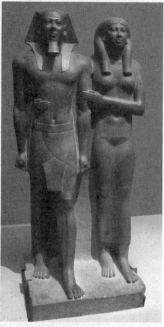

Figure 3.7: *Menkaura and His Queen*, 2490–2472 B.C.E., greywacke, Museum of Fine Arts, Boston

Temple of Amun-Re and Hypostyle Hall, 1550–1250 B.C.E., sandstone and mud brick, near Luxor, Egypt (Figures 3.8a, 3.8b, 3.8c)

- Huge columns, tightly packed together, admitting little light into the sanctuary
- Hypostyle halls
- Columns elaborately painted
- Massive lintels bind the columns together
- Axial plan
- Tallest columns have papyrus capitals; have a clerestory to allow some light and air into the darkest parts of the temple
- Lower columns have bud capitals
- Columns carved in sunken relief
- Enter complex through massive sloped pylon gateway into peristyle courtyard, then through a hypostyle hall and then into the sanctuary where few were allowed
- **Cross-Cultural Comparisons: Houses of Worship**
  - Lakshamana Temple (Figures 23.7a, 23.7b, 23.7c, 23.7d)
  - Santa Sabina (Figures 7.3a, 7.3b, 7.3c)
  - Great Mosque, Isfahan (Figures 9.13a, 9.13b, 9.13c)

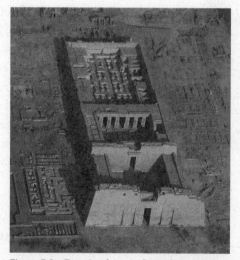

Figure 3.8a: Temple of Amun-Re and Hypostyle Hall, 1550–1250 B.C.E., sandstone and mud brick, near Luxor, Egypt

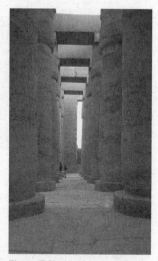

Figure 3.8b: Hypostyle Hall, 1550–1250 B.C.E., sandstone and mud brick, near Luxor, Egypt

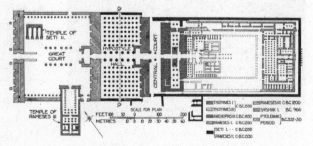

Figure 3.8c: Plan of Temple of Amun-Re and Hypostyle Hall, 1550–1250 B.C.E., sandstone and mud brick, near Luxor, Egypt

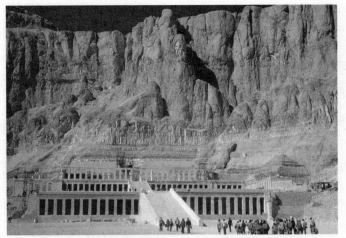

Figure 3.9a: Mortuary Temple of Hatshepsut, c. 1473–1458 B.C.E., sandstone, near Luxor, Egypt

Mortuary Temple of Hatshepsut, c. 1473–1458 B.C.E., sandstone, near Luxor, Egypt (Figure 3.9a)

- 3 colonnaded terraces and 2 ramps
- Visually coordinated with the natural setting; long horizontals and verticals of the terraces and colonnades repeat the patterns of the cliffs behind; patterns of dark and light in the colonnade are reflected in the cliffs
- Terraces were originally planted as gardens with exotic trees
- First time the achievements of a woman are celebrated in art history; her body is interred elsewhere

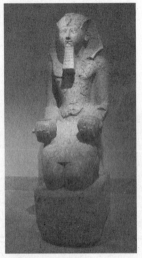

Figure 3.9b: *Queen Hatshepsut with Offering Jars*, 1473–1458 B.C.E., red granite, Metropolitan Museum of Art, New York

Queen Hatshepsut with Offering Jars, 1473–1458 B.C.E., red granite, Metropolitan Museum of Art, New York (Figure 3.9b)

- One of 200 statues placed around the complex
- One of ten statues of Queen Hatshepsut with offering jars, part of a ritual in honor of the sun god; pharaoh would only kneel before a god
- Statue of the god brought before sculpture in a procession
- Inscription on base says she is offering plants to Amun, the sun god
- Male pharaonic attributes: false beard, kilt
- Queen represented in male costume of a pharaoh, yet slender proportions and slight breasts indicate femininity
- Wears white crown of Upper Egypt
- **Cross-Cultural Comparisons: Guardian Figures**
  - Nio guardian figure (Figures 25.1c, 25.1d)
  - Staff God (Figures 28.5a, 28.5b)
  - *Lamassu* (Figure 2.5)

Akhenaton, Nefertiti, and Three Daughters, 1353–1335 B.C.E., limestone, Egyptian Museum, Berlin (Figure 3.10)

- Akhenaton holds eldest daughter (left), ready to be kissed
- Nefertiti holds daughter (right) with another daughter on her shoulder
- State religion changed by Akhenaton from Amun to Aton, symbolized by the sun-disk with a cobra
- At the end of the sun's rays, ankhs (the Egyptian symbol of life) points to the king and queen
- State religion shift indicated by an evolving style in Egyptian art:
  - smoother, curved surfaces
  - low hanging bellies
  - slack jaws

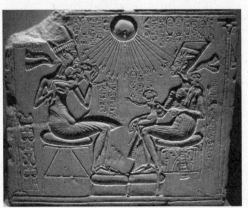

Figure 3.10: *Akhenaton, Nefertiti, and Three Daughters*, 1353–1335 B.C.E., limestone, Egyptian Museum, Berlin

- thin arms
- epicene bodies
- heavy-lidded eyes
- Domestic environment new in Egyptian art; panel is from an altar in a home
- Akhenaton and Nefertiti having a private relationship with their new god, Aton
- **Cross-Cultural Comparisons: Genre Scenes**
  - Vermeer, *Woman with a Balance* (Fig 17.10)
  - Courbet, *Stone Breakers* (Figure 21.1)
  - Stele of Hegeso (Figure 4.7)

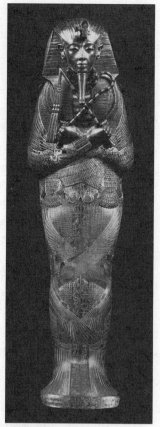

Figure 3.11: Innermost coffin of King Tutankhamun, c. 1323 B.C.E., gold, enamel, semiprecious stones, Egyptian Museum, Cairo

Innermost Coffin of King Tutankhamun, c. 1323 B.C.E., gold, enamel, semiprecious stones, Egyptian Museum, Cairo (Figure 3.11)

- Famous tomb discovered by Howard Carter in 1922
- Mummified body of King Tutankhamun buried with 143 objects on his head, neck, abdomen, and limbs; gold mask placed over head
- Gold coffin 6'7" long containing the body of the pharaoh
- Golden mask has smoothly idealized features of the boy–king
- Holds a crook and a flail, symbols of Osiris
- Son of Akhenaton, his father and mother were brother and sister; his wife his half-sister; perhaps physically handicapped caused by genetic inbreeding
- When Akhenaton died, two pharaohs ruled briefly, then Tutankhamun reigned for ten years from ages 9–19.
- **Cross-Cultural Comparisons: Commemoration**
  - Sarcophagus of the Spouses (Figure 5.4)
  - Moai (Figure 28.11)
  - Ndop (Figure 27.5a)

Last Judgment of Hu-Nefer, c. 1275 B.C.E., painted papyrus scroll, British Museum, London (Figure 3.12)

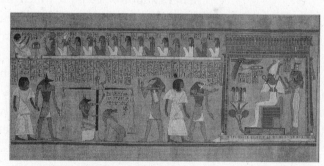

Figure 3.12: Last Judgment of Hu-Nefer, c. 1275 B.C.E., painted papyrus scroll, British Museum, London

- Illustration from the *Book of the Dead*, an Egyptian book of spells and charms
- The god of embalming, Anubis, has a jackal's head. He leads the deceased named Hu-Nefer into a hall where his soul is being weighed against a feather. If the sins weigh more than a feather, he will be condemned.
- The hippopotamus/lion figure between the scales will eat the heart of an evil soul.
- The god Thoth has the head of a bird. He is the stenographer writing down these events in the hieroglyphics that he invented.
- Osiris, god of the underworld, appears enthroned on the right to subject the deceased to a day of judgment.
- **Cross-Cultural Comparisons: Scrolls**
  - *Night Attack on the Sanjô Palace* (Figures 25.3a, 25.3b)
  - *Bayeux Tapestry* (Figures 11.7a, 11.7b)
  - Bing, *A Book from the Sky* (Figures 28.9a, 28.9b)

VOCABULARY

Amarna style: Art created during the reign of Akhenaton, which features a more relaxed figure style than in Old and Middle Kingdom art

Ankh: an Egyptian symbol of life

Axial plan: a building with an elongated ground plan (Figure 3.8c)

Clerestory: a roof that rises above lower roofs and thus has window space beneath

Engaged column: a column that is not freestanding but attached to a wall (Figure 3.2)

Ground line: a base line upon which figures stand (Figure 3.4)

Hierarchy of scale: a system of representation that expresses a person's importance by the size of his or her representation in a work of art (Figure 3.4)

Hieroglyphics: Egyptian writing using symbols or pictures as characters (Figure 3.12)

Hypostyle: a hall in an Egyptian temple that has a roof supported by a dense thicket of columns (Figure 3.8b)

In situ: a Latin expression that means that something is in its original location

Ka: the soul, or spiritual essence, of a human being that either ascends to heaven or can live in an Egyptian statue of itself

Mastaba: Arabic for "bench," a low, flat-roofed Egyptian tomb with sides sloping down to the ground (Figure 3.1)

Necropolis: literally, a "city of the dead," a large burial area

Papyrus: a tall aquatic plant whose fiber is used as a writing surface in ancient Egypt (Figure 3.12)

Peristyle: a colonnade surrounding a building or enclosing a courtyard (Figure 3.8a)

Pharaoh: a king of ancient Egypt (Figure 3.11)

Pylon: a monumental gateway to an Egyptian temple marked by two flat, sloping walls between which is a smaller entrance

Register: a horizontal band, often on top of another, that tells a narrative story (Figure 3.4)

Relief sculpture: sculpture which projects from a flat background. A very shallow relief sculpture is called a **bas-relief** (pronounced: bah-relief) (Figure 3.4)

Reserve column: a column that is cut away from rock but has no support function

Sarcophagus (plural, **sarcophagi**)**:** a stone coffin

Stylized: A schematic, non-realistic manner of representing the visible world and its contents, abstracted from the way that they appear in nature

Sunken relief: a carving in which the outlines of figures are deeply carved into a surface so that the figures seem to project forward

SUMMARY

Egyptian civilization covers a huge expanse of time that is marked by the building of monumental funerary monuments and expansive temple complexes. The earliest remains of Egyptian civilization show an interest in elaborate funerary practices, which resulted in the building of the great stone pyramids.

Egyptian figural style remained constant throughout much of its history, with its emphasis on broad frontal shoulders and profiled heads, torso, and legs. In the Old Kingdom the figures appear static and imperturbable. In the Amarna period the figures lose their motionless stances and have body types that are softer and increasingly androgynous.

The contents of the tomb of the short-lived King Tutankhamun give the modern world a glimpse into the spectacular richness of Egyptian tombs. One wonders how much more lavish the tomb of Ramses II must have been.

PRACTICE EXERCISES

Multiple-Choice

1. The purpose of the sculpture *The Seated Scribe* is to

   (A) illustrate the large retinue the pharaoh had
   (B) show how the pharaoh was literate and intelligent
   (C) indicate how the pharaoh used scribes to write down his deeds
   (D) attend to the pharaoh's needs in the afterlife

Question 2 refers to the following image.

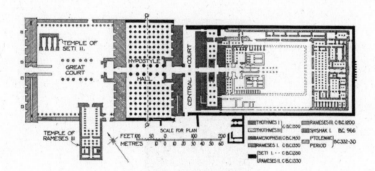

2. The ground plan of this building indicates that

   (A) vast spaces are vaulted for large interiors
   (B) there are four entrances, one for each cardinal point of the compass
   (C) the interior rooms are dominated by closely spaced, thick columns
   (D) the outside walls are low and shallow to allow the Nile to ceremonially flood the interior

3. The painting called The Last Judgment of Hu-Nefer shows the

   (A) eternal punishment proclaimed upon a damned soul
   (B) deceased being asked to account for the deeds in his life
   (C) might of the pharaoh in deciding life and death
   (D) rules of conduct imposed on the lowly and the mighty alike

4. Egyptian sculptors sometimes used sunken relief rather than bas-relief because of all of the following EXCEPT:

(A) sunken reliefs preserve the contours of the surfaces being carved so that columns still look round

(B) sunken reliefs are easier to carve, a necessity because Egyptians used soft bronze-age tools to carve into hard stones like greywacke

(C) sunken reliefs hide the function of columns as supporting elements, emphasizing instead their images and messages

(D) sunken reliefs cast deep shadows so that the images can be read more clearly in the Egyptian sun

5. Which historical event is represented on the *Palette of King Narmer*?

(A) The founding of the first Egyptian dynasty

(B) The conquering of the Assyrians

(C) The abandonment of the polytheistic Egyptian religion in favor of one god, Aton

(D) The unification of Upper and Lower Egypt

Short Essay

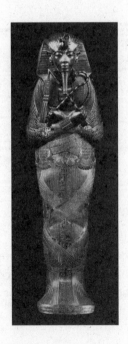

This is the inner coffin of King Tutankhamun from c. 1323 B.C.E.

Where was this coffin found?

Why was this site chosen for the burial of this coffin?

Using specific details, examine how this work is part of a tradition of pharaonic burial.

1. **D**   2. **C**   3. **B**   4. **B**   5. **D**

ANSWERS EXPLAINED

Multiple-Choice

1. **(D)** Images of scribes were placed in tombs to attend to the pharaoh's needs in the after-life. Whereas all of the other choices indicate how pharaohs used scribes, this sculpture of a seated scribe had the specific purpose of being placed in a tomb so that the ka could be accommodated, if necessary.

2. **(C)** There are thick round circles in linear order on the ground plan which represent columns placed very closely together.

3. **(B)** This painting is a last judgment scene, in which the deceased's soul is weighed against a feather to see if he is pure enough to face the gods.

4. **(B)** Sunken relief sculpture is no easier or more difficult to carve than any other sculpture no matter what tools are being used or what materials are being carved.

5. **(D)** The *Palette of King Narmer* symbolically represents a conflation of all the episodes leading to the unification of Upper and Lower Egypt.

Short-Essay Rubric

Question	Points	Key Points in a Good Response
Where was this coffin found?	1	The coffin was found in a tomb in the Valley of the Kings in Egypt.
Why was this site chosen for the burial of this coffin?	2	Answers could include: ■ This was the traditional burial ground for Egyptian kings. ■ The valley was naturally protected by cliffs against grave robbers. ■ The cliffs and tombs could be easily dug from the rock here.
Using specific details, examine how this work is part of a tradition of pharaonic burial.	2	Answers could include: ■ Elaborate funerary ceremonies; 143 objects found with the body ■ Gold symbolizes eternity, used extensively throughout the tomb ■ Holds a crook and a flail, symbols of Osiris ■ Above the head are symbols of upper and lower Egypt: the cobra and the falcon ■ Idealization of facial features of the king

Greek Art

4

TIME PERIOD	
Archaic Art	600–480 B.C.E.
Classical Art	480–323 B.C.E.
Hellenistic Art	323–30 B.C.E.

ENDURING UNDERSTANDING: Greek art is characterized by a pantheon of gods celebrated in large civic and religious buildings.

Essential Knowledge:

- Greek art is studied chronologically according to changes in style.
- Greek works are not studied according to dynastic rule, as in Egypt, but according to broad changes in stylistic patterns.
- Greek art is most known for its idealization and harmonic proportions, both in sculpture and in architecture.
- Greek art has had an important impact on European art, particularly in the eighteenth century.

ENDURING UNDERSTANDING: Much ancient writing survives in the fields of literature, law, politics, and business. These documents shed light on Greek civilization as a whole, and on Greek art in particular.

Essential Knowledge:

- Greek writing contains some of the earliest contemporary accounts about art and artists.
- Epics form the foundation of Greek writing. The texts were at first transmitted orally, but later were written down.

HISTORICAL BACKGROUND

The collapse of Aegean society around 1100 B.C.E. left a vacuum in the Greek world until a reorganization took place around 900 B.C.E. in the form of city-states. Places like Sparta, Corinth, and Athens defined Greek civilization in that they were small, competing political entities that were united only in language and the fear of outsiders.

In the fifth century B.C.E. the Persians threatened to swallow Greece, and the city-states rallied behind Athens' leadership to expel them. This was accomplished, but not before Athens itself was destroyed in 480 B.C.E. After the Persians were effectively neutralized, the Greeks then turned, once again, to bickering among themselves. The worst of these internal struggles happened during the Peloponnesian War (431–404 B.C.E.) when Athens was crushed by Sparta. Without an effective core, Greek states continued to struggle for another century.

This did not end until the reign of Alexander the Great, who, in the fourth century B.C.E., briefly united Macedonians and Greeks, by establishing a mighty empire that eventually toppled the Persians. But because Alexander died young and left no clear successor, his empire crumbled away soon after his death. The remnants of Greek civilization lasted for another hundred years or so, until it was eventually absorbed by Rome.

Patronage and Artistic Life

So many names of artists have come down to us that it is tempting to think that Greek artists achieved a distinguished status hitherto unknown in the ancient world. Artists signed their work, both as a symbol of accomplishment and as a bit of advertisement. Greek potters and painters signed their vases, usually in a formula that resembles "so and so made it" or "so and so decorated it."

Many artists were theoreticians as well as sculptors or architects. **Polykleitos** wrote a famous (no longer existing) book on the canon of human proportions. **Iktinos** wrote on the nature of ideal architecture. Phidias, who was responsible for the artistic program on the Acropolis, supervised hundreds of workers in a mammoth workshop and yet still managed to construct a complex with a single unifying artistic expression. This was a golden age for artists, indeed.

GREEK SCULPTURE

There are three ways in which Greek sculpture stands as a departure from the civilizations that have preceded it:

1. Greek sculpture is unafraid of nudity. Unlike the Egyptians, who felt that nudity was debasing, the Greeks gloried in the perfection of the human body. At first, only men are shown as nude; gradually women are also depicted, although there is a reluctance to fully accept female nudity, even at the end of the Greek period.
2. Large Greek marble sculptures are cut away from the stone behind them. Large-scale bronze works were particularly treasured; their lighter weight made compositional experiments more ambitious.
3. Greek art in the Classical and Hellenistic periods use **contrapposto**, which is a relaxed way of standing with knees bent and shoulders tilted. The immobile look of Egyptian art is replaced by a more informal and fluid stance, enabling the figures to appear to move.

Greek Archaic Sculpture

What survives of Greek Archaic art is limited to grave monuments, such as **kouros** and **kore** figures, or sculpture from Greek temples. Marble is the stone of choice, although Greek works survive in a variety of materials: bronze, limestone, terra cotta, wood, gold—even iron. Sculpture was often painted, especially if it were to be located high on the temple façade. Backgrounds are highlighted in red; lips, eyes, hair, and drapery are routinely painted. Sculpture often has metallic accessories: thunderbolts, harps, and various other attributes.

Bronze sculpture is hollow and made in the lost-wax process, call **cire perdue**. Eyes are inlaid with stone or glass, and lips, nipples, and teeth could be made of copper or silver highlights.

Kouros and **kore** figures stand frontally, bolt upright, and with squarish shoulders. Hair is knotted, and the ears are a curlicue. Figures are cut free from the stone as much as possible, although arms are sometimes attached to thighs. As in Egyptian works, kouros figures have one foot placed in front of the other, as if they were in mid-stride. The shins have a neat crease down the front, as Egyptian works do. To give the figures a sense of life, most kouros and kore figures smile.

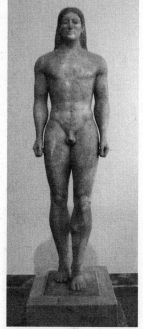

Figure 4.1: *Anavysos Kouros*, 530 B.C.E., marble and paint, National Archaeological Museum, Athens

Anavysos Kouros, 530 B.C.E., marble and paint, National Archaeological Museum, Athens (Figure 4.1)

- Grave marker, replacing huge vases of the Geometric period
- Not a real portrait, but a general representation of an ideal warrior
- Rigidly frontal
- Emulates stance of Egyptian sculpture, but is nude; arms and legs largely cut free from the stone
- Freestanding with legs appearing to stride forward, in contrast to many Egyptian works that are reliefs or are attached to stone
- Hair is knotted and falls in neatly braided rows down the back
- Eyes wide open; squarish shoulders
- Face is masklike
- Named after a young military hero Kroisos; inscription at base identifies him
- Some paint survives, which would have given the sculpture greater life
- "Archaic smile" meant to enliven the sculpture
- **Cross-Cultural Comparisons: Idealization**
  - Power Figure (Figure 27.6)
  - Staff God (Figure 28.5a)
  - Donatello, *David* (Figure 15.5)

Peplos Kore, c. 530 B.C.E., marble and paint, Acropolis Museum, Athens (Figure 4.2)

- Broken hand fitted in the socket and probably held an attribute; she may have been a goddess
- Hand emerges into our own space, breaks out of the mold of static Archaic statues
- Tightened waist
- Breasts revealed beneath drapery
- So-called because she is named for the *peplos*, traditionally thought to be one of the four garments she is wearing
- Rounded and naturalistic face
- Much of the paint still remains, animating the face and hair
- Hair falls naturally beside her body
- **Cross-Cultural Comparisons: Human Figure in Greek Art**
  - *Winged Victory of Samothrace* (Figure 4.8)
  - *Seated Boxer* (Figure 4.10)
  - *Victory Adjusting Her Sandal* (Figure 4.6)

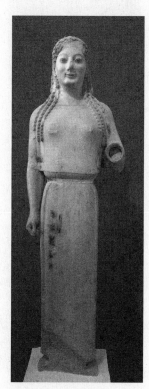

Figure 4.2: *Peplos Kore*, c. 530 B.C.E., marble and paint, Acropolis Museum, Athens

Greek Classical Sculpture

Classical sculpture is distinct from Archaic in the use of **contrapposto**, that is, the fluid body movement and relaxed stance that was unknown in freestanding sculpture before this. In addition, forms became highly idealized; even sculptures depicting older people have heroic bodies. In the fifth century B.C.E., this heroic form was defined by **Polykleitos**, a sculptor whose **canon** of proportions of the human figure had far-reaching effects. Polykleitos wrote that the head should be one-seventh of the body. He also favored a heavy musculature with a body expressing alternating stances of relaxed and stressed muscles. Thus, on his *Spear Bearer* (450–440 B.C.E.) (Figure 4.3), the right arm and the left leg are flexed, and the left arm and right leg are relaxed.

The crushing of Athens during the Peloponnesian War had a dramatic impact on the arts, which turned away from the idealizing canon of the fifth century B.C.E. In the Late Classical period of the fourth century B.C.E., gods were sculpted in a more humanized way. Praxiteles, the greatest sculptor of his age, carved figures with a sensuous and languorous appeal, and favored a lanky look to the bodies. Hallmarks of fourth-century work include heads that are one-eighth of the body and a sensuous S-curve to the frame.

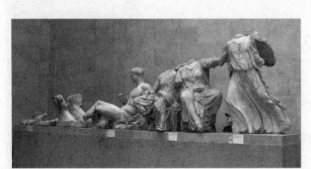

Figure 4.3: Polykleitos, *Spear Bearer*, c. 450–440 B.C.E., marble copy from a bronze original, National Archaeological Museum, Naples

Polykleitos, *Spear Bearer*, c. 450–440 B.C.E., marble copy from a bronze original, National Archaeological Museum, Naples (Figure 4.3)

- Greek name: *Doryphoros*
- Closed stance
- Alternating tense and relaxed elements of the body; left arm and right leg are relaxed, right arm and left leg are tensed
- Blocklike solidity
- Broad shoulders, thick torso, muscular body
- Movement restrained, Spartan ideal of body
- Warrior and athlete
- Hand once held a spear
- He averts his gaze; you may admire him, but he does not recognize the admiration
- Found in Pompeii in a place for athletic training
- **Cross-Cultural Comparisons: Human Figure**
  - Female Deity from Nukuoro (Figure 28.2)
  - Shiva as Lord of Dance (Figure 23.6)
  - Braque, *Portuguese* (Figure 22.6)

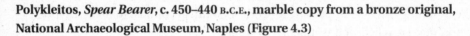

Figure 4.4: *Helios, Horses and Dionysos* c. 438–432 B.C.E., marble, British Museum, London

***Helios, Horses and Dionysos* c. 438-432 B.C.E., marble, British Museum, London (Figure 4.4)**

- Parthenon Sculptures, also called the Elgin Marbles
- East pediment of the Parthenon
- Shows the birth of Athena from the head of Zeus, and other deities watching
- Two seated figures are the goddesses Demeter and Persephone
- Sculptures comfortably sit in the triangular space of the pediment
- Classical art; contrapposto

Plaque of the Ergastines, c. 438-432 B.C.E., marble, Louvre, Paris (Figure 4.5)

- Scene from the Panathenaic Frieze depicting the Panathenaic Procession, held every four years to honor Athena
- First time in Greek art showing a depiction of a human event on a temple
- The higher up the relief placement, the more three-dimensional the relief was carved, to be seen better from below
- Procession began at the Dipylon Gate, passed through the agora, ended at the Parthenon
- Athenians placed a new peplos on the statue of Athena
- Six Ergastines, young women in charge of weaving Athena's peplos, are greeted by two priests
- Isocephalism: the tradition of depicting heads of figures on the same level
- New theory: not the Panathenaic Procession, but the story of the legendary Athenian king, Erechtheus, who sacrificed one of his daughters to save the city of Athens; told to do so by the Oracle of Delphi
- **Cross-Cultural Comparisons: Relief Sculpture**
  - _Churning of the Ocean of Milk_ (Figure 23.8c)
  - _Coyolxauhqui_ (Figure 26.5b)
  - Lintel 25 of Structure 23 from Yaxchilán (Figure 26.2b)

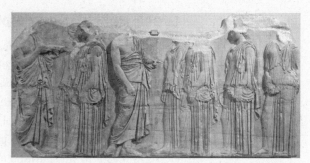

Figure 4.5: _Plaque of the Ergastines_, c. 438–432 B.C.E., marble, Louvre, Paris

Victory Adjusting Her Sandal, from the Temple of Athena Nike, c. 410 B.C.E., marble, Acropolis Museum, Athens (Figure 4.6)

- Graceful winged figure modeled in high relief
- Deeply incised drapery lines reveal body, wet drapery
- **Cross-Cultural Comparisons: Figure in Motion**
  - Shiva as Lord of Dance (Figure 23.6)
  - Nio guardian figure (Figures 25.1c, 25.1d)
  - _Churning of the Ocean of Milk_ (Figure 23.8c)

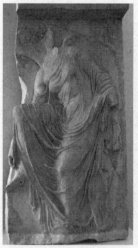

Figure 4.6: _Victory Adjusting Her Sandal_, from the Temple of Athena Nike, c. 410 B.C.E., marble, Acropolis Museum, Athens

Attributed to Kallimachos, _Grave Stele of Hegeso_, c. 410 B.C.E., painted marble, National Archaeological Museum, Athens (Figure 4.7)

- Attributed to the sculptor Kallimachos
- In Geometric period, Greeks used kraters to mark graves
- Archaic Greeks used kouroi or stelae; this is a classical work
- Erected in Dipylon cemetery in Athens
- Commemorates the death of Hegeso; inscription identifies her, and her father
- Genre scene: woman examining a piece of jewelry from a jewelry box handed to her by a standing servant; may represent her dowry
- Jewelry painted in, not visible
- **Cross-Cultural Comparisons: Funerary Markers and Materials**
  - Taj Mahal (Figures 9.17a, 9.17b)
  - Sarcophagus of the Spouses (Figure 5.4)
  - Tutankhamun's Tomb (Figure 3.11)

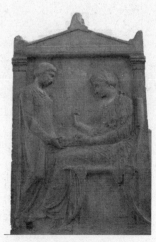

Figure 4.7: Attributed to Kallimachos, _Grave Stele of Hegeso_, c. 410 B.C.E., painted marble, National Archaeological Museum, Athens

Greek Hellenistic Sculpture

Hellenistic sculptors offer a wider range of realistic modeling and a willingness to show more movement than their classical colleagues. Figures have a great variety of expression from sadness to joy. Themes untouched before, such as childhood, old age, despair, anger, and drunkenness, are common subjects in Hellenistic art. To be certain, there are still Hellenistic beauties, but the accent is on a variety of expressions sweeping across the range of human emotion. Moreover, sculptors carve with greater flexibility, employing negative space more freely. The viewer is meant to walk around a Hellenistic sculpture and see it from many sides; hence, the work is often not meant to be placed against a wall.

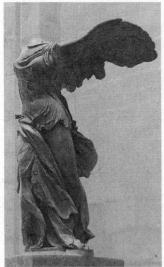

Figure 4.8: *Nike of Samothrace*, c. 190 B.C.E., marble, Louvre, Paris

Nike of Samothrace, c. 190 B.C.E., marble, Louvre, Paris (Figure 4.8)

- Meant to stand in or above a fountain cascading water around rocks below, similar to a figurehead of a boat
- Wet drapery look imitates the water playing on the wet body
- Shows evidence of invisible wind on her body
- Dramatic twist and contrapposto of the torso
- Monumentality of the figure
- Her missing right arm may have raised a victory crown or held an open hand in greeting; perhaps she was landing on the prow of a ship
- The boat at the base is a battleship with oarboxes and traces of a ram
- Probably built to commemorate a naval victory in 190 B.C.E.; Nike is a symbol of victory
- Found in 1863 *in situ* on Samothrace
- **Cross-Cultural References: Location**
  - Smithson, *Spiral Jetty* (Figure 22.26)
  - Dome of the Rock (Figures 9.12a, 9.12b)
  - Lanzón Stela (Figure 26.1b)

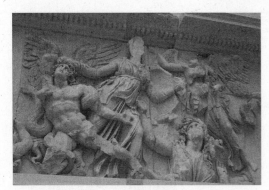

Figure 4.9: *Athena*, from the Pergamon Altar, c. 175 B.C.E., marble, State Museum, Berlin

Athena, from the Pergamon Altar, c. 175 B.C.E., marble, State Museum, Berlin (Figure 4.9)

- Gigantomachy
- Describes the battle between the gods and the giants; the giants, as helpless tools, were dragged up the stairs to worship the gods
- The gods' victory over the giants offers a parallel to Alexander the Great's defeat of the Persians
- Deeply carved figures overlap one another; masterful handling of spatial illusion
- Dramatic intensity of figures, movement; heroic musculature
- Athena grabs Alkyoneos by the hair and drags him up the stair to worship Zeus
- Nike on right crowns Athena in victory
- Gaia: earth goddess, looks on in horror and pleads for the fate of her sons, the giants
- **Cross-Cultural References: Relief Sculpture**
  - Narmer Palette (Figure 3.4)
  - Anthropomorphic Stele (Figure 1.2)
  - Pyxis of al-Mughira (Figure 9.4)

Seated Boxer, c. 100 B.C.E., bronze, National Roman Museum, Rome (Figure 4.10)

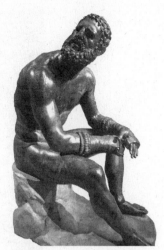

- Rare Hellenistic bronze
- May have been part of a group, or perhaps a single sculpture with a head turned to face an unseen opponent
- Older man, past his prime, mostly defeated look
- Smashed nose; lips sunken in to suggest broken teeth
- Cauliflower ears
- Nude fighter; hands wrapped in leather bands
- Blood denoted in copper; dripping from his face and onto his right arm and thigh
- Copper used as highlights on his lips, nipples, straps on leather gloves, wounds on head
- Great emotion
- May have been a good luck charm for athletes; evidence of toes worn away by touching
- **Cross-Cultural Comparisons: Individual vs. Society**
  - Goya, *And There's Nothing to Be Done* (Figure 20.2)
  - Kirchner, *Self-Portrait as a Soldier* (Figure 22.3)
  - Munch, *The Scream* (Figure 21.11)

Figure 4.10: *Seated Boxer*, c. 100 B.C.E., bronze, National Roman Museum, Rome

GREEK ARCHITECTURE

Like the Egyptians, the Greeks designed their temples to be the earthly homes of the gods. Also like the Egyptians, the Greeks preferred limited access to the deity. This is one reason why such grand temples had doors that were removed from public view. In fact, architecturally the front and back of Greek temples look almost identical; only the sculptural ornament is different. When Greeks came to worship they congregated at a temple near the building. Interiors of temples held huge statues whose forbidding presence allowed only those with appropriate credentials to enter.

There are three types of Greek temples: **Doric**, **Ionic**, and **Corinthian** (Figure 4.11). Greeks in mainland Greece and in the places they settled, like Sicily, preferred the Doric style, with its simplified capitals and columns with tapered **shafts** that sit, without a base, directly on the floor of the temple. **Doric** temples have unadorned **architraves** and alternating **triglyphs** and **metopes,** the latter depicting episodes from Greek mythology. Greek island architects preferred the **Ionic** style, with its volute-like capitals, columns that sit on bases, and **friezes** of sculpture

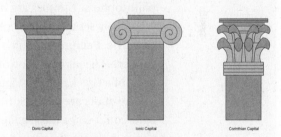

Figure 4.11: Greek orders of columns

placed along the **entablature**. Later, the **Corinthian** order was introduced, in which the capitals had leaves and the straight columns had bases that transitioned to the floor. The different orders of Greek architecture were occasionally freely mixed, as in the case of the **Parthenon**, where a Doric temple has Ionic features, like a frieze, introduced on the inside.

Elaborate Greek temple complexes were placed on a high hill, or **acropolis**, overlooking the city. Gateways, called **propylaea**, prepared the visitor for his or her entrance into the complex.

Greek temple architecture shows a reliance on few forms and develops these. However, there are two innovations of note. The first was the circular shrine, called a **tholos** (Figure

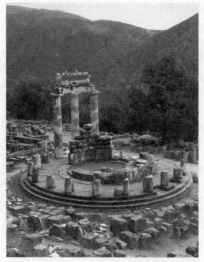

Figure 4.12: A tholos, a circular shrine

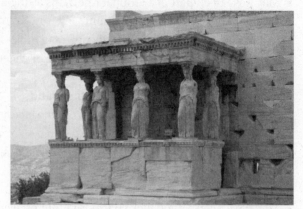

Figure 4.13: Caryatids act as columns holding up a building

4.12), which represents perfection to the geometry-minded Greeks. The second is the introduction of columns carved as figures, the female version of which are called **caryatids** (Figure 4.13). These columns have to be carefully executed because the weight of the building rests on the thin points of a body's structure: the neck and the legs. This means that all caryatids have long hair and solid gowns in order to stabilize the building above.

Besides temples, the Greeks built a number of other important buildings, such as shopping centers and theaters. The theaters are marvels of construction, possessing incredible acoustics, especially considering that the performances were held in the open air. Some 12,000 people seated at the theater at Epidauros could hear every word, even if they were seated 55 rows back.

Except for the rare **tholos** shrines, Greek temples are rectangular and organized on an inventive, although rigid, set of geometric principles, which tantalized Greek thinkers and philosophers. Temples are built with the post-and-lintel system in mind, the columns never too widely set apart. The columns completely surround the temple core in a design called a **peristyle**. **Pediments**, which project over the tops of columns, contain sculpture representing the heroic deeds of the god or goddess housed inside. A **cornice** separates the upper and lower parts of a Greek temple (Figure 4.14).

The doors are set back from the façade, sometimes by two rows of columns, so that little light could enter these generally windowless buildings. This increases the sense of mystery about the interior, where few could go and the deity serenely reigned.

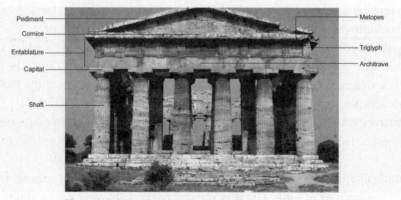

Figure 4.14: Parts of a Doric Greek temple

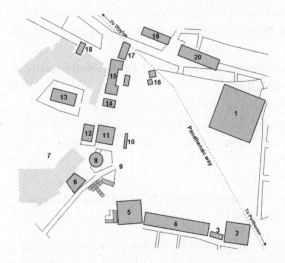

Figure 4.15: Athenian Agora, 600–150 B.C.E., Athens, Greece
1 Peristyle Court
2 Mint
3 Enneacrounos
4 South stoa
5 Heliaea
6 Strategeion
7 Colonos Agoraios
8 Tholos
9 Agora stone
10 Monument of the Eponymous Heroes
11 Old Bouleuterion
12 New Bouleuterion
13 Temple of Hephaestus (Hephaestion)
14 Temple of Apollo Patroos
15 Stoa of Zeus
16 Altar of the Twelve Gods
17 Royal stoa
18 Temple of Aphrodite Urania
19 Stoa of Hermes
20 Stoa poikile

Athenian Agora, 600–150 B.C.E., Athens, Greece (Figure 4.15)

- A plaza at the base of the Acropolis in Athens that contained commercial, civic, religious, and social buildings; ceremonies took place here
- Setting for the Panathenaic Festival, ceremonies and parades to honor Athena
- The Panathenaic Way cuts through the plaza from the northwest to the southeast corners
- Plaza surrounded by important buildings including:
  - a bouleuterion: a chamber used by a council of citizens
  - a tholos, a round temple
  - several stoas: a covered walkway with columns on one side and a wall on the other

Iktinos and Kallikrates, The Parthenon, 447–438 B.C.E., Athens, Greece (Figures 4.16a and 4.16b)

- Constructed under the leadership of Pericles after the Persian sack of Athens in 480 B.C.E. destroyed the original Acropolis
- Pericles used the extra funds in the Persian war treasury to build the Acropolis; Greek allies were furious
- Greek predilection for algebra and geometry omnipresent in the design of this building: Parts can be expressed as $x = 2y + 1$; thus, there are 17 columns on the side (x) and 8 columns in the front (y), and the ratio of the length to the width is 9:4; proportions are the same for the cella
- Unusually light interior had two windows in the cella
- Floor curves upward in the center of the façade to drain off rain water and to deflect appearance of sagging at the ends
- The columns at the ends are surrounded by light, which alters their appearance, so they are made thicker in order to look the same as the other columns
- Ionic elements in a Doric temple: rear room contains Ionic capitals, frieze on interior is Ionic

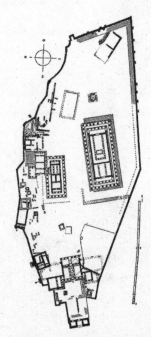

Figure 4.16a: Iktinos and Kallikrates, Acropolis, c. 447–424 B.C.E., marble, Athens, Greece

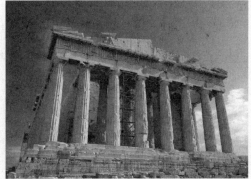

Figure 4.16b: Iktinos and Kallikrates, The Parthenon, 447–438 B.C.E., Athens, Greece

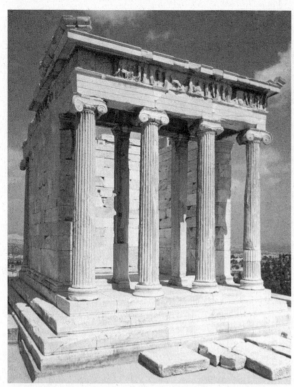

Figure 4.17: Kallikrates, Temple of Athena Nike, 425 B.C.E., Athens, Greece

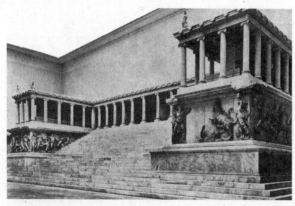

Figure 4.18a: Altar of Zeus and Athena at Pergamon, c. 175 B.C.E., marble, State Museum, Berlin

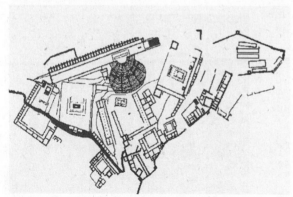

Figure 4.18b: Plan of the Altar of Zeus and Athena at Pergamon, c. 175 B.C.E., marble, Turkey

- Interior built to house a massive statue of Athena, to whom the building was dedicated; statue made of gold and ivory over a wooden core
- **Cross-Cultural Comparisons: Classical Influence on Later Buildings**
  - Jefferson, Monticello (Figures 19.5a, 19.5b)
  - Porta, Il Gesù (Figure 16.6a)
  - Venturi, House in New Castle County (Figures 22.7a, 22.7b)

Kallikrates, Temple of Athena Nike, 425 B.C.E., Athens, Greece (Figure 4.17)

- Amphiprostyle: having four columns in the front and four in the back
- Built to commemorate the Greek victory over the Persians in the Battle of Marathon
- Many images of victory on the temple

Altar of Zeus and Athena at Pergamon, c. 175 B.C.E., marble, State Museum, Berlin (Figures 4.18a and 4.18b)

- Altar placed on an elevated platform up a dramatic flight of stairs
- Conscious effort to be in dialogue with the Panathenaic Frieze on the Parthenon
- 7½-foot-high frieze over 400 feet long wraps around monument
- Contains an altar dedicated to Zeus
- Ionic columns frame monument
- Parallels made between King Attalos I's victories over the Gauls in a recent war, Alexander the Great's defeat of the Persians, and the gods' defeat over the giants in mythology

INNOVATIONS OF GREEK POTTERY

Much of what is known about Greek painting comes from pottery, which survives in surprising quantities, even though mural painting has almost totally disappeared. Professional pottery had been practiced in Greece from its origins in Aegean society throughout the entire span of the Greek period. Some vessels are everyday items, others serve as tomb monuments. Massive kraters have holes at the bottom so that when libations are poured liquid could run out the bottom of the pot and onto the grave itself. Pots that were used for these purposes often have a scene of the deceased lying on a bier surrounded by mourners. Chariots and warriors complete the grieving procession.

Form followed function in Greek pottery. Most pots were designed for a particular purpose and were so shaped. The portable **amphora** stored provisions like oil or wine with an opening large enough to admit a ladle. The **krater** was a bowl for mixing water and wine because the Greeks never drank their wine straight. A kylix, with its wide mouth and shallow dimensions, was a drinking cup, ideal for the display of scenes on the relatively flat bottom.

Painters wrote a myriad of inscriptions that were sometimes literally addressed to the viewer of the pot, saying things like "I greet you." Inscriptions could explain the narrative scene represented, or identify people or objects. The underside of vases usually indicated the selling transaction of the pot.

In the Archaic period, artists painted in a style called **black figure**, which emphasized large figures drawn in black on the red natural surface of the clay. Other colors would burn in the high temperature of the **kiln**, so after the pot had been fired, details were added in highlighting colors. The bright glazing of Greek pottery gives the surface a lustrous shine. At the end of the Archaic period, **red figure** vases were introduced by Andokides; in effect, they are the reversal of black figure style pots. The backgrounds were painted in black, and the natural red of the clay detailed the forms.

Archaic pottery has the same stiffness and monumentality of Archaic sculpture. Achievements in Classical sculpture, such as **contrapposto**, were paralleled in pottery as well. Similarly the dynamic movements of the Hellenistic period were reflected in Greek Hellenistic pottery.

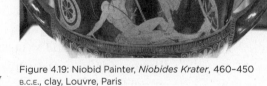

Niobid Painter, *Niobides Krater*, 460–450 B.C.E., clay, Louvre, Paris (Figure 4.19)

- Found in Orvieto, Italy
- Called the Niobid Krater because on one side is depicted the killing of Niobid's children
  - Niobid bragged about her fertility to the god Leto, who had only two children
  - Leto's two children, Apollo and Artemis, seek revenge by killing Niobid's twelve
  - Niobid punished for her hubris
- Other side of vase, story is subject of scholarly debate
  - One theory is that it represents Hercules surrounded by heroes in arms and Athena
  - Another theory is that the warriors of Marathon place themselves under the protection of Hercules
- First time in vase painting that isocephalism (the tradition of depicting heads of figures on the same level) has been jettisoned; may have been the influence of wall paintings
- **Cross-Cultural Comparisons: Ceramics**
  - Beaker with ibex motifs (Figure 1.10)
  - The David Vases (Figure 24.11)
  - Martínez, Black-on-black ceramic vessel (Figure 26.14)

Figure 4.19: Niobid Painter, *Niobides Krater*, 460–450 B.C.E., clay, Louvre, Paris

Greek Painting

Alexander Mosaic from the House of Faun, c. 310 B.C.E., Roman copy of c. 100 B.C.E., mosaic, National Archaeological Museum, Naples (Figure 4.20)

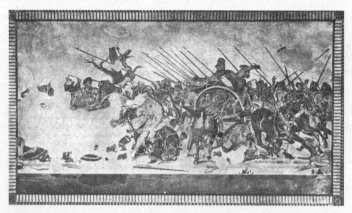

Figure 4.20: _Alexander Mosaic_ from the House of Faun, c. 310 B.C.E., Roman copy of c. 100 B.C.E., mosaic, National Archaeological Museum, Naples

- Alexander at left: young, brave, forthright, assured of success
- Darius in center right on chariot: horrified, weakly ceding the victory; his charioteer commands the horses to make their escape
- Crowded, with nervous excitement
- Roman floor mosaic based on an original Greek mural (?) painting, found at Pompeii
- Extremely complex interweaving of figures
- Perhaps a copy of a mural made by Philoxenos of Eretria for King Cassander
- Alternate theory: made by Helen of Egypt, one of the few female Greek artists who have come down to us
- **Cross-Cultural Comparisons: Battle and Glory**
  - Narmer Palette (Figure 3.4)
  - _Bayeux Tapestry_ (Figure 11.7a)
  - Delacroix, _Liberty Leading the People_ (Figure 20.4)

VOCABULARY

Acropolis: literally, a "high city," a Greek temple complex built on a hill over a city

Agora: a public plaza in a Greek city where commercial, religious, and societal activities are conducted (Figure 4.15)

Amphiprostyle: having four columns in the front and rear of a temple

Amphora: a two-handled ancient Greek storage jar

Architrave: a plain, unornamented lintel on the entablature (Figure 4.14)

Athena: Greek goddess of war and wisdom; patron of Athens

Canon: a body of rules or laws; in Greek art, the ideal mathematical proportion of a figure

Caryatid (male: **atlantid**): a building column that is shaped like a female figure (Figure 4.13)

Cella: the main room of a temple where the god is housed

Contrapposto: a graceful arrangement of the body based on tilted shoulders and hips and bent knees (Figure 4.3)

Corinthian: an order of ancient Greek architecture similar to the Ionic, except that the capitals are carved in tiers of leaves

Cornice: a projecting ledge over a wall (Figure 4.14)

Doric: an order of ancient Greek architecture that features grooved columns with no grooved bases and an upper story with square sculpture called metopes

Entablature: the upper story of a Greek temple (Figure 4.14)

Frieze: a horizontal band of sculpture (Figure 4.5)

Gigantomachy: a mythical ancient Greek war between the giants and the Olympian gods (Figure 4.9)

In Situ: a Latin expression that means that something is in its original location

Ionic: an order of Greek architecture that features columns with scrolled capitals and an upper story with sculptures that are in friezes

Isocephalism: the tradition of depicting heads of figures on the same level (Figure 4.5)

Kiln: an oven used for making pottery

Kouros (female: **kore**): an archaic Greek sculpture of a standing youth (Figures 4.1 and 4.2)

Krater: a large ancient Greek bowl used for mixing water and wine (Figure 4.19)

Metope: a small relief sculpture on the façade of a Greek temple (Figure 4.14)

Mosaic: a decoration using pieces of stone, marble, or colored glass, called **tesserae**, that are cemented to a wall or a floor (Figure 4.20)

Nike: ancient Greek goddess of victory (Figure 4.8)

Niobe: the model of a grieving mother; after boasting of her twelve children, jealous gods killed them

Panathenaic Way: a ceremonial road for a procession built to honor Athena during a festival (Figure 4.15)

Pediment: the triangular top of a temple that contains sculpture (Figure 4.14)

Peplos: a garment worn by women in ancient Greece, usually full length and tied at the waist (Figure 4.2)

Peristyle: a colonnade surrounding a building or enclosing a courtyard (Figure 4.16b)

Portico: an entranceway to a building having columns supporting a roof

Propylaeum (plural: **propylaea**): a gateway leading to a Greek temple

Relief sculpture: sculpture that projects from a flat background. A very shallow relief sculpture is called a **bas-relief** (pronounced: bah-relief) (Figure 4.5)

Shaft: the body of a column (Figure 4.14)

Stele (plural: **stelae**): an upright stone slab used to mark a grave or a site (Figure 4.7)

Stoa: an ancient Greek covered walkway having columns on one side and a wall on the other (Figure 4.15)

Tholos: an ancient Greek circular shrine (Figure 4.12)

Trigylph: a projecting grooved element alternating with a metope on a Greek temple (Figure 4.14)

Zeus: king of the ancient Greek gods; known as Jupiter to the Romans; god of the sky and weather

SUMMARY

The Greeks have had such a powerful influence on history that we have dubbed their art "classical," a word that means, among many other things, a standard of authority.

Greek temples are typically surrounded by an imposing set of columns that embrace the cella where the god is housed. The temple itself is often set apart from the rest of the city, sometimes located on an adjoining hill called an acropolis. Greek theaters, like the temples, are built of cut stone carefully carved into an important site.

Greek sculpture and pottery (little painting survives) are divided into a number of periods. Geometric pottery is characterized by linear designs and abstract patterns. The next style, called Orientalizing, shows an influence of Egyptian and Mesopotamian art.

Greek Archaic art is known for its bolt upright figures and animating smiles. The Classical period is characterized by the use of contrapposto, a figure placed in a relaxed pose and standing naturally. Fifth century B.C.E. art is known for its idealized body types; however, more humanizing expressions characterize fourth century B.C.E. work.

The last phase, called Hellenistic, shows figures with a greater range of expression and movement. Often sculptures look beyond themselves, at an approaching enemy perhaps, or in the face of an unseen wind.

Whatever the period, Greek art has provided a standard against which other classicizing trends in art history have been measured.

PRACTICE EXERCISES

Multiple-Choice

1. The tradition of depicting figures in isocephalism applied to all of the following works EXCEPT the

   (A) *Tomb of the Triclinium*
   (B) *Niobides Krater*
   (C) *Plaque of the Ergastines*
   (D) Last Judgment of Hu-Nefer

2. To emphasize realism seen in *The Seated Boxer*, the artist used

   (A) gold to symbolize the boxer's victory over his opponents
   (B) ivory to highlight the tousled nature of his hair during combat
   (C) copper to indicate wounds on the hands
   (D) blood to give a sense of the physical combat of boxing

3. *Helios, Horses and Dionysos* is a sculptural group placed on the pediment of the Parthenon because these figures

   (A) helped Athena defeat Neptune
   (B) were witnesses to Athena's birth
   (C) are associated with the Athenian king, Erechtheus
   (D) were part of the Panathenaic procession

4. The function of the *Anavysos Kouros is to*

   (A) mark the grave of a dead athlete
   (B) worship a Greek god
   (C) celebrate a military victory
   (D) honor athletes from the Olympics

5. The *Anavysos Kouros* has in common with Egyptian sculpture its

   (A) nudity
   (B) facial expression
   (C) contrapposto
   (D) stance

Short Essay

The images below show the Great Altar of Zeus at Pergamon and a detail of *Athena Battling Alkyoneos.*

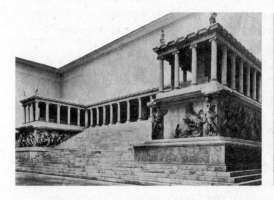 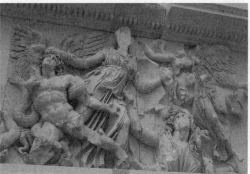

Describe the scene taking place on the frieze.

Why has this scene been placed on this monument?

What contemporary events are paralleled in the scenes depicted in this work?

What is the message this scene was meant to convey to the ancient Greek viewer?

ANSWERS EXPLAINED

Multiple-Choice

1. **(B)** Isocephalism is the tradition of depicting heads of figures on the same level, something that does not occur on the *Niobides Krater.*

2. **(C)** There are a number of copper highlights on the work, the most visible being the wounds on the hands of the boxer.

3. **(B)** *Helios, Horses and Dionysos* were witnesses to Athena's birth; therefore, they belong on the pediment of a temple dedicated to her.

4. **(A)** As an inscription at the base indicates, this sculpture was meant to honor a dead athlete.

5. **(D)** Both the *Anavysos Kouros* and Egyptian sculptures such as *Menkaura and His Queen* have the same stance, with one foot placed before the other, even as the torso remains rigid.

Short-Essay Rubric

Question	Points	Key Points in a Good Response
Describe the scene taking place on the frieze.	1	The frieze shows the battle between the Greek gods and the giants; the giants are defeated and brought up the stairs of the frieze to worship the gods.
Why has this scene been placed on this monument?	1	Answers could include: ■ This scene is here to show the power of the Greek gods (and the Greeks). ■ The architectural steps and the sculptural program act together to depict a mighty sanctuary in which the giants are literally dragged up the stairs to worship Athena and Zeus.
What contemporary events are paralleled in the scenes depicted in this work?	2	Answers could include: ■ The gods' victory over the giants offers a parallel to Alexander the Great's defeat of the Persians, and/or ■ King Attalos I's victories over the Gauls
What is the message this scene was meant to convey to the ancient Greek viewer?	1	Among the points to be mentioned, include: ■ The Greeks are mighty in war and can defeat larger enemies. ■ No matter how great the enemy is, the Greek gods protect the Greek people. ■ Foreigners will be taught to respect the Greeks and their gods.

Etruscan Art

5

TIME PERIOD

Tenth century B.C.E. to c. 270 B.C.E.
Height: seventh–sixth centuries B.C.E.

ENDURING UNDERSTANDING: Etruscan art is characterized by a pantheon of gods celebrated in large civic and religious buildings.

Essential Knowledge:

- Etruscan art is studied as a unit, rather than by individual city-states.
- Etruscan art shows a number of ancient influences.

ENDURING UNDERSTANDING: Etruscan art is known primarily through archaeology.

Essential Knowledge:

- The Etruscan literary tradition is mostly lost.

HISTORICAL BACKGROUND

The Etruscans are the people who lived in Italy before the arrival of the Romans. Although they heavily influenced the Romans, their language and customs were different. The ravages of time have destroyed much of what the Etruscans accomplished, but fortunately their sophisticated tombs in huge **necropoli** still survive in sufficient numbers to give us some idea of Etruscan life and art. Eventually the Romans swallowed Etruscan culture whole, taking from it what they could use.

ETRUSCAN ARCHITECTURE

Much of what is known about the Etruscans comes from their tombs, which are arranged in densely packed **necropoli** throughout the Italian region of Tuscany, an area named for the Etruscans. Most tombs are round structures with a door leading to a large interior chamber that is brightly painted to reflect the interior of an Etruscan home. These tombs frequently have symbols of the Etruscan lifestyle on their walls. Entire families, with their servants, are often buried in one tomb.

Little is known about Etruscan temples, except what can be gleaned from the Roman architect Vitruvius, who wrote about them extensively. Superficially, they seem to be inspired by

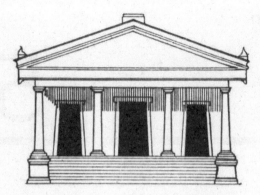

Figure 5.1a: Reconstruction drawing of the façade of the Temple of Minerva, 510–500 B.C.E., mud brick or tufa and wood, Veii, Italy

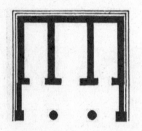
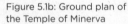

Figure 5.1b: Ground plan of the Temple of Minerva

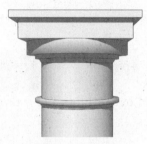

Figure 5.2: Tuscan capital

Greek buildings, with their pediments and columns, and the cella behind the porch. But Etruscan buildings were made of wood and **mud brick**, not stone. Moreover, there is a flight of stairs leading up to the principal entrance, not a uniform set of steps surrounding the whole building. Sculptures were placed on the rooftops, unlike in Greek temples, to announce the presence of the deity within.

Temple of Minerva, 510–500 B.C.E., mud brick or tufa and wood, Veii, Italy (Figures 5.1a and 5.1b)

- Little architecture survives; this model is drawn from descriptions by Vitruvius, a Roman architect during the first century B.C.E.
- Temple made of mud brick and wood
- Steps in front direct attention to the deep porch; entrances emphasized
- Influences of Greek architecture in the columns and capitals; columns are unfluted, made of wood
- Etruscan variation on Greek capitals, called the Tuscan order (Figure 5.2)
- Raised on a podium
- Three doors represent three gods; division of interior into three spaces

ETRUSCAN PAINTING

What survives of Etruscan painting is funerary, done on the walls and ceilings of tombs—some 280 painted chambers are still extant. Brightly painted frescoes reveal a world full of cheerful Etruscans celebrating, dancing, eating, and playing musical instruments. Much of the influence is probably Greek, but even less Greek painting from this period survives, so it is hard to draw firm parallels.

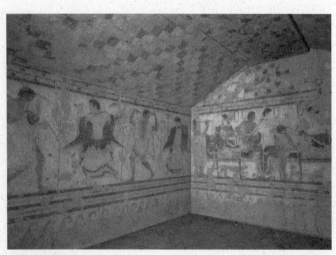

Figure 5.3: Tomb of the Triclinium. c. 480–470 B.C.E., tufa and fresco, Tarquinia, Italy

Tomb of the Triclinium, c. 480–470 B.C.E., tufa and fresco, Tarquinia, Italy (Figure 5.3)

- Named after a triclinium, an ancient Roman dining table, which appears in the fresco
- Banqueting couples recline, eating in the ancient manner
- Ancient convention of men painted in darker colors than women
- Trees spring up between the main figures, and shrubbery grows beneath the reclining couches—perhaps suggesting a rural setting
- Perhaps a funeral banquet is intended, but the emotions are of celebration

- Ceiling has polychrome checkerboard pattern; circles may symbolize time
- Dancing figures play musical instruments in festive celebration of the dead
- **Cross-Cultural Comparisons: Fresco murals**
  - Arena Chapel (Figure 13.1b)
  - Sistine Chapel (Figure 16.2a)
  - House of the Vettii (Figures 6.7a, 6.7b)

ETRUSCAN SCULPTURE

Etruscans prefered terra-cotta, **stucco**, and bronze for their sculpture; on occasion, stonework was introduced. Terra-cotta sculptures were modeled rather than carved. The firing of large-scale works in a kiln betray great technological prowess.

   Most Etruscan sculpture shows an awareness of Greek Archaic art, although the comparisons go only so far. In Greece, kouros figures were carved as stoic and proud, with an occasional smile to give life. For the Etruscans, whose terra-cotta work was brilliantly painted, figures move dynamically in space, aware of the world around them. Both cultures emphasize the broad shoulders of men and a stylization of the hair; however, the Etruscans avoid nudity.

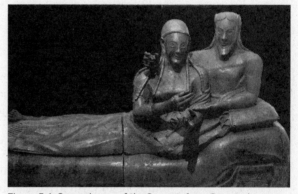

Figure 5.4: *Sarcophagus of the Spouses* from Cerveteri, c. 520 B.C.E., terra-cotta, Museo Nazionale di Villa Giulia, Rome

Sarcophagus of the Spouses **from Cerveteri, c. 520 B.C.E., terra-cotta, Museo Nazionale di Villa Giulia, Rome (Figure 5.4)**

- Sarcophagus of a married couple, whose ashes were placed inside
- Full-length portraits
- Both once held objects in their hands—perhaps an egg to symbolize life after death
- Great concentration on the upper body; less on the legs
- Bodies make an unrealistic L-turn to the legs
- Ancient tradition of reclining while eating; represents a banquet couch
- Symbiotic relationship: man has a protective gesture around the woman; the woman feeds the man; reflects the high standing women had in Etruscan society
- Broad shoulders; little anatomical modeling
- Emaciated hands
- Made in four separate pieces and joined together

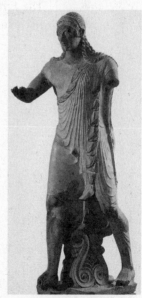

Figure 5.5: *Apollo from Veii*, c. 510 B.C.E., terra-cotta, Museo Nazionale di Villa Giulia, Rome

Apollo from Veii, **c. 510 B.C.E., terra-cotta, Museo Nazionale di Villa Giulia, Rome (Figure 5.5)**

- One of four large figures that once stood on the roof of the Temple at Veii, dedicated to Minerva (see Figure 5.1)
- Meant to be seen from below
- Figure has spirit, moves quickly as it strides forward
- Archaic Greek smile
- May have been carved by Vulcan of Veii, the most famous Etruscan sculptor of the age

■ **Cross-Cultural Comparisons: The Figure in Motion**
  - Shiva as Lord of Dance (Figure 23.6)
  - Nio guardian figures (Figures 25.1c, 25.1d)
  - Running Horned Woman (Figure 1.9)

VOCABULARY

Necropolis (plural: **necropoli**): a large burial area; literally, a "city of the dead"

Stucco: a fine plaster used for wall decorations or moldings

Terra-cotta: a hard ceramic clay used for building or for making pottery (Figures 5.4 and 5.5)

Triclinium: a dining table in ancient Rome that has a couch on three sides for reclining at meals

Tufa: a porous rock similar to limestone

Tumulus (plural: **tumuli**): an artificial mound of earth and stones placed over a grave

Tuscan order: an order of ancient architecture featuring slender, smooth columns that sit on simple bases; no carvings on the frieze or in the capitals (Figure 5.2).

SUMMARY

The Etruscans were a people who occupied central Italy before the arrival of the Romans—indeed, the region Tuscany is named for them. The remains of their civilization can be gleaned from written sources of later historians like Vitruvius or from what was buried in their expansive necropoli.

The Etruscans erected large mound-shaped tombs that contained a single large room in which the deceased were interred. The wall murals and stucco designs on the interior of the tombs are thought to parallel the interior of Etruscan homes. Large sarcophagi, made of terra-cotta, were placed within the tomb, usually containing the ashes of the deceased. The style of these works betrays a knowledge of Archaic Greek works from around the same time.

The Etruscans were eventually overwhelmed by the Romans, who continued to employ Etruscan artists well into the Roman Republic.

Multiple-Choice

Questions 1–2 refer to the image below.

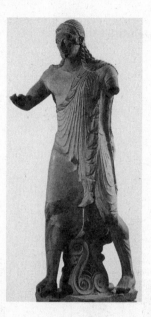

1. The sculpture of *Apollo from Veii* is inspired by ancient Greek works like kouroi figures EXCEPT that the

    (A)   Etruscan works have a smile that adds a lifelike quality to the sculpture
    (B)   Greek works are life-size
    (C)   Greek works have a more firmly articulated body
    (D)   Etruscan works move in space more dramatically

2. The *Apollo from Veii* was probably originally placed
    (A)   in a city square as a commemoration
    (B)   in a cemetery as a grave marker
    (C)   on a temple roof as part of a reenactment of a mythological story
    (D)   in a government building as a guiding spirit

---

3. Etruscans placed their tombs in tumuli, which were located in a necropolis. This was also done in which other ancient civilization?

    (A)   Egyptian
    (B)   Korean
    (C)   Persian
    (D)   Aztec

4. Etruscan art is unique in its

   (A)   use of painted terra-cotta
   (B)   ability to show contrapposto in large-scale sculpture
   (C)   tradition of depicting men and women together in a funerary monument
   (D)   painting of stone sculpture to give a work its lifelike quality

5. Etruscan tombs have fresco paintings that show

   (A)   funerary banquets
   (B)   mythological scenes
   (C)   historical panoramas
   (D)   last judgment scenes

Short Essay

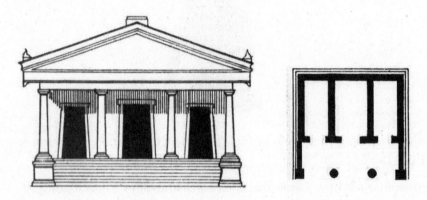

This is the reconstructed façade and ground plan of the Temple of Minerva from Veii, Italy, built around 510–500 B.C.E.

Temples like these were influenced by temple construction from ancient Greece. Identify an ancient Greek temple.

Using specific details, discuss how the ancient Greek temple influenced construction of the Etruscan temple.

Using specific details, discuss how Etruscan temples differ from Greek temples both in construction and function.

1. **D**   2. **C**   3. **B**   4. **C**   5. **A**

ANSWERS EXPLAINED

Multiple-Choice

1. **(D)** Etruscan works stride forward rather than stand at attention like kouroi from Archaic Greece.

2. **(C)** Sculptures like these were placed on the roofs of buildings, indicating important moments in mythological stories.

3. **(B)** Etruscan art is found in tumuli, like the gold and silver crown from the Silla Kingdom in Korea.

4. **(C)** The *Sarcophagus of the Spouses* is an Etruscan innovation depicting a relative parity between the sexes.

5. **(A)** Etruscan tombs, like those of the Triclinium in Tarquinia, Italy, depict people celebrating the life of the deceased with a funerary banquet.

Short-Essay Rubric

Question	Points	Key Points in a Good Response
Identify an ancient Greek temple.	1	Parthenon in Athens, Greece, by Iktinos and Kallikrates, c. 447–424 B.C.E., marble
Examining specific details, discuss how the ancient Greek temple influenced construction of the Etruscan temple.	2	Answers could include: ■ Greek elements of construction: pediment, columns, stairs, outdoor porch ■ Held a cult statue ■ Main room with subsidiary rooms ■ Decorated with sculpture ■ Both used to worship gods
Examining specific details, discuss how Etruscan temples are different from Greek temples both in construction and function.	2	Answers could include: ■ Made of wood, mud brick, and tufa; not marble as in Greek buildings ■ Sculpture made of terra-cotta, not marble as in Greek buildings ■ Flight of stairs in the front, not all around the sides as in Greek buildings ■ Interior porch leads to three chambers, indicating a different function for each, not one chamber as in Greek buildings ■ Four-column front, not eight or more as in Greek buildings ■ Walls around sides and back; columns all around the building as in Greek buildings ■ Capitals done in the Tuscan order, not Doric or Ionic as in the Greek buildings

Roman Art

6

TIME PERIOD: 753 B.C.E.–FIFTH CENTURY C.E.

Legendary founding of Rome by Romulus and Remus	753 B.C.E.
Roman Republic	509 B.C.E.–27 B.C.E.
Roman Empire	27 B.C.E.–410 C.E.

ENDURING UNDERSTANDING: Roman art is characterized by a pantheon of gods celebrated in large civic and religious buildings.

Essential Knowledge:

- Roman art can be subdivided into the following periods: Republican, Early Imperial, Late Imperial, and Late Antique.
- Roman architecture has a large public element and is influenced by Etruscan and Greek models. Roman architecture shows a great deal of variety and a willingness to experiment.
- Roman art was revived with an eighteenth-century interest in Roman laws, government, and philosophy.

ENDURING UNDERSTANDING: Much ancient writing survives in the fields of literature, law, politics, and business. These documents shed light on Roman civilization as a whole, and on Roman art in particular.

Essential Knowledge:

- Roman writing contains some of the earliest contemporary accounts about art and artists.
- Epics form the foundation of Roman writing. The texts were at first transmitted orally, but later were written down.

HISTORICAL BACKGROUND

From hillside village to world power, Rome rose to glory by diplomacy and military might. The effects of Roman civilization are still felt today in the fields of law, language, literature, and the fine arts.

According to legend, Romulus and Remus, abandoned twins, were suckled by a She-Wolf, and later established the city of Rome on its fabled seven hills. At first the state was ruled by kings, who were later overthrown and replaced by a Senate. The Romans then established a democracy of a sort, with magistrates ruling the country in concert with the Senate, an elected body of privileged Roman men.

Variously well-executed wars increased Rome's fortunes and boundaries. In 211 B.C.E., the Greek colony of Syracuse in Sicily was annexed. This was followed, in 146 B.C.E., by the absorption of Greece. The Romans valued Greek cultural riches and imported boatloads of sculpture, pottery, and jewelry to adorn the capital. Moreover, a general movement took hold to reproduce Greek art by establishing workshops that did little more than make copies of Greek sculpture.

Civil war in the late Republic caused a power vacuum that was filled by Octavian, later called Augustus Caesar, who became emperor in 27 B.C.E. From that time, Rome was ruled by a series of emperors as it expanded to faraway Mesopotamia and then retracted to a shadow of itself when it was sacked in 410 C.E.

The single most important archaeological site in the Roman world is the city of Pompeii, which was buried by volcanic ash from Mount Vesuvius in 79 C.E. In 1748, systematic excavation—actually more like fortune hunting—was begun. Because of Pompeii, we know more about daily life in Rome than we know about any other ancient civilization.

Patronage and Artistic Life

The Roman state and its wealthiest individuals were the major patrons of the arts. They could be known to spend lavishly on themselves and their homes, but they also felt a dedication to the general good and generously patronized public projects as well.

The homes of wealthy Romans, such as the ones that survive at Pompeii, were stage sets in which the influential could demonstrate their power and privilege. Elaborate social rituals inspired Romans to build their houses in order to impress and entertain. Consequently, Romans designed lavishly appointed interiors containing everything from finely executed fresco paintings to marble plumbing fixtures. Thus the interiors were grand domestic spaces that announced the importance of the owner. Artists, considered low members of the social scale, were treated poorly. Many were slaves who toiled in anonymity.

ROMAN ARCHITECTURE

The Romans were master builders. Improving upon nascent architectural techniques, they forged great roads and massive aqueducts as an efficient way of connecting their empire and making cities livable. Their temples were hymns to the gods and symbols of civic pride. Their arenas awed spectators both by their size and their engineering genius.

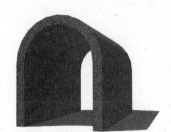

Figure 6.1: Barrel vault

The Romans understood the possibilities of the arch, an architectural device known before but little used. Because arches could span huge spaces, they do not need the constant support of the post-and-lintel system. Each wedge-shaped stone of a Roman arch is smaller at the bottom and wider at the top. This seemingly simple development allowed a stable arch to stand indefinitely because the wider top could not pass through the narrower bottom. Mortar is not needed because the shape of stones in the arch supports the structure unaided. Buildings without mortar are built in a technique known as **ashlar masonry.**

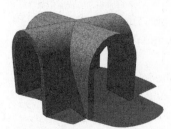

Figure 6.2: Groin vault

Roman architects understood that arches could be extended in space and form a continuous tunnel-like construction called a **barrel vault** (Figure 6.1). When two barrel vaults intersect, a larger, more open space is formed, called a **groin vault** (Figure 6.2). The latter is particularly important because the groin vault could be supported with only four corner **piers,** rather than requiring a continuous wall space that a barrel vault needed (Figure 6.3). The spaces between the arches on the piers are called **spandrels** (Figure 6.4).

Arches and vaults make enormous buildings possible, like the **Colosseum** (72–80 C.E.) (Figure 6.8), and they also make feasible vast interior spaces like the **Pantheon** (118–125 C.E.) (Figures 6.11a and 6.11b). Concrete walls are very heavy. To prevent the weight of a dome from cracking the walls beneath it, **coffers** (Figure 6.5) are carved into ceilings to lighten the load.

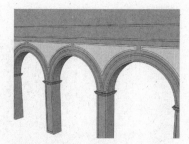

Figure 6.3: Piers

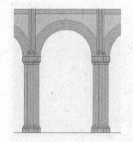

Figure 6.4: Spandrels are in the light areas

The Romans used concrete in constructing many of their oversized buildings. Although not their invention, once again they made this technique workable, using it initially as filler in buildings and then as the main support element. Romans thought that concrete was aestheticly displeasing, so although its flexibility and low cost were desirable, concrete was cloaked with another material, like marble, which seemed more attractive.

Much is known about Roman domestic architecture, principally because of what has been excavated at Pompeii. The exteriors of Roman houses have few windows, keeping the world at bay. A single entrance is usually flanked by stores which face the street. Stepping through the doorway one enters an open-air courtyard called an **atrium**, which has an **impluvium** to capture rainwater. Private bedrooms, called **cubicula**, radiate around the atrium. The atrium provides the only light and air to these windowless, but beautifully decorated, rooms.

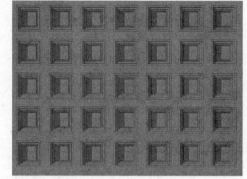

Figure 6.5: Coffers

The Romans placed their intimate rooms deeper into the house. Eventually another atrium, perhaps held up by columns called a **peristyle**, provided access to a garden flanked by more cubicula.

Grander Roman buildings, such as the **Colosseum** (Figure 6.8) and the **Pantheon** (Figure 6.11) use concrete, arches, and the various kinds of vaulting techniques to achieve grand and spacious effects.

The center of the Roman business world was the **forum**, a large public square framed by the principal civic buildings. The gods needed to be worshipped and appeased; therefore, the focus of all fora is the temple dedicated to the locally favorite god. Around the sides of the forum are bath houses, markets, and administrative buildings dealing with life's everyday essentials.

Although the Romans sometimes use Greek and Etruscan columns in their architecture, they are just as likely to use adapted forms that were inspired by their earlier counterparts. **Composite columns** first seen in the Arch of Titus have a mix of Ionic (the volute) and Corinthian (the leaf) motifs in the capitals. **Tuscan columns** as seen on the Colosseum are unfluted with severe Doric-style capitals (Figure 5.2).

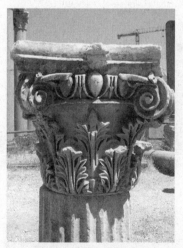

Figure 6.6: Composite capital

Both columns are raised on large pedestals to diminish the size of the viewers and increasing their sense of awe.

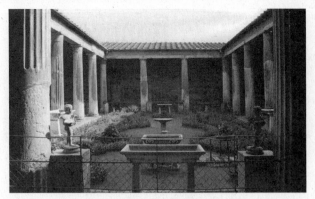

Figure 6.7a: House of the Vettii, 2nd century B.C.E.–1st century C.E., rebuilt c. 67–79 C.E., stone and fresco, Pompeii, Italy

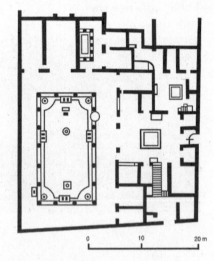

0   10   20 m

Figure 6.7b: House of the Vettii plan

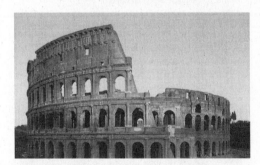

Figure 6.8a: The Colosseum, 72–80 C.E., stone and concrete, Rome

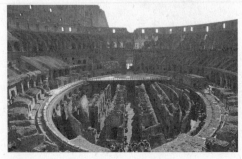

Figure 6.8b: The Colosseum, aerial view

Greek architecture remained a strong influence throughout Roman history. It was common for Roman temples to be fronted by Greek porches of columns and pediments, as in the **Pantheon**, even if the core of the building is completely Roman with its yawning domed interior.

House of the Vettii, second century B.C.E.–first century C.E., rebuilt c. 67–79 C.E., stone and fresco, Pompeii, Italy (Figures 6.7a and 6.7b)

- Two brothers owned the house; both were freedmen who made their money as merchants
- Narrow entrance sandwiched between several shops
- Large reception area, called the atrium, that is open to the sky and has a catch basin called an impluvium in the center; cubicula radiate around the atrium
- Peristyle garden in rear, with fountain, statuary, and more cubicula; this is the private area of the house
- Axial symmetry of house; someone entering the house can see all the way through to the peristyle garden in the rear
- Exterior of house lacks windows; interior lighting comes from the atrium and the peristyle

The Colosseum, 72–80 C.E., stone and concrete, Rome (Figures 6.8a and 6.8b)

- Real name is the Flavian Amphitheatre
- Accommodated 50,000 spectators
- Concrete core, brick casing, travertine facing
- 76 entrances and exits circle the façade
- Interplay of barrel vaults, groin vaults, arches
- Meant for wild and dangerous spectacles—gladiator combat, animal hunts, naval battles—but not, as tradition suggests, religious persecution
- Façade has engaged columns: first story Tuscan, second floor Ionic, third floor Corinthian, top flattened Corinthian; each thought of as lighter than the order below
- Above squared windows at top level are small brackets that are meant to hold flagstaffs; these staffs are the anchors for a retractable canvas roof used to protect the crowd on hot days
- Much of the marble was pulled off in the Middle Ages
- **Cross-Cultural Comparisons: Civic Spaces**
  - Hadid, MAAXI (Figures 29.2a, 29.2b)
  - Athenian Agora (Figure 4.15)
  - Mies van der Rohe, Seagram Building (Figure 22.18)

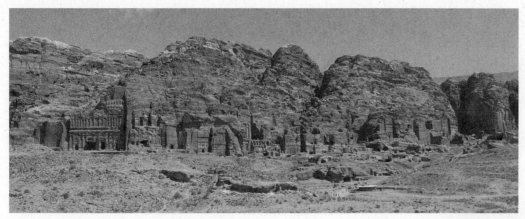

Figure 6.9a: Petra, 400 B.C.E.–100 C.E., cut rock, Jordan

Treasury, Monastery and Great Temple of Petra, Jordan, c. 400 B.C.E.–100 C.E., cut rock, Jordan (Figures 6.9a, 6.9b, and 6.9c)

- Petra as central city of the Nabataeans, a nomadic people
  - City built along a caravan route
  - Buried their dead in the tombs cut out of the sandstone cliffs
  - 500 royal tombs in the rock, but no human remains found; burial practices are unknown
- **Cross-Cultural Comparisons: City Planning**
  - Forum of Trajan (Figures 6.10a, 6.10b, 6.10c)
  - Persepolis (Figures 2.6a, 2.6b)
  - Hadid, MAAXI (Figures 29.2a, 29.2b)

Tomb named Al-Khazneh, "The Treasury"

- Lower story has the influence of Greek and Roman temples
- Columns not proportionally spaced
- Upper floor: broken pediment with a central tholos
- Combination of Roman and indigenous traditions
- Nabataean concept and Roman features like Corinthian columns
- Greek, Egyptian, Assyrian gods on the façade

Apollodorus of Damascus, Forum of Trajan, 106–112 C.E., Rome, Italy (Figure 6.10a)

- Built with booty collected from Trajan's victory over the Dacians
- Large central plaza flanked by stoa-like buildings on each flank
- Originally held an equestrian monument dedicated to Trajan in the center
- Part of a complex that included the Basilica of Ulpia, the Markets of Trajan, and the Column of Trajan

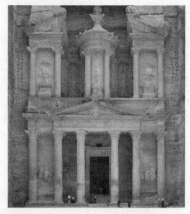

Figure 6.9b: Treasury at Petra, early second century, cut rock, Jordan

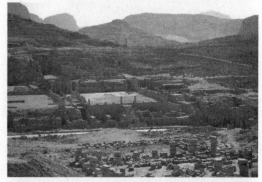

Figure 6.9c: Great Temple, early second century, cut rock, Jordan

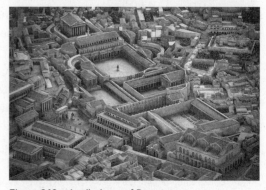

Figure 6.10a: Apollodorus of Damascus, Forum of Trajan, 106–112 C.E., Rome, Italy

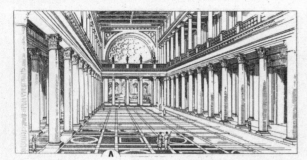

Figure 6.10b: Apollodorus of Damascus, Basilica of Ulpia, c.112 C.E., Rome, Italy

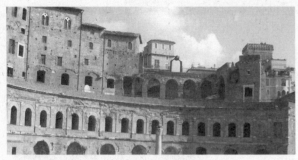

Figure 6.10c: Market of Trajan, 100–112 C.E., Rome

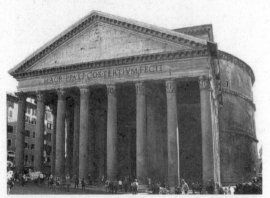

Figure 6.11a: Pantheon, 118–125 C.E., concrete with stone facing, Rome

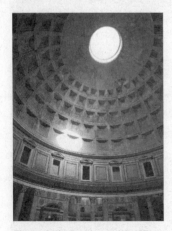

Figure 6.11b: Pantheon, 118–125 C.E., Rome

Apollodorus of Damascus, Basilica of Ulpia, c.112 C.E., Rome, Italy (Figure 6.10b)

- 385 feet by 182 feet, with two apses; grand interior space
- Nave is spacious and wide
- Double colonnaded side aisles
- Second floor had galleries or perhaps clerestory windows
- Timber roof 80 feet across
- Law courts held here; apses were a setting for the judges
- Said to have been paid for by Trajan's spoils taken from the defeat of the Dacians
- Ulpius was Trajan's family name

Market of Trajan, 106–112 C.E., brick and concrete, Rome (Figure 6.10)

- Original market had 150 shops
- Multilevel mall
- Semicircular building held several levels of shops
- Main space groin-vaulted; barrel-vaulted shops

Pantheon, 118–125 C.E., concrete with stone facing, Rome (Figures 6.11a and 6.11b)

- Dedicated to all the gods
- Inscription: "Marcus Agrippa, son of Lucius, having been consul three times, built it."
- Corinthian capital porch in front of building
- Façade has two pediments, one deeply recessed behind the other
- Square panels in floor and in coffers contrast with roundness of walls
- Coffers may have been filled with bronze rosette designs to simulate stars
- Cupola walls are enormously thick: 20 feet at base
- Oculus 27 feet across: allows for sunlight and air; acts as a moving spotlight across the interior
- Height of building equals its width; interior of building based on the circle, a hemisphere
- Walls have seven niches for statues of the gods
- Thickness of walls thinned at top, coffers take some weight pressure off walls
- Triumph of concrete construction
- Was brilliantly decorated
- Originally had a large atrium before it; originally built on a high podium; modern Rome has risen up to it
- **Cross-Cultural Comparisons: Houses of Worship**
  - Chartres Cathedral (Figures 12.4a, 12.4b)
  - Angkor Wat (Figure 23.8a)
  - Templo Mayor (Figure 26.5a)

ROMAN PAINTING

Interior wall paintings, created to liven up windowless Roman **cubicula**, were frescoed with mythological scenes, landscapes, and city plazas. Mosaics were favorite floor decorations—stone kept feet cool in summer. **Encaustics** from Egypt provided lively individual portraits of the deceased.

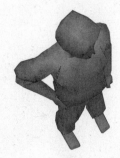

Figure 6.12a: Figure seen in foreshortening

Murals were painted with some knowledge of **linear perspective**—spatial relationships in landscape paintings appeared somewhat consistent. **Orthogonals** recede to multiple **vanishing points** in the distance. Sometimes, to present an object in the far distance, an artist used **atmospheric perspective**, a technique that employs cool pastel colors to create the illusion of deep recession. Figures were painted in **foreshortening** (Figures 6.12a and 6.12b), where they are seen at an oblique angle and seem to recede into space.

So much Pompeian wall painting survives that an early history of Roman painting can be reconstructed.

- First Pompeian Style is characterized by painted rectangular squares meant to resemble marble facing.
- Second Pompeian Style had large mythological scenes and/or landscapes dominating the wall surface. Painted stucco decoration of the First Style appears beneath in horizontal bands.
- Third Pompeian Style is characterized by small scenes set in a field of color and framed by delicate columns of tracery.
- Fourth Pompeian Style combine elements from the previous three: The painted marble of the First Style is at the base, the large scenes of the Second Style and the delicate small scenes of the Third Style are intricately interwoven. The frescos from the **Pentheus Room** (Figure 6.13) are from the Fourth Style.

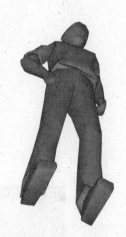

Figure 6.12b: Figure seen in foreshortening

Pentheus Room, 62–79 C.E., fresco, Pompeii, Italy (Figure 6.13)

- Triclinium: dining room in a Roman house
- Main scene is the death of the Greek hero Pentheus
- Pentheus opposed the cult of Bacchus and was torn to pieces by women, including his mother, in a Bacchic frenzy; two women pulling at his hair in this image
- Architecture seen through painted windows; imaginary landscape

Alexander Mosaic, **Roman mosaic copy of a Greek original, found in Pompeii:** *see under* **Greek Art, Figure 4.20**

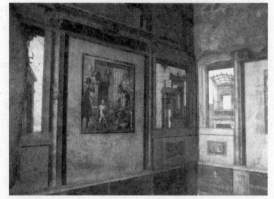

Figure 6.13: Pentheus Room, 62–79 C.E., fresco, Pompeii, Italy

ROMAN SCULPTURE

The Romans erected commemorative arches to celebrate military victories. Sculpture was applied to the surface to animate the architecture as well as to recount the story of Roman victories. A combination of painted relief and free-standing works was integrated into a coherent didactic program. Later arches used works from contemporary artists, as well as sculptures removed from arches of previous emperors, some two hundred years older. In this way the glory of the past was linked to the accomplishments of the present.

Another Roman innovation was the hollowed-out column with banded narrative relief sculptures spiraling around the exterior. The first, the *Column of Trajan* (112 C.E.) (Figure 6.16), had an entrance at the base, from which the visitor could ascend a spiral staircase and emerge onto a porch, where Trajan's architectural accomplishments would be revealed in all their glory. A statue of the emperor, which no longer exists, crowned the ensemble. The banded reliefs tell the story of Trajan's conquest of the Dacians. The spiraling turn of the narratives made the story difficult to read; scholars have suggested a number of theories that would have made the Column, and works like it, legible to the viewer.

Republican Sculpture

Republican **busts** of noblemen, called **veristic** sculptures, are strikingly and unflatteringly realistic, with the age of the sitter seemingly enhanced. This may have been a form of idealization: Republicans valued virtues such as wisdom, determination, and experience, which these works seem to possess.

Republican full-length statues concentrate on the heads, some of which are removed from one work and placed on another. The bodies were occasionally classically idealized, symbolizing valor and strength. The Romans had great respect for ancestors: Figures can sometimes be seen holding busts of their ancestors in their hands as a sign of their patrician heritage.

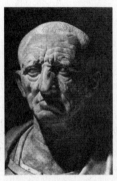

Figure 6.14: *Head of a Roman Patrician*, c. 75–50 B.C.E., marble, Museo Torlonia, Rome

Head of a Roman Patrician, c. 75–50 B.C.E., marble, Museo Torlonia, Rome (Figure 6.14)

- Realism of the portrayal shows influence of Greek Hellenistic art; late Etruscan art
- Extremely realistic face, called a veristic portrait
- Bulldog-like tenacity of features; overhanging flesh; deep crevices in face
- Full of experience and wisdom—traits Roman patricians would have desired
- Features may have been exaggerated by artist to enhance adherence to Republican virtues
- Busts are mostly of men; depicted as elderly
- **Cross-Cultural Comparisons: Portraits**
  - Mblo (Figure 27.7)
  - Sin Sukju (Figure 24.6)
  - Sherman, *Untitled #228* from the History of Portraits series (Figure 29.10)

Imperial Sculpture

While busts of senators conveyed the gruff virtues of Republican Rome, emperors, whose divinity descended from the gods themselves, were portrayed differently. Here, inspiration came from Classical Greece, and Roman sculptors adopted the contrapposto, ideal proportions, and heroic poses of Greek statuary. Forms became less individualized, iconography more associated with the divine.

At the end of the Early Imperial period, a stylistic shift begins to take place that transitions into the Late Imperial style. Perhaps reflecting the dissolution and anarchy of the Roman state, the classical tradition, so willingly embraced by previous emperors, is slowly abandoned by Late Imperial artists. Compositions are marked by figures that lack individuality and are crowded tightly together. Everything is pushed forward on the picture plane, as depth and recession were rejected along with the classicism they symbolize. Proportions are truncated—contrapposto ignored; bodies are almost lifeless behind masking drapery. Emperors are increasingly represented as military figures rather than civilian rulers.

Augustus of Prima Porta, 20 C.E., marble, copy of a bronze original, Vatican Museums, Rome (Figure 6.15)

- Idealized view of the Roman emperor
- Contrapposto, cf. *Spear Bearer* (Figure 4.3)
- Confusion between god and man intentional; sense of divine rule
- Standing barefoot indicates he is on sacred ground
- On his breastplate there are a number of gods participating in the return of Roman standards from the Parthians
- Breastplate indicates he is a warrior; judge's robes show him as a civic ruler
- Back not carved, meant to be placed against a wall
- Characteristic of Augustus is the part in the hair over the left eye, and two locks over the right
- May have carried a sword, pointing down, in his left hand
- Right hand in Roman orator pose, perhaps held laurel branches
- At base: Cupid on the back of a dolphin—a reference of Augustus's divine descent from Venus
- Found in the Villa of Livia, Augustus' wife
- **Cross-Cultural Comparisons: Power and Authority**
  - Ndop (Figure 27.5a)
  - Lindauer, *Tamati Waka Nene* (Figure 28.7)
  - Houdon, *George Washington* (Figure 19.7)

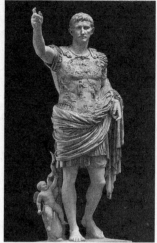

Figure 6.15: *Augustus of Prima Porta*, 20 C.E., marble copy of a bronze original, Vatican Museum, Rome

Column of Trajan, 112 C.E., marble, Rome (Figure 6.16)

- Burial chamber of Trajan, whose ashes were placed in the base
- Stood amid Trajan's Forum
- 128-feet high, 625-foot narrative cycle wrapped around the column, telling the story of Trajan's defeat of the Dacians
- 150 episodes; 2,500 figures; 23 registers; continuous narrative
- Crowded composition
- Low relief, few shadows to cloud what must have been a very difficult object to view in its entirety
- Scholarly debate over the way it was meant to be viewed
- Column meant to be entered; visitor to wander up the interior spiral staircase to the viewing platform at the top where a heroic nude statue of the Emperor was placed (now St. Peter has replaced him)
- View would impress visitor with Trajan's accomplishments, including his forum and his markets
- Two Roman libraries containing Greek and Roman manuscripts flanked the Column
- **Cross-Cultural Comparisons: Narrative in Art**
  - *The Bayeux Tapestry* (Figures 11.7a, 11.7b)
  - *Night Attack on the Sanjô Palace* (Figures 23.5a, 23.5b)
  - Walker, *Darkytown Rebellion* (Figure 29.21)

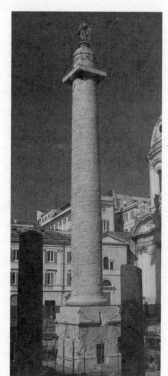

Figure 6.16: Column of Trajan, 112 C.E., marble, Rome, Italy

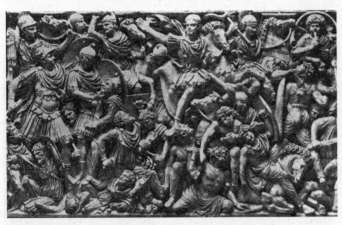

Figure 6.17: Ludovisi Battle Sarcophagus, c. 250–260 c.e., marble, National Roman Museum, Rome

Ludovisi Battle Sarcophagus, c. 250–260 C.E., marble, National Roman Museum, Rome (Figure 6.17)

- Extremely crowded surface with figures piled on top of one another
- Figures lack individuality
- Confusion of battle is echoed by congested composition
- Roman army trounces bearded and defeated barbarians
- Youthful Roman general appears center top with no weapons, and is the only Roman with no helmet indicating that he is invincible and needs no protection

- Rome at war throughout the third century
- **Cross-Cultural Comparisons: Relief Sculpture**
  - *Churning of the Ocean of Milk* (Figure 23.8c)
  - *Last Judgment* at Conques (Figure 11.6a)
  - Stele of Hammurabi (Figures 2.4a, 2.4b)

VOCABULARY

Ashlar masonry: carefully cut and grooved stones that support a building without the use of concrete or other kinds of masonry

Atrium (plural: atria): a courtyard in a Roman house or before a Christian church

Basilica: in Roman architecture, a large axially planned building with a nave, side aisles, and apses (Figure 6.10b)

Bust: a sculpture depicting a head, neck, and upper chest of a figure (Figure 6.14)

Coffer: in architecture, a sunken panel in a ceiling (Figure 6.5)

Composite column: one that contains a combination of volutes from the Ionic order and acanthus leaves from the Corinthian order

Continuous narrative: a work of art that contains several scenes of the same story painted or sculpted in a single frame

Contrapposto: a graceful arrangement of the body based on tilted shoulders and hips and bent knees (Figure 6.15)

Cubiculum (plural: cubicula): a Roman bedroom flanking an atrium; in Early Christian art, a mortuary chapel in a catacomb

Cupola: a small dome rising over the roof of a building; in architecture, a cupola is achieved by rotating an arch on its axis

Encaustic: an ancient method of painting that uses colored waxes burned into a wooden surface

Foreshortening: a visual effect in which an object is shortened and turned deeper into the picture plane to give the effect of receding in space (Figures 6.12a and 6.12b)

Forum (plural: fora): a public square or market place in a Roman city (Figure 6.10a)

Fresco: a painting technique that involves applying water-based paint onto a freshly plastered wall. The paint forms a bond with the plaster that is durable and long-lasting (Figure 6.13)

Impluvium: a rectangular basin in a Roman house that is placed in the open-air atrium in order to collect rainwater (Figure 6.7b)

Keystone: the center stone of an arch that holds the others in place

Oculus: a circular window in a church, or a round opening at the top of a dome (Figure 6.11b)

Peristyle: an atrium surrounded by columns in a Roman house (Figure 6.10a)

Perspective: depth and recession in a painting or a relief sculpture. Objects shown in **linear perspective** achieve a three-dimensionality in the two-dimensional world of the picture plane. All lines, called **orthogonals**, draw the viewer back in space to a common point, called the **vanishing point**. Paintings, however, may have more than one vanishing point, with orthogonals leading the eye to several parts of the work. Landscapes that give the illusion of distance are in **atmospheric** or **aerial perspective**

Pier: a vertical support that holds up an arch or a vault (Figure 6.3)

Spandrel: a triangular space enclosed by the curves of arches (Figure 6.4)

Triclinium: a dining table in ancient Rome that has a couch on three sides for reclining at meals

Tuscan order: an order of ancient architecture featuring slender, smooth columns that sit on simple bases.; no carvings on the frieze or in the capitals.

Vault: a roof constructed with arches. When an arch is extended in space, forming a tunnel, it is called a **barrel vault** (Figure 6.1). When two barrel vaults intersect at right angles, it is called a **groin vault** (Figure 6.2)

Veristic: sculptures from the Roman Republic characterized by extreme realism of facial features (Figure 6.14)

SUMMARY

Art was used to emphasize the power of the state in a society in which empire building was a specialty. Monumental buildings and sculptures graced the great cities of the Roman world. The introduction of new methods of vaulting and the use of new construction materials, like concrete, enabled the Romans to build structures that not only had impressive exteriors but also had unparalleled interiors of great spaciousness.

Much is known about Roman art because of the destruction of the city of Pompeii by the volcanic explosion of Vesuvius in 79 C.E. Remains of Roman paintings betray some knowledge of linear perspective and foreshortening. Frescoes dominate the walls of elaborate villas in this seaside resort.

The Romans greatly admired Greek sculpture and were inspired by it throughout their history; indeed, much is known about Greek art from Roman copies that survive. Republican veristic works were influenced by Hellenistic Greek art; Imperial sculptures are modeled more on the Greek Classical age. Even though Roman sculpture retained a grandeur until the end of the Empire, it increasingly took on a military character, as in works such as The Ludovisi Battle Sarcophagus.

PRACTICE EXERCISES

Multiple-Choice

1. Which of the following statements is true of both the Ludovisi Battle Sarcophagus and *Athena Battling Alkyoneos* from the Great Altar of Zeus and Athena at Pergamon?

(A)   They celebrate the victory of the gods over the giants.
(B)   They illustrate the conquest of barbarians.
(C)   They depict everyday events.
(D)   They show the defeat of Christian armies.

2. The form of the *Augustus of Prima Porta* is intended to recall

(A)   the majesty of Egyptian pharaohs as seen in works like *Menkaura and His Queen*
(B)   the idealization of the human form as seen in Greek classical sculptures such as the *Doryphoros*
(C)   the formal quality of Greek archaic sculptures like the *Anayvsos Kouros*
(D)   the Roman Republican veristic sculptures, such as the head of a Roman patrician

3. Which of the following works is a Roman copy of a Greek original?

(A)   *The Seated Boxer*
(B)   *The Winged Victory of Samothrace*
(C)   *The Peplos Kore*
(D)   *The Alexander Mosaic*

4. An atrium, such as the one seen in the House of Vettii, supplies light and air into the private spaces of a Roman home. Atriums can also function as

(A)   spaces conducive to family religious ceremonies
(B)   courtyards to conduct business in a more comfortable private setting
(C)   places to gather rainwater for household use
(D)   outdoor bedrooms in a protected space

5. The Column of Trajan had many functions, including all of the following EXCEPT:

(A)   it was the centerpiece of buildings surrounding the Forum of Trajan
(B)   it was used as a large sundial to indicate the time of day
(C)   it acted as the Emperor Trajan's tomb
(D)   it recounts the military victory of Emperor Trajan against the Dacians

Short Essay

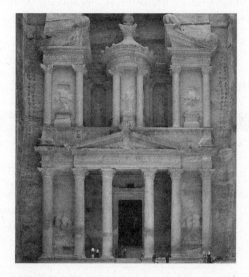

This is the Treasury at Petra, Jordan, dated between c. 400 B.C.E. and 100 C.E.

What was the function of this building?

Although built in the Roman period, it shows Greek influence. Which elements of the building are inspired from Greek architecture?

How has the design adapted the Greek elements in a non-traditional way to create a new architectural design?

ANSWER KEY

1. **B**   2. **B**   3. **D**   4. **C**   5. **B**

ANSWERS EXPLAINED

Multiple-Choice

1. **(B)** The Ludovisi Battle Sarcophagus illustrates a Roman victory over barbarians. The sculpture of *Athena Battling Alkyoneos* shows the victory of the gods over the giants. By implication, the Greeks were meant to see themselves as heroes over the barbarians who tried to conquer their land.

2. **(B)** *The Augustus of Prima Porta* is a Roman work whose idealization, contrapposto, and human form express a parallel with the works of the Greek classical period, particularly the *Doryphoros*.

3. **(D)** *The Alexander Mosaic* is a Roman copy of a Greek original, probably a fresco, that was found on the floor of a Roman villa at Pompeii.

4. **(C)** Interior atria often had impluvia, or basins, that were used to capture rainwater for household use.

5. **(B)** The Column of Trajan had many functions, including acting as a tomb for the emperor and as a glorification of his military victories. It also was the centerpiece in a vast complex of buildings that was built in central Rome. It did not tell time by acting as the point in a sundial.

Short-Essay Rubric

Question	Points	Key Points in a Good Response
What was the function of this building?	1	Although named a "treasury," the building was actually a tomb.
Which elements of the building are inspired from Greek architecture?	2	Answers could include: ■ Columns supporting an entablature ■ Pediment over the columns ■ Greek tholos structure ■ Door set back behind columns ■ Placement of sculpture in niches
How has the design adapted the Greek elements in a non-traditional way to create a new architectural design?	2	Answers could include: ■ Uneven and asymmetrical placement of columns ■ Tholos located on second story ■ Broken pediment on second story

Late Antique Art

7

TIME PERIOD: 200–500 C.E.

ENDURING UNDERSTANDING: Medieval art is studied according to geographic placement, styles, and traditions. There are frequent interconnections between religions, governments, and artistic influences that create a variety of approaches.

Essential Knowledge:

- Medieval periods are the following:
  - Late Antique and Early Christian: Chapter 7
  - Byzantine: Chapter 8
  - Islamic: Chapter 9
  - Early Medieval: Chapter 10
  - Romanesque: Chapter 11
  - Gothic: Chapters 12 and 13
- There is no uniform medieval style. Some periods revive ancient classicism; others use geometric and natural designs.
- Medieval artists are influenced by contemporaries in other parts of Europe, as well as ancient traditions.

ENDURING UNDERSTANDING: Medieval art is chiefly concerned with religious expression and court life. There is a strong culture of endorsing scholarship.

Essential Knowledge:

- Learning was centered on specific fields that were transmitted throughout Europe through trade, pilgrimage, and military activity.
- Medieval architecture is mostly religious.
- Medieval painting and sculpture avoids naturalistic depictions.
- At times medieval religions will reject images.

HISTORICAL BACKGROUND

Christianity, in the first century C.E., was founded by Jesus Christ, whose energetic preaching and mesmerizing message encouraged devoted followers like Saints Peter and Paul to spread the message of Christian faith and forgiveness across the Roman world through active missionary work. Influential books and letters, which today make up the New Testament, were powerful tools that fired the imagination of everyone from the peasant to the philosopher.

Literally an underground religion, Christianity had to hide in the corners of the Roman Empire to escape harsh persecutions, but the number of converts could not be denied, and gradually they became a majority. With Constantine's triumph at the Milvian Bridge in 312 C.E. came the Peace of the Church. Constantine granted restitution to Christians of state-confiscated property in the 313 C.E. Edict of Milan, which also granted religious toleration throughout the Empire. Constantine also favored Christians for government positions and constructed a series of religious buildings honoring Christian sites. Christianity was well on its way to becoming a state religion, with Emperor Constantine's blessing.

After emerging from the shadows, Christians began to build churches of considerable merit to rival the accomplishments of pagan Rome. However, pagan beliefs were by no means eradicated by the stroke of a pen, and ironically paganism took its turn as an underground religion in the Late Antique period.

Patronage and Artistic Life

It was not easy being a Christian in the first through third centuries. Persecutions were frequent; most of the early popes, including Saint Peter, were martyred. Those artists who preferred working for the more lucrative official government were blessed with great commissions in public places. Those who worked for Christians had to be satisfied with private church houses and burial chambers.

Most Christian art in the early centuries survives in the catacombs, buried beneath the city of Rome and other places scattered throughout the Empire. Christians were mostly poor—society's underclass. Artists imitated Roman works, but sometimes in a sketchy and unsophisticated manner. Once Christianity became recognized as an official religion, however, the doors of patronage sprang open. Christian artists then took their place alongside their pagan colleagues, eventually supplanting them.

EARLY CHRISTIAN ART

Christianity is an intensely narrative religion deriving its images from the various books of the New Testament. Christians were also inspired by parallel stories from the Old Testament, and they illustrated these to complement Christian ideology. Since there are no written accounts of what the men and women of the Bible looked like, artists recreated the episodes by relying on their imagination. The following episodes from the New Testament are most often depicted:

- *The Annunciation*: the Angel Gabriel announces to Mary that she will be the virgin mother of Jesus (Figure 14.1).
- *The Visitation*: Mary visits her cousin Elizabeth to tell her the news that she is pregnant with Jesus. Because she is elderly, Elizabeth's announcement of her own pregnancy is greeted as a miracle. Elizabeth gives birth to Saint John the Baptist.
- *Christmas* or *the Nativity*: the birth of Jesus in Bethlehem. Mary gives birth in a stable; her husband, Joseph, is her sole companion. Soon after, angels announce the birth to shepherds.
- *Adoration of the Magi*: Traditionally, three kings, who are also astrologers, are attracted by a star that shines over Jesus's manger. They come to worship him and present gifts.
- *Massacre of the Innocents:* After Jesus is born, King Herod issues an order to execute all male infants in the hope of killing him. His family takes him to safety in an episode called *The Flight into Egypt.*

- *Baptism of Jesus*: John the Baptist, Jesus's cousin, baptizes him in the Jordan River. Jesus's ministry officially begins.
- *Calling of the Apostles*: Jesus gathers his followers, including St. Matthew and St. Peter, as he proceeds in his ministry (Figure 17.5).
- *Miracles:* to prove his divinity, Jesus performs a number of miracles, like multiplying loaves and fishes, resurrecting the deceased Lazarus, and changing water into wine at the Wedding at Cana.
- *Giving the Keys*: sensing his own death, Jesus gives St. Peter the keys to the kingdom of Heaven, in effect installing him as his leader when he is gone, and therefore the first pope.
- *Transfiguration*: Jesus transfigures himself into God before the eyes of his apostles; this is the high point of his ministry.
- *Palm Sunday*: Jesus enters Jerusalem in triumph, greeted by throngs with palm branches.
- *Last Supper*: before Jesus is arrested he has a final meal with his disciples in which he institutes the Eucharist—that is, his body and blood in the form of bread and wine; at this meal he reveals that he knows that one of his apostles, Judas, has betrayed him for 30 pieces of silver (Figure 16.1).
- *Crucifixion*: after a brief series of trials, Jesus is sentenced to death for sedition. He is crowned with thorns, whipped with lashes, and forced to carry his cross through the streets of Jerusalem. At the top of a hill called Golgotha he is nailed to the cross and left to die. (Figure 14.4a)
- *Deposition/Lamentation/Entombment*: Jesus's body is removed from the cross by his relatives, cleaned, mourned over, and buried (Figure 16.5).
- *Resurrection*: On Easter Sunday, three days later, Jesus rises from the dead. On Ascension Day he goes to Heaven.

Also important are four author portraits of the Evangelists, who are the writers of the principal books, or gospels, of the New Testament. These books are arranged in the order in which it was traditionally believed they were written: Matthew, Mark, Luke, and John. Evangelist portraits appear often in Medieval and Renaissance art, each associated with an attribute:

- Matthew: angel or a man
- Mark: lion
- Luke: ox or calf (Figure 10.2b)
- John: eagle

These attributes derive from the Bible (Ezekiel 1:5–14; Revelations 4:6–8) and were assigned to the four evangelists by great philosophers of the early church such as St. Jerome.

Catacomb paintings, like the ones at **Priscilla** (Figure 7.1) from the fourth century, show a sensitivity toward artistic programs rather than random images. Jesus always maintains a position of centrality and dominance, but grouped around him are images that are carefully chosen either as Old Testament prefigurings or as subsidiary New Testament events. Early Christians learned from ancient paintings to frame figures in either **lunettes** or niches.

When Christianity was recognized as the official religion of the Roman Empire in 380 c.e., Christ was no longer depicted as the humble Good Shepherd; instead he took on imperial imagery. His robes become the imperial purple and gold, his crook a staff, his halo a symbol of the sun-king.

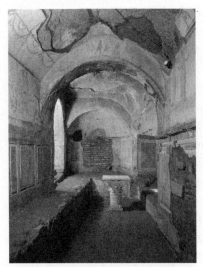

Figure 7.1a Greek Chapel in the Catacomb of Priscilla, 200–400, tufa and fresco, Rome, Italy

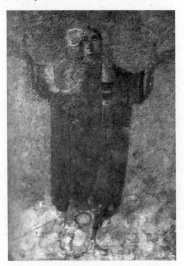

Figure 7.1b Orant Figure in the Catacomb of Priscilla

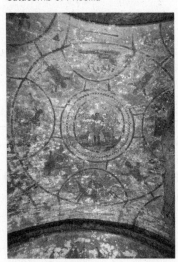

Figure 7.1c Good Shepherd Fresco in the Catacomb of Priscilla

Unlike Roman mosaics, which are made of rock, Christian mosaics are often of gold or precious materials and faced with glass. Christian mosaics glimmer with the flickering of mysterious candlelight to create an otherworldly effect.

Catacomb of Priscilla, 200–400, tufa and fresco, Rome, Italy (Figures 7.1a, 7.1b, and 7.1c)

- Catacombs beneath Rome have 4 million dead, and extend for about 100 miles
- Contains the tombs of seven popes and many early Christian martyrs
- Greek Chapel (Figure 7.1a):
  - Named for two Greek inscriptions painted on the right niche
  - Three niches for sarcophagi
  - Decorated with paintings in the Pompeian style; sketchy painterly brushstrokes
- Orants Figure (Figure 7.1b):
  - Fresco over a tomb niche set over an arched wall; cemetery of a family vault
  - Stand with arms outstretched in prayer
  - Figure is compact, dark, set off from a light background; terse angular contours; emphatic gestures
  - Left: painting of a teacher with children
  - Right: mother and child (perhaps Mary with Christ or the Church)
- Good Shepherd Fresco (Figure 7.1c):
  - Restrained portrait of Christ as a Good Shepherd, a pastoral motif in ancient art going back to the Greeks
  - Symbolism of the Good Shepherd: rescues individual sinners in his flock who stray
  - Stories of the life of the Old Testament Prophet Jonah often appear in the lunettes; Jonah's regurgitation from the mouth of a big fish is seen as prefiguring Christ's resurrection
  - Parallels between Old and New Testament stories feature prominently in Early Christian art; Christians see this as a fulfillment of the Hebrew scriptures
- **Cross-Cultural Comparisons: Ceiling paintings**
  - Sistine Chapel Ceiling (Figure 16.2a)
  - Arena Chapel (Figure 13.1b)
  - Gaulli, *Triumph of the Name of Jesus* (Figure 17.6)

EARLY CHRISTIAN ARCHITECTURE

Under the city of Rome can be found a hundred miles of **catacombs**, sometimes five stories deep, with millions of interred bodies. Christians, Jews, and pagans used these burial grounds because they found this a cheaper alternative to aboveground interment. Finding the Roman practice of cremation repugnant, Christians preferred burial because it symbolized Jesus's, as well as their own, rising from the dead—body and soul.

Catacombs were dug from the earth in a maze of passageways that radiated out endlessly from the starting point. The poor were placed in **loculi**, which were holes cut in the walls of the catacombs meant to receive the bodies of the dead. Usually the bodies were folded over to take up less room. The wealthy had their bodies blessed in mortuary chapels, called **cubicula**, and then often placed in extravagant sarcophagi.

After the Peace of the Church in 313 C.E., Christians understood how they could adapt Roman architecture to their use. Basilicas, with their large, groin-vaulted interiors and impressive naves, were meeting places for the influential under the watchful gaze of the emperor's statue. Christians reordered the basilica, turning the entrance to face the far end instead of the side, and focused attention directly on the priest, whose altar (meaning "high place") was elevated in the **apse**. The clergy occupied the perpendicular aisle next to the apse, called the **transept**. Male worshippers stood in the long main aisle called the **nave**; females were relegated to the side aisles with partial views of the ceremony. In this way, Christians were inspired by Jewish communities in which this sexual division was (and still is, in many cases) standard.

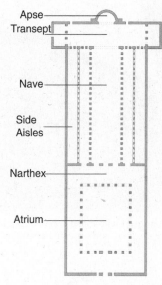

Figure 7.2: Early Christian basilica

A **narthex**, or vestibule, was positioned as a transitional zone in the front of the church. An atrium was constructed in front of the building, framing the façade. Atria also housed the *catechumens*, those who expressed a desire to convert to Christianity but had not yet gone through the initiation rites. They were at once inside the church precincts but outside the main building. On occasion this overall design had the symbolic effect of turning the church into a cross shape.

Early Christian art has a "love/hate" relationship with its Roman predecessors. On the one hand, these were the people who mercilessly cemented Christians into giant flowerpots, covered them with tar, ignited them, and used them to light the streets at night. On the other hand, this was the world they knew: the grandeur, the excitement, the eternal quality suggested by mythical Rome.

Early Christian art shows an adaptation of Roman elements—taking from their predecessors the ideas that best expressed Christianity, and using the remnants of their monuments to embellish the new faith. In this way, Christianity, like most religions, expressed dominance over the older forms of worship by forcing pagan architectural elements, like columns, to do service to a new god. **Santa Sabina** (Figures 7.3a, 7.3b, and 7.3c) employed a number of Roman columns from pagan temples. This type of reuse of architectural or sculptural elements is called **spolia**.

Early Christian churches come in two types, both inspired by Roman architecture: **centrally planned** and **axially planned** buildings. The exteriors of both church structures avoided decoration and sculpture that recall the façade of pagan temples.

The more numerous axially planned buildings, like **Santa Sabina**, had a long nave focusing on an apse. The nave, used for processional space, was usually flanked by side aisles. The first floor had columns lining the nave; the second floor contained a space decorated with mosaics; and the third floor had the **clerestory**, the window space. Early Christian **basilicas** have thin walls supporting wooden roofs with coffered ceilings (Figure 7.3b).

Centrally planned buildings were inspired by Roman buildings such as the Pantheon. The altar was placed in the middle of the building beneath a dome ringed with windows. Men stood around the altar, women in the side aisle, called an **ambulatory**.

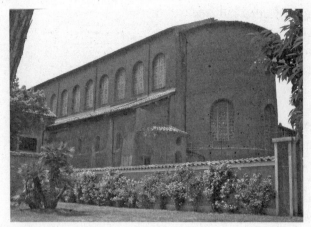

Figure 7.3a: Rear and flank exterior of Santa Sabina, 422–432, brick, stone and wooden roof, Rome, Italy

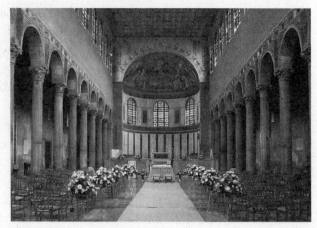

Figure 7.3b: Nave of Santa Sabina

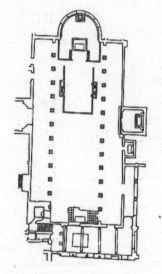

Figure 7.3c: Ground plan of Santa Sabina

Santa Sabina, 422–432, brick, stone, and wooden roof, Rome, Italy (Figures 7.3a, 7.3b, 7.3c)

- Three aisled basilica; no transepts
- Long, tall, broad nave; axial plan
- Spolia: tall slender columns taken from the Temple of Juno in Rome, erected on this site; a statement about the triumph of Christianity over paganism
- Windows not made of glass, but selenite, a type of transparent and colorless gypsum
- Flat wooden roof; coffered ceiling; thin walls support light roof
- Bare exterior, sensitively decorated interior: representing the Christian whose exterior may be gross, but whose interior soul is beautiful
- As in the Jewish tradition, men and women stood separately; the men stood in the main aisle, the women in the side aisles with a partial view
- Built by Peter of Illyria
- **Cross-Cultural Comparisons: Ground Plans**
  - Angkor Wat (Figure 23.8e)
  - Great Stupa (Figure 23.4d)
  - Great Mosque at Cordoba (Figure 9.14e)

VOCABULARY

Ambulatory: a passageway around the apse or altar of a church

Apse: the endpoint of a church where the altar is located

Atrium (plural: atria): a courtyard in a Roman house or before a Christian church

Axial plan (Basilican plan, Longitudinal plan): a church with a long nave whose focus is the apse, so-called because it is designed along an axis (Figure 7.3)

Basilica: In Christian architecture, an axially planned church with a long nave, side aisles, and an apse for the altar (Figure 7.3)

Catacomb: an underground passageway used for burial (Figure 7.1a)

Central plan: a church having a circular plan with the altar in the middle

Clerestory: the third, or window, story of a church

Coffer: in architecture, a sunken panel in a ceiling

Cubicula: small underground rooms in catacombs serving as mortuary chapels

Gospels: the first four books of the New Testament that chronicle the life of Jesus

Loculi: openings in the walls of catacombs to receive the dead

Lunette: a crescent-shaped space, sometimes over a doorway, that contains sculpture or painting

Narthex: the closest part of the atrium to the basilica, it serves as vestibule, or lobby, of a church (Figure 7.2)

Nave: the main aisle of a church (Figure 7.2)

Orant figure: a figure with its hands raised in prayer (Figure 7.1b)

Spolia: in art history, the reuse of architectural or sculptural pieces in buildings generally different from their original contexts

Transept: an aisle in a church perpendicular to the nave, where the clergy originally stood (Figure 7.2)

SUMMARY

Christianity was an underground religion for the first three hundred years of its existence. The earliest surviving artwork produced by Christians was buried in the catacombs far from the average Roman's view.

Imagery for Christian objects was derived from Roman precedents. Classical techniques such as fresco and mosaic flourished under Christian patronage, as did Roman figural compositions sometimes employing contrapposto. Moreover, Roman centrally and axially planned buildings found new life in Christian churches.

PRACTICE EXERCISES

Multiple-Choice

1. Construction of buildings like Santa Sabina relies on construction principles learned in the

   (A) Basilica Ulpia
   (B) Pantheon
   (C) Colosseum
   (D) Hagia Sophia

2. The painters of the catacombs preferred the fresco technique because

   (A) oil paint does not blend well on wall surfaces
   (B) mosaics were unavailable during this period
   (C) fresco forms a permanent bond with the wall
   (D) Christians have used fresco since Egyptian times

3. The Good Shepherd is an image in Early Christian catacombs that has its origins in the Bible, but pictorially the images are inspired by

  (A) Greek images of shepherding
  (B) Roman belief in agrarian virtues
  (C) Moslem cultivation of extensively planned gardens
  (D) prehistoric cave paintings of people and their animals

4. The division of painted spaces in the Good Shepherd fresco in the Catacombs of Priscilla is influenced by

  (A) Roman wall paintings as seen in the House of the Vettii
  (B) Greek vase painting as seen in the Niobides Krater
  (C) Greek friezes as seen in the Great Altar of Zeus and Athena at Pergamon
  (D) Etruscan wall paintings as seen in the Tomb of the Triclinium

5. After the catacombs in Rome were closed, legends grew around them that they were

  (A) haunted spaces
  (B) used to hide from Roman persecution
  (C) exclusively for the Roman elite
  (D) not really there, only the subject of legends

Short Essay

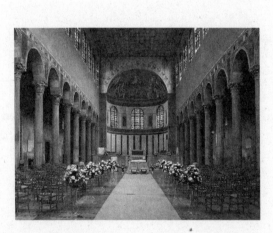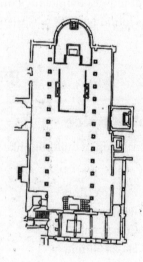

The images above show the interior and the ground plan of the church of Santa Sabina in Rome.

What are the principal architectural elements of this design?

Describe which elements of the Christian design were adapted from non-Christian sources.

Analyze how the design of the building is meant to accommodate the needs of the Christian ceremony.

1. **A**   2. **C**   3. **A**   4. **A**   5. **B**

ANSWERS EXPLAINED

Multiple-Choice

1. **(A)** The Basilica Ulpia and other Roman basilicas formed a general inspiration for Christian churches.

2. **(C)** Christians did not exist in the Egyptian period. Oil painting was invented much later in the Renaissance. Mosaics were available, but were very expensive. Fresco forms a permanent bond with the wall surfaces, and was comparatively easy to use.

3. **(A)** The Good Shepherd image is inspired by a story from the Bible, but it has its pictorial roots in the shepherding image dating back to the Greeks.

4. **(A)** Roman paintings, such as the ones in the House of the Vettii, are separated by lines that define the wall spaces.

5. **(B)** Legends grew up about the catacombs that Christians, who were persecuted under the Romans, used them for hideaways. In truth, everyone in the ancient world knew where they were, so no one would have escaped by hiding there.

Short-Essay Rubric

Question	Points	Key Points in a Good Response
What are the principal architectural elements of this design?	1	Answers could include: ■ Nave, side aisles, apse ■ Columns, clerestory ■ Thin walls support a light wooden roof ■ Coffered ceiling
Describe which elements of the Christian design were adapted from non-Christian sources.	2	Answers could include: ■ Windows made not of glass but of selenite, a type of transparent and colorless gypsum ■ Spolia: tall slender columns taken from the Temple of Juno in Rome, erected on this site; a statement about the triumph of Christianity over paganism ■ Wooden roof as seen in Roman basilicas ■ Upper story clerestory as seen in Roman basilicas ■ Building made of brick and stone as in Roman buildings
Analyze how the design of the building is meant to accommodate the needs of the Christian ceremony.	2	Answers could include: ■ Christians worship congregationally facing a priest ■ Long nave for congregation; rounded apse holds the altar and highlights the priest ■ As in the Jewish tradition, men and women stood separately; the men stood in the main aisle, the women in the side aisles with a partial view.

Byzantine Art

8

TIME PERIOD

Early Byzantine	500–726
Iconoclastic Controversy	726–843
Middle and Late Byzantine	843–1453, and beyond

ENDURING UNDERSTANDING: Medieval art is studied according to geographic placement, styles, and traditions. There are frequent interconnections between religions, governments, and artistic influences that create a variety of approaches.

Essential Knowledge:

- Medieval periods are the following:
  - Late Antique and Early Christian: Chapter 7
  - Byzantine: Chapter 8
  - Islamic: Chapter 9
  - Early Medieval: Chapter 10
  - Romanesque: Chapter 11
  - Gothic: Chapters 12 and 13
- There is no uniform medieval style. Some periods revive ancient classicism; others use geometric and natural designs.
- Medieval artists are influenced by contemporaries in other parts of Europe, as well as ancient traditions.

ENDURING UNDERSTANDING: Medieval art is chiefly concerned with religious expression and court life. There is a strong culture of endorsing scholarship.

Essential Knowledge:

- Learning was centered on specific fields that were transmitted throughout Europe through trade, pilgrimage, and military activity.
- Medieval architecture is mostly religious.
- Medieval painting and sculpture avoids naturalistic depictions.
- At times medieval religions will reject images.

HISTORICAL BACKGROUND

The term "Byzantine" would have sounded strange to residents of the Empire—they called themselves Romans. The Byzantine Empire was born from a split in the Roman world that occurred in the fifth century, when the size of the Roman Empire became too unwieldy for one ruler to manage effectively. The fortunes of the two halves of the Roman Empire could not have been more different. The western half dissolved into barbarian chaos, succumbing to hordes of migrating peoples. The eastern half, founded by Roman Emperor Constantine the Great at Constantinople (modern-day Istanbul), flourished for one-thousand years beyond the collapse of its western counterparts. Culturally different from their Roman cousins, the Byzantines spoke Greek rather than Latin, and promoted orthodox Christianity, as opposed to western Christianity, which was centered in Rome.

The porous borders of the Empire expanded and contracted during the Middle Ages, reacting to external pressures from invading armies, seemingly coming from all directions. The Empire had only itself to blame: The capital, with its unparalleled wealth and opulence, was the envy of every other culture. Its buildings and public spaces awed ambassadors from around the known world. Constantinople was the trading center of early medieval Europe, directing traffic in the Mediterranean and controlling the shipment of goods nearly everywhere.

Icon production was a Byzantine specialty (Figure 8.8). Devout Christians attest that **icons** are images that act as reminders to the faithful; they are not intended to actually be the sacred persons themselves. However, by the eighth century, Byzantines became embroiled in a heated debate over icons; some even worshipped them as idols. In order to stop this practice, which many considered sacrilegious, the emperor banned all image production. Not content with stopping images from being produced, iconoclasts smashed previously created works. Perhaps the iconoclasts were inspired by religions, such as Judaism and Islam, which discouraged images of sacred figures for much the same reasons. The unfortunate result of this activity is that art from the early Byzantine period (500–726) is almost completely lost. The artists themselves fled to parts of Europe where iconoclasm was unknown and Byzantine artists welcome. This so-called Iconoclastic Controversy serves as a division between the Early and Middle Byzantine art periods.

Despite the early successes of the iconoclasts, it became increasingly hard to suppress images in a Mediterranean culture such as Byzantium that had such a long tradition of creating paintings and sculptures of gods, going back to before the Greeks. In 843, iconoclasm was repealed and images were reinstated. This meant that every church and monastery had to be redecorated, causing a burst of creative energy throughout Byzantium.

Medieval Crusaders, some more interested in the spoils of war than the restoration of the Holy Land, conquered Constantinople in 1204, setting up a Latin kingdom in the east. Eventually the Latin invaders were expelled, but not before they brought untold damage to the capital, carrying off to Europe precious artwork that was simultaneously booty and artistic inspiration. The invaders also succeeded in permanently weakening the Empire, making it ripe for the Ottoman conquest in 1453. Even so, Late Byzantine artists continued to flourish both inside what was left of the Empire and in areas beyond its borders that accepted orthodoxy. A particularly strong tradition was established in Russia, where it remained until the 1917 Russian Revolution ended most religious activity. Even rival states, like Sicily and Venice, were known for their vibrant schools of Byzantine art, importing artists from the capital itself.

Patronage and Artistic Life

The church and state were one in the Byzantine Empire, so that many of the greatest works of art were commissioned, in effect, by both institutions at the same time. Monasteries were particularly influential, commissioning a great number of works for their private spaces. Interiors of Byzantine buildings were crowded with religious works competing with each other for attention.

A strong court atelier developed around a royal household interested in luxury objects. This atelier specialized in extravagant works in ivory, manuscripts, and precious metals.

Individual artists worked with great piety and felt they were executing works for the glory of God. They rarely signed their names, some feeling that pride was a sin. Many artists were monks, priests, or nuns whose artistic production was an expression of their religious devotion and sincerity.

BYZANTINE ARCHITECTURE

Byzantine architecture shows great innovation, beginning with the construction of the **Hagia Sophia** in 532 in Istanbul (Figures 8.3a, 8.3b, and 8.3c). The architects, Anthemius of Tralles and Isidorus of Miletus (actually a mathematician and a physicist rather than true architects), examined the issue of how a round dome, such as the one built for the Pantheon in Rome (Figure 6.11), could be placed on flat walls. Their solution was the invention of the **pendentive** (Figure 8.1), a triangle-shaped piece of masonry with the dome resting on one long side, and the other two sides channeling the weight down to a pier below. A pendentive allows the dome to be supported by four piers, one in each corner of the building. Since the walls between the piers do not support the dome, they can be opened up for greater window space. Thus the Hagia Sophia has walls of windows that flank the building on each side, unlike the Pantheon, which lacks windows, having only an oculus in the dome.

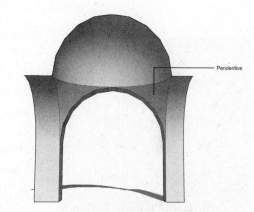

Figure 8.1: A dome supported by pendentives

Middle and Late Byzantine architects introduced a variation on the pendentive called the **squinch** (Figure 8.2). Although fulfilling the same function as a pendentive, that is, transitioning the weight of a dome onto a flat rather than a rounded wall, a squinch can take a number of shapes and forms, some corbelling from the wall behind, others arching into the center space. Architects designed pendentives and squinches so that artists could later use these broad and protruding surfaces as painted spaces.

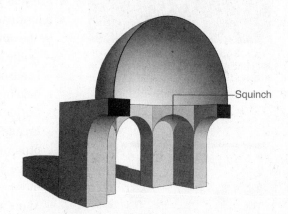

Figure 8.2: A dome supported by squinches

The Hagia Sophia's dome is composed of a set of ribs meeting at the top. The spaces between those ribs do not support the dome and are opened for window space. The Hagia Sophia has forty windows around the base of the dome, forming a great circle of light (or halo) over the congregation.

A further innovation in the Hagia Sophia involves its ground plan (Figure 8.3c). Churches in the Early Christian era concentrate on one of two forms: the circular building containing a centrally planned apse and the longer basilica with an axially planned nave facing an altar.

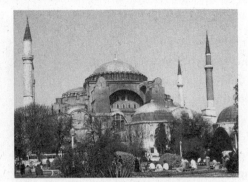

Figure 8.3a: Anthemius of Tralles and Isidorus of Miletus, Hagia Sophia, brick, ceramic, stone, mosaic, 532–537, Istanbul

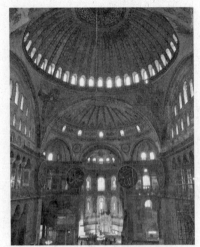

Figure 8.3b: Anthemius of Tralles and Isidorus of Miletus, Hagia Sophia, 532–537, Istanbul

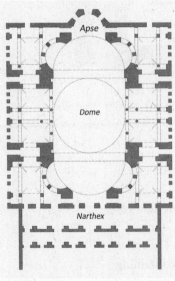

Figure 8.3c: Ground plan of Hagia Sophia

The Hagia Sophia shows a marriage of these two forms, with the dome emphasizing a centrally planned core and the long nave directing focus toward the apse.

Except for the Hagia Sophia, Byzantine architecture is not known for its size. Buildings in the Early period (500–726) have plain exteriors made of brick or concrete. In the Middle and Late periods (843–1453), the exteriors are richly articulated with a provocative use of various colors of brick, stone, and marble, often with contrasting vertical and horizontal elements. The domes are smaller, but there are more of them, sometimes forming a cross shape.

Interiors are marked by extensive use of variously colored marbles on the lower floors and mosaics or frescoes in the elevated portions of the buildings. Domes tend to be low rather than soaring, having windows around the base. Interior arches reach into space, creating mysterious areas clouded by half-lights and shimmering mosaics. These buildings usually set the domes on more elevated drums.

Greek Orthodox tradition dictates that important parts of the Mass take place behind a curtain or screen. In some buildings this screen is composed of a wall of icons called an **iconostasis**.

Anthemius of Tralles and Isidorus of Miletus, Hagia Sophia, 532–537, brick, ceramic, stone, mosaic, Istanbul (Figures 8.3a, 8.3b, and 8.3c)

- *Hagia Sophia* means "Holy Wisdom"
- Combination of centrally planned and axially planned church
- Exterior: plain and massive, little decoration
- Interior: altar at end of nave, but emphasis placed over the area covered by the dome
  - Dome supported by pendentives
  - Large central dome, with forty windows at base symbolically acting as a halo over the congregation when filled with light
  - Cornice unifies space
  - Arcade decoration: wall and capitals are flat and thin but richly ornamented
  - Large fields for mosaic decoration; at one time had four acres of gold mosaics on walls
  - Many windows punctuate wall spaces
- Minarets added in Islamic period, when Hagia Sophia functioned as a mosque; building now a museum
  - Marble columns appropriated from Rome, Ephesus, and other Greek sites
  - Capitals avoid classical allusions; surfaces contain deeply cut acanthus leaves
- Patrons were Emperor Justinian and Empress Theodora, who commissioned the work after the burning of the original building in the Nike Revolt of 532

- **Cross-Cultural Comparisons: Buildings that Have Changed Use**
  - Parthenon (Figure 4.16b)
  - Pantheon (Figures 6.11a, 6.11b)
  - Great Mosque at Cordoba (Figures 9.14a, 9.14b, 9.14c, 9.14d, 9.14e)

San Vitale, 526–547, brick, marble, stone, Ravenna, Italy (Figures 8.4a, 8.4b, and 8.4c)

- Eight-sided church
- Plain exterior except porch added later in Renaissance
- Large windows for illuminating interior designs
- Interior has thin columns and open arched spaces
- Interior elements dematerialize the mass of the structure
- A martyrium
- **Cross-Cultural Comparisons: Buildings with Circular Plans**
  - Pantheon (Figures 6.11a, 6.11b)
  - Dome of the Rock (Figures 9.12a, 9.12b)
  - Mosque of Selim II (Figures 9.16a, 9.16b, 9.16c)

BYZANTINE PAINTING

The most characteristic work of Byzantine art is the **icon**, a religious devotional image usually of portable size and hanging in a place of honor either at home or in a religious institution. An icon has a wooden foundation covered by preparatory undercoats of paint, sometimes composed of such things as fish glue or putty. Cloth is placed over this base, and successive layers of stucco are gently applied. A perforated paper sketch is placed on the surface, so that the image can be traced and then gilded and painted. The artist then applies varnish to make the icon shine, as well as to protect it, because icons are often touched, handled, and embraced. The faithful were encouraged to kiss icons and burn votive candles beneath them; as a result, icons have become blackened by candle soot and incense, their frames singed by flames. Consequently, many icons have been repainted and no longer have their original surface texture.

Icons were paraded in religious processions on feast days, and sometimes exhibited on city walls in times of invasion. Frequently they were believed to possess spiritual powers, and they held a sacred place in the hearts of Byzantine worshippers.

Byzantine painting is marked by a combination of the classical heritage of ancient Greece and Rome with a more formal and hieratic medieval style. Artists are trained in one tradition or the other, and it is common to see a single work of art done by a number of artists, some inspired by the classical tradition, and others by medieval formalism. *The Virgin and Child between Saints Theodore and George* (Figure 8.8) shows both traditions.

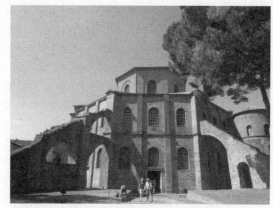
Figure 8.4a: San Vitale, 526–547, brick, marble, stone, Ravenna, Italy

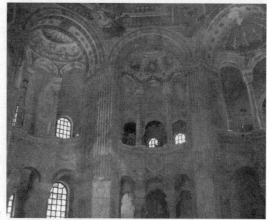
Figure 8.4b: San Vitale interior, 526–547, Ravenna, Italy

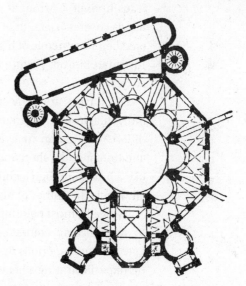
Figure 8.4c: San Vitale ground plan, 526–547, Ravenna, Italy

Those artists who were classically trained used a painterly brushstroke and an innovative way of representing a figure—typically from an unusual angle. These artists employed soft transitions between color areas and showed a more relaxed figure stance.

Those trained in the medieval tradition favored frontal poses, symmetry, and almost weightless bodies. The drapery is emphasized, so there is little effort to reveal the body beneath. Perspective is unimportant because figures occupy a timeless space, marked by golden backgrounds and heavily highlighted halos.

Whatever the tradition, Byzantine art, like all medieval art, avoids nudity whenever possible, deeming it debasing. Nudity also had a pagan association, connected with the mythological religions of ancient Greece and Rome.

One of the glories of Byzantine art is its jewel-like treatment of manuscript painting. The manuscript painter had to possess a fine eye for detail, and so was trained to work with great precision, rendering minute details carefully. Byzantine manuscripts are meticulously executed; most employ the same use of gold seen in icons and mosaics. Because so few people could read, the possession of manuscripts was a status symbol, and libraries were true temples of learning. The *Vienna Genesis* (Figure 8.7) is an excellent example of the sophisticated court style of manuscript painting.

Byzantine art continues the ancient traditions of fresco and mosaic painting, bringing the latter to new heights. Interior church walls are covered in shimmering tesserae made of gold, colored stones, and glass. Each piece of tesserae is placed at an odd angle to catch the flickering of candles or the oblique rays of sunlight; the interior then resembles a vast glittering world of floating golden shapes, perhaps echoing what the Byzantines thought heaven itself would resemble.

Court customs play an important role in Byzantine art. Purple, the color usually reserved for Byzantine royalty, can be seen in the mosaics of Emperor Justinian and Empress Theodora. However, in an act of transference, purple is sometimes used on the garments of Jesus himself. Custom at court prescribed that courtiers approach the emperor with their hands covered as a sign of respect. As a result, nearly every figure has at least one hand covered before someone of higher station, sometimes even when he or she is holding something. **Justinian** himself (Figure 8.5), in his famous mosaic in San Vitale, holds a **paten** with his covered hand.

Facial types are fairly standardized. There is no attempt at psychological penetration or individual insight: Portraits in the modern sense of the word are unknown. Continuing a tradition from Roman art, eyes are characteristically large and wide open. Noses tend to be long and thin, mouths short and closed. The Christ Child, who is a fixture in Byzantine art, is more like a little man than a child, perhaps showing his wisdom and majesty. Medieval art generally labels the names of figures the viewer is observing, and Byzantine art is no exception.

Typically, most paintings have flattened backgrounds, often with just a single layer of gold to symbolize an eternal space. This becomes increasingly pronounced in the Middle and Late Byzantine periods in which figures stand before a monochromatic of golden opulence, perhaps illustrating a heavenly world.

Justinian and Attendants, c. 547, mosaic from San Vitale, Ravenna (Figure 8.5)

- To his left the clergy, to his right the military
- Dressed in royal purple and gold
- Symmetry, frontality
- Holds a paten, a shallow bowl or plate, for the Eucharist
- Slight impression of procession forward
- Figures have no volume, seem to float, and overlap each other's feet
- Minimal background: green base at feet, golden background indicates timelessness
- Archbishop Maximianus identified, only participant labelled
- Halo indicates saintliness, a semidivinity as head of church and state
- Justinian and Theodora are actively participating in the Mass—their position over the altar enhances this allusion
- Banker Julianus Argentarius financed the building of San Vitale
- **Cross-Cultural Comparisons: Mosaics**
  - Alexander Mosaic (Figure 4.20)
  - Dome of the Rock interior (Figure 9.17b)
  - Taj Mahal interior (Figure 9.17b)

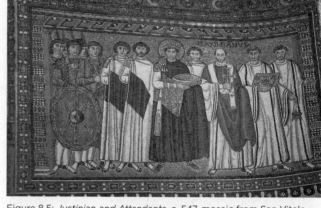

Figure 8.5: *Justinian and Attendants*, c. 547, mosaic from San Vitale, Ravenna

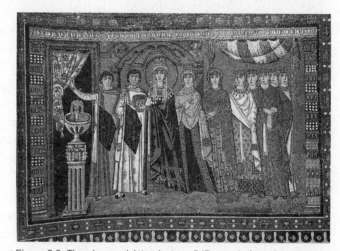

Figure 8.6: *Theodora and Attendants*, c. 547, mosaic from San Vitale, Ravenna

Theodora and Attendants, c. 547, mosaic from San Vitale, Ravenna (Figure 8.6)

- Slight displacement of absolute symmetry with Theodora—she plays a secondary role to her husband
- Richly robed empress and ladies at court
- She stands in an architectural framework, holding a chalice for the mass, and is about to go behind the curtain
- Figures are flattened and weightless, barely a hint of a body can be detected beneath the drapery
- Three Magi, who bring gifts to the baby Jesus, are depicted on the hem of her dress. This reference draws parallels between Theodora and the Magi.

Vienna Genesis, early sixth century, illuminated manuscript, pigment on vellum, Austrian National Library, Vienna (Figures 8.7a and 8.7b)

- Style:
  - Lively, softly modeled figures
  - Classical training of the artists: contrapposto, foreshortening, shadowing, perspective

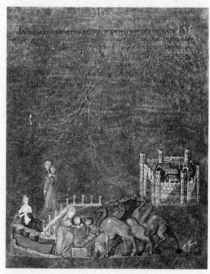

Figure 8.7a: *Rebecca and Eliezar at the Well*, from the *Vienna Genesis*, early sixth century, illuminated manuscript, pigment on vellum, Austrian National Library, Vienna

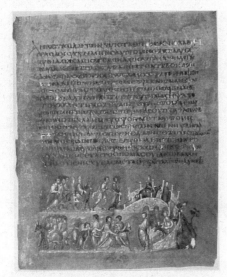

Figure 8.7b: *Jacob Wrestling the Angel*, from the *Vienna Genesis*, early sixth century, illuminated manuscript, pigment on vellum, Austrian National Library, Vienna

- Shallow settings
- Fluid movement of decorative figures
- Richly colored and shaded
- Two rows linked by a bridge or a pathway
- Text placed above illustrations, which are on lower half of the page

■ Technique and Origin:
- Manuscript painted on vellum
- Done in silver script, now oxidized and turned black
- Origin uncertain: Constantinople? Antioch?
- Perhaps done in a royal workshop; purple parchment is a hallmark of a royal institution
- Genesis stories are done in continuous narrative with genre details
- Written in Greek
- Partial manuscript: 48 of 192 (?) illustrations survive
- First surviving illustrations of the stories from Genesis

■ Rebecca and Eliezar at the Well
- Genesis 24: 15–61
- Rebecca emerges from the city of Nahor with a jar on her shoulder to go down to the spring
- She quenches the thirst of a camel driver and his camels
- Colonnaded road leads to the spring
- Roman water goddess personifies the spring

■ Jacob Wrestling the Angel
- Genesis 32: 22–31
- Jacob takes his two wives, two maids, and eleven children and crosses a river; number of children abbreviated
- Roman looking bridge
- At night he wrestles an angel; angel strikes him on the hip socket

■ **Cross-Cultural Comparisons: Narrative**
- *Night Attack on the Sanjô Palace* (Figures 25.3a, 25.3b)
- Last Judgment of Hu-Nefer (Figure 3.12)
- *Churning of the Ocean of Milk* (Figure 23.8c)

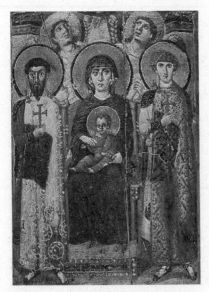

Figure 8.8: *Virgin (Theotokos) and Child between Saints Theodore and George*, sixth–early seventh centuries, encaustic on wood, Monastery of Saint Catherine, Mount Sinai, Egypt (Figure 8.8)

Virgin (Theotokos) and Child between Saints Theodore and George, sixth–early seventh centuries, encaustic on wood, Monastery of Saint Catherine, Mount Sinai, Egypt (Figure 8.8)

■ Icon placed in a medieval monastery
■ Virgin and Child centrally placed; firmly modeled
- Mary as Theotokos, Mother of God
- Mary looks beyond the viewer as if seeing into the future
- Christ Child looks away, perhaps anticipating his crucifixion
■ Saints Theodore and George; warrior saints; stiff and hieratic
- Engage the viewer directly
■ Angels look toward heaven
- Painted in a classical style with brisk brushwork
- Turned toward heaven, where the descending hand of God comes down to bless the scene

- Because the three groups have very different styles, it has been assumed that they were painted by three different artists
■ **Cross-Cultural Comparisons: A Work of Art Done by Many Artists**
  - Terra-cotta Warriors (Figures 24.8a, 24.8b)
  - Parthenon (Figures 4.16a, 4.16b)
  - Koons, *Pink Panther* (Figure 29.9)

VOCABULARY

Axial plan (Basilican plan, Longitudinal plan): a church with a long nave whose focus is the apse, so-called because it is designed along an axis

Cathedral: the principal church of a diocese, where a bishop sits (Figure 8.3)

Central plan: a church having a circular plan with the altar in the middle

Chalice: a cup containing wine, used during a Christian service (Figure 8.6)

Codex (plural: **codices**): a manuscript book (Figure 8.7)

Continuous narrative: a work of art that contains several scenes of the same story painted or sculpted in a single frame (Figure 8.7)

Cornice: a projecting ledge over a wall (Figure 8.3b)

Eucharist: the bread sanctified by the priest at the Christian ceremony commemorating the Last Supper

Genesis: first book of the Bible that details Creation, the Flood, Rebecca at the Well, and Jacob Wrestling the Angel, among other episodes (Figure 8.7)

Icon: a devotional panel depicting a sacred image (Figure 8.8)

Iconostasis: a screen decorated with icons, which separates the apse from the transept of a church

Martyrium (plural: **martyria**): a shrine built over a place of martyrdom or a grave of a martyred Christian saint (Figure 8.4)

Mosaic: a decoration using pieces of stone, marble or colored glass, called **tesserae**, that are cemented to a wall or a floor (Figures 8.5 and 8.6)

Paten: a plate, dish, or bowl used to hold the Eucharist at a Christian ceremony (Figure 8.5)

Pendentive: a construction shaped like a triangle that transitions the space between flat walls and the base of a round dome (Figure 8.1)

Squinch: the polygonal base of a dome that makes a transition from the round dome to a flat wall (Figure 8.2)

Theotokos: The Virgin Mary in her role as the Mother of God (Figure 8.8)

SUMMARY

The Eastern half of the Roman Empire lived for another one thousand years beyond the fall of Rome under a name we today call Byzantine. The Empire produced lavish works of art for a splendid court that resided in Constantinople—one of the most resplendent cities in history.

Byzantine art specialized in a number of diverse art forms. Walls were covered in shimmering gold mosaic that reflected a heavenly world of great opulence. Icons that were sometimes thought to have spiritual powers were painted of religious figures. Ivories were carved with consummate precision and skill.

Byzantine builders invented the pendentive, first seen at the Hagia Sophia. However, in later buildings the squinch was preferred.

The death of the Empire in 1453 did not mean the end of Byzantine art. Indeed, a second life developed in Russia, eastern Europe, and in occupied Greece lasting into the twentieth century.

PRACTICE EXERCISES

Multiple-Choice

1. Interior mosaic decoration is different in Late Antique and Byzantine buildings than in prior periods in that in the ancient world

   (A) mosaicists used large blocks of stone rather than miniature pieces called tesserae.
   (B) tiles were made from glass, whereas Byzantine tiles were made of metal
   (C) tiles depicted animals and vegetable forms; Byzantine mosaics depict people
   (D) tiles are colored in flat pastel shades; Byzantine tiles glow with a use of gold and sparkling colors

Questions 2–3 refer to the following images.

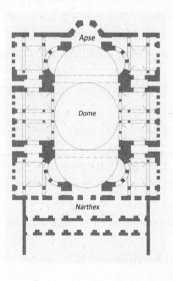
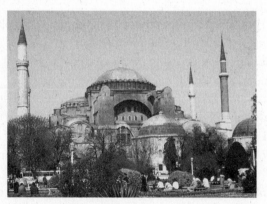

2. The ground plan of the Hagia Sophia suggests that

   (A) columns are used as decorative patterning rather than as internal supports
   (B) it is a combination of a central and a basilican plan
   (C) the mihrab faces Mecca
   (D) the Roman basilican type has been altered to create side aisles

3. The Hagia Sophia was added to after its initial construction, including the

(A) enlargement of windows
(B) development of rib vaults
(C) installation of underground catacombs
(D) addition of minarets

---

4. The mosaics of Justinian and Theodora have been placed in San Vitale

(A) to commemorate a state visit by the Emperor and Empress
(B) as a thank you for helping to construct the building
(C) as stand-ins to symbolize their semidivine status as participants in the Mass
(D) because they were declared saints after they died

5. After the fall of the Byzantine empire in 1453, its artistic tradition was carried on in

(A) Turkey
(B) Russia
(C) Austria
(D) Spain

Short Essay

The illustrations below are pages from the *Vienna Genesis: Rebecca and Eliezar at the Well* on the left and *Jacob Wrestling the Angel* on the right.

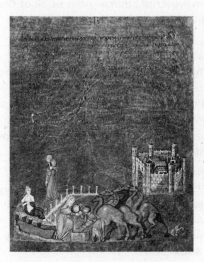 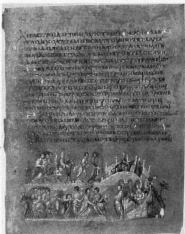

What is the source of the images in this manuscript?

Discuss the elements of the work that indicate an imperial or royal patronage.

The scenes have a number of motifs taken from classical art. Using specific details, analyze how *and* why these settings are incorporated into the text.

ANSWERS EXPLAINED

Multiple-Choice

1. **(D)** Byzantine mosaics are characterized by their glowing golden colors; Roman and Greek mosaicists use pastel colors.

2. **(B)** The Hagia Sophia was constructed as a combination of the central plan (dome sitting on pendentives) and a basilican plan (long nave terminating at an apse).

3. **(D)** The minarets were added by the Moslems when the building was turned into a mosque.

4. **(C)** There is no evidence that either Justinian or Theodora ever visited or financially supported San Vitale. Even though they wear halos, they were never declared saints after their death. Their presence and their halos suggest a semidivine presence at services.

5. **(B)** After the fall of the Byzantine Empire, the artistic tradition was carried on in Russia.

Short-Essay Rubric

Question	Points	Key Points in a Good Response
What is the source of the images in this manuscript?	1	The manuscript source is the Book of Genesis, Chapters 24 and 32.
Discuss the elements of the work that indicate an imperial or royal patronage.	2	Answers could include: ■ Work done on vellum, a luxurious expensive product ■ Painted with silver ink (now oxidized and turned black) ■ Purple parchment is a hallmark of a royal institution.

The scenes have a number of motifs taken from classical art. Using specific details, analyze how *and* why these settings are incorporated into the text.	2	Answers could include:
		■ Classical training of the artists: contrapposto, foreshortening, shadowing, perspective
		■ Classical style references the ancient world; great epic moments in ancient history
		■ In Rebecca:
		  – Roman water goddess personifies the spring.
		  – Colonnaded road leads to the spring.
		■ In Jacob:
		  – Roman-style bridge

Content Areas: Early Europe and Colonial Americas
West and Central Asia

Islamic Art

9

TIME PERIOD: 630 C.E. TO THE PRESENT

ENDURING UNDERSTANDING: Cultural exchanges on a vast scale take place in West Asia.

Essential Knowledge:

- The Silk Road connected distant lands culturally and economically.
- Intercultural exchanges cause a rich diversity of expression combining European, Asian, and Islamic sources.
- Islamic art dominates West Asia and South Europe.
- Patrons were royal and religious figures.
- Islamic art is influenced by trade with surrounding traditions.

ENDURING UNDERSTANDING: Islam is the dominant religion in North Africa, West Asia, and Spain.

Essential Knowledge:

- Islam unites a diverse region.
- Islamic architecture includes mosques, tombs, and monuments.
- Islamic art is spread though pilgrimages.

ENDURING UNDERSTANDING: The use of figural art varies in the Islamic tradition.

Essential Knowledge:

- Religious art contains no figures, but uses tessellation, calligraphy, and arabesques.
- Figural art flourishes in secular writings in Persia.

ENDURING UNDERSTANDING: Islamic art specializes in ceramics, book illumination, textiles, and metalwork.

Essential Knowledge:

- Islamic art tends to avoid perspective, be two-dimensional, and have arabesque and geometric designs.
- Ceramics were created for useful and decorative purposes.
- Metalwork was used for sculptures, armor, and utilitarian items.
- Carpets and tapestries are particularly prized examples of Islamic textiles.
- Islamic art excels in manuscript decoration, as well as wall paintings.

HISTORICAL BACKGROUND

The Prophet Muhammad's powerful religious message resonated deeply with Arabs in the seventh century, and so by the end of the Umayyad Dynasty in 750 C.E., North Africa, the Middle East and parts of Spain, India, and Central Asia were converted to Islam or were under the control of Islamic dynasties. The Islamic world expanded under the Abbasid Caliphate, which ruled a vast empire from their capital in Baghdad. After the Mongol sack of Baghdad in 1258, the Islamic world split into two great cultural divisions, the East, consisting of South and Central Asia, Iran, and Turkey; and the West, which included the Near East and the Arabic peninsula, North Africa, parts of Sicily and Spain.

Islam exists in two principal divisions, Shiite and Sunni, each based on a differing claim of leadership after Muhammad's death. Even though millions practice and continue to share a similar faith, there is great diversity in Islamic religious and artistic traditions.

Patronage and Artistic Life

Major artistic movements in the Islamic world are the result of patronage by secular and religious rulers and the social elite. Other objects much valued today, such as textiles, metalwork, and ceramics were produced for the art market, both at home and abroad.

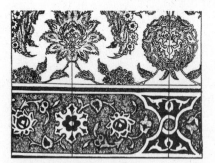

Figure 9.1: Arabesque

One of the most popular art forms in the Islamic world is **calligraphy**, which is based upon the Arabic script and varies in form depending on the period and region of its production. Calligraphy is considered to be the highest art form in the Islamic world as it is used to transmit the texts revealed from God to Muhammad. Calligraphers therefore were the most respected Islamic artists. Most early artists were humble handmaidens to the art form—and to God—therefore many remained anonymous. However, by the fourteenth and fifteenth centuries, writing examples are signed or attributed to specific calligraphers. Even royalty dabbled in calligraphy, raising the art form to new heights. Apprenticeships were exacting, making students master everything including the manufacture of ink and the correct posture for sitting while writing.

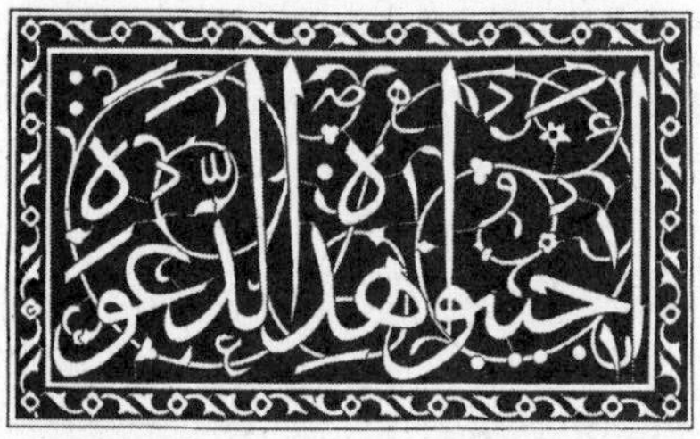

Figure 9.2: Islamic calligraphy with arabesque

ISLAMIC PAINTING AND SCULPTURE

Islamic art features three types of patterns—**arabesques**, **calligraphy**, and **tessellation** (Figures 9.1, 9.2, and 9.3, respectively)—used on everything from great monuments to simple earthenware plates; sometimes all three are used on the same item.

Favorite arabesque motifs include acanthus and split leaves, scrolling vines, spirals, wheels, and zigzags. Calligraphy is highly specialized, and comes in a number of recognized scripts, including **Kufic**. The Arabic alphabet has 28 letters from 17 different shapes, and is written from right to left. Arabic numerals, however, are written left to right as they are in the West. **Kufic** is highly distinguished, and has been reserved for official texts, indeed has been the traditional, but not the only, script for the **Qur'an**. It has evolved into a highly ornamental style, and therefore is difficult for the average reader to decipher. Tessellations, or the repetition of geometric designs, demonstrate the Islamic belief that there is unity in multiplicity.

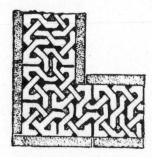

Figure 9.3: Tessellation

Their use can be found on objects as disparate as open metalwork and stone decorations. Perforated ornamental stone screens, called **jali**, were a particular Islamic specialty.

All of these designs, no matter how complicated, were achieved with only a straightedge and a compass. Islamic mathematicians were thinkers of the highest order; geometric elements reinforced their idea that the universe is based on logic and a clear design. Patterns seem to radiate from a central point, although any point can be thought of as the start. These patterns are not designed to fit a frame, rather to repeat until they reach the edge, and then by inference go beyond that.

Islamic textiles, carpets in particular, are especially treasured. Elaborate prayer rugs, often bearing the mihrab motif, are placed on mosque floors to provide a clean and comfortable spot for the worshipper to kneel on. Royal factories made elaborate carpets, in which it was usual to have hundreds of knots per square inch. In tribal villages, women were often the manufacturers of smaller carpets with designs created by either the knotting or the flat-weave technique.

Islamic art is intellectual, refined, and decorative; it contains no strong emotions and no pathos, but exhibits serene harmony.

Although the Qur'an does not ban images, there is an active tradition in many Islamic countries to avoid religious imagery whenever possible. Some societies strictly adhere to the prohibition, others allow floral designs and animal motifs, still others disregard the traditional ban.

Pyxis of al-Mughira, 968, ivory, Louvre, Paris (Figure 9.4)

- Calligraphic inscription in Arabic identifies the owner, asks for Allah's blessings, and tells us the function of the pyxis
- Function: container for expensive aromatics
- Gift for the caliph's younger son
- Horror vacui
- Vegetal and geometric motifs
- Eight medallion scenes showing pleasure activities of the royal court: hunting, falconry, sports, musicians
- From Muslim Spain
- **Cross-Cultural Comparisons: Relief Sculpture**
  - Relief Sculpture from Chavín (Figure 26.1c)
  - Narmer Palette (Figure 3.4)
  - Grave Stele of Hegeso (Figure 4.7)

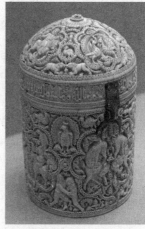

Figure 9.4: Pyxis of al-Mughira, 968, ivory, Louvre, Paris

Folio from the Qur'an, eighth–ninth century, ink and gold on parchment (Figure 9.5)

- Arabic read right to left
- Kufic script: strong uprights and long horizontals
- Great clarity of text important because several readers read book at once, some at a distance
- Consonants are scripted, vowels are indicated by dots or markings around the other letters
- Qur'ans were compiled and codified in the mid-seventh century; however, the earliest surviving Qur'an is from the ninth century

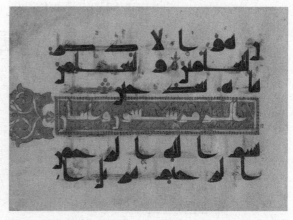

Figure 9.5 Folio from the Qur'an, eighth–ninth century, ink and gold on parchment

- **Cross-Cultural Comparisons: Calligraphy**
  - *Book of Lindisfarne* (Figure 10.2c)
  - *Night Attack on the Sanjô Palace* (Figures 25.3a, 25.3b)
  - *Vienna Genesis* (Figures 8.7a, 8.7b)

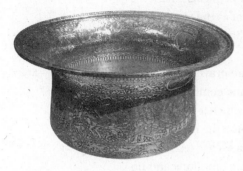

Figure 9.6: Muhammad ibn al-Zain, *Basin* or *Baptistère de St. Louis*, 1320–1340, brass inlaid with gold and silver, Louvre, Paris

Muhammad ibn al-Zain, *Basin* or *Baptistère de St. Louis*, 1320–1340, brass inlaid with gold and silver, Louvre, Paris (Figure 9.6)

- Signed by the artist six times
- Original use: washing hands at official ceremonies
- Later use: baptisms for French royal family (association with St. Louis fictional)
- Hunting alternate with battle scenes along side
- Mamluk hunters and Mongol enemies
- Bottom of bowl: decorated with fish, eels, crabs, frogs, and crocodiles

- **Cross-Cultural Comparisons: Works Reflecting a Cultural Diversity**
  - Miguel González, *Virgin of Guadelupe* (Figure 18.4)
- Quick-to-See-Smith, *Trade* (Figure 19.12)
- Kngwarreye, *Earth's Creation* (Figure 29.13)

Maqsud of Kashan, *The Ardabil Carpet*, 1539–1540, silk on wool, Victoria and Albert Museum, London (Figures 9.7a and 9.7b)

- Huge carpet, one of a matching pair, from the funerary mosque of Shayik Safial-Din; probably made when shrine was enlarged
- A prayer carpet
- Medallion in center perhaps represents the inside of a dome with sixteen pendants
- Mosque lamps hang from two of the pendants; one lamp smaller than the other, the larger lamp placed further away so that it would appear the same size as the smaller
- Corner squinches also have pendants completing the feeling of looking into a dome
- World's oldest dated carpet
- Wool carpet, woven by ten people, probably men; women did weaving in this period, but the importance of the location and the size of the project indicates that men were entrusted with its execution

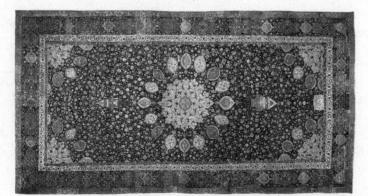

Figure 9.7a: Maqsud of Kashan, *The Ardabil Carpet*, 1539–1540, silk on wool, Victoria and Albert Museum, London

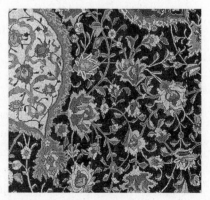

Figure 9.7b: Detail of 9.7a

- **Cross-Cultural Comparisons: Textiles**
  - Hiapo (Figure 28.6)
  - *The Bayeux Tapestry* (Figures 11.7a, 11.7b)
  - Ringgold, *Dancing at the Louvre* (Figure 29.11)

Persian Manuscripts

Persian painting descends from a rich and diverse heritage, including illustrated manuscripts from the western Islamic world and figural ceramics from pre-Mongol Iran. The Mongolian rulers who conquered Iran in 1258 introduced exotic Chinese painting to the Iranian court in the late Middle Ages. Persian manuscript paintings (sometimes called miniatures) gave a visual image to a literary plot, rendering a more enjoyable and easier-to-understand text. A number of diverse schools of manuscript painting were cultivated throughout Persia, some more, others less, under the spell of Chinese painting. Centuries after the Mongols, Chinese elements survive in the Asiatic appearance of figures, the incorporation of Chinese rocks and clouds, and the appearance of motifs such as dragons and chrysanthemums. Persian miniatures, in turn, influenced Mughal manuscripts in India.

Characteristics of many Persian manuscripts include a portrayal of figures in a relatively shadowless world, usually sumptuously dressed and occupying a richly decorative environment. Persian artists admire intricate details and multicolored geometric patterns. Space is divided into a series of flat planes. The marriage of text and calligraphy is especially stressed, as the words are often written with consummate precision in spaces reserved for them on the page.

The viewer's point of view shifts in a world perceived at various angles—sometimes looking directly at some figures, while also looking down at the floor and carpets. Artists depict a lavishly ornamented architectural setting with crowded compositions of doll-like figures distinguishable by a brilliant color palette.

Bahram Gur Fights the Karg, c. 1310–1340, ink and watercolor, gold, silver on paper, Harvard University Art Gallery, Cambridge, Massachusetts (Figure 9.8)

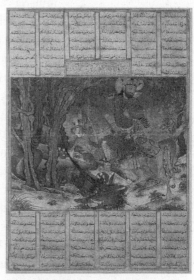

Figure 9.8: *Bahram Gur Fights the Karg*, c. 1310–1340, ink and watercolor, gold, silver on paper, Harvard University Art Gallery, Cambridge, Massachusetts

- Iranian manuscript
- Large painted surface area; calligraphy diminished
- Areas of flat color
- Spatial recession indicated by the overlapping planes
- Atmospheric perspective seen in the light bluish background
- Bahram Gur was an ancient Iranian king from the Sassanian dynasty
- Represents the ideal king; wears a crown and a golden halo
- Karg is a unicorn he fought during his trip to India
- Illustration from the *Book of Kings*
- Bahram Gur wears a garment of European fabric
- Chinese landscape conventions can be seen in background
- **Cross-Cultural Comparisons: Scenes of Conquering**
  - Athena from the Temple of Zeus (Figure 4.9)
  - Narmer Palette (Figure 3.4)
  - Ludovisi Battle Sarcophagus (Figure 6.17)

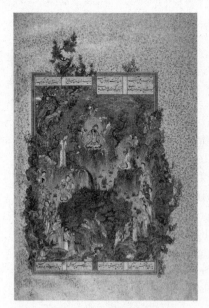

Sultan Muhammad, *The Court of Gayumars*, folio from the Shah Tashmasp, 1522–1525, ink, opaque watercolor, gold on paper, Aga Khan Museum, Toronto, Canada (Figure 9.9)

- The Shahnama (Book of Kings) is a Persian epic poem by Firdawsi (940–1025) telling the ancient history of Persia
- Whole book contains 258 illustrated pages
- This excerpt shows the first king, Gayumars, enthroned before his community
- On left: his son Siyamak; on right: his grandson Hushang
- His court appears in a semi-circle below him; they are all in court attire: wearing leopard skins
- Harmony between man and landscape
- Minute details do not overwhelm the harmony of the scene
- The angel, Surush, tells Gayumars that his son will be murdered by the Black Div, son of the demon Ahriman
- **Cross-Cultural Comparisons: King and Court**
  - Bichitr, *Jahangir Preferring a Sufi Shaikh to Kings* (Figure 23.9)
  - Presentation of Fijian mats and tapa cloths (Figure 28.10)
  - Velázquez, *Las Meninas* (Figure 17.7)

Figure 9.9: Sultan Muhammad, *The Court of Gayumars*, folio from the Shah Tashmasp, 1522–1525, ink, opaque watercolor, gold on paper, Aga Khan Museum, Toronto, Canada

ISLAMIC ARCHITECTURE

All mosques are oriented toward Mecca because Muslims must pray five times a day facing the holy city. The **qiblah**, or direction, to Mecca is marked by the **mihrab** (Figure 9.10), an empty niche, which directs the worshipper's attention.

To remind the faithful of the times to pray, great **minarets** (Figure 9.16a) are constructed in every corner of the Muslim world, from which the call to prayer is recited to the faithful.

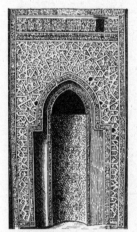

Minarets are composed of a base, a tall shaft with an internal staircase, and a gallery from which **muezzins** call people to prayer. Galleries are often covered with canopies to protect the occupants from the weather.

Mosques come in many varieties. The most common designs are either the hypostyle halls like the **Great Mosque at Córdoba** (eighth–tenth centuries) (Figures 9.14a–9.14e) or the unified open interior as the **Mosque of Selim II** (1568–1575) (Figures 9.16a–9.16c). The former is characterized by an interior that is a forest of columns, sometimes invested with an open central courtyard. The arches at Córdoba are horseshoe-shaped with alternating striped stonework. The focus of all prayer is the mihrab, which points the direction to Mecca.

In contrast, the Mosque of Selim II has a unified central core with a brilliant dome surmounting a centrally organized ground plan. Works like this were inspired by Byzantine architecture. The domes of mosques and tombs employ squinches, which in Islamic hands can be made to form an elaborate orchestration of suspended facets called **muqarnas**.

Figure 9.10: A mihrab

In Iran mosques evolved around a centrally placed courtyard. Each side features a centrally placed half-dome open at one end called an **iwan**. The Great Mosque in Isfahan, Iran (Figure 9.13) might be the first example of this architectural arrangement.

The Kaaba, 631–632, granite masonry, covered with silk curtain, gold and silver thread, Mecca, Saudi Arabia (Figures 9.11a and 9.11b)

- Mecca is the spiritual center of Islam
- Said to have been built by Ibrahim and Ishamel for God
- Existing structure encases the blackstone in the eastern corner, the only part of the original structure by Ibrahim that survives
- Has been repaired and reconstructed many times since Mohammed's time
- Cube-like in shape; covered by textiles
- Destination for those making the hajj; circumambulate the Kaaba counterclockwise, seven times
- **Cross-Cultural Comparisons: Buildings Built on Important Sites**
    - Dome of the Rock (Figures 9.12a, 9.12b)
    - Lin, Vietnam Veterans Memorial (Figure 29.4a)
    - Tutankhamun's Tomb (Figure 3.11)

Dome of the Rock, 691–692, stone masonry and wood roof decorated with glazed ceramic tile, mosaics, and gilt aluminum and bronze dome, Jerusalem (Figures 9.12a and 9.12b)

- Domed wooden octagon
- Influenced by centrally planned buildings
- Columns taken from Roman monuments
- Sacred rock where Adam was buried, Abraham nearly sacrificed Isaac, Muhammad ascended to heaven, Temple of Jerusalem was located
- Meant to rival the Christian church of the Holy Sepulcher in Jerusalem, although it was inspired by its domed rotunda
- Mosaic Arabic calligraphy urges Moslems to embrace Allah as one god, and indicates that the Christian notion of the Trinity is an aspect of polytheism
- Oldest surviving Qur'an verses; first use of Qur'an verses in architecture
- Pilgrimage site for the faithful
- Erected by Abd al-Malik, caliph of the Umayyad Dynasty
- **Cross-Cultural Connections: Domes**
    - Taj Mahal (Figures 9.17a, 9.17b)
    - Pantheon (Figures 6.11a, 6.11b)
    - Hagia Sophia (Figures 8.3a, 8.3b)

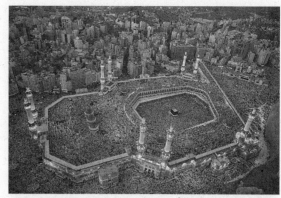

Figure 9.11a: The Kaaba, 631–632, Granite masonry, covered with silk curtain, gold and silver thread, Mecca, Saudi Arabia

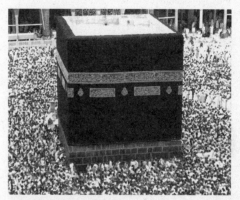

Figure 9.11b: Detail of 9.11a

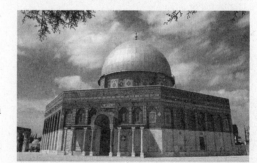

Figure 9.12a: Dome of the Rock, 691–692, stone masonry and wood roof decorated with glazed ceramic tile, mosaics, and gilt aluminum and bronze dome, Jerusalem

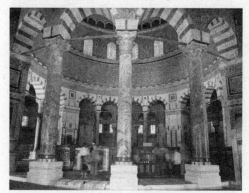

Figure 9.12b: Interior of the Dome of the Rock

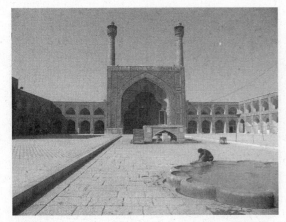

Figure 9.13a: Great Mosque (Masjid-e Jameh), c. 700 and following, mostly eleventh–seventeenth centuries, brick, wood, plaster, ceramic tile, Isfahan, Iran

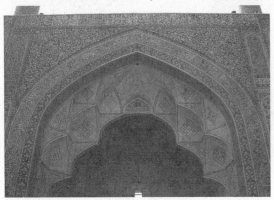

Figure 9.13b: Detail of 9.13a

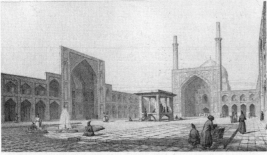

Figure 9.13c: Courtyard of 9.13a

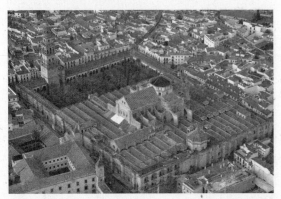

Figure 9.14a: Great Mosque, aerial view, eighth–tenth centuries, stone, Córdoba, Spain

Great Mosque (Masjid-e Jameh), c. 700 and following, mostly eleventh–seventeenth centuries, brick, wood, plaster, ceramic tile, Isfahan, Iran (Figures 9.13a, 9.13b, 9.13c, and 9.13d)

- Large central rectangular courtyard surrounded by a two-story arcade
- Each side of courtyard has a centrally placed iwan; may be first mosque to have this feature
- One iwan is an entry for a private space used by the sultan and his retinue; dome adorned by tiles
- The qibla iwan is the largest and most decorative; its size indicates the direction to Mecca
- **Cross-Cultural Comparisons: Houses of Worship**
  - Chartres Cathedral (Figures 12.4a, 12.4b, 12.4c)
  - Great Stupa at Sanchi (Figures 23.4a, 23.4b)
  - White Temple and its ziggurat (Figures 2.1a, 2.1b)

Great Mosque, eighth–tenth centuries, stone, Córdoba, Spain (Figures 9.14a–e)

- Double-arched columns, brilliantly articulated in alternating bands of color; voussoirs
- A light and airy interior
- Horseshoe-shaped arches have a tradition in Visigothic Spain and Roman architecture
- Hypostyle mosque: no central focus, no congregational worship
- Original wooden ceiling replaced by vaulting
- Complex dome over mihrab with elaborate squinches
- Columns are spolia from ancient Roman structures
- Relatively short columns made ceilings low; doubling of arches enhances interior space; perhaps influenced by the Roman aqueduct in Mérida, Spain
- Kufic calligraphy on walls

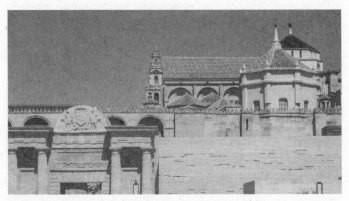

Figure 9.14b: Flank view of Great Mosque, Córdoba, Spain

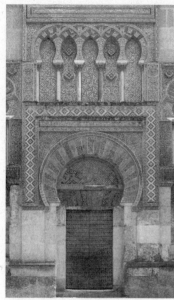

Figure 9.14c: Detail of façade of 9.14a

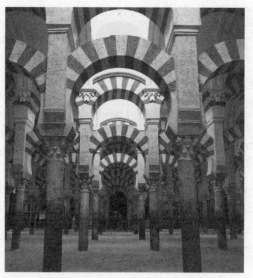

Figure 9.14d: Great Mosque, 8th–10th centuries, stone, Córdoba, Spain

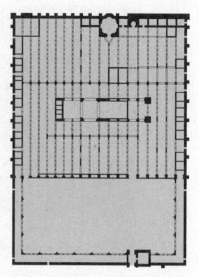

Figure 9.14e: Ground plan for Great Mosque, Córdoba, Spain

- Built on the site of a church; after Christian reconquest center of the mosque was used for a church
- **Cross-Cultural Comparisons: Architectural Plans**
  - Sullivan, Carson Pirie Scott building (Figure 21.14c)
  - Chartres Cathedral (Figure 12.4c)
  - Temple of Amun-Re (Figure 2.8c)

Alhambra, 1354–1391, whitewashed adobe stucco, wood, tile, paint, and gilding, Granada, Spain (Figures 9.15a, and 9.15d)

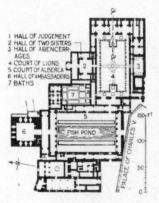

Figure 9.15a: Alhambra, 1354–1391, whitewashed adobe stucco, wood, tile, paint, and gilding, Granada, Spain

- Palace of the Nasrid sultans of Southern Spain
- Light, airy interiors; fortress-like exterior
- Built on a hill overlooking the city of Granada
- Contains palaces, gardens, water pools, fountains, courtyards
- Small, low bubbling fountains in each room provide cool temperatures in the summer

Court of the Lions (Figure 9.15b)

- Thin columns support heavy roofs; a feeling of weightlessness
- Intricately patterned and sculpted ceilings and walls
- Central fountain supported by protective lions; animal imagery permitted in secular monuments
- Parts of the walls are chiseled through to create vibrant light patterns within

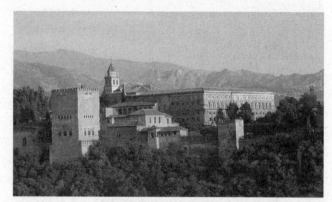

Figure 9.15d: Plan of the Alhambra, Granada, Spain

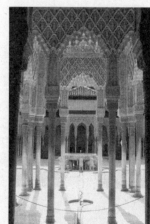

Figure 9.15b: Court of the Lions

Hall of the Sisters (Figure 9.15c)

- Sixteen windows at top of hall, light dissolves into a honeycomb of stalactites that dangle from the ceiling
- Abstract patterns, abstraction of forms
- 5,000 muqarnas refract light; carved in stucco onto ceiling
- Highly sophisticated and refined interior
- Perhaps used as a music room or for receptions
- **Cross-Cultural Comparisons: Interiors**
  - House of the Vettii (Figure 6.13)
  - Wright, Fallingwater (Figure 22.16b)
  - Hall of Mirrors, Versailles (Figure 17.3d)

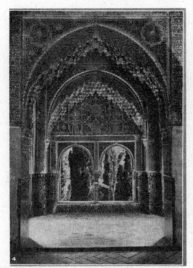

Figure 9.15c: Hall of the Sisters, Alhambra, Spain

Sinan, Mosque of Selim II, 1568–1575, brick and stone, Edirne, Turkey (Figures 9.16a, 9.16b, and 9.16c)

- Extremely thin soaring minarets
- Abundant window space makes for a brilliantly lit interior
- Decorative display of mosaic and tile work
- Inspired by Hagia Sophia (Figure 9.4), but a centrally planned building
- Octagonal interior, with 8 pillars resting on a square set of walls
- Open airy interior contrasts with conventional mosques that have partitioned interiors
- Part of a complex including a hospital, school, library, etc.
- Sinan was chief court architect for Suleyman the Magnificent (c. 1520–1566)
- Transitions from square ground plan to round dome achieved by inserting smaller domes into the corners
- Huge piers support the dome
- **Cross-Cultural Comparisons: Domes**
  - Pantheon (Figures 6.11a, 6.11b)
  - Dome of the Rock (Figures 9.12a, 9.12b)
  - Hagia Sophia (Figures 8.3a, 8.3b, 8.3c)

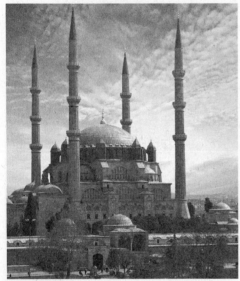

Figure 9.16a: Sinan, Mosque of Selim II, 1568–1575, brick and stone, Edirne, Turkey

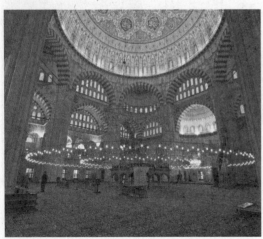

Figure 9.16b: Sinan, Mosque of Selim II, interior

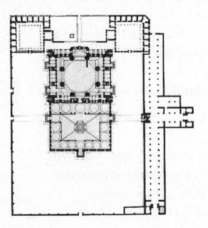

Figure 9.16c: Ground plan of Sinan, Mosque of Selim II

Taj Mahal, c. 1632–1648, stone, marble, precious and semi-precious stones, Agra, India (Figures 9.17a and 9.17b)

- Translated in English as "Crown Palace"
- Named for Mumtaz Mahal, deceased wife of Shah Jahan; she died while giving birth to her fourteenth child
- Built to serve as Mumtaz Mahal's tomb, centrally placed under dome. Shah Jahan was interred next to her after his death, placed asymmetrically next to her
- Symmetrical harmony of design
- Typical Islamic feature of one large arch flanked by two smaller arches
- Square plan with chamfered corners
- Onion-shaped dome rises gracefully from the square façade
- Small kiosks around dome lessen severity
- Intricate floral and geometric inlays on façade
- Grounds represent a vast funerary garden, the gardens found in heaven in the Islamic tradition
- Minarets act like a picture frame, directing our view and sheltering the monument
- Once formed part of a larger ensemble of buildings
- May have been built to salute the grandeur of the Shah Jahan and his royal kingdom, as much as to honor his wife's memory
- **Cross-Cultural Comparisons: Gardens**
  - Versailles (Figure 17.3e)
  - Kusama, *Narcissus Garden* (Figures 22.25a, 22.25b)
  - Ryoan-ji (Figures 25.2a, 25.2b, 25.2c)

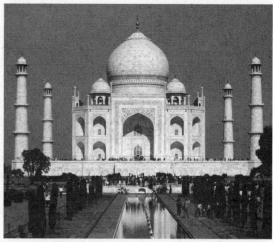

Figure 9.17a: Taj Mahal, c. 1632–1648, stone, marble, precious and semi-precious stones, Agra, India

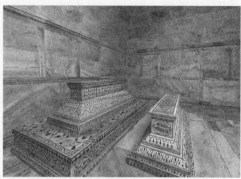

Figure 9. 17b: Interior of Taj Mahal, Agra, India

VOCABULARY

Arabesque: a flowing, intricate, and symmetrical pattern deriving from floral motifs (Figure 9.1)

Calligraphy: decorative or beautiful handwriting (Figure 9.2)

Hajj: an Islamic pilgrimage to Mecca that is required as one of the five pillars of Islam

Iwan: a rectangular vaulted space in a Muslim building that is walled on three sides and open on the fourth (Figure 9.13)

Jali: perforated ornamental stone screens in Islamic art

Kufic: a highly ornamental Islamic script

Mausoleum: a building, usually large, that contains tombs (Figure 9.17)

Mecca, Medina: Islamic holy cities; Mecca is the birthplace of Muhammad and the city all Muslims turn to in prayer; Medina is where Muhammad was first accepted as the Prophet, and where his tomb is located

Mihrab: a central niche in a mosque, which indicates the direction to Mecca (Figure 9.10)

Minaret: a tall, slender column used to call people to prayer (Figure 9.14)

Minbar: a pulpit from which sermons are given

Mosque: a Muslim house of worship (Figure 9.14)

Muezzin: an Islamic official who calls people to prayer traditionally from a minaret

Muhammad (570?–632): The Prophet whose revelations and teachings form the foundation of Islam

Muqarna: a honeycomb-like decoration often applied in Islamic buildings to domes, niches, capitals, or vaults. The surface resembles intricate stalactites

Pyxis (pronounced "pick-sis"): a small cylinder-shaped container with a detachable lid used to contain cosmetics or jewelry (Figure 9.4)

Qiblah: the direction toward Mecca which Muslims face in prayer

Qur'an: the Islamic sacred text, dictated to the Prophet Muhammad by the Angel Gabriel

Tessellation: decoration using polygonal shapes with no gaps (Figure 9.3)

Voussoirs (pronounced "vōō-swar"): a wedge-shaped stone that forms the curved part of an arch; the central voussoir is called a **keystone** (Figure 9.14d)

SUMMARY

Although not specifically banned by the Qur'an, a traditional prohibition against figural art dominates much of the Islamic movement. This did not prove to be an impediment for Muslim artists, who formed an endless creative expression of abstract designs based on calligraphy, arabesques, and tessellations. Figural art occurs mostly in Persian manuscripts that depict lavishly costumed courtiers recreating famous stories from Arabic literature.

Islamic architecture borrows freely from Byzantine, Sassanian, and Early Christian sources. Mosques all have niches, called mihrabs, which direct the worshipper's attention to Mecca. Religious symbolism dominates mosques, but is also richly represented in secular buildings such as tombs or palaces.

Multiple-Choice

Questions 1–3 refer to this picture of a basin.

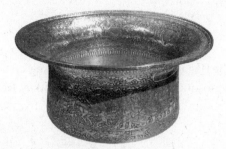

1. The decoration on the basin called the *Baptistère de St. Louis* is noted for its use of

   (A) calligraphy
   (B) contrapposto
   (C) horror vacui
   (D) tessellation

2. The original function of the basin called the *Baptistère de St. Louis* was for

   (A) the baptisms of infants in the royal household
   (B) coronation rituals of royalty
   (C) retelling mythological stories of the ancient past
   (D) washing hands during official ceremonies

3. The importance of the item is alluded to in the

   (A) rich material used to create it
   (B) depiction of royal family members and their entourage
   (C) use of lions and peacocks as royal symbols
   (D) purple color which symbolized royalty

   _____

4. How has the Great Mosque at Córdoba been altered by Christians after the reconquest of Spain?

   (A) The interior arches were taken down to make a vast unified space.
   (B) The mihrab was destroyed and an altar was placed in its stead.
   (C) The interior was reroofed using European vaulting techniques.
   (D) The building was turned into a church and then back into a mosque again.

5. The kufic script used in Islamic calligraphy is read in the same way as which of the following works?

(A) *The Golden Haggadah*
(B) *The Book of Lindisfarne*
(C) *The Vienna Genesis*
(D) *The Bayeux Tapestry*

Short Essay

The building at the left is the Hagia Sophia in Istanbul, Turkey, created from 532–537. The building on the right is the Mosque of Selim II in Edirne, Turkey, from 1568–1575.

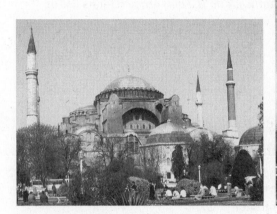
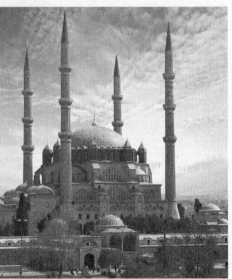

What were the original religious contexts for each building?

How has the building on the right been retrofitted to a different religious context?

Using specific evidence, explain how the Hagia Sophia influenced the design of the Mosque of Selim II.

1. **C**   2. **D**   3. **A**   4. **C**   5. **A**

ANSWERS EXPLAINED

Multiple-Choice

1. **(C)** All of the surfaces on the basin are covered with decoration. The definition of horror vacui (Latin for "fear of empty spaces") suggests that artists intentionally filled the whole surface with patterns, as is the case with this basin.

2. **(D)** Originally this basin functioned as a bowl for washing hands during ceremonies. It was later brought into the French royal court and used for baptisms.

3. **(A)** The basin is made of brass, inlaid with gold and silver—rich items indicating court patronage.

4. **(C)** After Spain was reconquered from the Moors in 1492, this building had its original wooden ceiling removed, and European-style vaulting was installed.

5. **(A)** Kufic script is read right to left, the way Hebrew is. *The Golden Haggadah* is written in Hebrew.

Short-Essay Rubric

Question	Points	Key Points in a Good Response
What were the original religious contexts for each building?	1	Hagia Sophia was originally designed for Christian worship; the Mosque of Selim II was originally designed, and is still used, for Islamic worship.
How has the building on the right been retrofitted to a different religious context?	2	The building on the right has had all of the Christian images either destroyed or covered over. The altar and the Christian imagery have been removed. A mihrab has been installed. Islamic calligraphy and medallions have been added. Minarets have been placed on the outside to call people to prayer.
Using specific evidence, explain how the Hagia Sophia influenced the design of the Mosque of Selim II.	2	The design of Selim has the following ideas taken from the Hagia Sophia: ■ Dome resting on pendentives ■ Base of dome surrounded by windows ■ Large window spaces on interior walls ■ Large open interior space ■ Large exterior massings to support the dome ■ Decoration on the walls of the interior

Early Medieval Art

10

TIME PERIOD: 450–1050		
Merovingian Art	481–714	France
Hiberno-Saxon Art	6th–8th centuries	British Isles

ENDURING UNDERSTANDING: Medieval art is studied according to geographic placement, styles, and traditions. There are frequent interconnections between religions, governments, and artistic influences that create a variety of approaches.

Essential Knowledge:

■ Medieval periods are the following:
  – Late Antique and Early Christian: Chapter 7
  – Byzantine: Chapter 8
  – Islamic: Chapter 9
  – Early Medieval: Chapter 10
  – Romanesque: Chapter 11
  – Gothic: Chapters 12 and 13
■ There is no uniform medieval style. Some periods revive ancient classicism, others use geometric and natural designs.
■ Medieval artists are influenced by contemporaries in other parts of Europe, as well as ancient traditions.

ENDURING UNDERSTANDING: Medieval art is chiefly concerned with religious expression and court life. There is a strong culture of endorsing scholarship.

Essential Knowledge:

■ Learning was centered on specific fields that were transmitted throughout Europe through trade, pilgrimage, and military activity.
■ Medieval architecture is mostly religious.
■ Medieval painting and sculpture avoids naturalistic depictions.
■ At times medieval religions will reject images.

HISTORICAL BACKGROUND

In the year 600, almost everything that was known was old. The great technological break-throughs of the Romans were either lost to history or beyond the capabilities of the migratory people of the seventh century. This was the age of mass migrations sweeping across Europe, an age epitomized by the fifth-century king, Attila the Hun, whose hordes were famous for despoiling all before them.

Certainly Attila was not alone. The Vikings from Scandinavia, in their speedy boats, flew across the North Sea and invaded the British Isles and colonized parts of France.

Other groups, like the notorious Vandals, did much to destroy the remains of Roman civilization. So desperate was this era that historians named it the "Dark Ages," a term that more reflects our knowledge of the times than the times themselves.

However, stability in Europe was reached at the end of the eighth century when a group of Frankish kings, most notably Charlemagne, built an impressive empire whose capital was centered in Aachen, Germany.

Patronage and Artistic Life

Monasteries were the principal centers of learning in an age when even the emperor, Charlemagne, could read, but not write more than his name. Therefore, artists who could both write and draw were particularly honored for the creation of manuscripts.

The modern idea that artists should be original and say something fresh or new in each work is a notion that was largely unknown in the Middle Ages. Scribes copied great works of ancient literature, like the Bible or medical treatises; they did not record contemporary literature or folk tales. Scribes were expected to maintain the wording of the original, while illustrators painted important scenes, keeping one eye on traditional approaches, and another on his or her own creative powers. Therefore, the text of a manuscript is generally an exact copy of a continuously recopied book; the illustrations allow the artist some freedom of expression.

EARLY MEDIEVAL ART

One of the great glories of Medieval art is the decoration of manuscript books, called **codices**, which were improvements over ancient scrolls both for ease of use and durability. A codex was made of resilient antelope or calf hide, called **vellum**, or sheep or goat hide, called **parchment**. These hides were more durable than the friable papyrus used in making ancient scrolls. Hides were cut into sheets and soaked in lime in order to free them from oil and hair. The skin was then dried and perhaps chalk was added to whiten the surface. Artisans then prepared the skins by scraping them down to an even thickness with a sharp knife; each page had to be rubbed smooth to remove impurities. The hides were then folded to form small booklets of eight pages. Parchment was so valued as a writing surface that it continued to be used for manuscripts even after paper became standard.

The backbone of the hide was arranged so that the spine of the animal ran across the page horizontally. This minimized movement when the hide dried and tried to return to the shape of the animal, perhaps causing the paint to flake.

Illuminations were painted mostly by monks or nuns who wrote in rooms called **scriptoria**, or writing places, that had no heat or light, to prevent fires. Vows of silence were maintained to limit mistakes. A team often worked on one book; scribes copied the text and illustrators drew capital letters as painters illustrated scenes from the Bible. Eventually, the booklets were sewn together to create a manuscript.

Manuscript books had a sacred quality. This was the word of God, and had to be treated with appropriate deference. The books were covered with bindings of wood or leather, and gold leaf was lavished on the surfaces. Finally, precious gems were inset on the cover.

A spectacular hoard of medieval gold and silverwork was discovered on a farm in Shropshire, England, in 2009. This find is so large that it has forced scholars to reconsider everything that is known about the Anglo-Saxon kingdoms of medieval Britain.

Objects are done in the **cloisonné** technqiue, with **horror vacui** designs featuring **animal style** decoration. Interlace patternings are common. Images enjoy an elaborate symmetry, with animals alternating with geometric designs. Most of the objects that survive are portable.

MEROVINGIAN ART

The Merovingians were a dynasty of Frankish kings who, according to tradition, descended from Merovech, chief of the Salian Franks. Power was solidified under Clovis (reigned 481–511) who ruled what is today France and southwestern Germany. The Frankish custom of dividing property among sons when a father died led to instability because Clovis's four male descendants fought over their patrimony. With the constant division of land after a king's death, Merovingian history became marked by internal struggles and civil wars.

Even so, court life and art production could be quite splendid. Merovingian rulers treated their kingdom as private property and exploited its wealth as much as possible, spending lavishly on themselves.

Royal burials supply almost all our knowledge of Merovingian art. A wide range of metal objects were interred with the dead, including personal jewelry items like brooches, discs, pins, earrings and bracelets. Garment clasps, called fibulae, were particular specialties. They were often inlaid with hard stones, like garnets, and were made using chasing and cloisonné techniques.

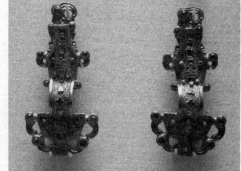

Looped fibulae, mid-sixth century, silver gilt with semiprecious stones, inlays of garnets and other stones, Cabinet des Médailles, Paris (Figure 10.1)

- Fibula: a pin or brooch used to fasten garments; showed the prestige of the wearer
- Cloisonné and chasing techniques
- Zoomorphic elements
- Small portable objects
- Decline of the classical tradition

Figure 10.1: Looped fibulae, mid-sixth century, silver gilt with semiprecious stones, inlays of garnets and other stones, Cabinet des Médailles, Paris

HIBERNO-SAXON ART

Hiberno-Saxon art refers to the art of the British Isles in the Early Medieval period; Hibernia is the ancient name for Ireland. The main artistic expression is illuminated manuscripts, of which a particularly rich collection still survives.

Hiberno-Saxon art relies on complicated interlace patterns in a frenzy of horror vacui. The borders of these pages harbor animals in stylized combat patterns, sometimes called the animal style. Each section of the illustrated text opens with huge initials that are rich fields for

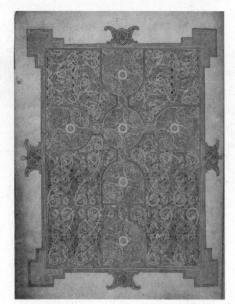

Figure 10.2a: Cross Page from the *Book of Matthew* from *The Book of Lindisfarne*, c. 700, illuminated manuscript, ink, pigments, and gold on vellum, British Library, London

ornamentation. The Irish artists who worked on these books had an exceptional handling of color and form, featuring a brilliant transference of polychrome techniques to manuscripts.

The Book of Lindisfarne, c. 700, illuminated manuscript, ink, pigments, and gold on vellum, British Library, London (Figures 10.2a, 10.2b, and 10.2c)

- Written by Eadrith, bishop of Lindisfarne
- Unusual in that it is the work of an individual artist and not a team of scribes
- Written in Latin, with annotations in English between the lines
- English added around 970 and is the oldest surviving manuscript of the Bible in English
- Uses Saint Jerome's translation of the Bible, called "The Vulgate"
- Latin script is called half-uncial
- English script called Anglo-Saxon miniscule
- 130 calf skins used to make the manuscript
- Colophon at end of book discusses the making of the manuscript

Cross Page from the *Book of Matthew* from *The Book of Lindisfarne*

- Cross depicted on a page filled with horror vacui decoration
- Dog-headed snakes intermix with birds with long beaks
- Cloisonné style used in the bodies of the birds
- Elongated figures lost in a maze of "S" shapes
- Symmetrical arrangement
- Black background makes patterning stand out
- Mixture of traditional Celtic imagery and Christian theology

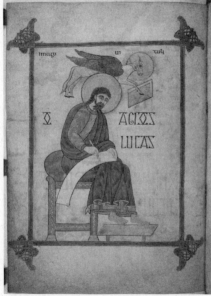

Figure 10.2b: Saint Luke Portrait from *The Book of Lindisfarne*, c. 700, illuminated manuscript, ink, pigments, and gold on vellum, British Library, London

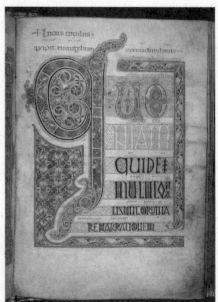

Figure 10.2c: Saint Luke Incipit Page from *The Book of Lindisfarne*, c. 700, illuminated manuscript, ink, pigments, and gold on vellum, British Library, London

Saint Luke Portrait from *The Book of Lindisfarne*

- Traditional symbol associated with Saint Luke is the calf (a sacrificial animal)
- Identity of the calf is acknowledged in the Latin phrase "imago vituli"
- Saint Luke is identified by Greek words using Latin characters: "Hagios Lucas"
- Heavily bearded Saint Luke gives weight to his authority as an author, but he appears as a younger man
- Saint Luke sits with legs crossed holding a scroll and a writing instrument

Saint Luke Incipit Page from *The Book of Lindisfarne*

- "Incipit," meaning opening words of Saint Luke's gospel: "Quoniam Quidem…"
- Numerous Celtic spiral ornaments; step patterns appear in the enlarged "O"
- Lower right corner: naturalistic detail of a cat who has eaten eight birds
- **Cross-Cultural Comparisons: Manuscripts**
  - *Golden Haggadah* (Figures 12.10a, 12.10b, 12.10c)
  - *Bahrum Gur Fights the Karg* (Figure 9.8)
  - Folio from the Qur'an (Figure 9.5)

VOCABULARY

Animal style: a medieval art form in which animals are depicted in a stylized and often complicated pattern, usually seen fighting with one another (Figure 10.2)

Chasing: to ornament metal by indenting into a surface with a hammer (Figure 10.1)

Cloissonné: enamelwork in which colored areas are separated by thin bands of metal, usually gold or bronze (Figure 10.1)

Codex (plural: **codices**)**:** a manuscript book (Figure 10.2a)

Colophon: 1) a commentary on the end panel of a Chinese scroll, 2) an inscription at the end of a manuscript containing relevant information on its publication

Fibula (plural: **fibulae**)**:** a clasp used to fasten garments (Figure 10.1)

Gospels: the first four books of the New Testament that chronicle the life of Jesus Christ (Figure 10.2b)

Horror vacui: (Latin, meaning "fear of empty spaces") a type of artwork in which the entire surface is filled with objects, people, designs, and ornaments in a crowded, sometimes congested way (Figure 10.2a)

Parchment: a writing surface made from animal skins; particularly fine parchment made of calf skin is called **vellum** (Figure 10.2)

Scriptorium (plural: **scriptoria**)**:** a place in a monastery where monks wrote manuscripts

Zoomorphic: having elements of animal shapes

SUMMARY

The political chaos resulting from the Fall of Rome set in motion a period of migrations. The unifying force in Europe was Christianity, whose adherents established powerful centers of learning, particularly in places like Ireland.

Artists concentrated on portable objects that intermixed the animal style of Germanic art with horror vacui and strong interlacing patterns.

Fibulae and other personal jewelry became a sign of status and wealth.

PRACTICE EXERCISES

Multiple-Choice

1. *The Book of Lindisfarne* shows classical influence in its

    (A)   animals depicted in margins
    (B)   figures shown in contrapposto
    (C)   calligraphy written in Latin
    (D)   interlace patterning with interweaving forms

2. A fibula can be seen worn in which of the following images?

    (A)   *Sarcophagus of the Spouses*
    (B)   *Augustus of Prima Porta*
    (C)   *Justinian from San Vitale*
    (D)   *Head of a Roman Patrician*

3. The Merovingian looped fibula shows the horror vacui and cloisonné and chasing techniques common in which of the following traditions?

    (A)   Roman
    (B)   Byzantine
    (C)   Greek
    (D)   Celtic

4. Zoomorphic designs, as seen in *The Lindisfarne Gospels*, are similar to those found on

    (A)   Camelid sacrem in the shape of a canine
    (B)   Anthropomorphic Stele
    (C)   Jade cong from Liangzhu, China
    (D)   Tlatilco female figure

5. Gospel books

    (A)   are biographies of Jesus

    (B)   foretell the coming of Jesus

    (C)   discuss apocalyptic visions of the Last Judgment

    (D)   are letters written by saints after the death of Jesus

Short Essay

These are two pages from *The Lindisfarne Gospels*.

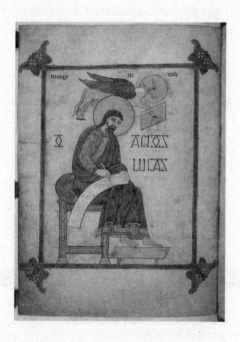 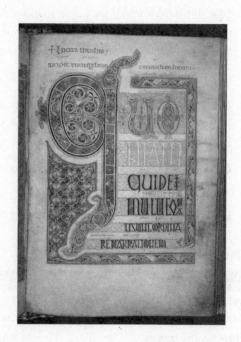

What is the subject of this book?

How do the pages depicted here illustrate the subject of the book?

Describe how this book was used.

How does this book show the influence of the classical and non-classical traditions?

1. **C**   2. **C**   3. **D**   4. **C**   5. **A**

ANSWERS EXPLAINED

Multiple-Choice

1. **(C)** Both (A) and (D) are Celtic inspirations in *The Book of Lindisfarne.* Choice (B) would be correct except that there is no trace of contrapposto in the drawing of this book. The book is written in Latin, a classical language.

2. **(C)** Justinian wears a fibula in the Byzantine mosaics in San Vitale.

3. **(D)** Merovingian looped fibulae show a decline in the classical tradition in Western Europe. Byzantine, Greek, and Roman art are aspects of the classical tradition. Celtic art from Northern Europe developed separately and is from a different tradition.

4. **(C)** Zoomorphic designs, those having elements of animal shapes, are seen in the jade cong from Liangzhu, China.

5. **(A)** The four gospels books are, among other things, biographies of the life of Jesus.

Short-Essay Rubric

Question	Points	Key Points in a Good Response
What is the subject of this book?	1	The Gospel of Saint Luke, from the New Testament of the Bible
How do the pages depicted here illustrate the subject of the book?	1	Answers could include: ■ Saint Luke is shown in an author portrait with his symbol, a calf, in the left illustration ■ Saint Luke's name appears next to him. ■ The calf is identified near him. ■ The opening words in Latin of Saint Luke's gospel appear in the right illustration.
Describe how this book was used.	1	Used during the Christian mass for readings from the New Testament

How does this book show the influence of the classical and non-classical traditions?	2	Answers could include:
		■ Classical:
		  – Latin calligraphy
		  – author portrait
		  – scroll
		  – Saint Luke symbolized by a calf (or an ox)
		■ Non-Classical:
		  – margins written in Gaelic
		  – zoomorphic designs
		  – interlace patterning
		  – stylized figures

Romanesque Art

11

> **TIME PERIOD: 1050–1150, SOME OBJECTS DATE AS EARLY AS 1000 AND AS LATE AS 1200**

To nineteenth-century art historians, Romanesque architecture looked like a derivative of ancient Roman art, and they titled the period "Romanesque," or "in the Roman manner." Although there are some superficial resemblances in the roundness of architectural forms, the Romanesque period is very different from its namesake.

ENDURING UNDERSTANDING: Medieval art is studied according to geographic placement, styles, and traditions. There are frequent interconnections between religions, governments, and artistic influences that create a variety of approaches.

Essential Knowledge:

- Medieval periods are the following:
  - Late Antique and Early Christian: Chapter 7
  - Byzantine: Chapter 8
  - Islamic: Chapter 9
  - Early Medieval: Chapter 10
  - Romanesque: Chapter 11
  - Gothic: Chapters 12 and 13
- There is no uniform medieval style. Some periods revive ancient classicism, others use geometric and natural designs.
- Medieval artists are influenced by contemporaries in other parts of Europe, as well as ancient traditions.

ENDURING UNDERSTANDING: Medieval art is chiefly concerned with religious expression and court life. There is a strong culture of endorsing scholarship.

Essential Knowledge:

- Learning was centered on specific fields that were transmitted throughout Europe through trade, pilgrimage, and military activity.
- Medieval architecture is mostly religious.
- Medieval painting and sculpture avoids naturalistic depictions.
- At times medieval religions will reject images.

HISTORICAL BACKGROUND

By 1000, Europe had begun to settle down from the great migration that characterized the Early Medieval period. Wandering seafarers like the Vikings were Christianized, and their descendants colonized Normandy, France, and southern Italy and Sicily. Islamic incursions from Spain and North Africa were neutralized; in fact, Europeans began a counterinvasion of Muslim lands called the Crusades. The universal triumph of Christianity in Europe with the pope cast as its leader was a spiritual empire not unlike the Roman secular one.

Even though Europeans fought with equal ardor among themselves, enough stability was reached so that trade and the arts could flourish; cities, for the first time in centuries, expanded. People began to crisscross Europe on religious pilgrimages to Rome and even Jerusalem. The most popular destination was the shrine dedicated to Saint James in the northwestern Spanish town of Santiago de Compostela. A magnificent Romanesque cathedral was built as the endpoint of western European pilgrimages.

The journey to Santiago took perhaps a year or longer to make. Shrines were established at key points along the road, so that pilgrims could enjoy additional holy places, many of which still survive today. This pilgrimage movement, with its consequent building boom, is one of the great revitalizations in history.

Patronage and Artistic Life

Medieval society centered on feudalism, which can be expressed as a symbiotic relationship between lords and peasants. Peasants worked the land, sustaining all with their labor. Lords owned the land, and they guaranteed peasants security. Someplace between these stations, artists lived in what eventually became a middle class. Painting was considered a higher calling compared to sculpture or architecture because painters worked less with their hands.

Women were generally confined to the "feminine arts" such as ceramics, weaving, or manuscript decoration. Powerful and wealthy women (queens, abbesses, and so on) were active patrons of the arts, sponsoring the construction of nunneries or commissioning illuminated manuscripts. Hrotswitha of Gandersheim, a nun, wrote plays that were reminiscent of Roman playwrights and poets. One of the most brilliant people of the period was Hildegard von Bingen, who was a renowned author, composer, and patroness of the arts.

Although Christian works dominate the artistic production of the Romanesque period, a significant number of beautifully crafted secular works also survives. The line between secular and religious works in medieval society was not so finely drawn, as objects for one often contain symbolism of the other.

The primary focus of medieval architecture is on the construction of castles, manor houses, monasteries, and churches. These were conceived not by architects in the modern sense of the word, but by master builders, who oversaw the whole operation from designing the building to contracting the employees. These master builders were often accompanied by master artists, who supervised the artistic design of the building.

ROMANESQUE ARCHITECTURE

Cathedrals were sources of civic pride as well as artistic expression and spiritual devotion. Since they sometimes took hundreds of years to build and were extremely expensive, great care was lavished on their construction and maintenance. Church leaders sought to preserve structures from the threat of fire and moved away from wood to stone roofs. Those that were originally conceived with wood were sometimes retrofitted. This revival of structures entirely in stone is one reason for the period's name, "Romanesque."

But stone caused problems. It is heavy—which means that the walls have to be extra thick to sustain the weight of the roof. Windows are small, so that there are as few holes in the walls as possible. The interiors are correspondingly dark. To bring more light into the buildings, the exterior of the windows are often narrow and the interior of the window wider—this way the light would come in through the window and ricochet off its thick walls and appear more luminous. However, the introduction of stained glass darkened attempts at lightening the interiors.

To help support the roofs of these massive buildings, master builders designed a new device called the **rib vault** (Figure 11.1). At first, these ribs were decorative moldings placed on top of groin vaults, but eventually they became a new way of looking at roof support. While they do not carry its full weight, they help channel the stresses of its load down to the walls and onto the massive piers below, which serve as functional buttresses. Rib vaults also open up the ceiling spaces more dramatically, allowing for larger windows to be placed in the clerestory. During construction, rib vaults were the first part of the roof to be built, the stones in the spaces between were added later (Figure 11.1).

Besides the advantage of being fireproof, stone has several other positive properties. It is easy to maintain, durable, and generally weatherproof. It also conducts sound very well, so that medieval music, characterized by Gregorian chant, could be performed, enabling even those in the rear of these vast buildings to hear the service.

The basic unit of medieval construction is called the **bay**. This spatial unit contains an arch on the first floor, a triforium with smaller arches on the second, and windows in a clerestory on the third. The bay became a model for the total expression of the cathedral—its form is repeated throughout the building to render an artistic whole (Figure 11.2).

In order to accommodate large crowds who came to Romanesque buildings during feast days or for pilgrimages, master builders designed an addition to the east end of the building, called an **ambulatory**, a feature that was also present in Early Christian churches. This walkway had the benefit of directing crowds around the church without disturbing the ceremonies taking place in the apse. Chapels were placed at measured intervals around the ambulatory so that pilgrims could admire the displays of relics and other sacred items housed there. The ambulatory at **St. Sernin** (Figure 11.3) is a good example of how they work in this context.

After six hundred years of relatively small buildings, Romanesque architecture with its massive display of cut stone comes as a surprise. The buildings are characterized as being uniformly large, displaying

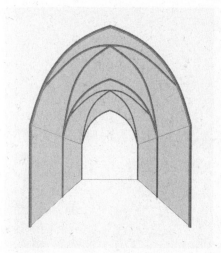

Figure 11.1: Rib vaults

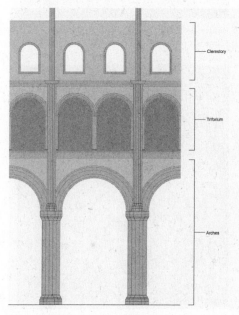

Figure 11.2: A bay is a vertical section of a church often containing arches, a triforium, and a clerestory.

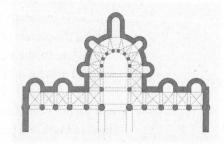

Figure 11.3: An ambulatory is the passageway that winds around an apse. Romanesque buildings often have chapels that radiate from them. Ambulatories can be found in buildings as early as the Early Christian period.

monumentality and solidity. Round arches, often used as **arcades**, are prominent features on façades. Concrete technology, a favorite of the ancient Romans, was forgotten by the tenth century.

Interiors are dark; façades are sometimes punctured with round oculus-type windows.

Although some buildings were built with wood ceilings, the tendency outside Italy is to use Roman stone-vaulting techniques, such as the barrel and groin vault to cover the interior spaces as at **Sainte-Foy** (Figures 11.5 and 11.6). However, later buildings employ rib-covered groin vaults to make interiors seem taller and lighter.

Italian buildings have separate bell towers called **campaniles** to summon people to prayer. Northern European buildings incorporate this tower into the fabric of the building often over the crossing (as at **Sainte-Foy**).

Church of Sainte-Foy, c. 1050–1130, stone, Conques, France (Figures 11.4a and 11.4b)

- A church built along the pilgrimage road to Santiago de Compostela
- Church built to handle the large number of pilgrims: wide transepts, large ambulatory with radiating chapels
- Massive heavy interior walls, unadorned
- No clerestory; light provided by windows over the side aisles and galleries
- Barrel vaults in nave, reinforced by transverse arches
- Cross-like ground plan
- **Cross-Cultural Comparisons: Pilgrimages**
    - Great Stupa, Sanchi (Figures 23.4a, 23.4b, 23.4c, 23.4d, 23.4e)
    - Kaaba (Figures 9.11a, 9.11b)
    - Bamiyan Buddha (Figures 23.2a, 23.2b)

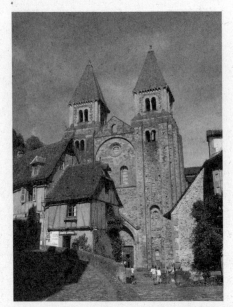

Figure 11.4a: Church of Sainte-Foy, c. 1050–1130, stone, Conques, France

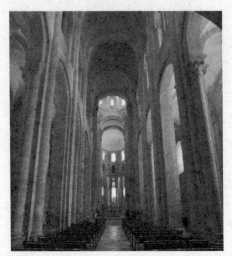

Figure 11.4b: Nave of Church of Sainte-Foy

ROMANESQUE SCULPTURE AND PAINTING

Large-scale stone sculpture was generally unknown in the Early Medieval period—its revitalization is one of the hallmarks of the Romanesque. Sculptors took their inspiration from goldsmiths and other metal workers, but expanded the scale to almost life-size works. Most characteristically, sculpture was placed around the portals of medieval churches so that worshippers could understand, among other things, the theme of a particular building (Figure 11.5). Small-scale works, such as ivories, wooden objects, and metalwork continued to flourish as they did in earlier periods.

Most of what we know about Romanesque painting comes from illuminated manuscripts and an occasional surviving ceiling or wall mural. Characteristically, figures tend to be outlined in black and then vibrantly colored. Gestures are emphatic; emotions are exaggerated—therefore, heads and hands are proportionally the largest features. Figures fill a blank surface rather than occupy a three-dimensional reality; hence they seem to float. Sometimes they are on tiptoe or glide across a surface, as they do in the **Bayeux Tapestry** (Figure 11.7). People are most important; they dominate buildings which seem like props or stage sets in the background of most Romanesque illustrations.

Painted stone sculpture is a trademark of Romanesque churches. Capitals are elaborately, and often fancifully, carved with scenes from the Bible. The chief glory of Romanesque sculpture is the portal. These are works of so prominent a location that sculptors vied for the honor of carving in so important a site. As artists became famous for their work, towns competed to hire them. Some have prominently placed signatures that proclaim their glory.

Although there are regional variations, there are some broad characteristics that generally define Romanesque sculpture. Figures tend to have a flattened look with zigzagging drapery that often hides body form rather than defines it. Scale is carefully articulated, with a hierarchy of figures being presented according to their importance. Figures are placed within borders, usually using them as isolated frames for scenes to be acted out in. They rarely push against these frames, preferring to be defined by them.

Smaller, independent sculptures were also produced at this time. Among the most significant are **reliquaries** (Figure 11.6c) that contain venerated objects, like the bones of saints; they are richly adorned and highly prized.

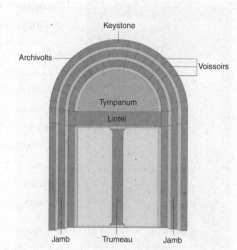

Figure 11.5: A Romanesque portal

Last Judgment, 1107–1125, painted stone, Sainte-Foy, Conques (Figures 11.6a and 11.6b)

- Largest Romanesque tympanum
- Christ as a strict judge, dividing the world into those going to Heaven and those going to Hell
- Christ's welcoming right hand, cast down left hand
- Dividing line runs vertically through the cross in the middle of the composition
- Archangel Michael and the devil at Christ's feet, weighing the souls
- Hell with damned on right; saved on left; people enter the church on the right and exit saved, on left
- Subject of the tympanum reminds pilgrims of the point of their pilgrimage
- 124 figures originally richly painted, densely packed together
- The saved move towards Christ, Mary and Saint Peter in the lead
- Paradise, on lower level, portrayed as the heavenly Jerusalem
- In left triangle, arches of Conques Abbey with dangling chains—Sainte Foy interceded for those enslaved by the Moslems in Spain; she herself appears kneeling before a giant hand of God
- On right lower level, the devil presides over a chaotic tangle of tortured condemned sinners
- Inscription on lintel: "O Sinners, change your morals before you might face a cruel judgment."
- **Cross-Cultural Comparisons: Last Judgment Scenes**
  - Giotto, Arena Chapel (Figure 13.1b)
  - Michelangelo, Sistine Chapel (Figure 16.2e)
  - Last Judgment of Hu-Nefer (Figure 3.12)

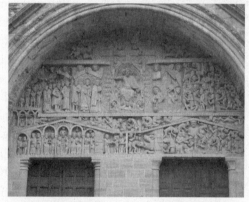

Figure 11.6a: *Last Judgment*, 1107–1125, painted stone, Sainte-Foy, Conques

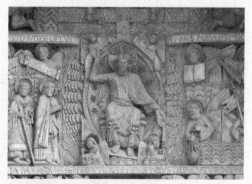

Figure 11.6b: Detail of 11.6a

Reliquary of Sainte-Foy, gold, silver, gemstones, and enamel over wood, ninth century, Sainte-Foy, Conques (Figure 11.6c)

■ Reliquary of a young girl martyred in the early fourth century; she refused to sacrifice to the Roman gods in a pagan ritual
■ Relics of her body stolen from a nearby town and enthroned in Conques in 866
■ One of the earliest large scale sculptures in the Middle Ages
■ Jewels, gems, and crown added over the years by the faithful
■ Child's skull is housed in the rather mannish looking enlarged head

Bayeux Tapestry, 1066–1080, embroidery on linen, Bayeux Tapestry Museum, Bayeux, France (Figures 11.7a and 11.7b)

■ Tapestry a misnomer; actually an embroidery
■ Commissioned by Bishop Odo, half-brother of William the Conqueror
■ Tells the story (in Latin) of William's conquest of England at the Battle of Hastings in 1066
■ Probably designed by a man; executed by women
■ Fanciful beasts in upper and lower registers
■ Borders sometimes comment on the main scenes, or show scenes of everyday life
■ Color used in a non-natural manner; different parts of a horse are colored variously

■ Neutral background
■ Flatness of figures; no shadows
■ Narrative tradition going back to the *Column of Trajan* (Figure 7.34)
■ 75 scenes, over 600 people
■ 230-feet long; continues narrative tradition of Medieval art
■ Uncertainty over how this work was meant to be displayed
■ **Cross-Cultural Comparisons: Battle Scenes**
  – Ludovisi Battle Sarcophagus (Figure 6.17)
  – *Night Attack on the Sanjô Palace* (Figures 25.3a, 25.3b)
  – Delacroix, *Liberty Leading the People* (Figure 20.4)

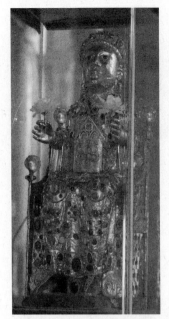

Figure 11.6c: *Reliquary of Sainte-Foy*, gold, silver, gemstones, and enamel over wood, ninth century, Sainte-Foy, Conques

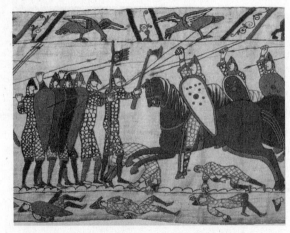

Figure 11.7a: Cavalry scene from *The Bayeux Tapestry*, c. 1066–1080, embroidery on linen, Bayeux Tapestry Museum, Bayeux, France

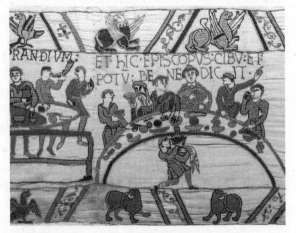

Figure 11.7b: Banquet scene from *The Bayeux Tapestry*

VOCABULARY

Abbey: a monastery for monks, or a convent for nuns, and the church that is connected to it (Figure 11.4a)

Ambulatory: a passageway around the apse of a church (Figure 11.3)

Apse: the end point of a church where the altar is (Figure 11.3)

Arcade: a series of arches supported by columns. When the arches face a wall and are not self-supporting, they are called a **blind arcade**

Archivolt: a series of concentric moldings around an arch (Figure 11.5)

Axial plan (Basilican plan, Longitundinal plan): a church with a long nave whose focus is the apse, so-called because it is designed along an axis (Figure 11.4b)

Baptistery: in medieval architecture, a separate chapel or building in front of a church used for baptisms

Bay: a vertical section of a church that is embraced by a set of columns and is usually composed of arches and aligned windows (Figure 11.2)

Campanile: a bell tower of an Italian building

Cathedral: the principal church of a diocese, where a bishop sits

Clerestory: the third, or window, story of a church (Figure 11.2)

Embroidery: a woven product in which the design is stitched into a premade fabric (Figures 11.7a and 11.7b)

Jamb: the side posts of a medieval portal (Figure 11.5)

Last Judgment: in Christianity, the judgment before God at the end of the world (Figure 11.6a)

Narthex: the vestibule, or lobby, of a church

Portal: a doorway. In Medieval art they can be significantly decorated (Figure 11.5)

Reliquary: a vessel for holding a sacred relic. Often reliquaries took the shape of the objects they held. Precious metals and stones were the common material (Figure 11.6c)

Rib vault: a vault in which diagonal arches form riblike patterns. These arches partially support a roof, in some cases forming a weblike design (Figure 11.1)

Tapestry: a woven product in which the design and the backing are produced at the same time on a device called a **loom**

Transept: an aisle in a church perpendicular to the nave

Transverse arch: an arch that spans an interior space connecting opposite walls by crossing from side to side (Figure 11.4b)

Triforium: A narrow passageway with arches opening onto a nave, usually directly below a clerestory (Figure 11.2)

Trumeau (plural: **trumeaux**): the central pillar of a portal that stabilizes the structure. It is often elaborately decorated (Figure 11.5)

Tympanum (plural: **tympana**): a rounded sculpture placed over the portal of a medieval church (Figure 11.6a)

Voussoir (pronounced "vōō-swar"): a wedge-shaped stone that forms the curved part of an arch. The central voussoir is called a **keystone** (Figure 11.5)

SUMMARY

In a way, the monumentality, rounded arches, and heavy walls of Roman architecture are reflected in the Romanesque tradition. However, the liturgical purpose of Romanesque buildings, their use of ambulatories and radiating chapels and their dark interiors give these churches a religious feeling quite different from their Roman predecessors.

Romanesque builders reacted to the increased mobility of Europeans, many of whom were now traveling on pilgrimages, by enlarging the size of their buildings. As Romanesque art progresses increasingly sophisticated vaulting techniques are developed. Hallmarks of the Romanesque style include thick walls and piers that give the buildings a monumentality and massiveness lacking in Early Medieval art.

Most great Romanesque sculpture was done around the main portals of churches, usually on themes related to the Last Judgment and the punishment of the bad alongside the salvation of the good. French sculptors carved energetic and elongated figures that often look flattened against the surface of the stone. Although regional variations are common, most Romanesque sculpture is content within the frame of the work it is conceived in, and rarely presses against the sides or emerges forward.

Although religious themes dominate Romanesque art, occasionally works of secular interest, like the *Bayeux Tapestry*, were created.

PRACTICE EXERCISES

Multiple-Choice

1. The subject matter in the *Bayeux Tapestry* is similar to

   (A)   scenes from the *Vienna Genesis*
   (B)   the Temple of Zeus and Athena at Pergamon
   (C)   the *Niobides Krater*
   (D)   the Column of Trajan

2. Pilgrims entering Romanesque churches such as Sainte-Foy were expected to

   (A)   walk to the chapels in the rear where the relics were housed
   (B)   worship around a centrally planned altar where services would be held
   (C)   travel to the top of the bell towers to ceremonially ring the bells
   (D)   place offerings at the foot of a statue of Jesus

3. The scene over the doorway of the Church of Sainte-Foy of the Last Judgment shows the damned condemned to hell on the right and the saved rising to heaven on the left because

   (A) in the middle are those who were noncommittal about religion and salvation
   (B) one enters the church as a sinner on the right but emerges saved on the left
   (C) in the Christian tradition, the damned are unwelcome in church
   (D) a parallel is drawn between sinners who must use the right door and saints who must use the left door

4. The *Reliquary of Sainte-Foy* and the *Reliquary Figure (Nlo bieri)* are similar in that they

   (A) are both meant to ward off evil
   (B) are both male figures in the shape of females
   (C) both held skulls of important deceased people
   (D) are both part of an extensive pilgrimage site for many to come to

5. Romanesque architecture can be characterized as

   (A) small, intimate, and warm
   (B) soaring, vertical, and uplifting
   (C) thick, heavy, and massive
   (D) irregular, unbalanced, and asymmetrical

Short Essay

This is the Romanesque church at Sainte-Foy.

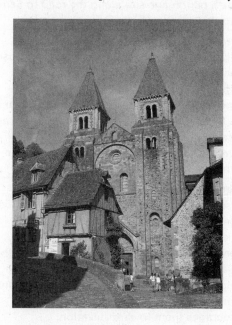
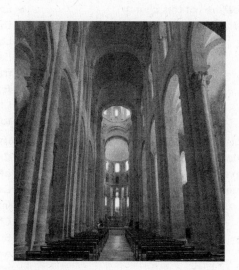

Why was this church built?

Discuss how the design features of this church reflect its use.

Discuss how the design elements contributed to a religious experience for medieval Christians.

1. **D**   2. **A**   3. **B**   4. **C**   5. **C**

ANSWERS EXPLAINED

Multiple-Choice

1. **(D)** Both the *Bayeux Tapestry* and the *Column of Trajan* have narrative retellings of real historical events.

2. **(A)** Pilgrims treasured seeing relics of the saints, which were placed in chapels in the ambulatory around the altar of a church.

3. **(B)** One enters the church a sinner and leaves absolved of sins.

4. **(C)** Both reliquary figures hold skulls. The Sainte-Foy holds one within the head of the saint; the Reliquary Figure holds one in a container he is resting on.

5. **(C)** Romanesque architecture is thick, heavy, and massive, and often very dark.

Short-Essay Rubric

Question	Points	Key Points in a Good Response
Why was this church built?	1	Answers could include: ■ To house the relics of Sainte-Foy ■ To be a pilgrimage site along the road to Santiago de Compostela
Discuss how the design features of this church reflect its use.	2	Answers could include: ■ Long nave, wide transept, and ambulatory used to accommodate large numbers of pilgrims ■ Long nave used for processions ■ Large ambulatory around the altar allows for a free flow of pilgrims to the various chapels, and relics on display. ■ Church is nestled amid other buildings downtown, symbolically mixing with the people.
Discuss how the design elements contributed to a religious experience for medieval Christians.	2	Answers could include: ■ Cross-like ground plan reflects the Crucifixion of Jesus. ■ Lack of nave windows contributes to a dark interior, which symbolizes the mysteries of the Christian faith. ■ Sculpture on the façade of the Last Judgment warns pilgrims of the dangers of Hell and encourages them toward salvation. ■ Stone walls enhance the echo effect that characterized medieval chanting.

Content Area: Early Europe and Colonial Americas

Gothic Art

12

TIME PERIOD: 1140–1400, UP TO 1550 IN SOME SECTIONS OF EUROPE

ENDURING UNDERSTANDING: Medieval art is studied according to geographic placement, styles, and traditions. There are frequent interconnections between religions, governments, and artistic influences that create a variety of approaches.

Essential Knowledge:

- Medieval periods are the following:
  - Late Antique and Early Christian: Chapter 7
  - Byzantine: Chapter 8
  - Islamic: Chapter 9
  - Early Medieval: Chapter 10
  - Romanesque: Chapter 11
  - Gothic: Chapters 12 and 13
- There is no uniform medieval style. Some periods revive ancient classicism; others use geometric and natural designs.
- Medieval artists are influenced by contemporaries in other parts of Europe, as well as ancient traditions.

ENDURING UNDERSTANDING: Medieval art is chiefly concerned with religious expression and court life. There is a strong culture of endorsing scholarship.

Essential Knowledge:

- Learning was centered on specific fields that were transmitted throughout Europe through trade, pilgrimage, and military activity.
- Medieval architecture is mostly religious.
- Medieval painting and sculpture avoids naturalistic depictions.
- At times medieval religions will reject images.

HISTORICAL BACKGROUND

The beginning of the Gothic period cannot be dated precisely, although the place of its creation, Paris, can. The change in thinking that we call "Gothic" is the result of a number of factors:

1. An era of peace and prosperity in the region around Paris, owing to an increasingly centralized monarchy, new definition of the concepts of "king" and "kingship," together with the peaceful succession of kings from 987 to 1328.
2. Increasing growth and wealth of cities and towns, encouraged by the sale of royal charters that bound the cities to the king rather than to local lords and the increased wealth of the king.
3. The gradual development of a money economy in which cities played a role in converting agricultural products to goods and services.
4. The emergence of the schools in Paris as the intellectual center of western Europe that brought together the teachers and scholars who transformed western thinking by changing the way questions were asked and by arguing using logic.

The late Gothic period is marked by three crucial historical events:

1. The Hundred Years' War between France and England (1337–1453). This conflict devastated both countries socially and economically, and left vast regions of France ruined.
2. The Babylonian Captivity (1304–1377). French popes moved the headquarters of the Christian church to Avignon, France, creating a spiritual crisis that had far-reaching effects on European society, and on Rome in particular. With the popes away, there was little reason to maintain Saint Peter's; indeed Rome itself began to decay. When the pope finally returned to Rome in 1377, a schism developed as rival popes set up competing claims of authority, none of which was resolved until 1409. This did much to undermine the authority of the church in general.
3. The Black Death of 1348. This was the greatest cataclysm in human history: A quarter to a third of the world perished in a misdiagnosed pulmonary plague. The consequences for art history were enormous; in many towns there were not enough living to bury the dead: Consequently, architecture came to a standstill. Artists interpreted the plague as a punishment from God, thus painting became conservative and began to look backward to earlier styles. Europe spent generations recovering from the plague's devastating effects.

Patronage and Artistic Life

Master builders coordinated hundreds of laborers and artisans—masons, stonecutters, sculptors, haulers, carpenters—in the building of a cathedral. Indeed, the cathedral was the public works project of its day, keeping the local economies humming and importing artists as needed from everywhere.

Similarly, manuscripts were organized by a chef d'atelier who was responsible for establishing an overall plan or vision of a book so that the workshop could execute his or her designs. A scribe copied the text, but in so doing left room for decorative touches, such as initials, borders, and narrative scenes. Embellishments were added by artists who could express themselves more fully than scribes, who had to stick to the text. Artists often rendered fanciful designs to an initial or a border. Lastly, a bookbinder had the manuscript bound.

GOTHIC ARCHITECTURE

Gothic architecture developed advances made in the Romanesque:

1. The rib vault. Invented at the end of the Romanesque period, and became the standard vaulting practice of the Gothic period.
2. Bays. The Romanesque use of repeated vertical elements in bays also became standard in the Gothic period.
3. The rose window. Begun as an oculus on the façade of Romanesque buildings, the rose window becomes an elaborate circular feature that opens up wall spaces by allowing more light in through the façade and transepts.
4. The pointed arch. First seen in Islamic Spain, this arch directs thrusts down to the floor more efficiently than rounded arches. More fanciful "S" shaped arches, called **ogee** arches, are developed at this time (Figure 12.3).

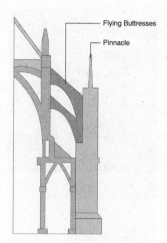

Figure 12.1: Flying buttress and pinnacle on a Gothic cathedral

What is new in the Gothic period is the **flying buttress** (Figure 12.1). These stone arches support a roof by having the weight bypass the walls and travel down to piers outside the building. This enabled the building to be opened up for more window space and to display more stained glass. Most importantly, flying buttresses also help to stabilize the building, preventing wind stresses from damaging these very vertical and narrow structures.

Ground plans of Gothic buildings denote innovations in the east end, or **chevet** (Figure 12.2). Increasingly elaborate ceremonies called for a larger space to be introduced between the transept and the apse, called the **choir**. While allowing for greater clergy participation, it also had the side effect of removing the public further from the main altar and keeping the ceremony at arm's length.

Another innovation is the introduction of decorative **pinnacles** on the roof of Gothic churches. Long thought to be mere ornaments on flying buttresses, pinnacles are now understood to be essential architectural components that act as stabilizing forces in a wind storm.

Gothic buildings are tall and narrow, causing the worshipper to look up upon entering. The architecture, therefore, reinforces the religious symbolism of the building.

French Gothic buildings tend to be nestled downtown, surrounded by other buildings, and rising above the city landscape as a point of civic and religious pride. In sort of a competition, each town built successively taller buildings, seeking to outdo its neighbors.

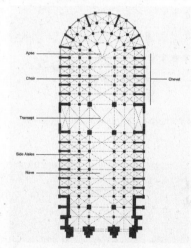

Figure 12.2: Plan of Notre Dame, Paris

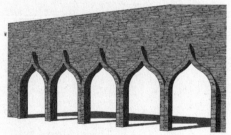

Figure 12.3: Ogee arches

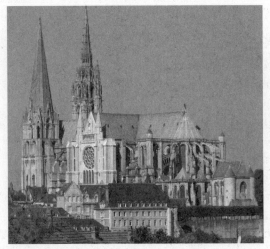

Figure 12.4a: Chartres Cathedral flank, c. 1145–1155, later additions, limestone and stained glass, Chartres, France

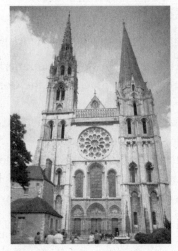

Figure 12.4b: Chartres Cathedral façade

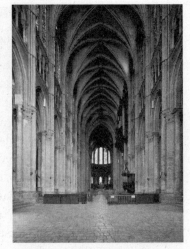

Figure 12.4c: Chartres Cathedral interior

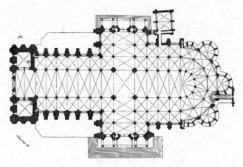

Figure 12.4d: Chartres Cathedral ground plan

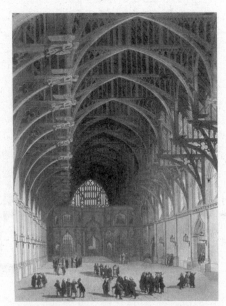

Figure 12.5: Westminster Hall, 1097–1099; ceiling 1390s, stone and wood, London, England

Chartres Cathedral, c. 1145–1155, later additions, limestone and stained glass, Chartres, France (Figures 12.4a, 12.4b, 12.4c, and 12.4d)

- Started in 1145; fire in 1194 forced reconstruction of everything except the façade
- Dedicated to Mary; a Marian shrine
- Mary's tunic worn at Jesus' birth is most sacred relic; it escaped the fire and was seen as signal to rebuild cathedral
- Right spire is from 1160; left spire is late Gothic from 1507–1513—conceived in a different style: more elaborate and decorative
- Importance of church reflected in the speed of construction: 26 years
- Enlarged chevet accommodated elaborate church ceremonies
- Tall vertical nature of the interior pulls the viewer's eyes up to the ceiling and symbolically to heaven
- Dark, mysterious interior increases spiritual feeling
- Stained glass enlivens the interior surfaces of the church

Westminster Hall, 1097–1099; ceiling 1390s, stone and wood, London, England (Figure 12.5)

- Started under William II as largest hall in England at the time
- Meant for grand ceremonial occasions: coronations, feasts; later used as law court to dispense justice
- Bare walls were probably decorated with tapestries
- Windows placed high up surrounded by Romanesque arches
- Original roof replaced; debate over how the roof was originally vaulted, perhaps with beams that came down to the floor denoting a main aisle and two side aisles
- Remodeled roof under Richard II

- Hammerbeam style; made of oak; beams curve to meet in center of roof like a corbelled arch
- Richard II also placed six statues of kings at one entrance, along with his emblems
- When the old Houses of Parliament were burned to the ground, this remained as the last vestige of the medieval parliament building
- Cf. Houses of Parliament (Figure 20.1a)

GOTHIC SCULPTURE

Although Romanesque buildings had sculpture on the portals and on parts of building façades, its role was subsidiary to architecture. In the Gothic period, sculpture begins to emerge more forcefully on church façades.

Saint-Denis (c. 1140–1144) was the first building to have statue columns on the jambs, now mostly destroyed. Although still attached to the columns, jamb figures have rounded volumes that set them apart from their architectural background. The statue columns at the **Royal Portals** at Chartres (1145–1155) (Figure 12.6) appear to imitate the verticality of the church itself, but contain a robust three-dimensionality lacking in the Romanesque period.

There is also a change in the subject matter from the Romanesque to the Gothic portals. Romanesque sculptural programs stress the Last Judgment and the threat of being damned to hell. Gothic sculpture concentrates on the possibility of salvation; the believer is empowered with the choice of salvation.

In Romanesque sculpture, figures are flattened into the wall space of tympana or jambs, being content to be defined by that space. In Gothic sculpture, the statue columns progress away from the wall, building a space seemingly independent of the wall surface. The **Royal Portals of Chartres** (Figure 12.6) begin this process by bringing figures forward, although they are still columnar.

As Gothic art advances, the columns become increasingly three-dimensional and free-standing. In the thirteenth century, the figures are defining their own space, turning to one another with humanizing expressions and engaging in a narrative interplay.

By the fourteenth century, Gothic sculpture and painting develops a courtly S-curve to the bodies.

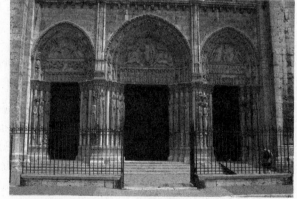

Figure 12.6: Royal Portals, 1145–1155, limestone, Chartres Cathedral, Chartres, France

Royal Portals, 1145–1155, limestone, Chartres Cathedral, Chartres, France (Figure 12.6)

- So-called Royal Portals because the jamb sculptures depict kings and queens from the Old Testament; connection made between French and Biblical royalty
- Portals used by church hierarchy, not commoners
- Originally 24 statues, 19 survive
- Jamb statues stand in front of the wall, almost fully rounded; cf. Romanesque figures which are flat against the surface
- Upright, rigid, elongated figures reflect the vertical columns behind, and the vertical nature of the cathedral itself
- Rich courtly dress with vertical folds
- Robes are almost hypnotic in their concentric composition, cf. Romanesque nervous excitement to drapery

- Heads: serenity; slightly heavy eyes; benevolent; humanized faces
- Heads lined up in a row, but feet of different lengths
- Central tympanum: Christ as Judge of the World, no menacing Last Judgment as at Conques (Figure 11.6a)
- Three portals linked by lintels, and by 24 capitals that contain the life of Christ

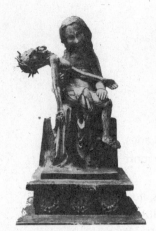

Figure 12.7: *Röttgen Pietà*, 1300–1325, painted wood, Rheinisches Landesmuseum, Bonn, Germany

Röttgen Pietà, 1300–1325, painted wood, Rheinisches Landesmuseum, Bonn, Germany (Figure 12.7)

- An andachtsbild, used for private devotion
- Christ emaciated, drained of all blood, all tissue, all muscle
- Horror of the Crucifixion manifest
- Humanizing of religious themes
- Grape-like drops of Christ's blood a reference to Christ as "mystical vineyard"
- Cross-Cultural Comparisons: Images of Suffering
  - *Coyolxauhqui Stone* (Figure 26.5b)
  - Munch, *The Scream* (Figure 21.11)
  - *Seated Boxer* (Figure 4.10)

GOTHIC PAINTING

Stained glass has existed for centuries; the earliest surviving examples are from the seventh century in England. It became an industry in the Gothic period. Craftsmen made the glass, while glaziers cut the big panels into the desired shapes, wrapping the leading around them. Details (i.e., facial expressions or folds of drapery) were then painted on the glass before it was refired and then set into the window frame.

Stained glass windows became the illustrations of a sophisticated theological program. Generally, larger images of saints appeared in the clerestory so that they could be read from the floor. Narratives appeared in side aisle windows where they could be read more clearly at a closer distance.

Illuminated manuscripts continue to be important, some seeking to emulate the luminous colors of stained glass windows. Forms have borders much like the leading of windows, and are painted in brilliant colors.

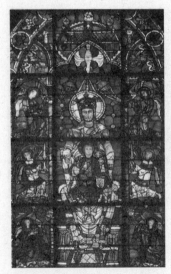

Figure 12.8: *Notre Dame de la Belle Verriere*, c. 1170, stained glass, Chartres Cathedral

Notre Dame de la Belle Verriere, "*Our Lady of the Beautiful Window,*" c. 1170, stained glass, Chartres Cathedral (Figure 12.8)

- Mary is crowned as Queen of Heaven with the Christ Child in her lap
- Light as a manifestation of the divine; shades color patterns across the grey stone of the cathedral
- Part of a lancet window
- Undamaged by the fire of 1194; reset with framing angels on either side of the main scene
- Bands across the surface are typical of early Gothic stained glass
- Cross-Cultural Comparisons: Transparency and Reflection
  - Kusama, *Narcissus Garden* (Figures 22.25a, 22.25b)
  - Mies van der Rohe, Seagram Building (Figure 23.18)
  - Versailles, Hall of Mirrors (Figure 17.3d)

Scenes from the Apocalypse, **from a Bible moralisée (Moralized Bible), c. 1226–1234, illuminated manuscript, ink, tempera, and gold leaf on vellum, Cathedral, Toledo (Figure 12.9a)**

- Eight medallions, format derives from stained glass windows
- Two vertical columns of four painted scenes
- Each scene has a text with a summary of the event depicted in the roundel
- **Cross-Cultural Comparisons: Gold**
  - Golden Stool (Figure 27.4)
  - Ogat Korin, *White and Red Plum Blossoms* (Figures 25.4a, 25.4b)
  - Gold and Jade Crown (Figure 24.10)

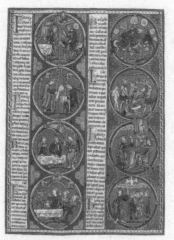

Figure 12.9a: *Scenes from the Apocalypse,* from a Bible moralisée, c. 1226–1234, illuminated manuscript, ink, tempera, and gold leaf on vellum, Cathedral, Toledo

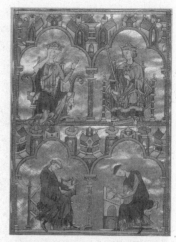

Figure 12.9b: *Blanche of Castile and Louis IX,* 1226–1234, illuminated manuscript, ink, tempera, and gold leaf on vellum, Morgan Library, New York

Blanche of Castile and Louis IX, **1226–1234, illuminated manuscript, ink, tempera and gold leaf on vellum, Morgan Library, New York (Figure 12.9b)**

- Moralized Bible
- Top left: Blanche of Castile, mother and regent to the king
- Top right: teenage King Louis IX
- Bottom: older monk dictates to younger scribe
- Luminosity of stained glass windows, strong black outlining of forms
- Modeling is minimal

JEWISH ART

Although Jews almost universally ban images in temples today, their ancient and medieval ancestors did not always follow this prohibition. Perhaps they were inspired by episodes in the Old Testament that mention incidents in which images could be valid; for example, in Exodus 25: 18–22, God orders Moses to install two cherubim above the Arc of the Covenant in the Holy of Holies.

Jews living in the Greco-Roman world were also influenced by pagan artists who created sweeping narratives of the heroic deeds of their gods. This is perhaps why there are a few ancient synagogues that have illustrations of episodes from the Old Testament. In the Middle Ages, wealthy Jewish patrons often commissioned luxury objects like illuminated manuscripts the same way their Christian or Muslim neighbors would. Jewish patrons often used Christian painters to decorate important sacred books, mostly for personal use.

Golden Haggadah **(The Plagues of Egypt, Scenes of Liberation and Preparation for Passover), c. 1320, illuminated manuscript, pigment on vellum, British Library, London (Figures 12.10a, 12.10b, and 12.10c)**

- Illustrates the story of the Jewish exodus from Egypt under Moses and its subsequent celebration
- To be read at a Passover seder

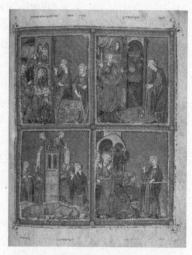

Figure 12.10a: *Golden Haggadah: The Plagues of Egypt*
Upper right: plague of frogs initiated here by Moses, not Aaron as depicted in the Bible
Upper left: plague of lice: Pharaoh and his magicians are covered with lice
Lower left: Moses looks on as Pharaoh is attacked by wild beasts
Lower right: plague on livestock

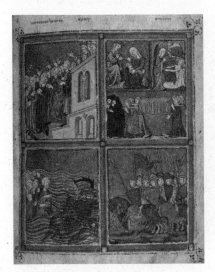

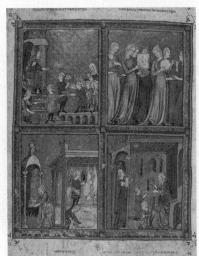

Figure 12.10c: *Golden Haggadah: Preparation for Passover*
Upper right: Miriam, Moses' sister, holds a tambourine decorated with an Islamic motif and is joined by maidens dancing and playing contemporary musical instruments
Upper left: master of the house, sitting under a canopy, orders the distribution of *matzah* (unleavened bread) and *haroset* (sweetmeats) to the children
Lower right: a family prepares the house for Passover; women clean and the man searches for leaven
Lower left: people are preparing for Passover: sheep are being slaughtered and utensils are being purified

Figure 12.10b: *Golden Haggadah: Scenes of Liberation*
Upper right: Plague and death of the first-born Egyptian child
Upper left: Pharaoh orders Israelites to leave Egypt
Lower right: Egyptians dressed in medieval armor attack the Israelites
Lower left: Israelites safely cross the Red Sea; Egyptians drown

- Haggadah means "narration"; fulfills the Jewish requirement to tell the story of the Jews' escape from Egypt as a reminder of God's mercy
- Narrative cycle of events from the Books of Genesis and Exodus
- This haggadah used primarily at home; avoids the more stringent restriction against holy images in a synagogue
- Haggadot (plural) are generally the most lavishly painted of Jewish manuscripts
- Two unknown artists, probably Christian, illustrated the Golden Haggadah; a Jewish scribe wrote the Hebrew script
- Style similarities to French Gothic manuscripts in the handling of space, architecture, figure style, facial/gestural expression, and the manuscript medium itself
- Painted in the Barcelona area of Spain
- 56 miniatures using gold leaf background
- Book read right to left according to the manner of Hebrew texts; vellum pages
- **Cross-Cultural Comparisons: Works as Part of a Series**
  - Rubens, *Henry IV Receives the Portrait of Marie de'Medici* from the Marie de'Medici Cycle (Figure 17.8)
  - Lawrence, *The Migration of the Negro, Panel no. 49* (Figure 22.19)
  - Giotto, *Lamentation* from the Arena Chapel (Figures 13.1b, 13.1c)

VOCABULARY

Andachtsbild: an image used for private contemplation and devotion (Figure 12.7)

Apocalypse: The last book of the Christian Bible, sometimes called Revelations, which details God's destruction of evil and consequent raising to heaven of the righteous (Figure 12.9a)

Chevet: the east end of a Gothic church (Figure 12.2)

Choir: a space in a church between the transept and the apse for a choir or clergymen (Figure 12.2)

Close: an enclosed gardenlike area around a cathedral (Figure 12.2)

Compound pier: a pier that appears to be a group or gathering of smaller piers put together (Figure 12.3c)

Flying buttress: a stone arch and its pier that support a roof from a pillar outside the building. Flying buttresses also stabilize a building and protect it from wind sheer (Figure 12.1)

Haggadah (plural: **Haggadot**): literally "narration"; specifically a book containing the Jewish story of Passover and the ritual of the Seder (Figure 12.10)

Hammerbeam: a type of roof in English Gothic architecture, in which timber braces curve out from walls and meet high over the middle of the floor (Figure 12.5)

Lancet: a tall narrow window with a pointed arch usually filled with stained glass (Figure 12.8)

Moralized Bible: a Bible in which the Old and New Testament stories are paralleled with one another in illustrations, text, and commentary (Figure 12.8)

Ogee arch: an arch formed by two S-shaped curves that meet at the top (Figure 12.3)

Passover: an eight day Jewish festival that commemorates the exodus of Jews from Egypt under the leadership of Moses. So-called because an avenging angel of the Lord knew to "pass over" the homes of Jews who, in order to distinguish their houses from those of the pagan Egyptians, had sprinkled lamb's blood over their doorways, thus preserving the lives of their first-born sons.

Pietà: a painting or sculpture of a crucified Christ lying on the lap of a grieving Mary (Figure 12.6)

Pinnacle: a pointed sculpture on piers or flying buttresses

Portal: a doorway. In medieval art they can be significantly decorated (Figure 12.5)

Rib vault: a vault in which diagonal arches form riblike patterns; these arches partially support a roof, in some cases forming a weblike design (Figure 12.3c)

Rose window: a circular window, filled with stained glass, placed at the end of a transept or on the façade of a church (Figure 12.3b)

Seder: a ceremonial meal celebrated on the first two nights of Passover that commemorates the Jewish flight from Egypt as told in the Bible; marked by a reading of the Haggadah

Spire or **Steeple:** a tall pointed tower on a church (Figure 12.4b)

SUMMARY

A century of peace and prosperity brought architectural greatness to Northern France, where the Gothic style of architecture exploded on the scene around 1140. New buildings were built with great verticality, pointed arches, and large expanses of stained glass windows. The introduction of flying buttresses made taller and thinner buildings possible.

Gothic portal sculpture became more humanized than its Romanesque counterparts, stressing salvation and resurrection rather than judgment and fear. Figures are still attached to the wall space, but are more three-dimensional. As Gothic sculpture progresses, the body is increasingly revealed beneath the drapery.

Multiple-Choice

1. The cathedral at Chartres is typical of Gothic churches in that it

    (A) contains references of classical architecture
    (B) has an oculus to admit light
    (C) uses flying buttresses to stabilize tall naves
    (D) provides a separate space for coronations

2. Christian worshippers at Chartres had their attention drawn to

    (A) the relics displayed in the crypt
    (B) the mihrab pointing the way to Mecca
    (C) the royal tombs that line the side aisles
    (D) the apse, which was elevated from the nave

3. The great portal of the west façade of Chartres is similar to the Lamassu of ancient Assyria in that they

    (A) are both guardian figures protecting what is inside
    (B) are both attached to the walls behind the figure
    (C) both have the faces of the religious leaders of their day, forming a divine connection with the earthly
    (D) both show a military presence to frighten the viewer

4. The architectural achievement that, in part, makes Gothic buildings so tall and yet so stable is the use of

    (A) rib vaults
    (B) stained glass windows
    (C) a dome on pendentives
    (D) ashlar masonry

5. Perpendicular Gothic is a style of architecture unique to

    (A) Spain
    (B) France
    (C) Germany
    (D) England

Short Essay

The building on the left is the interior of the Cathedral at Durham, England, founded in 1093, and built in the twelfth century. The building on the right is the interior of Chartres Cathedral, built between 1145 and 1155, and then rebuilt from 1194 to 1220.

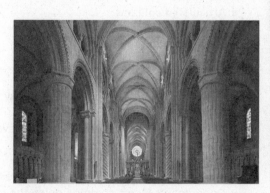 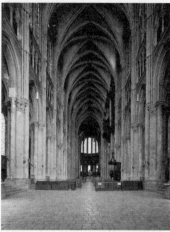

What architectural style is the building on the left done in?

Using specific examples, explain how buildings like the one on the left influenced the design of buildings like Chartres.

How do both works demonstrate a Christian sense of a spiritual space?

ANSWER KEY

1. **C**   2. **D**   3. **B**   4. **A**   5. **D**

ANSWERS EXPLAINED

Multiple-Choice

1. **(C)** Flying buttresses were first introduced at Notre Dame in Paris and were used to stabilize naves that were getting increasingly tall.

2. **(D)** In order for the altar to be seen more effectively in a darkened church, it was generally elevated above the floor of the nave.

3. **(B)** Both the Lamassu and the great portals at Chartres are attached to the walls behind them and, therefore, are not entirely free-standing.

4. **(A)** Rib vaults stabilize the stone roofs and help pass pressure down to the walls below. Gothic buildings do not have domes, and ashlar masonry is rarely used. Stained glass windows do not have a supporting function in a building.

5. **(D)** Perpendicular, a form of late Gothic architecture, is unique to England. Westminster Hall is Perpendicular Gothic.

Short-Essay Rubric

Question	Points	Key Points in a Good Response
What architectural style is the building on the left done in?	1	The building on the left is Romanesque.
Using specific examples, explain how buildings like the one on the left influenced the design of buildings like Chartres.	2	Answers could include: ■ Rib vaults ■ Articulated columns ■ Open central space that faces an altar ■ Rose windows ■ Side aisles
How do both works demonstrate a Christian sense of a spiritual space?	2	Answers could include: ■ Dark interiors connoted an otherworldly experience ■ Stone surfaces acoustically echo medieval chanting ■ Stained glass depicts religious images casting colored lights across the wall surface ■ Congregants face a common point, the apse, where the ceremonies take place

Gothic Art in Italy

13

TIME PERIOD: 1250–1400

ENDURING UNDERSTANDING: Medieval art is studied according to geographic placement, styles, and traditions. There are frequent interconnections between religions, governments, and artistic influences that create a variety of approaches.

Essential Knowledge:

- Medieval periods are the following:
  - Late Antique and Early Christian: Chapter 7
  - Byzantine: Chapter 8
  - Islamic: Chapter 9
  - Early Medieval: Chapter 10
  - Romanesque: Chapter 11
  - Gothic: Chapters 12 and 13
- There is no uniform medieval style. Some periods revive ancient classicism; others use geometric and natural designs.
- Medieval artists are influenced by contemporaries in other parts of Europe, as well as ancient traditions.

ENDURING UNDERSTANDING: Medieval art is chiefly concerned with religious expression and court life. There is a strong culture of endorsing scholarship.

Essential Knowledge:

- Learning was centered on specific fields that were transmitted throughout Europe through trade, pilgrimage, and military activity.
- Medieval architecture is mostly religious.
- Medieval painting and sculpture avoids naturalistic depictions.
- At times medieval religions will reject images.

HISTORICAL BACKGROUND

Italy did not exist as a unified entity the way it does today. The peninsula was divided into a spectrum of city-states, some quite small, ruled by an assortment of princes, prelates, and the occasional republic, like Venice. Citizens identified themselves as Sienese or Florentines, not as Italians. The varied topography and differences in the local dialects of the Italian language often made the distinction from one state to another even more profound. Sometimes, as in the case of modern Sicilian, the linguistic differences are enough to be classified as a separate language.

Nothing seems more complicated to the modern viewer than Italian medieval politics, characterized as it is by routinely shifting allegiances that break into splinter groups and reform into new alliances. Those who lost power were either killed or driven from their city. Sometimes they regrouped and returned for revenge. Add to this military interventions from outside forces, such as the Holy Roman Empire or France, and medieval Italy becomes a complicated network of splintering associations.

With such instability it is a wonder that any works of art were completed, but this behavior does explain why many pieces come down to us in fragmentary condition, and why artists who were favored by one monarch may not have completed a work when another ruler came to power.

Patronage and Artistic Life

Medieval artists worked within an elaborate network called the guild system, in which artwork was regulated as an industry like any other. Guilds were artist associations that determined, among other things, how long apprenticeships should take, how many apprentices an artist could have, and what the proper route would be for an artist trying to establish him- or herself on his or her own. However, female artists were rare, because apprentices lived with their teacher, creating a situation unthinkable for females.

After a successful internship, former apprentices entered the guild as mature artists and full members. The guild helped to regulate commissions as well as ensure that not too many people entered the field, a situation that would have driven down prices. The guild system remained in effect until replaced by the free-market approach that took hold in the eighteenth century.

Artistic patronage was particularly strong among preaching orders of friars, such as the Franciscans, the devoted followers of St. Francis of Assisi, and the Dominicans, the faithful followers of St. Dominic de Guzman. Coalescing early in the thirteenth century, both groups abstained from material concerns and committed themselves to helping the poor and the sick. Since the Dominicans stressed teaching, they were instrumental in commissioning narrative pulpits and altarpieces for their churches so that the faithful could learn important Christian tenets. The Franciscan mother church in Assisi has a program of frescoes unequalled in **trecento** art, in part devoted to the life of the charismatic St. Francis.

Italian citizens had a strong devotional attachment to their local church, sometimes being buried inside. Families commissioned artists to decorate private chapels, occasionally with members of the family serving as models in a religious scene. If a family could not afford a whole chapel, they perhaps could sponsor a sculpture or an altarpiece. Analogously, rulers, church leaders, and civic-minded institutions led by laypersons commissioned works for public display, using them to legitimize their reign or express their public generosity.

The modern approach to art, as a business run by professionals, has its origins in the late Gothic period. Contracts between artists and patrons were drawn up, bookkeeping records of transactions between the two were maintained, and artists self-consciously and confidently began signing works more regularly. Artists' signatures indicate their rising status—a radical break from the general anonymity in which earlier medieval artists had toiled—and a self-conscious need publicly to associate their names with works of art of which they were particularly proud.

ITALIAN GOTHIC PAINTING

The trend in Gothic sculpture is to liberate works from the wall, allowing them to occupy space independent of their architectural framework. Concurrently, Italian painting of the late Gothic period is characterized by large scale panels that stand on their own.

Wall paintings in the Middle Ages, including frescoes and mosaics, emphasize the flatness of the wall surface, encouraging artists to produce compositions that are frontal and linear. Late Gothic artists prefer fresco and tempera, techniques that enabled them to shade figures convincingly and reach for a three-dimensional reality.

At first, artists accepted Byzantine formulas for pictorial representation, commonly referred to as the **maniera greca**. Subsequent Florentine painters, however, particularly under the guidance of **Giotto** and his followers, began to move away from this tradition and toward a different concept of reality that substantiated masses and anchored figures to ground lines. Through expressive faces and meaningful gestures, emotions become more palpable and dynamic. Florentine painting dares to experiment with compositional arrangements, moving the focus away from the center of the painting.

Arena (Scrovegni) Chapel, c. 1303, brick, Padua, Italy (Figure 13.1a)

- Arena Chapel built over an ancient Roman arena, hence the name
- Also called the Scrovegni Chapel after the name of the patron, Enrico Scrovegni
- Built to expiate the sin of usury through which Scrovegni's father amassed a fortune
- Some narrative scenes illustrate Biblical episodes of ill-gotten gains

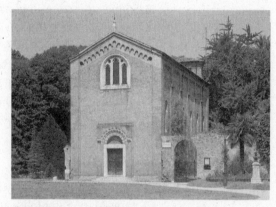

Figure 13.1a: Arena (Scrovegni) Chapel, c. 1303, brick, Padua, Italy

Giotto, *Last Judgment* from the Arena Chapel, 1305–1306, fresco, Padua, Italy (Figure 13.1b)

- Christ as Judge, coming at the end of the world
- Heavenly powers arranged in an organized chorus; heads aligned in a row
- Twelve apostles arranged symmetrically around Christ
- Cross at bottom center divides the saved from the damned
- On the side of the saved is Enrico Scrovegni as a donor presenting a model of the church to angels
- At right is the devil who eats and excretes sinners
- Those guilty of usury or money-related sins like prostitution are particularly noted

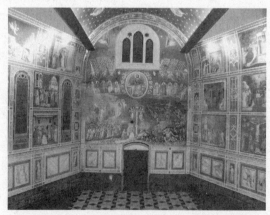

Figure 13.1b: Giotto, *Last Judgment* from the Arena Chapel, 1305–1306, fresco, Padua, Italy

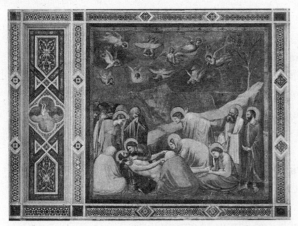

Figure 13.1c: Giotto, *Lamentation* from the Arena Chapel, 1305–1306, fresco, Padua, Italy

Giotto, *Lamentation* from the Arena Chapel, 1305–1306, fresco, Padua, Italy (Figure 13.1c)

- Lamentation shows scenes of Jesus' followers mourning his death: usually scene contains Mary, Saint John, and Mary Magdalene
- St. John throws his head back; Mary Magdalene cradles Jesus' feet; Mary holds Jesus' head
- At left is the Old Testament scene of Jonah being swallowed by the whale and returning to life; parallel with New Testament scene of Christ dying and rising from the dead
- Shallow stage, figures occupy a palpable space pushed forward toward the picture plane
- Diagonal cliff formation points to main action daringly placed in lower left-hand corner
- Modeling indicates direction of light, light falls from above right
- Range of emotions: heavy sadness, quiet resignation, flaming outbursts, despair
- Sadness of scene emphasized by grieving angels, barrenness of tree
- Figures on the lower left are seen from the back and isolate the main action
- Clear foreground, middle ground, and background
- **Cross-Cultural Comparisons: Pathos**
  - *Seated Boxer* (Figure 4.10)
  - Kollwitz, Kollwitz, *Memorial Sheet for Karl Liebknecht* (Figure 22.4)
  - Abakanowicz, *Androgyn III* (Figure 29.7)

VOCABULARY

Lamentation: shows scenes of Jesus' followers mourning his death. Usually the scene contains Mary, Saint John, and Mary Magdalene (Figure 13.1c)

Last Judgment: in Christianity, the judgment before God at the end of the world (Figure 13.1b)

Maniera greca: (Italian for "Greek manner") a style of painting based on Byzantine models that was popular in Italy in the twelfth and thirteenth centuries

Tempera: a type of paint employing egg yolk as the binding medium that is noted for its quick drying rate and flat opaque colors

Trecento: the 1300s, or fourteenth century, in Italian art

SUMMARY

It is not degrading to trecento artists to say that Late Gothic art in Italy is a bridge period between the Middle Ages and the Renaissance. Italian artists were inspired by Roman works, broke away from Byzantine traditions, and established strong schools of painting in the trecento. Florentine artists like **Giotto** concentrate on mass and solidity, often using shading to create the suggestion of three dimensions.

Multiple-Choice

Questions 1 and 2 refer to the image below.

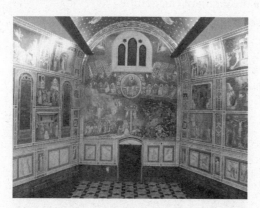

1. Among the innovations seen in this work is the artist's

    (A) combination of fresco, tempera, and oil paint, which allowed for greater detail
    (B) affinity for human emotions in Christian subject matter
    (C) ability to paint works in a series
    (D) referencing of Old and New Testament scenes side by side

2. The scene in the back of the Arena Chapel over the main door is the same scene depicted in

    (A) the tympanum of the church of Sainte-Foy, Conques
    (B) the Great Portal, west façade, Chartres
    (C) the *Golden Haggadah*
    (D) Blanche of Castile and King Louis IX of France in a moralized Bible

---

3. The artistic revival known as the Renaissance began with painters like Giotto and was stimulated in part by the

    (A) use of fresco, which had fallen into disuse
    (B) building of Gothic cathedrals
    (C) preaching of the Franciscans
    (D) discovery of the ancient city of Pompeii

4. The fresco technique, as seen in Giotto's work *The Lamentation,* is the same used in all of the following EXCEPT

    (A) Tomb of the Triclinium
    (B) (attributed to) Juan Rodríguez Juárez's *Spaniard and Indian Produce a Mestizo*
    (C) Diego Rivera's *Dream of a Sunday Afternoon at Alameda Park*
    (D) Raphael's *School of Athens*

5. Enrico Scrovegni, the patron of the Arena Chapel, had the building built and decorated to

(A) expiate the sin of usury, which his family had committed
(B) honor the memory of Saint Francis of Assisi
(C) commemorate the Virgin of Guadalupe
(D) house the tombs of his family and his descendants

Short Essay

The illustration below is the *Lamentation* by Giotto from the Arena Chapel, dated around 1305.

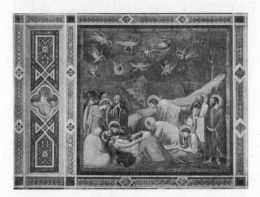

What is the scene in the margin on the left?

How does this marginal scene represent a parallel to the main scene?

Using specific examples, analyze the innovation in Giotto's technique that makes his style revolutionary.

1. **B**   2. **A**   3. **C**   4. **B**   5. **A**

ANSWERS EXPLAINED

Multiple-Choice

1. **(B)** Giotto's techniques include painting figures with profoundly human expressions.

2. **(A)** Both the Arena Chapel and the tympanum of Sainte-Foy have scenes of the Last Judgment.

3. **(C)** Franciscan preaching was an important element in the revival of Renaissance art.

4. **(B)** The painting of a *Spaniard and Indian Produce a Mestizo* is an oil on canvas.

5. **(A)** Enrico Scrovegni had the chapel built, in part, to expiate the sin of usury. His father amassed a considerable fortune at this practice, and Scrovegni felt the need to atone.

Short-Essay Rubric

Question	Points	Key Points in a Good Response
What is the scene in the margin on the left?	1	The scene on the left is of Jonah and the Whale, from the book of Jonah in the Old Testament.
How does this marginal scene represent a parallel to the main scene?	2	Answers could include: ■ Jonah is swallowed by a whale but later comes out of the whale's belly and is reborn. ■ Jesus has died on the cross but has risen from the dead three days later. ■ In a sense they are both reborn; hence, the parallel of the Old and New Testament scenes.
Using specific examples, analyze the innovation in Giotto's technique that makes his style revolutionary.	2	Answers could include: ■ Shallow stage, figures occupy a palpable space pushed forward toward the picture plane ■ Diagonal cliff formation points to main action daringly placed in lower left-hand corner ■ Modeling indicates direction of light; light falls from above right ■ Range of emotions: heavy sadness, quiet resignation, flaming outbursts, despair ■ Figures seen from the back seem to isolate the main action ■ Sadness of scene emphasized by grieving angels, barrenness of tree

Content Area: Early Europe and Colonial Americas

Renaissance in Northern Europe

14

TIME PERIOD: 1400–1600

ENDURING UNDERSTANDING: Modern European art emerges from an interaction with cultures on a global scale. Prior studies highlighted a more narrow geographic or chronological approach.

Essential Knowledge:

- Western Europe and the American colonies are at the center of Renaissance and Baroque studies.
- Europe and the Americas are brought into closer alignment with this new course of study. One is not considered more important than the other.
- Europeans brought goods and culture to the Western hemisphere with their trade and conquest.
- Europeans began to collect and organize knowledge from their various expansions around the globe. European influence is on the rise at home and abroad.

ENDURING UNDERSTANDING: There is an interest in returning to classical ideals in the fifteenth century, with a greater emphasis on formal education and artistic training.

Essential Knowledge:

- There is a greater exploration of the formal elements of painting, like perspective, composition, and color.
- Artistic training is enhanced by the birth of academies.
- The display of artwork often meant a glorification of the patron.

ENDURING UNDERSTANDING: The Reformation and Counter-Reformation caused a rift in Christian art of Western Europe.

Essential Knowledge:

- In Northern Europe there was an emphasis on non-religious subjects, like portraits, genre paintings, and still lifes. In Southern Europe there was an emphasis on religious subjects with much more active and dynamic compositions.

HISTORICAL BACKGROUND

The prosperous commercial and mercantile interests in the affluent trading towns of Flanders stimulated interest in the arts. Emerging capitalism was visible everywhere, from the first stock exchange established in Antwerp in 1460 to the marketing and trading of works of art. Cities vied with one another for the most sumptuously designed cathedrals, town halls, and altarpieces—in short, the best Europe had to offer.

Political and religious turmoil began with the Reformation, which is traditionally dated to 1517 when a German monk and scholar named Martin Luther nailed a list of his complaints to the doors of All Saints Church in Wittenberg, Germany. Perhaps unknowingly, he began one of the greatest upheavals in European history, causing a split in the Christian faith and political turmoil that would last for centuries. Those countries that were Christian the shortest period of time (Germany, Scandinavia, and the Netherlands) became Protestant. Those with longer Christian traditions (Spain, Italy, Portugal, and Poland) remained Catholic.

With a Protestant wave of anti-Catholic feeling came an iconoclastic movement attacking paintings and sculptures of holy figures, which only a short while before were considered sacred. Calvinists, in particular, were staunchly opposed to what they saw as blasphemous and idolatrous images; they spearheaded the iconoclastic movement.

Patronage and Artistic Life

The conflict between Protestant iconoclasm and Catholic images put artists squarely in the middle. On the one hand, the Church was an excellent source of employment; on the other, what if the contentions of the Protestants were true?

Many, like **Dürer**, tried to resolve the issue by either turning to other types of painting, like portraits, or by seeking a middle road by playing down religious ecstasies or the lives of the saints. Protestants thought that God could be reached directly through human intercession, so paintings of Jesus, when permitted, were direct and forceful. Catholics wanted intermediaries, such as Mary, the saints, or the priesthood to direct their thoughts, so these images were more permissible to them. However, Catholics always insisted that a sculpture of Mary was just a reminder of the figure one was praying to. Idolatry was not endorsed by either.

The Northern European economy can be characterized by a capitalist market system that flourished due to expansive trade across the Atlantic. This brought with it a parallel emphasis on buying and selling works of art as commodities. New technologies in printmaking made artists internationally popular, and more courted than ever before.

NORTHERN RENAISSANCE PAINTING

One of the most important inventions in the last thousand years, if not history, is the development of movable type by Johann Gutenberg. The impact was enormous. This device could mass produce books, make them available to almost anyone, and have them circulated on a wide scale.

However, mechanically printed books looked cheap and artificial to those who were used to having their books handmade over the course of years, as the *Golden Haggadah* (Figure 12.10) did for the super-wealthy patrons. Gutenberg's first book, *The Bible*, was printed mechanically, but the decorative flourishes—mostly initial letters before each chapter—were hand painted by calligraphers. Meanwhile, a similar mechanical process gave birth to the print, first as a **woodcut**, then as an **engraving**, and later as an **etching**. Prints were mass produced and relatively inexpensive, since the artist made a prototype that was reprinted many times. Although individually cheaper than a painting, the artist made his profit on the number of reproductions. Indeed, fame could spread more quickly with prints, because these products went everywhere, whereas paintings were in the hands of single owners.

The second important development in the fifteenth century was the widespread use of oil paint. Prior to this, wall paintings were done in fresco and panel paintings in tempera. Oil paint was developed as an alternative in a part of Europe in which fresco was never that popular.

Oil paint produces exceptionally rich colors, having the notable ability to accurately imitate natural hues and tones. It can generate enamel-like surfaces and sharp details. It also preserves well in wet climates, retaining its luster for a long time. Unlike tempera and fresco, oil paint is not quick drying and requires time to set properly, thereby allowing artists to make changes onto what they previously painted. With all these advantages, oil paint has emerged as the medium of choice for most artists since its development in Flanders in the early Renaissance.

The great painted altarpieces of medieval art were the pride of accomplished painters whose works were on public view in the most conspicuous locations. Italian altarpieces from the age of Giotto tend to be flat paintings that stand directly behind an altar, often with gabled tops.

Alternatively, Northern European altarpieces are cupboards rather than screens, with wings that open and close, folding neatly into one another. The large central scene is the most important, sometimes carved rather than painted; sculpture was considered a higher art form. Small paintings such as *The Mérode Triptych* of 1425–1428 (Figure 14.1) were designed for portability. Larger works were meant to be housed in an elaborate Gothic frame that enclosed the main scenes. Sometimes the frame alluded to the architecture of the building in which the painting resided.

Altarpieces usually have a scene painted on the outside, visible during the week. On Sundays, during key services, the interior of the altarpiece is exposed to view. Particularly elaborate altarpieces may have had a third view for holidays.

Northern European artists were heavily influenced by International Gothic Painting, a courtly elegant art form, begun by Italian artists such as Simone Martini in the fourteenth century. This style of painting features thin, graceful figures that usually have an S-shaped curve as does Late Gothic sculpture. Natural details abound in small bits of reality that are carefully rendered. Costumes are splendidly depicted with the latest fashions and most stylish fabrics. Gold is used in abundance to indicate the wealth of the figures and the patrons who sponsored these works. Architecture is carefully rendered, frequently with the walls of buildings opened up so that the viewer can look into the interior. International Gothic paintings often have elaborate frames that match the sumptuous painting style.

Regardless of whether artists worked in the International Gothic tradition, Northern European painters generally continued the practice of opening up wall spaces to see into rooms as in *The Mérode Triptych* (Figure 14.1). Typically, figures are encased in the rooms they occupy, rather than being proportional to their surroundings. Ground lines tilt up dramatically, as do table tops and virtually any flat surface. High horizons are the norm. Although symbolism can be seen in virtually any work of art in any art historical period, it seems to be particularly a part of the fabric of Northern European painting. Items that appear casually placed as a bit of naturalism can be construed as part of a symbolic network of interpretations existing on several important levels. Scholars have spilled a great deal of ink in decoding possible readings of important works.

Northern European art during the sixteenth century is characterized by the assimilation of Italian Renaissance ideas into a Northern European context. Michelangelo was enormously popular in Northern Europe, even though he never went there, and only one of his works did. However, many other Italian artists made the journey, including the elderly Leonardo da Vinci.

Northern European painting had a fondness for nature unknown in Italian art—whether it is seen in sweeping Alpine landscape views or the study of a rabbit or even a clump of earth. Landscapes, no matter how purely represented, generally have a trace of human involvement, sometimes shown by the presence of buildings or farms, or the rendering of small people in an overwhelming setting.

Northern artists continued to use high horizon lines that enabled a large area of the canvas to be filled with earthbound details. In general, there is a reluctance to use linear perspective in paintings, although atmospheric perspective is featured in landscapes.

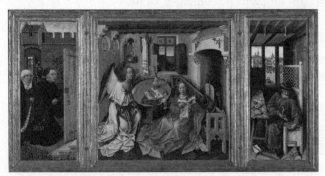

Figure 14.1: Robert Campin (?) or workshop, *The Annunciation Triptych* (also called *The Merode Altarpiece*), 1425–1428, oil on wood, Metropolitan Museum of Art, New York

Robert Campin (?) or workshop, *The Annunciation Triptych* (also called *The Merode Altarpiece*), 1425–1428, oil on wood, Metropolitan Museum of Art, New York (Figure 14.1)

- Left panel: donors, middle-class people kneeling before the holy scene; wife added later perhaps because of the donor's marriage
- Center panel: Annunciation taking place in an everyday Flemish interior
- Humanization of traditional themes: no halos, domestic interiors, view into a Flemish cityscape
- Symbolism:
  - Towels and water stand for Mary's purity; water is a baptism symbol
  - Flowers have three buds symbolizing the Trinity; unopened bud is the unborn Jesus; lilies also symbolize Mary's purity
  - Mary seated on floor symbolizing her humility
  - Mary blocks the fireplace, or the entrance to hell
  - Candlestick: Mary holds Christ in the womb
  - Figure with a cross comes in through the window: the divine birth
- Right panel: Joseph in his carpentry workshop; mousetrap symbolizes the capturing of the devil
- Meticulous handling of paint; intricate details
- Steeply rising ground line; figures too large for the architecture they sit in

Jan van Eyck, *Arnolfini Portrait*, 1434, oil on wood, National Gallery, London (Figure 14.2)

- Many theories as to the meaning of the work:
  - Traditionally assumed to be wedding portrait of Giovanni Arnolfini and his wife
  - Theory that it is a memorial to a dead wife
  - Theory that is represents a betrothal
  - Theory that Arnolfini is conferring legal and business privileges on his wife during an absence

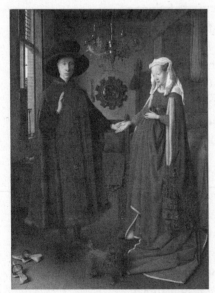

Figure 14.2: Jan van Eyck, *Arnolfini Portrait*, 1434, oil on wood, National Gallery, London

- Symbols of weddings:
  - Custom of burning a candle on the first night of a wedding
  - Shoes cast off indicates they are standing on holy ground
  - Prayerful promising pose of a groom
  - Dog symbolizes fidelity
- Two witnesses in the convex mirror; perhaps the artist himself, since the inscription reads "Jan van Eyck was here 1434"
- Wife pulls up dress to symbolize childbirth, although she is not pregnant
- Statue of Saint Margaret, patron of childbirth, appears on the bedpost
- Man appears near the window symbolizing his role as someone who makes his way in the outside world; the woman appears farther in the room to emphasize her role as a homemaker
- Meticulous handling of paint; great concentration of minute details
- **Cross-Cultural Comparisons: Couples in Art**
  - *Menkaura and His Queen* (Figure 3.7)
  - Veranda post (Figure 27.14)
  - *Justinian and Attendants* and *Theodora and Attendants* (Figures 8.5 and 8.6)

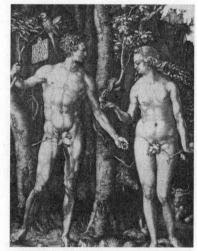

Figure 14.3: Albrecht Dürer, *Adam and Eve*, 1504, engraving, Museum of Fine Arts, Boston

Albrecht Dürer, *Adam and Eve*, 1504, engraving, Museum of Fine Arts, Boston (Figure 14.3)

- Influenced by classical sculpture; Adam looks like the ancient Greek sculpture called *The Apollo Belvedere*; Eve like *Medici Venus*; Italian massing of forms
- Ideal image of humans before the Fall of Man
- Contrapposto of figures from the Italian Renaissance
- Four humors are represented in the animals below: cat (choleric or angry), rabbit (sanguine or energetic), elk (melancholic or sad), ox (phlegmatic or lethargic); four humors were kept in balance before the Fall of Man
- Mouse represents Satan
- Parrot a symbol of cleverness
- Adam tries to dissuade Eve; he grasps the mountain ash, a tree from which snakes recoil
- Northern European devotion to detailed paintings
- **Cross-Cultural Comparisons: The Human Figure**
  - Polykleitos, *Spear Bearer* (Figure 4.3)
  - Botticelli, *Birth of Venus* (Figure 15.4)
  - Braque, *Portuguese* (Figure 22.6)

Matthias Grünewald, Isenheim Altarpiece, 1512–1516, oil on panel, Musée d'Unterlinden, Colmar (Figures 14.4a and 14.4b)

- Placed in a monastery hospital where people were treated for "Saint Anthony's Fire," or ergotism—a disease caused by eating a fungus that grows on rye flour
- St. Anthony's Fire explains the presence of St. Anthony on the first and third views

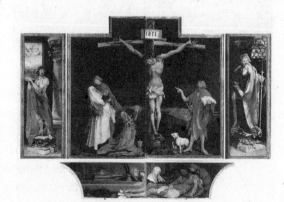

Figure 14.4a: Matthias Grünewald, first view, Isenheim Altarpiece, 1510-1515, oil on panel, Musée d'Unterlinden, Colmar

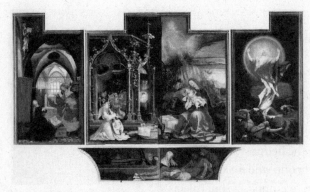

Figure 14.4b: Matthias Grünewald, Isenheim Altarpiece, second view, 1512–1516, oil on panel, Musée d'Unterlinden, Colmar

- Ergotism causes convulsions and gangrene
- *First view:*
  - Crucifixion: dark background
  - dead, decomposing flesh
  - arms almost torn from sockets
  - lashed and whipped body
  - agony of the body unflinchingly shown
  - symbolizes the agony of ergotism
  - swooning Mary dressed like the nuns who worked in the hospital
  - when panels open to reveal next scene, Christ is amputated as patients suffering ergotism would be
  - same true in the predella: Christ's legs seem amputated below the kneecaps
- *Second view:*
  - Marian symbols: the enclosed garden, closed gate, rosebush, rosary
  - Christ rises from the dead on right—his rags changed to glorious robes, showing his wounds, which do not harm him now
  - message to patients is that earthly diseases will vanish in the next world
- *Third view:* symbols of ergotism: oozing boils, withered arm, distended stomach (not illustrated)
- **Cross-Cultural Comparisons: Pathos**
  - *Seated Boxer* (Figure 4.10)
  - Munch, *The Scream* (Figure 21.11)
  - Kollwitz, *Memorial Sheet for Karl Liebknecht* (Figure 22.4)

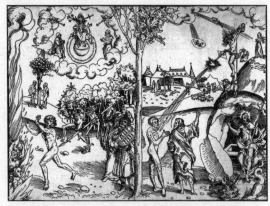

Figure 14.5: Lucas Cranach the Elder, *Allegory of Law and Grace*, c. 1530, woodcut

Lucas Cranach the Elder, *Allegory of Law and Grace*, c. 1530, woodcut (Figure 14.5)

- Protestantism: faithful achieve salvation by God's grace; guidance can be achieved using the Bible
- Done in consultation with Martin Luther, a leader in the Protestant movement
- Left: Last Judgment
  - Moses holds Ten Commandments
  - Ten Commandments represents the Old Law, Catholicism
  - Law of Moses not enough; not enough to live a good life
  - Skeleton chases a person into Hell
- Right: Figure bathed in Christ's blood
  - Faith in Christ alone is needed for salvation
- **Cross-Cultural Comparisons: Ideas and Rebellion**
  - Lawrence, *The Migration of the Negro, Panel no. 49* (Figure 22.19)
  - Michel Tuffery, *Pisupo Lua Afe* (Figure 29.16)
  - Neshat, *Rebellious Silence* (Figure 29.14)

Pieter Bruegel, *Return of the Hunters*, 1565, oil on wood panel, Art History Museum, Vienna (Figure 14.6)

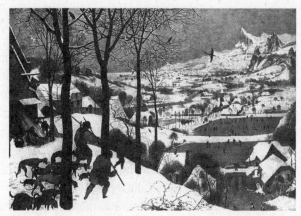

Figure 14.6: Pieter Bruegel, *Return of the Hunters*, 1565, oil on wood panel, Art History Museum, Vienna

- One of a series of paintings representing the months— this is November/December
- Alpine landscape, winter scene
- Strong diagonals lead the eye deeper into the painting
- Figures are peasant types, not individuals
- Landscape has high horizon line, a Northern European tradition
- Many details; nothing is static
- Hunters have had little success in the winter hunt; dogs are skinny and hang their heads
- **Cross-Cultural Comparisons: Hardship**
  - Turner, *The Slave Ship* (Figure 20.5)
  - Neshat, *Rebellious Silence* (Figure 29.14)
  - Stieglitz, *Steerage* (Figure 22.8)

VOCABULARY

Altarpiece: a painted or sculpted panel set on an altar of a church (Figure 14.1)

Annunciation: in Christianity, an episode in the Book of Luke 1:26–38 in which Angel Gabriel announces to Mary that she would be the Virgin Mother of Jesus (Figure 14.1)

Donor: a patron of a work of art, who is often seen in that work (Figure 14.1 left panel)

Engraving: a printmaking process in which a tool called a **burin** is used to carve into a metal plate, causing impressions to be made in the surface. Ink is passed into the crevices of the plate and paper is applied. The result is a print with remarkable details and finely shaded contours (Figure 14.3)

Etching: a printmaking process in which a metal plate is covered with a ground made of wax. The artist uses a tool to cut into the wax to leave the plate exposed. The plate is then submerged into an acid bath, which eats away at the exposed portions of the plate. The plate is removed from the acid, cleaned, and ink is filled into the crevices caused by the acid. Paper is applied and an impression is made. Etching produces the finest detail of the three types of early prints

Oil paint: a paint in which pigments are suspended in an oil-based medium. Oil dries slowly allowing for corrections or additions; also allows for a great range of luster and minute details

Polyptych: a many-paneled altarpiece

Triptych: a three-paneled painting or sculpture (Figure 14.1)

Woodcut: a printmaking process by which a wooden tablet is carved into with a tool, leaving the design raised and the background cut away (very much as how a rubber stamp looks). Ink is rolled onto the raised portions, and an impression is made when paper is applied to the surface. Woodcuts have strong angular surfaces with sharply delineated lines. (Figure 14.5)

SUMMARY

Northern European art from the fifteenth century is dominated by monumental altarpieces prominently erected in great cathedrals. Flemish artists delight in symbolically rich compositions that evoke a visually enticing experience along with a religiously sincere and intellectually challenging interpretation. Flemish emphasis on minute details does not minimize the total effect. The introduction of oil paint provides a new luminous glow to Northern European works.

The invention of movable type brought about a revolution in the art world. Instead of producing individual items, artists could now make multiple images whose portability and affordability would ensure their widespread fame.

The achievements of Italian Renaissance painters had a profound effect on their Northern European counterparts in the sixteenth century. The monumentality of forms, particularly in the works of Michelangelo, were of great interest to Northern European artists, who traveled to Italy in great numbers. Even so, most Northern painters continued their own tradition of meticulously painting details, high horizon lines, and colorful surfaces that characterize their art.

The civil unrest that was an outgrowth of the Reformation caused many churches to be violated as works of art were smashed and destroyed because they were thought to be pagan. Protestants in general sought more austere church interiors in reaction against the perceived lavishness of their Catholic counterparts.

PRACTICE EXERCISES

Multiple-Choice

Questions 1 and 2 refer to this image.

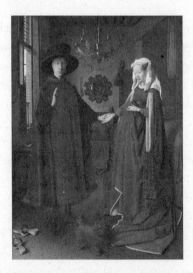

1. This work is both signed and dated, showing the growing status of artists. Which of the following works are also signed?

    (A) Basin (*Baptistère de St. Louis*)
    (B) *Virgin and Child with Saints Theodore and George*
    (C) *Lamentation* by Giotto
    (D) *Last Supper* by Leonardo da Vinci

2. This painting has been traditionally thought of as a wedding portrait. All of the following have been interpreted as wedding symbols EXCEPT

(A) the burning candle, a custom on the first night of a wedding
(B) the shoes cast off, indicating they are standing on holy ground
(C) the prayerful promising pose of the groom
(D) the convex mirror, which reflects God's blessing on this event

---

3. Traditions of double portraits are common in all of the following cultures EXCEPT

(A) Etruscan
(B) Egyptian
(C) Baroque
(D) Romanesque

4. Woodcuts, such as Cranach's *Allegory of Law and Grace*, enabled

(A) the artist to reach a wider audience with his ability to mass produce images
(B) the collector to display works that were resistant to fading and peeling
(C) the artist to use color in printmaking; before, only black and white was possible
(D) the artist for the first time to represent a scene three-dimensionally

5. Albrecht Dürer's engraving of *Adam and Eve* references works of classical art for the forms of the two figures because it shows them as

(A) pagan and corrupt
(B) idealized before the Fall of Man
(C) saintly and holy
(D) concerned only about their physical appearance

Short Essay

Attribute this painting to the artist who painted it.

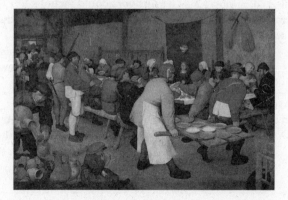

Identify a painting by the same artist in the art history curriculum using the title, artist, date, and medium.

Using specific details, justify your attribution by comparing the two works.

How do both works reflect the artist's rejection of classical models?

1. **A**   2. **D**   3. **D**   4. **A**   5. **B**

ANSWERS EXPLAINED

Multiple-Choice

1. **(A)** The Basin (*Baptistère de St. Louis)* is signed (six times!) by Muhammad ibn al-Zain.

2. **(D)** There are indeed things reflected in the convex mirror between the two main figures, but God is not one of them.

3. **(D)** Etruscan: *Sarcophagus of the Spouses*; Egyptian: *Menkaura and His Queen*; Baroque: Rembrandt's *Self-Portrait with Saskia*. There is no tradition of double portraits in Romanesque art that have come down to us.

4. **(A)** Woodcuts made cheap mass-produced images available for a fraction of the cost of paintings. This enabled an artist's reputation to spread very quickly.

5. **(B)** Dürer is representing people before the Fall of Man, and therefore perfect as God originally created them. It was after they sinned that their bodies became mortal and corruptible.

Short-Essay Rubric

Question	Points	Key Points in a Good Response
Attribute this painting to the artist who painted it.	1	Pieter Bruegel the Elder
Identify a painting by the same artist in the art history curriculum using the title, artist, date, and medium.	1	*Hunters in the Snow*, Pieter Bruegel the Elder, 1565, oil on wood
Using specific details, justify your attribution by comparing the two works.	2	Answers could include: ■ Peasants in everyday activities ■ Very detailed paintings ■ Strong receding diagonals ■ Gruff but picturesque view of country life ■ No central focus
How do both works reflect the artist's rejection of classical models?	1	Answers could include: ■ Not interested in symmetry and balance ■ Gives the impression of the immediate and spontaneous; moment in time ■ No classical idealization of forms ■ Avoiding nudity

Content Area: Early Europe and Colonial Americas

Early Renaissance in Italy: Fifteenth Century

15

TIME PERIOD: 1400–1500

The early Renaissance takes place in the courts of Italian city-states:
Ferrara, Florence, Mantua, Naples, Rome, Venice, and so on.

ENDURING UNDERSTANDING: Modern European art emerges from an interaction with cultures on a global scale. Prior studies highlighted a more narrow geographic or chronological approach.

Essential Knowledge:

- Western Europe and the American colonies are at the center of Renaissance and Baroque studies.
- Europe and the Americas are brought into closer alignment with this new course of study. One is not considered more important than the other.
- Europeans brought goods and culture to the Western hemisphere with their trade and conquest.
- Europeans began to collect and organize knowledge from their various expansions around the globe. European influence is on the rise at home and abroad.

ENDURING UNDERSTANDING: There is an interest in returning to classical ideals in the fifteenth century, with a greater emphasis on formal education and artistic training.

Essential Knowledge:

- There is a greater exploration of the formal elements of painting, like perspective, composition, and color.
- Artistic training is enhanced by the birth of academies.
- The display of artwork often meant a glorification of the patron.

ENDURING UNDERSTANDING: The Reformation and Counter-Reformation caused a rift in Christian art of Western Europe.

Essential Knowledge:

- In Northern Europe there was an emphasis on non-religious subjects, like portraits, genre paintings, and still lifes. In Southern Europe there was an emphasis on religious subjects with much more active and dynamic compositions.

HISTORICAL BACKGROUND

Italian city-states were controlled by ruling families who dominated politics throughout the fifteenth century. These princes were lavish spenders on the arts, and great connoisseurs of cutting-edge movements in painting and sculpture. Indeed, they embellished their palaces with the latest innovative paintings by artists such as **Lippi** and **Botticelli**. They commissioned architectural works from the most pioneering architects of the day. Competition among families and city-states encouraged a competition in the arts, each state and family seeking to outdo the other.

Princely courts gradually turned their attention away from religious subjects to more secular concerns, in a spirit today defined as **humanism**. It became acceptable, in fact encouraged, to explore Italy's pagan past as a way of shedding light on contemporary life. The exploration of new worlds, epitomized by the great European explorers, was mirrored in a new growth and appreciation of the sciences, as well as the arts.

Patronage and Artistic Life

The influence of the patrons of this period can be seen in a number of ways, including such things as specifying the amount of gold lavished on an altarpiece or which family members the artist was required to prominently place in the foreground of a painting. It was also customary for great families to have a private chapel in the local church dedicated to their use. Artists would often be asked to paint murals in these chapels to enhance the spirituality of the location.

EARLY RENAISSANCE ARCHITECTURE

Renaissance architecture depends on order, clarity, and light. The darkness and mystery, indeed the sacred sense of Gothic cathedrals, was deemed barbaric. In its place were created buildings with wide window spaces, limited stained glass, and vivid wall paintings.

Although all buildings need mathematics to sustain the engineering principles inherent in their design, Renaissance buildings seem to stress geometric designs more demonstrably than most. Harmonies were achieved by a system of ideal proportions learned from an architectural treatise by the Roman Vitruvius. The ratios and proportions of various elements of the interior of Florentine Renaissance churches were interpreted as expressions of humanistic ideals. The Early Christian past was recalled in the use of unvaulted naves with coffered ceilings.

Thus, the crossing is twice the size of the nave bays, the nave twice the width of the side aisles, and the side aisles twice the size of side chapels. Arches and columns take up two-thirds of the height of the nave, and so on. This logical expression is often strongly delineated by the floor patterns in the nave, in which white and grey marble lines demarcate the spaces, as at Brunelleschi's **Pazzi Chapel** (Figures 15.1a and 15.1b).

Florentine palaces, such as Alberti's **Palazzo Rucellai** (Figure 15.2), have austere dominating façades that rise three stories from street level. Usually the first floor is reserved as public areas; business is regularly transacted here. The second floor rises in lightness, with a strong stringcourse marking the ceiling of one story and the floor of another. Here is where the family gathered in their private quarters. The third floor is capped by a heavy cornice in the style of a number of Roman temples.

Filippo Brunelleschi, Pazzi Chapel, designed 1423, built 1429–1461, masonry, Florence, Italy (Figures 15.1a and 15.1b)

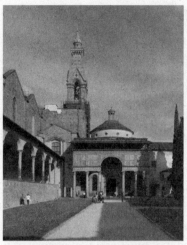
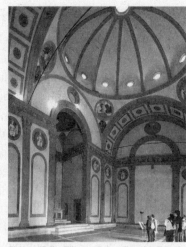

- Rectangular chapel attached to the church of Santa Croce, Florence
- Two barrel vaults on the interior, small dome over crossing
- Interior has a restrained sense of color, muted tones, punctuated by glazed terra-cotta tiles
- Chapter House: a meeting place for the Franciscan monks
- Attribution to Brunelleschi has been questioned

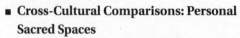

Figure 15.1a: Filippo Brunelleschi, Pazzi Chapel, 1429–1461, masonry, Florence

Figure 15.1b: Filippo Brunelleschi, Pazzi Chapel interior, 1429–1461, Florence

- **Cross-Cultural Comparisons: Personal Sacred Spaces**
  - Bernini, Cornaro Chapel (Figures 17.4a, 17.4b)
  - Giotto, Arena Chapel (Figures 13.1a, 13.1b, 13.1c)
  - Ryoan-ji (Figures 25.2a, 25.2b)

Leon Battista Alberti, Palazzo Rucellai, c. 1450, stone, masonry, Florence (Figure 15.2)

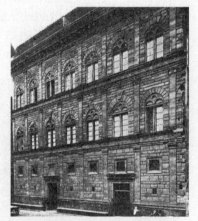

Figure 15.2: Leon Battista Alberti, Palazzo Rucellai, c. 1450, stone, masonry, Florence

- Three horizontal floors of equal height separated by a strongly articulated stringcourse
- Pilasters rise vertically and divide the spaces into squarish shapes
- Strong classical cornice caps the building
- Rejects rustication of earlier Renaissance palaces; instead used beveled masonry joints
- First floor pilasters are Tuscan (derived from Doric); second are Alberti's own invention (derived from Ionic); third are Corinthian
- Friezes contain Rucellai family symbols: billowing sails
- Square windows on the first floor; windows with mullions on second and third floors
- Original building had five bays on the left, with a central door; second doorway bay and right bay added later; eighth bay fragmentary: owners of house next door refused to sell
- Patron was Giovanni Ruccelai, a wealthy merchant
- **Cross-Cultural Comparisons: City Buildings**
  - Gehry, Guggenheim Bilbao (Figures 29.1a, 29.1b)
  - Sullivan, Carson Pirie Scott building (Figure 21.14a)
  - Trajan's Market (Figure 6.10a)

FIFTEENTH-CENTURY ITALIAN PAINTING AND SCULPTURE

The most characteristic development of Italian Renaissance painting is the use of linear perspective, a technique some scholars say was known to the Romans. Other scholars have attributed its revitalization, if not invention, to **Filippo Brunelleschi**, who developed perspective while drawing the Florence Cathedral Baptistery in the early fifteenth century. Some artists were fascinated with perspective, showing objects and people in proportion with one another, unlike medieval art which has people dominating compositions. Artists who were trained prior to this tradition were quick to see the advantages to linear perspective and incorporated it into their later works.

Later in the century, perspective becomes an instrument that some artists would use, or exploit, to create different artistic effects. The use of perspective to intentionally fool the eye, the **tromp l'oeil technique**, is an outgrowth of the ability of later fifteenth-century painters who employed it as one tool in an arsenal of techniques.

In the early part of the fifteenth century, religious paintings dominated, but by the end of the century, portraits and mythological scenes proliferated, reflecting humanist ideals and aspirations.

Interest in humanism and the rebirth of Greco–Roman classics also spurs an interest in authentic Greek and Roman sculptures. The ancients gloried in the nude form in a way that was interpreted by medieval artists as pagan. The revival of nudity in life-size sculpture is begun in Florence with **Donatello's *David*** (Figure 15.5), and continued throughout the century.

Nudity is one manifestation of an increased study of human anatomy. Drawings of people with heroic bodies are sketched in the nude and transferred into stone and bronze. Some artists show the intense physical interaction of forms in the twisting gestures and straining muscles of their works.

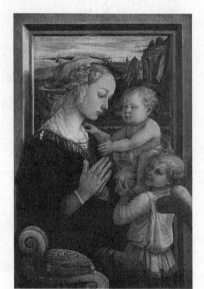

Figure 15.3: Fra Filippo Lippi, *Madonna and Child with Two Angels*, c. 1465, tempera on wood, Uffizi, Florence

Fra Filippo Lippi, *Madonna and Child with Two Angels*, c. 1465, tempera on wood, Uffizi, Florence (Figure 15.3)

- Mary seen as a young mother
- Model may have been the artist's lover
- Landscape inspired by Flemish painting
- Symbolic landscape
  - Rock formations indicate the Church
  - City near the Madonna's head is the Heavenly Jerusalem
- Motif of a pearl: seen in headdress and pillow as products of the sea (in upper left corner)
- Pearls used as symbols in scenes of the Immaculate Conception of Mary and the Incarnation of Christ
- Scene depicted as if in a window in a Florentine home
- Humanization of a sacred theme
- **Cross-Cultural Comparisons: Virgin Mary**
  - *Notre Dame de la Belle Verriere* (Figure 12.8)
  - *Röttgen Pietá* (Figure 12.7)
  - Miguel González, *Virgin of Guadelupe* (Figure 18.4)

Sandro Botticelli, *Birth of Venus*, c. 1484–1486, tempera on canvas, Uffizi, Florence (Figure 15.4)

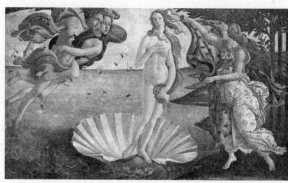

Figure 15.4: Sandro Botticelli, *Birth of Venus*, c. 1484–1486, tempera on canvas, Uffizi, Florence

- Venus emerges fully grown from the foam of the sea; faraway look in her eyes
- Roses scattered before her; roses created at the same time as Venus, symbolizing that love can be painful
- Left: zephyr (west wind) and chloris (nymph)
- Right: handmaiden rushes to clothe her
- Figures float, not anchored to the ground
- Crisply drawn figures; pale colors
- Landscape flat and unrealistic, simple V-shaped waves
- A Medici commission
- **Cross-Cultural Comparisons: Classical References**
  - David, *The Oath of the Horatii* (Figure 19.6)
  - Raphael, *School of Athens* (Figure 16.3)
  - Dürer, *Adam and Eve* (Figure 14.3)

Donatello, *David*, c. 1440–1460, bronze, National Museum, Bargello, Florence (Figure 15.5)

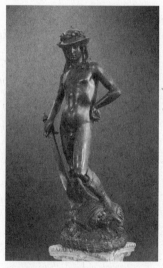

Figure 15.5: Donatello, *David*, c. 1440–1460, bronze, National Museum, Bargello, Florence

- First large bronze nude since antiquity
- Exaggerated contrapposto of the body
- Life-size work probably meant to be housed in the Medici Palace, not for public viewing
- Androgynous figure
- Stance: nonchalance, contemplating the victory over Goliath—Goliath's head at David's feet; David's head is lowered to suggest humility
- Laurel on hat indicates David was a poet; hat a foppish Renaissance design
- **Cross-Cultural Comparisons: Nudity**
  - Female Deity from Nukuoro (Figure 28.2)
  - *Seated Boxer* (Figure 4.10)
  - Ingres, *The Grand Odalisque* (Figure 20.3)

VOCABULARY

Bottega: the studio of an Italian artist

Chapter House: a building next to a church used for meetings

Humanism: an intellectual movement in the Renaissance that emphasized the secular alongside the religious. Humanists were greatly attracted to the achievements of the classical past, and stressed the study of classical literature, history, philosophy, and art

Madonna: the Virgin Mary, mother of Jesus Christ (Figure 15.3)

Mullion: a central post or column that is a support element in a window or a door (Figure 15.2)

Orthogonal: lines that appear to recede toward a vanishing point in a painting with linear perspective

Pilaster: a flattened column attached to a wall with a capital, a shaft, and a base (Figure 15.2)

Quattrocento: the 1400s, or fifteenth century, in Italian art

Trompe l'oeil: (French, meaning "fools the eye") a form of painting that attempts to represent an object as existing in three dimensions, and therefore resembles the real thing

Humanist courts of Renaissance Italy patronized artists who rendered both religious compositions and secular works. After 1450 it is common to see contemporary events, ancient mythology, or portraits of significant people take their place side by side with scenes of the Annunciation and Crucifixion.

Brunelleschi's development of one-point perspective revolutionized Italian painting. At first, artists faithfully used the formula in their compositions, creating realistic three-dimensional spaces on their surfaces. Later, painters used perspective as a tool to manipulate the viewer's impression of a particular scene.

Sculptors competed with the glory of ancient artists by creating monumental figures and equestrian images, and revived antiquity's interest in nudity and idealized human proportion.

Architecture was dominated by spatial harmony and light interiors that contrasted markedly with the mystical stained glass-filled Gothic buildings.

PRACTICE EXERCISES

Multiple-Choice

1. Leon Battista Alberti's architectural style represents a scholarly interpretation of classical elements seen in buildings such as

    (A) the Mortuary Temple of Hatshepsut
    (B) the Parthenon
    (C) the Forum of Trajan
    (D) the Colosseum

Questions 2–4 refer to the following picture.

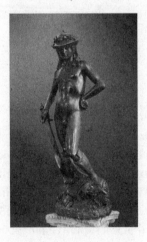

2. The nudity in Donatello's *David*

    (A) would have been considered heroic in Islamic art
    (B) is inspired by Gothic portal sculpture
    (C) references the ideal human proportions expressed in Polykleitos's canon
    (D) recalls the nudity of public sculptures from the ancient Mediterranean

3. The laurel wreath on the head of the *David* refers to his

   (A) oneness with nature
   (B) victory over Goliath
   (C) role as a shepherd
   (D) author of a book in the Bible

4. Before the creation of Donatello's *David*, nude sculptures were not executed because

   (A) they represented the pagan world of mythological gods
   (B) artists were influenced by a general ban on images in Jewish art
   (C) they showed man in a primitive and bestial state
   (D) they were not suitable for churches

   ———————————

5. Fra Filippo Lippi's *Madonna and Child with Two Angels* reflects the Renaissance's attitude toward a more

   (A) ethereal and heavenly vision of Mary and Jesus
   (B) formal and forbidding image of divine figures
   (C) human and approachable interpretation of heavenly figures
   (D) pagan and mythological approach to Christian imagery

SHORT ESSAY

This work is Sandro Botticelli's *Birth of Venus*. The work references a mythological story cast in a Renaissance light.

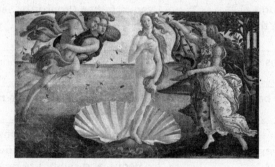

Describe the mythological story occurring in this painting.

Who were the patrons of this work?

What is this painting based on?

What symbolism did Botticelli use to convey the meaning of this story?

ANSWER KEY

1. **D**   2. **D**   3. **D**   4. **A**   5. **C**

ANSWERS EXPLAINED

Multiple-Choice

1. **(D)** The three floors with rounded arches interspersed by columns recalls an arrangement on the Colosseum in Rome.

2. **(D)** Greek and Roman cities are often characterized by a preponderance of large-scale heroic nude figures. Islamic art would have considered nudes as blasphemous and debasing. Gothic portal sculptures are typically entirely covered by drapery except for the extremities. This work does not have the ideal human proportions expressed by Polykleitos.

3. **(D)** David was a poet. The Book of Psalms is ascribed to his authorship.

4. **(A)** Nudity was associated with the pagan world; Christians sought to avoid association with pagan gods.

5. **(C)** The Renaissance was mostly interested in making human the divine image. This painting has a particularly affectionate view of a young mother as Mary, and a suitably human child accompanied by impish angels.

Short-Essay Rubric

Question	Points	Key Points in a Good Response
Describe the mythological story occurring in this painting.	1	Venus' father, Cronos (or Saturn) casts his genitals into the sea, from which Venus is born, fully grown.
Who were the patrons of this work?	1	The Medici were the patrons of this work.
What is this painting based on?	1	The painting is based on a popular court poem by the writer Poliziano.
What symbolism did Botticelli use to convey the meaning of this story?	2	The symbols to be mentioned include: ■ Roses were created at the same time as Venus, and symbolize beauty. ■ Roses have thorns, and are symbols that love can be painful. ■ Venus is modest, and therefore is immediately covered up. ■ The wind god blows at Venus and gently propels her to shore.

High Renaissance and Mannerism

16

> **TIME PERIOD: HIGH RENAISSANCE: 1495–1520,**
> **ROME, FLORENCE, VENICE**
> **MANNERISM: 1520–1600, ITALY**

ENDURING UNDERSTANDING: Modern European art emerges from an interaction with cultures on a global scale. Prior studies highlighted a more narrow geographic or chronological approach.

Essential Knowledge:

- Western Europe and the American colonies are at the center of Renaissance and Baroque studies.
- Europe and the Americas are brought into closer alignment with this new course of study. One is not considered more important than the other.
- Europeans brought goods and culture to the Western hemisphere with their trade and conquest.
- Europeans began to collect and organize knowledge from their various expansions around the globe. European influence is on the rise at home and abroad.

ENDURING UNDERSTANDING: The Reformation and Counter-Reformation caused a rift in Christian art of Western Europe.

Essential Knowledge:

- In Northern Europe there was an emphasis on non-religious subjects, like portraits, genre paintings, and still lifes. In Southern Europe there was an emphasis on religious subjects with much more active and dynamic compositions.

HISTORICAL BACKGROUND

Italian city-states with their large bankrolls and small populations were easy pickings for Spain and France, as they began their advances over the Italian peninsula. Venice alone remained an independent power, with its incomparable fleet bringing goods and profits around the Mediterranean.

The High Renaissance flourished in the cultivated courts of princes, doges, and popes—each wanting to make his city-state greater than his neighbor's. Unfortunately, most of this came to a temporary halt with the sack of Rome in 1527—a six-month rape of the city that did much to undo the achievements of one of the most creative moments in art history. What emerged from the ruins of Rome was a new period, Mannerism, which took art on a different path.

When Martin Luther nailed his theses to the doors of a church in Wittenberg, Germany in 1517, he touched off a religious and political upheaval that had long-lasting repercussions throughout Europe. Even if this movement, called the Protestant Reformation, was treated as a heresy in Italy, it had a dramatic impact on Italian art. No longer was the High Renaissance sense of perfection a representation of the world as it is, or could ever be. Mannerist distortions were more appropriate in this highly contentious period. Indeed, the basic tenets of Mannerism concern the tension between the ideal, the natural, and the symmetrical against the real, the artificial, and the unbalanced.

The schism that the Reformation caused was met by a Catholic response, framed at the Council of Trent (1545–1563) and later termed the Counter-Reformation. At the Council a new order of priests was created, called the Jesuits, whose missionary activity and commitment to education is still visible around the world today. The Jesuits quickly saw the power of art as a teaching tool and a religious statement, and became great patrons of the arts.

The religious and political upheaval that characterized the sixteenth century was exemplified by the sacking of the city of Rome in 1527. The unpaid army of the Holy Roman Empire, after defeating the French troops in Italy, sought restitution in looting and pillaging the holy city. The desecration of Rome shook all Christendom, especially since it proved that its chief holy place could so easily fall victim to the undisciplined and the greedy.

Patronage and Artistic Life

Most Renaissance artists came from humble origins, although some like **Titian** and **Michelangelo** came from families of limited influence. Every artist had to join a trade guild, which sometimes made them seem equivalent to house painters or carpenters. Even so, artists could achieve great fame, so great that monarchs competed to have them in their employ. Francis I of France is said to have held the dying **Leonardo da Vinci** in his arms, Charles V of the Holy Roman Empire lavished praise upon **Titian**, and **Michelangelo** was called "divino" by his biographers.

The dominant patron of the era was Pope Julius II, a powerful force in European religion and politics. It was Julius's ambition that transformed the rather ramshackle medieval town of Rome into an artistic center and capital of the Renaissance. It was Julius's devotion to the arts that inspired **Raphael** and **Michelangelo** to do their greatest work.

The first permanent painting academy was established by Cosimo I of Florence in 1563; its function was to train artists and improve their status in society. The best artists, however, did not need academies, nor did they need patrons. Although some preferred to work for a duke and stay in his graces, the reality was that a duke usually did not have enough commissions to keep a painter occupied. Famous artists did not need this security, and most achieved success by keeping their important patrons satisfied. Michelangelo's relationship with Pope Julius II was successful in part because Julius became his preferred, although by no means his only, customer. Mannerist painters saw nothing about this situation worth changing.

HIGH RENAISSANCE PAINTING

Northern European artists discovered the durability and portability of canvas as a painting surface. This was immediately taken up in Venice, where the former backing of choice—wood—would often warp in damp climate. Since canvas is a material with a grainy texture, great care was made to prepare it in such a way as to minimize the effect the cloth would have on the paint. Canvas, therefore, had to be primed properly to make it resemble the enamel-like surface of wood. In modern art, the grainy texture is often maintained for the earthy feel it lends a painting.

Leonardo da Vinci used a painting technique known as **sfumato**, in which he rendered forms in a subtly soft way to create a misty effect across the painted surface. Sfumato has the effect of distancing the viewer from the subject by placing the subject in a hazy world removed from us.

Artists also employed **chiaroscuro**, which provides soft transitions between light and dark. Chiaroscuro often heightens modeling effects in a work by having the light define the forms.

Venetian artists, particularly **Titian**, increased the richness of oil-painted surfaces by applying **glazes**. Glazes had been used on pottery since ancient times, when they were applied to ceramics to give them a highly polished sheen. In painting, as in pottery, glazes are transparent so that the painted surface shows through. However, glazes subtly change colors by brightening them, much as varnish brightens wood.

In portrait painting, instead of profiles, which were popular in the quattrocento, three-quarter views became fashionable. This view obscures facial defects that profiles enhance. With Leonardo da Vinci's *Mona Lisa*, portraits become psychological paintings. It was not enough for artists to capture likenesses; artists were expected to express the character of the sitter.

The idealization that characterizes **Raphael's** work becomes the standard High Renaissance expression. Raphael specialized in balanced compositions, warm colors, and ideally proportioned figures. He favored a triangular composition: The heavy bottom anchors forms securely and then yields to a lighter touch as the viewer's eye ascends.

Works like **Leonardo da Vinci's *The Last Supper*** (Figure 16.1) show a High Renaissance composition, with the key figure, in this case Jesus, in the center of the work, alone and highlighted by the window behind. The twelve apostles are grouped in threes, symmetrically balanced around Jesus, who is the focal point of the orthogonals. Even so, the work's formal structure does not dominate because the Biblical drama is rendered so effectively on the faces of the individuals.

Leonardo da Vinci, *The Last Supper*, 1494–1498, tempera and oil, Santa Maria delle Grazie, Milan (Figure 16.1)

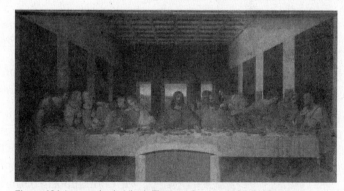

Figure 16.1: Leonardo da Vinci, *The Last Supper*, 1494–1498, tempera and oil, Santa Maria delle Grazie, Milan

- Commissioned by the Sforza of Milan for the refectory, or dining hall, of a Dominican abbey
- Relationship between the friars eating and a Biblical meal
- Only Leonardo work remaining *in situ*
- Linear perspective; orthogonals of ceiling and floor point to Jesus
- Apostles in groupings of three; Jesus is alone but before a group of three windows symbolizing the Trinity
- Leonardo used an experimental combination of paints to yield a greater chiaroscuro; however, the paints began to peel off the wall in Leonardo's lifetime. As a result, the painting has been restored many times.
- Great drama of the moment: Jesus says, "One of you will betray me." (Matthew 26:21)

- Various reactions on the faces of the apostles: surprise, fear, anger, denial, suspicion; anguish on the face of Jesus
- Judas falls back clutching his bag of coins, face in darkness
- **Cross-Cultural Comparisons: Composition**
  - *Justinian* and *Theodora* (Figures 8.5, 8.6)
  - Basquiat, *Horn Players* (Figure 29.5)
  - *Niobid Krater* (Figure 4.19)

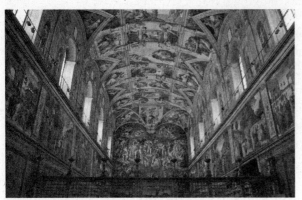

Figure 16.2a: Michelangelo, Sistine Chapel, 1508–1512, fresco, Vatican City, Italy

Michelangelo, Sistine Chapel Ceiling, 1508–1512, fresco, Vatican City, Italy (Figures 16.2a and 16.2d)

- Sistine Chapel erected in 1472 and painted by quattrocento masters including Botticelli and Perugino, as well as Michelangelo's teacher Ghirlandaio
- Function of Sistine Chapel: the place where new popes are elected
- Michelangelo chose a complicated arrangement of figures for the ceiling, broadly illustrating the first few chapters of Genesis, with accompanying Old Testament figures and antique sibyls—many based on antique sculptures
- Three hundred figures on ceiling, no two in the same pose; Michelangelo's lifelong preoccupation with the male nude in motion
- Enormous variety of expression
- Painted cornices frame groupings of figures in a highly organized way
- Many figures, like the Ignudi, are done for artistic expression rather than to enhance the narrative
- Acorns are a motif on the ceiling, inspired by the crest of the patron, Pope Julius II

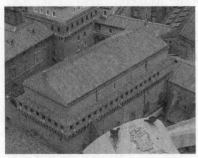

Figure 16.2d: Sistine Chapel, begun 1472, Vatican City, Italy

Michelangelo, *Delphic Sybil*, c. 1508–1512, fresco, Sistine Chapel, Vatican City, Italy (Figure 16.2b)

- One of five sibyls (prophetesses) on the ceiling
- Greco–Roman figures whom Christians felt foretold the coming of Jesus Christ
- Wears a Greek style turban
- Turns head as if listening
- Expression seems sorrowful
- Contrapposto of the body
- Holds the scroll containing her prophecy
- Combination of Christian religious and pagan mythological imagery
- **Cross-Cultural Connections: Time and Memory**
  - Calendar Stone (Figure 26.5c)
  - Lukasa Memory Board (Figure 27.11)
  - Lin, Vietnam Veterans Memorial (Figures 29.4a, 29.4b)

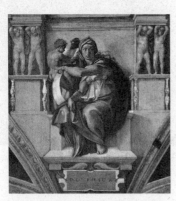

Figure 16.2b: Michelangelo, *Delphic Sybil*, c. 1508–1512, fresco, Sistine Chapel, Vatican City, Italy

Michelangelo, *The Flood*, c. 1508–1512, fresco, Sistine Chapel, Vatican City, Italy (Figure 16.2c)

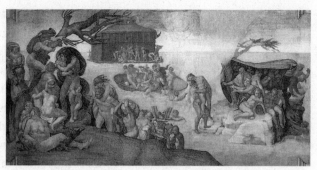

- Story details Noah and his family's escape of rising flood waters as told in Genesis 7
- Few remaining survivors cling to mountain tops
- Man carrying drowned son to safety, will only meet his son's fate
- Over 60 figures; crowded composition
- Sculptural intensity of the figure style
- Ark in background is the only safe haven

Figure 16.2c: Michelangelo, *The Flood*, c. 1508–1512, fresco, Sistine Chapel, Vatican City, Italy

Michelangelo, *Last Judgment*, 1536–1541, fresco, Sistine Chapel, Vatican City, Italy (Figure 16.2e)

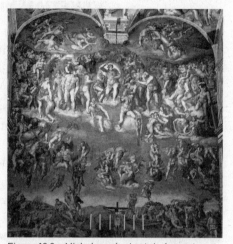

- In contrast to the ceiling, there are no cornice divisions; it is one large space with figures more casually grouped
- Mannerism shown in the distortions of the body, elongations, crowded groups
- Four broad horizontal bands act as the unifying element:
    1. Bottom: left: dead rising, right: the mouth of hell
    2. Second level: ascending elect, descending sinners, trumpeting angels
    3. Third level: those rising to heaven gathered around Jesus
    4. Top lunettes: angels carrying the Cross and the Column, instruments used at Christ's death

Figure 16.2e: Michelangelo, *Last Judgment*, fresco from the Sistine Chapel, 1536–1541, Vatican City, Italy

- Christ in center and gestures defiantly with right hand; complex pose
- Justice is delivered: the good rise, the evil fall
- Lower right-hand corner has figures from Dante's *Inferno*: Minos and Charon
- Saint Bartholomew's face is modeled on a contemporary critic. Saint Bartholomew holds his skin, a symbol of his martyrdom, but the skin's face is Michelangelo's. An oblique remark about critics who skin him alive with their criticism
- Spiraling composition is a reaction against the High Renaissance harmony of the Sistine Chapel ceiling, and reflects the disunity of Christendom caused by the Reformation
- **Cross-Cultural Comparisons: Group Compositions**
    - Leonardo DaVinci, *Last Supper* (Figure 16.1)
    - Rivera, *Dream of a Sunday Afternoon* (Figure 22.20)
    - Lam, *The Jungle* (Figure 22.12)

Raphael, *School of Athens*, 1509–1511, fresco, Apostolic Palace, Vatican City, Italy (Figure 16.3)

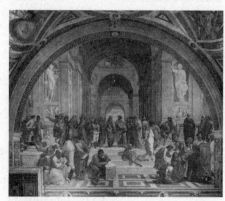

- Commissioned by Pope Julius II to decorate his library
- Painting originally called "Philosophy" because the pope's philosophy books were meant to be housed on shelving below
- One painting in a complex program of works that illustrates the vastness and variety of the papal library
- Open, clear light uniformly spread throughout composition

Figure 16.3: Raphael, *School of Athens*, 1509–1511, fresco, Apostolic Palace, Vatican City, Italy

- Nobility and monumentality of forms parallel to the greatness of the figures represented; figures gesture to indicate their philosophical thought
- Building behind might reflect Bramante's plan for Saint Peter's
- In center are the two greatest figures in ancient Greek thought: Plato (with the features of Leonardo on left, pointing up) and Aristotle
- Bramante, the Pope's architect, is the bald figure of Euclid on the lower right
- Raphael is in the corner at extreme right
- Michelangelo resting on the stone block writing a poem
- Raphael's overall composition influenced by Leonardo da Vinci's *The Last Supper* (Figure 16.1)

VENETIAN HIGH RENAISSANCE PAINTING

In contrast to the Florentines and Romans, whose paintings valued line and contour, the Venetians bathed their figures in a soft atmospheric ambiance highlighted by a gently modulated use of light. Bodies are sensuously rendered. While Florentines and Venetians both paint religious scenes, Florentines choose to see them as heroic accomplishments, whereas Venetians imbue their saints with a more human touch, setting them in bucolic environments that show a genuine interest in the beauty of the natural world. This natural setting is often called **Arcadian**.

The damp Venetian climate caused wooden paintings to warp and crack, frescoes to peel and flake. Artists opted for **canvas**, a more secure and lightweight surface that could maintain the integrity of a work for an indefinite period.

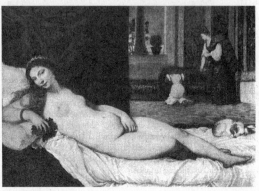

Figure 16.4: Titian, *Venus of Urbino*, 1538, oil on canvas, Uffizi, Florence

Titian, *Venus of Urbino*, 1538, oil on canvas, Uffizi, Florence (Figure 16.4)

- May not have been a Venus, may have been a courtesan
- Sensuous delight in the skin tones
- Looks at us directly
- Complex spatial environment: figure placed forward on the picture plane, servants in middle space; open window with plants in background
- Roses contribute to the floral motif carried throughout the work
- Dog perhaps symbolizes faithfulness
- Cassoni: trunks intended for storage of clothing for a wife's trousseau
- Patron Guildobaldo della Rovere of Urbino
- Painting became a standard for future reclining female nudes, cf. Ingres, *The Grand Odalisque* (Figure 20.3); Manet, *Olympia* (Figure 21.3)

MANNERIST PAINTING

Typical High Renaissance paintings have a perspective grid on a plaza that leads the eye to a central point (cf. *School of Athens*) (Figure 16.3). Mannerists chose to discard conventional theories of perspective by having the eye wander around a picture plane—as in **Pontormo**

(Figure 16.5)—or use perspective to create an interesting illusion. Although heavily indebted to High Renaissance forms, the Mannerist uses these as starting points to freely vary the ideals of the previous generation. It is the ability of the Mannerists to defy the conventional classical order and rationality that gives the style much of its appeal.

A new artistic subject, the **still life**, is born in the Mannerist period. Although understood as the lowest form of painting, it gradually becomes an accepted art form in seventeenth-century Holland. **Genre** paintings are introduced as scenes of everyday life become acceptable in finished works of art.

For many years scholars saw the demanding compositions of Mannerist paintings as crude reflections of High Renaissance art—the aftermath of a great period. But scholars have slowly come to realize that the unusual complexities and ambiguous spaces—the artifice—of Mannerist art is its most endearing quality. This is an intensely intellectual art form that is deliberately complex, seeking refinement in unusual compositions and contrived settings. The irrational spatial effects rely on an exaggeration of forms, obscure imagery, and symbolic enigmas whose consequence is puzzling, stimulating, and challenging. It is the calculated ambiguity of Mannerist painting that gives it its enduring value.

Jacopo da Pontormo, *Entombment of Christ*, 1525–1528, oil on wood, Santa Felicità, Florence (Figure 16.5)

- Center of the circular composition is a grouping of hands
- Elongation of bodies
- High-keyed colors, perhaps taking into account the darkness of the chapel it is placed in
- No ground line for many figures; what is Mary sitting on?
- Hands seem disembodied
- Some androgynous figures
- No weeping, just yearning
- Linear bodies twisting around one another
- Anti-classical composition
- The painting is called *Entombment of Christ*, although there is no tomb, just the carrying of Jesus' lifeless body
- **Cross-Cultural Comparisons: Composition**
  - Picasso, *Les Demoiselles d'Avignon* (Figure 22.5)
  - Bichitr, *Jahangir Preferring a Sufi Sheikh to Kings* (Figure 23.9)
  - Neshat, *Rebellious Silence* (Figure 29.14)

MANNERIST ARCHITECTURE

Mannerist architecture invites us to question the use of classical vocabulary on a sixteenth-century building. Drawing on a wealth of antique elements, the Mannerist architect playfully engages the viewer in the reuse of these elements independent of their original function. These are commonly seen in works in which a bold interlocking of classical forms is arranged in a way to make us ponder the significance of ancient architecture in the Renaissance.

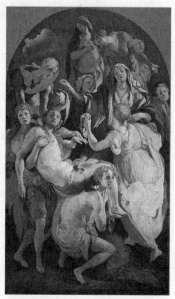

Figure 16.5: Jacopo da Pontormo, *Entombment of Christ*, 1525–1528, oil on wood, Santa Felicità, Florence

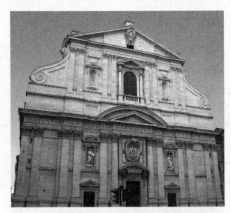

Figure 16.6a: Giacomo della Porta, Il Gesù façade, 1575–1584, brick and marble, Rome

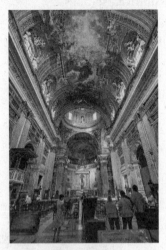

Figure 16.6b: Giacomo da Vignola, Il Gesù nave, sixteenth century, Rome, Italy

Giacomo della Porta, Il Gesù façade, 1575–1584, brick and marble, Rome (Figure 16.6a); nave by Giacomo da Vignola, sixteenth century

- Principal church of the Jesuit order
- Column groupings emphasize central doorway
- Tympana and pediment over central door
- Slight crescendo of forms toward the center
- Two stories separated by cornice; united by scrolls
- Framing niche acts as a unifying device
- Interior has no aisles, meant for grand ceremonies

VOCABULARY

Arcadian: a simple rural and rustic setting used especially in Venetian paintings of the High Renaissance; named after Arcadia, a district in Greece to which poets and painters have attributed a rural simplicity and an idyllically untroubled world

Canvas: a heavy woven material used as the surface of a painting; first widely used in Venice (Figure 16.4)

Cassone: (plural: **cassoni**): a trunk intended for storage of clothing for a wife's trousseau (Figure 16.4)

Chiaroscuro: a gradual transition from light to dark in a painting. Forms are not determined by sharp outlines, but by the meeting of lighter and darker areas (Figure 16.1)

Cinquecento: the 1500s, or sixteenth century, in Italian art

Entombment: a painting or sculpture depicting Jesus Christ's burial after his crucifixion (Figure 16.5)

Flood Story: as told in Genesis 7 of the Bible, Noah and his family escape rising waters by building an ark and placing two of every animal aboard

Genre painting: painting in which scenes of everyday life are depicted

Glazes: thin transparent layers put over a painting to alter the color and build up a rich sonorous effect

Ignudi: nude corner figures on the Sistine Chapel ceiling (Figure 16.2c)

Last Supper: a meal shared by Jesus Christ with his apostles the night before his death by Crucifixion (Figure 16.1)

Sfumato: a smoke-light or hazy effect that distances the viewer from the subject of a painting (Figure 16.1)

Sibyl: a Greco-Roman prophetess whom Christians saw as prefiguring the coming of Jesus Christ (Figure 16.2b)

Still Life: a painting of a grouping of inanimate objects, such as flowers or fruit

SUMMARY

The Papal Court of Julius II commissioned some of the greatest works of Renaissance art to beautify the Vatican, including starting construction on the new Saint Peter's. Artists sought to rival the ancients with their accomplishments, often doing heroic feats like carving monumental sculptures from a single block of marble, or painting vast walls in fresco.

The Venetian School of painting was at its height during this period, realizing works that have a soft, sensuous surface texture layered with glazes. Sfumato and chiaroscuro are widely used to enhance this sensuous effect.

Mannerist artists broke the conventional representations of Italian Renaissance art by introducing intentionally distorted figures, acidy colors, and unusual compositions to create evocative and highly intellectual works of art that challenge the viewer's perceptions and ideals. Perspective was used as a tool to manipulate a composition into intriguing arrangements of spatial forms.

The questioning of artistic values extends to the types of paintings as well. Still lifes and genre paintings, long considered too low for sophisticated artists, make their first appearance.

Mannerist architects seek to combine conventional architectural elements in a refined and challenging interplay of forms. It is this ambiguity that gives Mannerism a fascination today.

PRACTICE EXERCISES

Multiple-Choice

Questions 1–3 refer to the image below.

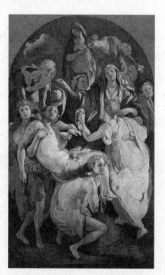

1. The literary source for this work is

   (A) The New Testament
   (B) *The Odyssey*
   (C) The Qur'an
   (D) *The Metamorphosis*

2. This type of painting is a departure from High Renaissance painting in that it

   (A) relies on symbolism to convey its meaning
   (B) has exaggerated and elongated figures
   (C) is painted with a quick and visible brushstroke
   (D) is meant for private viewing rather than public display

3. Paintings from this period are often seen as all of the following EXCEPT

   (A) satiric and filled with contemporary commentary
   (B) coded in layers of meaning defying one simple explanation
   (C) intentionally confusing in order to create a sense of imbalance
   (D) highly intellectual and deliberately complex

   _____

4. The Venetian High Renaissance differs from the Florentine High Renaissance in its great emphasis on

   (A) foreshortening
   (B) chiaroscuro
   (C) warm and rich colors
   (D) mythological scenes

5. Leonardo Da Vinci's *Last Supper* provided a general inspiration for Raphael's *School of Athens*. This can be particularly seen in their use of

   (A) strict symmetry, which adds balance to the composition
   (B) self-portraits in discreet locations
   (C) linear perspective, which creates a unified architectural framework
   (D) contemporary faces placed on people from the past

Short Essay

This work is the ceiling of the Sistine Chapel, painted by Michelangelo from 1508–1512.

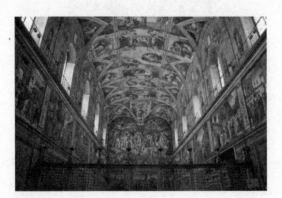

What is the subject of the ceiling painting?

Who was the patron for this painting?

Why was this subject chosen for the ceiling of the Sistine Chapel?

How does the painting reflect the ambitions of the patron?

Answer Key

1. **A**   2. **B**   3. **A**   4. **C**   5. **C**

ANSWERS EXPLAINED

Multiple-Choice

1. **(A)** This painting is Pontormo's *Entombment of Christ*, a scene taken from the New Testament.

2. **(B)** This painting is different from High Renaissance art in that it shows a Mannerist delight in "mannered" figure styles: exaggerated and elongated poses.

3. **(A)** Mannerist paintings are highly intellectual exercises that enjoy creating imbalances and layers of meaning. They are not satiric commentaries on the contemporary world.

4. **(C)** Venetian High Renaissance paintings, like those by Titian, are often painted in warm and rich colors.

5. **(C)** All of these characteristics are true of one or the other painting, but the only one that characterizes both works is the unified architectural setting based on linear perspective.

Short-Essay Rubric

Question	Points	Key Points in a Good Response
What is the subject of the ceiling painting?	1	The subject is the first few chapters of the Book of Genesis.
Who was the patron for this painting?	1	Pope Julius II
Why was this subject chosen for the ceiling of the Sistine Chapel?	1	The walls of the chapel were already painted with scenes from the life of Christ and the life of Moses. It was natural, then, to fill the ceiling with other Biblical narratives, the most dramatic involving the creation story.
How does the painting reflect the ambitions of the patron?	2	Answers could include: ■ Pope Julius II wanted to revive Rome; this was part of a grand scheme to fill the city with great projects. ■ Julius II is named after Julius Caesar, reviving imperial visions. ■ The Ceiling is a heroic, grand painting of huge dimensions, meant to glorify its patron. ■ Acorns from the crest of Julius II are placed on the ceiling as a motif.

Baroque Art

17

TIME PERIOD: 1690–1700

The term "Baroque" means "irregularly shaped" or "odd,"
a negative word that evolved in the eighteenth century to
describe the Baroque's departure from the Italian Renaissance.

ENDURING UNDERSTANDING: Modern European art emerges from an interaction with cultures on a global scale. Prior studies highlighted a more narrow geographic or chronological approach.

Essential Knowledge:

- Western Europe and the American colonies are at the center of Renaissance and Baroque studies.
- Europe and the Americas are brought into closer alignment with this new course of study. One is not considered more important than the other.
- Europeans brought goods and culture to the Western hemisphere with their trade and conquest.
- Europeans began to collect and organize knowledge from their various expansions around the globe. European influence is on the rise at home and abroad.

ENDURING UNDERSTANDING: Seventeenth century art can be characterized by a taste for the theatrical and a stress on movement and compositional variety. Many artists experiment with psychological and emotional portrayals.

ENDURING UNDERSTANDING: The Reformation and Counter-Reformation caused a rift in Christian art of Western Europe.

Essential Knowledge:

- In Northern Europe there was an emphasis on non-religious subjects like portraits, genre paintings, and still lifes. In Southern Europe there was an emphasis on religious subjects with much more active and dynamic compositions.

HISTORICAL BACKGROUND

In 1600, the artistic center of Europe was Rome, particularly at the court of the popes. The completion of Saint Peter's became a crusade for the Catholic Church, both as an evocation of faith and as a symbol of the Church on earth. By 1650, however, the increased power and influence of the French kings, first at Paris and then at their capital in Versailles, shifted the art world to France. While Rome still kept its allure as the keeper of the masterpieces for both the ancient world and the Renaissance, France became the center of modern art and innovation, a position it kept unchallenged until the beginning of World War II.

The most important political watershed of the seventeenth century was the Thirty Years' War, which ended in 1648. Ostensibly started over religion, and featuring a Catholic resurgence called the Counter-Reformation, the Thirty Years' War also had active political, economic, and social components as well. The war succeeded in devastating central Europe so effectively that economic activity and artistic production ground to a halt in this region for the balance of the seventeenth century.

The Counter-Reformation movement reaffirmed all the things the Protestant Reformation was against. Protestants were largely iconoclasts, breaking painted and sculpted images in churches; Catholics endorsed the place of images and were reinspired to create new ones. Protestants derided saints; Catholics reaffirmed the communion of saints and glorified their images. Protestants played down miracles; Catholics made them visible and palpable as in the *Ecstasy of Saint Teresa* (Figures 17.4a and 17.4b).

Patronage and Artistic Life

Even with all the religious conflict, the Catholic Church was still the greatest source of artistic commissions in the seventeenth century, closely followed by royalty and their autocratic governments. Huge churches and massive palaces had big spaces that needed to be filled with large paintings commanding high prices. However, artists were not just interested in monetary gain; many Baroque artists such as **Rubens** and **Bernini** were intensely religious people, who were acting out of a firm commitment to their faith as well as to their art. Credit must be given to the highly cultivated and farsighted patrons who allowed artists to flourish; Pope Urban VIII, for example, sponsored some of Bernini's best work.

BAROQUE ARCHITECTURE

Landscape architecture becomes an important artistic expression in the Baroque. Starting at **Versailles** (Figure 17.3e) and continuing throughout the eighteenth century, palaces are envisioned as the principal feature in an ensemble with gardens that are imaginatively arranged to enhance the buildings they framed. Long views are important. Key windows are viewing stations upon which gardens spread out before the viewer in an imaginatively orchestrated display that suggests man's control over his environment. Views look down extended avenues carpeted by lawns and embraced by bordering trees, usually terminating in a statue or a fountain. The purpose is to impress the viewer with a sense of limitlessness.

Baroque architecture relies on movement. Façades undulate, creating symmetrical cavities of shadow alternating with projecting pilasters that capture the sun. Emphasis is on the center of the façade with wavelike forms that accentuate the entrance. Usually entrances are topped by pediments or tympana to reinforce their importance. A careful interplay of concave and convex shapes marks the most experimental buildings by **Borromini**. Interiors are richly designed to combine all the arts; painting and sculpture service the architectural members in a choreographed ensemble. The aim of Baroque buildings is a dramatically unified effect.

Baroque architecture is large; it seeks to impress with its size and its elaborate ornamentation. In this regard, the Baroque style represents the imperial or papal achievements of its patrons—

proclaiming their power and wealth. Buildings are erected at high points accessible by elaborately carved staircases, ones that spill out toward the spectator and change direction—and view—as they rise.

Carlo Maderno, Santa Maria della Vittoria, 1605–1620, Rome (Figure 17.1)

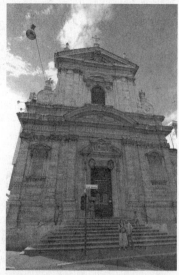

- Church was originally dedicated to Saint Paul
- Rededicated to the Virgin Mary in gratitude for a military victory in Bohemia in 1620
- Turkish standards captured in Siege of Vienna in 1683 on display
- Single wide nave; one of the side chapels houses Bernini's *Ecstasy of Saint Teresa* (Figures 17.4a and 17.4b)
- First story: six Ionic pilasters; emphasis placed on center of façade
- Round and triangular pediments; broken pediments; swags and scrollwork

Figure 17.1: Carlo Maderno, Santa Maria della Vittoria, 1605–1620, Rome

Francesco Borromini, Saint Charles of the Four Fountains (San Carlo alle Quattro Fontane), 1638–1646, stone and stucco, Rome (Figures 17.2a, 17.2b, and 17.2c)

- So named because it is on a square in Rome with four fountains
- Unusually small site
- Alternating convex and concave patterns and undulating volumes in ground plan and façade
- Façade higher than the rest of the building
- Interior side chapels merge into central space
- Interior dome oval shaped and coffered
- Walls treated sculpturally
- Borromini worked in shades of white, avoided colors used in many Baroque buildings
- **Cross-Cultural Comparisons: Architectural Sculpture**
  - Temple of Amun-Re (Figures 3.8a, 3.8b, 3.8c)
  - Parthenon (Figures 4.4, 4.16b)
  - Lakshmana Temple (Figures 23.7a, 23.7b)

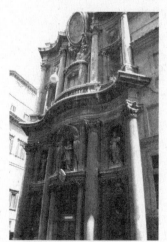

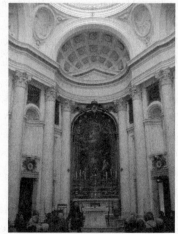

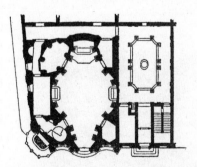

Figures 17.2a: Francesco Borromini, Saint Charles of the Four Fountains (San Carlo alle Quattro Fontane), 1638–1646, stone and stucco, Rome

Figure 17.2b: Francesco Borromini, interior of Saint Charles of the Four Fountains (San Carlo alle Quattro Fontane), 1638–1646, stone and stucco, Rome, Italy

Figure 17.2c: Francesco Borromini, plan of Saint Charles of the Four Fountains (San Carlo alle Quattro Fontane)

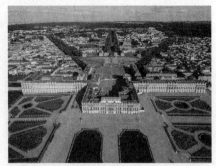

Figure 17.3a: Louis Le Vau and Jules Hardouin-Mansart, Versailles, begun 1669, masonry, stone, wood, iron, and gold leaf, Versailles, France

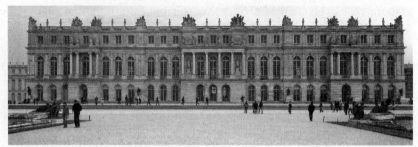

Figure 17.3b: Louis Le Vau and Jules Hardouin-Mansart, Versailles façade, begun 1669, masonry, stone, wood, iron, and gold leaf, Versailles, France

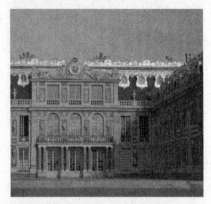

Figure 17.3c: Louis Le Vau and Jules Hardouin-Mansart, Versailles courtyard, begun 1669, masonry, stone, wood, iron, and gold leaf, Versailles, France

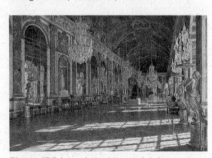

Figure 17.3d: Louis Le Vau and Jules Hardouin-Mansart, Versailles, Hall of Mirrors, begun 1669, masonry, stone, wood, iron, and gold leaf, Versailles, France

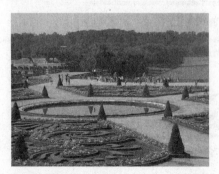

Figure 17.3e: Versailles gardens, begun 1669, Versailles, France

Louis Le Vau and Jules Hardouin-Mansart, Versailles, begun 1669, masonry, stone, wood, iron, and gold leaf; gardens, Versailles, France (Figures 17.3a–17.3e)

- Reorganization and remodeling of a hunting lodge into an elaborate palace
- Center of the building was Louis XIV's bedroom, or audience chamber, from which all aspects of the design radiate like rays from the sun (hence Louis's sobriquet "the Sun King")
- Versailles corresponds to Louis XIV's political and economic ambitions
- Building was centered in a vast garden and town complex radiating from it
- Subdued exterior decoration on façade; undulation of projecting members is understated
- Hall of Mirrors: 240-feet long; barrel-vaulted painted ceiling; light comes in from one side and ricochets off the largest panes of glass that could be made at the time; flickering use of light in an architectural setting; ceiling paintings illustrate civil and military achievements of Louis XIV
- **Cross-Cultural Comparisons: National Capitals**
  - Nan Madol (Figures 28.1a, 28.1b)
  - Great Zimbabwe (Figures 27.1a, 27.1b)
  - Forbidden City (Figures 24.2a, 24.2b, 24.2c, 24.2d)
- Gardens:
  - Classically and harmoniously arranged
  - Formal gardens near palace; more wooded and less elaborate plantings at distances farther from palace
  - Baroque characteristics:
    - size
    - long vistas
    - terminal views in fountains and statuary
  - Mile-long canal crossed by another canal forms the main axis of the gardens
  - Only the fountains near the palace played all the time; others turned on for the king if he progressed through the gardens

BAROQUE PAINTING AND SCULPTURE

Baroque artists explored subjects born in the Renaissance but previously considered too humble for serious painters to indulge in. These subjects, still life, genre, and landscape painting, flourished in the seventeenth-century as never before. While religious and historical paintings were still considered the highest form of expression, even great artists such as **Rembrandt** and **Rubens** painted landscapes and genre scenes. Still lifes were a specialty of the Dutch school.

Landscapes and still lifes exist not in and of themselves, but to express a higher meaning. Still lifes frequently contain a **vanitas** theme, which stresses the brevity of life and the folly of human vanity. Broad open landscapes feature small figures in the foreground acting out a Biblical or mythological passage. Genre paintings often had an allegorical commentary on a contemporary or historical issue.

Landscapes were never actual views of a particular site; instead they were composed in a studio from sketches done in the field. The artist was free to select trees from one place and put them with buildings from another. Landscape painters felt they had to reach beyond the visual into a world of creation that relies on the thoughtful combination of disparate elements to make an artistic statement.

Painters were fascinated by **Caravaggio's** use of **tenebrism**—even the greatest painters of the century experiment with it. The handling of light and shadow became a trademark of the Baroque, not only for painters, but for sculptors and architects as well. Northern artists specialized in **impasto** brushwork, which created a feeling of spontaneity with a vibrant use of visible brushwork. Similarly, sculptors animated the texture of surfaces by variously polishing or abrading surfaces.

Painters like **Caravaggio** painted with an expressive sense of movement. Figures are dramatically rendered, even in what would appear to be a simple portrait. Light effects are key, as offstage sources illuminated parts of figures in a strong dark light contrast called **tenebroso**. Colors are descriptive and evocative. Inspiration comes from the Venetian Renaissance, and passes through **Caravaggio** and onto **Rubens** and his followers, who are called **Rubénistes.** Naturalists reject what they perceive as the contortions and artificiality of the Mannerists.

As in the other arts, Baroque sculpture stressed movement. Figures are caught in mid-motion, mouths open, with the flesh of one figure yielding to the touch of another. Some large works, particularly those by **Bernini**, were often meant to be placed in the middle of the floor or at a slight distance from a wall and be seen in the round. Sculptors employ negative space, carving large openings in a work so that the viewer can contemplate a multiplicity of angles. Marble is treated with a tactile sense: human skin given a high polish, angel wings shown with a feathery touch, animal skins reveal a coarser feel. Baroque sculptors found inspiration in the major works of the Greek Hellenistic period.

Italian Baroque Art

Gian Lorenzo Bernini, *Ecstasy of Saint Teresa*, 1647–1652, marble, stucco and gilt bronze, Santa Maria della Vittoria, Rome (Figures 17.4a and 17.4b)

■ A sculptural interpretation of Saint Teresa's diary in which she tells of her visions of God, many involving an angel descending with an arrow and plunging it into her

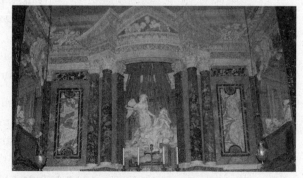

Figure 17.4a: Gian Lorenzo Bernini, Cornaro Chapel, *Ecstasy of Saint Teresa*, 1647–1652, marble, stucco, and gilt bronze, Santa Maria della Vittoria, Rome

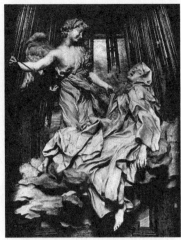

Figure 17.4b: Gian Lorenzo Bernini, *Ecstasy of Saint Teresa*, 1647–1652, marble, Santa Maria della Vittoria, Rome

- Natural light redirected onto the sculpture from a window hidden above the work
- Marble handled in a tactile way to reveal textures: skin is high gloss, feathers of angel are rougher, drapery is animated and fluid, clouds are roughly cut
- Carved from a single block of marble
- Figures seem to float in their space, with the rays of God's light symbolically illuminating the scene from behind
- Saint Teresa's pose suggests sexual exhaustion, a feeling that is consistent with her description of spiritual ecstasy described in her diary entries
- Stagelike setting with the patrons, members of the Cornaro family, sitting in theatre boxes looking on and commenting
- **Cross-Cultural Connections: Use of Light and Dark**
  – Lanzón Stele (Figure 26.1b)
  – Court of the Lions (Figure 9.15b)
  – Pantheon (Figures 6.11a, 6.11b)

Caravaggio, *Calling of Saint Matthew*, 1597–1601, oil on canvas, San Luigi dei Francesi, Rome (Figure 17.5)

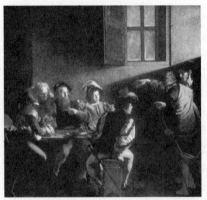

Figure 17.5: Caravaggio, *Calling of Saint Matthew*, 1597–1601, oil on canvas, San Luigi dei Francesi, Rome

- One of three paintings illustrating the life of Saint Matthew in a chapel dedicated to him by the Contarelli family
- Light comes in from two sources on right, creating a tenebroso effect on figures
- Diagonal shaft of light points directly to Saint Matthew, who points to himself as if unsure that Christ would select a tax collector, depicting a moment in time
- Christ's hand gesture similar to Adam's on the Sistine Chapel ceiling
- Foppishly dressed figures are in the latest Baroque fashion
- Narrow stage for figures to sit and stand on
- Only slight suggestion of halo on Christ's head indicates sanctity of the scene
- Sensual figures, everyday characteristics
- Naturalist approach to the Baroque
- **Cross-Cultural Connections: Light Effects**
  – Viola, *Crossing* (Figures 29.18a, 29.18b)
  – Walker, *Darkytown Rebellion* (Figure 29.21)
  – *Notre Dame de la Belle Verriere* (Figure 12.8)

Giovanni Battista Gaulli, *Triumph of the Name of Jesus*, 1676–1679, Il Gesù, Rome (Figure 17.6)

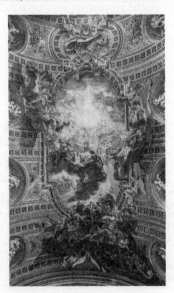

Figure 17.6: Giovanni Battista Gaulli, *Triumph of the Name of Jesus*, 1676–1679, fresco and stucco, Il Gesù, Rome

- On the ceiling in the main nave of Il Gesù, Rome (Figure 16.6b)
- Monogram of Jesus's "IHS" in a brilliantly lit sea of golden color
- Figures tumbling below the name; some carved in stucco enhancing the three-dimensional effect
- Some cast long shadows across the barrel vault
- Some painted figures are not stucco, but maintain a vibrant three-dimensional illusion

- As if the ceiling were open to the sky and the figures were spiraling around Jesus's name
- Di sotto in sù
- The damned are cast into hell; the saved rise heavenward; a Last Judgment
- Influence of Bernini's dramatic emotionalism in the style; Gaullì was Bernini's pupil
- **Cross-Cultural Connections: Ceiling Paintings**
  - Michelangelo, *Flood* (Figure 16.2c)
  - Catacomb of Priscilla Good Shepherd (Figure 7.1c)
  - Lascaux Caves (Figure 1.8)

Spanish Baroque Art

Diego Velázquez, *Las Meninas*, 1656, oil on canvas, Prado, Madrid (Figure 17.7)

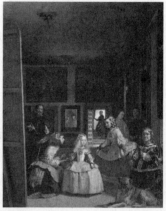

Figure 17.7: Diego Velázquez, *Las Meninas*, 1656, oil on canvas, Prado, Madrid

- Group portrait of the artist in his studio at work; he steps back from the canvas and looks at the viewer
- Velázquez wears the cross of the Royal Order of Santiago, elevating him to knighthood
- Central is the Infanta Margharita of Spain with her meninas, or attendants, a dog, a dwarf, and a midget. Behind are two chaperones in half-shadow. In the doorway is perhaps José Nieto, who was head of the queen's tapestry works (hence his hand on a curtain)
- King and queen appear in a mirror. But what is the mirror reflecting: Velázquez's canvas? The king and queen standing in our space (is this why people have turned around)? Or is it reflecting a painting of the king and queen on our wall of the room?
- Alternating darks and lights draw us deeper into the canvas; the mirror simultaneously reflects out into our space
- Dappled effect of light on shimmering surfaces
- Painting originally hung in Philip IV's study
- **Cross-Cultural Connections: Self-Portraits**
  - Morie, *Pure Land* (Figure 29.19)
  - Raphael, *School of Athens* (Figure 16.3)
  - Bichitr, *Jahangir Preferring a Sufi Sheikh to Kings* (Figure 23.9)

Flemish Baroque Art

Peter Paul Rubens, *Marie de' Medici Cycle*, 1621–1625, oil on canvas, Louvre, Paris (Figure 17.8)

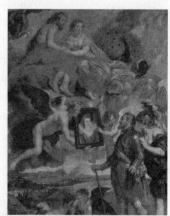

Figure 17.8: Peter Paul Rubens, *Henry IV Receives the Portrait of Marie de'Medici*, 1621–1625, oil on canvas, Louvre, Paris

- Heroic gestures, demonstrative spiraling figures
- Mellow intensity of color, inspired by Titian and Caravaggio
- Sumptuous full-fleshed women
- Twenty-one huge historical paintings allegorically retelling the life of Marie de' Medici, Queen of France, wife of Henry IV
- Splendid costumes suggest opulent theatrical production
- Allegories assist in telling the story and mix freely with historical people

- *Henry IV Receives the Portrait of Marie de'Medici*
  - Henry IV is smitten by the portrait of his intended
  - Portrait held by Cupid (god of love) and Hymen (god of marriage)
  - Jupiter and Juno look down from below; symbolic of marital harmony; they express support
  - Royalty considered demi-gods; approval of mythological gods in concert with their beliefs about themselves
  - Portraits were exchanged before the marriage
  - Married by proxy in 1600
  - Behind Henry is the personification of France
    - France is a female figure with a masculine helmet and manly legs
    - Whispers to Henry to take love over war
  - **Cross-Cultural Connections: Relationships**
    - Klimt, *The Kiss* (Figure 21.12)
    - Veranda post (Figure 27.14)
    - *Akhenaton, Nefertiti, and Three Daughters* (Figure 3.10)

Dutch Baroque Art

While the Baroque is often associated with stately court art, it also flourished in mercantile Holland. Dutch paintings are harbingers of modern taste: landscapes, portraits, and genre paintings flourished; religious ecstasies, great myths, and historical subjects were avoided. In contrast to the massive buildings in other countries, Dutch houses are small and wall space scarce, so painters designed their works to hang in more intimate settings. Even though commerce and trade boomed, the Dutch did not want industry portrayed in their works. Ships are sailboats, not merchant vessels, which courageously braved the weather, not unloaded cargo. Animals are shown quietly grazing rather than giving milk or being shorn for wool. A featureless flat Dutch landscape is animated by powerful and evocative skies.

Dutch painting, however, has several things in common with the rest of European art. Most significantly, Dutch art features many layers of symbolism that provokes the viewer to intellectual consideration. Still life paintings, for example, are not the mere arrangement of inanimate objects, but a cause to ponder the passing and fleetness of life. Stark church interiors often symbolized the triumph of Protestantism over Catholicism. Indeed, while Dutch art may seem outside the mainstream of the Baroque, it does have important parallels with contemporary art in the rest of Europe.

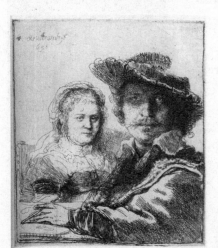

Figure 17.9: Rembrandt, *Self-Portrait with Saskia*, 1636, etching, Los Angeles County Museum of Art

Rembrandt, *Self-Portrait with Saskia*, 1636, etching, Los Angeles County Museum of Art (Figure 17.9)

- Only image of Rembrandt with his wife together in an etching
- 30-year-old Rembrandt with his new bride
- Not wearing contemporary dress; fanciful dress
- Images of Saskia abundant in Rembrandt's output, a source of inspiration for him
- Marital harmony, Saskia as a muse inspiring him
- Wife and mother of four
- Rembrandt is drawing, or perhaps making an etching

- Rembrandt painted 50 self-portraits; 32 self-portrait etchings; 7 self-portrait drawings
- Not for general sale, but for private purposes
- **Cross-Cultural Comparisons: Graphic Arts**
  - Dürer, *Adam and Eve* (Figure 14.3)
  - Cranach, *Allegory of Law and Grace* (Figure 21.7)
  - Kollwitz, *Memorial Sheet for Karl Liebknecht* (Figure 22.4)

Johannes Vermeer, *Woman Holding a Balance*, c. 1664, oil on canvas, National Gallery of Art, Washington (Figure 17.10)

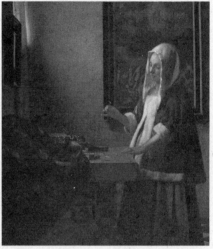

Figure 17.10: Johannes Vermeer, *Woman Holding a Balance*, c. 1664, oil on canvas, National Gallery of Art, Washington

- Small number of Vermeer works in existence
- Except for two landscapes, Vermeer's works portray intimate scenes in the interior of Dutch homes
- Viewer looks into a private world in which seemingly small gestures take on a significance greater than what first appears
- Figures seem unaware of our presence
- Light enters from the left and warmly highlights textures and surfaces: the woman's garments, wood table, marble checkerboard floor, jewelry, painting, etc.
- A moment in time: stillness and timelessness
- A moment of weighing and judging
- Behind a painting of the Last Judgment: a time of weighing souls
- Balance has nothing in it; pearls and coins on the table waiting to be measured
- Balancing reference perhaps to the unborn child
- Allegory
- Vanitas: gold should not be a false allure
- Geometric lines focus on a central point at the pivot of the balance
- Dressed in fine clothing: fur-trimmed
- Perhaps a Vermeer family member posed for the painting; theories that it may have been his wife, Caterina
- **Cross-Cultural Comparisons: Genre Scenes**
  - *Stele of Hegeso* (Figure 4.7)
  - Cassatt, *The Coiffure* (Figure 21.7)
  - *Bayeux Tapestry, First Meal* (Figure 11.7b)

Rachel Ruysch, *Fruits and Insects*, 1711, oil on wood, Uffizi, Florence (Figure 17.11)

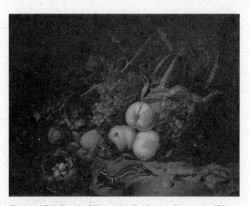

Figure 17.11: Rachel Ruysch, *Fruits and Insects*, 1711, oil on wood, Uffizi, Florence

- Not a depiction of actual flowers, but a construct of perfect specimens all in bloom at the same time
- Asymmetrical arrangement; artful arrangement
- Probably used illustrations in botany textbooks as a basis for painting
- Her father was a professor of anatomy and botany as well as an amateur painter
- In a phase in which the artist produced still lifes in a woodland setting

VOCABULARY

Di sotto in sù: ("from the bottom up"), a type of ceiling painting in which the figures seem to be hovering above the viewers, often looking down at us (Figure 17.6).

Genre painting: painting in which scenes of everyday life are depicted

Impasto: a thick and very visible application of paint on a painting surface

Tenebroso/Tenebrism: a dramatic dark and light contrast in a painting (Figure 17.5)

Vanitas: a theme in still life painting that stresses the brevity of life and the folly of human vanity (Figure 17.11)

SUMMARY

The Baroque has always symbolized the grand, the majestic, the colorful, and the sumptuous in European art. While the work of Rubens and Bernini and the architecture of Versailles certainly qualify as this view of the Baroque, the period is equally famous for small Dutch paintings of penetrating psychological intensity and masterful interplays of light and shadow.

Illusion is a key element of the Baroque aesthetic. Whether it be the floating of Saint Teresa on a cloud or the tromp l'oeil ceilings of Roman palaces, the Baroque teases our imagination by stretching the limits of the space deep into the picture plane. The same complexity of thought is applied to intriguing and symbolic still lifes, known as vanitas paintings, or intricate groupings of figures such as *Las Meninas* (Figure 17.7).

The Baroque is characterized by a sense of ceaseless movement. Building façades undulate, sculptures are seen in the round, and portraits show sitters ready to speak or interact with the viewer. Naturalist painters, like Caravaggio, use dramatic contrasts of light and dark to highlight the movement of the figures.

The Baroque achieves a splendor through an energetic interaction reminiscent of Hellenistic Greek art, which serves as its original role model.

PRACTICE EXERCISES

Multiple-Choice

1. The theatrical illusionism of Baroque works is similar to those seen in which of the following periods?

   (A) Roman Republic
   (B) Chinese Ming
   (C) Cambodian Khmer
   (D) Greek Hellenistic

2. Vanitas paintings are usually seen as symbolic elements in

   (A) still lifes, where they demonstrate the passing nature of human life
   (B) genre paintings, where they show the foibles of human interactions
   (C) landscapes, where they stress the changing nature of the seasons
   (D) historical paintings, where they indicate the folly of greatness and triumph

3. An innovation seen in the architecture of Francesco Borromini is his

    (A) use of non-Western elements in his Catholic churches
    (B) massing of forms on a grand scale to achieve a powerful effect
    (C) use of gardens to enhance the setting of his buildings
    (D) creation of stone buildings that are not linear but curvilinear and undulating in form

4. Which of the following is the prime reason why Caravaggio's public and patrons found his art objectionable?

    (A) He copied directly from great masters of the Renaissance and was considered derivative rather than inventive.
    (B) He worked for discredited bishops, popes, and kings and was tainted by association.
    (C) He made saintly figures have earthly characteristics, which shocked church officials.
    (D) He showed the harsh glare of direct sunlight on his figures, which illuminated them in an uncompromising light.

5. The union of mythological gods and allegorical figures with real people as seen in the Peter Paul Rubens painting *Henry IV Receives the Portrait of Marie de'Medici* from the *Marie de'Medici Cycle* can also be seen in

    (A) *Akhenaton, Nefertiti, and Three Daughters*
    (B) Code of Hammurabi
    (C) *Night Attack on the Sanjô Palace*
    (D) Rodin's *The Burghers of Calais*

Short Essay

This work is *Woman Holding a Balance* by Johannes Vermeer from 1664.

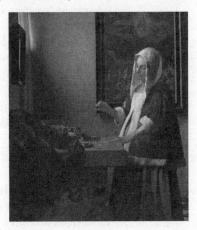

What culture is this work from?

Using specific details in the painting, explain how this work is representative of the culture it is from.

Using specific details, explain how this work is different from many other works in the Baroque period.

1. **D**   2. **A**   3. **D**   4. **C**   5. **B**

ANSWERS EXPLAINED

Multiple-Choice

1. **(D)** Works like the *Winged Victory of Samothrace* show a theatrical illusionism, similar to that of Bernini's *Ecstasy of Saint Teresa*.

2. **(A)** Vanitas paintings are still lifes, generally still lifes that stand alone, although they can be part of larger compositions. They usually have symbols of the passing of time, like clocks, skulls, or hourglasses, which symbolize—among other things—the folly of human endeavor.

3. **(D)** Borromini's buildings, like San Carlo alle Quattro Fontane, show his interest in cutting stone into undulating and curvilinear forms.

4. **(C)** Caravaggio was famous for using models who were not glorious or saintly looking for images of angels, the Virgin Mary, and various saints.

5. **(B)** In the *Code of Hammurabi*, the god Shamash has contact with Hammurabi by literally handing him the code.

Short-Essay Rubric

Question	Points	Key Points in a Good Response
What culture is this work from?	1	This work is Dutch.
Using specific details in the painting, explain how this work is representative of the culture it is from.	2	Some of the details that could be mentioned include: ■ Genre scene; interior domestic scene ■ Small scale work ■ Delicate handling of light ■ Drapery ■ Captures a moment in time ■ Short mercantile activity in a symbolic sense
Using specific details, explain how this work is different from many other works in the Baroque period.	2	Some of the details that could be mentioned include: ■ It is not grand, large, or overwhelming, but small and concentrated ■ It does not have religious or historical associations ■ It is seemingly simple, but asks us to contemplate its meaning ■ It is not theatrical, but poignant ■ The drapery is still rather than active ■ The meaning is captured in a simple gesture and a moment suspended in time

Content Area: Early Europe and Colonial Americas

Art of New Spain: Spanish Colonies in the Americas

18

TIME PERIOD: c. 1500–1820

ENDURING UNDERSTANDING: Seventeenth century art can be characterized by a taste for the theatrical and a stress on movement and compositional variety. Many artists experiment with psychological and emotional portrayals.

Essential Knowledge:

- In colonial Latin America there is a mixing of indigenous art forms with European formulas and materials.
- There is also an influence from Asia and Africa.
- In addition to religious subjects found in Europe at the time, there are other types of paintings, including portraits, history paintings, and genre scenes.

ENDURING UNDERSTANDING: The Reformation and Counter-Reformation caused a rift in Christian art of Western Europe.

Essential Knowledge:

- Latin American colonial art closely aligns with art production from Spain and the rest of southern Europe.

HISTORICAL BACKGROUND

Following the news that Columbus landed in what is now the Bahamas in 1492, European powers immediately set upon a mission of conquest and colonization. Spanish and Portuguese adventurers occupied vast expanses of territory in an area we today call Latin America. The great Native American civilizations of the Aztecs and Inkas rapidly fell before the more technologically advanced and disease-bearing Europeans.

Within a short time, local populations were made to work for their European overlords, artists included. Some Native Americans married into the established Spanish hierarchy and produced children called **mestizos**.

The Spanish extracted much the New World had to offer: silver, gold, and new crops, like potatoes and corn. They also established a world-wide trading empire in which ships slowly trekked across the Pacific connecting Mexico with Asia. These voyages, called the Manila Galleon, enabled trade vessels to make the four-month journey unimpeded. The Mexican market could boast Asian spices, ceramics, silks, ivory, and other precious items long before they became available in the colonial United States. Artistic life became enriched by the contact of East and West layered onto a Native American population.

Instability in Europe during the Napoleonic wars, however, inspired Spain's colonies to seek independence. As quickly as Spain gained her territories, she lost them to very capable generals like Simón Bolivar and José de San Martin. By 1822 most of Latin America was a patchwork of independent states; colonial rule was over.

Patronage and Artistic Life

The Spanish brought Roman Catholicism, a religion rich in imagery, to the New World. Ecclesiastical patrons sponsored an astonishing degree of high quality religious works. Unlike English colonists, the Spanish were not reluctant to use native artists. Works from New Spain combine Roman Catholicism with Native American traditions in a pictorial landscape that often uses new materials from Asia. Concurrently, English Protestants in what is now the United States limited their artistic expression to portraits.

In the beginning, the Spanish brought over late medieval artistic conventions that were often combined with provincial Renaissance works. Soon thereafter efforts were made to establish local schools that were inspired by the more current Baroque style. Many Mexican portraits show men dressed in the latest Madrid styles to prove they had aristocratic sensibilities.

The first center of European art in the Americas was established in Cusco, Peru. Spanish painters taught local Quechan and mestizo artists the newly imported style. In addition to religious images, patrons also were interested in portraits, as well other subjects current in European painting like historical paintings of battle scenes and Arcadian landscapes.

Painting in New Spain

Religious painting of the colonial Spanish era is generally marked by a combination of Old and New World skills. Spain contributed the oil technique and Catholic imagery to American painting. Native artists, working within their own traditions, showed less interest in European painting formulas such as perspective. They favored a flattened surface with earthen tones. This is particularly evident in the works of the Cusco School.

Many works of art were created anonymously, in service of religion rather than in service of the fame of the artist. Today it is oftentimes impossible to establish the name of the artist because the style of a given school is so closely united.

The Manila Galleon brought trade from Asia, and new materials as well, so it is not unusual to see works of Latin American art that use ivory, silk, or ceramics.

Frontispiece of the Codex Mendoza, c. 1542, pigment on paper, Bodleian Library, Oxford University (Figure 18.1)

- Named after Antonio de Mendoza, viceroy of New Spain
- Intended as a history of the Aztecs for Charles V of the Holy Roman Empire
- Created twenty years after the Spanish conquest
- Shows Aztec rulers and daily life in Mexico
- Uses pictograms created by Aztec artists that were later annotated in Spanish
- This scene depicts the founding of Tenochtitlan and the conquest of Colhuacan and Tenayucan on the bottom
- Enemy temples are on fire while Aztec warriors carry clubs and shields

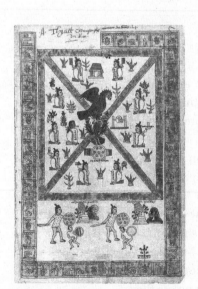

Figure 18.1: Frontispiece of the Codex Mendoza, c. 1542, pigment on paper, Bodleian Library, Oxford University

- Small representation of the Templo Mayor above the eagle (Figure 26.5a)
- Skulls represent sacrificial victims
- Eagle landing on a cactus at the intersection of the two waterways commemorates the division of Tenochtitlan into four quarters
- Current Mexican flag has an eagle perched on a cactus that rests on a rock, as seen in this work
- **Cross-Cultural Comparisons: National Symbols**
  - Delacroix, *Liberty Leading the People* (Figure 20.4)
  - Golden Stool (Figure 27.4)
  - Quick-to-See-Smith, *Trade* (Figure 29.12)

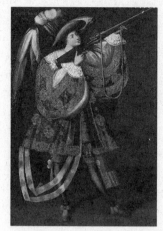

Figure 18.2: Master of Calamarca, *Angel with Arquebus, Asiel Timor Dei*, c. 1680, oil on canvas, National Art Museum, La Paz, Bolivia

Master of Calamarca, *Angel with Arquebus, Asiel Timor Dei*, c. 1680, oil on canvas, National Art Museum, La Paz, Bolivia (Figure 18.2)

- Angel depicted with an arquebus (a form of a rifle) instead of traditional sword
- Military poses derived from European engravings of military exercises
- Probably one in a series of angel drummers, buglers, standard bearers, and holders of swords
- Drapery of a seventeenth century Spanish aristocrat; rich costuming
- Mannerist influence in the stiffness of the figure; dance-like pose
- Latin inscription: "Asiel, fear of God"
- Angel appears in an androgynous stance
- Gold embroidered on fabric favored by indigenous people
- Relationship between these images and the winged warriors of Pre-Columbian art
- May have originated in the region around Lake Titicaca in the Collao region of Peru
- **Cross-Cultural Comparisons: Guardian Figures**
  - Nio guardian figure (Figures 25.1c, 25.1d)
  - *Lamassu* (Figure 2.5)
  - *Jayvaraman VII as Buddha* (Figure 23.6d)

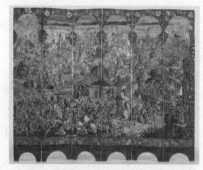

Figure 18.3a: Circle of the Gonzalez Family, Screen with the Siege of Belgrade, 1697–1701, tempera and resin on wood inlaid with mother-of-pearl, Brooklyn Museum, New York

Circle of the Gonzalez Family, Screen with the Siege of Belgrade and Hunting Scenes, 1697–1701, tempera and resin on wood inlaid with mother-of-pearl, Brooklyn Museum, New York (Figures 18.3a and 18.3b)

- Screen commissioned by José Sarmiento de Valladares, viceroy of New Spain
- Displayed in Viceregal Palace in Mexico City
- Only known example of an art work that combines biombos and enconchados
- Two faces of the screen: one has hunting screen; other has a war scene
- The hunting scene suited to an intimate space for small receptions
- War scene more suited for a grander room with political importance
- War scene depicts the contemporary event of the Great Turkish War 1683–1699; Dutch print used for inspiration
- Illustrates a scene of Hapsburg power

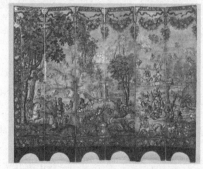

Figure 18.3b: Circle of the Gonzalez Family, Screen with Hunting Scenes, 1697–1701, tempera and resin on wood inlaid with mother-of-pearl, Brooklyn Museum, New York

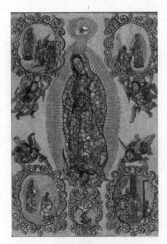

Figure 18.4: Miguel González, *Virgin of Guadelupe*, 1698, oil on canvas on wood with mother-of-pearl, Los Angeles County Museum of Art, Los Angeles, California

Miguel González, *Virgin of Guadelupe*, 1698, oil on canvas on wood with mother-of-pearl, Los Angeles County Museum of Art, Los Angeles, California (Figure 18.4)

- Painting describes an event in which Mary appeared to Native Americans on a hill called Tepeyac, a shrine sacred to a pre-Columbian goddess
- Mary ordered a Native American convert, Juan Diego in 1531, to tell the local archbishop to build a sanctuary on this site
- Mary made the hilltop flower and Juan Diego brought the flowers to the archbishop; Juan Diego's cloth revealed the Virgin's image
- Virgin of Guadelupe the most revered symbol in Mexico; patroness of New Spain
- Symbol of Mexico: eagle perched on a cactus at bottom center
- In Guadelupe images Mary always stands on a crescent moon; surrounded by sunrays; clouds behind her
- Cf. Revelations 12:1: "A great sign appeared in heaven: a woman clothed with the sun, with the moon under her feet and a crown of twelve stars on her head."
- Surrounded by four roundels depicting the apparition to Juan Diego at the moment the Virgin's image is revealed in his tunic

- Brocade on Virgin's robes made of enconchados
- Enconchados: influence of Asian decorative arts
- Image in demand: many made for export around New Spain
- **Cross-Cultural Connections: Images of Mary**
  - *Notre Dame de la Belle Verriere* (Figure 12.8)
  - Lippi, *Madonna and Child with Two Angels* (Figure 15.3)
  - *Virgin and Child between Saints Theodore and George* (Figure 8.8)

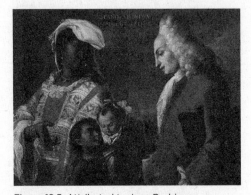

Figure 18.5: Attributed to Juan Rodriguez, *Spaniard and Indian Produce a Mestizo*, c. 1715, oil on canvas, Private Collection, London

Attributed to Juan Rodriguez, *Spaniard and Indian Produce a Mestizo*, c. 1715, oil on canvas, Private Collection, London (Figure 18.5)

- Panel from the first known series of casta paintings; may not have been a completed set
- Spanish social hierarchy with the European ancestry at the top; sixteen different gradations of social scale
- Spanish blood linked to civilizing forces; wearing lavish costumes
- Africans and Indians are rendered with respect; showing harmony and mixing of the classes
- Many Africans and Indians are rendered with South European features: slim noses, curly hair, almond-shaped eyes

- Spanish colonists commissioned with works to be sent abroad to show how the caste system of the New World works
- Not considered art objects but illustrations of ethnic groups
- **Cross-Cultural Connections: Meeting of Cultures**
  - Quick-to-See-Smith, *Trade* (Figure 29.12)
  - Bandolier Bag (Figure 26.11)
  - Bichitr, *Jahangir Preferring a Sufi Sheikh to Kings* (Figure 23.9)

Miguel Cabrera, *Portrait of Sor Juana Inés de la Cruz,* **1750, oil on canvas (Figure 18.6)**

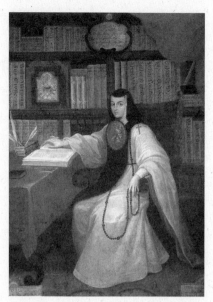

- Sor Juana Inés (Sister Juana Agnes), a child prodigy (1651–1695)
- Creole woman, became a nun in 1669
- Feminist culture survived in Mexican convents where privileged nuns lived in comfort with servants and households
- Literary figure, published books that were widely read; wrote poetry and theatrical pieces
- Maintained a great library
- Instrumental in giving girls an education in a male-dominated world
- Wearing the habit of the religious order of the Hermits of St. Jerome nuns of Mexico City; including the escudo—a framed vellum painting
- Seated in her library surrounded by symbols of her faith and her learning
- Many portraits survive, but all images derive from a now lost self-portrait
- Painting done 55 years after her death for her admirers
- **Cross-Cultural Comparisons: Portraits**
    – Mblo (Figure 27.7)
    – *Sin Sukju* (Figure 24.6)
    – Smith, *Lying with the Wolf* (Figure 29.20)

Figure 18.6: Miguel Cabrera, *Portrait of Sor Juana Inés de la Cruz*, 1750, oil on canvas

VOCABULARY

Biombos: folding free-standing screens (Figures 18.3a and 18.3b)
Casta Paintings: paintings from New Spain showing people of mixed races (Figure 18.5)
Enconchados: shell-inlay paintings; tiny fragments of mother-of-pearl placed onto a wooden
    support and canvas and covered with a yellowish tint and thin glazes of paint (Figure 18.4)
Escudo: a framed painting worn below the neck in a colonial Spanish painting (Figure 18.6)
Mestizo: someone of mixed European and Native American descent (Figure 18.5)

SUMMARY

Spanish colonists combined European Baroque traditions with Native American labor and Asian imports to create a multi-layered artistic experience. Patrons sponsored a wide range of subjects: religious images, portraits, painted screens, landscapes, and historical episodes. While many of the artistic formulas remain European in inspiration, the appeal of art from this period is its ability to wed disparate artistic experiences into a coherent whole.

Multiple-Choice

Questions 1–3 refer to the image below.

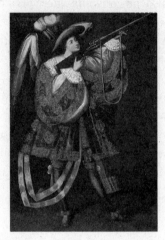

1. The formal quality of this work shows that it was influenced by

   (A) Byzantine art in its extensive use of gold
   (B) Gothic art in its angularity and frontality
   (C) Mannerism in its awkwardness of poses
   (D) Rococo art in its light-hearted humor

2. This image of an angel differs from other angels in other contexts in that

   (A) the body is covered in drapery
   (B) this face looks human rather than divine
   (C) this angel is carrying a gun rather than a sword
   (D) there is no suggestion of an episode from the Bible being depicted

3. The materials used in this work show the influence of

   (A) Aztec sculptures
   (B) Mayan frescoes
   (C) Aztec feather work
   (D) Spanish painting

   _____

4. The Codex Mendoza was created for

   (A) the Aztecs as an official account of their history
   (B) the Aztecs as a record of their civilization before the conquest by Spain
   (C) Antonio de Mendoza as a keepsake to remember his time spent in Mexico
   (D) Europeans to show them this history of the Aztecs

5. *The Virgin of Guadalupe* by Miguel González shows the influence of Asian art in its

   (A) use of exotic materials, such as mother-of-pearl
   (B) subject matter, which included the Chinese shrine at Guadalupe
   (C) Chinese calligraphy identifying the images
   (D) abstract formulae for depicting the human body

Short Essay

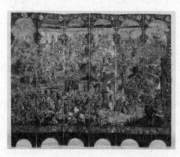 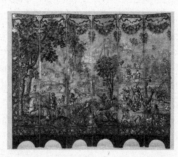

This screen was done by artists associated with the González family from 1697 to 1701.

What are the scenes depicted on each side?

Where was this screen originally displayed?

Discussing specific features, analyze what each side of the screen was meant to face.

What symbolism did the patrons see in the events portrayed on this screen?

ANSWER KEY

1. **C**   2. **C**   3. **D**   4. **D**   5. **A**

ANSWERS EXPLAINED

Multiple-Choice

1. **(C)** The stiff and awkward nature of the pose shows influence from Mannerist artists.

2. **(C)** It is not unusual for an angel to carry a weapon, like a sword. It is highly unusual for him to carry a gun.

3. **(D)** This work is an oil on canvas, the same technique as that used in Spain.

4. **(D)** The purpose of The Codex Mendoza is to show Europeans the life and history of the Aztec people.

5. **(A)** Exotic materials were brought from Asia through a shipping route called the Magellan Galleon. Spanish artists were particularly attracted to the widespread use of mother-of-pearl, as seen in this screen.

Short-Essay Rubric

Question	Points	Key Points in a Good Response
What are the scenes depicted on each side?	1	The left side is a war scene that depicts the contemporary event of the Great Turkish War, 1683–1699: the Siege of Belgrade. The right side is a hunting scene.
Where was this screen originally displayed?	1	It was originally displayed in Viceregal Palace in Mexico City, separating two rooms: an intimate space and a grand salon.
Discussing specific features, analyze what each side of the screen was meant to face.	1	The grand salon, for formal occasions, would be an appropriate setting for the battle scene; the hunting scene would face a more intimate setting meant for smaller gatherings.
What symbolism did the patrons see in the events portrayed on this screen?	2	The Viceregal Mexicans were connected with the Habsburgs in Europe, and saw the conquering of the Turks as a reflection of their own greatness. The war scene proved their mettle in battle in Europe and, by extension, in America. The hunting scene shows a leisure activity of the upper classes.

Content Area: Early Europe and Colonial Americas
Later Europe and Americas

19

Rococo and Neoclassicism

TIME PERIOD: ROCOCO: 1700–1750 AND BEYOND
NEOCLASSICISM: 1750–1815

The Rococo derives its name from a combination of the French *rocaille*,
meaning "pebble" or "shell," and the Italian *barocco*, meaning "baroque."
Thus, motifs in the Rococo were thought to resemble ornate shell or pebble work.

ENDURING UNDERSTANDING: Art is influenced by changes in society. It is affected by economic forces which cause widespread migration, war, and a concentration of population in cities. New countries emerge and social movements gain strength.

Essential Knowledge:

- The late eighteenth century is known as the Enlightenment, a period of scientific advance. It is followed by the revolutionary principles of the Romantic period.
- New philosophies, particularly those by Marx and Darwin, spread throughout the world. These views were supplemented by a new understanding of worldwide cultures.

ENDURING UNDERSTANDING: Artists become more prominent members of society. Art movements come in a rapid succession.

Essential Knowledge:

- Modern movements include Neoclassicism and Romanticism.
- Artists belong to academies and show their work in salons.
- Architecture is characterized by a series of revivals.

ENDURING UNDERSTANDING: Art is seen in a new, often provoking, way by the public.

Essential Knowledge:

- The salons of Paris grow in importance.
- Artists work less in the service of religion, more for corporations.

HISTORICAL BACKGROUND

Center stage in early-eighteenth-century politics was the European conquest of the rest of the world. The great struggles of the time took place among the colonial powers, who at first merely established trading stations in the lands they encountered, but later occupied distant places by layering new settlers, new languages, new religions, and new governments onto an indigenous population. At first, Europeans hoped to become wealthy by exploiting these new territories, but the cost of maintaining foreign armies soon began to outweigh the commercial benefits.

As European settlers grew wistful for home, they built Baroque- and Rococo-inspired buildings, imported Rococo fashions and garments, and made the New World seem as much like the Old World as they could.

In France, the court at Versailles began to diminish after the death of Louis XIV, leaving less power in the hands of the king and more in the nobility. Therefore, the Rococo departs from the Baroque interest in royalty, and takes on a more aristocratic flavor, particularly in the decoration of lavish townhouses that the upper class kept in Paris—not in Versailles.

The late eighteenth century was the age of the Industrial Revolution. Populations boomed as mass-production, technological innovation, and medical science marched relentlessly forward. The improvements in the quality of life that the Industrial Revolution yielded were often offset by a new slavery to mechanized work and inhumane working conditions.

At the same time, Europe was being swept by a new intellectual transformation called The Enlightenment, in which philosophers and scientists based their ideas on logic and observation, rather than tradition and folk wisdom. Knowledge began to be structured in a deliberate way: Denis Diderot (1713–1784) organized and edited a massive 52-volume French encyclopedia in 1764, Samuel Johnson (1709–1784) composed the first English dictionary singlehandedly in 1755, and Jean-Jacques Rousseau discussed how a legitimate government was an expression of the general will in his 1762 *Social Contract*.

With all this change came political ferment—the late eighteenth century being a particularly transformational moment in European politics. Some artists, like David, were caught up in the turbulent politics of the time and advocated the sweeping societal changes that they thought the French Revolution espoused.

Patronage and Artistic Life

Rome was the place to be—to see the past. New artistic life was springing up all over Europe, leaving Rome as the custodian of inspiration and tradition, but not of progress. Italy's seminal position as a cultural cornucopia was magnified in 1748 by the discovery of the buried city of Pompeii. Suddenly genuine Roman works were being dug up daily, and the world could admire an entire ancient city.

The discovery of Pompeii inspired art theorist Johann Winckelmann (1717–1768) to publish *The History of Ancient Art* in 1764, which many consider the first art history book. Winckelmann heavily criticized the waning Rococo as decadent, and celebrated the ancients for their purity of form and crispness of execution.

Because of renewed interest in studying the ancients, art academies began to spring up around Europe and in the United States. Artists were trained in what the Academy viewed as the proper classical tradition—part of that training sent many artists to Rome to study works firsthand.

The French Academy showcased selected works by its members in an annual or biannual event called the **Salon**, so-called because it was held in a large room, the Salon Carrè, in the Louvre. Art critics and judges would scout out the best of the current art scene, and accept a limited number of paintings for public view at the Salon. If an artist received this critical endorsement, it meant his or her prestige greatly increased, as well as the value of his paintings.

The Salons had very traditional standards, insisting on artists employing a flawless technique with emphasis on established subjects executed with conventional perspective and drawing. History paintings, that is, those paintings dealing with historical, religious, or mythological subjects, were most prized. Portraits were next in importance, followed by landscapes, genre paintings, and then still lifes.

No education was complete without a **Grand Tour** of Italy. Usually under the guidance of a connoisseur, the tour visited cities like Naples, Florence, Venice, and Rome. It was here that people could immerse themselves in the lessons of the ancient world and perhaps collect an antiquity or two, or buy a work from a contemporary artist under the guidance of the connoisseur. The blessings of the Neoclassical period were firmly entrenched in the mind of art professionals and educated amateurs.

ROCOCO PAINTING

Just as in architecture, Rococo painting shuns straight lines, even in the frames of paintings. It is typical to have curved frames with delicate rounded forms in which the limbs of several of the figures spill over the sides so that the viewer is hard-pressed to determine what is painted and what is sculpted.

Rococo art is flagrantly erotic, sensual in its appeal to the viewer. The curvilinear characteristics of Rococo paintings enhance their seductiveness. Unlike the sensual paintings of the Venetian Renaissance, these paintings tease the imagination by presenting playful scenes of love and romance with overt sexual overtones.

Although the French are most noted for the Rococo, there were also active centers in England, central Europe, and Venice.

Rococo painting is the triumph of the Rubénistes over the Poussinistes. Artists, particularly those of Flemish descent like **Watteau**, were captivated by Rubens's use of color to create form and modeling.

Figures in Rococo painting are slender, often seen from the back. Their light frames are clothed in shimmering fabrics worn in bucolic settings like park benches or downy meadows. Gardens are rich with plant life and flowers dominate. Figures walk easily through forested glens and flowery copses, contributing to a feeling of oneness with nature reminiscent of the Arcadian paintings of the Venetian Renaissance.

Colors are never thick or richly painted; instead, **pastel** hues dominate. Some artists specialized in pastel paintings that possessed an extraordinary lifelike quality. Others transferred the spontaneous brushwork and light palette of pastels to oils.

By and large, Rococo art is more domestic than Baroque, meaning it is more for private rather than public display. **Fête galante** painting features the aristocracy taking long walks or listening to sentimental love songs in garden settings.

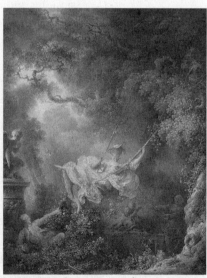

Figure 19.1: Jean-Honoré Fragonard, *The Swing*, 1767, oil on canvas, Wallace Collection, London

Jean-Honoré Fragonard, *The Swing*, 1767, oil on canvas, Wallace Collection, London (Figure 19.1)

- Figures are small in a dominant gardenlike setting
- Atmospheric perspective
- Puffy clouds; rich vegetation; abundant flowers; sinuous curves
- Patron in lower left looking up the skirt of a young lady who swings flirtatiously, boldly kicking off her shoe at a Cupid sculpture
- Unsuspecting bishop swings her from behind

- An intrigue painting; patron hides in a bower; Cupid asks the young lady to be discreet and/or may be a symbol for the secret hiding of the patron
- **Cross-Cultural Comparisons: Figures Set in a Landscape**
  - Fan Kuan, *Travelers Among Mountains and Streams* (Figure 24.5)
  - Dürer, *Adam and Eve* (Figure 14.3)
  - Cotsiogo, Hide Painting of a Sun Dance (Figure 26.13)

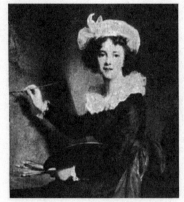

Figure 19.2 : Louise Élisabeth Vigée Le Brun, *Self-Portrait*, 1790, oil on canvas, Uffizi, Florence

Louise Élisabeth Vigée Le Brun, *Self-Portrait*, 1790, oil on canvas, Uffizi, Florence (Figure 19.2)

- Forty self-portraits exist, all highly idealized
- Looks at the viewer as she paints a portrait of Marie Antoinette, who is rendered from memory since she was killed during the French Revolution; subject in painting looks admiringly upon the painter
- Light Rococo touch to the coloring
- Inspired by the portraits of Rubens
- **Cross-Cultural Comparisons: Individual, Status, and Society**
  - *Augustus of Primaporta* (Figure 6.15)
  - *Sin Sukju* (Figure 24.6)
  - Mblo (Figure 27.7)

EIGHTEENTH-CENTURY ENGLISH PAINTING

Freedom of expression swept through France and England at the beginning of the eighteenth century and found its fullest expression in the satires of Jonathan Swift's *Gulliver's Travels* and Voltaire's *Candide*. The visual arts responded by painting the first overt satires, the most famous of which are by the English painter **Hogarth**. Satirical paintings usually were done in a series to help spell out a story as in *Marriage à la Mode* (Figure 19.3). Afterward the paintings were transferred to prints, so that the message could be mass-produced. Themes stem from exposing political corruption to spoofs on contemporary lifestyles. Hogarth knew that the pictorial would reach more people than the written, and he hoped to use his prints to didactically expose his audience to abuses in the upper class. Society had changed so much that by now those in power grew more tolerant of criticism so as to allow satirical painting to flourish, at least in England. Today, the political cartoon is the descendant of these satirical prints.

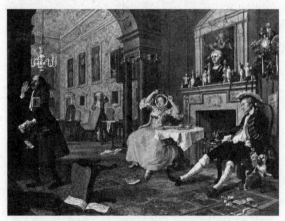

Figure 19.3: William Hogarth, *The Tête à Tête* from *Marriage à la Mode*, c. 1743, oil on canvas, National Gallery, London

William Hogarth, *The Tête à Tête* from *Marriage à la Mode*, c. 1743, oil on canvas, National Gallery, London (Figure 19.3)

- One of six scenes in a suite of paintings called *Marriage à la Mode*
- Narrative paintings; later turned into a series of prints
- Highly satiric paintings about aristocratic English society and those who would like to buy their way into it
- *The Tête à Tête*: shortly after the marriage, each partner has been pursuing pleasures without the other
  - Husband has been out all night with another woman (the dog sniffs suspiciously at another bonnet); the broken sword means he has been in a fight and probably lost (and may also be a symbol for sexual inadequacy)

- The wife has been playing cards all night, the steward (at left) indicating by his expression that she has lost a fortune at whist; he holds nine unpaid bills in his hand, one was paid by mistake
- Turned-over chair indicates that the violin player made a hasty retreat when the husband came home

■ **Cross-Cultural Comparisons: Personal Relationships**
  - van Eyck, *Arnolfini Portrait* (Figure 14.2)
  - Veranda post (Figure 27.14)
  - Sultan Muhammad, *Court of the Gayumars* (Figure 9.9)

Joseph Wright of Derby, *A Philosopher Giving a Lecture on the Orrery*, 1763–1765, oil on canvas, Derby Museum and Art Gallery, Derby, U.K. (Figure 19.4)

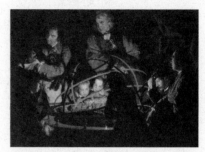

Figure 19.4: Joseph Wright of Derby, *A Philosopher Giving a Lecture on the Orrery*, 1763–1765, oil on canvas, Derby Museum and Art Gallery, Derby, U.K.

■ Influenced by the meeting of a provincial group of intellectuals called the Lunar Society, who met once a month to discuss current scientific discoveries and developments
■ Orrery is an early form of a planetarium, imitating the motion of the solar system
■ Lamp in the center (out of view) is the sun
■ Mixed group of middle class people in attendance representing all ages of men; young woman seated to the left
■ Some curious, some contemplate, some in wonder, some fascinated
■ The philosopher is based loosely on a portrait of Isaac Newton; he is demonstrating an eclipse
■ The philosopher stops to clarify a point to the note-taker on the left
■ To complete the celestial theme: each face in the painting is an aspect of the phases of the moon
■ One of a series of candlelight pictures by Wright; inspired by Caravaggio's use of tenebrism
■ **Cross-Cultural Comparisons: Knowledge**
  - Bichitr, *Jahangir Preferring a Sufi Sheikh to Kings* (Figure 23.9)
  - Cabrera, *Portrait of Sor Juana Inés de la Cruz* (Figure 18.6)

Neoclassical Architecture

The best Neoclassical buildings were not dry adaptations of the rules of ancient architecture, but a clever revision of classical principles onto a modern framework. While many buildings had the outward trappings of Roman works, they were also efficiently tailored to living in the eighteenth century.

Ancient architecture came to Europe distilled through the books written by the Renaissance architect Andrea Palladio, and reemphasized by the classicizing works of Inigo Jones. From these sources Neoclassicists learned about symmetry, balance, composition, and order. Greek and Roman columns, with their appropriate capitals, appeared on the façades of most great houses of the period, even in the remote hills of Virginia. Pediments crown entrances and top windows. Domes grace the center of homes, often setting off gallery space. The interior layout is nearly or completely symmetrical, with rectangular rooms mirroring one another on either side of the building. Each room is decorated with a different theme, some inspired by the

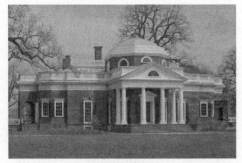

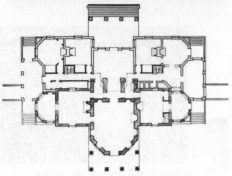

Figures 19.5a and 19.5b: Thomas Jefferson, Monticello, 1770–1806, Charlottesville, Virginia

ancient world, others with a dominant color in wallpaper or paint. It is common for an eighteenth-century home.

Thomas Jefferson, Monticello, 1768–1806, brick, glass, stone, and wood, Charlottesville, Virginia (Figures 19.5a and 19.5b)

- "Little mountain" in Italian
- Chief building on Jefferson's plantation
- Symmetrical interior design
- Brick building, stucco applied to trim to give the effect of marble
- Tall French doors and windows to allow circulation in hot Virginia summers
- Appears to be a one-story building with a dome, but the balustrade hides the second floor
- Inspired by Palladian villas in Italy and Roman ruins in France
- Octagonal dome
- Jefferson obsessed with saving space in his home: very narrow spiral staircases, beds in alcoves or in walls between rooms
- **Cross-Cultural Comparisons: Classical Revival**
  - Houdon, *George Washington* (Figure 19.7)
  - Donatello, *David* (Figure 15.5)
  - Alberti, Palazzo Rucellai (Figure 15.2)

NEOCLASSICAL PAINTING

Stories from the great epics of antiquity spoke meaningfully to eighteenth-century painters. Mythological or Biblical scenes were painted with a modern context in mind. The retelling of the story of the Horatii would be a dry academic exercise if it did not have the added implication of self-sacrifice for the greater good. A painting like this was called an **exemplum virtutis**.

Even paintings that did not have mythological references had subtexts inviting the viewer to take measure of a person, a situation, and a state of affairs.

Compositions in Neoclassical paintings were symmetrical, with linear perspective leading the eye into a carefully constructed background. The most exemplary works were marked by invisible brushwork and clarity of detail.

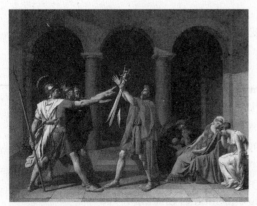

Figure 19.6: Jacques-Louis David, *The Oath of the Horatii*, 1784, oil on canvas, Louvre, Paris

Jacques-Louis David, *The Oath of the Horatii*, 1784, oil on canvas, Louvre, Paris (Figure 19.6)

- Exemplum virtutis
- Story of three Roman brothers (the Horatii) who do battle with three other brothers (the Curiatii—not painted) from a nearby city; they pledge their fidelity to their father and to Rome
- One of the three women on right is a Horatii engaged to one of the Curiatii brothers; another woman is the sister of the Curiatii brothers
- Forms are vigorous, powerful, animated, emphatic
- Gestures are sweeping and unified
- Figures pushed to the foreground

- Neoclassical drapery and tripartite composition
- Not Neoclassical in its Caravaggio-like lighting and un-Roman architectural capitals
- Painted under royal patronage
- Created a sensation at the Salon of 1785
- **Cross-Cultural Comparisons: Historicism**
  - Rivera, *Dream of a Sunday Afternoon in the Alameda Park* (Figure 27.20)
  - Shonibare, *The Swing* (Figure 29.22)
  - Sherman, *Untitled* (Figure 29.10)

NEOCLASSICAL SCULPTURE

Before the Industrial Revolution, bronze was the most expensive and most highly prized sculptural medium. Mass production of metal made possible by factories in England and Germany caused the price of bronze to fall, while simultaneously causing the price of marble to rise. Stonework relied on manual labor, a cost that was now going up. However, because it was felt that the ancients preferred marble, it still seemed more authentic, possessing an authoritative appeal. It was also assumed that the ancients preferred an unpainted sculpture, because the majority of marbles that have come down to us have lost their color.

The recovery of artifacts from Pompeii increasingly inspired sculptors to work in the classical medium. This reached a fever pitch with the importation of the Parthenon sculptures, the Elgin Marbles, to London, where they were eventually purchased by the state and ensconced in the Neoclassical British Museum. Sculptors like **Houdon** saw the Neoclassical style as a continuance of an ancient tradition.

Sculpture, while deeply affected by classicism, also was mindful of the realistic likeness of the sitter. Sculptors moved away from figures wrapped in ancient robes to more realistic figural poses in contemporary drapery. Classical allusions were secondary influences. Still, Neoclassical sculpture was carved from white marble with no paint added, the way it was felt the ancients worked.

Jean-Antoine Houdon, *George Washington*, 1788–1792, marble, State Capitol, Richmond, Virginia (Figure 19.7)

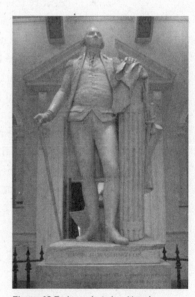

- Washington dressed as an eighteenth century gentleman
- Military associations minimized: epaulettes on shoulder and sword cast to the side
- Naturalistic details: missing button on his jacket; tightly buttoned vest around a protruding stomach
- Seen as a man of vision and enlightenment
- Badge of Cincinnatus on this belt: Washington as gentleman–farmer who left Mount Vernon to take up the American cause the way Cincinnatus from the Roman Republic left his farm to command Roman armies, and then returned to his farm
- Plow behind Washington symbolizes his plantation
- Washington leans on the Roman fasces: a group of rods bound together on top and bottom
- Thirteen rods symbolize thirteen colonies
- Washington leans on the thirteen colonies, from which he gets his support

Figure 19.7: Jean-Antoine Houdon, *George Washington*, 1788-1792, marble, State Capitol, Richmond, Virginia

- **Cross-Cultural Comparisons: Rulers**
  - Menkaura and His Queen (Figure 3.7)
  - Lindauer, *Tamati Waka Nene* (Figure 28.7)
  - *Augustus of Prima Porta* (Figure 6.15)

VOCABULARY

Academy: an institution whose main objectives include training artists in an academic tradition, ennobling the profession, and holding exhibitions

Exemplum virtutis: a painting that tells a moral tale for the viewer (Figure 19.6)

Fête galante: an eighteenth-century French style of painting that depicts the aristocracy walking through a forested landscape

Grand Tour: in order to complete their education young Englishmen and Americans in the eighteenth century undertook a journey to Italy to absorb ancient and Renaissance sites

Pastel: a colored chalk that when mixed with other ingredients produces a medium that has a soft and delicate hue

Salon: a government-sponsored exhibition of artworks held in Paris

SUMMARY

The early eighteenth century saw the shift of power turn away from the king and his court at Versailles to the nobles in Paris. The royal imagery and rich coloring of Baroque painting was correspondingly replaced by lighter pastels and a theatrical flair. Watteau's lighthearted compositions, called *fête galantes*, were symbolic of the aristocratic taste of the period.

Partly inspired by the French Rococo, a strong school of portrait painting under the leadership of Gainsborough and Reynolds emerged in England. In addition, English painters and patrons delighted in satirical painting, reflecting a more relaxed attitude in the eighteenth century toward criticism and censorship.

The aristocratic associations of the Rococo caused the style to be reviled by the Neoclassicists of the next generation, who thought that the style was decadent and amoral. Even so, the Rococo continued to be the dominant style in territories occupied by Europeans in other parts of the world—there it symbolized a cultured and refined view of the world in the midst of perceived pagans.

Intellectuals influenced by the Enlightenment were quick to reject the Rococo as decadent, and espoused Neoclassicism as a movement that expressed the "Liberty, Equality, and Fraternity" of the French Revolution. Moreover, the discovery of Pompeii and the writings of Johann Winckelmann, the first art historian, did much to revive interest in the classics and use them as models for the modern experience.

PRACTICE EXERCISES

Multiple-Choice

1. *The Swing* by Jean-Honoré Fragonard is similar to other Rococo paintings in that it

    (A) uses tenebrism to sharply contrast dark and light
    (B) is concerned with the classical ideals of Polykleitos
    (C) is innovative and experimental in painting techniques
    (D) uses a pastel palette

2. The structure of Monticello is heavily influenced by Thomas Jefferson's

    (A) trip to Spain to study Renaissance architecture
    (B) work as an archaeologist uncovering the ancient ruins of Pompeii
    (C) study of classical temples in the south of France
    (D) friendship with George Washington and by his architectural theories

3. The columns and the pediment of Monticello are meant to recall the

    (A) ancient Egyptian pharaohs and their expression of eternity
    (B) Greek gods and their mythological stories
    (C) Roman Republic and its governmental ideals
    (D) Gothic churches and their spirituality

4. Jacques-Louis David's *The Oath of the Horatii* is based on an ancient Roman story, but the painting technique owes a great deal to

    (A) Peter Paul Rubens
    (B) Caravaggio
    (C) Johannes Vermeer
    (D) Jacopo Pontormo

5. William Hogarth's satiric paintings are a reflection of a movement in the eighteenth century called

    (A) the Enlightenment
    (B) Naturalism
    (C) the Industrial Revolution
    (D) the Grand Tour

Short Essay

Attribute this painting to the artist who painted it.

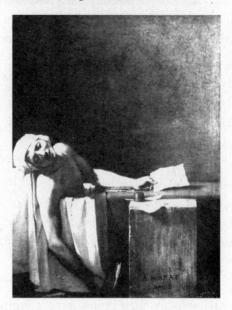

Identify a painting by the same artist in the art history curriculum using the title, artist, date and medium.

Using specific details, justify your attribution by comparing the two works.

How do both works combine the artist's interest in antiquity and contemporary politics?

Answer Key

1. **D**   2. **C**   3. **C**   4. **B**   5. **A**

ANSWERS EXPLAINED

Multiple-Choice

1. **(D)** Rococo paintings can be characterized by their soft, delicate, pastel color schemes.

2. **(C)** Jefferson admired the Roman ruins in the south of France erected during the Roman Republic.

3. **(C)** Jefferson felt that the Roman Republic embodied the spirit of democracy.

4. **(B)** The dark/light contrast called tenebrism is associated with artists like Caravaggio. David's mysteriously darkened background in *The Oath of the Horatii* is indebted to this artist.

5. **(A)** European painting was affected by the Enlightenment. For the first time, artists experienced a new freedom to lampoon political and social conventions in a public way. All the other choices are events that took place in the eighteenth century but don't apply to this question.

Short-Essay Rubric

Question	Points	Key Points in a Good Response
Attribute this painting to the artist who painted it.	1	Jacques-Louis David
Identify a painting by the same artist in the art history curriculum using the title, artist, date, and medium.	1	*The Oath of the Horatii*, by Jacques-Louis David, 1784, oil on canvas
Using specific details, justify your attribution by comparing the two works.	2	Answers could include: ■ Greco-Roman imagery ■ Classical compositions ■ Firm, robust, idealized figure styles ■ Minimum of extraneous detail ■ Tenebrism
How do both works combine the artist's interest in antiquity and contemporary politics?	1	Answers could include: ■ Roman stories are a reflection of contemporary politics. ■ Antique drapery ■ Strong advocate of the French Revolution ■ French Revolution seen as a mythical moment in politics ■ Both works indicate a dedication to patriotic causes.

Romanticism

20

TIME PERIOD: 1789-1848

The French Revolution of 1789 and the European revolts of 1848 form
a neat, although not completely accurate, boundary for Romanticism.

ENDURING UNDERSTANDING: Art is influenced by changes in society. It is affected by economic forces which cause widespread migration, war, and a concentration of population in cities. New countries emerge and social movements gain strength.

Essential Knowledge:

- The late eighteenth century is known as the Enlightenment, a period of scientific advance. It is followed by the revolutionary principles of the Romantic period.
- New philosophies, particularly those by Marx and Darwin, spread throughout the world. These views were supplemented by a new understanding of worldwide cultures.

ENDURING UNDERSTANDING: Artists become more prominent members of society. Art movements come in a rapid succession.

Essential Knowledge:

- Modern movements include Neoclassicism and Romanticism.
- Artists belong to academies and show their work in salons.
- Architecture is characterized by a series of revivals.

ENDURING UNDERSTANDING: Art was seen in a new, often provoking, way by the public.

Essential Knowledge:

- The salons of Paris grow in importance.
- Artists work less in the service of religion, more for corporations.

HISTORICAL BACKGROUND

The revolutionary spirit of casting off oppressors and installing "Liberty, Equality, and Fraternity" created a dynamic for freedom not just in France, but throughout Europe, and in North and South America as well. However, the French Revolution itself, even though well-intentioned, devolved into the chaos of the Reign of Terror and eventually the Napoleonic Wars.

Nonetheless, the philosophical powers that were unleashed by these revolutionary impulses had long-term positive effects on European life, which are embodied in the Romantic spirit.

Romantics espoused social independence, freedom of individual thought, and the ability to express oneself openly. This was manifest not only in the political battles of the day, but also in the societal changes in general education, social welfare, and a newfound expression in the arts. As a reaction against the Enlightenment, the Romantics would argue that you should trust your heart, not your head.

Patronage and Artistic Life

The Romantic artist was a troubled genius, deeply affected by all around him or her—temperamental, critical, and always exhausted. Seeking pleasure in things of greatest refinement, or adventures of audacious daring, the Romantic was a product of the extremes of human endeavor. **Turner**, for example, liked to be tied to the deck of a ship in a storm so that he could bring a greater sense of the **sublime** to his paintings.

Stereotypically, Romantic artists were loners who fought for important causes. **Delacroix** painted a number of great political paintings, and **Goya** understood that human folly exists on the side of the villain and the hero alike.

Romantics enjoyed a state of melancholy, that is, a gloomy, depressed, and pensive mindset that is soberly thoughtful. This can be seen in a series of nineteenth century portraits. Romantics also championed the antihero, a protagonist who does not have the typical characteristics of a hero, often shunning society and rarely speaking, but capable of great heroic deeds.

The greatest artistic invention of the period was the development of photography. Since this was a new art form, there were no academies, no salons, and no schools from which to learn the craft. Even so, the mechanical nature of the camera prejudiced the public against viewing photographs as works of art. Anyone with a camera and a how-to book could open a photo shop. Because of photography's universality, and because there were no preconceived notions about photographers creating great art, marginalized populations, including women, easily entered the field. Some of the most important advances in the history of photography were made by these groups; it was the first instance of equal opportunity in the arts.

REVIVAL ARCHITECTURE

Nineteenth-century architecture is characterized by a revival of nearly every style of the past. Historicism and yearning for past ideals fueled a reliance on the old, the tried, and the familiar.

There was symbolism in this. The Middle Ages represented a time when religion was more devout and sincere, and life was more centered around faith. Modern living, it was felt, was corrupted by the Industrial Revolution. People were so nostalgic for medieval ruins that when there were none handy, they had ruins built so that Romantic souls could ponder the loss of civilization.

Medieval art may have been the favorite theme to revive, but it was by no means the only one. Egyptian, Islamic, and even Baroque architecture was updated and grafted onto structures that had no connection with their original inspiration. Bath houses in England are done in the Islamic style; opera houses in Paris are Baroque; office buildings in the United States are Gothic; a monument to George Washington in Washington, D.C., is an Egyptian obelisk.

The use of iron in architecture, which started in the Neoclassical period, became more important in the Romantic. Architects concerned with reviving past architectural styles like Gothic or Romanesque used ironwork, but hid it under the skin of the building. More adventuresome architects used stone on the exterior, but were unafraid of iron as an exposed structural element on the interior. Progressive architects found the elegance and malleability of ironwork irresistible, especially when combined with walls of glass.

Charles Barry and Augustus Pugin, Palace of Westminster (The Houses of Parliament), 1840–1870, limestone, masonry, and glass, London (Figures 20.1a and 20.1b)

- Competition held in 1835 for a new Houses of Parliament after the old one burned down
- 97 entrants in the contest; 91 in the Perpendicular Gothic, 6 in the Elizabethan style; thought to be native English styles
- Enormous structure of 1,100 rooms, 100 staircases, 2 miles of corridors
- Modern office building cloaked in medieval clothes
- Barry a classical architect, accounts for regularity of plan
- Pugin a Gothic architect, added Gothic architectural touches to the structure
- Profusion of Gothic ornament is greater than would appear in an original Gothic building
- Big Ben is a clock tower, in a sense a village clock for all of England
- **Cross-Cultural Comparisons: Government Centers**
  - Nan Madol (Figures 28.1a, 28.1b)
  - Versailles (Figures 17.3a, 17.3b, 17.3c)
  - Forbidden City (Figures 24.2a, 24.2b, 24.2c, 24.2d)

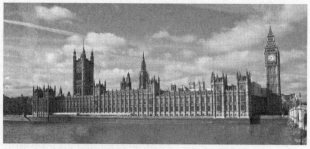

Figure 20.1a: Charles Barry and Augustus Pugin, Palace of Westminster (The Houses of Parliament), 1840–1870, limestone, masonry, and glass, London

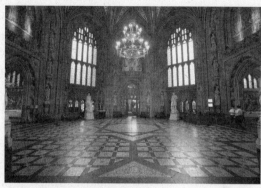

Figure 20.1b: Central lobby of the Houses of Parliament

Central Lobby

- Situated between the House of Commons and the House of Lords
- Meant to be a space where constituents can meet their member of Parliament
- Metal grills on doorways were originally in the House of Commons and marked off the spots where women could be seated to watch Parliament; now they are symbols of the suffrage movement
- Central octagonal space with statues of the Kings and Queens of England and Scotland
- Four large mosaics over each doorway represents the four saints who represent different areas of the UK
  - England is St. George
  - Scotland is St. Andrew
  - Wales is St. David
  - Northern Island is St. Patrick

Westminster Hall

- When the old Houses of Parliament were burned to the ground, this remained as the last vestige of the medieval parliament building
- See Figure 12.5.

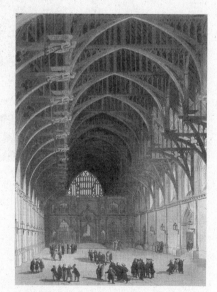

Figure 20.1c: Westminster Hall, 1097–1099; ceiling 1390s, stone and wood, London, England

ROMANTIC PAINTING

Artists were impressed by the **sublime** in art. What the Enlightenment saw as ordered, symmetrical, logical, and scientific—and therefore beautiful—the Romantics viewed with disdain.

Artists wanted to create the fantastic, the unconscious, the haunted, and the insane. Some visited asylums and depicted their residents. Others painted the underside of the subconscious state a hundred years before Freud.

Photography had an enormous impact on painters. Some fled painting, feeling that their efforts could not match the precision and speed of a photograph. Others more wisely saw that pictures could be a great aid in a painter's work, from hiring a model to capturing a landscape. Painters eventually learned that photography was a new art form that was not in competition with the long-standing tradition of painting.

Artists, like everyone else, were caught up in European and American revolutions. The fight for Greek independence was particularly galvanizing for European intellectuals. Political paintings became important, expressing the artist's solidarity with a social movement or a political position. **Delacroix** and **Goya** are among many who create memorable political compositions.

Even landscape painting had a political agenda. No longer content to paint scenes for their physical beauty or artistic arrangement, landscape painters needed to make a contemporary statement. Perhaps the paintings were expressions against the Industrial Revolution, or as in the case of **Cole**, an answer to criticism on how Americans had polluted their land.

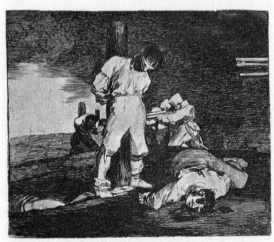

Figure 20.2: Francisco de Goya, *And There's Nothing to Be Done (Y no hai remedio)*, from the *Disasters of War*, 1810–1823, drypoint etching

Francisco de Goya, *And There's Nothing to Be Done (Y no hai remedio)*, from the *Disasters of War*, 1810–1823, drypoint etching (Figure 20.2)

Disasters of War
- Eighty etchings and aquatints
- Published in 1863, thirty-five years after the artist's death
- Art work was critical of the French occupation of Spain and the subsequent Spanish rulers
- Influenced by Spain's continuous warfare
- Original title: "Fatal Consequences of Spain's Bloody War with Bonaparte and Other Emphatic Caprices"
- Explores themes of war, famine, and politics

And There's Nothing to Be Done
- Bitterly ironic and sardonic
- Guns at very close range point toward victims, assumedly Spanish patriots, who will be summarily killed by French soldiers
- Mangled body on the ground
- Are they civilians or soldiers who are being shot?

Jean-Auguste Ingres, *La Grand Odalisque (The Grand Odalisque)*, 1814, oil on canvas, Louvre, Paris (Figure 20.3)

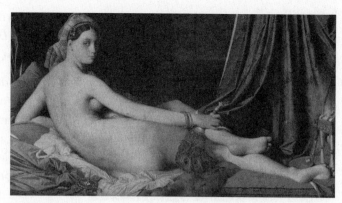

Figure 20.3: Jean-Auguste Ingres, *La Grand Odalisque (The Grand Odalisque)*, 1814, oil on canvas, Louvre, Paris

- Raphael-like face
- Turkish elements: incense burner, peacock fan, tapestrylike turban, hashish pipe, hence the name "odalisque"
- Inconsistent arrangement of limbs: rubbery arm, elongated back, placement of leg, one arm is longer than the other
- Heavily influenced by Italian Mannerism in the exaggerated body forms
- A further development of the female nude form
- **Cross-Cultural Comparisons: Female Figure**
  - Tlatilco Female Figure (Figure 1.5)
  - Neshat, *Rebellious Silence* (Figure 29.14)
  - Pwo Mask (Figure 27.8)

Eugène Delacroix, *Liberty Leading the People*, 1830, oil on canvas, Louvre, Paris (Figure 20.4)

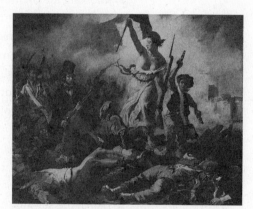

Figure 20.4: Eugène Delacroix, *Liberty Leading the People*, 1830, oil on canvas, Louvre, Paris

- July Revolution of 1830; Liberty with French tricolor marches over the barricades to overthrow government soldiers
- Red/white/blue echo throughout the painting
- Strong pyramidical structure
- Child with pistols symbolizes the role of students in the revolt; middle class by man in top hat and carrying rifle; lower class represented by man at extreme left with sword in hand and pistol in belt
- Liberty wears a red Phrygian cap, worn in the ancient world by freed slaves
- Notre Dame Cathedral seen through the smoke on the far right; French tricolor raised on its tower
- The Parisian landmark of Notre Dame is mixed with the true historical event and the allegorical and symbolic figures
- Memorializes the overthrow of the French government in favor of the "Citizen King" Louis-Philippe
- Acquired by the French state in 1831, but not exhibited publicly for 25 years because of its subversive message
- **Cross-Cultural Comparisons: National Symbols**
  - Menkaura and His Queen (Figure 3.7)
  - *Chairman Mao En Route to Anyuan* (Figure 24.7)
  - Golden Stool (Figure 27.4)

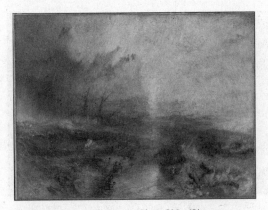

Figure 20.5: Joseph Turner, *Slave Ship (Slavers Throwing Overboard the Dead and Dying, Typhoon Coming On)*, 1840, oil on canvas, Museum of Fine Arts Boston

Joseph Turner, *Slave Ship (Slavers Throwing Overboard the Dead and Dying, Typhoon Coming On)*, 1840, oil on canvas, Museum of Fine Arts, Boston (Figure 20.5)

- Exhibited at the Royal Academy in 1840, with an excerpt from Turner's own poem called "The Fallacies of Hope"

    "Aloft all hands, strike the top-masts and belay;
    Yon angry setting sun and fierce-edged clouds
    Declare the Typhon's coming.
    Before it sweeps your decks, throw overboard
    The dead and dying - ne'er heed their chains
    Hope, Hope, fallacious Hope!
    Where is thy market now?"

- Based on the true story of an event in 1781 in which a slave ship, *The Zong*, sailed for the Americas full of slaves
- The slaves were insured against accidental drowning but not against sickness; a policy instituted to force captains to treat slaves humanely
- Knowing that he would not collect insurance money on sick and dying slaves, the captain cast them overboard
- Turner's painting inspired by account of the scandal published in a book by Thomas Clarkson which had been reprinted in 1839
- England freed the slaves in 1833 by an act of Parliament; however, there were exceptions which were not addressed until 1843
- Emotional use of color
- Rapid brushwork
- Recognizable forms—the ship, the hands, the chains—are reduced in size and pale in comparison to the mightiness of the turbulent seascape
- Bloody sunset acts as a symbol of the scene taking place
- Use of the sublime enhances dramatic impact

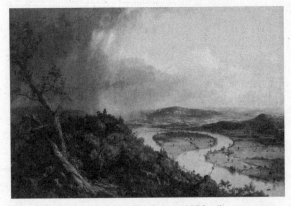

Figure 20.6: Thomas Cole, *The Oxbow*, 1836, oil on canvas, Metropolitan Museum of Art, New York

Thomas Cole, *The Oxbow*, 1836, oil on canvas, Metropolitan Museum of Art, New York (Figure 20.6)

- Founder of the Hudson River School
- Actual view in Massachusetts
- Cole's division of landscape into two clearly contrasting areas: the Romantic on the left and the Classical landscape on the right
- Cole's self-portrait in the foreground amid a dense forest that is impenetrably thick, with broken trees, and a wild landscape with storms; the sublime
- On the right, man's touch is seen in light, cultivated fields, boats drifting down the river
- Painted as reply to a British book that alleged that Americans had destroyed a wilderness with industry
- Painted for an exhibit and the National Academy of Design, accounts for the unusually large size

- **Cross-Cultural Comparisons: Nature**
  - Korin, *White and Red Plum Blossoms* (Figures 25.4a, 25.4b)
  - Su-nam, *Summer Trees* (Figure 29.6)
  - Ryoan-ji (Figures 25.2a, 25.2b, 25.2c)

THE DEVELOPMENT OF PHOTOGRAPHY

Experiments in photography go back to the seventeenth century, when artists used a device called a **camera obscura** (Figure 20.7) to focus images in a box so that artists could render accurate copies of the scene before them. Gradually, photosensitive paper was introduced that could replicate the silhouette of an object when exposed to light. These objects were called **photograms**, which yielded a primitive type of photography that captured outlines of objects and little else.

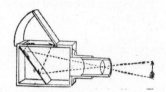

Figure 20.7: Camera obscura

Modern photography was invented in two different places at the same time: France and England. The French version, called the **daguerreotype** after its inventor Louis Daguerre, was a single image that is characterized by a sharp focus and great clarity of detail. Englishman William Talbot invented the **calotype**, which, though at first inferior in quality to the French version, was less costly to make and had an accompanying negative that could generate an unlimited number of copies from the original. Both men showed their inventions to scientific conventions in January 1839.

Photography spread quickly, and technological advances followed almost as fast. For example, shutter speeds were made faster so that sitters could pose for pictures without blurring, and the cameras themselves became increasingly portable and user-friendly. The advantages to photography were obvious to everyone: It went everywhere a person could go, capturing and illustrating everything from the exotic to the commonplace.

Louis Daguerre, *Still Life in Studio*, 1837, daguerreotype, French Photographic Society, Paris (Figure 20.8)

- Still life inspired by painted still lifes, like vanitas paintings
- Variety of textures: fabric, wicker, plaster, framed print, metal, wood, and so on
- New art form inspired by older art forms
- Daguerreotypes have a shiny surface with great detail
- **Cross-Cultural Comparisons: Still Lifes**
  - Ruysch, *Fruits and Insects* (Figure 17.11)
  - Matisse, *Goldfish* (Figure 22.1)

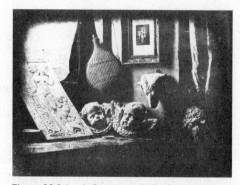

Figure 20.8: Louis Daguerre, *Still Life in Studio*, 1837, daguerreotype, French Photographic Society, Paris

VOCABULARY

Calotype: a type of early photograph, developed by William H. F. Talbot that is characterized by its grainy quality. A calotype is considered the forefather of all photography because it produces both a positive and a negative image

Camera obscura: (Latin, meaning "dark room") a box with a lens which captures light and casts an image on the opposite side (Figure 20.7)

Caprice: usually a work of art that is an architectural fantasy; more broadly any work that has a fantasy element (Figure 20.2)

Daguerreotype: a type of early photograph, developed by Louis Daguerre that is characterized by a shiny surface, meticulous finish, and clarity of detail. Daguerreotypes are unique photographs; they have no negative (Figure 20.8)

Odalisque: a woman slave in a harem (Figure 20.3)

Photogram: an image made by placing objects on photosensitive paper and exposing them to light to produce a silhouette

School: a group of artists who share the same philosophy, work around the same time, but not necessarily together

The sublime: any cathartic experience from the catastrophic to the intellectual that causes the viewer to marvel in awe, wonder, and passion (Figure 20.5)

SUMMARY

A spirited cultural movement called Romanticism inspired artists to move beyond former boundaries and express themselves as individuals. Romantic artists introduce new subjects such as grand political canvases, the world of the unconscious, and the awesome grandeur of nature.

Romantics were influenced by the invention of photography, which was used by some artists as a tool for preserving such things as a model's pose or a mountain landscape. Photography's immediacy and realistic impact made it a sensation from its inception, causing the art form to spread quickly among all classes of people.

Early nineteenth-century architects sought to revive former artistic styles and graft them onto modern buildings. It is common to see an office building, like the Houses of Parliament, wrapped in Gothic clothes. This yearning for the past is a reaction against the mechanization of the Industrial Revolution and a way of life that seemed to have permanently passed from the scene.

PRACTICE EXERCISES

Multiple-Choice

1. *The Grand Odalisque* by Jean-Auguste-Dominique Ingres from 1814 was inspired by all of the following EXCEPT

   (A) an exoticism derived from depicting a Middle Eastern setting
   (B) the facial formulas used by Raphael
   (C) a figure style reminiscent of Italian Mannerist
   (D) a brushstroke used in the Rococo

2. *Liberty Leading the People* by Eugène Delacroix depicts in allegorical terms a moment from the

   (A) French Revolution of 1789
   (B) American Revolution of 1776
   (C) Parisian uprising of 1830
   (D) Franco-Prussian War of 1870

3. *The Slave Ship* by Joseph W.M. Turner is based on

   (A)   the novels of Herman Melville
   (B)   the sinking of the French frigate *The Medusa*
   (C)   events related to the eighteenth century ship called *The Zong*
   (D)   the American Civil War and the passage of the Emancipation Proclamation

4. Thomas Cole's paintings have historical allusion to contemporary issues concerning

   (A)   slavery in the American South
   (B)   Manifest Destiny
   (C)   the building of the railroads and their effect on American culture
   (D)   the treatment of American Indians as anthropological specimens

5. Joseph Turner's theories about landscape painting are most closely akin to those of

   (A)   Ogata Korin
   (B)   Thomas Cole
   (C)   Claude Monet
   (D)   Hokusai

Short Essay

Both of these buildings are in the same location in London, England. The building on the left is the central lobby of the Houses of Parliament. Identify the building on the right.

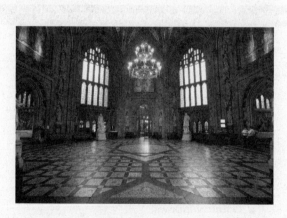 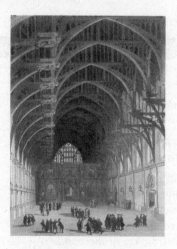

What period is the building on the right from?

What event caused the construction of the building on the left?

Using specific examples, analyze how the building on the right influenced the construction of the building on the left.

1. **D**   2. **C**   3. **C**   4. **B**   5. **D**

ANSWERS EXPLAINED

Multiple-Choice

1. **(D)** Ingres was influenced by a great many sources, but he rejected the Rococo as frivolous.

2. **(C)** *Liberty Leading the People* depicts the Parisian uprising of 1830, which installed Louis-Philippe as "Citizen King" of France.

3. **(C)** *The Slave Ship* depicts the journey of an actual ship, *The Zong*, which traveled to the New World laden with slaves. The slaves were insured against accidental drowning, but they weren't insured against sickness. Knowing that he would not collect insurance money on sick and dying slaves, the captain cast them overboard.

4. **(B)** The notion of Manifest Destiny, that it was in the United States' interests to expand across the North American continent, is expressed in many of Cole's works.

5. **(D)** The routine violence seen in Turner's landscapes can be equated to Hokusai's *The Great Wave*.

Short-Essay Rubric

Question	Points	Key Points in a Good Response
Identify the building on the right.	1	Westminster Hall, 1097–1099; ceiling 1390s, stone and wood
What period is the building on the right from?	1	Perpendicular Gothic
What event caused the construction of the building on the left?	1	A fire caused the old Houses of Parliament to burn to the ground.
Using specific examples, analyze how the building on the right influenced the construction of the building on the left.	2	Answers could include: ■ Both done in Perpendicular Gothic ■ Elaborate ceilings using detailed arches ■ Gothic windows ■ Pointed arches ■ Pronounced vertical bays ■ Both contain (or contained) statues of English royalty

Late Ninteenth-Century Art

21

TIME PERIOD: 1848–1900	

Movement	Dates
Realism	1848–1860s
Impressionism	1872–1880s
Post-Impressionism	1880s–1890s
Symbolism	1890s
Art Nouveau	1890s–1914

ENDURING UNDERSTANDING: Art is influenced by changes in society. It is affected by economic forces which cause widespread migration, war, and a concentration of population in cities. New countries emerge and social movements gain strength.

Essential Knowledge:

■ New philosophies, particularly those by Freud and Einstein, spread throughout the world. These views were supplemented by a new understanding of worldwide cultures.

ENDURING UNDERSTANDING: Artists become more prominent members of society. Art movements come in a rapid succession.

Essential Knowledge:

■ Modern movements include Realism, Impressionism, and Post-Impressionism.
■ Artists joined groups and worked for galleries.
■ Artists used new media like photography and lithography.
■ Architects use new technology in construction.

ENDURING UNDERSTANDING: Art was seen in a new, often provoking, way by the public.

Essential Knowledge:

■ Commercial galleries become important. Museums open and display art. Art sells to an ever widening market.
■ Artists work for private and public institutions to a sometimes critical public.

HISTORICAL BACKGROUND

The year 1848 was busy. Europe was shaken by revolutions in Sicily, Venice, Germany, Austria, and Lombardy—each challenging the old order and seeking to replace aristocracies with democracies. In France, Louis-Philippe, the great victor of the Revolution of 1830 and self-styled "Citizen King," faced internal pressure and deposed himself. He was soon replaced by Napoleon III, who led France down a path of belligerency culminating in the Franco-Prussian War of 1870. When the dust cleared, the Germans were masters of continental Europe, but by that time everyone had had enough of turmoil, and settled down for a generation of peace.

Social reformers were influenced by a concept called **positivism** promulgated by Auguste Comte (1798–1857). This theory allowed that all knowledge must come from proven ideas based on science or scientific theory. Comte said that only tested concepts can be accepted as truths. Key nineteenth-century thinkers like Charles Darwin (1809–1882) and Karl Marx (1818–1883) added to the spirit of positivism by exploring theories about human evolution and social equality. These efforts shook traditional thinking and created a clamor in intellectual circles. New inventions such as telephones, motion pictures, bicycles, and automobiles shrank the world by opening communication to a wider audience.

Artists understood these powerful changes by exchanging traditional beliefs for the "**avant-garde**," a word coined at this time. The academies, so carefully set up in the eighteenth century, were abandoned in the late nineteenth century. Artists used the past for inspiration, but rejected traditional subject matter. Gone are religious subjects, aristocratic portraits, history paintings, and scenes from the great myths of Greece and Rome. Instead the spirit of **modernism** prevailed, artists chose to represent peasant scenes, landscapes, and still lifes. Systematic and scientific archaeology began during this period as well, with excavations in Greece, Turkey, and Egypt.

Patronage and Artistic Life

Even though most artists wanted to exhibit at the Salon of Paris, many found the conservative nature of the jury to be stifling, and began to look elsewhere for recognition. Artists whose works were rejected by the Salon, such as **Courbet** or **Manet**, set up oppositional showcases, achieving fame by being antiestablishment. The Impressionist exhibitions of the 1870s and 1880s fall into this category.

One of the greatest changes in the marketing of art came about with the emergence of the art gallery. Here was a more comfortable viewing experience than the Salon: No great crowds, no idly curious—just the art lover with a dealer in tastefully appointed surroundings. Galleries featured carefully selected works of art from a limited number of artists, and were not the artistic impluvia that the Salon had become.

Paul Cézanne cultivated the persona of the struggling and misunderstood artist. He fought the conventional aspirations of his family, escaped to a bohemian lifestyle, and worked for years without success or recognition. The more he suffered, and the cruder he grew, the more people were attracted to him and found his artwork intriguing. He was one of the first to exploit the stereotype of the artist as rebel. Other artists follow suit: Gauguin escaped to Tahiti, van Gogh to the south of France.

European artists were greatly influenced by an influx of Japanese art, particularly their highly sophisticated prints of genre scenes or landscapes. These broke European conventional methods of representation, but were still sophisticated and elegant. Japanese art relies on a different sense of depth, enhancing a flatness that dominates the background. Subjects appear at odd angles or on a tilt. This interest in all things Japanese was called **Japonisme**.

Painters felt that the artificial atmosphere of the studio inhibited artistic expression. In a movement that characterizes Impressionism, called **plein-air**, artists moved their studio outdoors seeking to capture the effects of atmosphere and light on a given subject.

A new creative outlet for printmakers was the invention of **lithography** in 1798. Great Romantic artists such as Delacroix and Goya saw the medium's potential and made effective prints. By the late nineteenth century, those politically inclined, such as **Daumier**, used the lithography to critique society's ills. Others, like **Toulouse-Lautrec**, used the medium to mass-produce posters of the latest Parisian shows.

Characteristics of Realism

Courbet's aphorism "Show me an angel, and I'll paint one" sums up the Realist philosophy. Inspired by the **positivism** movement, Realist painters believe in painting things that one could experience with the five senses, which often translated into painting the lower classes in their environment. Usually peasants are depicted with reverence, their daily lives touched with a basic honesty and sincerity thought to be missing among the middle and upper classes. They are shown at one with the earth and the landscape; brown and ochre are the dominant hues.

Gustave Courbet, *The Stone Breakers*, 1849, oil on canvas, formerly in Gemäldgalerie, Dresden, destroyed in World War II (Figure 21.1)

- Submitted to the Salon of 1850–1851
- Breaking stones down to rubble to be used for paving
- Poverty emphasized
- Figures were born poor, will remain poor their whole lives
- Reaction to labor unrest of 1848: demanding better working conditions
- Large size of painting usually reserved for grand historical paintings; elevating the commonplace into the realm of legend and history

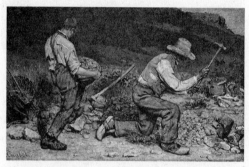

Figure 21.1: Gustave Courbet, *The Stone Breakers*, 1849, oil on canvas, formerly in Gemäldgalerie, Dresden, destroyed in World War II

- Courbet's words: "I stopped to consider two men breaking stones on the highway. It's rare to meet the most complete expression of poverty, so an idea of a picture came to me on the spot. I made an appointment with them at my studio for the next day…. On the one side is an old man, seventy….On the other side is a young fellow…in his filthy tattered shirt. Alas, in labor such as this, one's life begins that way, and it ends the same way."
- **Cross-Cultural Comparisons: Genre Scenes**
  - Vermeer, *Woman Holding a Balance* (Figure 17.10)
  - Breughel, *Hunters in the Snow* (Figure 14.6)
  - Cassatt, *The Coiffure* (Figure 21.7)

Honoré Daumier, *Nadar Raising Photography to the Height of Art*, 1862, lithograph, Brooklyn Museum, Brooklyn, New York (Figure 21.2)

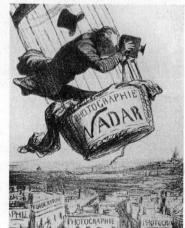

- Nadar was famous for taking aerial photos of Paris beginning in 1858
- Presents Nadar as a quacky photographer; in his excitement to get a daring shot he almost falls out of his balloon and loses his hat
- Every building has the word "*photographie*" on it
- Mocks the claims that photography can be a "high art"; irony implied in title
- Done after a court decision in 1862 that determined that photographs could be considered works of art

Figure 21.2: Honoré Daumier, *Nadar Raising Photography to the Height of Art*, 1862, lithograph, Brooklyn Museum, Brooklyn, New York

- Originally appeared in a journal: *Le Boulevard*
- Intrusive photography: Nadar's balloon reused in the 1870 Siege of Paris
- Foreshadows modern surveillance photographs
- **Cross-Cultural Comparisons: Humor in Art**
  - Hogarth, *The Tête à Tête* (Figure 19.3)
  - Fragonard, *The Swing* (Figure 19.1)
  - Duchamp, *Fountain* (Figure 22.9)

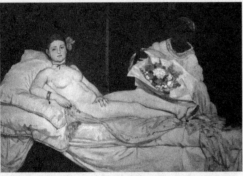

Figure 21.3: Édouard Manet, *Olympia*, 1863, oil on canvas, Musée d'Orsay, Paris

Édouard Manet, *Olympia*, 1863, oil on canvas, Musée d'Orsay, Paris (Figure 21.3)

- Created a scandal at the Salon of 1865
- Traditional subject of a reclining nude; inspired by Titian's *Venus of Urbino* (Figure 16.4)
- Figure is cold and uninviting, no mystery, no joy
- Maid delivers flowers from an admirer
- Olympia is a common name for prostitutes of the time
- Olympia's frank, direct, uncaring, and unnerving look startled viewers
- Simplified modeling; active brushwork

- Stark contrast of colors
- A mistress was common to upper class Parisian men
- **Cross-Cultural Comparisons: Female Form**
  - Ingres, *The Grand Odalisque* (Figure 20.3)
  - Titian, *Venus of Urbino* (Figure 16.4)
  - DeKooning, *Woman I* (Figure 22.21)

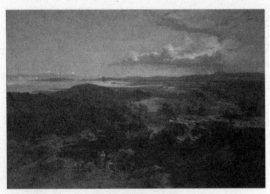

Figure 21.4: José Maria Velasco, *The Valley of Mexico from the Hillside of Santa Isabel*, 1882, oil on canvas, National Art Museum, Mexico City

José Maria Velasco, *The Valley of Mexico from the Hillside of Santa Isabel*, 1882, oil on canvas, National Art Museum, Mexico City (Figure 21.4)

- Primarily an academic landscape painter
- Specialized in broad panoramas of the Valley of Mexico
- Keen observer of nature: rocks, foliage, clouds, waterfalls
- Rejected realist landscapes of Courbet; romantic landscapes of Turner
- Settled in Villa Guadalupe with an overview of the Valley of Mexico
- Dramatic perspective; small human figures
- Glorifies Mexican countryside

- **Cross-Cultural Comparisons: Landscape**
  - Cole, *The Oxbow* (Figure 20.6)
  - Korin, *White and Red Plum Blossoms* (Figures 25.4a, 25.4b)
  - Su-nam, *Summer Trees* (Figure 29.6)

Eadweard Muybridge, *The Horse in Motion*, 1878, photograph (Figure 21.5)

- Photography now advanced enough that it can capture moments the human eye cannot
- Cameras snap photos at evenly spaced points along a track, giving the effect of things happening in sequence
- These motion studies bridge the gap between still photography and movies
- Used a device called a zoopraxiscope
- Great influence on painters
- **Cross-Cultural Comparisons: Multiple Images**
  - Terra-Cotta Warriors (Figures 24.8a, 24.8b)
  - Warhol, *Marilyn Diptych* (Figure 22.23)
  - Christo and Jeanne Claude, *The Gates* (Figures 29.3a, 29.3b)

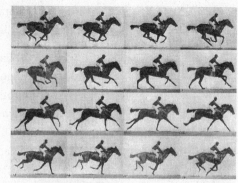

Figure 21.5: Eadweard Muybridge, *The Horse in Motion*, 1878, photograph

Impressionism

Impressionism is a true modernist movement symbolized by the **avant-garde** artists who spearheaded it. Relying on the transient, the quick and the fleeting, Impressionist brushstrokes seek to capture the dappling effects of light across a given surface. The knowledge that shadows contain color, that times of day and seasons of the year affect the appearance of objects—these are the basic tenets of Impressionism. Often working in **plein-air**, Impressionists use a spectacular color range, varying from subtle harmonies to stark contrasts of brilliant hues.

Impressionists concentrate on landscape and still-life painting, imbuing them with an urban viewpoint, even when depicting a country scene. Some make the human figure in movement a specialty, others, like **Monet**, eventually abandon figure painting altogether.

The influence of Japanese art cannot be underestimated. Artists like **Cassatt** were struck by the freedom that Japanese artists used to show figures from the back, or solid blocks of color without gradations of hues. Others signed their names in a Japanese anagram and imitated the flatness and off-center compositional qualities Japanese prints typically have.

Impressionism originally prided itself on being both antiacademic and antibourgeois; ironically, today it is the hallmark of bourgeois taste.

Claude Monet, *The Saint-Lazare Station*, 1877, oil on canvas, Musée d'Orsay, Paris (Figure 21.6)

- Exhibited at the Impressionist exhibition of 1877
- One of a series depicting this train station
- Monet famous for painting series of paintings on the same subject at different times of day and different days of the year
- Originally meant to be hung together for effect: Haystacks were his first group to hang this way
- Effects of steam, light, and color; not really about the machines or travelers
- Subtle gradations of light on the surface
- Forms dissolve and dematerialize; color overwhelms the forms

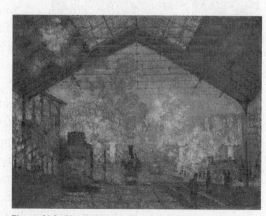

Figure 21.6: Claude Monet, *The Saint-Lazare Station*, 1877, oil on canvas, Musée d'Orsay, Paris

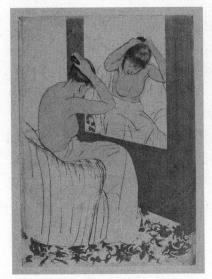

Figure 21.7: Mary Cassatt, *The Coiffure*, 1890–1891, drypoint and aquatint, National Gallery of Art, Washington

Mary Cassatt, *The Coiffure*, 1890–1891, drypoint and aquatint, National Gallery of Art, Washington (Figure 21.7)

- Casssatt's world is filled with women; women as independent and not needing men to complete themselves; women who enjoy company of other women
- No posing or acting; figures possess a natural charm
- Decorative charm influenced by Japanese art
- Japanese hair style; Japanese point-of-view: figure seen from the back
- Tenderness foreign to other Impressionists
- Part of a series of ten prints exhibited together
- Contrasting sensuous curves of female figure with straight lines of the furniture and wall
- Pastel color scheme
- **Cross-Cultural Comparisons: Domestic Scenes**
  - Vermeer, *Woman with a Balance* (Figure 17.10)
  - Velázquez, *Las Meninas* (Figure 17.7)
  - *Stele of Hegeso* (Figure 4.7)

Post-Impressionism

While the Impressionists stressed light, shading, and color, the Post-Impressionists—that is, those painters of the next generation—moved beyond these ideals to combine them with an analysis of the structure of a given subject. **Paul Cézanne**, the quintessential Post-Impressionist, said that he wished to "make Impressionism something solid and durable, like the art of the museums." It is common for Post-Impressionists to move toward abstraction in their work, and yet seemingly paradoxically retaining solid forms, exploring underlying structure, and preserving traditional elements such as perspective.

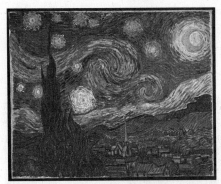

Figure 21.8: Vincent van Gogh, *The Starry Night*, 1889, oil on canvas, Museum of Modern Art, New York

Vincent van Gogh, *The Starry Night*, 1889, oil on canvas, Museum of Modern Art, New York (Figure 21.8)

- Thick short brushstrokes
- Mountains in the distance that Van Gogh could see at his hospital room in St.-Rémy, steepness exaggerated
- Composite landscape: Dutch church, cresent moon, Mediterranean cypress tree
- At one with the forces of nature
- Parts of the canvas can be seen through the brushwork; artist need not fill in every space of the composition
- Strong left-to-right wavelike impulse in the work, broken only by tree and church steeple
- Tree looks like green flames reaching into the sky exploding with stars over a placid village; cypress tree a traditional symbol of death and eternal life
- **Cross-Cultural Comparisons: Landscape**
  - Kngwarreye, *Earth's Creation* (Figure 29.13)
  - Fan Kuan, *Travelers among Mountains and Streams* (Figure 24.5)
  - Cole, *The Oxbow* (Figure 20.6)

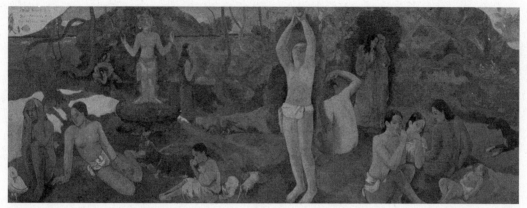

Figure 21.9: Paul Gauguin, *Where Do We Come From? What Are We? Where Are We Going?*, 1897–1898, oil on canvas, Museum of Fine Arts, Boston

Paul Gauguin, *Where Do We Come From? What Are We? Where Are We Going?*, 1897–1898, oil on canvas, Museum of Fine Arts, Boston (Figure 21.9)

- Painted during his second stay in Tahiti between 1895–1901
- Suffered from poor health and poverty; obsessed by thoughts of death
- He learned of the death of daughter, Aline, in April 1897; was deeply shaken; determined to commit suicide and have this painting be his artistic last will and testament
- Story of life, read right to left
- Right: birth, infant and three adults
- Center: mid-life; picking of the fruit of the world
- Left: death (a figure derived from a Peruvian mummy exhibited in Paris, cf. *The Scream*)
- Blue Idol represents "The Beyond"
- Figures in foreground represent Tahiti and an Eden-like paradise; background figures are anguished darkened figures
- A rejection of Greco–Roman influence
- Many non-traditional influences:
  - Egyptian figures used for inspiration
  - Japanese prints in the solid fields of color and unusual angles
  - Tahitian imagery in the Polynesian idol
- Gauguin thought of the painting as a summation of his artistic and personal expression
- **Cross-Cultural Comparisons: European Encounters with the World**
  - Frontispiece of the Codex Mendoza (Figure 18.1)
  - Bandolier Bag (Figure 26.11)
  - Rodriguez, *Spanish and Indian Produce a Mestizo* (Figure 18.5)

Paul Cézanne, *Mont Saint-Victoire* (Figure 21.10)
1902–1904, oil on canvas, Philadelphia Museum of Art, Philadelphia

- One of eleven canvases of this view, series dominates Cézanne's mature period
- Had contempt for flat painting, wanted rounded and firm objects, but ones that were geometric constructions made from splashes of undiluted color

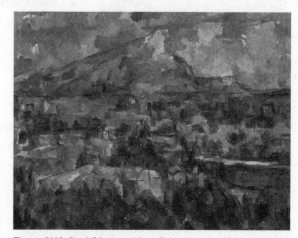

Figure 21.10: Paul Cézanne, *Mont Saint-Victoire*, 1902–1904, oil on canvas, Philadelphia Museum of Art, Philadelphia

- Used perspective through juxtaposing forward warm colors with receding cool colors
- Landscape rarely contains humans
- Not the countryside of Impressionism, more interested in geometric forms rather than dappled effects of light
- Not a momentary glimpse of atmosphere as in the Impressionists, but a solid and firmly constructed mountain and foreground
- Landscape seen from an elevation
- Invited to look at space, but not enter
- **Cross-Cultural Comparisons: Interpretations of the Natural World**
  - Su-nam, *Summer Trees* (Figure 29.6)
  - Hokusai, *Under the Wave off Kanagawa,* also known as the "Great Wave" (Figure 25.5)
  - Silver and gold maize cobs, Inka (Figure 26.7)

Symbolism

As a reaction against the literal world of Realism, Symbolist artists felt that the unseen forces of life, the things that are deeply felt rather than merely seen, were the guiding influences in painting. Symbolists embraced a mystical philosophy in which the dreams and inner experiences of an artist's life became the source of inspiration. Hence, Symbolists vary greatly in their painting styles from the very flat primitive quality of a work by **Rousseau** to the expressionistic swirls of **Munch's** art.

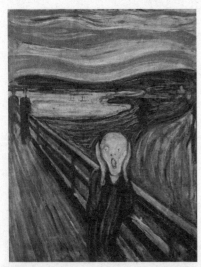

Figure 21.11: Edvard Munch, *The Scream*, 1893, tempera and pastel on cardboard, National Gallery, Oslo

Edvard Munch, *The Scream*, 1893, tempera and pastel on cardboard, National Gallery, Oslo (Figure 21.11)

- Figure walking along a wharf, boats are at sea in the distance
- Long thick brushstrokes swirl around composition
- Figure cries out in a horrifying scream, the landscape echoes his emotions
- Said to have been inspired by an exhibit of a Peruvian mummy in Paris
- Discordant colors symbolize anguish
- Emaciated twisting stick figure with skull-like head
- Prefigures Expressionist art
- Painted as part of a series called *The Frieze of Life*
- Art Nouveau swirling patterns
- **Cross-Cultural Comparisons: Individual vs. Society**
  - *Chairman Mao En Route to Anyuan* (Figure 24.7)
  - Neshat, *Rebellious Silence* (Figure 29.14)
  - Salcedo, *Shibboleth* (Figure 29.26)

Art Nouveau

Art Nouveau developed in a few artistic centers in Europe—Brussels, Barcelona, Paris, and Vienna—and lasted from about 1890 to the outbreak of World War I in 1914. Art Nouveau seeks to eliminate the separation among various artistic media and combine them into one unified experience. Thus, an Art Nouveau building was designed, furnished, and decorated by the same artist or artistic team as an integrated whole.

Stylistically, Art Nouveau relies on vegetal and floral patterns, complexity of design, and undulating surfaces. Straight lines are assiduously avoided; the accent is on the curvilinear.

Designers particularly enjoy using elaborately conceived wrought iron-work for balconies, fences, railings, and structural elements.

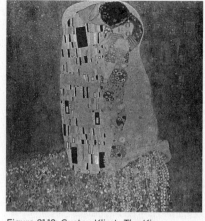

Figure 21.12: Gustav Klimt, *The Kiss*, 1907–1908, oil on canvas, Austrian Gallery, Vienna

Gustav Klimt, *The Kiss*, 1907–1908, oil on canvas, Austrian Gallery, Vienna (Figure 21.12)

- Little of the human form is actually seen: two heads, four hands, two feet
- The bodies are suggested under a sea of richly designed patterning
- Male figure has large rectangular boxes; female figure has circular forms
- Suggests all-consuming love; passion; eroticism
- Spaced in an indeterminate location against a flattened background
- Gold leaf reminiscent of Byzantine mosaics
- **Cross-Cultural Comparisons: Couples**
  - *Akhenaton, Nefertiti, and Three Daughters* (Figure 3.10)
  - Sarcophagus of the Spouses (Figure 5.4)
  - van Eyck, *Arnolfini Portrait* (Figure 14.2)

Late Nineteenth-Century Architecture

The movement toward skeletal architecture increased in the late nineteenth century. Architects and engineers worked in the direction of a curtain wall, that is, a building that is held up by an interior framework, called a **skeleton**, the exterior wall being a mere curtain made of glass or steel that keeps out the weather.

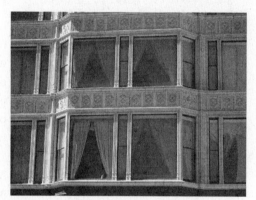

Figure 21.13: Chicago windows on Daniel Burnham's Reliance Building, 1890–1894, Chicago

The emphasis is on the vertical. Land values soar in modern cities, and architects respond by building up. Buildings emphasized their verticality by placing tall pilasters and setting back windows behind them. Still, architects conceived their buildings as works of art, and covered them in traditional terra-cotta or ironwork.

During this period, the greatest advances in architecture were made by the Chicago School, formed shortly after the Great Fire burned much of the city to the ground in 1871. This disaster exposed not only the faults of building downtown structures out of wood, but also demonstrated the weaknesses of iron, which melts and bends under high temperatures. What survived quite nicely is building ceramic, especially when steel or iron is wrapped in terra-cotta casings. This became the mainstay of Chicago buildings built in the late nineteenth century, such as **Carson Pirie Scott** (Figure 21.14). These buildings demanded open and wide window spaces for light and air, as well as allowing passersby to admire window displays. Thus, the Chicago window was developed with a central immobile windowpane flanked by two smaller double-hung windows that opened for ventilation (Figure 21.13).

The single most important development in the history of early modern architecture is the invention of the elevator by Elisha Otis. This made buildings of indefinite height a reality.

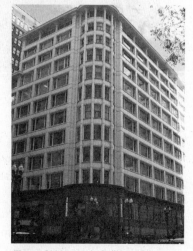

Figure 21.14a: Louis Sullivan, Carson Pirie Scott, 1899–1904, iron, steel, glass, and terra-cotta, Chicago

Louis Sullivan, Carson Pirie Scott, 1899–1904, iron, steel, glass, and terra-cotta, Chicago (Figures 21.14a, 21.14b, and 21.14c)

- Horizontal emphasis symbolizes continuous flow of floor space
- Maximum window areas to admit light, also to display store wares

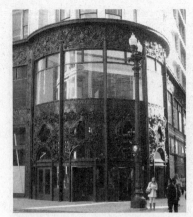

Figure 21.14b: Louis Sullivan, Carson Pirie Scott, detail of main entrance

- Nonsupportive role of exterior
- Cast iron decorative elements transformed the store into a beautiful place to buy beautiful things
- Influence of Art Nouveau in decorative touches
- Sullivan motto: "Form follows function"
- Exterior coated in decorative terra-cotta tiles; original interior ornament elaborately arranged around lobby areas, hallways, elevator
- Some historical touches in the round entrance arches and the heavy cornice at the top of the building
- **Cross-Cultural Comparisons: City Planning**
  - Gehry, Guggenheim Bilbao (Figures 29.1a, 29.1b)
  - Trajan Market (Figure 6.10c)
  - Mies van der Rohe, Seagram Building (Figure 22.18)

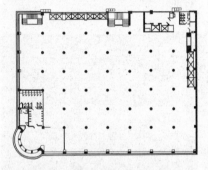

Figure 21.14c: Louis Sullivan, Carson Pirie Scott, plan

Late Nineteenth-Century Sculpture

Late nineteenth-century sculpture, symbolized by **Rodin**, visibly represented the imprint of the artist's hand on a given work. Most works were hand molded first in clay, and then later cast in bronze or cut in marble, usually by a workshop. The sculptor then put finishing touches on a work he or she conceived, but never executed. The physical imprint of the hand is analogous to the visible brushstroke in Impressionist painting.

Auguste Rodin, *The Burghers of Calais*, 1884–1895, bronze, Metropolitan Museum of Art, New York (Figure 21.15)

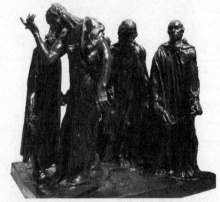

Figure 21.15: Auguste Rodin, *The Burghers of Calais*, 1884–1895, bronze, Metropolitan Museum of Art, New York

- Six burghers offer their lives to the English king in return for saving their besieged city during the Hundred Years' War
- English king insisted burghers wear sackcloths and carry the key to the city
- Parallels between Paris besieged during the Franco-Prussian War of 1870 and Calais besieged by the English in 1347
- Figures sculpted individually, then arranged as the artist thought best
- Figures suffer from privation, are weak and emaciated
- Each figure has a different emotion: some fearful, resigned, or forlorn
- Central figure is Eustache de Saint-Pierre, who has large swollen hands and a noose around his neck, ready for his execution
- Details reduced to emphasize overall impression
- Meant to be placed at ground level so that people could see it close up
- Rejected by town council of Calais as being inglorious; they wanted a single allegorical figure
- **Cross-Cultural Comparisons: Public Sculpture**
  - Christo and Jeanne Claude, *The Gates* (Figures 29.3a, 29.3b)
  - *Queen Hatshepsut with Offering Jars* (Figure 3.9b)
  - Bamiyan Buddha (Figure 23.2a and 23.2b)

VOCABULARY

Aquatint: a kind of print that achieves a watercolor effect by using acids that dissolve onto a copper plate

Avant-garde: an innovative group of artists who generally reject traditional approaches in favor of a more experimental technique

Caricature: a drawing that uses distortion or exaggeration of someone's physical features or apparel in order to make that person look foolish

Drypoint: a printmaking technique in which the artist uses a needle to incise into a metal plate; different from etching in that it does not use acid to create the image

Japonisme: an attraction for Japanese art and artifacts that were imported into Europe in the late nineteenth century

Lithography: a printmaking technique that uses a flat stone surface as a base. The artist draws an image with a special crayon that attracts ink. Paper, which absorbs the ink, is applied to the surface and a print emerges

Modernism: a movement begun in the late nineteenth century in which artists embraced the current at the expense of the traditional in both subject matter and in media. Modernist artists often seek to question the very nature of art itself.

Plein-air: painting in the outdoors to directly capture the effects of light and atmosphere on a given object (Figure 21.6)

Positivism: a theory that expresses that all knowledge must come from proven ideas based on science or scientific theory; a philosophy promoted by French philosopher Auguste Comte (1798–1857)

Skeleton: the supporting interior framework of a building

Zoopraxiscope: a device that projects sequences of photographs to give the illusion of movement (Figure 21.5)

SUMMARY

The late nineteenth century is known for a series of art movements, one following quickly upon another: Realism, Impressionism, Post-Impressionism, Symbolism, and Art Nouveau. Each movement expresses a different philosophy demonstrating the richness and diversity of artistic expression in this period.

Realism relied on the philosophy of positivism, which made paintings of mythological and religious scenes seem not only outdated but archaic. Many Impressionist artists painted in the outdoors, seeking to draw inspiration from nature. Post-Impressionists explored the underlying structural foundation of images, and laid the groundwork for much of modern art. Symbolists drew upon personal visions to create works resembling a dreamworld. Lastly, Art Nouveau was a stylish and creative art form that put emphasis on sinuous shapes and curvilinear forms.

The late nineteenth century saw a revival of sculpture under the command of Auguste Rodin, who molded works in clay giving a very tactile quality to his works.

The direction of late nineteenth-century architecture was vertical. Architects responded to increased land values and advances in engineering by designing taller and thinner. For the first time in history, cities began to be defined by their skylines, which rose dramatically in downtown areas.

Multiple-Choice

1. Late nineteenth-century European painting had a fascination for all of the following EXCEPT

   (A) trains, canals, and other forms of modern transportation
   (B) light atmospheric effects achieved by short brushstrokes
   (C) still lifes and landscapes
   (D) historical and religious subjects done on commission

2. Painters achieved fame in the nineteenth century by having their works

   (A) realize success at the Salons of Paris
   (B) photographed for posterity
   (C) enter royal collections
   (D) shipped to eager buyers in non-Western countries

3. Manet's *Olympia* horrified contemporary critics as well as the public because

   (A) the central figure was a prostitute, which was new in art history
   (B) the inclusion of a black woman was bold and experimental
   (C) it relied on the Renaissance view of formal composition, and that was deemed outdated
   (D) it depicted the main figure as shameless and defiant in her role

4. Eadweard Muybridge's experiments using the zoopraxiscope enabled him to

   (A) draw onto a negative to create special effects
   (B) freeze the action of a fast-moving object
   (C) introduce color for the first time in a world of black and white photography
   (D) make multiple copies from a single negative

5. Post-Impressionist artists differed from the Impressionists a generation earlier by rejecting the Impressionist use of

   (A) everyday people and situations in their work
   (B) paintings in a series
   (C) the transitory effect of changing atmospheric conditions
   (D) solid massing of forms

Short Essay

Attribute this painting to the artist who created it.

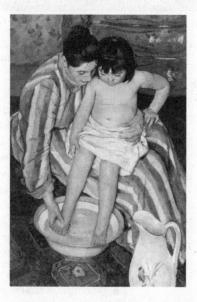

Identify a painting by the same artist in the art history curriculum.

Using specific details, justify your attribution by comparing the two works.

How do both works show an interest in non-Western cultural traditions?

ANSWERS EXPLAINED

Multiple-Choice

1. **(D)** Historical and religious paintings were out; still lifes, landscapes, trains, and atmospheric effects were in.

2. **(A)** Without success at the Paris salon, an artist's career could not go anywhere.

3. **(D)** Both prostitutes and black women have appeared in art history before, so there was nothing shocking about this. This painting uses a Renaissance notion of composition in that it references Titian's *Venus of Urbino*. What is new is the representation of the prostitute in a bold and confrontational manner rather than as a secretive and demure individual.

4. **(B)** A zoopraxiscope freezes the motion of a fast-moving person, animal, or object, and presents images in a sequence.

5. **(C)** Post-Impressionists wanted to return to a solid form of representation; therefore, they rejected Impressionists' interest in the transitory and the fleeting.

Short-Essay Rubric

Question	Points	Key Points in a Good Response
Attribute this painting to the artist who created it.	1	Mary Cassatt
Identify a painting by the same artist in the art history curriculum.	1	Mary Cassatt, *The Coiffure*, 1890–1891, drypoint and aquatint
Using specific details, justify your attribution by comparing the two works.	1	Answers could include: ■ Casssatt's world is filled with women: women as independent and not needing men to complete themselves; women who enjoy the company of other women ■ No posing or acting; figures possess a natural charm ■ Decorative charm influenced by Japanese art ■ Tenderness foreign to other Impressionists ■ Pastel color scheme
How do both works show an interest in non-Western cultural traditions?	2	Answers could include: ■ Decorative charm influenced by Japanese art ■ Japanese hairstyle ■ Japanese point of view: figure seen from the back or from above ■ Simple decorative color patterns ■ Japanese-style furniture in painting

Content Area: Later Europe and Americas

Early and Mid-Twentieth-Century Art

22

Movement	Dates	Major Artists
Fauvism	c. 1905	Matisse
Expressionism	1905–1930s	Kollwitz
▪ The Bridge	1905	Kirchner
▪ The Blue Rider	1911	Kandinsky
Cubism	1907–1930s	Picasso, Braque
Constructivism	1914–1920s	Stepanova
Dada	1916–1925	Duchamp
DeStijl	1917–1930s	Mondrian
Mexican Muralists	1920s–1930s	Rivera
International Style	1920s–1930s	Le Corbusier
Surrealism	1924–1930s	Kahlo, Oppenheim, Lam
Harlem Renaissance	1930s	Lawrence
Abstract Expressionism	Late 1940s–1950s	DeKooning
Pop Art	1955–1960s	Warhol, Oldenburg
Color Field Painting	1960s	Frankenthaler
Happenings	1960s	Kusama
Site Art	1970s–1990s	Lin, Smithson
Postmodern	1975–today	Venturi

ENDURING UNDERSTANDING: Art is influenced by changes in society. It is affected by economic forces which cause widespread migration, war, and a concentration of population in cities. New countries emerge and social movements gain strength.

Essential Knowledge:

▪ New philosophies, particularly those by Freud and Einstein, spread throughout the world. These views were supplemented by a new understanding of worldwide cultures.

ENDURING UNDERSTANDING: Artists become more prominent members of society. Art movements come in a rapid succession.

Essential Knowledge:

- Modern movements include Expressionism, Cubism, Surrealism, etc.
- Women artists become more recognized.
- Artists publish manifestos.
- Artists and architects use new materials such as acrylic, earthworks, and cantilevers.

ENDURING UNDERSTANDING: Art was seen in a new, often provoking, way by the public.

Essential Knowledge:

- Commercial galleries become important. Museums open and display art. Art sells to an ever widening market.
- Artists work for private and public institutions to a sometimes critical public.

HISTORICAL BACKGROUND

With the cataclysmic events of World War I and World War II, as well as the Great Depression, one would never suspect that the early twentieth century was an intensely creative period in the arts. But in nearly every artistic venue—literature, music, dance, and the fine arts—artistic expression flourished. Some movements fed on these very cataclysms for inspiration, others sought to escape the visceral world. Whatever the reason, the early twentieth century is one of the most creative periods in art history.

Patronage and Artistic Life

Early twentieth-century art was sponsored by extremely cultivated and intellectual patrons who were members of the avant-garde. They saw art as a way to embrace the modern spirit in a cultured way. These influential patrons, like Gertrude Stein, promoted great artists through their sponsorship and connections.

New to the art world is the patronage of museums. It has become standard for a great museum to hire the finest architectural firms to handle expansion projects and turn the museum into a work of art in its own right. Museums also commission works of sculpture and painting from contemporary artists to be showcased in their public spaces.

Not all modern art, however, was greeted with enthusiasm. The **Armory Show** of 1913, which introduced modern art to American audiences, was generally reviled by American audiences. **Picasso's** *Les Demoiselles d'Avignon* (Figure 22.5) horrified the public. **Duchamp's** *Fountain* (Figure 22.9) even upset the promoters of the gallery who were supposed to allow anyone to be able to exhibit, provided he or she paid the six-dollar admission fee.

One of the results of World War II was the abandonment of Paris as the art capital of the world, a position it had retained since about 1650. New York, the financial and cultural capital of the United States, took over that position, in part because that is where so many fleeing Europeans settled, and in part because it had an active artistic community that was unafraid of experimentation. Mondrian, Duchamp, and Kandinsky moved to New York, not so much to continue their work, most of which was well behind them, but to galvanize modern American artists in what has been called The New York School. **De Kooning** and **Frankenthaler** settled here to do their most impressive works.

EARLY AND MID-TWENTIETH-CENTURY ART

All of the characteristic painter's tools of expression were under question in the early twentieth century. Color was not only used to describe a setting or an artist's impression, but also to evoke a feeling and challenge the viewer. Perspective was generally discarded, or violently tilted for dramatic impact. Compositions were forcefully altered in a new and dynamic way.

Most radically, the introduction of pure form, **abstraction**, became the feature of modern art. Actually, abstract art has always existed, usually in marginal areas of works of art, sometimes in frames or as decorative designs. New is the placement of the abstract form directly in the center of the composition—a statement averring that abstraction has a meaning independent of realistically conveyed representations.

Artists moved beyond the traditional oil-on-canvas approach to great art, and were inspired by **frottage** and **collage**, techniques formerly relegated to children's art. Such fervent experimentation led Europeans to draw inspiration from African cultures, hitherto ignored or labeled as primitive. Europeans were stimulated by African artists' ability to create works in geometric, even abstract, terms, unafraid of a lack of conventional reality. This freedom of expression inspired Europeans to rethink traditional representations, sometimes by writing their thoughts down in artistic manifestos, which served as a call to arms for their movement.

The Armory Show, named after the building in New York where it was held, was mounted in 1913 to introduce Americans to the current trends in European art. Many contemporary artists, such as Duchamp and Picasso, were showcased in America for the first time. The show also exhibited prominent American artists.

The adventurous spirit that epitomizes modern painting and architecture also characterizes modern sculpture. Artists used new materials, such as plastic, and new formats, such as collages, to create dynamic compositions. Artists also dangled metal shapes from a ceiling and called them **mobiles**.

In the Dada movement, artists saw a found object and turn it into a work of art. These **ready-mades** became works of art simply because the artist said they were.

Fauvism

Fauvism is an art movement that debuted in 1905 at Salon d'Automne in Paris. It was so named because a critic, Louis Vauxcelles, thought that the paintings looked as if they were created by "Wild Beasts." Fauvism was inspired by Post-Impressionist painters like Gauguin and Van Gogh, whose work was exhibited in Paris around this time. Fauves stressed a painterly surface with broad flat areas of violently contrasting color. Figure modeling and color harmonies were suppressed so that expressive effects could be maximized. Fauvism all but died out by 1908.

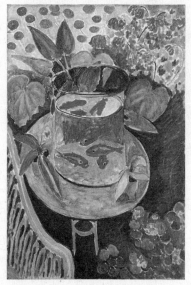

Figure 22.1: Henri Matisse, *Goldfish*, 1912, oil on canvas, Hermitage, Saint Petersburg, Russia

Henri Matisse, *Goldfish*, 1912, oil on canvas, Hermitage, Saint Petersburg, Russia (Figure 22.1)

- Still life painting
- Violent contrasts of color
- Thinly applied colors; white of canvas shows through
- Energetic painterly brushwork
- May have been influenced by the decorative quality of Asian art
- Broad patches of color anticipate Color-Field painting later in century

Expressionism

Inspired by the Fauve movement in Paris, a group of German artists in Dresden gathered around **Kirchner** and formed Die Brüke, **The Bridge**, in 1905, so named because they saw themselves as a bridge from traditional to modern painting. They emphasized the same Fauve ideals expressed in violent juxtapositions of color, which so purposely roused the ire of critics and the public.

A second Expressionist group, called **Der Blaue Reiter**, **The Blue Rider**, formed in Munich, Germany, in 1911. This group (so named because of an affection the founders had for horses and the color blue) began to forsake representational art and move toward abstraction. Highly intellectual, and filled with theories of artistic representation, artists like **Kandinsky**

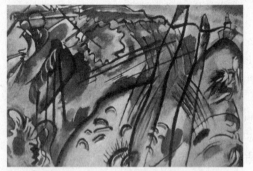

saw abstraction as a way of conceiving the natural world in terms that went beyond representation. Kandinsky's theories were best expressed in his influential essay, *Concerning the Spiritual in Art*, which outlined his theories on color and form for the modern movement.

Figure 22.2: Vassily Kandinsky, *Improvisation 28 (second version)*, 1912, oil on canvas, Guggenheim Museum, New York

Vassily Kandinsky, *Improvisation 28 (second version)*, 1912, oil on canvas, Guggenheim Museum, New York (Figure 22.2)

- Movement toward abstraction; representational objects suggested rather than depicted
- Title derived from musical compositions
- Strongly articulated use of black lines
- Colors seem to shade around line forms
- Felt that sound and color were linked
- Gave musical titles to his works like "Composition" and "Improvisation"
- Kandinsky wanted the viewer to respond to a painting the way one would to an abstract musical composition like a concerto, sonata, or symphony
- **Cross-Cultural Comparisons: Composition**
  - David, *The Oath of the Horatii* (Figure 19.6)
  - Ringgold, *Dancing at the Louvre* (Figure 29.11)
  - Giotto, *Lamentation* (Figure 13.1c)

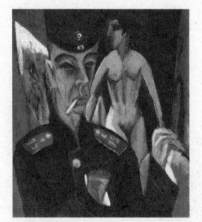

Figure 22.3: Ernst Kirchner, *Self-Portrait as a Soldier*, 1915, oil on canvas, Allen Memorial Art Museum, Oberlin College, Oberlin, Ohio

Ernst Kirchner, *Self-Portrait as a Soldier*, 1915, oil on canvas, Allen Memorial Art Museum, Oberlin College, Oberlin, Ohio (Figure 22.3)

- Kirchner was an "unwilling volunteer" driver in the artillery in World War I, rather than be drafted into the infantry
- Declared unfit for service; lung problems and weakness; mental breakdown—scholarly debate as to whether or not he faked these to avoid service
- Painted this work during a recuperation period

- Drawn face; loss of right hand indicates his feeling that he has an inability to paint
- Nude model represents what he used to paint, but no longer can
- Nightmarish quality
- Colors are non-representational, but symbolic, and chosen to provide a jarring impact
- Expressive quality of horrified facial features and grim surroundings
- Tilted perspective moves things closer to the picture plane
- His life was plagued by drug abuse, alcoholism, and then paralysis
- **Cross-Cultural Comparisons: Self-Portraits**
  - Rembrandt, *Self-Portrait with Saskia* (Figure 17.9)
  - Vigée Le Brun, *Self-Portrait* (Figure 19.2)
  - Kahlo, *The Two Fridas* (Figure 22.11)

Käthe Kollwitz, *Memorial Sheet for Karl Liebknecht,* 1919–1920, woodcut. Private Collection (Figure 22.4)

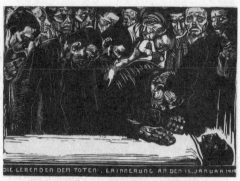

Figure 22.4: Käthe Kollwitz, *Memorial Sheet for Karl Liebknecht*, 1919–1920, woodcut, Private Collection

- Themes of war and poverty dominate her oeuvre
- Theme of women grieving over dead children; her son died in World War I, then she became a socialist
- Karl Liebknecht among the founders of the Berlin Spartacus League that became the German Communist Party
- In 1919 Liebknecht shot to death during a Communist uprising in Berlin called the Spartacus Revolt (named for the slave who led a revolt against the Romans in 73 B.C.E.)
- No political reference in the woodcut
- Human grief dominates
- Stark black and white of the woodcut used to magnify the grief
- **Cross-Cultural Comparisons: Memorials**
  - Taj Mahal (Figures 9.17a, 9.17b)
  - The Sphinx and the Pyramids (Figure 3.6a)
  - Terra-Cotta Warriors (Figures 24.8a, 24.8b)

Cubism

Cubism was born in the studio of **Pablo Picasso**, who in 1907 revealed the first cubist painting, *Les Demoiselles d'Avignon* (Figure 22.5). Perhaps influenced by the simple geometries of African masks, then the rage in Paris, Picasso was inspired to break down the human form into angles and shapes, achieving a new way of looking at the human figure from many sides at once. This use of multiple views shows parts of a face, for example, from a number of angles. Cubism is dominated by wedges and facets that are sometimes shaded to simulate depth.

The first phase of Cubism, from 1907–1912, called **Analytical**, was highly experimental, showing jagged edges and sharp multifaceted lines. The second phase, after 1912, called **Synthetic Cubism**, was initially inspired by collages and found objects and featured flattened forms. The last phase, **Curvilinear Cubism**, in the 1930s, was a more flowing rounded response to the flattened and firm edges of Synthetic.

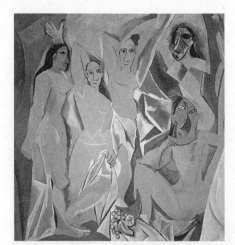

Figure 22.5: Pablo Picasso, *Les Demoiselles d'Avignon*, 1907, oil on canvas, Museum of Modern Art, New York

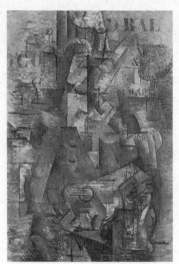

Figure 22.6: Georges Braque, *The Portuguese*, 1911, oil on canvas, Art Museum, Basel, Switzerland

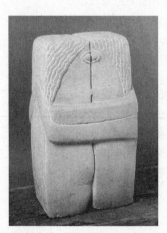

Figure 22.7: Constantin Brancusi, *The Kiss*, 1907–1908, limestone, Philadelphia Museum of Art, Philadelphia

Major Works of Cubism

Pablo Picasso, *Les Demoiselles d'Avignon*, 1907, oil on canvas, Museum of Modern Art, New York (Figure 22.5)

- First Cubist work, influenced by late Cézanne, and perhaps African masks
- Represents five prostitutes in a bordello on Avignon Street in Barcelona, each posing for a customer
- Poses are not traditionally alluring but awkward, expressionless, and uninviting
- Three on left more conservatively painted, two on right more radical; reflects a dichotomy in Picasso
- Multiple views expressed at the same time
- No real depth
- Influenced by Gauguin's primitivism
- **Cross-Cultural Comparisons: Group Figures**
  - Velázquez, *Las Meninas* (Figure 17.7)
  - Basquiat, *Horn Players* (Figure 29.5)
  - Sultan Muhammad, *Court of the Gayumars* (Figure 9.9)

Georges Braque, *The Portuguese*, 1911, oil on canvas, Art Museum, Basel, Switzerland (Figure 22.6)

- Analytical Cubism; worked in concert with Pablo Picasso to develop this style
- Rejected naturalistic and conventional painting
- Fractured forms; breaking down of objects into smaller forms
- Clear-edged surfaces sit on the picture plane, not recessed in space
- Nearly monochrome
- Not a portrait of a Portuguese musician, but rather an exploration of shapes
- Only realistic elements are the stenciled letters and numbers; perhaps they suggest a dance hall poster behind the guitarist; a café atmosphere

Constantin Brancusi, *The Kiss*, 1907–1908, limestone, Philadelphia Museum of Art, Philadelphia (Figure 22.7)

- Symbolic, almost Cubist, rendering of the male and female bodies
- Intertwined and enveloped figures
- Two eyes become one, almost Cyclops-like
- Interlocked forms
- Brancusi worked in Rodin's studio; cf. Rodin's *The Kiss*
- This is the fourth stone version of this subject, done as a commission
- First version was one of Brancusi's earliest efforts at stone carving (Craiova Art Museum, Romania)
- Second version of *The Kiss* (a plaster cast) exhibited at the Armory Show

- Third version used as tombstone in Montparnasse Cemetery in Paris over the body of a suicide victim: a young Russian anarchist; artist asked by a friend of the deceased, who had jilted her, for a marking of her grave; artist said take what you want; he took this
- There may be many more undocumented versions
- **Cross-Cultural Comparisons: Schematic Human Forms**
  - Anthropomorphic Stele (Figure 1.2)
  - Female Deity from Nukuoro (Figure 28.2)
  - Ikenga Shrine (Figure 27.10)

Photo-Secession

From 1902 through 1917 Alfred Stieglitz's gallery, called Gallery 291, was the most progressive gallery in the United States, showcasing photographs as works of art beside avant-garde European paintings and modern American works.

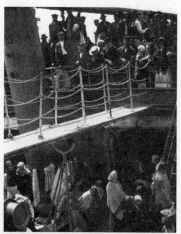

Figure 22.8: Alfred Stieglitz, *The Steerage*, 1907, photograph, Private Collection

Alfred Stieglitz, *The Steerage*, 1907, photograph, Private Collection (Figure 22.8)
- Stieglitz photographed the world as he saw it, arranged little and allowed people and events to make their own compositions
- Interested in compositional possibilities of diagonals and lines acting as framing elements
- Diagonals and framing effects of ladders, sails, steam pipes, and so on
- Depicts the poorest passengers on a ship traveling from the United States to Europe in 1907
- Some may have been people turned away from entrance to the United States, more likely artisans whose visas had expired and were returning home
- Published in October 1911 in *Camera Work*
- Influenced by experimental European painting; compared to a Cubist drawing by Picasso; Cubist-like in arrangement of shapes and tonal values
- Represents social divisions of society
- Steerage: the part of a ship reserved for passengers with the cheapest tickets
- **Cross-Cultural Comparisons: Disadvantaged Persons**
  - Turner, *Slave Ship* (Figure 20.5)
  - Courbet, *The Stone Breakers* (Figure 21.1)
  - Rodin, *The Burghers of Calais* (Figure 21.15)

Dada

Dada, a nonsense word that literally means "hobby horse," is a term directed at a movement in Zurich, Cologne, Berlin, Paris, and New York from 1916 to 1925. Disillusioned by the useless slaughter of World War I, the Dadaists rejected conventional methods of representation and the conventional manner in which they were exhibited. Oil and canvas were abandoned. Instead, Dadaists accepted **ready-mades** as an art form, and often did their work on glass. Dadaists challenged the relationship between words and images, often incorporating words prominently in their works. The meaning of Dada works is frequently contingent on location or accident. If a glass should shatter, as a few did, it was hailed as an enhancement, acknowledging the hand of chance in this achievement. In sum, Dada accepts the dominance of the artistic concept over the execution.

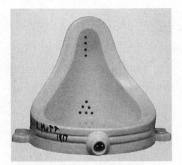

Figure 22.9: Marcel Duchamp, *Fountain*, original 1917, this version 1950, china with black paint, Philadelphia Museum of Art, Pennsylvania

Marcel Duchamp, *Fountain*, original 1917, this version 1950, china with black paint, Philadelphia Museum of Art, Pennsylvania (Figure 22.9)

- Ready-made sculpture, actually a found object that Duchamp deemed to be a work of art
- Entered in an unjuried show, but the work was refused
- Signed by the "artist" R. Mutt, a pun on the *Mutt and Jeff* comic strip and Mott Iron Works
- Title *Fountain* a pun; fountains spout liquid, a urinal is meant to collect it
- Added irony of placing the urinal upside down

Surrealism

Inspired by the psychological studies of Freud and Jung, Surrealists sought to represent an unseen world of dreams, subconscious thoughts, and unspoken communication. Starting with the theories of Andre Breton in 1924, the movement went in two directions: The abstract tradition of **biomorphic** and suggestive forms, and the veristic tradition of using reality-based subjects put together in unusual ways. Those who seek to understand the inscrutable world of Surrealism by looking at a painting's title will find themselves even more confused than when they started. Surrealism is meant to puzzle, challenge, and fascinate; its sources are in mysticism, psychology, and the symbolic. It is not meant to be clearly understood and didactic.

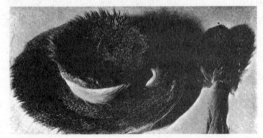

Figure 22.10: Meret Oppenheim, *Object*, 1936, fur-covered cup, saucer, and spoon, Museum of Modern Art, New York

Meret Oppenheim, *Object*, 1936, fur-covered cup, saucer, and spoon, Museum of Modern Art, New York (Figure 22.10)

- Said to have been done in response to Picasso's claim that anything looks good in fur
- Combination of unlike objects: fur-covered teacup, saucer, and spoon
- Erotic overtones
- An assemblage
- Combined traditionally female and genteel objects vs. masculinity of sculpture done in hard surfaces in great scale and made vertically
- Chosen by visitors of a Surrealist show in New York as the quintessential Surrealist work of art
- Fame came to her young (she was 22 when she produced the work), and it inhibited her growth as an artist
- **Cross-Cultural Comparisons: Found Objects**
  - Camelid Sacrem (Figure 1.1)
  - Duchamp, *Fountain* (Figure 22.9)

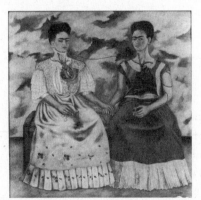

Figure 22.11: Frida Kahlo, *The Two Fridas*, 1939, oil on canvas, Museum of Modern Art, Mexico City

Frida Kahlo, *The Two Fridas*, 1939, oil on canvas, Museum of Modern Art, Mexico City (Figure 22.11)

- Juxtaposition of two self-portraits
- Left: Kahlo dressed as a Spanish lady in white lace
- Right: Kahlo dressed as a Mexican peasant—the stiffness and provincial quality of Mexican folk art serves as a direct inspiration for the artist

- Her two hearts are twined together by veins that are cut by scissors at one end and lead to a portrait of her husband, artist Rivera, at the other; painted at the time of their divorce
- Barren landscape, two figures sit against a wildly active sky
- Kahlo rejected the label of Surrealism to her artwork
- The vein acts as an umbilical cord, symbolically associating Rivera as a husband and son
- Blood on her lap suggests many abortions and miscarriages, also her surgeries related to her polio
- **Cross-Cultural Comparisons: Self-Portraits**
  - Bichitr, *Jahangir Preferring a Sufi Shaikh to Kings* (Figure 23.9)
  - Rembrandt, *Self-Portrait with Saskia* (Figure 17.9)
  - Vigée Le Brun, *Self-Portrait* (Figure 19.2)

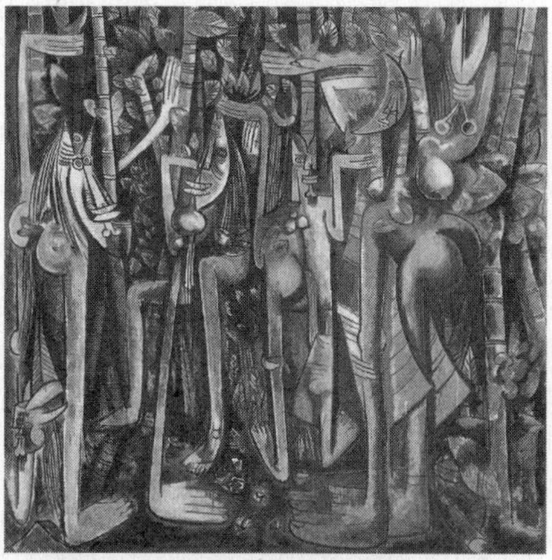

Wifredo Lam, *The Jungle*, 1943, gouache on paper mounted on canvas, The Museum of Modern Art, New York (Figure 22.12)

- Cuban-born artist whose career took him to Europe and United States
- Interested in Cuba's mixture of Hispanic and African cultures
- Influenced by African sculpture; Cubist works; Surrealist paintings (he was a member of the Surrealist movement in Paris)
- This work "intended to communicate a psychic state"
- Addresses the history of slavery in colonial Cuba
- Crescent-shaped faces suggest African masks
- Rounded backs, thins arms and legs, pronounced hands and feet
- Meant to suggest sugarcane, which are grown in fields, not jungles
- **Cross-Cultural Comparisons: Art Inspired from Diverse Cultural Traditions**
  - Petra (Figures 6.9a, 6.9b)
  - *Golden Haggadah* (Figures 12.10a, 12.10b, 12.10c)
  - Kngwarreye, *Earth's Creation* (Figure 29.13)

Figure 22.12: Wifredo Lam, *The Jungle*, 1943, gouache on paper mounted on canvas, The Museum of Modern Art, New York

Constructivism

Constructivists experimented with new architectural materials and assembled them in a way devoid of historical reference. Beginning in 1914, Stepanova and others saw the new Russia as an idealistic center removed from historical reference and decoration. Influenced by the Cubists, Constructivism designed buildings with no precise façades. Emphasis was placed on the dramatic use of the materials used to create the project.

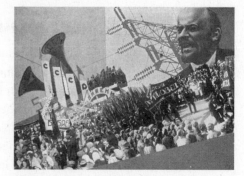

Figure 22.13: Varvara Stepanova, Illustration from *The Results of the First Five-Year Plan*, 1932, photomontage, Museum of the Revolution, Moscow, Russia

Varvara Stepanova, Illustration from *The Results of the First Five-Year Plan*, 1932, photomontage, Museum of the Revolution, Moscow, Russia (Figure 22.13)

- Stepanova one of the main figures in the Russian avant-garde movement
- Graphic art for political and propaganda purposes
- Influenced by Cubism and Futurism
- Five year plan: Soviet practice of increasing agricultural and industrial output in five years; launched in 1928; considered complete in 1932

- Emphasis on growth of heavy industry rather than consumer goods
- Huge increases in electrical output (dominant industrial symbol in the work)
- A double page spread in a book
- Red dominates: the color of Communist Soviet Union
- CCCP (Союз Советских Социалистических Республик) is a Russian abbreviation for the Soviet Union
- Large portrait of Lenin dominates; although deceased, his image is used to stimulate patriotism
- **Cross-Cultural Comparisons: Social Commentary**
  - Delacroix, *Liberty Leading the People* (Figure 20.4)
  - Sherman, *Untitled #228* (Figure 29.10)
  - Walker, *Darkytown Rebellion* (Figure 29.21)

DeStijl

DeStijl, a movement symbolized by the Dutch painter **Mondrian**, reached its height between 1917 and the 1930s. At its purest, DeStijl paintings are completely abstract; even the titles make no reference to nature. They are painted on a white background and use black lines to shape the rectangular spaces. Only the three primary colors are used: red, yellow, and blue, and they are painted without modulation. Lines can only be placed perpendicularly—diagonals are forbidden.

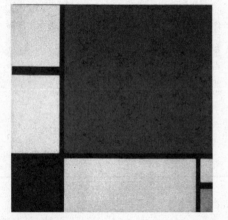

Figure 22.14: Piet Mondrian, *Composition with Red, Blue and Yellow*, 1930, oil on canvas, Private Collection

Piet Mondrian, *Composition with Red, Blue and Yellow*, 1930, oil on canvas, Private Collection (Figure 22.14)

- Only primary colors used: red, yellow, blue and the neutrals, white and black
- Severe geometry of form, only right angles; gridlike forms
- No shading of colors
- Assymetrical composition
- **Cross-Cultural Comparisons: Composition**
  - Su-nam, *Summer Trees* (Figure 29.6)
  - Navigation Chart (Figure 28.3)
  - Martínez, Black-on-black ceramic vessel (Figure 26.14)

EARLY AND MID-TWENTIETH-CENTURY ARCHITECTURE

Early twentieth-century architecture is marked by a complete embrace of technological advances. **Ferroconcrete** construction, particularly in Europe, allowed for new designs employing skeleton frameworks and glass walls. The **cantilever** (Figure 22.15) helped push building elements beyond the solid structure of the skeletal framework.

In general, architects avoided historical associations: There are few columns and fewer flying buttresses. Architects prefer clean sleek lines that stress the building's underlying structure and emphasize the impact of the machine and technology.

The Prairie Style

The Prairie School of architecture concerns a group of architects working in Chicago from 1900 to 1917, of which **Frank Lloyd Wright** is the most famous. They rejected the idea that buildings should be done in historic styles of architecture; however, they insisted that they should be in harmony with their site. Wright employed complex irregular plans and forms that seemed to reflect the abstract shapes of contemporary painting: Rectangles, triangles, squares, and circles. Stylized botanical shapes were particularly prized. Wright used **cantilever** construction to have porches and terraces extend out from the main section of a structure (Figure 22.15). Cantilevers give the impression of forms hovering over open space, held up by seemingly weightless anchors.

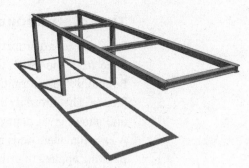

Figure 22.15: Cantilever

The organic qualities of the materials—concrete with pebble aggregate, sand-finished stucco, rough-hewn lumber, and natural woods—were believed to be the most beautiful. The horizontal nature of the prairie is stressed in the alignment of these houses. Although **Fallingwater** was designed well after The Prairie School peaked, it still reflects many of the same characteristics.

Frank Lloyd Wright, Kaufmann House "Fallingwater," 1936–1939, reinforced concrete, sandstone, steel, and glass, Bear Run, Pennsylvania (Figures 22.16a, 22.16b, and 22.16c)

- Cantilevered porches extend over waterfall; accent on horizontal lines; architecture in harmony with site
- Living room contains glass curtain wall around three of the four sides; embraces the woods around it
- Floor of living room and walls of building are made from stone of the area
- Hearth is the center of the house, an outcropping of natural stones surrounds it
- Suppression of space devoted to hanging a painting; Wright wanted architecture to dominate
- Irregularity and complexity of ground plan and design
- **Cross-Cultural Connections: Homes**
  – Jefferson, Monticello (Figures 19.5a, 19.5b)
  – Ryoan-ji (Figures 25.2a, 25.2b, 25.2c)
  – House of the Vettii (Figures 6.7a, 6.7b)

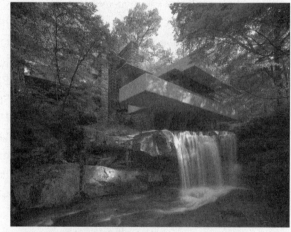

Figure 22.16a: Frank Lloyd Wright, Kaufmann House "Fallingwater," 1936–1939, Bear Run, Pennsylvania

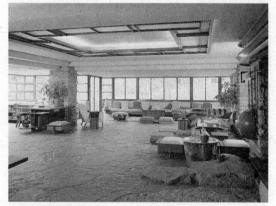

Figure 22.16b: Frank Lloyd Wright, Kaufmann House, "Fallingwater," living room

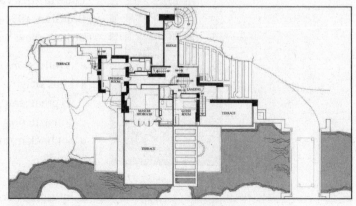

Figure 22.16c: Frank Lloyd Wright, Kaufmann House, "Fallingwater," plan

The International Style

Le Corbusier's dictum that a house should be a "machine for living" sums up the International Style from the 1920s to the 1950s. Greatly influenced by the streamlined qualities of the Bauhaus, the International Style celebrates the clean spacious white lines of a building's façade. The internal structure is a skeleton system which holds the building up from within and allows great planes of glass to wrap around the walls using **ferroconcrete** construction. A key characteristic is the lack of architectural ornament and an avoidance of sculpture and painting applied to exterior surfaces.

Le Corbusier, Villa Savoye, 1929, steel and reinforced concrete, Poissy-sur-Seine, France (Figure 22.17)

- Three-bedroom villa with servant's quarters
- Boxlike horizontal quality; an abstraction of a house
- Main part of house lifted off the ground by narrow pilotis—thin freestanding posts
- Turning circle on bottom floor is a carport, so that family members can enter the house directly from their car
- All space is utilized, including the roof which acts as a patio

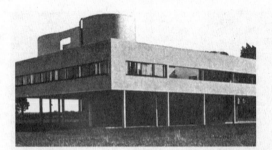

Figure 22.17: Le Corbusier, Villa Savoye, 1929, steel and reinforced concrete, Poissy-sur-Seine, France

- No historical ornamentation
- Subtle colors: white on exterior symbolized modern cleanliness, the new, simplicity, healthful living
- Open interior free of many walls
- Furniture built into the walls
- Ribbon windows wind around second floor
- Streamlined look
- House appears to float on pilotis
- Living spaces around an open courtyard-type setting on second floor; surrounded by glass
- Patrons: Pierre and Emilie Savoye, wanted a country house
- **Cross-Cultural Comparisons: Houses**
  - House of the Vettii (Figures 6.7a, 6.7b)
  - Alberti, Palazzo Rucellai (Figure 5.2)
  - Alhambra (Figures 9.15a, 9.15b)

Ludwig Mies van der Rohe and Philip Johnson, Seagram Building, 1954–1958, steel frame with glass curtain wall and bronze, New York (Figure 22.18)

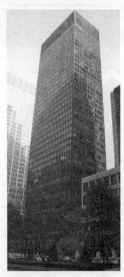

Figure 22.18: Ludwig Mies van der Rohe and Philip Johnson, Seagram Building, 1954–1958, New York

- A reflection of the Minimalist movement in painting
- Mies's saying "Less is more" can be see in this building with its great simplicity, geometry of design, and elegance of construction
- Set back from the street on a wide plaza balanced by reflecting pools
- Bronze veneer gives the skyscraper a monolithic look
- Interplay of vertical and horizontal accents
- Steel-and-glass skyscraper became the model after World War II
- A triumph of the International Style of architecture

The Harlem Renaissance

In the early twentieth century African-Americans moved in great numbers to a New York City neighborhood called Harlem. This migration, and its subsequent infusion of talent, created a deep cultural center that reached its fullest expression in painting, theatre, music, writing, and photography. The movement began after World War I, around 1919, and reached its peak in the 1920s and early 1930s, but its influence extended well into the later twentieth century. The movement's general themes, which extended across the arts, include racial pride, civil rights, and the influence of slavery on modern culture.

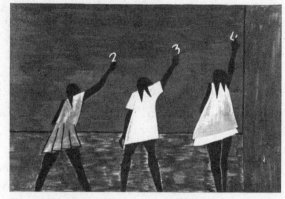

Figure 22.19: Jacob Lawrence, *The Migration of the Negro, Panel no. 49*, tempera on hardboard, 1940–1941, Museum of Modern Art, New York

Jacob Lawrence, *The Migration of the Negro, Panel no. 49*, tempera on hardboard, 1940–1941, Museum of Modern Art, New York (Figure 22.19)

- A series of sixty paintings that depicts the migration of African-Americans from the rural South to the urban North after World War I.
- Overall color unity in the series unites each painting
- Forms hover in large spaces
- Flat simple shapes
- Unmodulated colors
- Collective African-American experience, little individuality to the figures
- Goes back to tempera paint; influenced by Italian masters of the fourteenth and fifteenth centuries
- Collective unity achieved by painting one color across many panels before going on to the next color
- Angularity of forms
- This scene involved a public restaurant in the North; segregation emphasized by yellow poles that zigzag down the center
- Tilted table tops show the surface of the table
- Narrative painting in an era of increasing abstraction
- **Cross-Cultural Comparisons: Social Criticism**
  - Salcedo, *Shibboleth* (Figure 29.26)
  - Smith, *Lying with the Wolf* (Figure 29.20)
  - Quick-to-See-Smith, *Trade* (Figure 29.12)

Mexican Muralists

A major revival of Mexican art took place in the 1920s and 1930s by artists whose training was in the age-old tradition of fresco painting. Using large murals that all could see and appreciate, the Mexican Muralists usually promoted a political or a social message. These didactic paintings have an unmistakable meaning rendered in an easy-to-read format. The themes generally promote the labor and struggle of the working classes, and usually have a socialist agenda.

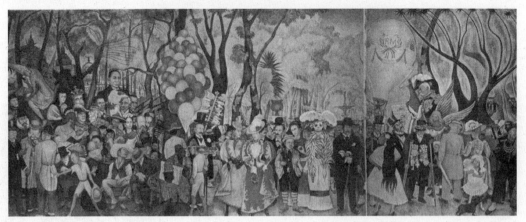

Figure 22.20: Diego Rivera, *Dream of a Sunday Afternoon in the Alameda Park*, 1947–1948, fresco, Museo Mural Diego Rivera, Mexico City

Diego Rivera, *Dream of a Sunday Afternoon in the Alameda Park*, 1947–1948, fresco, Museo Mural Diego Rivera, Mexico City (Figure 22.20)

■ Fifty-foot-long fresco; thirteen feet high
■ Originally in lobby of the Hotel Del Prado
■ After 1985 earthquake that destabilized the hotel it was placed in Alameda Park, Mexico City's first city park; built on the grounds of an Aztec marketplace
■ Three eras of Mexican history depicted:
  – Conquest and colonization of Mexico by the Spanish
  – Porfirio Diaz dictatorship
  – Revolution of 1910
■ Depicts a who's who of Mexican politics, culture, and leadership:
  – Sor Juana (Figure 18.6)
  – Benito Juárez, five term president of Mexico
  – General Santa Ana handing the Keys of Mexico to General Winfield Scott
  – Emperor Maximilian and Empress Carlota
  – José Marti, father of Mexican independence (tipping his hat)
  – General Porfirio Díaz with medals, asleep
  – A police officer ordering a family out of an elitist park
  – Francisco Madero, a martyred president
  – Artist in center, at age ten, holding hands with Caterina ("Death") dreaming of a perfect love (Kahlo is behind him)
■ Horror vacui; didactic painting
■ Colorful painting
■ Revival of fresco painting, a Mexican specialty
■ **Cross-Cultural Comparisons: Historicism**
  – Delacroix, *Liberty Leading the People* (Figure 20.4)
  – Raphael, *School of Athens* (Figure 16.3)
  – Olmec Style Mask (Figure 26.5d)

Abstract Expressionism

Sometimes called **The New York School**, Abstract Expressionism of the 1950s is the first American avant-garde art movement. It developed as a reaction against artists like **Mondrian**, who took the Minimalist approach to abstraction. Abstract Expressionists seek a more active representation of the hand of the artist on a given work. Hence, **action painting** is a big component of Abstract Expressionism.

Willem de Kooning, *Woman, I*, 1950–1952, oil on canvas, Museum of Modern Art, New York (Figure 22.21)

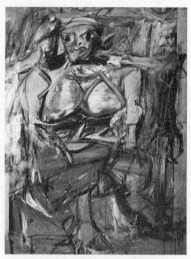

- Ferocious woman with great fierce teeth and huge eyes
- Large bulbous breasts are a satire on women who appear in magazine advertising; smile said to be influenced by an ad of a woman selling Camel cigarettes
- Slashing of paint onto canvas
- Jagged lines create an overpowering image
- Smile is a cut out of a female smile from an magazine advertisement
- Blank stare; frozen grin
- Ambiguous environment: vagueness, insecurity
- Combination of stereotypes; ironic comment on the banal and artificial world of film and advertising
- One of a series of six on the woman theme
- Influenced by everything from Paleolithic goddesses to pin-up girls
- Thick and thin black lines dominate
- **Cross-Cultural Comparisons: Images of Women**
  - Manet, *Olympia* (Figure 21.3)
  - Titian, *Venus of Urbino* (Figure 16.4)
  - Neshat, *Rebellious Silence* (Figure 29.14)

Figure 22.21: Willem de Kooning, *Woman, I*, 1950–1952, oil on canvas, Museum of Modern Art, New York

Color Field Painting

Color Field Painting lacks the aggression of Abstract Expressionism. It relies on subtle tonal values that are often variations of a monochromatic hue. With **Frankenthaler** the images are mysteriously hovering in an ambiguous space. With artists like Barnett Newman, there is a more clear-cut definition of forms with lines descending through the composition. Color Field Painting was popular in the 1960s.

Helen Frankenthaler, *The Bay*, 1963, acrylic on canvas, Detroit Institute of Arts, Detroit, Michigan (Figure 22.22)

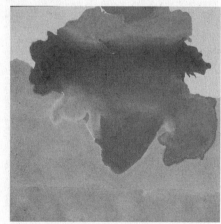

- Painted directly on unprimed canvas; canvas absorbs paint more directly
- Uses a runny paint, sometimes thinned with turpentine
- Uses landscape as a starting point; basis for imagery in the works
- Accentuates the two-dimensionality of the canvas
- Worked in the avant-garde New York School at mid-century
- **Cross-Cultural Comparisons: Nature**
  - Su-nam, *Summer Trees* (Figure 29.6)
  - Hokusai, *Great Wave* (Figure 25.5)
  - Breughel, *Hunters in the Snow* (Figure 14.6)

Figure 22.22: Helen Frankenthaler, *The Bay*, 1963, acrylic on canvas, Detroit Institute of Arts, Detroit, Michigan

Pop Art

Pop, or Popular, Art is a term coined by an English critic in 1955 about a movement that gathered momentum in the 1950s and then reached its climax in the 1960s. It draws on materials of the everyday world, items of mass popular culture like consumer goods or famous singers—the Pop artist saw no distinction between "high" art or the design of mass-produced items. It glorifies, indeed magnifies, the commonplace, bringing the viewer face to face with everyday reality. Most Pop Artists proclaim that their art is not satirical, although sometimes this is hard to believe given the images they used and the scale used to dislpay them. It is generally thought that Pop Art is a reaction against Abstract Expressionism.

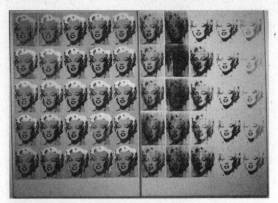

Figure 22.23: Andy Warhol, *Marilyn Diptych*, 1962, oil, acrylic, silkscreen enamel on canvas, Tate Gallery, London

Andy Warhol, *Marilyn Diptych,* 1962, oil, acrylic, silkscreen enamel on canvas, Tate Gallery, London (Figure 22.23)

- Screen-printing photographic images onto backgrounds of rectangular shapes
- Repeated imagery drains the image of Monroe of meaning
- Fifty images from a film still from a movie, *Niagara* (1953)
- Reproduction of many denies the concept of the unique work of art
- Cult of celebrity

- Left, in color, represents her in life; right, in black and white, represents her death; work done four months after her tragic death
- Marilyn's public face appears highlighted by bold, artificial colors
- Private persona of the individual submerged beneath the public face
- Social characteristics magnified: brilliance of blonde hair, heavily applied lipstick, seductive expression

- **Cross-Cultural Comparisons: Human Identity**
  - Tlatilco Female Figure (Figure 1.5)
  - Rodriguez, *Spaniard and Indian Produce a Mestizo* (Figure 18.5)
  - Neshat, *Rebellious Silence* (Figure 29.14)

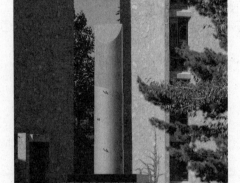

Figure 22.24: Claes Oldenburg, *Lipstick (Ascending) on Caterpillar Tracks*, 1969–1974, cor-ten steel, aluminum, and cast resin, painted with polyurethane enamel, Yale University, New Haven, Connecticut

Claes Oldenburg, *Lipstick (Ascending) on Caterpillar Tracks,* 1969–1974, cor-ten steel, aluminum, and cast resin, painted with polyurethane enamel, Yale University, New Haven, Connecticut (Figure 22.24)

- First installed on Beinecke Plaza, New Haven, in 1969
- Intended as a platform for public speakers; rallying point for anti-Vietnam era protests
- Erected secretly
- Tank-shaped platform base with lipstick ascending—anti-war symbolism
- Male and female forms unite: themes of death, power, desire, and sensuality
- Sculpture made of inexpensive and perishable materials (plywood tracks and an inflatable vinyl balloon tip)

- Refurbished with steel, aluminum, fiberglass; reinstalled in 1974 in front of Morse College at Yale
- First monumental sculpture by Oldenburg
- **Cross-Cultural Comparisons: War and Battle Commemorations**
  - Column of Trajan (Figure 6.16)
  - Lin, Vietnam Veterans Memorial (Figures 29.4a, 29.4b)
  - *Siege of Belgrade* (Figures 18.3a, 18.3b)

HAPPENINGS

The word "happening" was coined in the late 1950's to describe an act of performance art that is initially planned, but involves spontaneity, improvisation, and often audience participation. Happenings continue today in various formats, including Flash Mobs, Improvisational Theatre, and Performance Art.

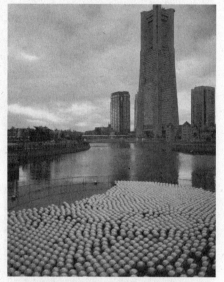

Yayoi Kusama, *Narcissus Garden*, first seen in 1966, installation of mirrored balls, Venice (Figures 22.25a and 22.25b)

- Internationally renowned Japanese-born artist
- Got her start showing large works of art featuring huge polka dots
- One of the foremost innovators of Happenings
- Works in a wide variety of media, including installations

Narcissus Garden
- Artist originally featured the work as a non-participant in the 1966 Venice Biennale

Figure 22.25a: Yayoi Kusama, *Narcissus Garden*, 2001, mirrored balls, this installation at Yokohama Triennale entitled "Narcissus Sea."

- 1500 large, mirrored, stainless steel balls placed on a lawn under a sign that said "Your Narcissism for Sale"
- Artist offered the balls for sale for 1200 lira ($2 dollars each) as a commentary on the commercialism and vanity of the current art world
- Narcissus Garden references the ancient myth of Narcissus, a young man who is so enraptured by his image in reflecting water that he stares at it indefinitely until he becomes a flower
- Installation later moved to water, where the floating balls reflect the natural environment—and the viewers—around the work; water placement makes a stronger connection to the ancient myth
- Balls move with the currents of the water and wind, reflecting organically made ever-changing viewpoints
- Installation has been exhibited in many places around the world, both in water and in dry spaces
- **Cross-Cultural Comparisons: Human Identity and Image**
  - Sherman, *Untitled 228* (Figure 29.10)
  - Wall Plaque from Oba's Palace (Figure 27.3)
  - Narmer Palette (Figures 3.4a and 3.4b)

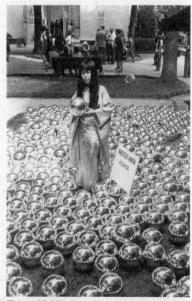

Figure 22.25b: Yayoi Kusama, *Narcissus Garden*, artist sells balls at the Venice Biennale 1966

Site Art

Sometimes called Earth Art, Site Art is dependent on its location to render full meaning. Often works of Site Art are temporary, as in the works of **Christo** and **Jeanne-Claude**. Other times the works remain, but need the original environment intact in order for it to be fully understood. Such items are often called **earthworks**. Site Art dates from the 1970s and is still being done today.

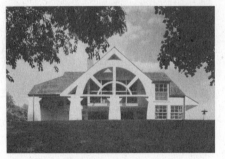

Figure 22.26: Robert Smithson, *Spiral Jetty*, 1970, mud, salt crystals, rocks, water coil, Great Salt Lake, Utah

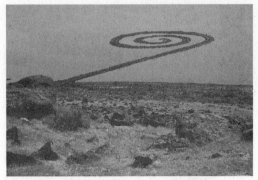

Figure 22.27a: Robert Venturi, John Rauch, and Denise Scott Brown, House in New Castle County, 1978-1983, wood frame and stucco, Delaware

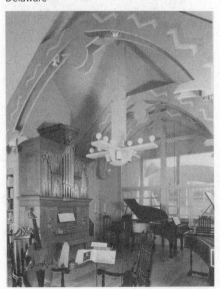

Figure 22.27b: Music Room of House in New Castle County

Robert Smithson, *Spiral Jetty*, 1970, mud, salt crystals, rocks, water coil, Great Salt Lake, Utah (Figure 22.26)

- Coil of rock in a part of the Great Salt Lake; located in an extremely remote and inaccessible area that features abandoned mines and mining equipment
- Upon walking on the jetty, the twisting and curling path changes the participant's view from every angle
- Artist used a tractor with native stone to create the jetty
- A jetty is supposed to be a pier in the water; here it is transformed into a curl of rocks sitting silently in a vast empty wilderness
- Coil is an image seen in North American earthworks, cf. Serpent Mound, Ohio
- Artist liked the blood red color of the water due to the presence of bacteria that live in the high salt content
- **Cross-Cultural Comparisons: Spirals and Circular Constructions**
  - Christo and Jeanne-Claude, *The Gates* (Figures 29.3a, 29.3b)
  - Great Serpent Mound (Figure 26.4)
  - Stonehenge (Figures 1.12a, 1.12b)

POSTMODERN ARCHITECTURE

Postmodern architecture, generally thought to emerge in the late 1970s and early 1980s sees the achievements of the International Style as cold and removed from the needs of modern cities with their cosmopolitan populations. Postmodernists see nothing wrong with incorporating ornament, traditional architectural expressions, and references to past styles in a modern context. Philip Johnson, himself a contributor to the International Style, as well as someone who worked on the Seagram Building (Figure 22.18), began the shift away to a Postmodern ideal with the AT&T building.

Robert Venturi, John Rauch, and Denise Scott Brown, House in New Castle County, 1978–1983, wood frame and stucco, Delaware (Figures 22.27a and 22.27b)

- House designed for a family of three
- Wife: musician; hence music room with two pianos, an organ, and a harpsichord
- Husband: bird watcher; large windows facing the woods

- Post-modern mix of historical styles
- Venturi's comment on the International Style: "Less is a bore."
- **Cross-Cultural Comparisons: Homes**
  - Jefferson, Monticello (Figures 19.5a, 19.5b)
  - Alberti, Palazzo Rucellai (Figure 15.2)
  - LeCorbusier, Villa Savoye (Figure 22.17)

VOCABULARY

Abstract: works of art that may have form, but have little or no attempt at pictorial representation (Figure 22.14)

Action Painting: an abstract painting in which the artist drips or splatters paint onto a surface like a canvas in order to create the work

Assemblage: a three-dimensional work made of various materials such as wood, cloth, paper, and miscellaneous objects

Biomorphism: a movement stressing organic shapes that hint at natural forms

Cantilever: a projecting beam that is attached to a building at one end, but suspended in the air at the other (Figure 22.15)

Collage: a composition made by pasting together different items onto a flat surface

Color field painting: a style of abstract painting characterized by simple shapes and monochromatic color

Documentary photography: a type of photography that seeks social and political redress for current issues by using photographs as a way of exposing society's faults

Earthwork: a large outdoor work in which the earth itself is the medium (Figure 22.26)

Ferroconcrete: steel reinforced concrete; the two materials act together to resist building stresses

Frottage: a composition made by rubbing a crayon or a pencil over paper placed over a surface with a raised design

Happening: an act of performance art that is intially planned but involves spontaneity, improvisation, and often audience participation

Harlem Renaissance: a particularly rich artistic period in the 1920s and 1930s that is named after the African-American neighborhood in New York City where it emerged. It is marked by a cultural resurgence by African-Americans in the fields of painting, writing, music, and photography

Installation: a temporary work of art made up of assemblages created for a particular space, like an art gallery or a museum (Figure 22.25b)

Mobile: a sculpture made of several different items that dangle from a ceiling and can be set into motion by air currents

Ready-made: a commonplace object selected and exhibited as a work of art

Silkscreen: a printing technique that passes ink or paint through a stenciled image to make multiple copies (Figure 22.23)

Venice Biennale: a major show of contemporary art that takes place every other year in various venues throughout the city of Venice; begun in 1895 (Figure 22.25b)

SUMMARY

Early modern art is characterized by the birth of radical art movements. Avant-garde artists, with the help of their progressive patrons, broke new ground in rethinking the traditional figure, and in the use of color as a vehicle of expression rather than description.

Artists moved in many directions; for example, abstract art was approached in entirely different ways by artists as diverse as Kandinsky and Mondrian. Other artists, such as Brancusi, come close to the abstract form, using representational ideas as a starting point. Still others, such as Surrealists, see conventional painting as a beginning, but expanded their horizons immediately after that.

Modern architects embrace new technology, using it to cantilever forms over open space, imitate the machine aesthetic of Art Deco, or espouse the complete artistic concept of the Bauhaus. Whatever the motivations, modern architecture is dominated by clear, clean, simple lines, paralleling some of the advances made in painting and sculpture.

PRACTICE EXERCISES

Multiple-Choice

1. Robert Smithson's works, like *Spiral Jetty*, were inspired by

   (A) Surrealist paintings
   (B) Aztec temple structures and complexes
   (C) Buddhist stupas and toranas
   (D) American Indian earthworks

2. The *Memorial Sheet for Karl Liebknecht* commemorates a moment in the

   (A) Franco-Prussian War of 1980
   (B) Communist uprising in 1919
   (C) erection of the Berlin Wall in 1961
   (D) collapse of the Stock Market in 1929

3. Cuban artist Wifredo Lam sought to combine his Hispanic heritage with

   (A) flat areas of color used in Japanese prints
   (B) facial designs inspired by African masks
   (C) abstract patterning popularized by painters of the New York School
   (D) found objects used by the Dadists

4. Alfred Stieglitz's photographs have been compared to

   (A) Surrealist paintings because of their odd juxtapositions
   (B) Cubist paintings because of the tonal values and the arrangement of shapes
   (C) Impressionist paintings because of their atmospheric effects
   (D) Realist paintings because of the concentration on the plight of the hard-working poor

5. Frida Kahlo's artwork expresses all of the following concerns EXCEPT

(A) Mexican and Pre-Columbian motifs

(B) European-style Surrealism

(C) frescos and Mexican muralism

(D) autobiographical episodes translated into personal visions

Short Essay

This work is Yayoi Kusama's *Narcissus Garden*. The photo on the right shows the artist at its first installation.

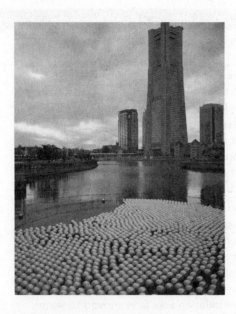 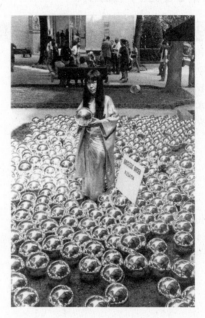

Where was this work first shown?

Why did this work cause a scandal when it was first shown?

How has the media used in this work created a variety of interpretations?

ANSWER KEY

1. **D**   2. **B**   3. **B**   4. **B**   5. **C**

ANSWERS EXPLAINED

Multiple-Choice

1. **(D)** The circular patterns seen in such earthworks as Great Serpent Mound formed a general inspiration for Smithson's works.

2. **(B)** The *Memorial Sheet for Karl Liebknecht* commemorates a moment in the Communist uprising in 1919 in Berlin, Germany.

3. **(B)** Cuban artist Wifredo Lam was influenced by African masks. Cuban ancestry is a mixture of European and African heritages, and his work often mirrors that combination.

4. **(B)** The development of Cubism is simultaneous with Stieglitz's experiments in photography. There is a strong parallel between Cubism's refined artistic palette and the subtle tonal shades in Stieglitz's photographs. Moreover, there is a comparison between Cubism's sharp angles and thoughtful compositional varieties in Stieglitz.

5. **(C)** Frida Kahlo did not paint murals or work in fresco.

Short-Essay Rubric

Question	Points	Key Points in a Good Response
Where was this work first shown?	1	Artist originally featured the work as a non-participant in the 1966 Venice Biennale
Why did this work cause a scandal when it was first shown?	2	Answers could include: ■ 1,500 large-mirrored, stainless steel balls placed on a lawn under a sign that said "Your Narcissism for Sale" ■ Artist offered the balls for sale for 1,200 lira ($2 dollars each) as a commentary on the commercialism and vanity of the current art world
How has the media used in this work created a variety of interpretations?	2	Answers could include: ■ Narcissus Garden references the ancient myth of Narcissus, a young man who is so enraptured by his image in reflecting water that he stares at it indefinitely until he becomes a flower. ■ The installation was later moved to water, where the floating balls reflect the natural environment—and the viewers—around the work; water placement makes a stronger connection to the ancient myth. ■ Balls move with the currents of the water and wind, reflecting organically made, ever-changing viewpoints. ■ The installation has been exhibited in many places around the world, both in water and in dry spaces.

Indian and Southeast Asian Art

23

ENDURING UNDERSTANDING: South, East, and Southeast Asia have ancient artistic traditions.

Essential Knowledge:

- Ancient ceramics survive from China and India.
- Religious beliefs developed locally, but spread throughout Asia.
- Rich artistic traditions were exchanged throughout the great civilizations of Asia.

ENDURING UNDERSTANDING: Great religions were established in Asia.

Essential Knowledge:

- Ancient belief systems, called Indic, spread throughout the region, eventually developing into religions like Hinduism and Buddhism.
- Buddhism spread through East Asia. Chinese religions were influenced by Buddhism and stressed living in harmony with nature and one another. Daoism and Confucianism emphasized living ethically within society's boundaries.
- Buddhism is a visual art form, noted for its religious images and narratives.
- Islam, Christianity, and ancient European cultures play a role in Asian art.
- Architecture is best expressed by religious temples, shrines, and rock-cut caves.

ENDURING UNDERSTANDING: Asian art is a reflection of Asian aesthetics.

Essential Knowledge:

- Indian art is characterized by Buddhist temples and shrines.
- There is a wide range of materials used in this region.
- Uniquely Asian art forms include Buddhist and Hindu images and buildings.
- Indian painting was often done in miniatures for court patrons.

ENDURING UNDERSTANDING: Asian art spreads throughout the world through trade.

Essential Knowledge:

- The Silk Road was key to the spread of artistic styles.
- Asian art shows evidence of the interconnectivity of regional schools with the wider world.
- Asian art heavily influenced the art of Europe.

HISTORICAL BACKGROUND

The fertile Indus and Ganges valleys were too great a temptation for outsiders, and thus the history of India has become a history of invasions and assimilations. But those who invaded came to stay, and so Indian life today is a layering of disparate populations to create a cosmopolitan culture. There are eighteen official languages in India—Hindi, the one foreigners think of as the national language, is spoken natively by only 20 percent of the population. Along with Hindus and Muslims, there are many concentrations of Jains, Buddhists, Christians, and Sikhs, as well as myriad tribal religions. Geographically, India has enormous range as well, from the world's tallest mountains to vast deserts and tropical forests. This is one of the most diverse countries on earth.

Patronage and Artistic Life

The arts play a critical role in Indian life. Most rulers have been extremely generous patrons, commissioning great buildings, sculptures, and murals to enhance civic and religious life, as well as their own glory. The interconnectiveness of the arts in India is crucial to understanding Indian artistic life. Monuments are conceived as a combination of the arts; the artists who work on them carry out their work at the behest of an artist who acts as a team leader with a single artistic vision. Thus, Indian monuments have a surprising uniformity of style. The design of religious art and architecture may have also been determined by a priest or other religious advisor, who ensured that proportions and iconography of monuments agreed with descriptions supplied in canonical texts and diagrams.

Much as in the European tradition, artists were trained as apprentices in workshops. The process was comprehensive; the artist learned everything from how to make a brush to how to create intricate miniatures or vast murals. Indians are highly organized in their approach to artistic training.

BUDDHIST PHILOSOPHY AND ART

Still practiced today as the dominant religion of Southeast Asia, Buddhism is a spiritual force that teaches individuals how to cope in a world full of misery. The central figure, Buddha (563–483 B.C.E.), who is not a god, rejected the worldly concerns of life at a royal court, and sought fulfillment traveling the countryside and living as an ascetic.

In Buddhism, life is believed to be full of suffering that is compounded by an endless cycle of birth and rebirth. The aim of every Buddhist is to end this cycle and achieve oneness with the supreme spirit, which involves a final release or extinguishing of the soul. This can only happen by accumulating spiritual merit through devotion to good works, charity, love of all beings, and religious fervor.

Buddhist art has a rich cultural iconography. Some of the most common symbols include:

- The Lion: a symbol of Buddha's royalty
- The Wheel: Buddha's law
- Lotus: a symbol of Buddha's pure nature. The lotus grows in swamps, but mud slides off its surface.
- Columns surrounded by a wheel: Buddha's teaching
- Empty Throne: Buddha, or a reminder of a Buddha's presence.

There is a surprising uniformity in the way in which Buddhas are depicted, given that they were produced over thousands of years and across thousands of miles. Typically Buddhas have a compact pose with little negative space (Figure 23.1). They are often seated, although standing and lying down are occasional variations. When seated, a Buddha is usually posed in a lotus position with the balls of his feet turned straight up, and a wheel marking on the souls of the feet is prominently displayed.

The treatment of drapery varies from region to region. In Central India, Buddhist drapery is extremely tight-fitting, and resting on one shoulder with folds slanting diagonally down the chest. In Gandhara, a region that spreads across northwest India, Pakistan, and Afghanistan, Buddhist figures wear heavy robes that cover both shoulders, similar to a Roman toga, showing a Hellenistic influence.

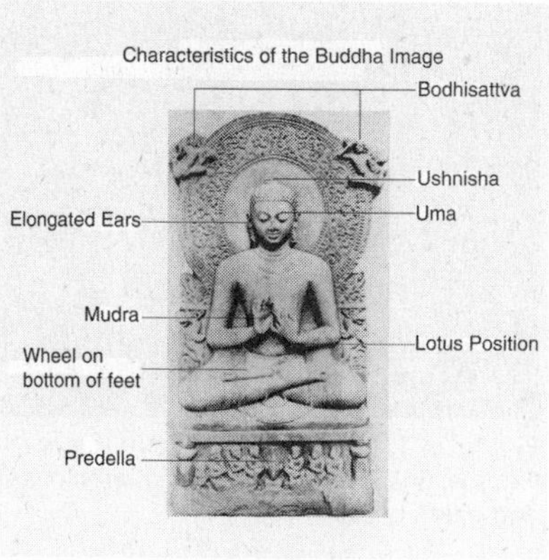

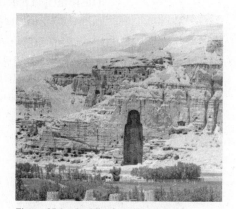

Figure 23.1: Principal characteristics of the Buddha

Buddhas are generally frontal, symmetrical, and have a nimbus, or halo, around their heads. Helpers, called **bodhisattvas**, are usually near the Buddha, sometimes attached to the nimbus.

Buddhas' moods are many, but most have a detached, removed quality that suggests meditation. Buddhas' actions and feelings are revealed by hand gestures called **mudras**.

The head has a top knot, or **ushnisha**, and the hair has a series of tight-fitting curls. Extremely long ears dangle almost to his shoulders. A curl of hair called an **urna** appears between his brows. His rejection of courtly life explains his disdain for personal jewelry.

Beneath statues of Buddha there usually is a base or a **predella**, which can include donor figures and may have an illustration of one of his teachings or a story from his life.

Buddhist art also depicts distinctive figures called **yakshas** (males) and **yakshis** (females), which are nature spirits that appear frequently in Indian popular religion. Their appearance in Buddhist art indicates their incorporation into the Buddhist pantheon. The females often stand in an elaborate dancelike poses, almost nude, with their breasts prominently displayed. The depiction of yakshas accentuates male characteristics such as powerful shoulders and arms.

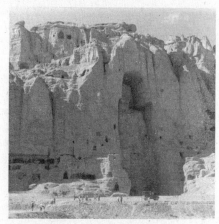

Figure 23.2a: Buddha from Bamiyan, 400–800, destroyed 2001, cut rock with plaster and polychrome paint, Afghanistan

Buddha from Bamiyan, 400–800, destroyed 2001, cut rock with plaster and polychrome paint, Afghanistan (Figures 23.2a and 23.2b)

- Bamiyan at the western end of the silk route; trading and religious center
- Two huge standing Buddhas, one 175 feet tall, the other 115 feet tall
- First colossal Buddhas
- Niche shaped like a halo—or mandorla—around the body
- Smaller Buddha: Sakyamuni, the historical Buddha
- Larger Buddha: Vairocana, the universal Buddha
- Buddhas originally covered with pigment and gold
- Cave galleries weave through the cliff face; some painted with wall paintings and images of the seated Buddha
- Pilgrims can walk through the cave galleries into passageways that lead to the level of the Buddha's shoulders
- Models for later large-scale rock-cut images in China
- Destroyed by the Taliban in an act of iconoclasm in March 2001

Figure 23.2b: Buddha from Bamiyan, oblique view

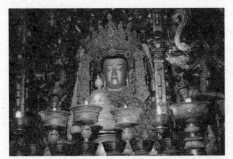

Figure 23.3: Jowo Rinpoche from the Jokhang Temple, 641, gilt metal with semiprecious stones and paint, Lhasa, Tibet

Jowo Rinpoche from the Jokhang Temple, 641, gilt metal with semiprecious stones and paint, Lhasa, Tibet (Figure 23.3)

- Enshrined in the Jokhang Temple; Tibet's earliest and foremost Buddhist temple
- Temple founded in 647 by the first ruler of a unified Tibet
- *Jowo* means "lord," *khang* means "house"
- Statue thought to have been blessed by the Buddha himself; believed to have been crafted in India during his lifetime
- Depiction of Buddha Sakyamuni as a young man, around the age of twelve
- Disappeared in 1960s during China's "Cultural Revolution"
- In 1983 lower part found in a rubbish heap; upper part in Beijing; restored in 2003
- **Cross-Cultural Comparisons: Sacred Images**
  - Moai (Figure 28.11)
  - *Apollo from Veii* (Figure 5.5)
  - *Reliquary of Sainte-Foy* (Figure 11.6c)

BUDDHIST ARCHITECTURE

The principal place of early Buddhist worship is the **stupa**, a mound-shaped shrine that has no interior. A stupa is a reliquary; worshippers gain spiritual merit through being in close proximity to its contents. A staircase leads the worshipper from the base to the drum. Buddhists pray while walking in a clockwise or easterly direction, that is, the direction of the sun's course. Because of the its distinctive shape, that of a giant hemisphere, and because one walks and prays with the sun, the stupa has cosmic symbolism. It is also conceived as being a symbol of Mt. Meru, the mountain that lies at the center of the world in Buddhist cosmology and serves as an axis connecting the earth and the heavens.

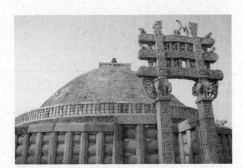

Figure 23.4a: Great Stupa, 3rd century B.C.E.–1st century C.E., stone masonry, sandstone on dome, Sanchi, Madhya Preadesh, India

Stupas, like one at **Sanchi** (Figure 23.4a), have a central mast of three umbrellas at the top of the monument, each umbrella symbolizing the three jewels of Buddhism: The Buddha, the Law, and the Community of Monks. The square enclosure around the umbrellas symbolizes a sacred tree surrounded by a fence.

Four **toranas**, at the cardinal points of the compass, act as elaborate gateways to the structure.

Great Stupa, third century B.C.E.–first century C.E., stone masonry, sandstone on dome, Sanchi, Madhya Preadesh, India (Figures 23.4a–23.4e)

- A Buddhist shrine, mound shaped, and faced with dressed stone
- Three umbrellas at the top representing Buddha, Buddha's Law, and Monastic Orders
- Railing at crest of mound surrounds the umbrellas, symbolically a sacred tree
- Double stairway at south end leads from base to drum where there is a walkway for circumambulation
- Originally painted white

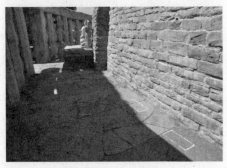

Figure 23.4b: Interior ambulatory

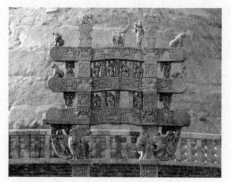

Figure 23.4c: North Gate, or Torana

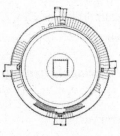

Figure 23.4d: Great Stupa plan

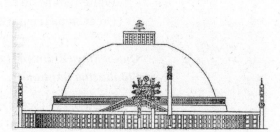

Figure 23.4e: Great Stupa elevation

- Hemispherical dome is a replication of the dome of heaven
- Four toranas grace entrances, at cardinal points of the compass
- Torana: richly carved scenes on architraves; Buddha does not appear himself, but is symbolized by an empty throne or a tree under which he meditated; some of these reliefs may also represent the sacred sites where Shakyamuni Buddha visited or taught; horror vacui of composition; high-relief sculptures
- 600 donors have inscriptions carved into the stupa revealing the project was funded by women as well as men; common people as well as monks
- **Cross-Cultural Comparisons: Integration of Sculpture and Architecture**
  - Angkor Wat (Figures 3.8a, 3.8b, 3.8c, 3.8d)
  - Parthenon (Figures 4.5, 4.6b)
  - Mortuary Temple of Hatshepsut (Figure 3.9a)

Borobudur, c. 750–842, volcanic stone masonry, Java, Indonesia (Figures 23.5a, 23.5b, and 23.5c)

- Massive Buddhist monument contains 504 life-size Buddhas, 1,460 narrative relief sculptures on 1,300 panels 8,200 feet long; there are 1,500 stupas and one million carved blocks of stone
- Iconographically complex and intricate; many levels of meaning; may reflect Buddhist cosmology
- Meant to be walked around (circumambulated) on each terrace; six concentric square terraces topped by three circular tiers with a great stupa at the summit
- Pyramidal in form, aligned with the four cardinal points of the compass
- Lower stories represent the world of desire and negative impulses; middle areas represent the world of forms, people have to control these negative impulses; the top story is the world of formulas, where the physical world and worldly desire are expunged
- A place of pilgrimage
- Five terraces of identical stepped square plan
- 72 openwork Buddhas each with a preaching mudra
- On top an enclosed stupa
- Rubble faced with carved volcanic stone

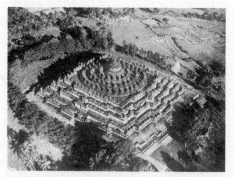

Figure 23.5a: Borobudur Temple, c. 750–842, volcanic stone masonry, Java, Indonesia

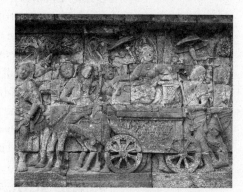

Figure 23.5b: Borobudur Temple: Queen Maya Riding a Horse Carriage Retreating to Lumbini to Give Birth to Prince Siddhartha Gautama

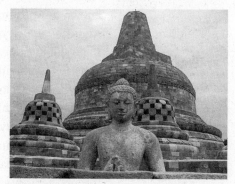

Figure 23.5c: Borobudur Temple, Buddha

- **Cross-Cultural Comparisons: Pyramid-Shaped Monuments**
  - Great Pyramids of Gizeh (Figure 3.6a)
  - White Temple on Its Ziggurat (Figures 2.1a, 2.1b)
  - Great Stupa (Figure 23.4a)

Queen Maya Riding a Horse Carriage Retreating to Lumbini to Give Birth to Prince Siddhartha Gautama

- Densely packed scene; horror vacui
- Queen majestic and at rest before giving birth
- She is brought to the city in a great ceremonial procession
- Ready to give birth to her son, Prince Siddhartha Gautama, the Buddha
- **Cross-Cultural Comparisons: Relief Sculpture**
  - Plaque of the Ergastines (Figure 4.5)
  - Wall Plaque from Oba's Palace (Figure 27.3)
  - Anthropomorphic Stele (Figure 1.2)

HINDU PHILOSOPHY AND ART

To outsiders, Hinduism is a bewildering religion with myriad sects, each devoted to the worship of one of its many gods. The complexity and multiplicity of the practices and beliefs associated with Hinduism are evident in the name of the religion, which is an umbrella term meaning, "the religions of Hindustan (India)." Folk beliefs exist side by side with sophisticated philosophical schools. But all forms of Hinduism concentrate on the infinite variety of the divine, whether it is expressed in the gods, in nature, or in other human beings. Those who proclaim to be orthodox Hindus accept the Vedic texts as divine in origin, and many maintain aspects of the Vedic social hierarchy, which assigns a caste of ritual specialists, known as Brahmins, to officiate between the gods and humankind.

As in the case of Buddhism, every Hindu is to lead a good life through prayer, good deeds, and religious devotion, because only in that way can he or she break the cycle of reincarnation. **Shiva** is one of the principal Hindu deities, who periodically dances the world to destruction and rebirth. Other important deities include Brahma, the creator god; Vishnu, the preserver god; and the great goddesses who are manifest as peaceful consorts, like Laksmi and Parvati.

HINDU SCULPTURE

Temple sculpture is a complete integration with the architecture to which it is attached—sometimes the buildings are thought of as a giant work of sculpture. Pairs of divine couples, known as **mithuna**, appear upon the exterior and doorways of some temples. Sexual allusions dominate and are expressed with candor, but not obscenity. Hindu sculptures accentuate sinuous curves and the lines of the body. Dance poses are common. Temple surfaces are also ornamented with organic and geometric designs, including lateral bands that depict subjects such as lotus flowers, temple bells, and strings of pearls.

Images placed in the "womb" of the temple are idols in that they are invoked with the essence of divinity that the figure represents. To touch the image is to touch the god himself or herself; few can do this. Instead the image is treated with the utmost respect and deference, and is occasionally exposed to public viewing. Worshippers experience the divine through actively seeing the invoked image, an experience known as **darshan** and performing **puja**, a ritual offering to the deity, which is mediated by temple priests.

Shiva as Lord of Dance (Nataraja) with a nimbus, c. eleventh century c.e., cast bronze, Musée Guimet, Paris (Figure 23.6)

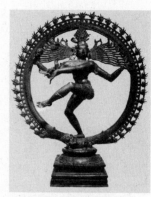

Figure 23.6: Shiva as Lord of Dance (Nataraja), with a nimbus, c. 11th century c.e., cast bronze, Musée Guimet, Paris

- Vigorously dancing with one foot on a dwarf, the Demon of Ignorance; often depicted in a flaming nimbus
- Flying locks of hair terminate in rearing cobra heads
- One hand sounds the drum that he dances to, another has a flame
- Shiva has four hands
- Epicene quality
- Periodically destroys the universe so it can be reborn again
- He unfolds the universe out of the drum held in one of his right hands; he preserves it by uplifting his other right hand in a gesture indicating "do not be afraid"
- Shiva has a third vertical eye barely suggested between his other two eyes. He once burned the god Kama with this eye.
- **Cross-Cultural Comparisons: Sacred Images**
  - Bernini, *Ecstasy of Saint Teresa* (Figures 17.4a, 17.4b)
  - Saint Luke from the *Lindisfarne Gospels* (Figure 10.2b)
  - Great Buddha from Todai-ji (Figure 25.1b)

HINDU ARCHITECTURE

The Hindu temple is not a hall for congregational worship; instead it is the residence of a god. The temples are solidly built with small interior rooms, just enough space for a few priests and individual worshippers. At the center is a tiny interior cella that is called the "Womb of the World" where the sacred statue invoked with the main deity is placed. Although Indians knew the arch, they preferred corbelled-vaulting techniques to create a cavelike look on the inside. Thick walls protect the deity from outside forces. An antechamber, where ceremonies are prepared, precedes the cella, and a hypostyle hall is visible from the outside where congregants can participate. Hindu temples are constructed amid a temple complex that includes subsidiary buildings.

In northern India, temples have a more vertical character, with large towers setting the decorative scheme, and other subsidiary towers imitating the shape but at various scales. Placed on high pedestals, temples have a sense of grandeur as they command the countryside. Major temples form "temple cities" in south India, where layers of concentric gated walls surround a network of temples, shrines, pillared halls, and colonnades. The Hindu temples found in Cambodia are based upon a pyramidal plan with a central shrine surrounded by subshrines and enclosed walls.

Temple exteriors are covered with sculpture, almost in a feverish frenzy to crowd every blank spot on the surface.

Lakshmana Temple, 930–950, sandstone, Khajuraho, India (Figures 23.7a, 23.7b, 23.7c, 23.7d)

- Placed on a high pedestal
- A series of shapes that build to become a large tower; complicated intertwining of similar forms
- In the center is the "embryo" room containing the shrine, very small, only space enough for the priest

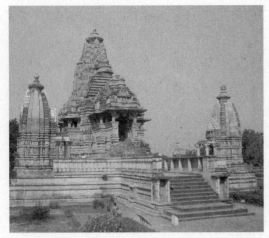
Figure 23.7a: Lakshmana Temple, 930–950, sandstone, Khajuraho, India

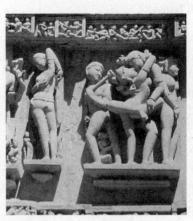
Figure 23.7b: Detail of façade of Lakshmana Temple

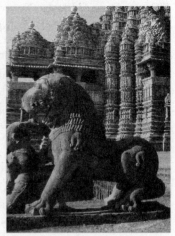
Figure 23.7c: Detail of Lakshmana Temple

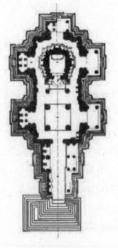
Figure 23.7d: Plan of Lakshmana Temple

- Corbelled roofs have a beehive quality
- Hindu temple grouped with a series of other temples in Khajuraho
- Made of ashlar masonry
- Bands of horizontal moldings unite the temple
- Made of fine sandstone
- Compact proportions
- Sandhara: an inner ambulatory
- East/west axis: receives direct rays from the rising sun
- Sculpture has a harmonious integration with the architecture
- Figures are sensuous with revealing clothing
- Erotic poses symbolize regeneration
- **Cross-Cultural Comparisons: Ashlar Masonry**
  - Parthenon (Figure 4.16b)
  - Persepolis (Figures 2.6a, 2.6b)
  - Petra (Figures 6.9a, 6.9b, 6.9c)

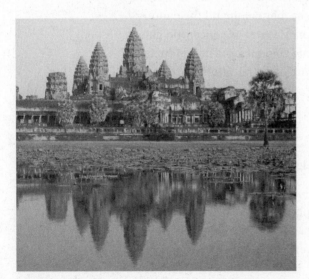
Figure 23.8a: Angkor Wat, c. 800–1400, stone masonry, sandstone, Cambodia

Angkor, the temple of Angkor Wat, and the city of Angkor Thom, c. 800–1400, stone masonry, sandstone, Cambodia (Figures 23.8a–23.8e)

- Capital of medieval Cambodia built by Suryavarman II
- Main pyramid is surrounded by four corner towers; temple–mountain
- Corbelled gallery roofs
- Dedicated to Vishnu, most sculptures represent Vishnu's incarnations
- Horror vacui of sculptural reliefs
- Sculpture in rhythmic dance poses; repetition of shapes
- Complex built by successive kings installing various deities in the complex
- Complex has a mixed Buddhist/Hindu character
- Kings often identified themselves with the gods they installed

- Influenced by Indian use of corbelled vaulting
- Mountain-like towers symbolize the five peaks of Mount Meru, a sacred mountain said to be the center of the spiritual and physical universe in both Buddhism and Hinduism
- **Cross-Cultural Comparisons: Water and Art**
  - Versailles Gardens (Figure 17.3e)
  - Kusama, *Narcissus Garden* (Figures 22.25a, 22.25b)
  - Alhambra (Figure 9.15b)
- ***Churning of the Ocean of Milk***
  - Story from Hindu religion
  - Churning of the Ocean of the Stars to obtain Amrita, the nectar of immortal life
  - Both the gods (the devas) and the devils (asuras) churn the ocean to guarantee themselves immortality
  - To churn the ocean they used the Serpent King, Vasuki
  - A bas-relief at Angkor Wat depicts devas and asuras churning the Ocean of Milk
  - Vishnu wraps a serpent around Mount Mandara; the mountain rotates around the sea and churns it
- ***Jayavarman VII***, Khmer King, reigned c.1181–1218
  - Most famous and powerful Khmer monarch
  - Heavily influenced by his two wives, who were sisters. He married one after the other's death
  - Patron of Angkor Thom
  - Devoted to Buddhism, although his monuments show a mixture of Buddhist and Hindu iconography
- **Cross-Cultural Comparisons: Gardens**
  - Versailles Gardens (Figure 17.3e)
  - Ryoan-ji (Figures 25.2a, 25.2b, 25.2c)
  - Kusama, *Narcissus Garden* (Figures 22.25a, 22.25b)

HINDU PAINTING

Indians excel at painting miniatures, illustrations done with water-color on paper, used either to illuminate books or as individual leaves kept in an album. One of the most famous schools of Indian painting is the Rajput School, which enjoyed illustrating Hindu myths and legends, especially the life of Krishna. Care is also lavished on individual portraits, which were done with immediacy and freshness.

As in most Indian art, compositions tend to be both crowded and colorful. Perspective is tilted upward so that the surface of objects, like tables or rugs, can be seen in their entirety. Floral patterns contribute to the richness of expression. Figures are painted with great delicacy and generally seem small compared to the landscape around them. They have a doll-like character that adds to the fairy-tale–like nature of the stories being illustrated.

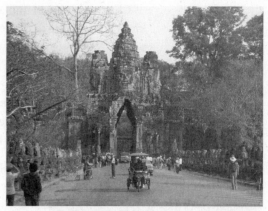

Figure 23.8b: South Gate of Angkor Thom

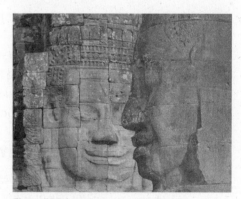

Figure 23.8c: *Churning of the Ocean of Milk*

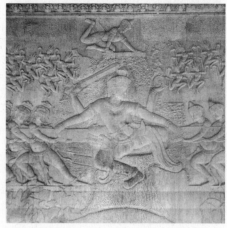

Figure 23.8d: *Jayavarman VII as Buddha*

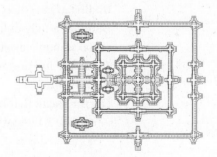

Figure 23.8e: Angkor Wat plan

Characteristics of Indian painting include a heightened and intense use of color, with black lines outlining figures. Humans have a wide range of emotion; figures often gesticulate wildly. Nature is seen as friendly and restorative. Few names of Indian artists have come down to us; the works are generally anonymous, even among the greatest masters.

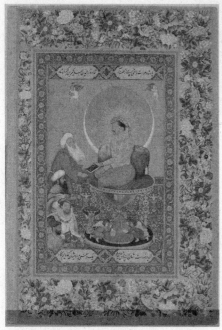

Figure 23.9: Bichitr, *Jahangir Preferring a Sufi Shaikh to Kings*, c. 1620, watercolor, gold, and ink on paper, Freer Gallery of Art, Washington D.C.

Bichitr, *Jahangir Preferring a Sufi Shaikh to Kings*, c. 1620, watercolor, gold, and ink on paper, Freer Gallery of Art, Washington D.C. (Figure 23.9)

- Jahangir had many artists follow him wherever he went; wanted everything recorded
- He sought to bring together things from distant lands
- Seated on an hourglass throne; sands of time run out; Jahangir near the end
- Surrounded by a halo of the sun and moon; Jahangir is the source of all light
- Cross-cultural influences: sits on a Renaissance carpet; figures of small cherubs copied from European paintings
- Artist in lower left corner; symbolically signs his name on the footstool beneath Jahangir
- Artist holds a miniature with two horses and an elephant—perhaps gifts from his patron
- James I of England in lower left corner
- Ottoman sultan (not a real portrait)
- Holy Man is handed a book by Jahangir, or perhaps the Holy Man is handing Jahangir the book; Holy men placed above and ranks higher than all others
- Quotation says: "Though outwardly shahs stand before him, he fixes his gazes on dervishes."
- **Cross-Cultural Comparisons: Works that Show Western Influence**
  - Cotsiogo, Hide Painting of a Sun Dance (Figure 26.13)
  - Cabrera, *Sor Juana Inés de la Cruz* (Figure 18.6)
  - Lindauer, *Tamati Waka Nene* (Figure 28.7)

VOCABULARY

Ashlar masonry: carefully cut and grooved stones that support a building without the use of concrete or other kinds of masonry (Figure 23.7a)

Bas-relief: a very shallow relief sculpture (Figure 23.5b)

Bodhisattva: a deity who refrains from entering nirvana to help others

Buddha: a fully enlightened being. There are many Buddhas, the most famous of whom is Sakyamuni, also known as Gautama or Siddhartha (Figure 23.5c)

Darshan: in Hinduism, the ability of a worshipper to see a deity and the deity to see the worshipper

Horror vacui: (Latin, meaning "fear of empty spaces"), a type of artwork in which the entire surface is filled with objects, people, designs, and ornaments in a crowded and sometimes congested way (Figure 23.5b)

Iconoclasm: the destruction of religious images that are seen as heresy (Figure 23.3)

Mandorla: (Italian for "almond"), an almond-shaped circle of light around the figure of Christ or Buddha (Figure 23.2)

Mithuna: in India, the mating of males and females in a ritualistic, symbolic, or physical sense (Figure 23.7b)

Mudra: a symbolic hand gesture in Hindu and Buddhist art (Figure 23.1)

Nirvana: an afterlife in which reincarnation ends and the soul becomes one with the supreme spirit

Puja: a Hindu prayer ritual

Sakyamuni: the historical Buddha, named after the town of Sakya, Buddha's birthplace (Figure 23.3)

Shiva: the Hindu god of creation and destruction (Figure 23.6)

Stupa: a dome-shaped Buddhist shrine (Figure 23.4a)

Torana: a gateway near a stupa that has two upright posts and three horizontal lintels. They are usually elaborately carved (Figure 23.4a)

Urna: a circle of hair on the brows of a deity, sometimes represented as focal point (Figure 23.1)

Ushnisha: a protrusion at the top of the head, or the top knot of a Buddha (Figure 23.1)

Vairocana: the universal Buddha, a source of enlightenment; also known as the Supreme Buddha who represents "emptiness," that is, freedom from earthly matters to help achieve salvation (Figure 23.2a)

Vishnu: the Hindu god worshipped as the protector and preserver of the world (Figure 23.8c)

Wat: a Buddhist monastery or temple in Cambodia (Figure 23.8a)

Yakshi (masculine: **yaksha**): female and male figures of fertility in Buddhist and Hindu art

SUMMARY

The diversity of the Indian subcontinent is reflected in the wide range of artistic expression one finds there. Indians typically unify the arts, so that one large monument is realized as a single creative expression involving painting, sculpture, and architecture.

Buddhist images dominate early Indian art. Buddha himself is often depicted in a meditative state, with his various mudras revealing his inner thoughts. Hindu sculptures feature a myriad of gods, with Shiva as the most dominant. Both Buddhist and Hindu temples are mound-shaped, the Buddhist works being a large, solid hemisphere, and the Hindu a sculpted mountain with a small interior.

Both Hindu and Buddhist art are marked by horror vacui, forms piled one atop the other in crowded compositions.

Multiple-Choice

Questions 1–3 refer to these images.

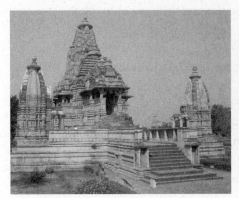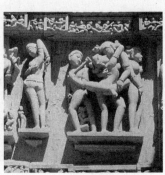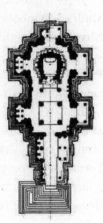

1. The Lakshmana temple is a Hindu temple that has a narrow interior because

   (A) it is only for the high priests to enter and address the god inside
   (B) vaulting techniques were unknown
   (C) the narrow passageway symbolizes the journey to salvation
   (D) the interior darkness symbolizes the evil in the world

2. The outside is addressed with erotic sculptures that connote

   (A) inspiration
   (B) regeneration
   (C) subjugation
   (D) intolerance

3. The highly carved exterior is similar to the complex at

   (A) Borobudur, Java
   (B) Persepolis, Iran
   (C) Todai-ji, Japan
   (D) Ryoan-ji, Japan

---

4. In Bichitr's *Jahangir Preferring a Sufi Shaikh to Kings*, the artist shows the influence of European art in all of the following details EXCEPT the use of

   (A) baby angels
   (B) a foreign king
   (C) a self-portrait of the artist
   (D) a Renaissance-type carpet

5. The Bamiyan Buddhas were destroyed in 2001 in an act of

(A) iconography
(B) impluvium
(C) isocephalism
(D) iconoclasm

Short Essay

This is the Great Stupa in Sanchi, India, dated between 300 B.C.E. AND 100 C.E.

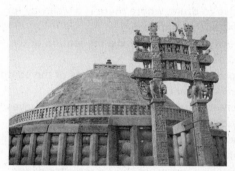 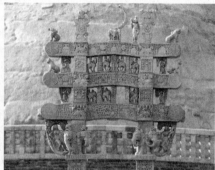

With what religion is this monument associated?

Using specific examples, explain the symbolism of the features of the monument.

How was the worshipper intended to use this monument for practicing his or her faith?

ANSWER KEY

1. **A**   2. **B**   3. **A**   4. **C**   5. **D**

ANSWERS EXPLAINED

Multiple-Choice

1. **(A)** The interiors of these temples are quite small, so only high priests were permitted to enter into the presence of the god inside.

2. **(B)** The erotic sculptures are done with frankness to symbolize regeneration. They are not done to be lurid or sinful.

3. **(A)** Borobudur has many sculptures, both in relief and free standing, wrapped around its exterior.

4. **(C)** All of these choices are things that appear in the painting, but the self-portrait is the only one that is not just from Europe but could also be Indian.

5. **(D)** Iconoclasm is defined as the destruction of images. The Bamiyan Buddhas were blown up because they were considered false idols.

Short-Essay Rubric

Question	Points	Key Points in a Good Response
With what religion is this monument associated?	1	Buddhism
Using specific examples, explain the symbolism of the features of the monument.	2	Answers could include: ■ Three umbrellas at the top representing Buddha, Buddha's Law, and Monastic Orders ■ Railing at crest of mound surrounds the umbrellas, symbolically a sacred tree ■ Double stairway at south end leads from base to drum, where there is a walkway for circumambulation ■ Hemispherical dome is a replication of the dome of heaven ■ Four toranas, at cardinal points of the compass, grace entrances ■ *Torana*: richly carved scenes on architraves; Buddha does not appear himself but is symbolized by an empty throne or a tree under which he meditated; some of these reliefs may also represent the sacred sites where Sakyamuni Buddha visited or taught
How was the worshipper intended to use this monument for practicing his or her faith?	2	Answers could include: ■ A stupa is a reliquary, and worshippers gain spiritual merit through being in proximity to its contents. ■ A staircase leads the worshipper from the base to the drum. ■ Buddhists pray while walking in a clockwise or easterly direction, which is the direction of the sun's course. ■ Because of its distinctive shape, that of a giant hemisphere, and because one walks and prays with the sun, the stupa has cosmic symbolism. ■ The stupa is also conceived as being a symbol of Mt. Meru, the mountain that lies at the center of the world in Buddhist cosmology and serves as an axis connecting the earth and the heavens.

Chinese and Korean Art

24

TIME PERIOD: FROM PREHISTORIC TIMES TO THE PRESENT

ENDURING UNDERSTANDING: South, East, and Southeast Asia have ancient artistic traditions.

Essential Knowledge:

- Ancient ceramics survive from China and India.
- Religious beliefs developed locally, but spread throughout Asia.
- Rich artistic traditions were exchanged throughout the great civilizations of Asia.

ENDURING UNDERSTANDING: Great religions were established in Asia.

Essential Knowledge:

- Ancient belief systems, called Indic, spread throughout the region, eventually developing into religions like Hinduism and Buddhism.
- Buddhism spread through east Asia. Chinese religions were influenced by Buddhism and stressed living in harmony with nature and one another. Daoism and Confucianism emphasized living ethically within society's boundaries.
- Buddhism is a visual art form, noted for its religious images and narratives.
- Islam, Christianity, and ancient European cultures play a role in Asian art.
- Architecture is best expressed by religious temples, shrines, and rock-cut caves.

ENDURING UNDERSTANDING: Asian art is a reflection of Asian aesthetics.

Essential Knowledge:

- Chinese art is characterized by paintings on scrolls with limited color.
- There is a wide range of materials used in this region.
- Uniquely Asian art forms include Buddhist and Hindu images and buildings.
- Calligraphy is a central art form in Chinese art.

ENDURING UNDERSTANDING: Asian art spreads throughout the world through trade.

Essential Knowledge:

- The Silk Road was key to the spread of artistic styles.
- Asian art shows evidence of the interconnectivity of regional schools with the wider world.
- Asian art heavily influenced the art of Europe.

HISTORICAL BACKGROUND

Although Chinese culture seems monolithic to those in the West, China has the size and population of Europe, with the same ethnic diversity and the same number of languages. To speak in general terms of Chinese art, therefore, has the same validity as speaking in general terms about European art.

To make such a diverse subject more manageable, Chinese art is divided into historical periods named after the families who ruled China for vast stretches of time. These families, united by blood and tradition, formed dynasties, and their impact on Chinese culture has been enormous.

The first ruler of a united China was Emperor **Shih Huangdi**, who reigned in the third century B.C.E. He not only unified China politically, but was also responsible for codifying written Chinese, standardizing weights and measures, and establishing a uniform currency. Moreover, he started the famous Great Wall and began his majestic tomb. While historians have taken a more critical look at Shi Huangdi's accomplishments, his insistence on government promotion based on achievement rather than family connections had far-reaching effects on Chinese society.

Dynastic fortunes reached their greatest height during the Tang Dynasty (618–906 C.E.). Brilliant periods were also achieved under the Yuan of Kublai Khan (1215–1294) and the Ming Dynasty (1368–1644), which built the **Forbidden City** (Figure 24.2).

A particularly long-lasting and artistically rich period in Korea was formed during the Silla Dynasty (57 B.C.E.–935 C.E.). Silla rulers united with the Tang Dynasty to solidify territorial gains on the Korean peninsula. They later waged a successful war to expel the Chinese who had intended to form puppet governments throughout Korea. Silla rulers established a royal burial ground in present-day Gyeongju. The largest tomb measures over 260 feet in diameter and 400 feet long, and contains a wide array of imperial gold regalia, jewelry, pottery, and metalwork.

East Asia has been marked by a great deal of turbulence in the twentieth century. The Qing Dynasty collapsed in 1911, replaced by a chaotic rule under the Republic of China. The Japanese invasion in the 1930s caused more upheaval, as did the eventual triumph of the communist forces under Mao Tse-tung in 1949. Peace still did not settle over China since internal struggles, such as the Cultural Revolution and the Great Leap Forward, ended up being political motives to enforce purges and persecutions.

Similarly in Korea, occupation by Japan left great scars on the Korean physical and mental landscape. The 1945 Japanese collapse left Korea as a nation divided in two. The subsequent Korean War achieved little—the country lay in ruins, and is still divided roughly the same way it was before the war. Today South Korea has a vibrant economy and is a world leader in many scientific and economic related fields. North Korea, however, remains economically stagnant.

Patronage and Artistic Life

Calligraphy is the central artistic expression in traditional China, standing as it does at a midpoint between poetry and painting. Those who wanted important state positions had to pass a battery of exams that included calligraphy. Even emperors were known to have been accomplished calligraphers, painters, and poets. Standard written Chinese is often at variance with the more cursive or running script used in paintings, some of which is so artistically rendered that modern Chinese readers cannot decipher it. Rather than letters, which are used in European languages, Chinese employs characters, each of which represents a word or an idea. Therefore, the artistic representation of a word inherently carries more meaning than a creatively written individual letter in English.

Artists worked under the patronage of religion or the state, although a counterculture was developed by a group called the **literati** who painted for themselves, eschewing public commissions and personal fame. These artists produced paintings of a highly individualized nature, not caring what the world at large would think.

At first the Korean language was written with adapted Chinese characters called **hanja**. A native alphabet was invented in 1444 during the reign of Kong Sejong, a king of the Joseon Dynasty. However, many Koreans preferred to remain loyal to the Chinese script, seeing the native writing as common and for the uneducated. During the twentieth century, standard Korean began to adopt the native script as its own. Today, it is more likely to be written in a western style—that is, horizontally and from left to right—in contrast to other Asian scripts.

CHINESE PHILOSOPHIES

Daoism and **Confucianism**, the two great philosophies of ancient China, dominate all aspects of Chinese art, from the original artistic thought to the final execution. Dao, meaning "the Way," can be characterized as a religious journey that allows the pilgrim to wander meaningfully in search of self-expression. It was begun by **Laozi** (604–531 B.C.E.), a philosopher who believed in escaping society's pressures, achieving serenity, and working toward a oneness with nature. Daoists emphasize individual expression and strongly embrace the philosophy of doing unto others. The yin and the yang are well-known Daoist symbols (Figure 24.3c).

The great Chinese philosopher **Confucius** (551–479 B.C.E.) wrote about behavior, relationships, and duty in a series of precepts called *The Analects*. Built on a system of mutual respect, the Confucian model presents an ideal man whose attributes include loyalty, morality, generosity, and humanity. An important ingredient in Confucianism is respect for traditional values.

CHINESE ARCHITECTURE

The design of the stupa, a Buddhist building associated with India, moved eastward with missionaries along the Great Silk Road, transforming itself into the **pagoda** when it reached China. Built for a sacred purpose, the pagoda characteristically has one design that is repeated vertically on each level, each smaller than the design below it. In this way, pagodas achieve substantial height through a repetition of forms.

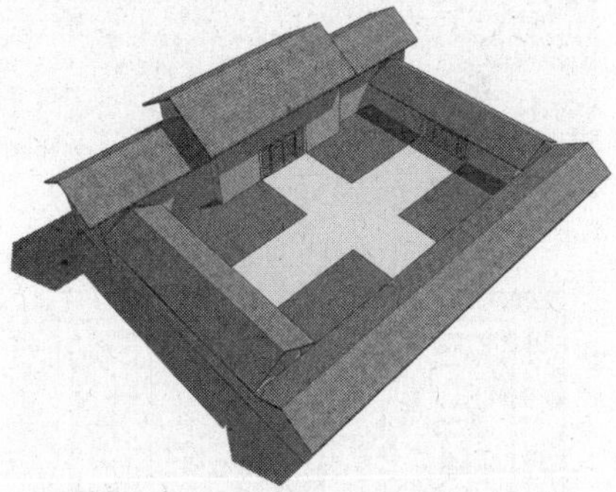

The exterior walls of a courtyard style residence (Figure 24.1) kept the crowded outside world away and framed an atrium in which family members resided in comparative tranquility. In harmony with Confucian thought, elders were to be honored and so were to live in a suite of rooms on the warmer north end of the courtyard. Children

Figure 24.1: Chinese courtyard-style residence with the principal structure on the north side facing south.

lived in the wings, servants in the south end. The southeast corner usually functioned as an entrance, the southwest as a lavatory.

This courtyard-style arrangement is reflected on a massive scale in the **Forbidden City**. The emperor's seat is in the Hall of Supreme Harmony, itself on the north end of a courtyard; the throne faces south. The entire Forbidden City is a rectangular grid with its southern entrance and its high walls keeping the concerns of the multitude at a safe distance.

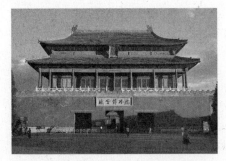

Figure 24.2a: Forbidden City, 15th century and later, stone masonry, marble, brick, wood, and ceramic tile, Beijing, China

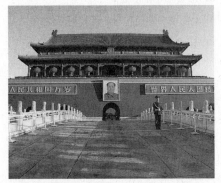

Figure 24.2b: Front Gate of the Forbidden City

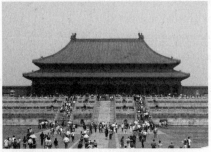

Figure 24.2c: Hall of Supreme Harmony

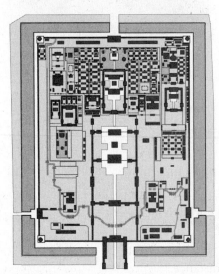

Figure 24.2d: Plan of Forbidden City

The Chinese, both in the Forbidden City and in less lavish projects, used wood for their principal building material. Tiled roofs seem to float over structures with eaves that hang away from the wall space and curve up to allow light in and keep rain out. Walls protect the interior from the weather, but do not support the building. Instead, support comes from an interior fabric of wooden columns that are grooved together rather than nailed. Corbeled brackets are used to transition the tops of columns to the swinging eaves. Wooden architecture is painted both to preserve the wood and enhance artistic effect.

Forbidden City, fifteenth century, Ming Dynasty, stone masonry, marble, brick, wood, ceramic tile, Beijing, China (Figures 24.2a–24.2d)

- Largest and most complete Chinese architectural ensemble in existence
- 9,000 rooms
- Walls 30 feet high to keep people out and those inside in
- Forbidden City so named because only the royal court could enter
- Each corner of the rectangular plan has a tower representing the four corners of the world
- Focus is the Hall of Supreme Harmony, the throne room and seat of power; wood structure made with elaborately painted beams; meant for grand ceremonies
- Yellow tile roofs and red painted wooden beams placed on marble foundations unify the structures in the Forbidden City into an artistic whole
- Hall of Supreme Harmony ceremonies: new year, the winter solstice, emperor's birthday
- Surrounding wall of the Forbidden City characteristic of a Chinese city: privacy within provides protection; containment part of Chinese culture
- **Cross-Cultural Comparisons: Centers of Power**
  - Versailles (Figure 17.3a)
  - Nan Madol (Figures 28.1a, 28.1b)
  - Barry and Pugin, Houses of Parliament (Figures 20.1a, 20.1b)

CHINESE AND KOREAN PAINTING

East Asian painting appears in many formats, including album leaves, fans, murals, and scrolls. Scrolls come in two formats: The handscroll (Figure 24.3a), which is horizontal and can be read on a desk or table, and the hanging scroll (Figure 24.3b), which is supported by a pole or hung for a time on a wall and unraveled vertically. No scrolls were allowed on permanent view in a home—they were something to be admired, studied, and analyzed, not hung for mere decorative qualities. Scrolls were stored away in specifically designed cabinets.

Handscrolls are read right to left. Although paper is sometimes used as a painting surface, silks are preferred and specially chosen by the artist for their color and texture to evoke a mood. The silk is then attached to wooden dowels and secured at the ends. When the scrolls are unwound, a title panel first appears, much like the title page in a book. As the scroll is carefully unrolled a section at a time, the viewer encounters both text and painting intertwined. Square red markings, made by artistically rendered seals, identify either the artist or the owners of the painting. In Chinese art, it is considered acceptable to comment on a work by writing poetry in praise of what has been read or seen. The commentaries are written on the last panel, called the **colophon**.

Landscape paintings are highly prized in Chinese art. Like European paintings of the same date, they do not seek to represent a particular forest or mountain, but reflect an artistic construct yielding a philosophical idea. Typically, some parts of a painting are empty and barren, suggesting openness and space. Other parts are crowded, almost impenetrable. This intertwining of crowded and empty spaces is a reflection of the Daoist theory of **yin** and **yang** (Figure 24.3c), in which opposites flow into one another.

Another specialty is **porcelain**. Subtle and refined vase shapes are combined with imaginative designs to create works of art that appear to be utilitarian, but are actually objects that stand alone. To achieve maximum gloss and finish, sophisticated glazing techniques are applied to the surface. Glazing has the added benefit of protecting the vase from wear.

The Literati

Some artists rejected the restrictive nature of court art and developed a highly individualized style. These artists, called **literati**, worked as painters, furniture makers, and landscape architects, as well as in other fields. The literati were often scholars rather than professional artists, and by tradition did not sell their works, but gave them to friends and connoisseurs.

Funeral Banner of Lady Dai (Xin Zhui), 180 B.C.E., painted silk, Hunan Provincial Museum, Changsha (Figure 24.4)

- Lady Dai died 168 B.C.E. in Hunan province; Han Dynasty
- Tomb found with over 100 objects in 1972
- T-shaped silk banner covering the inner coffin of the intact body
- Probably carried in a procession to the tomb then placed over the body to speed its journey to the afterlife
- Yin symbols at left; yang symbols at right; the center mixes the two philosophies
- Painted in three distinct regions
- Top: Heaven with crescent moon at left, and the legend of the ten suns at the right; in the center two seated officers guard the entrance to the heavenly world
- Middle: earth with Lady Dai in center on white platform about to make her journey to heaven with a walking stick that was found in her tomb;

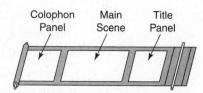

Figure 24.3a: A Chinese handscroll read right to left. It starts with the title panel, moves to the main scene, and ends with a colophon.

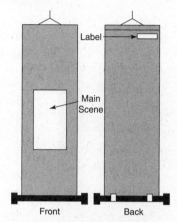

Figure 24.3b: A Chinese hanging scroll with the main scene on the front and the title on the top back.

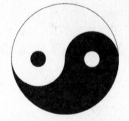

Figure 24.3c: Yin and yang

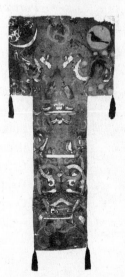

Figure 24.4: Funeral Banner of Lady Dai (Xin Zhui), 180 B.C.E., painted silk, Hunan Provincial Museum, Changsha

mourners and assistants appear by her side; dragons' bodies are symbolically circled through a bi in a yin and yang exchange
  - Bottom: the underworld; symbolic low creatures frame the underworld scene: fish, turtles, dragon tails; tomb guardians protect the body
- **Cross-Cultural Comparisons: Fabric Arts**
  - Hiapo (Figure 28.6)
  - All-T'oqapu Tunic (Figure 26.10)
  - Ringgold, *Dancing at the Louvre* (Figure 29.11)

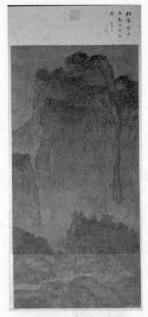

Figure 24.5: Fan Kuan, *Travelers among Mountains and Streams*, c. 1000, ink on silk, National Palace Museum, Taipei, Taiwan

Fan Kuan, *Travelers among Mountains and Streams*, c. 1000, ink on silk, National Palace Museum, Taipei, Taiwan (Figure 24.5)

- Artist isolated himself away from civilization to be with nature and study it, for his landscapes; Daoist philosophy
- Produced very complex landscapes
- Different brushstrokes describe different kinds of trees: coniferous, deciduous, etc.
- Long waterfall on right balanced by mountain on left; waterfall accents the height of the mountain
- Not a pure landscape: donkeys laden with firewood are driven by two men; a small temple appears in the forest; man seen as small and insignificant in a vast natural world
- Mists created by ink washes; silhouette the roofs of the temple
- Might be his only surviving work; signature hidden in the bushes on the lower right
- Hanging scroll
- **Cross-Cultural Comparisons: Figures Set in Landscape**
  - Cole, *The Oxbow* (Figure 20.6)
  - Breughel, *Hunters in the Snow* (Figure 14.6)
  - Circle of the Gonzalez Family, Screen with Hunting Scenes (Figure 18.3b)

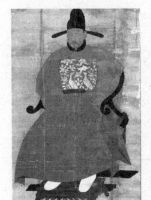

Figure 24.6: *Portrait of Sin Sukju*, 1417–1475, ink and color on silk

Portrait of Sin Sukju, 1417–1475, ink and color on silk (Figure 24.6)

- Korean prime minister (1461–1464 and from 1471–1475) and soldier
- Portrait made when he was a second grade civil officer: insignia designed with clouds and a wild goose
- Korean portraits emphasize how the subject made a great contribution to the country and how the spirit of loyalty to king and country was valued by Confucian philosophy
- Repainted over the years, especially in 1475, when he died
- Great scholar
- Hanging scroll
- **Cross-Cultural Comparisons: Painting Technique**
  - Oil: Campin (?), *Annunciation Triptych* (Figure 14.1)
  - Fresco: Rivera, *Dream of a Sunday Afternoon in the Alameda Park* (Figure 22.30)
  - Ink and pencil: Smith, *Lying with the Wolf* (Figure 29.20)

Chairman Mao En Route to Anyuan, **based on an oil painting by Liu Chunhua, 1969, color lithograph, Private Collection (Figure 24.7)**

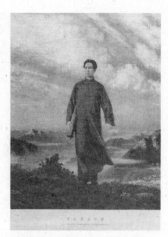

Figure 24.7: *Chairman Mao En Route to Anyuan*, based on an oil painting by Liu Chunhua, 1969, color lithograph, Private Collection

- Painted during the Cultural Revolution of 1966-76; high art was dismissed as feudal or bourgeois
- Poster-like; vivid colors, dramatic and obvious political message
- Dominated by pictorial representation
- Art was done anonymously; individual artistic fame seen as counter-cultural in a collectivist society
- A moment in the 1920s; Mao on his way to Anyuan to lead a miner's strike
- Mao worked for reforms for miners; supported a local strike for better wages, working conditions, and education
- For many people this action formed a permanent bond with the Communist party
- Iconic representation of the Great Leader's career
- May be the most reproduced image ever made: 900,000,000 copies were generated
- **Cross-Cultural Comparisons: Non-Western Works Using Western Ideas**
  - Bandolier Bag (Figure 26.11)
  - Lindauer, *Tamati Waka Nene* (Figure 28.7)
  - Frontispiece from the Codex Mendoza (Figure 18.1)

CHINESE SCULPTURE

China is a monumental civilization that has produced large-scale sculpture as a sign of grandeur. Enormous scale, without sacrificing artistic integrity, is a typical Chinese characteristic epitomized by the terra-cotta army of **Shi Huangdi** (Figures 24.8a and 24.8b) and the huge **seated Buddha at Longmen** (Figure 24.9a). The Chinese have created a dazzling number of sculptures cut from the rock *in situ*, a technique probably imported from India.

At the same time, Chinese sculpture is known for intricately designed miniature objects. Those made of jade are especially prized for their beauty; they are durable and polish to a high shine in a matte green-gray color.

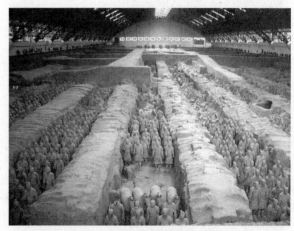

Figure 24.8a: Army of Emperor Shi Huangdi, painted terra-cotta, c. 221–209 B.C.E., Qin Dynasty, Lintong, China

Army of Emperor Shi Huangdi, painted terra-cotta, c. 221–209 B.C.E., Qin Dynasty, Lintong, China (Figures 24.8a and 24.8b)

- About 8,000 terra-cotta warriors, 100 wooden chariots, 2 bronze chariots, 30,000 weapons buried as part of the tomb of Emperor Shi Huangdi
- Soldiers are six-feet tall, some fierce, some proud, some confident; taller than the average person of the time
- A representation of a Chinese army marching into the next world

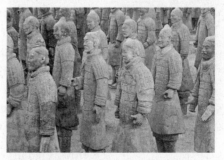

Figure 24.8b: Army of Emperor Shi Huangdi, painted terra-cotta, c. 221–209 B.C.E., Qin Dynasty, Lintong, China

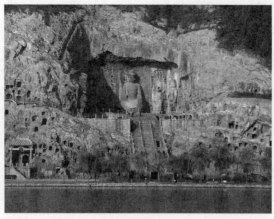

Figure 24.9a: Longmen Caves with Vairocana Buddha, 493–1127, Tang Dynasty, limestone, Luoyang, China

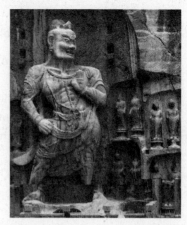

Figure 24.9b: Longmen Caves detail

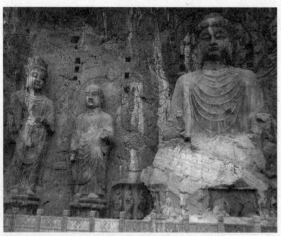

Figure 24.9c: Longmen Caves detail

- Daoism seen in the individualization of each soldier despite their numbers
- Originally colorfully painted
- Discovered in 1974
- **Cross-Cultural Comparisons: Buried Works**
  - Tomb of Tutankhamun (Figure 3.11)
  - Catacomb of Priscilla (Figure 7.1a)
  - Tomb of the Triclinium (Figure 5.3)

Longmen Caves, 493–1127, Tang Dynasty, limestone, Luoyang, China (Figures 24.9a, 24.9b, and 24.9c)

- Caves along the banks of the Yi River
- Sculptures and reliefs carved from the existing rock; some colossal, some small
- Documents attest that 800,000 people worked on the site; 110,000 Buddhist stone statues, more than 60 stupas, and 2,800 inscriptions on steles
- Buddha arranged as if on an altar of a temple, deeply set into the rock face
- Inscription states that Empress Wu Zetian was the principal patroness of the site, and she used her private funds to finance the project
- Vairocana Buddha having monk attendants, bodhisattvas, and guardians flanking
- Elongated legs and exaggerated poses
- **Cross-Cultural Comparisons: Grand Outdoor Sculpture**
  - Great Altar of Zeus and Athena at Pergamon (Figures 4.18a, 4.18b)
  - Bamiyan Buddha (Figure 23.2)
  - Moai (Figure 28.11)

Gold and jade crown, fifth–sixth century, metalwork, National Museum of Korea, Seoul, South Korea (Figure 24.10)

- Uncovered in Gyeongju, Korea from a royal tomb
- Symbolizes geometric trees
- Antler forms influenced by Shamanistic practices in Siberia

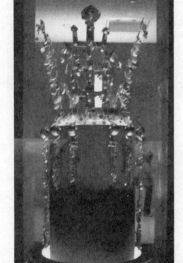

Figure 24.10: Gold and jade crown, fifth-sixth century, metalwork, National Museum of Korea, South Korea

- Very light weight; had limited use; maybe for ceremonial occasions, perhaps only for burial
- **Cross-Cultural Comparisons: Metalwork**
  - Merovingian Looped Fibula (Figure 10.1)
  - Golden Stool (Figure 27.4)
  - El Anatsui, *Old Man's Cloth* (Figure 29.23)

PORCELAIN

Almost every world culture has a tradition of ceramics, few as fine as those from China. Originally most ceramics were made by the **coiling** method, in which clay was rolled onto a long, flat surface so that it resembles a long cord. The cords were wrapped around themselves creating a sculpture, sometimes of considerable size. To remove the appearance of the coils, the edges were often smoothed out with the artist's hands or an instrument.

Later the clay was placed on a round tray and made to revolve using a pedal; this began the invention of the **potter's wheel**. The process of making pottery on a wheel is called **throwing**. The potter uses his or her hands to shape the pottery as it revolves.

Yuan Dynasty (1279–1368) vases have a distinctive blue and white color. The cobalt used to make the iridescent blue was imported from Iran and greatly prized by the Chinese.

The David Vases, 1351, white porcelain with cobalt blue underglaze, British Museum, London (Figure 24.11)

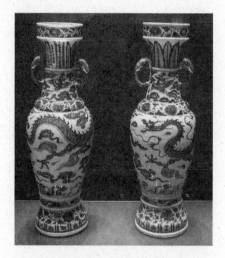

- One of the most important examples of blue and white porcelain in existence
- Made for the altar of a Daoist temple, along with an incense burner which has not been found; a typical altar set
- Dedication on the side of the neck of the vessels; believed to be earliest known blue and white porcelain dedication
- Inscription on one of the vases: "Zhang Wenjin, from Jingtang community, Dejiao village, Shuncheng township, Yushan county, Xinzhou circuit, a disciple of the Holy Gods, is pleased to offer a set comprising one incense burner and a pair of flower vases to General Hu Jingyi at the Original Palace in Xingyuan, as a prayer for the protection and blessing of the whole family and for the peace of his sons and daughters. Carefully offered on an auspicious day in the Fourth Month, Eleventh year of the Zhizheng reign."

Figure 24.11: The David Vases, 1351, white porcelain with cobalt blue underglaze, British Museum, London

- Blue color imported from Iran; Chinese expansion into western Asia makes the cobalt blue available
- Vases were modeled after bronzes
- Elephant-head-shaped handles
- Neck and foot of vases: leaves and flowers
- Central section: Chinese dragons with traditional long bodies and beards; dragons have scales and claws and are set in a sea of clouds
- Named after Sir Percival David, a collector of Chinese art
- **Cross-Cultural Connections: Porcelain and Ceramic**
  - Martínez, Black-on-black ceramic vessel (Figure 26.14)
  - Niobid Krater (Figure 4.19)
  - Terra-Cotta Warriors (Figures 24.8a, 24.8b)

VOCABULARY

Bi: a round ceremonial disk found in ancient Chinese tombs; characterized by having a circular hole in the center, which may have symbolized heaven (Figure 24.4)

Bodhisattva: a deity who refrains from entering nirvana to help others (Figure 24.9c)

Coiling: a method of creating pottery in which a rope-like strand of clay is wrapped and layered into a shape before being fired in a kiln

Colophon: a commentary on the end panel of a Chinese handscroll; an inscription at the end of a manuscript containing relevant information on its publication (Figure 24.4)

Confucianism: a philosophical belief begun by Confucius that stresses education, devotion to family, mutual respect, and traditional culture

Daoism: a philosophical belief begun by Laozi that stresses individual expression and a striving to find balance in one's life

Hanja: Chinese characters used in Korean script with a Korean pronunciation

Literati: a sophisticated and scholarly group of Chinese artists who painted for themselves rather than for fame and mass
acceptance. Their work is highly individualized

Pagoda: a tower built of many stories. Each succeeding story is identical in style to the one beneath it, only smaller. Pagodas typically have dramatically projecting eaves that curl up at the ends

Porcelain: a ceramic made from clay that when fired in a kiln produces a product that is hard, white, brittle, and shiny

Potter's wheel: a device that usually has a pedal used to make the flat circular table spin, so that a potter can create pottery

Throwing: to mold forms on a potter's wheel

Vairocana: the universal Buddha, a source of enlightenment; also known as the Supreme Buddha who represents "emptiness," that is, freedom from earthly matters to help achieve salvation (Figure 24.9c)

Yin and yang: complementary polarities. The yin is a feminine symbol that has dark, soft, moist, and weak characteristics. The yang is the male symbol that has bright, hard, dry, and strong characteristics (Figure 24.3)

SUMMARY

The great Chinese philosophies of Daoism and Confucianism dominate the fine arts, as well as all intellectual thought in China. They express the relationship of buildings to one another in courtyard-style residences from the most humble to the Forbidden City. They also articulate a relationship of the forms in Chinese painting.

Chinese artists apprenticed under a master and worked under a system of patronage controlled by religion or government. A powerful minority, the literati, deliberately chose to walk away from traditional artistic venues and cultivate a more individualized type of art.

Chinese art has a penchant for the monumental and the grand, epitomized by the Great Wall, the Colossal Buddhas, and the Tomb of Shi Huangdi. Considerable attention, however, is paid to smaller items such as delicate porcelains, finely cut jade figures, and laquered wooden objects.

Multiple-Choice

1. The tomb of the terra-cotta warriors from the First Qin emperor of China has more than 6,000 soldiers who are

    (A) alike to show their uniformity in protecting the emperor
    (B) unpainted to contrast with the colorful image of the emperor more forcefully
    (C) subtly different to show their ethnic diversity of China
    (D) from every social class, gender, and age in China

Questions 2–4 refer to this image.

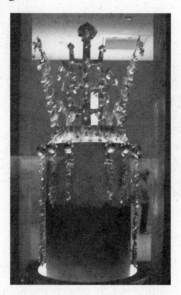

2. This Korean crown was found

    (A) in a royal sanctuary placed with other religious objects
    (B) on the head of a large sculpture of Buddha
    (C) in a royal tomb buried in a mound
    (D) in Japan, given as a diplomatic gift to the Japanese emperor

3. The crown was probably not meant to be worn because

    (A) the gold is too precious and would have been easily stolen
    (B) gold is a soft metal that could be easily bent if worn
    (C) the gold applied here is extremely thin and fragile
    (D) the whole crown was too heavy to be worn comfortably

4. The uprights probably symbolized

    (A) a distinctive royal lineage of "family tree" that came from the gods to the wearer
    (B) a stylized tree with antler forms that denoted spiritual power
    (C) everlasting peace achievable through the gods and the divinely appointed emperor
    (D) the riches of an earthly kingdom reflecting the glory of an eternal world

5. Which of the following Chinese art forms inspired contemporary artwork?

    (A) Chinese music as seen in *Horn Players*.
    (B) Chinese porcelains as seen in *Pink Panther*.
    (C) Chinese photography as seen in *Rebellious Silence*.
    (D) Chinese writing as seen in *A Book from the Sky*.

Short Essay

These images depict a view and a ground plan of the Forbidden City in Beijing, China.

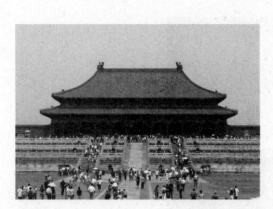 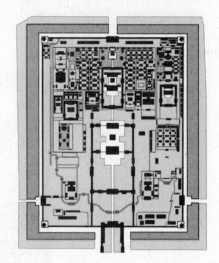

What is the design of the Forbidden City based on?

Analyze how the design of the Forbidden City reflects its function.

Analyze how the design of the Forbidden City reflects the political aspirations of the Chinese royal court.

ANSWER KEY

1. **C**   2. **C**   3. **C**   4. **B**   5. **D**

ANSWERS EXPLAINED

Multiple-Choice

1. **(C)** Each of the figures is subtly different to depict various ethnic features in different regions of China. There are no women, or old or young people.

2. **(C)** The crown was found in a tumulus, or burial mound.

3. **(C)** The gold is extremely thin and very fragile; it was meant only for limited occasions or mostly likely burial.

4. **(B)** The uprights symbolize a stylized tree reaching up to the sky. They have connections with spiritual forces.

5. **(D)** Xu Bing's *Book from the Sky* contains references to traditional Chinese art, bookmaking, and calligraphy, although much of the calligraphy is made up.

Short-Essay Rubric

Question	Points	Key Points in a Good Response
What is the design of the Forbidden City based on?	1	The traditional court-style residence in Chinese architecture
Analyze how the design of the Forbidden City reflects its function.	2	Answers could include: ■ Walls 30 feet high to keep people out and those inside in ■ Forbidden City so-called because only the royal court could enter ■ Each corner of the rectangular plan has a tower representing the four corners of the world. ■ Focus is the Hall of Supreme Harmony, the throne room and seat of power; wood structure made with elaborately painted beams; meant for grand ceremonies ■ Yellow tile roofs and red painted wooden beams placed on marble foundations unify the structures in the Forbidden City into an artistic whole.
Analyze how the design of the Forbidden City reflects the political aspirations of the Chinese royal court.	2	Answers could include: ■ The Emperor and his court saw themselves as divine monarchs; the Forbidden City is a miniature celestial world. ■ They sought grandeur and a lavish lifestyle to project an image of power and wealth. ■ The Chinese court projected an image of being removed from the world, remote, unattainable; the Forbidden City had huge walls to keep people out.

Japanese Art

25

TIME PERIOD: 1789–1848

ENDURING UNDERSTANDING: Asian art is a reflection of Asian aesthetics.

Essential Knowledge:

- Japanese art is characterized by its influence from Shintoism and Zen philosophy.
- Calligraphy is a central art form in Japanese art.

ENDURING UNDERSTANDING: Asian art spreads throughout the world through trade.

Essential Knowledge:

- Asian art shows evidence of the interconnectivity of regional schools with the wider world.
- Asian art, particularly Japanese prints, heavily influenced the art of Europe.

HISTORICAL BACKGROUND

Japan is one of the few countries in the world that has never been successfully invaded by an outside army. There are those who have tried, like the Mongols in 1281, whose fleet was destroyed by a typhoon called a kamikaze, or divine wind, and there are those who have defeated the Japanese without invading, like the Allies in World War II, who never landed a force on the four principal islands, until the war was over.

Because of the relatively sheltered nature of the Japanese archipelago, and the infrequency of foreign interference, Japan has a greater proportion of its traditional artistic patrimony than almost any other country in the world. It was Commodore Perry who opened Japan, to outside influence in 1854. One by-product of Perry's intervention was the shipment of **ukiyo-e** prints to European markets, first as packing material and then in their own right. They achieved enduring fame in nineteenth-century Europe and America, but were looked down upon by the upper classes in Japan, who were more than willing to send them off for export.

Patronage and Artistic Life

Japanese artists worked on commission, some for the royal court, others in the service of religion. Masters ran workshops with a range of assistants—the tradition in Japan usually marking this as a family-run business with the eldest son inheriting the trade. Assistants learned from the ground up, making paper and ink, for example. The master created the composition by brushing in key outlines and his assistants worked on the colors and details.

Painting is highly esteemed in Japan. Aristocrats of both sexes not only learned to paint, but became distinguished in the art form.

ZEN BUDDHISM

Zen is a school of Buddhism that is deeply rooted in all East Asian societies, and was imported from China in the late twelfth century. It had a particularly great impact on the art of Japan, where the Zen philosophy was warmly embraced.

Zen adherents reject worldliness, the collection of goods for their own sake, and physical adornment. Instead, the Zen world is centered on austerity, self-control, courage, and loyalty. Meditation is key to enlightenment; for example, samurai warriors reach deeply into themselves to perform acts of bravery and great physical endurance.

Zen teaches through intuition and introspection, rather than through books and scripture. Warriors as well as artists were quick to adopt a Zen philosophy.

THE JAPANESE TEA CEREMONY

The tea ceremony is a ritual of greater importance than it at first seems to the Westerner. The simple details, the crude vessels, the refined tea, the uncomplicated gestures—these alluring items are all part of a seemingly casual, but in fact, highly sophisticated tea ceremony that endures because of its minimalism. Teahouses have bamboo and wooden walls with floor mats of woven straw. Everything is carefully arranged to give the sense of straightforwardness and delicacy.

Visitors enter through a low doorway—symbolizing their humbleness—into a private setting. Rectangular spaces are broken by an unadorned alcove that houses a Zen painting done in a free and monochromatic style, selected to enhance an intimate atmosphere of warm and dark spaces.

Participants sit on the floor in a small space usually designed for about five people, and drink tea. The ceremony requires four principles: Purity, harmony, respect, and tranquility. All elements of the ceremony are proscribed, even the purification ritual of hand washing and the types of conversation allowed.

JAPANESE ARCHITECTURE AND SCULPTURE

The austerity of **Zen** philosophy can be most readily seen in the simplicity of architectural design that dominates Japanese buildings. A traditional structure is usually a single story, made of wood, and meant to harmonize with its natural environment. The wood is typically undressed—the fine grains appreciated by the Japanese. Because wood is relatively light, the pillars could be placed at wide intervals to support the roof, opening the interior most dramatically to the outdoors.

Floors are raised above the ground to reduce humidity by allowing the air to circulate under the building. Eaves are long to generate shady interiors in the summer, and steeply pitched to allow the quick runoff of rain and snow.

Interiors have mobile spaces created by sliding screens, which act as room dividers, by changing its dimensions at will. Particularly lavish homes may have gilded screens, but most are of wooden materials. The floors are overlaid with removable straw mats.

A principal innovation in Japanese design is the Zen garden, which features meticulous arrangements of raked sand circling around prominently placed stones and plants (Figure 25.2b). Each garden suggests wider vistas and elaborate landscapes. Zen gardens contain no water, but the careful placement of rocks often suggests a cascade or a rushing stream.

Ultimately these gardens serve for spiritual refreshment, a place of contemplation and rejuvenation.

There is a deep respect for the natural world in Japanese thought. The native religion, Shintoism, believes in the sacredness of spirits inherent in nature. In a heavily forested and rocky terrained country like Japan, wood becomes the natural choice for building, and stone for Zen gardens.

Todai-ji, Nara, Japan

Todai-ji, 743, rebuilt c. 1700, wood with ceramic tile roofing, Nara, Japan (Figure 25.1a)

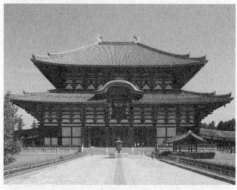

Figure 25.1a: Todai-ji, 743, rebuilt c. 1700, wood with ceramic tile roofing, Nara, Japan

- Great Eastern Temple, refers to its location on the eastern edge of the city of Nara, Japan
- Noted for its colossal sculpture of seated image of the Vairocana Buddha
- Temple and Buddha have been razed several times during military unrest
- Seven external bays on façade
- Influenced by monumental Chinese sculptures (cf. Longmen)
- Largest wooden building in the world

Great Buddha, base eighth century, upper portion including head twelfth century, copper (Figure 25.1b)

- Monumental feat of casting
- Emperor Shōmu embraced Buddhism and erected sculpture as a way of stabilizing Japanese population during a time of economic crisis
- Largest metal statue of Buddha in the world
- Mudra: right hand means "do not fear"; left hand means "welcome"
- **Cross-Cultural Comparisons: Images of Buddha Across Asia**
  - Bamiyan Buddha (Figure 23.2)
  - Jowo Rinpoche (Figure 23.3)
  - Longmen Caves (Figures 24.9a, 24.9b, 24.9c)

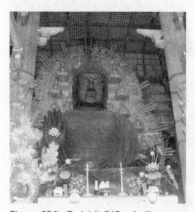

Figure 25.1b: Todai-ji, 743, rebuilt c. 1700, wood with ceramic tile roofing, Nara, Japan

Nio Guardian Figures, c. 1203, wood, by Unkei, Tankei, and Jokahu (Figures 25.1c and 25.1d)

- One on either side of the gate
- Complex joined woodblock construction
- Intricate swirling drapery
- Fierce forbidding looks and gestures
- Masculine, frightening figures that protect the Buddha

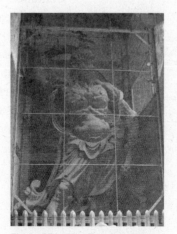 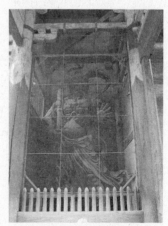

Figure 25.1c: Nio Guardian Figure, c. 1203, wood, by Unkei, Tankei, and Jokahu

Figure 25.1d: Nio Guardian Figure, c. 1203, wood, by Unkei, Tankei, and Jokahu

Great South Gate, 1181–1203, wood with ceramic tile roofing (Figure 25.1e)

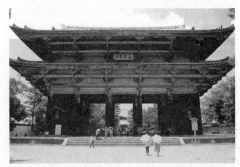

Figure 25.1e: Great South Gate, 1181–1203, wood with ceramic tile roofing

- Nandaimon: great south gate, with five bays, three central bays for passing, and two outer that are closed
- Two stories are same size; unusual in Japanese architecture (usually upper story is smaller)
- Deep eaves supported by the six-stepped bracket complex, which rise in tiers with no bracketed arms
- Roof supported by huge pillars
- Unusual in that it has no ceiling; roof is exposed from below
- Overall effect is of proportion and stateliness
- **Cross-Cultural Comparisons: Entrances**
  - Great Portal, Chartres (Figure 12.6)
  - North Gate of the Great Stupa (Figure 23.4c)
  - Front Gate of the Forbidden City (Figure 24.2b)

Ryoan-ji, c. 1480, current design eigthteenth century, rock garden, Kyoto, Japan (Figures 25.2a, 25.2b, 25.2c)

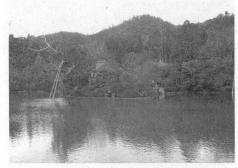

Figure 25.2a: Ryoan-ji, c. 1480, current design eighteenth century, wet garden, Kyoto, Japan

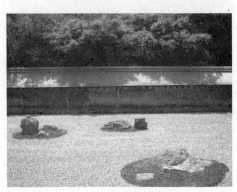

Figure 25.2b: Ryoan-ji, dry garden

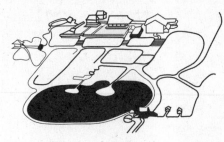

Figure 25.2c: Ryoan-ji, plan

- Garden as a microcosm of nature
- Zen dry garden:
  - Gravel acts as water; gravel racked in wavy patterns
  - Rocks are mountain ranges
  - Meant to be viewed from a veranda in a nearby building
  - Fifteen rocks arranged in three groups
  - Interpreted as islands in a floating sea; mountain peaks above clouds; constellations in the sky
  - From no viewpoint is the entire garden viewable at once
  - Served as a focus for meditation
  - Asymmetrical arrangement
  - Bounded on two sides by a low, yellow wall
- Wet Garden:
  - Contains a tea house
  - Seemingly arbitrary in placement, the plants are actually placed in a highly organized and structured environment symbolizing the natural world
  - Water symbolizes purification; used in rituals
- **Cross-Cultural Comparisons: People and Nature**
  - Weiwei, *Sunflower Seeds* (Figure 29.27)
  - Velasco, *Valley of Mexico* (Figure 21.4)
  - Turner, *The Slave Ship* (Figure 20.5)

JAPANESE PAINTING AND PRINTMAKING

Chinese painting techniques and formats were popular in Japan as well, so it is common to see the Japanese as masters of the handscroll, the hanging scroll, and the decorative screen.

Characteristics of the Japanese style include elevated viewpoints, diagonal lines, and depersonalized faces.

A Japanese specialty is **haboku** or **ink-splashed** painting that involved applying in a free and open style that gives the illusion of being splashed on the surface. The preponderance of Chinese imagery and painting techniques caused a reaction in Japan, as artists and patrons sought to find a national voice, independent of other Asian traditions. **Yamato-e**, developed in the twelfth century, features tales from Japanese history and literature depicted usually in long narrative scrolls. There is a depersonalization of figures in yamato-e works, often with just a line to indicate the eyes and mouth, and many times the nose is missing or just suggested. Strong diagonals dominate compositions that feature buildings with their roofs missing so we can see inside. Clouds are used to divide compositions into sections so they become more manageable to the viewer.

Genre painting from the seventeenth to the nineteenth centuries was dominated by **ukiyo-e**, a term that means "pictures of the floating world." The word "floating" is meant in the Buddhist sense of the passing or transient nature of life; therefore ukiyo-e works depict scenes of everyday life or pleasure: festivals, theatre (i.e., the kabuki), domestic life, geishas, brothels, and so on. Ukiyo-e is most famously represented in woodblock prints, although it can be found on scrolls and painted screens.

Ukiyo-e was immensely popular; millions of prints were sold to the middle class during its heyday, usually put between 1658 and 1858. Although disdained by the Japanese upper classes for being popular, they won particular affection in Europe and in the Americas as an example of innovative Japanese art.

Printmaking was a collaborative process between the artist and the publisher. The publisher determined the market, dictated the subject matter and style, and employed the woodblock carver and the printer. At first, all prints were in black and white, but the popularity encouraged experimentation, and a two-color system was introduced in 1741.

By 1765, a polychrome print was created, and while this made the product more time-consuming to create and therefore more expensive, it was wildly popular and sold enthusiastically. Colors are subtle and delicate, and separated by black lines. Each color was applied one at a time, requiring a separate step in the printmaking process. This made the steps complicated with precise alignments critical to a successful print. Suzuki Harunobu was the first successful ukiyo-e artist in the polychrome tradition. **Hokusai** explored the relationship of ukiyo-e and landscape painting.

Western artists were taken with ukiyo-e prints. They particularly enjoyed the flat areas of color, the largely unmodulated tones, the lack of shadows, and the odd compositional angles, with figures occasionally seen from behind. Forms are often unexpectedly cut off and cropped by the frame of the work. The Western interest in realistic subject matter found agreement in ukiyo-e prints.

Figure 25.3a: *Night Attack on the Sanjô Palace*, c. 1250–1300, handscroll (ink and color on paper), Museum of Fine Arts, Boston.

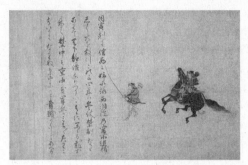

Figure 25.3b: *Night Attack on the Sanjô Palace*, detail

Night Attack on the Sanjô Palace, c. 1250–1300, Handscroll (ink and color on paper), Museum of Fine Arts, Boston (Figures 25.3a and 25.3b)

- Painted 100 years after the civil war depicted in the scene
- Elevated viewpoint
- Strong diagonals emphasizing movement and action
- Swift active brushstrokes
- Narratives read from right to left as the scroll is unrolled
- Depersonalized figures, many with only one stroke for the eyes, ears, and mouth
- Tangled mass of forms accentuated by Japanese armor
- Lone archer leads the escape from the burning palace with equestrian Japanese commander behind him
- Military rule in Japan from 1185 on had an interest in the code of the warrior; reflected in the large quantity of war-related literature and paintings
- Unrolls like a film sequence; as one unrolls, time advances
- Burning of the imperial palace at Sanjô in Kyoto as rebel forces try to sieze power by capturing the emperor
  - Coup staged in 1159 as Emperor Go-Shirakawa is taken prisoner
  - Imperial palace in flames; rebels force the emperor to board a cart waiting to take him into captivity
  - Rebels kill those opposed and place their heads on sticks and parade them as trophies
  - **Cross-Cultural Comparisons: Historical Events**
    - Lin, Vietnam Veterans Memorial (Figures 29.4a, 29.4b)
    - Goya, *And There's Nothing to Be Done* (Figure 20.2)
    - Column of Trajan (Figure 6.16)

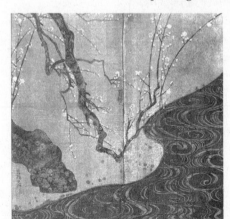

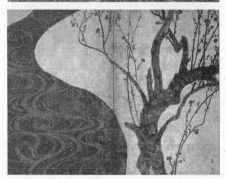

Figures 25.4a and 25.4b: Ogata Korin, *White and Red Plum Blossoms*, 1710–1716, watercolor on paper, MOA Museum of Art, Atami, Japan

Ogata Korin, *White and Red Plum Blossoms*, 1710–1716, watercolor on paper, MOA Museum of Art, Atami, Japan (Figures 25.4a and 25.4b)

- Japanese rinpa style named for Ogata (*Rin* for "Ko-rin" and *pa* meaning "school")
- Influenced by the yamato-e style of painting
- Stream cuts rhythmically through the scene; swirls in paint surface indicate water currents
- White plum blossoms on left; red on right
- Tarashikomi technique in which paint is applied to a surface that has not already dried from a previous application; creates a dripping effect useful in depicting streams or flowers

- **Cross-Cultural Comparisons: Multi-Panel Paintings**
  - Campin (?), *Annunciation Triptych* (Figure 14.1)
  - Grünewald, *Isenheim Altarpiece* (Figures 14.4a, 14.4b)
  - Circle of the Gonzalez Family, *Screen with the Siege of Belgrade and Hunting Scene* (Figures 18.3a, 18.3b)

Hokusai, *Under the Wave off Kanagawa (Kanagawa oki nami ura),* called "The Great Wave," from "Thirty-six Views of Mount Fuji," 1830–1833, polychrome woodblock print; ink and color on paper, Metropolitan Museum of Art, New York (Figure 25.5)

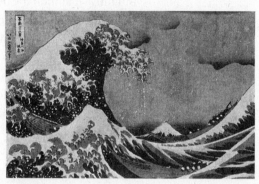

Figure 25.5: Hokusai, *Under the Wave off Kanagawa (Kanagawa oki nami ura)*, called "The Great Wave," from "Thirty-Six Views of Mount Fuji," 1830–1833, polychrome woodblock print, ink and color on paper, Metropolitan Museum of Art, New York

- First time landscape is a major theme in Japanese prints
- Last of a series of prints called *Thirty-Six Views of Mount Fuji*
- Personification of nature, it seems intent on drowning the figures in boats
- Mount Fuji, sacred mountain to the Japanese, seems to be one of the waves
- Striking design contrasts water and sky with large areas of negative space
- **Cross-Cultural Comparisons: Images of the Sea and Water**
  - Michelangelo, *The Flood* (Figure 16.2c)
  - Turner, *The Slave Ship* (Figure 20.5)
  - Kusama, *Narcissus Garden* (Figures 22.25a, 22.25b)

VOCABULARY

Genre painting: painting in which scenes of everyday life are depicted

Haboku (splashed ink): a monochrome Japanese ink painting done in a free style in which ink seems to be splashed on a surface

Kondo: a hall used for Buddhist teachings (Figure 25.1a)

Mandorla (Italian, meaning "almond"): a term that describes a large almond-shaped orb around holy figures like Christ and Buddha (Figure 25.1b)

Tarashikomi: a Japanese painting technique in which paint is applied to a surface that has not already dried from a previous application

Ukiyo-e: translated as "pictures of the floating world," a Japanese genre painting popular from the seventeenth to the nineteenth century (Figure 25.5)

Yamato-e: a style of Japanese painting that is characterized by native subject matter, stylized features, and thick bright pigments

Zen: a metaphysical branch of Buddhism that teaches fulfillment through self-discipline and intuition

With much of its tradition intact, a firm history of Japanese artistic production can be studied from its earliest roots. Scultpures often survive in their original architectural settings.

The Japanese are particularly sensitive to the properties of wood construction. The earliest buildings maintain the beauty of untreated wood and show a great emphasis on harmonizing with the natural surrounding environment. Japanese buildings are meant to be viewed as part of an overall balance in nature. Japanese buildings never intrude upon a setting, but complement it fully.

Traditional Chinese forms of painting, such as scrolls, were admired in Japan. Nevertheless, uniquely Japanese artistic styles, such as ukiyo-e prints, were popular as well, particularly with the middle classes. The impact of ukiyo-e prints on nineteenth-century European art cannot be overstated.

PRACTICE EXERCISES

Multiple-Choice

1. The Nio Guardian Figures and the *Lamassu* from the Assyrian culture have in common that they are both

    (A) meant to symbolically protect the areas behind them
    (B) combinations of human and animal forms
    (C) made of stone and symbolize permanence
    (D) carved with the image of the ruler on their faces

2. The Great Buddha in Todai-ji's Great East Temple was probably influenced by similar works, such as

    (A) the Terra-Cotta Warriors
    (B) Longmen Caves
    (C) Angkor Wat
    (D) the Great Stupa

3. Japanese woodblock prints can be seen as directly influencing works like Mary Cassatt's *The Coiffure* in that they both

    (A) share an affinity for brilliant coloring
    (B) place figures at odd angles to the picture plane
    (C) are concerned with solid modeling and massing of forms
    (D) use the conventional three-dimensional linear perspective

4. The yamato-e technique is characterized by all of the following EXCEPT

    (A) the artists used stories from Japanese history and literature
    (B) the figures are depersonalized with just one stroke for facial details
    (C) compositions are dominated by diagonals
    (D) the artists were the first in Japan to specialize in the Western oil painting technique

5. Dry landscape gardens in Japanese art carry great symbolic value. The viewer was meant to

    (A) arrange the rocks and the sand in an artful display to suggest a real landscape

    (B) sit directly in the center of the garden and meditate on the natural environment

    (C) use the garden as a place to refresh the spirit by painting, writing poetry, or composing music

    (D) be refreshed through reflection, contemplation, and meditation

Short Essay

Attribute this painting to the artist who painted it.

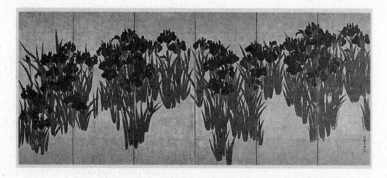

Identify a work by the same artist in the art history curriculum.

Using specific details, justify your attribution by comparing the two works.

How do both works demonstrate the Japanese view of landscape?

ANSWER KEY

1. **A**   2. **B**   3. **B**   4. **D**   5. **D**

ANSWERS EXPLAINED

Multiple-Choice

1. **(A)** Both the Nio Guardian Figures and the *Lamassu* are images at gateways, which act to shield the areas behind them.

2. **(B)** The grandeur of the Great Buddha in Todai-ji's Great East Temple is equal to the great Buddha statues at the Longmen Caves.

3. **(B)** Mary Cassatt's compositions were influenced by the unusual compositional angles seen in many Japanese woodblock prints.

4. **(D)** Yamato-e is more about Japanese history and literature depicted with diagonal compositions and depersonalized faces than about oil paint. Yamato-e was developed in Japan in the twelfth century, well before European contact.

5. **(D)** Viewers never entered a Japanese dry garden. They were enclosed environments meant for reflection, contemplation, and meditation.

Short-Essay Rubric

Question	Points	Key Points in a Good Response
Attribute this painting to the artist who painted it.	1	Ogata Korin
Identify a work by the same artist in the art history curriculum.	1	Ogata Korin, *White and Red Plum Blossoms*, 1710–1716, watercolor on paper
Using specific details, justify your attribution by comparing the two works.	2	Answers could include: ■ Diagonals influenced by the yamato-e style of painting ■ Rhythmic composition ■ Painted on a screen ■ View limited to a few details that are carefully painted rather than grand landscapes ■ Tarashikomi technique in which paint is applied to a surface that has not already dried from a previous application; creates a dripping effect useful in depicting streams or flowers
By examining both works, discuss what aspects of landscape painting the artist was most interested in.	1	Answers could include: ■ Concentration of a few details ■ Deeply personal view of nature ■ Emphasis on a fragile, tender, and gentle nature—rather than awesome, threatening, or overwhelming ■ Organizes natural forms into patterned compositions

Art of the Americas

26

TIME PERIOD: 3500 B.C.E.–1492 C.E. AND BEYOND

Some of the main periods are these:

Civilization	Date	Location
Chavín	900–200 B.C.E.	Coastal Peru
Mayan	300–900 C.E. and later	Belize, Guatemala, Honduras, Yucatán
Anasazi	550–1400 C.E.	American Southwest
Mississippian	800–1500 C.E.	Eastern United States
Aztec	1400–1521	Central Mexico, centered in Mexico City
Inka	1438–1532	Peru
North American Indian	18th century to present	North America

ENDURING UNDERSTANDING: The indigenous Americas have among the oldest art traditions in the world.

Essential Knowledge:

- Ancient America can be divided into many cultural and historical groupings both in North and South America.
- Art in these regions is often animal based (feathers, hides, etc.) and used in shamanistic rituals. Art carved from stone is also important.

ENDURING UNDERSTANDING: Mesoamerican art (from Mexico to Guatemala, Honduras, and Belize) is characterized by architectural structures such as pyramids, a strong influence of astronomy and calendars on ritual objects, and great value placed on green objects, such as jade or feathers.

Essential Knowledge:

- Pyramids began as earthworks and then grew to multi-level structures. Sites were often added to over many years. Most architecture is made of stone, using the post and lintel system and faced with painted sculpture. There are usually large plazas before the pyramids.

- Sculpture relates the deeds of rulers and epic stories of the gods. Artists generally worked under a united vision in a workshop. The audience for art could be an entire city or an intimate religious circumstance.
- Mesoamericans have had an influence on the Spanish who occupied the area, both commercially and artistically.
- Mesoamerican objects were valued and treasured in Europe by connoisseurs and collectors. Increased recognition of their value today has led to a greater understanding of their contribution to world art.

ENDURING UNDERSTANDING: Andean art (from Peru, Bolivia, and Ecuador) relies on shamanistic rituals involving a special veneration for the natural world.

Essential Knowledge:

- Geography plays a key role in understanding Andean art. People of the coastal plains often acted individually; those in the mountains united against the elements. The geographic diversity accounts for the differing materials used in the creation of works of art.
- Most Andean art seems to have been a workshop system whereby many collaborate on a single piece.
- Most common Andean findings have been in graves; a great many works were done for funerary purposes.
- Andean art has had an influence on modern European and Latin American artists.

ENDURING UNDERSTANDING: North American Indians have undergone widespread persecution and cultural reshaping since the arrival of Europeans.

Essential Knowledge:

- Many interdisciplinary sources are used to piece together the major monuments of Native North Americans.
- Archaeology, oral and written history, documents, and museum records form the basis of North American Indian research.

ENDURING UNDERSTANDING: Modern Native Americans maintain active cultural identities today.

Essential Knowledge:

- There is no uniform naming structure for the original people of this area.
- In addition to traditional North American materials and techniques used in artwork (weaving, basketry, wood, bone, hides, and ceramic), objects that have been traded with outsiders (beads, ribbons) have become part of the Indian artistic experience.
- Many motifs, such as animals and geometric designs, appear in North American art. Respect for nature, religion, and elders are dominant themes.
- Art was created mostly for groups, as the patrons were likely important tribal leaders. Artists worked in groups in an apprentice-type relationship.
- Native North American art has had a minimal impact on European and American styles. However, a revival movement has invigorated cultural traditions and opened them up to a wider market.

HISTORICAL BACKGROUND

Humans are not native to the "New World"; Americans do not have an ancestry dating back millions of years, the way they do in Africa or Asia. People migrated from Asia to America over a span of perhaps 30,000 years, crossing over the Bering Strait when the frozen winters made the way walkable. Eventually people understood that the climate was good enough to raise crops, particularly in what is today Mexico and Central America, and the population boomed.

As in other parts of the world, local rivalries and jealousies have played their part in the ebb and flow of American civilizations. Some civilizations are intensely cultivated and technological, refining metal ore and developing a firm understanding of astronomy and literature. Others remained nomadic and limited their activities as hunter–gatherers. In any case, when the European colonizers arrived at the end of the fifteenth century, they encountered in some ways a very sophisticated society, but in others, one that did not even possess a functioning wheel and refined metals mostly for jewelry rather than for use.

Each succeeding civilization buried or destroyed the remains of the civilization before, so only the hardiest ruins have survived the test of time. Most of what can be gleaned about pre-Columbian American society is ascertained by archaeologists working on elaborate burial grounds or digging through the ruins of once-great ancient cities.

Patronage and Artistic Life

Artists were commoners, as was true in most societies in the ancient world. Because of their special abilities, however, artists were employed by the state to work at important sites instead of doing menial labor. Some were even members of the royalty. Artists were trained in an apprenticeship program, and reached fame through the rendering of beautifully crafted items.

Ancient Americans used an extremely wide variety of materials in their artwork, usually capitalizing on what was locally available. Since they did not have draught animals, and since wheeled carts were unknown, artists were reliant on what was locally produced, or on objects small enough to trade and carry. Even so, Aztecs, for example, carved in obsidian, jade, copper, gold, turquoise, basalt, sandstone, granite, rock crystal, wood, limestone, and amethyst, among many other media.

Tropical cultures profited from the skins of animals and feathers of birds and produced great works using brilliant plumage. Featherwork became a distinguished art form in the hands of Pre-Columbian artists.

CHAVÍN ART

Chavín is a civilization named after its main archaeological site, preserved in coastal Peru. Chavín art is dominated by figural compositions, often shown in a combination of human and animal motifs. Many figures unite various animal forms into one being: fanged mouths are merged with serpents in the hair, for example. Figures are generally heavily rendered with an eye to monumentality. Symmetry is desired; works are carved in low relief on polished surfaces that use rectangular formats.

Chavín architects chose sites that were dramatic, sometimes on mountain tops. Often buildings, such as those at Chavín de Huántar, were built around a U-shaped plan that embraced a plaza and faced out toward an expansive view. Stepped platforms rise to support ceremonial buildings. Some sites are oriented to the cardinal points on the compass,

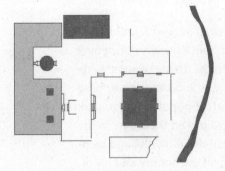
Figure 26.1a: Plan of Chavín de Huántar, 900–200 B.C.E., Peru

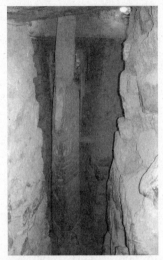
Figure 26.1b: Lanzón Stone, 900–200 B.C.E., granite, Peru

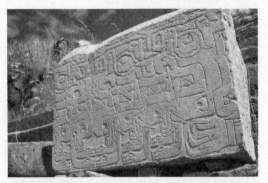
Figure 26.1c: Relief sculpture, granite, 900–200 B.C.E., Peru

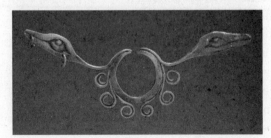
Figure 26.1d: Nose ornament, gold alloy, Cleveland Museum of Art

but at Chavín the site seems to be coordinated with an adjacent river, which some say was a reference to water sources and their importance to society.

Chavín de Huántar, 900–200 B.C.E., Peru

- A religious capital
- Temple was 60 meters tall adorned by a jaguar sculpture, a symbol of power
- Hidden entrance to the temple led to stone corridors

Plan and Lanzón Stone, granite (Figures 26.1a and 26.1b)

- Inside the Old Temple of Chavín there is a maze-like system of hallways
- At the center, underground, is the *Lanzón* (Spanish for "blade") stone
- Fifteen feet tall; blade shaped
- Depicts a powerful figure that is part human (body) and part animal (claws, fangs)
- Head of snakes and face of a jaguar
- Eyebrows terminate in snakes
- Flat relief; designs in a curvilinear pattern
- Served as a cult figure
- Center of pilgrimage; however, few had access to the Lanzón Stone
- Modern scholars hypothesize that the stone acted as an oracle, hence a point of pilgrimage

Relief sculpture, granite, Chavín de Huántar (Figure 26.1c)

- Located on the ruins of a stairway at Chavín
- Shows jaguars in shallow relief

Nose ornament, gold alloy, Cleveland Museum of Art (Figure 26.1d)

- Worn by males and females under the nose
- Held in place by the semi-circular section at top
- Two snake heads on either end
- Makes the wearer into a supernatural being during ceremonies

MAYAN ART

Mayan sculpture is easy to recognize, because of the unusual Mayan concept of ideal beauty. The model seems to have been a figure with an arching brow, with the indentation above the nose filled in as a continuous bridge between forehead and nose. Most well-to-do Mayans put their children in head braces to create this symbol of beauty if the child was not born with it. Facial types are long and narrow, with full lips and mouths ready to speak. It is common to see figures elaborately dressed with costumes composed of feathers, jade, and jaguar skin. The Mayans preferred narrative art done in relief sculpture. Their relief work has crisp outlines with little attention given to modeling.

Mayan sculpture is typically related to architectural monuments: Lintels, facades, jambs, and so on. Figures of gods are stylized and placed in conventional hieratic poses possessing symbols of beauty, most notably tattooing and crossed eyes. Most Mayan sculptures were painted.

A typical work that appears everywhere in Mayan cities is the **chacmool**, a figure that is half-sitting and half-lying on his back. The unusual pose of the figure is balanced by the face which turns 90 degrees from the body. Elbows firmly rest on the ground, lending a sloping sense to the body. On his stomach is a plate, which has made some scholars deduce that the figure was meant to receive offerings. Sculptures such as these influenced modern artists such as Henry Moore.

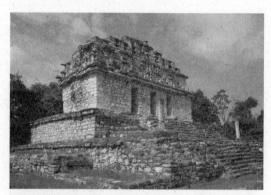

Figure 26.2a: Structure 40, Yaxchilán, 725 c.e., limestone, Chiapas, Mexico

Mayan pyramids are set in wide plazas as a center of civic focus. Grandly proportioned temples accompany pyramids, although their interiors are narrow and tall, giving a certain claustrophobic effect enhanced by the use of corbelled vaulting. Temples had long roof combs on the roof to accentuate their verticality.

Yaxchilán, 725 c.e., limestone, Chiapas, Mexico (Figures 26.2a, 26.2b, and 26.2c)

- City set on a high terrace; plaza surrounded by important buildings
- Flourished c. 300–800 c.e.

Structure 40, Yaxchilán, 725 c.e., limestone, Chiapas, Mexico (Figure 26.2a)

- Built by ruler Bird Jaguar IV, or his son who dedicated it to him
- Overlooks the main plaza
- Three doors leading to a central room decorated with stucco
- Roof remains nearly intact, with a large roof comb (ornamented stone tops on roofs)
- Corbel arch interior

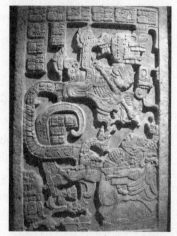

Figure 26.2b: Lintel 25, Structure 23, Yaxchilán, 725 c.e., limestone, British Museum, London

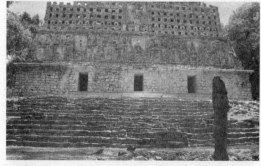

Figure 26.2c: Structure 33, Yaxchilán, 725 c.e., limestone, Chiapas, Mexico

Lintel 25, Structure 23, Yaxchilán, 725 C.E., limestone, British Museum, London (Figure 26.2b)

- Lintel originally set above the central doorway of Structure 23
- Building dedicated to Lady Xoc
- Lady Xoc (bottom right) invoking the Vision Serpent to commemorate her husband's rise to the throne
- She holds a bowl with bloodletting ceremonial items: stinging spine and bloodstained paper
- Vision Serpent has two heads: one has a warrior emerging from its mouth; the other has Tlaloc, a war god
- Inscription written as a mirror image—extremely unusual in Mayan script; uncertain meaning, perhaps indicating she has a vision from the other side of existence, and she is acting as an intercessor or shaman

Structure 33, Yaxchilán, 725 C.E., limestone, Chiapas, Mexico (Figure 26.2c)

- Restored temple structure
- Remains of roof comb with perforations
- Three central doorways lead to a large single room
- Corbel arch interior
- **Cross-Cultural Comparisons: Temples**
  - White Temple on Its Ziggurat (Figure 2.1a)
  - Lakshmana Temple (Figures 23.7a, 23.7b)
  - Todai-ji (Figure 25.1a)

ANASAZI ART

Anasazi is a term that means "ancient ones" or "ancient enemies" in the Navajo language. They are most famous for their meticulously rendered **pueblos**, which are composed of local materials. A core of rubble and mortar is usually faced with a veneer of polished stone. The thickness of the base walls were used to determine the size of the overall superstructure, with some pueblos daring to raise themselves five or six stories tall. All pueblos faced a well-defined plaza that was the religious and social center of the complex.

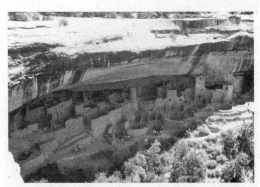

Figure 26.3 Mesa Verde cliff dwellings, Anasazi, 450–1300 C.E., sandstone, Montezuma County, Colorado

Mesa Verde cliff dwellings, Anasazi, 450–1300 C.E., sandstone, Montezuma County, Colorado (Figure 26.3)

- Pueblo built into the sides of a cliff, housed about 250 people
- Clans moved together for mutual support and defense
- Top-ledge stores all supplies, cool and dry area out of the way, accessible only by ladder
- Plaza in front of abode structure; kivas face the plaza
- Each family received one room in the dwelling
- Farming done on plateau above pueblo, everything had to be imported into the structure, including water
- **Cross-Cultural Comparisons: Cliffside**
  - Bamiyan Buddhas (Figures 23.2a. 23.2b)
  - Longmen Caves (Figures 24.9a, 24.9b)
  - Petra (Figure 6.9b)

MISSISSIPPIAN ART

An increase in agriculture meant a population boom, as sustained communities evolved in fertile areas. Eastern Native Americans were mound-builders and created an impressive series of earthworks that survive in great numbers even today. Huge mound complexes, such as Cahokia, Illinois, were impressive city–states that governed wide areas. Other mounds, such as **Great Serpent Mound** (Figure 26.4), were built in effigy shapes of uncertain meaning. Many of these mounds have baffled archaeologists, because they clearly could only be fully appreciated from the air or a high vantage point, which mound builders did not possess.

Great Serpent Mound, Mississippian (Eastern Woodlands), c. 1070 c.e., earthwork, Adams County, southern Ohio (Figure 26.4)

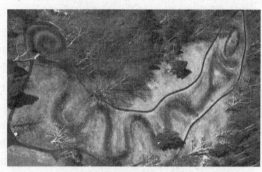

Figure 26.4: Great Serpent Mound, Mississippian (Eastern Woodlands), c. 1070 c.e., earthwork, Adams County, southern Ohio

- Many mounds were enlarged and changed over the years, not built in one campaign
- Effigy mounds popular in Mississippian culture
- Influenced by comets? Astrological phenomenon? Head pointed to summer solstice sunset?
- Rattlesnake as a symbol in Mississippian iconography; could this play a role in interpreting this mound?
- Snakes associated with crop fertility
- There are no burials or temples associated with this mound
- Theory that it could be a representation of Halley's Comet in 1066
- **Cross-Cultural Comparisons: Earthworks**
  - Smithson, *Spiral Jetty* (Figure 22.26)

AZTEC ART

Aztec art is most famously represented by gold jewelry that survives in some abundance, and jade and turquoise carvings of great virtuosity. The aggressive nature of Aztec religions, with its centering on violent ceremonies of blood-letting, was often manifest in great stone sculptures of horrifying deities such as **Coyolxauhqui**, whose characteristics include human remains from bloody sacrifices.

Templo Mayor (Main Temple), 1375–1520, stone, Tenochtitlán, Mexico City, Mexico (Figure 26.5a)

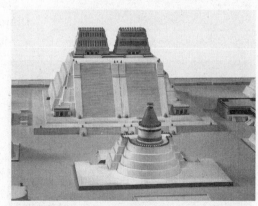

Figure 26.5a: Templo Mayor (Main Temple), 1375–1520, stone, Tenochtitlán, Mexico City, Mexico

- Tenochtitlán laid out on a grid; city seen as the center of the world
- Two temples atop pyramid, each with a separate staircase
- North: dedicated to Tlaloc: god of rain, agriculture
- South: dedicated to Huitzilopochtli: god of sun and war
- Spring and autumn equinoxes: sun rises between the two
- Large braziers put on top where the sacred fires burned
- Temples begun in 1375, rebuilt six times, destroyed by the Spanish in 1520

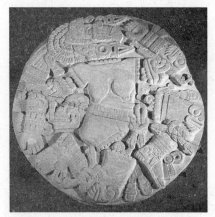

Figure 26.5b: Coyolxauhqui Stone, volcanic stone

Coyolxauhqui "She of the Golden Bells," 1469 (?), volcanic stone, Museum of the Templo Mayor, Mexico City (Figure 26.5b)

- So-called because of the bells she wears as earrings
- Aztecs similarly dismembered enemies and threw them down the stairs of the great pyramid to land on the disk of Coyolxauhqui
- Circular relief sculpture
- Coyolxauhqui and her many brothers plotted the death of her mother Coatlicue, who became pregnant after tucking a ball of feathers down her bosom. When Coyolxauhqui chopped off Coatlicue's head, a child popped out of the severed body fully grown, and dismembered Coyolxauhqui, who fell dead at the base of the shrine
- Represents the dismembered moon goddess who is placed at the base of the twin pyramids of Tenochtitlán
- Aztec sacrificed people and then threw them down the steps of the temple dismembered; Huitzilopochtli did this to Coyolxauhqui
- Relationship between the death and decapitation of Coyolxauhqui with the sacrifice of enemies at the top of Aztec pyramids
- Once brilliantly painted
- **Cross-Cultural Comparisons: Human Figure in Relief**
  - *Akhenaton, Nefertiti, and Three Daughters* (Figure 3.10)
  - *Victory Adjusting Her Sandal* (Figure 4.6)
  - Anthropomorphic stele (Figure 1.2)

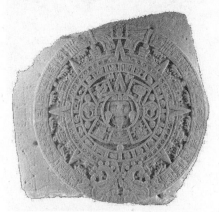

Figure 26.5c: Calendar Stone, basalt

Calendar Stone, basalt (Figure 26.5c)

- Circular shape reflects the cyclic nature of time
- Place where rituals took place on certain days
- Aztecs felt they needed to feed the Sun god human hearts and blood regularly
- Tongue in the center of the stone coming from the god's mouth was a sacrificial flint knife used to slash open the victims
- Used the Calendar Stone as an altar to murder victims, and then threw them down the steps of the temple to the base where the Coyolxauhqui Stone rests

Olmec-style mask, jadeite (Figure 26.5d)

- Found on the site; actually a much older work executed by the Olmecs
  - Olmec works have a characteristic frown on the face; pugnacious visage; heavy lidded eyes; headgear suggested
  - Shows that the Aztecs collected and embraced art work from other cultures

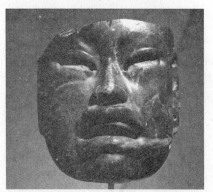

Figure 26.5d: Olmec-style mask, jadeite

Ruler's feather headdress (probably of Motecuhzoma II), 1428–1520, feathers (quetzal and blue cotinga) and gold, Museum of Ethnology, Vienna (Figure 26.6)

- 400 long green feathers are the tails of sacred quetzal birds; male birds produce only two such feathers each
- 400 symbolizes eternity

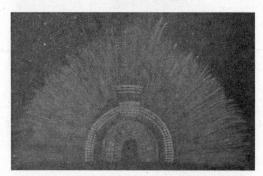

Figure 26.6: Ruler's feather headdress (probably of Motecuhzoma II), 1428–1520, feathers (quetzal and cotinga) and gold, Museum of Ethnology, Vienna

- Only known feather headdress in the world
- Headdress probably part of a collection of artifacts given by Motechuzoma (Montezuma) to Cortez for Charles V of the Holy Roman Empire
- **Cross-Cultural Comparisons: Exotic Materials**
  - 'Ahu 'ula (Figure 28.4)
  - Circle of the González Family, *Screen with the Siege of Belgrade and Hunting Scene* (Figures 18.3a, 18.3b)
  - González, *Virgin de Guadalupe* (Figure 18.4)

INKAN ART

Inkan architecture defies the odds by building impressive and well-designed cities in some of the most inaccessible or inhospitable places on earth. Typically Inkan builders used **ash-lar masonry** of perfectly grooved and fitted stones placed together in almost a jigsaw puzzle arrangement. All stones have slightly beveled edges that emphasize the joints. The buildings tend to taper upward like a trapezoid, the favorite building shape of early Americans.

The impressive Inka empire stretched from Chile to Colombia and was well-maintained by an organized system of roads that united the country in an efficient communication network. The Inka had no written language, so much of what we know about the civilization has been deduced from archaeological remains.

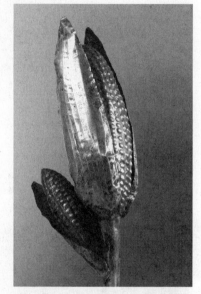

Maize cobs, c. 1400–1533, sheet metal/repoussé, gold and silver alloys, Staatliche Museen zu Berlin (Figure 26.7)

- Maize was the principal food source in the Andes
- Maize was celebrated by having sculptures fashioned out of sheet metal
- Black maize common in Peru; oxidized silver reflects that
- May have been part of a garden in which full sized metal sculptures of maize plants, and other items, were put in place alongside plants
- May have been used to ensure a successful harvest
- Repoussé technique
- **Cross-Cultural Comparisons: Metalwork**
  - Merovingian Looped Fibula (Figure 10.1)
  - Golden Stool (Figure 27.4)
  - Muhammad ibn al-Zain, *Baptistère de St. Louis* (Figure 9.6)

Figure 26.7: Maize cobs, c. 1400–1533, sheet metal/repousée, gold and silver alloys, Staatliche Museen zu Berlin

City of Cusco plan, Peru, c. 1440 (Figure 26.8a)

- Historic capital of the Inkan empire
- In the shape of the puma, a royal animal
- Modern plaza is in the place where the puma's belly would be
- Head a fortress; heart a central square
- **Cross-Cultural Comparisons: City Planning**
  - Athenian Agora (Figure 4.15)
  - Forum of Trajan (Figure 6.10a)
  - Forbidden City (Figures 24.2a, 24.2b, 24.2c, 24.2d)

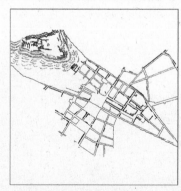

Figure 26.8a: Plan of the City of Cusco, c. 1440

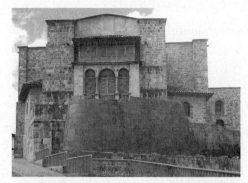

Figure 26.8b: Qorikancha: main temple, church and convent of Santo Domingo, c. 1440, sandstone, Peru

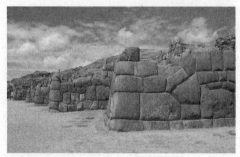

Figure 26.8c: Walls at Saqsa Waman (Sacsayhuaman), c. 1440, sandstone, Peru

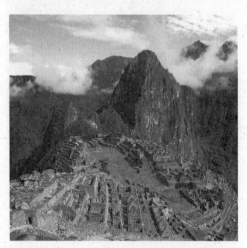

Figure 26.9a: Machu Picchu, 1450–1540, granite, Peru

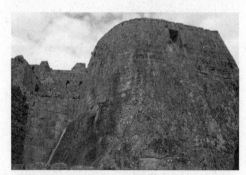

Figure 26.9b: Observatory, 1450–1540, granite, Peru

Qorikancha: main temple, church, and convent of Santo Domingo, c. 1440, sandstone, Peru (Figure 26.8b)

- Remains of the Inkan Temple of the Sun form the base of the Santo Domingo convent built on top
- Original exterior walls of the Temple decorated in gold to symbolize sunshine
- Ashlar masonry; carefully grooved and beveled edges of the stone fitted together
- Qorikancha: golden enclosure; once was the most important temple in the Inkan world
- Once was an observatory for priests to chart the skies
- Interior courtyard said to have been entirely covered in gold
- Walls taper upward; examples of Inkan trapezoidal architecture

Walls at Saqsa Waman (Sacsayhuaman), c. 1440, sandstone, Peru (Figure 26.8c)

- Complex outside the city of Cusco, Peru, at the head of the puma-shaped plan of the city
- Ashlar masonry
- Ramparts contain stones weighing up to seventy tons, brought from a quarry two miles away

Machu Picchu, 1450–1540, granite, Peru (Figure 26.9a)

- Originally functioned as a royal retreat
- Estate of fifteenth century Inkan rulers
- So remote that it was probably not used for administrative purposes in the Inka world
- Buildings built of stone with perfectly carved rock rendered in precise shapes and grooved together; thatched roofs
- Two hundred buildings, mostly houses, some temples, palaces, baths, even an astronomical observatory; most using the basic trapezoidal shape
- People farmed on terraces
- **Cross-Cultural Comparisons: Public spaces**
  - Acropolis (Figure 2.16a)
  - Persepolis (Figure 2.6a, 2.6b)
  - Mesa Verde (Figure 26.3)

Observatory, 1450–1540, granite, Peru (Figure 26.9b)

- Used to chart the sun's movements
- Ashlar masonry

Intihuatana Stone, 1450–1540, granite, Peru (Figure 26.9c)

- Intihuatana means "Hitching Post of the Sun," aligns with the sun at the spring and the autumn equinoxes when the sun stands directly over the pillar, creating no shadow
- Inkan ceremonies held in concert with this event

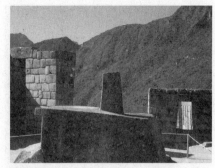

Figure 26.9c: Intihuatana Stone, 1450–1540, granite, Peru

All-T'oqapu tunic, 1450–1540, camelid fiber and cotton, Dumbarton Oaks, Washington D.C. (Figure 26.10)

- Rectangular shape; a slit in the center for the head, then the tunic is folded in half and the sides are sewn for the arms
- Composition is comprised of small rectangular shapes called *t'oqapu*
- Individual *t'oqapu* may be symbolic of individuals, events or places
- This tunic contains a large number of *t'oqapu*
- Wearing such an elaborate garment would indicate the status of the individual
- May have been worn by an Inkan ruler
- Exhibits Inkan preference for abstract designs, standardization of designs, and an expression of unity and order
- **Cross-Cultural Comparisons: Fabric Arts**
  - Funeral Banner of Lady Dai (Figure 24.4)
  - Hiapo (Figure 28.6)
  - *The Bayeux Tapestry* (Figures 11.7a, 11.7b)

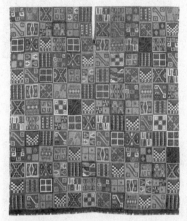

Figure 26.10: All-T'oqapu tunic, 1450–1540, camelid fiber and cotton, Dumbarton Oaks, Washington D.C.

NORTH AMERICAN INDIAN ART

Local products form the basis of most North American art forms: wood in the Pacific Northwest; clay, plant fibers, and wool in the American Southwest; and hides in areas populated by large animals like bison and deer. As with most nomadic or semi-nomadic peoples (although the Southwest Indians lived in large pueblos or cliff dwellings with fairly sophisticated agricultural programs), geometric designs on ceramics and utilitarian objects and highly decorated fabric with beading and weaving mark their art. Plains Indians even illustrated hides to relate myths and events pertinent to their tribal histories. As the influence of the European settlers spread throughout the Indian nations, native Indian artists were keen to adapt their traditional art forms to new media introduced from abroad. The Europeans also brought with them a curiosity about native art forms, and acted as collectors and patrons for works that appealed to their sensibilities. Thus native American artists, like Cadzi Cody in hide painting and Maria Martínez in ceramics, began serving an emerging tourist industry that appreciated their artistry.

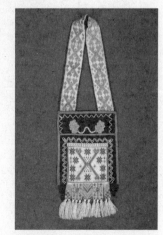

Figure 26.11: Bandolier bag, Lenape tribe, c. 1850, beadwork on leather, Children's Museum of Indianapolis, Indianapolis, Indiana

Bandolier bag, Lenape (eastern Delaware) tribe, c. 1850, beadwork on leather, Children's Museum of Indianapolis, Indianapolis, Indiana (Figure 26.11)

- Bandolier bag has a large heavily beaded pouch with a slit on top
- Bag held at hip level; strap across the chest
- Bag constructed of trade cloth: cotton, wool, velvet, or leather
- Beadwork not done in the Americas before European contact
- Beads imported from Europe

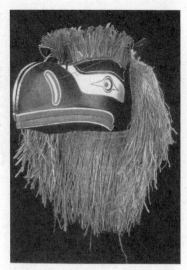

Figure 26.12a: Transformation mask, Kwakiutl, Northwest coast of Canada, late 19th century, wood, paint, and string, Children's Museum of Indianapolis, Indianapolis, Indiana

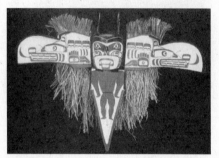

Figure 26.12b: Interior of Transformation mask

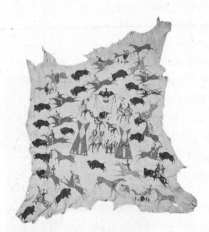

Figure 26.13: Attributed to Cotsiogo (Cadzi Cody), Hide Painting of a Sun Dance, c. 1890–1900, painted elk hide, Cowan's Auctions, Inc., Cincinnati, Ohio

- Made for women; objects of prestige
- Native American and European motifs
- Functional and beautiful
- **Cross-Cultural Comparisons: Functional Works of Art**
  - *Niobid Krater* (Figure 4.19)
  - Navigation Chart (Figure 28.3)
  - Duchamp, *Fountain* (Figure 22.9)

Transformation Mask, Kwakiutl, Northwest coast of Canada, late nineteenth century, wood, paint, and string, Children's Museum of Indianapolis, Indianapolis, Indiana (Figures 26.12a and 26.12b)

- Masks worn by native people of the Pacific Northwest, western Canada, and Alaska
- Worn over the head as part of a complete body costume
- During a ritual performance the wearer opens and closes the transformation mask using strings
- Opening the mask reveals another face inside
- Bird exterior opens to reveal human face on interior
- At the moment of transformation, the performer turns his back to the audience to conceal the action and heighten the mystery
- **Cross-Cultural Comparisons: Human and Animal Hybrids**
  - Sphinx (Figure 3.6a)
  - Running Horned Woman (Figure 1.9)
  - Mutu, *Preying Mantra* (Figure 29.25)

Attributed to Cotsiogo (Cadzi Cody), Hide Painting of a Sun Dance, Eastern Shoshone, Wind River Reservation, Wyoming, c. 1890–1900, painted elk hide, Cowan's Auctions, Inc., Cincinnati, Ohio (Figure 26.13)

- Worn as a robe over the shoulders of the warrior
- Warrior's deeds are celebrated on the hide
- Conveyed biographical details; personal accomplishments; heroism; battles
- Men painted hides to narrate an event
- Eventually painted hides for European and American markets
- Depicted traditional aspects of the Plains people culture that were nostalgic rather than practical: bison hunt with bow and arrow—nomadic hunting gone; bison nearly extinct
- Bison considered to be gifts from the Creator
- Horses in common use around 1750, liberated the Plains people
- Sun Dance conducted around a bison head—outlawed by the U.S. government; viewed as a threat to order
- Sun Dance: men dance; others sing, prepare the feast, drum, construct a lodge
- Teepee: made of hide stretched over poles
- Exterior poles reach the spirit world or sky

- Fire represents the heart
- Doorway faces east to greet the new day
- **Cross-Cultural Comparisons: Animal Imagery**
  - Apollo 11 Stones (Figure 1.7)
  - Aka Elephant Mask (Figure 27.12)
  - Muybridge, *Horse in Motion* (Figure 21.5)

Maria Martínez and Julian Martínez, black-on-black ceramic vessel, Tewa, Puebloan, San Ildefonso Pueblo, New Mexico, mid-twentieth century, Andrea Fisher Fine Pottery (Figure 26.14)

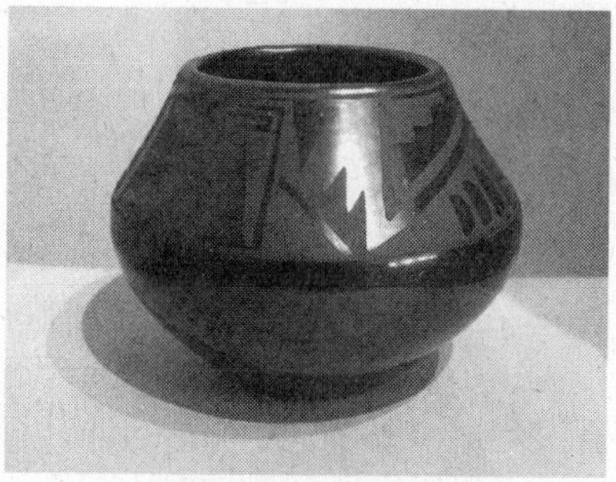

Figure 26.14: Maria Martínez and Julian Martínez, black-on-black ceramic vessel. Tewa, Puebloan, San Ildefonso Pueblo, New Mexico, mid-twentieth century, Andrea Fisher Fine Pottery

- Black on black vessels
- Highly polished surfaces
- Contrasts of shiny black and matte black finishes
- Comes from the 1000-year-old tradition of pottery making in the Southwest
- At the time of production, pueblos were in decline; modern life replacing traditional life
- Their work sparked a revival of pueblo techniques
- Maria made the pots; developed and invented more shapes than traditional pueblos used
- Julian painted the pots; uses a revival of ancient mythic figures and designs
- Exceptional symmetry; walls of even thickness; surfaces are free of imperfections
- **Cross-Cultural Comparisons: Limited Color**
  - Weiwei, *Sunflower Seeds* (Figure 29.27)
  - Mblo (Figure 27.7)
  - *Shiva as Lord of Dance* (Figure 23.6)

VOCABULARY

Ashlar masonry: carefully cut and grooved stones that support a building without the use of concrete or other kinds of masonry (Figure 26.8b)

Bandolier bag: a large heavily beaded pouch with a slit on top (Figure 26.11)

Chacmool: a Mayan figure that is half-sitting and half-lying on his back

Corbel arch: a vault formed by layers of stone that gradually grow closer together as they rise and eventually meet

Coyolxauhqui: an Aztec goddess who died when she tried to assassinate her mother, Coatlicue (Figure 26.5b)

Huitzilopochtli: an Aztec god of the sun and war; sometimes represented as an eagle or as a hummingbird

Kiva: a circular room wholly or partly underground used for religious rites

Pueblo: a communal village of flat-roofed structures of many stories that are stacked in terraces; made of stone or adobe (Figure 26.3)

Relief sculpture: a sculpture which projects from a flat background (Figure 26.1c)

Repoussé: (French, meaning "to push back") a type of metal relief sculpture in which the back side of a plate is hammered to form a raised relief on the front (Figure 26.7)

Roof comb: a wall rising from the center ridge of a building to give the appearance of greater height (Figure 26.2a)

Teepee: a portable Indian home made of stretched hides placed over wooden poles

Tlaloc: ancient American god who was highly revered; associated with rain, agriculture, and war

T'oqapu: small rectangular shapes in an Inkan garment (Figure 26.10)

Transformation mask: A mask worn in ceremonies by people of the Pacific Northwest, Canada, or Alaska. The chief feature of the mask is its ability to open and close, going from a bird-like exterior to a human-faced interior (Figures 26.12a and 26.12b)

SUMMARY

It is difficult to condense into a simple format the complex nature of ancient American civilizations. Some societies were nomadic and produced portable works of art that were meant for ceremonial use. Others established great cities in which ceremonial centers were carefully designed to enhance religious and secular concerns.

Each society of Indians used the local available materials to create their works. Indians from rich forest lands produced huge totem poles that symbolized the spirit of the living tree as well as the gods or legends carved upon them. Those from drier climates made use of adobe for their building material, as in the desert Southwest, or earthenware for fancifully decorated jugs and pitchers. The great cities of Mesoamerica are hewn from stone to create a symbol of permanence and stability in cultures that were more often than not dynamic and in flux.

It is common in ancient America for societies to build on the foundations of earlier cultures. Thus new cities spring from the ruins of the old, as pyramids are built over smaller structures on the same site.

PRACTICE EXERCISES

Multiple-Choice

1. Transformation masks are best understood as works

    (A) used as centerpieces in homes
    (B) that are seen as part of a larger ceremony
    (C) used to recall ancestral spirits to act on the wearer's behalf
    (D) used as a display much the same way that totem poles are used

2. Native American artworks often show the influence of Europeans in that they

    (A) used European materials in their work
    (B) portrayed European historical events with their own histories
    (C) adapted European faith traditions and abandoned Native American imagery in their work
    (D) experimented with European artistic techniques such as contrapposto and chiaroscuro

3. The image of Coyolxauhqui was carved on a round disk and placed

   (A) at the top of an Aztec pyramid so people could worship it
   (B) at the entrance to an Aztec temple complex so people could see to whom the complex was dedicated
   (C) at the base of a pyramid so sacrificial victims could reenact the fate of Coyolxauhqui
   (D) in the coronation room of the king so that his ancestral lineage could be observed by all

4. The Hide Painting of a Sun Dance attributed to Cotsiogo has a similar painting format to

   (A) *Night Attack on the Sanjô Palace*
   (B) *The Book of Lindisfarne*
   (C) *Folio from a Qur'an*
   (D) *The Court of Gayumars*

5. The Hide Painting of a Sun Dance attributed to Cotsiogo draws on Native American traditions

   (A) in its use of the repoussé technique
   (B) in that it shows great virtuosity in the handling of classical forms
   (C) of articulating forms by placing them in an active sequence around a given space
   (D) that place humans on an exaggerated scale dominating all other figures in a work

Short Essay

This is the Lanzón Stela from Chavín de Hunántar.

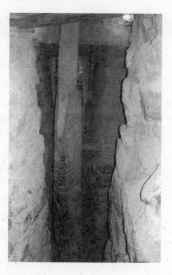

Where was this stela originally placed within the complex at Chavín?

Discuss the symbolism of its placement.

What is depicted on the stela *and* how does this depiction reflect the meaning of the work at this site?

1. **B**   2. **A**   3. **C**   4. **B**   5. **C**

ANSWERS EXPLAINED

Multiple-Choice

1. **(B)** Transformation masks were only one part of a much larger ceremony of Kwakiutl Indians.

2. **(A)** When the Europeans settled in America, they often traded their materials for things the Indians valued. The Bandolier bag, for example, is made from beads imported from Europe.

3. **(C)** The disk containing the image of Coyolxauhqui was placed at the bottom of a pyramid. The Aztecs sacrificed people and then threw them down the pyramid the way Huitzilopochtli did to Coyolxauhqui. There was a relationship established between the death and decapitation of Coyolxauhqui and the sacrifice of Aztec enemies at the top of the pyramid.

4. **(B)** Both the hide painting and *The Book of Lindisfarne* were executed on animal skins.

5. **(C)** Native American art often places figures in an active sequence around a given space.

Short-Essay Rubric

Question	Points	Key Points in a Good Response
Where was this stela originally placed within the complex at Chavin?	1	Inside the Old Temple of Chavín there is a maze-like system of hallways. At the center, underground, is the Lanzón (Spanish for blade) stone.
Discuss the symbolism of its placement.	2	Modern scholars hypothesize that the stone acted as an oracle, hence a point of pilgrimage. Few people had access to the stone itself.
What is depicted on the stela and how does this depiction reflect the meaning of the work at this site?	2	It depicts a powerful figure that is part human (body) and part animal (claws, fangs), with the head of snakes and a face of a jaguar. Eyebrows terminate in snakes. It served as a cult figure that was awesome and ferocious to behold.

African Art

27

TIME PERIOD: FROM PREHISTORIC TIMES TO THE PRESENT

Some chief African civilizations include:

Civilization	Time Period	Location
Great Zimbabwe	11th–15th Centuries	Zimbabwe
Bamileke	11th–21st Centuries	Cameroon
Benin	13th–19th Centuries	Nigeria
Luba	16th–21st Centuries	Congo
Kuba	17th–19th Centuries	Congo
Ashanti	17th–21st Centuries	Ghana
Chokwe	17th–21st Centuries	Congo
Yoruba	17th–21st Centuries	Nigeria
Baule	19th–21st Centuries	Côte d'Ivoire
Ibgo	19th–21st Centuries	Nigeria
Fang	19th–21st Centuries	Cameroon, Gabon, Equatorial Guinea
Mende	19th–21st Centuries	Sierra Leone

ENDURING UNDERSTANDING: Human life began in Africa.

Essential Knowledge:

- Rock art is the earliest art form found in Africa. It depicts animals and human activity.
- The spreading Sahara caused migrations to southern Africa where the arts flourished.

ENDURING UNDERSTANDING: African art is active and interactive with other art forms.

Essential Knowledge:

- African art is truly interdisciplinary, encompassing a wide variety of media, materials, and performances.
- African art addresses the spiritual world. It can be seen on everyday items, as well as on items associated with royalty.
- Art can be commissioned by a shaman or a worshiper. It is often used as part of an elaborate and prescribed ritual.

ENDURING UNDERSTANDING: African art is meant to be used, not just viewed.

Essential Knowledge:

- Art permeates all important aspects of society. Rituals initiate coming of age, leadership, or family communion, and often have elements of contact with ancestors.
- Art objects are often manipulated and interpreted in rituals. Historic accomplishments are orally preserved by poets and historians who use objects to identify with their stories.
- Large leadership centers, as in Zimbabwe, show that Africans sometimes used monumental structures to mark settlements and territory.

ENDURING UNDERSTANDING: Formerly thought of as static and primitive, today African art is seen as interactive with many cultures and ever changing.

Essential Knowledge:

- African history has been preserved in an oral tradition. Outsiders have used a written record of historical events.
- Collectors of African art have often ignored the usual data associated with art history: the names of artists and the dates of creation.
- African art has had a global impact.

HISTORICAL BACKGROUND

Despite the incredible vastness of the African continent, there are a number of similarities in the way in which African artists create art, stemming from common beliefs they share.

Africans believe that ancestors never die and can be addressed; hence a sense of family and a respect for elders are key components of the African psyche. Many African sculptures are representations of family ancestors and were carved to venerate their spirits.

Fertility, both of the individual and the land, is highly regarded. Spirits who inhabit the forests or are associated with natural phenomenon have to be respected and worshipped. Sculptures of suckling mothers are extremely common; it is implied that everyone suckles from the breast of God.

Great ancient civilizations in Nubia, Egypt, and Carthage dominated politics in North Africa for centuries before empires began to develop in southern Africa, or much of the rest of the world.

African kingdoms came and went with regularity; more populous and dominant people occupied wide swaths of African territory. Strong indigenous states were established in Christian Aksum in present-day Ethiopia in the fourth century, and in the Luba Empire concentrated in central Africa beginning in the fifteenth century. In the twelfth century an important center evolved in southern Africa on the Zimbabwe plateau. Whatever the location, African states developed strong cultural traditions yielding a great variety of artistic expression.

African affairs were largely internal struggles because outsiders were held back by natural barriers like the Sahara Desert and the Indian Ocean. However, by the fifteenth century African politics became greatly complicated by Asian and European incursions on both the east and west coasts of the continent. In general, outsiders restricted themselves to coastal areas that afforded the most access to African goods, and few bothered with the interior of the continent. All this changed in the late nineteenth century when a large series of invasions called the "Scramble for Africa" divided the continent into colonies.

The era of European control spanned less than a century. Most states achieved independence in the 1960s, with the Portuguese colonies waiting until the 1970s. Colonization brought

African cultural affairs in direct contact with the rest of the world. Today African artists work both at home and abroad, using native and foreign materials, and marketing their work on a global scale.

Patronage and Artistic Life

Since traditional Africans rely on an oral tradition to record their history, African objects are unsigned and undated. Although artists were famous in their own communities and were sought after by princes, written records of artistic activity stem principally from European or Islamic explorers who happened to encounter artists in their African journeys.

African artists worked on commission, often living with their patrons until the commission was completed. The same apprenticeship training that was current in Europe was the standard in Africa as well. Moreover, Africans also had guilds that promoted their work and helped elevate the profession.

As a rule, men were builders and carvers and were permitted to wear masks. Women painted walls and created ceramics. Both sexes were weavers. There were exceptions; for example, in Sierra Leone and Liberia women wore masks during important coming-of-age ceremonies.

The most collectable African art originated in farming communities rather than among nomads, who desired portability. To that end, the more nomadic people of East Africa in Kenya and Tanzania produced a fine school of body art, and the more agricultural West Africans around Sierra Leone and Nigeria achieved greatness with bronze and wood sculpture.

African art was imported into Europe during the Renaissance more as curiosities than as artistic objects. It was not until the early twentieth century that African art began to find true acceptance in European artistic circles.

AFRICAN ARCHITECTURE

Traditional African architecture is built to be as cool and comfortable as a building could get in the hot African sun, and therefore is made of mud-brick walls and thatched roofs. While mud-brick is certainly easy and inexpensive to make, it has inherent problems. All mud-brick buildings have to be meticulously maintained in the rainy season; otherwise, much would wash away. Nonetheless, Africans build huge structures of mud-brick with horizontally placed timbers as maintenance ladders.

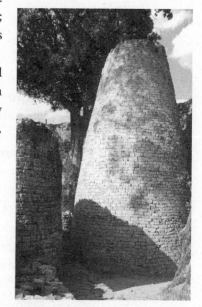

In a culture that generally eschews stonework, both in its architecture and its sculpture, the royal complex at **Zimbabwe** (Figure 27.1) from the fourteenth century is most unusual. The sophisticated handling of this type of masonry implies a long-standing tradition of construction of permanent materials, traces of which have all but been lost.

Great Zimbabwe, c. 1000–1400, granite, Zimbabwe (Figures 27.1a and 27.1b)

- Zimbabwe derives from a Shona term meaning "venerated houses" or "houses of stone"
- Prosperous trading center and royal complex
- Stone enclosure, probably a royal residence
- Walls: 800 feet long, 32 feet tall, 17 feet thick at base
- Conical tower modeled on traditional shapes of grain silos; control over food symbolized wealth, power, and royal largesse

Figure 27.1a: Conical tower of Great Zimbabwe, c. 1000–1400, granite, Zimbabwe

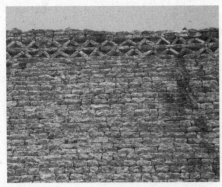

Figures 27.1b: Circular Wall of Great Zimbabwe

- Walls slope inward toward the top, made of exfoliated granite blocks
- Internal and external passageways are tightly bounded, narrow, and long, forcing occupants to walk in single file, paralleling experiences in the African bush
- Tower resembles a granary; represented a good harvest and prosperity
- **Cross-Cultural Comparisons: Ashlar Masonry**
  - Saqsa Waman (Figure 26.8c)
  - Angkor Wat (Figure 23.8a)
  - Parthenon (Figures 6.11a, 6.11b)

Great Mosque, c. 1200, rebuilt 1906–1907, adobe, remodeled in 1907, Djenné, Mali (Figure 27.2)

- Three tall towers, one in center is a mihrab
- Crowning ornaments have ostrich eggs: symbols of fertility and purity
- Torons: wooden beams projecting from walls
- **Cross-Cultural Comparisons: Other Mosques**
  - Great Mosque, Córdoba (Figures 9.14a, 9.14b, 9.14c)
  - Mosque of Selim II (Figures 9.16a, 9.16b, 9.16c)
  - Great Mosque, Isfahan (Figures 9.13a, 9.13b, 9,13c)
- Made of adobe, a baked mixture of clay and straw

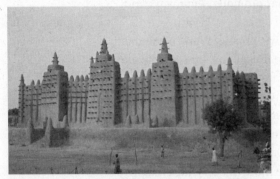

Figure 27.2: Great Mosque, c. 1200, rebuilt 1906–1907, adobe, remodeled in 1907, Djenné, Mali

- Wooden beams act as permanent ladders for the maintenance of the building
- Vertical fluting drains water off the surfaces quickly
- Largest mud-brick mosque in the world

AFRICAN SCULPTURE

Despite the number of sculptural traditions in Africa, there are certain similarities.

- African art is basically portable. Large sculptures, the kind that grace the plazas of ancient Egypt or Rome, are unknown.
- Wood is the favorite material. Trees were honored and symbolically repaid for the branches taken from them. Ivory is used as a sign of rank or prestige. Metal shows strength and durability, and is restricted to royalty. Stone is extremely rare.
- Figures are basically frontal, drawn full-face, with attention paid to the sides. Symmetry is occasionally used, but more talented artists vary their approach on each side of the object.
- Africans did no preliminary sketches and worked directly on the wood. There is a certain stiffness to all African works.
- Heads are disproportionately large, sometimes one-third of the whole figure. Sexual characteristics are also enlarged. Bodies are immature and small. Hands and feet are very small; fingers are rare.
- Multiple media are used. It is common to see wood sculptures adorned with feathers, fabric, or beads.
- African sculpture prefers geometrization of forms. It generally avoids physical reality, representing the spirits in a more timeless world. Proportions are therefore manipulated.

Important sculpture is never created for decoration, but for a definite purpose. African masks are meant to be part of a costume that represents a spirit, and can only come alive when ceremonies are initiated. Every mask has a purpose and represents a different spirit. When the masks are worn in a ceremony, the spirit takes over the costumed dancer and his identity remains unknown—every part of his body is hidden from view. Moved by the beat of a drum, the masked dancer connects with the spirit world and can transmit messages to villagers who are witnesses.

BENIN

Wall plaque from Oba's palace, sixteenth century, brass, Metropolitan Museum of Art, New York (Figure 27.3)

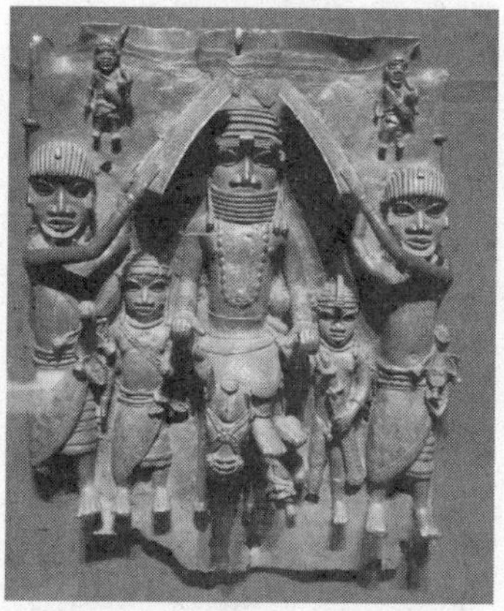

- 900 brass plaques produced; between 16 and 18 inches
- Decorated walls of royal palace in Benin
- Part of a sprawling palace complex; wooden pillars covered with brass plaques
- Show aspects of court life in the Benin culture
- Oba ("king") believed to be direct descendant of Oranmiyan, the legendary founder of the dynasty
- Only the Oba was allowed to be shielded in the way depicted on the plaque
- Hierarchical proportions: largest figure was the greatest
- Symbols of high rank are emphasized
- Stepping on a fallen leader
- Emphasis on heads; bodies are often small and immature
- Lost wax process
- Ceremonial scene at court
- High relief sculpture
- **Cross-Cultural Comparisons: Bronze and Brass Work**
  - Donatello, *David* (Figure 15.5)
  - Great Buddha at Todai-ji (Figure 25.1b)
  - *Shiva as Lord of Dance* (Figure 23.6)

Figure 27.3: Wall plaque from Oba's palace, sixteenth century, brass, Metropolitan Museum of Art, New York

ASHANTI

Golden Stool (Skia dwa kofi), c. 1700, gold over wood, location unknown (Figure 27.4)

- Symbol of the Ashanti nation; held in Ghana
- Contains the soul of the nation
- Never actually used as a stool; never allowed to touch the ground
- New king is raised over the stool
- Carried to the king on a pillow; he alone is allowed to touch it
- Taken out on special occasions
- Entire surface inlaid with gold
- Bells hang from the side to warn the king of danger
- Replicas often used in ceremonies, but each replica is different
- War of the Golden Stool: March–September 1900
- Conflict over British sovereignty in Ghana (formerly Gold Coast)
- British representative tried to sit on the stool; caused an uproar and subsequent rebellion
- War ended in British annexation and Ashanti de facto independence

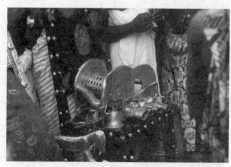

Figure 27.4: Golden Stool (Skia dwa kofi), c. 1700, gold over wood, location unknown

■ **Cross-Cultural Comparisons: Sacred Objects**
- Kaaba (Figure 9.11a)
- Lanzón Stela (Figure 26.1b)
- Gold and Jade Crown (Figure 24.10)

KUBA

Ndop (portrait figure) of King Mishe miShyaang maMbul, 1760–1780, wood, Brooklyn Museum, Brooklyn, New York (Figure 27.5a)

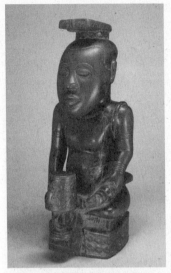

Figure 27.5a: Ndop (portrait figure) of King Mishe miShyaang maMbul, 1760–1780, wood, Brooklyn Museum, Brooklyn, New York

- Ndop figures are commemorative portraits of Kuba rulers, presented in an ideal state
- Not an actual representation of a deceased king, but his spirit
- Made after death of the king
- Each king is commemorated by symbols on the base of the figure; this king has a sword in his left hand in a non-aggressive pose, handle facing out
- One of the earliest existing African wood sculptures; oldest ndop in existence
- Rubbed with oil to protect them from insects
- Acted as a surrogate for the king in his absence
- Characteristics of ndop figures:
  - Cross-legged pose
  - Sits on a base
  - Face seems uninvolved; above mortal affairs
  - A peace knife in left hand
- Kept in the king's shrine with other works called a set of "royal charms"
■ Royal regalia: bracelets, arm bands, belts, headdress
■ **Cross-Cultural Comparisons: Authority Figures**
- Houdon, *George Washington* (Figure 19.7)
- Lindauer, *Tamati Waka Nene* (Figure 28.7)
- Stele of Hammurabi (Figures 2.4a, 2.4b)

CONTEXTUAL IMAGE

Kuba Nyim (ruler) Kot a Mbweeky III in state dress with royal drum in Mushenge, Congo (Figure 27.5b)

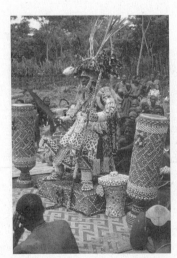

Figure 27.5b: Kuba Nyim (ruler) Kot a Mbweeky III in state dress with royal drum in Mushenge, Congo

- Photo of a Kuba ruler enthroned wearing royal regalia
- Headdress
- Necklace of leopard teeth
- Sword
- Lance
- Drums of reign
- Basket
- Photo made in 1971 capturing a royal event
- Continuous tradition of honoring a Kuba king
- Costuming extremely elaborate; could weigh 185 pounds, he needed help to move
- Costuming represents the splendor of his court, his greatness, and his responsibilities
- Symbolizes the ruler's wealth, status, power

- Kuba taste of accumulation of objects
- Ruler often buried with the material after his death

KONGO

Power figure (Nkisi n'kondi), c. late nineteenth century, wood and metal (Figure 27.6)

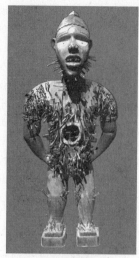

Figure 27.6: Power figure (Nkisi n'kondi), c. late 19th century, wood and metal

- Spirits are embedded in the images
- Spirits can be called upon to bless or harm others, cause death, or give life
- In order to prod the image into action, nails and blades are often inserted into the work or removed from it
- Medical properties are inserted into the body cavity, thought to be a person's life or soul
- Nails pounded into the figure
- Alert pose
- **Cross-Cultural Comparisons: Wood Sculpture**
  - *Röttgen Pietà* (Figure 12.7)
  - Transformation mask (Figures 26.12a, 26.12b)
  - Nio guardian figure (Figures 25.1c, 25.1d)

BAULE

Portrait mask (Mblo), late nineteenth to early twentieth century, wood and pigment (Figure 27.7)

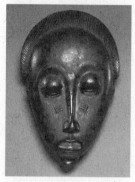

Figure 27.7: Portrait mask (Mblo), late 19th to early 20th century, wood and pigment

- Presented at Mblo performances in which an individual is honored by having ritual dances and tributes are performed in someone's honor
- Honoree receives mask as a gift that reflects an artistic double
- Masks commissioned by a group of admirers, not by an individual
- Dancer who wears the mask and wears the clothes of the honored person is accompanied by the actual person during the performance
- Idealized representation of a real person; not a portrait in the modern sense of the term
- Portraits of real people, even if commemorative, are rare in African art
- Broad foreheads, pronounced eye sockets, column-shaped nose
- Quiet faces; introspective look; peaceful face; meditative; eyebrows in an arch

CHOKWE

Female (Pwo) mask, late nineteenth to early twentieth century, wood, fiber, pigment, and metal, National Museum of African Art, Washington D.C. (Figure 27.8)

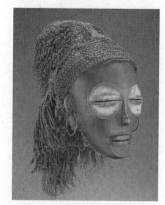

Figure 27.8: Female (Pwo) mask, late nineteenth to early twentieth century, wood, fiber, pigment, and metal, National Museum of African Art, Washington D.C.

- Female masks used by men in ritual dances
- Male dancers are covered with their identities masked; dressed as women with braided hair
- Ritual in which men move like women
- Chokwe a matriarchal society
- Depicts female ancestors

- Mask is discarded when not in use; can be buried with the dancer
- Characteristics:
  - Enlarged eye sockets
  - Pushed in chin
  - Slender nose
  - High forehead
  - Balanced features
  - Almost closed eyes
- **Cross-Cultural Connections: Faces**
  - Roman Patrician (Figure 6.14)
  - Transformation mask (Figures 26.12a, 26.12b)
  - Lindauer, *Tamati Waka Nene* (Figure 28.7)

MENDE

Bundu mask, Sande Society, nineteenth to early twentieth century, wood, cloth, and fiber, Private Collection (Figure 27.9)

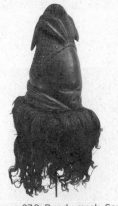

Figure 27.9: Bundu mask, Sande Society, 19th to 20th century, wood, cloth, and fiber, Private Collection

- Only African wooden masks worn by women
- Idealized female beauty
- Elaborate hairstyle symbolizes wealth; worn by women of status
- Large forehead
- Small eyes in the shape of slits
- Tight-lipped mouth symbolizing secrets not revealed
- Sande society is a group of women who prepare girls for adulthood and their role in society
- Costumed women wear a black gown made of raffia that hides the body
- Costumed as a Sowei, the water spirit; rings around neck symbolize concentric waves from which Sowei breaks through the surface
- Mask rests on her head; head not placed inside the mask
- Mask coated with palm oil for a lustrous effect
- Black color symbolizes water, coolness, and humanity
- Individuality of each mask is stressed
- **Cross-Cultural Comparisons: Art as Part of a Performance**
  - Presentation of Fijian mats … (Figure 28.10)
  - Viola, *The Crossing* (Figures 29.18a, 29.18b)
  - Plaque of the Ergastines (Figure 4.5)

IGBO

Ikenga (shrine figure), c. nineteenth to twentieth century, wood, Brooklyn Museum, Brooklyn, New York (Figure 27.10)

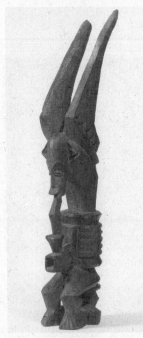

Figure 27.10: *Ikenga* (shrine figure), c. nineteenth–twentieth century, wood, Brooklyn Museum, New York

- *Ikenga* means "strong right arm," thus physical prowess
- Honors the right hand, which holds tools or weapons, makes sacrifices, conducts rituals, and alerts to speak at public forums
- Traditional masculine associations of strength and potency
- Carved from hardwoods considered masculine
- It tells of the owner's morality, prosperity, achievements, genealogy, social rank

- Personal god of achievement and success
- Requires blessings before use; consecrated with offerings before kinsmen
- Enormous horns symbolize power
- As man achieves more success he might commission a more elaborate version
- It is maintained in the man's home; destroyed when the owner dies; another can reuse it if not destroyed
- **Cross-Cultural Comparisons: Sculpture in the Round**
  - *Queen Hatshepsut with Offering Jars* (Figure 3.9)
  - Rodin, *The Burghers of Calais* (Figure 21.15)
  - Abakanowicz, *Androgyn III* (Figure 29.7)

LUBA

Memory Board (Lukasa), Mbudye Society, c. nineteenth to twentieth century, wood, beads, and metal, Brooklyn Museum, Brooklyn, New York (Figure 27.11)

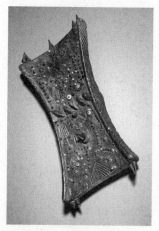

Figure 27.11: Memory Board (Lukasa), Mbudye Society, c. nineteenth to twentieth century, wood, beads, and metal, Brooklyn Museum, Brooklyn, New York

- Memory Board, or lukasa, helps the user remember key elements in a story, for example:
  - Court ceremonies
  - Migrations
  - Heroes
  - Kinship
  - Genealogy
  - Lists of kings
- Carved from wood in an hourglass shape; then adorned with shells, beads, or metal
- Reader holds lukasa in left hand and traces the designs with the right index finger
- Ability to read the board is limited to a few people
- Back resembles a tortoise
- Reading example:
  - One colored bead can stand for an individual
  - Large beads surrounded by smaller beads is a king and his court
  - Lines of beads are journeys or paths
- Each board's design is unique and represents the divine revelations of a spirit medium expressed in sculptural form
- Memory Boards are controlled by the *mbudye,* a council of men and women who interpret the political and historical aspects of Luba society
- Zoomorphic elements symbolize the crocodile, an animal that lives on both land and water; dual nature of crocodile is a metaphor for the Luba's political organization which has two interdependent leaders: the *kikungulu* (head of the *mbudye*) and the *kaloba* ("owner of the land," or chief).

BAMILEKE

Aka elephant mask, c. nineteenth to twentieth century, wood, woven raffia, cloth, and beads (Figure 27.12)

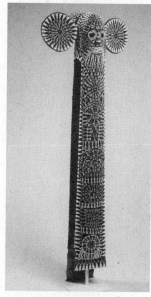

Figure 27.12: Aka elephant mask, c. nineteenth to twentieth century, wood, woven raffia, cloth, and beads

- Only important people in society can own and wear an aka, or elephant mask; used at a royal court

- Elite Kuosi masking society owns and wears the masks; worn on important ceremonial occasions
- Beadwork a symbol of power
- Symbolizes features of an elephant: long trunk, large ears (symbolizes strength and power)
- Mask fits over the head and two folds hang down in front (symbolizing the trunk) and behind the body
- Performance art: maskers dance barefoot to a drum and gong; they wave spears and horsetails
- Human face
- **Cross-Cultural Comparisons: Spiritual World**
  - Bernini, *Ecstasy of Saint Teresa* (Figures 17.4a, 17.4b)
  - Staff God (Figures 28.5a, 28.5b)
  - *Queen Hatshepsut with Offering Jars* (Figure 3.9)

FANG

Reliquary guardian figure (nlo bieri), c. 19th to 20th century, wood, Brooklyn Museum, Brooklyn, New York (Figure 27.13)

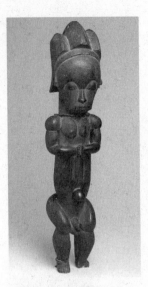

Figure 27.13: Reliquary guardian figure (nlo bieri), c. nineteenth to twentieth century, wood, Brooklyn Museum, Brooklyn, New York

- Figures placed on top of cylinder-like containers made of bark that hold skulls and other bones of important clan leaders
- Feet dangling over the rim in a gesture of protecting the contents
- The reliquary figure guards the head box against the gaze of women or young boys
- Bieri figures are composed of characteristics the Fang people place high value on: tranquility, introspection, vitality
- Surfaces were ritually rubbed with oils to add luster and protect against insects
- Prominent belly button and genitals emphasize life; the prayerful gesture and somber look emphasize death
- Abstraction of human body an attraction for the early twentieth century artists
- **Cross-Cultural Comparisons: Male Figure**
  - Apollo from Veii (Figure 5.5)
  - Donatello, *David* (Figure 15.5)
  - Nio guardian figure (Figures 25.1c, 25.1d)

YORUBA

Olowe of Ise, Veranda post of enthroned king and senior wife (Opo Ogoga), 1910–1914, wood and pigment, Art Institute of Chicago, Chicago, Illinois (Figure 27.14)

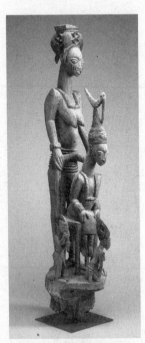

Figure 27.14: Olowe of Ise, Veranda post of enthroned king and senior wife (Opo Ogoga), 1910–1914, wood and pigment, Art Institute of Chicago, Chicago, Illinois

- Olowse of Ise carved posts for the rulers of the Ekiti-Yoruba kingdom in Nigeria
- One of four carved for the palace at Ikere
- Negative space creates an openness in the composition
- King is the focal point in relationship between his figure and others represented on this post
- Behind him his large-scale senior wife supporting the throne
- She crowns the king during the coronation; protects him during his reign

- Small figures: junior wife; flute player is Esu, the trickster god; a now missing fan bearer
- Most veranda posts were painted; traces of paint remain
- **Cross-Cultural Comparisons: Multi-Figure Sculptures**
  - Helios, Horses and Dionysos (Figure 4.4)
  - Rodin, *The Burghers of Calais* (Figure 21.15)
  - Menkaura and His Queen (Figure 3.7)

VOCABULARY

Adobe: a building material made from earth, straw, or clay dried in the sun (Figure 27.2)

Aka: an elephant mask of the Bamileke people of Cameroon (Figure 27.12)

Bieri: in the art of the Fang people, a reliquary guardian figure (Figure 27.13)

Bundu: masks used by the women's Sande society to bring girls into puberty (Figure 27.9)

Cire perdue: the lost wax process. A bronze casting method in which a figure is modeled in clay and covered with wax and then recovered with clay. When fired in a kiln, the wax melts away, leaving a channel between the two layers of clay which can be used as a mold for liquid metal (Figure 27.3)

Fetish: an object believed to possess magical powers

Ikenga: a shrine figure symbolizing traditional male attributes of the Igbo people (Figure 27.10)

Lukasa: a memory board used by the Luba people of central Africa (Figure 27.11)

Mblo: a commemorative portrait of the Baule people (Figure 27.7)

Ndop: a Kuba commemorative portrait of a king in an ideal state (Figure 27.5a)

Nkisi n'kondi: a Kongo power figure (Figure 27.6)

Pwo: a female mask worn by women of the Chokwe people (Figure 27.8)

Scarification: scarring of the skin in patterns by cutting with a knife: when the cut heals, a raised pattern is created, which is painted

Torons: Wooden beams projecting from walls of adobe buildings (Figure 27.2)

SUMMARY

African artists operated under the same general conditions of artists everywhere—learning their craft in a period of apprenticeship, working on commission from the powerful and politically connected, and achieving a measure of international fame. However, because African artists relied on the oral tradition, little written documentation of their achievements has been recorded.

Africans achieved great distinction in the carving of masks, both in wood and metal. Costumed dancers don the mask and assume the powers of the spirit that it represents. The role of the mask, therefore, indeed the role of African art, is never merely decorative, but functional and spiritual; works are imbued with powers that are symbolically much greater than the merely visible representation.

Multiple-Choice

Questions 1–3 refer to the image below.

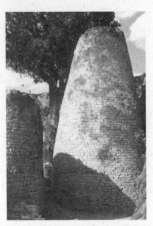

1. Great Zimbabwe had many functions, including all of the following EXCEPT

   (A) a storehouse for grain used for dispersal in times of need
   (B) a military fortress used to keep invaders out
   (C) a royal residence of the king and his court
   (D) an open area for ceremonial activities to take place

2. Visitors who entered Great Zimbabwe were meant

   (A) to be left with the feeling that they were in a major city and transportation hub
   (B) to be impressed that this was the center of commerce and industry
   (C) to admire the impressive and extensive use of stone in a part of the world that specialized in more perishable types of construction
   (D) to admire the painted friezes depicting the military exploits of the king

3. The stone walls of Great Zimbabwe exemplify the Southern African architectural practices of

   (A) using ashlar masonry to create force-dependent structures
   (B) making the stones from mud-backed bricks, similar to adobe construction
   (C) spanning large interior spaces with great arches
   (D) employing flying buttresses to support the massive walls

---

4. Each Kongo power figure (Nkisi n'kondi) had a unique function ascribed to an individual sculpture. They could be used for all of the following purposes EXCEPT:

   (A) recovery from disease
   (B) helping communities out of difficulties
   (C) destroying enemies
   (D) insuring a successful mate

5. The power of Nkisi n'kondi figures is activated by

    (A) nailing blades into the surface of a figure

    (B) carrying a figure in a procession around a village square

    (C) "marrying" the image to a second power figure

    (D) masking the figure to allow its powers to work unseen

Short Essay

The work on the left is a Pwo mask from the Congo, around the early twentieth century.

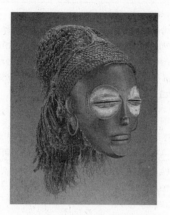 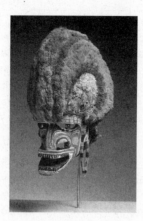

Identify the work on the right.

Both masks are used in ceremonies. Describe the purpose of each ceremony.

What else was used in these ceremonies besides the masks?

Analyze how the form of the mask is meant to convey important elements in the rituals.

ANSWER KEY

1. **B**   2. **C**   3. **A**   4. **D**   5. **A**

ANSWERS EXPLAINED

Multiple-Choice

1. **(B)** There is no evidence that this building was used for military activity, even though the stone walls suggest that this was an option available to those who lived inside.

2. **(C)** Stone buildings are rare in traditional African culture, making this complex admirable from both architectural and engineering points of view.

3. **(A)** No mortar is used in the construction of Great Zimbabwe; therefore, it is made of ashlar masonry.

4. **(D)** Power figures have many functions, but insuring a successful mate is not one of them, as evidenced by the very brutal nature of hammering blades into the surface.

5. **(A)** The power figure is activated by nailing blades into the surface.

Short-Essay Rubric

Question	Points	Key Points in a Good Response
Identify the work on the right.	1	Malagan mask, New Ireland province, Papua New Guinea, c. twentieth century, wood, pigment, fiber, and shell.
Both masks are used in ceremonies. Describe the purpose of each ceremony.	1	Pwo mask: ■ Female masks used by men in ritual dances ■ Male dancers are covered with their identities masked; dressed as women with braided hair ■ Ritual in which men move like a woman ■ Depicts female ancestors Malagan mask: ■ Malagan ceremonies send the souls of the deceased on their way to the otherworld
What else was used in these ceremonies besides the masks?	1	Answers could include: ■ Dance, music ■ Costume ■ Chanting ■ Scent

Analyze how the form of the mask is meant to convey important elements in the rituals.	2	Pwo mask:
		■ Chokwe, a matriarchal society
		■ Depicts female ancestors
		  – Enlarged eye sockets
		  – Pushed-in chin
		  – Slender nose
		  – High forehead
		  – Balanced features
		  – Almost closed eyes
		
		Malagan mask:
		■ Masks are extremely intricate in their carving
		■ Mask indicates the relationship of a particular deceased person to a clan and to living members of the family
		■ Large hair comb reflects a hairstyle of the time, but masks are not physical portraits, only portraits of the soul
		■ Painted black, yellow, and red: important colors denoting violence, war, and magic

Oceanic Art

28

Except for the Easter Island sculptures, which date from the tenth century, most surviving Oceanic Art dates from the nineteenth and twentieth centuries.

ENDURING UNDERSTANDING: Since the region is so big, the arts of the Pacific are hard to classify.

Essential Knowledge:

- Art is created using available materials such as bone, shell, wood, coral, fiber, and stone.
- Australia was populated about 30,000 years ago. The islands were populated about 4,000 years ago. Europeans began arriving in the sixteenth century.
- Some objects symbolize family or clan history; others celebrate history and were meant to be destroyed afterwards.

ENDURING UNDERSTANDING: Pacific art, across all spectrums, is influenced by the sea, which separates and connects each island.

Essential Knowledge:

- The Lapita culture began the Pacific pattern of migration, bringing their plants, animals, customs, and culture with them.
- Ship building and navigation became essential communication lines in the vast distances involved.

ENDURING UNDERSTANDING: Pacific art deals with complex belief systems controlled by powerful members of society.

Essential Knowledge:

- Sculptures representing forces in the supernatural world were often wrapped to be protected. One's *mana* or vital force needs to be defended and protected. Sometimes *mana* could represent a whole community. The act of protecting the *mana* through rituals or wrapping is called *tapu.*
- Each community in the Pacific had a different way of conducting spiritual exercises and commanding a social structure.

ENDURING UNDERSTANDING: Pacific arts are performed using costumes, dance, song, and cosmetics.

Essential Knowledge:

- Ritual performances each have a different purpose: e.g., celebration, war.
- The act of performance contains the work's meaning. The objects in that performance contain no meaning unless brought to life by the rituals.
- Rituals and performances often involve exchanging pre-arranged items that have symbolic value.
- A symmetry of relationships is often sought. Opposing forces, such as gender, are placed within a balancing situation in many rituals.

HISTORICAL BACKGROUND

Certain areas of the Pacific are some of the oldest inhabited places on earth, and yet, paradoxically, some areas are among the newest. Aborigines reached Australia around 50,000 years ago, but the remote islands of the Pacific, like Hawaii, Easter Island, and New Zealand were occupied only in the last thousand years or so.

Around 1300 B.C.E. seafarers reached across the vast oceanic expanses to chart their way toward Fiji in the central South Pacific. Technological development of sailing craft meant greater territories could be mapped and charted for possible occupation. The particularly effective twin-hulled sailing canoe was used to traverse hundreds of nautical miles; Tonga was reached in 420 B.C.E., and then Samoa in 200 B.C.E.

The final push to populate the Pacific came with the discovery of New Zealand. This happened perhaps as early as the tenth century, but certainly by the thirteenth century by the ancestors of the Maori.

European involvement in the Pacific began with the circumnavigation of the globe by Portuguese explorer Ferdinand Magellan and his crew. Explorers of the eighteenth century were followed by occupiers from the nineteenth century, who implanted European customs, values, religions, and technologies onto the indigenous population. Many areas of the Pacific, however, achieved independence in the twentieth century.

Patronage and Artistic Life

Men and women had clearly defined roles in Pacific society, including which sex could create works of art in which media. Men carved in wood, woman sewed and made pottery.

One of the most characteristic works still done by Pacific women is the weaving of bark-cloth, or **tapa** (Figure 28.6). The inner bark of the mulberry tree is harvested and small strips are made malleable by repeated soakings. Each strip is placed in a pattern and then beaten in order to fuse them together. Designs were added by stenciling or painting directly onto the surface. The result is a cloth of refined geometric organization and intricate patterning.

MICRONESIA

Nan Madol, c. 700–1600, basalt boulders and prismatic columns, Pohnpei, Micronesia (Figures 28.1a and 28.1b)

- Ancient city that acted as the capital of the Saudeleur Dynasty of Micronesia
- 92 small artificial islands connected by canals, about 170 acres in total
- Built out into the water on a lagoon; similar to Venice, Italy

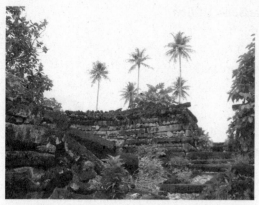

Figure 28.1a: Nan Madol, c. 700–1600, basalt boulders and prismatic columns, Pohnpei, Micronesia

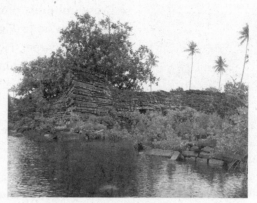

Figure 28.1b: Nan Madol, c. 700–1600, basalt boulders and prismatic columns, Pohnpei, Micronesia

- Seawalls act as breakwaters; fifteen feet high, thirty-five feet thick
- Canals were flushed clean with the tides
- Islands are arranged SW to NE to take advantage of the trade winds
- City built to separate the upper classes from the lower classes
- King arranged for the upper classes to live close to him, to keep an eye on them
- Curved outer walls point upward at edges giving the complex a symbolic boat-like appearance
- **Cross-Cultural Comparisons: Water and Architecture**
  - Ryoan-ji (Figures 25.2a, 25.2b, 25.2c)
  - Gehry, Guggenheim Bilbao (Figures 29.1a, 29.1b)
  - Wright, Fallingwater (Figures 22.16a, 22.16b, 22.16c)

Female deity, c. eighteenth to nineteenth century, wood, Nukuoro, Micronesia (Figure 28.2)

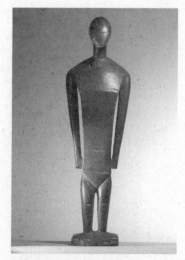

- Many kept in religious buildings belonging to the community
- Represent individual deities
- Sometimes dressed in garments; may have been decorated with flowers
- Simple geometric forms
- Erect pose; long arms; broad chest
- Chin drawing to a point; no facial features
- Horizontal lines used to indicate knee caps, navel, waistline

Figure 28.2: Female deity, c. eighteenth to nineteenth century, wood, Nukuoro, Micronesia

Navigation chart, Marshall Islands, nineteenth to early twentieth century, wood and fiber (Figure 28.3)

- Marshall Islands are low-lying and hard to see from a distance
- Charts composed to steer through the many islands to get to a destination
- Horizontal and vertical sticks support the chart
- Diagonal lines indicate wind and water currents
- Small shells indicate the position of the islands on the chart
- Chart is made of wood, therefore waterproof and buoyant
- Charts meant to be memorized prior to a voyage; not necessarily used during a voyage

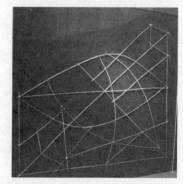

Figure 28.3: Navigation chart, Marshall Islands, nineteenth to early twentieth century, wood and fiber

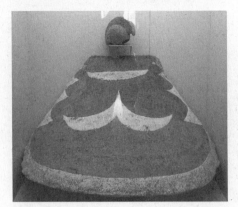

Figure 28.4: 'Ahu 'ula (feather cape), late 18th century, feathers and fiber, Museum of the Americas, Madrid

- **Cross-Cultural Comparisons: Utility**
  - Ambum Stone (Figure 1.4)
  - Ardabil Carpet (Figure 9.7a)
  - *Pyxis of al-Mughira* (Figure 9.4)

HAWAII

'Ahu 'ula (feather cape), late eighteenth century, feathers and fiber, Museum of the Americas, Madrid (Figure 28.4)

- Coat made of thousands of bird feathers; worn by men
- 500,000 feathers; some birds had only seven usable feathers
- Red considered a royal color in Polynesia
- Coconut fiber used as a base; feathers tied to it
- Cloak created by artists who chanted the wearer's ancestors to imbue their power on it
- Protected the wearer from harm
- **Cross-Cultural Comparisons: Regalia**
  - Ruler's Feathered Headdress (Figure 26.6)
  - Gold and Jade Crown (Figure 24.20)
  - Ndop Contextual Photograph (Figure 27.5b)

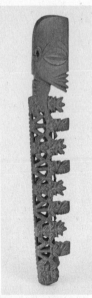
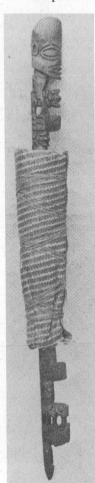

Figure 28.5a: Staff god, Rarotonga, Cook Islands, late eighteenth to early nineteenth century, wood, tapa, fiber, and feathers, British Museum, London

Figure 28.5b: Staff god, Rarotonga

COOK ISLANDS

Staff god, Rarotonga, Cook Islands, late eighteenth to early nineteenth century, wood, tapa, fiber, and feathers, British Museum, London (Figures 28.5a and 28.5b)

- Large column-like wooden shaft placed upright in a village common
- Large head placed on top; several smaller heads carved below it
- Shaft in the form of an elongated body
- Central carved wooden shaft around which a roll of tapa is placed
- The soul of the god is represented by polished pearl shells and red feathers that are placed inside the bark cloth next to the interior shaft
- Most staff gods were destroyed, only the top ends were retained as trophies
- In contextual image (not shown) the staff gods have been thrown down in the village square in front of a European-style church; represents the fall of one faith and the adoption of another
- Figure 28.5b shows the god wrapped, or protected.

POLYNESIA

Hiapo (tapa) from Niue, c. 1850–1900, tapa or bark cloth, freehand painting, Aukland War Memorial Museum, New Zealand (Figure 28.6)

- Hiapo is the word used in Niue for "tapa" or "bark cloth"
- Tapa is cloth made from tree bark; the pieces are beaten and pasted together
- Using stencils, the artists dye the exposed parts of the tapa with paint

- After the tapa is dry, designs are sometimes repainted to enhance the effect
- Traditionally worn as clothing before the importation of cotton
- Tapa take on a special meaning: commemorating an event; honoring a chief; noting a series of ancestors
- Each set of designs is meant to be interpreted symbolically; many of the images have a rich history
- **Cross-Cultural Comparisons: Abstraction**
  - Braque, *Portuguese* (Figure 22.6)
  - Ambum Stone (Figure 1.4)
  - Mehretu, *Stadia II* (Figure 29.24)

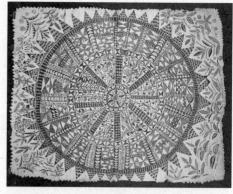

Figure 28.6: Hiapo (tapa) from Niue, c. 1850–1900, tapa or bark cloth, freehand painting, Aukland War Memorial Museum, New Zealand

NEW ZEALAND

Gottfried Lindauer, *Tamati Waka Nene*, 1890, oil on canvas, Aukland Art Gallery, Aukland, New Zealand (Figure 28.7)

- New Zealand painter, famous for portraits of Maori chieftains
- Journeyman painter-tradesman who worked on commission
- Subject is Tamati Waka Nene (c.1780–1871), Maori chief and convert to the Wesleyan faith
- Painting is posthumous based on a photograph by John Crombie
- Emphasis placed on symbols of rank: elaborate tattooing, staff with an eye in the center, feathers dangling from the staff
- **Cross-Cultural Comparisons: Rulers**
  - Houdon, *George Washington* (Figure 19.7)
  - Wall plaque from Oba's palace (Figure 27.3)
  - *Augustus of Prima Porta* (Figure 6.15)

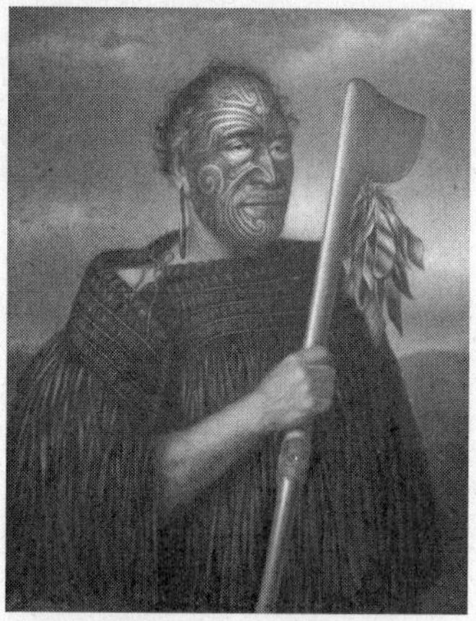

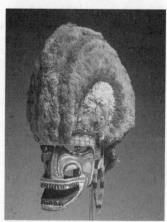

Figure 28.7: Gottfried Lindauer, *Tamati Waka Nene*, 1890, oil on canvas, Aukland Art Gallery, Aukland, New Zealand

PAPUA NEW GUINEA

Malagan mask, Papua New Guinea, c. twentieth century, wood, pigment, fiber, and shell, Brooklyn Museum, Brooklyn, New York (Figure 28.8)

- Malagan ceremonies send the souls of the deceased on their way to the otherworld
- Sometimes ceremonies begin months after death, and can last an extended period of time
- Ceremonies free the living of the obligation of serving the dead
- Erect structures suited to the purpose; after the ceremony the structures are considered useless; usually destroyed or allowed to rot
- Sculptures of the deceased are commissioned; they represent the individual's soul or life force, not physical presence
- Masks are extremely intricate in their carving
- Mask indicates the relationship of a particular deceased person to a clan, and living members of the family
- Large hair comb reflects a hairstyle of the time, but masks are not physical portraits, only portraits of the soul
- Painted black, yellow, and red: important colors denoting violence, war, and magic

Figure 28.8: Malagan mask, Papua New Guinea, c. twentieth century, wood, pigment, fiber, and shell, Brooklyn Museum, Brooklyn, New York

- Artists are specialists in using negative space
- **Cross-Cultural Comparisons: Faces**
  - Mblo (Figure 27.7)
  - Roman Patrician (Figure 6.14)
  - Reliquary of Sainte-Foy (Figure 11.6c)

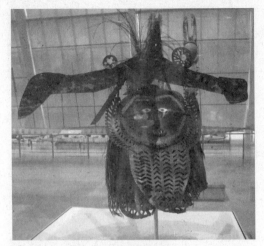

Figure 28.9: Buk (mask), Torres Strait, mid-to-late nineteenth century, turtle shell, wood, fiber, feathers, and shell, Metropolitan Museum of Art, New York

Buk (mask), Torres Strait, mid-to-late nineteenth century, turtle shell, wood, fiber, feathers, and shell, Metropolitan Museum of Art, New York (Figure 28.9)

- Torres Strait is the water passageway between Australia and New Guinea
- Turtle shell masks unique to this region
- Used with grass costumes in ceremonies about death, fertility, or male initiation
- Ceremonies involved fire, drum beats, and chanting; recreating mythical ancestral beings and their impact on these people in everyday activities
- Some masks combine human and animal forms; this mask shows a bird placed on top
- **Cross-Cultural Comparisons: Masks**
  - Aka elephant mask (Figure 27.12)
  - Olmec mask (Figure 26.5d)
  - Transformation mask (Figures 26.12a, 26.12b)

FIJI

Presentation of Fijian mats and tapa cloths to Queen Elizabeth II during the 1953–1954 royal tour, 1953, multimedia performance, photographic documentation (Figure 28.10)

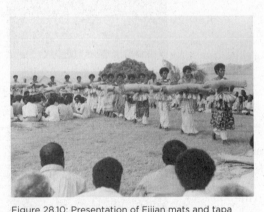

Figure 28.10: Presentation of Fijian mats and tapa cloths to Queen Elizabeth II during the 1953–1954 royal tour, 1953, multimedia performance, photographic documentation

- Enormous tapa cloth made for the visit of Queen Elizabeth II in 1953 to Fiji, on the occasion of her coronation as Queen of England
- Presentation to the Queen is an example of performance art
- Imagery of royal crowns, geometric patterns, and a floral motif
- Men oversee the growth of the mulberry trees that produce the tapa; women turn the bark into cloth
- Bark removed from tree, soaked in water, and treated to make it pliable
- Clubs are used to beat the strips into a long rectangular block to form pieces of cloth
- The edges of these smaller pieces are then glued or felted together to produce large sheets.
- Decorated according to a local tradition: sometimes stenciled, sometimes printed or dyed
- Cf. Lapita geometric motifs (Figure 1.6)
- Fiji ceremony with mats viewable on this webpage: *http://hmonghot.com/WFR6Tnk5Qnhmc2sz*
- **Cross-Cultural Comparisons: Performance**
  - Viola, *The Crossing* (Figures 29.18a, 29.18b)
  - Lukasa Memory Board (Figure 27.11)

EASTER ISLAND (RAPA NUI)

Moai on platform (ahu), c. 1100–1600, volcanic tuff figures on basalt base, Easter Island (Rapa Nui) (Figure 28.11)

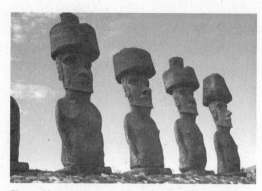

Figure 28.11: Moai on platform (ahu), c. 1100–1600, volcanic tuff figures on basalt base, Easter Island (Rapa Nui)

- About nine hundred statues in all, mostly male, almost all facing inland; fifty tons apiece
- Erected on large platforms of stone mixed with ashes from cremations; the platforms are as sacred as the statues on them
- Images represent personalities deified after death, or commemorated as the first settler-kings
- Prominent foreheads, large broad noses, thin pouting lips, ears that reach to the top of their heads
- Short thin arms falling straight down; hands across lower abdomen below navel
- Chests and navels delineated
- Topknots added to some statues
- White coral placed in eyes to "open" them

VOCABULARY

'Ahu 'ula: Hawaiian feather cloaks (Figure 28.4)
Moai: large stone sculptures found on Easter Island (Figure 28.11)
Tapa: a cloth made from bark that is soaked and beaten into a fabric (Figure 28.6)

SUMMARY

The great expanses of the Pacific were peopled gradually over thousands of years. Indeed, the vast stretch of ocean is matched by the immense variety of artwork produced by disparate people speaking a myriad of languages.

A few generalities about Oceanic Art can be stated with foundation. Many items are portable, usually created for use in a ceremony, and made of wood or bark. When large wooden objects are introduced, they are carved with great precision using the whole of a wooden log. Intricately woven fabrics made of natural materials are a particular Pacific specialty. In all cases, intricate line definition is a hallmark of Oceanic artistic output.

None of these characteristics apply to the art of Easter Island, a unique place in which giant stone sculptures dominate a windswept landscape. These large torsos and heads find their closest artistic affinities with the cultures of ancient America, but the connection between the two cultures is still largely unproven.

Multiple-Choice

Questions 1 and 2 refer to the illustration below.

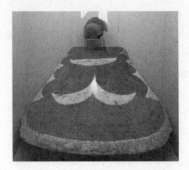

1. This type of garment is used in which of the following contexts?
   (A) It established a royal lineage by discrediting rivals to the throne.
   (B) It linked the wearer to the gods.
   (C) It made a connection between the human world and the animal world.
   (D) It cast a spell on enemies.

2. This garment belonged to

   (A) Hawaiian royalty
   (B) Motecuhzoma II
   (C) King Mishe miShyaang maMbul
   (D) Coyolxauhqui

   ───────────────────

3. The *Processional Welcoming Queen Elizabeth II* is analogous in content to

   (A) *The Plaque of the Ergastines*
   (B) *The Column of Trajan*
   (C) *The Bayeux Tapestry*
   (D) *The Grave Stele of Hegeso*

4. The weaving technique used to make tapa requires

   (A) a heating process whereby the fabric is covered with wax and the threads are melted in place
   (B) the use of silk threads to be woven onto a background of sheep's wool
   (C) beating soaked strips of tree bark into a flat surface to be later woven into a cloth-like fabric
   (D) stitching thread into a pre-made backing to form a design

5. Prehistoric works from the Pacific, such as the *Ambum Stone,* illustrate the ongoing tradition of using animal motifs that appear in such works as

   (A) the Moai from Rapa Nui (Easter Island)
   (B) Malagan Masks
   (C) Buk Masks
   (D) the Female Deity from Nukuoro

Short Essay

This work is *Tamati Waka Nene* by Gottfried Lindauer.

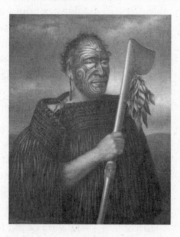

Who is the subject of this painting?

How was the painting viewed by contemporaries?

Using specific details, analyze how elements of this painting are put together to create a particular image of the sitter.

What elements of the work betray a European influence?

ANSWER KEY

1. **B**   2. **A**   3. **A**   4. **C**   5. **C**

ANSWERS EXPLAINED

Multiple-Choice

1. **(B)** The cloak was created by artists who chanted to the wearer's ancestors to imbue their power on it. Wearers chanted to create a link between the wearer and the world of spirits.

2. **(A)** The garment is associated with Hawaiian royalty.

3. **(A)** *Processional Welcoming Queen Elizabeth II* is akin to the *Plaque of the Ergastines* because in both cases offerings are being made in a ceremonial procession.

4. **(C)** Tapa is made by beating soaked strips of tree bark into a flat surface to be later woven into a cloth-like fabric.

5. **(C)** Buk masks contain many animal motifs. The one on the curriculum guide has a turtle shell topped by a bird.

Short-Essay Rubric

Question	Points	Key Points in a Good Response
Who is the subject of this painting?	1	The subject is Tamati Waka Nene, a Maori chief and convert to the Wesleyan faith.
How was the painting viewed by contemporaries?	1	Answers could include: ■ Painting is posthumous, based on a photograph by John Crombie. ■ Subject was revered, and people wanted to memorialize him after death. ■ Surrounding dramatic sky indicates his place in history.
Using specific details, analyze how elements of this painting are put together to create a particular image of the sitter.	1	Answers could include: ■ Emphasis placed on symbols of rank: elaborate tattooing, staff with an eye in the center, feathers dangling from the staff ■ Details contribute to the interpretation of a majestic, yet kindly, figure
What elements of the work betray a European influence?	2	Answers could include: ■ Oil on canvas technique ■ Atmospheric perspective ■ Shading and modeling ■ Three-dimensional, solid figure ■ Figure turned to 3/4 view

Contemporary Art

29

TIME PERIOD: 1980-PRESENT

ENDURING UNDERSTANDING: Traditional forms of art history have been enhanced by technology.

Essential Knowledge:

- Traditional skills have been challenged by digital works, works that were meant to last only a short time, works captured on video, computer generated works, etc.
- Diverse art forms are created that reflect and challenge the environment in which they were made.
- Artists appropriate works from the past which reveal layers of meaning beyond what was perhaps intended.
- Cities seek to be defined by an iconic landmark.

ENDURING UNDERSTANDING: Contemporary art is global.

Essential Knowledge:

- Art history has traditionally ignored contemporary art from non-American and European sources. Excellent contemporary art is being produced globally.
- Eurocentric views have been downplayed by the rise of the Internet and political power shifts around the globe.
- Artists now come from a multitude of backgrounds, not just the traditional white heterosexual male.
- There are many more venues for displaying art in the world today than ever. Galleries, exhibits, and annual exhibitions proliferate.

HISTORICAL BACKGROUND

The devastation of World War II formed the backdrop for much of the rest of the twentieth century. Far from solving the world's problems, it just replaced the Fascist menace with smaller conflicts no less deadly in the world's traditional hot spots. With the invention of television, global issues were brought into the living rooms of millions as never before. One disillusioning world problem after another—racism, the environment, weapons of mass destruction—has contributed to a tense atmosphere, even in parts of the world not physically touched by conflict. Artists are quick to pick up on social and political issues, using them as springboards to create artwork.

But not all is bleak in the contemporary world. The rapid growth of technology has brought great advances in medical science and everyday living. Inventions formerly beyond the realm of possibility, like home computers or cell phones, have turned into the necessities of modern life. New media has become fertile ground for artistic exploration. Artists exploit materials, like plastics, for their elastic properties. Video projections, computer graphics, sound installations, fiberglass products, and lasers are new technologies for artists to investigate. One challenge posed to the artist concerns how these media will be used in a way that will thoughtfully provoke the audience. Certainly the modern world has much to offer the artist.

MODERN ARCHITECTURE

Everything about architecture has changed since 1980, and most of the changes have been brought about by the computer. No longer are blueprints painstakingly drawn by hand to exacting specifications. Programs like AutoCAD and MicroStation not only assist in drawing ground plans, but also automatically check for errors. They also make feasible designs that heretofore existed only in the mind. Frank Gehry's **Guggenheim Bilboa Museo** (Figure 29.1) is a good example of how computers can help architects render shapes and meaningful designs in an imaginative way.

New age technology has produced an array of products that make buildings lighter, cheaper, and more energy efficient than before. All these developments, however, come aligned with new challenges for architects. How can cost efficiency and expensive new technology be brought into a meaningful architectural plan? The resources are there for the future to explore.

One would be hard-pressed to find a modern building with pediments, Doric columns, or flying buttresses; historical associations have been downplayed in modern architecture. What exists is a proud display of technology: Innovative materials like titanium in **Gehry's** work, or unusual shapes like the buildings of **Hadid**.

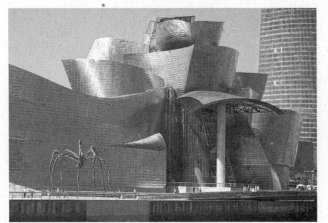

Figure 29.1a: Frank Gehry, Guggenheim Bilboa Museo, 1997, titanium, glass, and limestone, Bilboa, Spain

Dark interiors, as in Gothic or Romanesque buildings, are out. Natural light supplemented by artificial light is in. Domes presage a modern fascination, almost obsession, with glass and its properties.

Frank Gehry, Guggenheim Bilboa Museo, 1997, titanium, glass, and limestone, Bilboa, Spain (Figures 29.1a and 29.1b)

- Canadian-American architect based in Los Angeles
- Swirling forms and shapes mark a contract with the industrial landscape of Bilbao
- From the river side, the building resembles a boat, referencing the Bilbao's past as a shipping and commercial center
- Curving forms designed by a computer software program called Catia
- Fixing clips make a shallow dent in the titanium surface; effect of having a shimmering surface that changes according to atmospheric conditions
- Revitalized the port area of Bilbao; "Bilbao effect" refers to the impact that a museum can have on a local economy
- Appearance of asymmetrical exterior with outside walls giving no hint to interior spaces

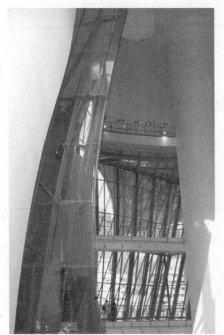

Figure 29.1b: Detail of interior of Guggenheim Bilbao Museo

- Irregular masses of titanium walls
- Sweeping curved lines
- Called Deconstructionist architecture—architecture that seeks to create a seemingly unstable environment with unusual spatial arrangements
- **Cross-Cultural Connections: Curvilinear Forms**
  - Borromini, San Carlo alle Quattro Fontane (Figures 17.2a, 17.2b)
  - Walls of Saqsa Waman (Figure 26.8c)
  - Great Zimbabwe (Figures 27.1a, 27.1b)

Zaha Hadid, MAXXI National Museum of XXI Century Arts, 2009, glass, steel, and cement, Rome, Italy (Figures 29.2a and 29.2b)

- Iraqi-born, British-based architect
- Two museums (MAXXI Art and MAXXI Architecture), a library, auditorium, and cafeteria
- Internal spaces covered by a glass roof; natural light admitted into the interior, filtered by louvered blinds
- Walls flow and melt into one another, creating new and dynamic interior spaces
- Constantly changing interior and exterior views
- Transparent roof, modulate natural light
- **Cross-Cultural Comparisons: Public Spaces**
  - Forum of Trajan (Figure 6.10a)
  - Angkor Wat (Figures 23.8a, 23.8b, 23.8c, 23.8d)
  - Forbidden City (Figures 24.2a, 24.2b, 24.2c, 24.2d)

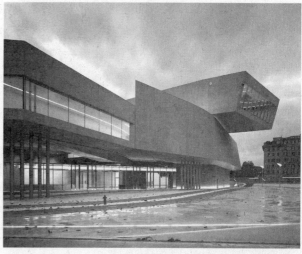

Figure 29.2a: Zaha Hadid, MAXXI National Museum of XXI Century Arts, 2009, glass, steel, and cement, Rome, Italy

MODERN PAINTING AND SCULPTURE

Oil on canvas is still the preferred medium. In the 1950s, however, a new type of paint—**acrylic**—was developed to wide popular appeal. Acrylics take very little time to dry, unlike oils, which can take weeks or even months, and unlike watercolor, acrylics do not change color when they dry. However, acrylics crack with time much faster than other paints do. Contemporary artists who are working "for the ages" still prefer oils, although commercially available extenders can prolong the life of acrylics.

While traditional painting techniques are still popular, many modern artists have abandoned the canvas for the computer screen and have reached into cyberspace to create new forms and modes of representation. Computer programs make the process easier, bringing with them a dizzy array of applications and alternatives. The computer has revolutionized the creative spirit of fine art.

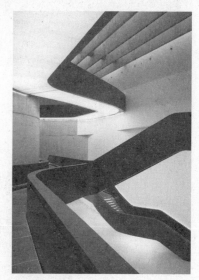

Figure 29.2b: Interior of MAXXI

Marble carving is dead. All the great advantages to marble—its permanence, durability, and lustrous shine—have been cast into the dustbin of history. Few artists want to spend years studying marble carving in a world that will offer no commissions for laboring over an art form that is associated with the ancients and has seemingly nothing to offer beyond that. Marble is also unforgiving; once chipped, it cannot be repaired without showing the damage.

Modern forms of sculpture are faster to produce and even easier to reproduce. Unlike marble or bronze they come in a variety of textures, from the high-polish porcelains by Jeff Koons

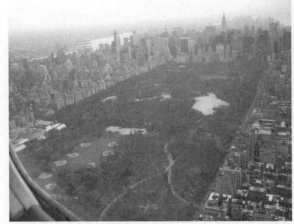

Figure 29.3a: Christo and Jean-Claude, *The Gates*, 1979–2005, mixed media installation, New York City

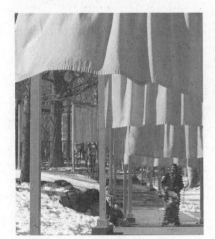

Figure 29.3b: Detail of *The Gates*

to the knotty fabrics of Magdalena Abakanowicz. Anything that can be molded, like beeswax, is experimented with to make a visceral impact.

On occasion, sculptors will combine objects into works of art, called **assemblages**. If the assemblages are large enough, they are called **installations** and can take up a whole room in a museum or gallery.

Christo and Jean-Claude, *The Gates*, 1979–2005, mixed media installation, New York City (Figures 29.3a and 29.3b)

- Christo is Bulgarian born; Jean-Claude is of French descent, born in Morocco
- 7,503 "gates" of free-hanging saffron colored fabric panels
- Framed all the pathways in Central Park, New York City
- 16-foot-tall gates formed a continuous river of color
- Covered 23 miles of footpaths
- Temporary installation, left up for sixteen days
- After the exhibition closed the materials were recycled
- **Cross-Cultural Comparisons: Gateways**
  - Great Portal, Chartres (Figure 12.6)
  - Todai-ji (Figure 25.1e)
  - Forbidden City (Figures 24.2a, 24.2b, 24.2c, 24.2d)

Maya Lin, Vietnam Veterans Memorial, 1982, black granite, Washington, D.C. (Figures 29.4a and 29.4b)

- Artist an Ohio-born Chinese-American
- V-shaped monument cut into the earth with 60,000 casualties of the Vietnam War listed in the order they were killed or reported missing
- One arm of the monument points to the Lincoln Memorial, the other to the Washington Monument

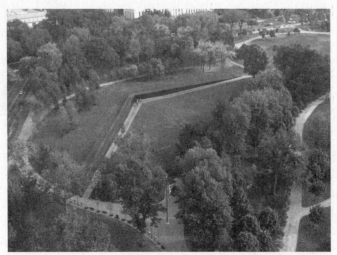

Figure 29.4a: Maya Lin, Vietnam Veterans Memorial, 1982, black granite, Washington D.C.

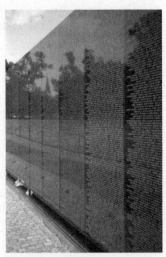

Figure 29.4b: Maya Lin, Vietnam Veterans Memorial, 1982, black granite, Washington, D.C.

- Black granite as a highly reflective surface so that viewers can see themselves in the names of the veterans; black is an appropriate somber color for the memorial
- Strongly influenced by the Minimalist movement

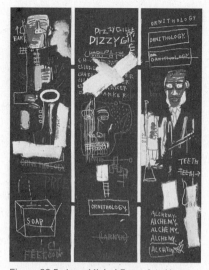

Figure 29.5: Jean-Michel Basquiat, *Horn Players*, 1983, acrylic and oil paintstick on canvas panels, Broad Art Foundation, Santa Monica, California

Jean-Michel Basquiat, *Horn Players*, 1983, acrylic and oil paintstick on canvas panels, Broad Art Foundation, Santa Monica, California (Figure 29.5)

- Artist born in Brooklyn, New York, of Puerto Rican and Haitian parents
- Artist rebelled against the middle class upbringing he was born into
- Some traditional forms: triptych, canvas, oil paint
- Modernist expression: influence of graffiti art
- Flattened darkened background; flat patches of color; thick lines
- Glorifies African-American musicians: salute to jazz musicians Charlie Parker and Dizzy Gillespie in either wing
- Heads seem to float over outlined bodies and dissolve as you go down the body
- Focus is on contrast and juxtaposition, not on balance or scale
- Words are those attributed to the musicians (ornithology misspelled; reference to Charlie "The Bird" Parker)

Song Su-nam, *Summer Trees*, 1983, ink on paper, British Museum, London (Figure 29.6)

- Korean artist using traditional ink on paper
- Large vertical lines of various thickness
- Subtle tonal variations of ink wash
- One of the leaders of the "Sumukhwa," a new type of ink painting in the 1980s
- Ink painting a traditional form of artist expression in Korea; this movement revitalizes ink painting in a modern context
- **Cross-Cultural Comparisons: Ink Technique**
  - Folio from the Qur'an (Figure 9.5)
  - Bichitr, *Jahangir Preferring a Sufi Shaikh to Kings* (Figure 23.9)
  - *Bahrum Gur Fights the Karg* (Figure 9.8)

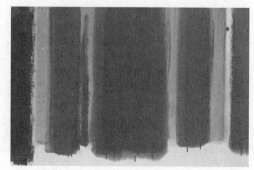

Figure 29.6: Song Su-nam, *Summer Trees*, 1983, ink on paper, British Museum, London

Magdalena Abakanowicz, *Androgyn III*, 1985, burlap, resin, wood, nails, and string, Metropolitan Museum of Art, New York (Figure 29.7)

- Polish artist
- Since 1974 artist makes figures often without heads or arms in large groups or singly
- Figure sits on a low stretcher of wooden legs, substituting for human legs
- Figure hollowed out, just a shell, hardened fiber casts made from plaster molds
- Figure placed to be seen in the round: the complete back, the hollow front
- Hardened fiber has the appearance of crinkled human skin set in earth tones

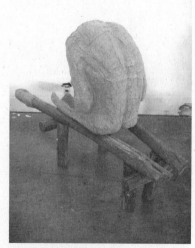

Figure 29.7: Magdalena Abakanowicz, *Androgyn III*, 1985, burlap, resin, wood, nails, and string, Metropolitan Museum of Art, New York

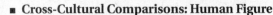

- **Cross-Cultural Comparisons: Human Figure**
  - Tlatilco Female Figure (Figure 1.5)
  - Lakshmana Temple detail (Figure 27.3b)
  - Nlo Bieri (Figure 27.13)

Xu Bing, *A Book from the Sky*, 1987–1991, 100 boxed sets of 4-volume woodblock printed books, variable numbers of scrolls hanging from the ceiling, and variable number of wall panels, installation, Elvehjem Museum of Art, University of Wisconsin-Madison, Madison, Wisconsin (Figures 29.8a and 29.8b)

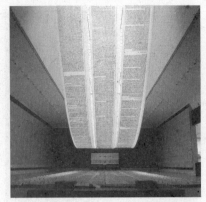

Figure 29.8a: Xu Bing, *A Book from the Sky*, mixed media installation, Elvehjem Museum of Art, University of Wisconsin-Madison, Madison, Wisconsin

- Chinese-born artist; U.S. resident
- Original title "An Analyzed Reflection of the End of This Century"
- Originally in the National Museum of Fine Arts in Beijing; filled a large exhibition space
  - 400 handmade books placed in rows on the ground
  - One walks beneath fifty printed scrolls which hang from the ceiling
  - Uses traditional Asian wood block techniques
  - Many of the Chinese characters are inventions of the artist and have no meaning
  - Artist lost favor with the Communist government over this work
  - Criticized as "bourgeois liberation" and it was claimed that its meaninglessness hid secret subversions
  - **Cross-Cultural Comparisons: Book Making**
    - *Book of Lindisfarne* (Figures 10.2a, 10.2b.10.2c)
    - *Golden Haggadah* (Figures 12.10a, 12.10b, 12.10c)
    - Frontispiece of the Codex Mendoza (Figure 18.1)

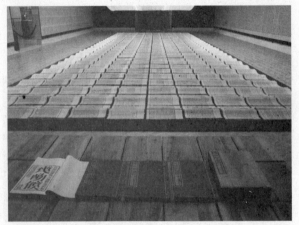

Figure 29.8b: Alternate view of Figure 29.8a

Jeff Koons, *Pink Panther*, 1988, glazed porcelain, Museum of Modern Art, New York (Figure 29.9)

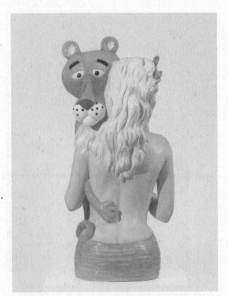

Figure 29.9: Jeff Koons, *Pink Panther*, 1988, glazed porcelain, Museum of Modern Art, New York

- Pennsylvania-born artist, working in New York
- Work exists as a commentary on celebrity romance, sexuality, commercialism, stereotypes, pop culture, sentimentality
- Artificially idealized female form: overly yellow hair, bright red lips, large breasts, pronounced red fingernails; overtly fake look
- Life-size
- Kitsch
- Creates a permanent reality out of something that is ephemeral and never meant to be exhibited
- Woman is Jayne Mansfield, a popular screen star
- Pink Panther, a cartoon character derived from a series of American movies
- Tender delicacy of the panther's gesture
- Part of a series called "The Banality" at a show in the Sonnenbend Gallery in NY in 1988

- **Cross-Cultural Comparisons: Porcelain and Ceramic**
  - The David Vases (Figure 24.11)
  - Apollo from Veii (Figure 5.5)
  - Terra-cotta Fragment (Figure 1.6)

Cindy Sherman, *Untitled #228* from the History Portraits series, 1990, photograph, Broad Art Foundation, Santa Monica, California (Figure 29.10)

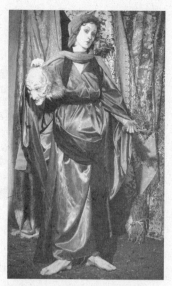

Figure 29.10: Cindy Sherman, *Untitled #228* from the History Portraits series, 1990, photograph, Broad Art Foundation, Santa Monica, California

- New Jersey born, American artist
- Artist appears as the photographer, subject, costumer, hairdresser, and makeup artist in each work
- Artist's work comments on gender, identity, society, and class distinction
- This series sheds a modern light on the great masters
- Uses old master paintings as a starting point, but the works are not derivative
- This image explores the theme of Salome decapitating Saint John the Baptist
- Richness of costuming and setting acts as a commentary on late nineteenth-century versions of this subject
- Richly decorative drapes hang behind the figure
- Salome lacks any emotional attachment to the murder that has taken place
- Saint John the Baptist appears mask-like, alert, and nearly bloodless
- **Cross-Cultural Comparisons: References to the Past**
  - Jefferson, Monticello (Figures 19.5a, 19.5b)
  - Ringgold, *Dancing at the Louvre* (Figure 29.11)
  - Shinobare, *The Swing* (Figure 29.22)

Faith Ringgold, *Dancing at the Louvre* from the series *The French Collection, Part I; #1*, 1991, acrylic on canvas, with fabric borders, Private Collection (Figure 29.11)

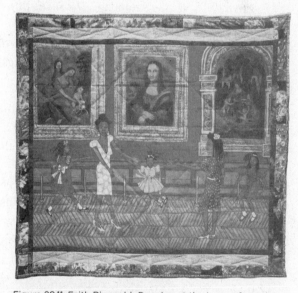

Figure 29.11: Faith Ringgold, *Dancing at the Louvre* from the series *The French Collection, Part I; #1*, 1991, acrylic on canvas, with fabric borders, Private Collection

- New York-born African-American artist
- Artist uses the American slave art form of the quilt to create her works
- Quilts were originally meant to be both beautiful and useful; works of applied art
- Quilting seen as a traditionally female art form
- Combines the traditional use of oil paint with the quilting technique
- These quilts are not meant to be placed on beds
- Quilt has a narrative element
- Feminist issues dominate
- Often figures in Ringgold works act out a history that might never have taken place, but the artist would have liked to take place
- Artist created a character named Willia Marie Simone, who takes her friend and three daughters to the Louvre museum and dances in front of three paintings by Leonardo DaVinci
- **Cross-Cultural Comparisons: Woven Arts**
  - Bandolier Bag (Figure 26.11)
  - Hiapo (Figure 28.6)
  - *The Bayeux Tapestry* (Figures 11.7a, 11.7b)

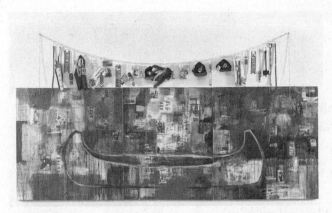

Figure 29.12: Jaune Quick-to-See-Smith, *Trade (Gifts for Trading Land with White People)*, 1992, oil and mixed media, Chrysler Museum of Art, Norfolk

Jaune Quick-to-See-Smith, *Trade (Gifts for Trading Land with White People)*, 1992, oil and mixed media, Chrysler Museum of Art, Norfolk (Figure 29.12)

- Member of the Salish and Kootenai American Indian tribes of the Flathead Nation
- Work meant as the "Quincentenary Non-Celebration" of European occupation of North America
- Collage elements and abstract expressionist brushwork
- Red paint symbolic of shedding of American Indian blood
- Newspaper clippings, images of conquest placed over a large dominant canoe
- American Indian social issues caused by European occupation stressed: poverty, unemployment, disease, alcoholism
- Array of objects sardonically representing Indian culture in the eyes of Europeans: sports teams, Indian-style knickknacks like toy tomahawks, dolls, and arrows
- **Cross-Cultural Comparisons: Multi-Media Works and Installations**
  - Paik, *Electronic Superhighway* (Figure 29.17)
  - Osario, *No Crying Allowed in the Barbershop* (Figure 29.15a)
  - Shonibare, *The Swing (after Fragonard)* (Figure 29.22)

Emily Kame Kngwarreye, *Earth's Creation*, 1994, synthetic polymer, paint on canvas, Mbantua Gallery, Alice Springs, Australia (Figure 29.13)

- Australian aborigine artist
- Simulates the color and lushness of the "green time" in Australia after the rains when the outback flourishes
- Dump dot technique using the brush to pound the color into the canvas and create layers of color and movement
- Four panels, eleven meters wide
- **Cross-Cultural Comparisons: Landscape**
  - Fan Kuan, *Travelers among Mountains and Streams* (Figure 24.5)
  - Cézanne, *Mont Sainte-Victoire* (Figure 21.10)
  - Cole, *Oxbow* (Figure 20.6)

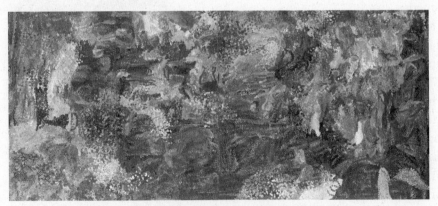

Figure 29.13: Emily Kame Kngwarreye, *Earth's Creation*, 1994, synthetic polymer, paint on canvas, Mbantua Gallery, Alice Springs, Australia

Shirin Neshat, photo by Cynthia Preston, *Rebellious Silence*, from the Women of Allah series, 1994, ink on photograph, Barbara Gladstone Gallery, New York (Figure 29.14)

- Iranian-born artist, raised in the United States
- Chador: a type of outer garment, like a cloak, that allows only the face and hands of Iranian women to be seen
- Chador keeps women's bodies from being seen as sexual objects
- Poem on face written in Farsi, the Persian language; poem expresses piety
- Poem by an Iranian woman who writes poetry on gender issues
- Gun divides body into a darker and lighter side
- Gun adds a note of ominous tension in the work
- Westerners view the work as an expression of female oppression
- Iranians could view the work as an obedient right-minded woman who is ready to die defending her faith and customs
- Black and white photograph
- **Cross-Cultural Comparisons: Portraits**
  - *Sin Sukju* (Figure 24.6)
  - Roman Patrician (Figure 6.14)
  - Vigée Le Brun, *Self-Portrait* (Figure 19.2)

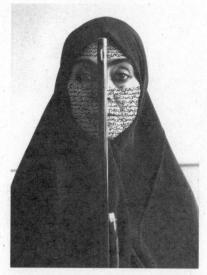

Figure 29.14: Shirin Neshat, photo by Cynthia Preston, *Rebellious Silence*, from the Women of Allah series, 1994, ink on photograph, Barbara Gladstone Gallery, New York

Pepón Osorio, *En la Barberia no se Llora (No Crying Allowed in the Barbershop)*, 1994, mixed media installation (Figures 29.15a and 29.15b)

- Puerto Rican-born artist living in New York
- Large installation recreating the center of Latino male culture: the barbershop
- Challenges the viewer to question issues of identity, masculinity, culture, and attitudes
- Interior of a barbershop in which "no crying is allowed"—a masculine attribute
- Photos of Latino men on the walls
- Video screens on the headrests depict men playing, a baby being circumcised, and men crying
- Appropriately tacky and grimy setting
- Kitsch items used everywhere as symbols of consumer culture
- **Cross-Cultural Comparisons: Gender Identification**
  - Veranda post (Figure 27.14)
  - Delacroix, *Liberty Leading the People* (Figure 20.4)
  - Hogarth, *The Tête à Tête* (Figure 19.3)

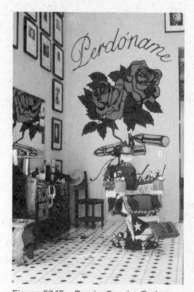

Figure 29.15a: Pepón Osorio, *En la Barberia no se Llora (No Crying Allowed in the Barbershop)*, 1994, mixed media installation

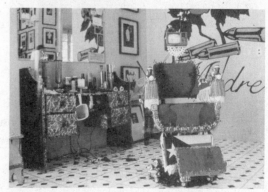

Figure 29.15b: Alternate view of Figure 29.15a

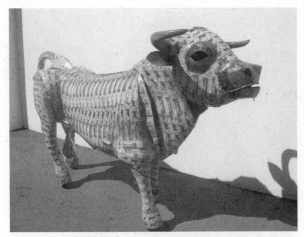

Figure 29.16: Michel Tuffery, *Pisupo Lua Afe (Corned Beef 2000)*, 1994, mixed media, Collection of the Artist

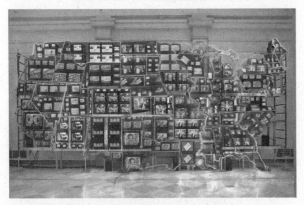

Figure 29.17: Naum June Paik, *Electronic Superhighway*, 1995, mixed media, Smithsonian American Art Museum

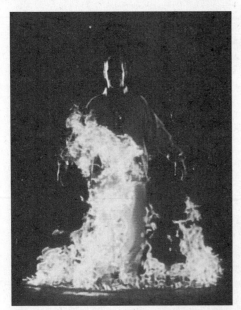

Figure 29.18a: Bill Viola, *The Crossing*, 1996, video and sound installation, room dimensions: 16 × 27.5 × 57 ft, performer: Phil Esposito, photo: Kira Perov

Michel Tuffery, *Pisupo Lua Afe (Corned Beef 2000)*, 1994, mixed media, Collection of the Artist (Figure 29.16)

- Artist born in New Zealand of Samoan, Cook Islands, and Tahitian descent
- Interest in Polynesian heritage
- Life-size sculpture of a bull made from flattened cans of corned beef
- Canned corned beef a favorite food in Polynesia; exported from New Zealand
- Canned meat (pisupo) given as gifts on special occasions in Polynesia
- Canned meat a major contributor to Polynesian obesity
- Introduction of canned meat caused a fall in traditional cultural skills of fishing, cooking, and agriculture
- Static sculpture with small concealed wheels at the feet for ease of movement
- Theme of recycling emphasized by the reuse of these cans
- Two motorized bulls often engage in multi-media performance art called *The Challenge*

Naum June Paik, *Electronic Superhighway*, 1995, mixed media (49-channel closed-circuit video installation, neon, steel, and electronic components), Smithsonian American Art Museum (Figure 29.17)

- Korean-born artist who lived in New York City
- Neon lighting outlines fifty states and District of Columbia (Alaska and Hawaii are on side walls)
- Each state has a separate video feed; total of 313 monitors
- A camera is turned on the spectator and its TV feed appears in the monitors for New York State; it turns the spectator into a participant in the artwork
- Paik intrigued by maps and travel: neon outlines symbolize multi-colored maps of each state; fascination with the interstate highway system; neon symbolizes motel and restaurant signs
- **Cross-Cultural Comparisons: New Media for Its Time**
  - Daguerre, *Still Life in Studio* (Figure 20.8)
  - The Colosseum (Figures 6.8a, 6.8b)
  - Cranach, *Allegory of Law and Grace* (Figure 14.5)

Bill Viola, *The Crossing*, 1996, video and sound installation, room dimensions: 16 × 27.5 × 57 ft, performer: Phil Esposito, photo: Kira Perov (Figures 29.18a and 29.18b)

- Artist born in Queens, New York
- Promoted video as an art form
- Video installations are total environments

- Two channels of color video projections from opposite sides of large dark gallery onto two large back-to-back screens suspended from ceiling and mounted to floor; four channels of amplified stereo sound, four speakers
- *The Crossing* is two channels of video projected on to a twelve-foot-tall double-sided screen. On one side, a figure approaches from a long distance. As he stops, a small flame appears at his feet and spreads rapidly to engulf him in a roaring fire. When it subsides, the man is gone.
- On the opposite side a similar scene unfolds. But when the figure stops, a stream of water begins to pour upon his head. It quickly turns into a raging torrent, inundating the man. When the water slows, the man is gone.
- Two video screens: free-standing, double-sided projections
- Fire: flames consume the figure of a man, beginning at his feet
- Water: man walks toward the viewer and water falls from above
- Figures walk in extremely slow motion
- Actions repeat again and again
- Interested in sense perceptions
- Implied cycle of purification and destruction
- Evokes eastern and western spiritual traditions: Zen Buddhism, Islamic Sufism, Christian mysticism
- **Cross-Cultural Comparisons: Motion**
  - Muybridge, *The Horse in Motion* (Figure 21.5)
  - *Nike of Samothrace* (Figure 4.8)
  - Presentation of Fijian mats (Figure 2.10)

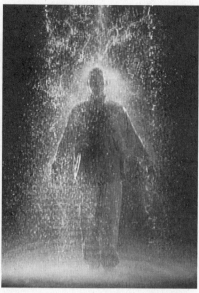

Figure 29.18b: Bill Viola, *The Crossing*

Mariko Mori, *Pure Land*, 1998, color photograph on glass, Los Angeles County Museum of Art, Los Angeles, California (Figure 29.19)

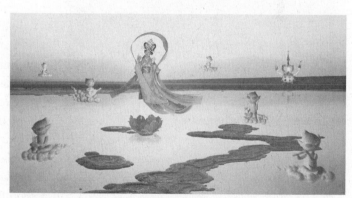

Figure 29.19: Mariko Mori, *Pure Land*, 1998, color photograph on glass, Los Angeles County Museum of Art, Los Angeles, California

- Japanese artist
- Artist uses a creative interpretation of traditional Japanese art forms
- Romanticized views of popular culture
- Mori herself appears as if in a vision in the guise of the Heian deity Kichijōten
- Kichijōten is the essence of beauty and harbinger of prosperity and happiness
- She holds a wish-granting jewel, a *nyoi hōju*, which has the power to deny evil and fulfill wishes
- Jewel symbolizes Buddha's universal mind
- Animated figures of lighthearted aliens play musical instruments on clouds
- Merging of consumer entertainment fantasies with traditional Japanese imagery
- **Cross-Cultural Comparisons: Photography**
  - Daguerre, *Still Life in Studio* (Figure 20.8)
  - Muybridge, *The Horse in Motion* (Figure 21.5)
  - Stieglitz, *The Steerage* (Figure 22.8)

Kiki Smith, *Lying with the Wolf*, 2001, ink and pencil on paper (Figure 29.20)

- American artist, born in Germany, lives in New York City
- Nude female figure; theme of Smith's work is the human body
- Large wrinkled drawing, pinned to a wall; reminiscent of a table cloth or bed sheet
- Female strength emphasized in the woman lying down with the wild beast
  - Wolf seems tamed by the woman's embrace
  - Wolf seen as a traditionally evil or dangerous symbol, but not here
  - **Cross-Cultural Comparisons: Stereotypes**
    - Osario, *No Crying Allowed in the Barbershop* (Figure 29.15a)
    - Salcedo, *Shibboleth* (Figure 29.26)
    - Lawrence, *The Migration of the Negro, Panel no. 49* (Figure 22.19)

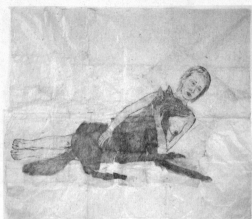

Figure 29.20: Kiki Smith, *Lying with the Wolf*, 2001, ink and pencil on paper

Kara Walker, *Darkytown Rebellion*, 2001, cut paper and projection on wall, Collection Musée d'Art Moderne Grand-Duc Jean, Luxembourg (Figure 29.21)

- California-born, New York-based, African-American artist
- Technique:
  - draws images with a greasy white pencil or soft pastel crayon on large pieces of black paper; cuts paper with a knife
  - images adhered to gallery wall with wax
  - traditional silhouette forms
  - overhead projectors throw colored light onto the walls, ceilings, floor
  - cast shadows of the viewer's body that mingle with the black paper images
- Exploration of African-Americans in the antebellum South: teenager holds a flag that resembles a colonial ship sail; one man has his leg cut off; a woman aborting a child; a woman caring for newborns
- Viewer interacts with the work, walking around it, engaging in elements of it; we are part of the history of the piece
- **Cross-Cultural Comparisons: Wall Surfaces**
  - Lascaux Caves, Great Hall of the Bulls (Figure 1.8)
  - Tomb of the Triclinium (Figure 5.3)
  - Michelangelo, *Sistine Chapel Ceiling* (Figure 16.2a)

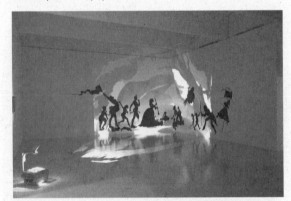

Figure 29.21: Kara Walker, *Darkytown Rebellion*, 2001, cut paper and projection on wall, Collection Musée d'Art Moderne Grand-Duc Jean, Luxembourg

Yinka Shonibare, *The Swing (after Fragonard)*, 2001, mixed media installation, Tate, London (Figure 29.22)

- Artist is British born of Nigerian descent; lives and works in London
- Inspired by Fragonard's *The Swing* (Figure 19.1)
- Life-size headless mannequin

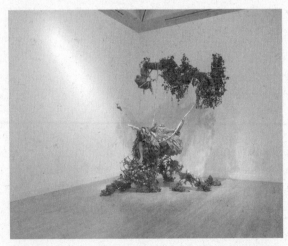

Figure 29.22: Yinka Shonibare, *The Swing (after Fragonard)*, 2001, mixed media installation, Tate, London

- Dress made of African print fabric
- Flowering vines cast to the floor
- Two men in the Fragonard painting are not included; audience takes the place of the men; erotic voyeurism
- Headless figure: guillotined by the French Revolution

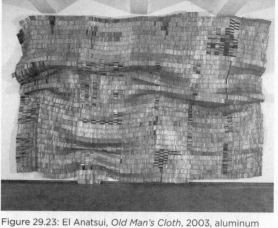

Figure 29.23: El Anatsui, *Old Man's Cloth*, 2003, aluminum liquor bottle caps and copper wire

El Anatsui, *Old Man's Cloth*, 2003, aluminum liquor bottle caps and copper wire (Figure 29.23)

- Artist born in Ghana, spent much of his career in Nigeria
- 1000 drink tops joined by wire to form a cloth-like hanging
- Bottle caps from a distillery in Nigeria
- Artist uses power tools like chain saws and welding torches
- Converts found materials into a new type of media that lies someplace between painting and sculpture
- Recycling of found objects
- Colorful textured wall hangings; relates to West African textiles
- Combines aesthetic traditions of his home country of Ghana, his adopted country of Nigeria, and the global art movement of abstract art
- **Cross-Cultural Comparisons: Cloth**
  - All-T'oqapu Tunic (Figure 26.10)
  - Hiapo (Figure 28.6)
  - Funeral Banner of Lady Dai (Figure 24.4)

Julie Mehretu, *Stadia II*, 2004, ink and acrylic on canvas, Carnegie Museum of Art, Pittsburgh (Figure 29.24)

- Artist born in Ethiopia, lives and works in New York City
- Paints large scale paintings
- Although paintings done with abstract elements, titles allude to meaning
- Stylized renderings of stadium architecture
- Forms suggest the excitement, almost frenzy, of a competition held in a circular space surrounded by international images

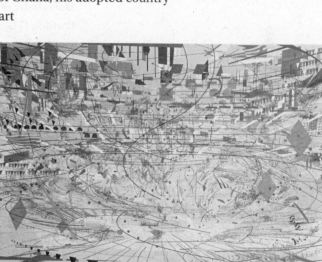

Figure 29.24: Julie Mehretu, *Stadia II*, 2004, ink and acrylic on canvas, Carnegie Museum of Art, Pittsburgh

- Dynamic competition suggested in sweeping lines that create a vibrant pulse
- Uses multi-layered lines to create animation in the work
- Sweeping lines create depth, focus of attention around a central core from which colors, icons, flags, and symbols resonate
- Cf. Kandinsky's abstractions (Figure 22.2)
- **Cross-Cultural Comparisons: Images of Entertainment**
  - The Colosseum (Figure 6.8a, 6.8b)
  - *Seated Boxer* (Figure 4.10)
  - Basquiat, *Horn Players* (Figure 29.5)

Wangechi Mutu, *Preying Mantra*, 2006, mixed media on mylar, Brooklyn Museum, Brooklyn, New York (Figure 29.25)

- Kenya-born, New York-based artist
- Collaged female figures composed of human, animal, object, and machine parts
- Commentary on the female persona in art history
- Cyborg: a person whose function is aided by a mechanical device or whose powers are enhanced by computer implants
- Reclines in a relaxed position
- Green snake interlocks with her fingers; bird feathers in the back of the head
- Left ear lobe has chicken feet, insect legs, and pinchers
- Blotched skin
- Ironic twist on the praying mantis:
  - suggests religious rituals
  - *mantis* means "prophet" in Greek
  - insects use camouflage; this figure seems camouflaged

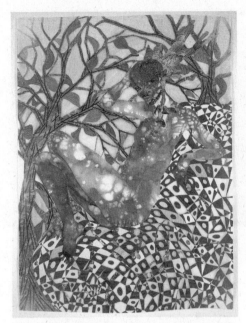

Figure 29.25: Wangechi Mutu, *Preying Mantra*, 2006, mixed media on mylar, Brooklyn Museum, Brooklyn, New York

Doris Salcedo, *Shibboleth*, 2007–2008, installation, Tate Modern, London (Figure 29.26)

- Colombian sculptor
- Installation that features a large crack that begins as a hairline and then widens to two feet in depth
- Floor of the museum was opened and a cast of Colombian rock faces was inserted
- Stresses the interaction between sculpture and space
- *Shibboleth*: a word or custom that a person not familiar with a language may mispronounce; used to identify foreigners or people of another class
- Shibboleth is meant to exclude people from joining a group
- The crack emphasizes the gap in relationships; a reminder of the disruption in spaces
- References racism and colonialism; keeping people away or separating them
- Installation now sealed, but exists as a scar, commemorates life of the underclasses
- **Cross-Cultural Comparisons: Works on the Ground**
  - Smithson, *Spiral Jetty* (Figure 22.26)
  - Great Serpent Mound (Figure 26.4)
  - Weiwei, *Sunflower Seeds* (Figure 29.27)

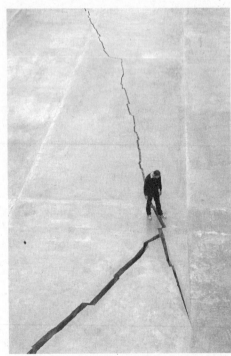

Figure 29.26: Doris Salcedo, *Shibboleth*, 2007–2008, installation, Tate Modern, London

Ai Weiwei, *Kui Hua Zi (Sunflower Seeds)*, 2010–2011, sculpted and painted porcelain, Tate Modern, London (Figure 29.27)

- Chinese artist
- Installation containing millions of individually handcrafted ceramic pieces resembling sunflower seeds
- They symbolically represent an ocean of fathomless depth; each seed is made in Jingdezhen, a city known for its porcelain production in Imperial China
- 600 artisans worked for two years, each seed hand-painted
- Sunflower seeds were eaten as a source of food during the famine era under Mao Tze-tung
- Ideology of Chairman Mao: he was the sun, his followers were the seeds
- Originally you could walk on the installation, but it raised harmful ceramic dust, viewing was then limited to the sidelines
- **Cross-Cultural Comparisons: Installations**
  - Osario, *No Crying Allowed in the Barbershop* (Figures 29.15a, 29.15b)
  - Bing, *A Book from the Sky* (Figures 29.8a, 29.8b)
  - Shonibare, *The Swing (after Fragonard)* (Figure 29.22)

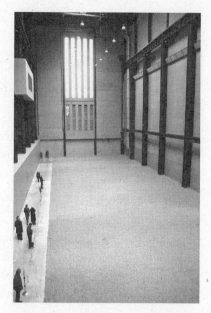

Figure 29.27: Ai Weiwei, *Kui Hua Zi (Sunflower Seeds)*, 2010–2011, sculpted and painted porcelain, Tate Modern, London

VOCABULARY

Action Painting: an abstract painting in which the artist drips or splatters paint onto a surface like a canvas in order to create his or her work (Figure 22.26)

Assemblage: a three-dimensional work made of various materials such as wood, cloth, paper, and miscellaneous objects (Figure 29.13)

Earthwork: a large outdoor work in which the earth itself is the medium (Figure 22.26)

Installation: a temporary work of art made up of assemblages created for a particular space, like an art gallery or a museum (Figure 29.22)

Kitsch: something of low quality that appeals to popular taste (Figure 29.9)

SUMMARY

Contemporary art defies categorization because artists easily adapt to new styles and artistic impulses. Therefore, movements are intense but fleeting, and influenced by current politics and culture. Minimalists designed works that show a modern predilection for clean, open, and simple forms. Site Art expresses an awareness of the surroundings a work of art may have, and insists on a mutual coexistence of the object and its environment. Awareness of feminist issues influenced not only the production of Feminist Art, but also spurred the growth of female collectors, artists, and gallery owners.

Contemporary artists have a great range of materials and venues to express themselves—perhaps more than any other time in history. Artists experiment both with new art forms and with new ideas to create a dynamic range of effects. Architecture has been particularly affected by the growth of technology, both in the planning stages by using a computer, and in the construction phases by using new types of metal and glass.

Modern art is sensitive to all contemporary issues—setting, world politics, technological advances, new techniques, and to the dynamics of the art market itself.

Multiple-Choice

1. All of the following are site specific works EXCEPT

    (A) Maya Lin, Vietnam Veterans Memorial
    (B) Robert Smithson, *Spiral Jetty*
    (C) Doris Salcedo, *Shibboleth*
    (D) Bill Viola, *The Crossing*

2. Song Su-nam's *Summer Trees* references the

    (A) Asian tradition of painting with ink
    (B) Chinese tradition of painting on the scroll format
    (C) Korean tradition of painting screens that separate rooms
    (D) Japanese tradition of woodblock prints popular in Europe

3. Australian aboriginal artists such as Emily Kame Kngwarreye rely on their traditions for their work, while maintaining a presence in the contemporary global art world. Kngwarreye's work differs from traditional Pacific art in that it

    (A) has no emphasis on color
    (B) does not use patterns and markings
    (C) is not done for display
    (D) does not have figures

4. The Vietnam Veterans Memorial is designed so that the viewer would

    (A) think about the glory of war and ultimate victory
    (B) descend into a grave-like setting to remember the dead
    (C) commemorate the ultimate sacrifice people made to ensure peace
    (D) be able to protest American involvement in foreign wars

5. The anthropomorphized human figure in Wangchi Mutu's *Preying Mantra* symbolizes

    (A) the ancient tradition of combining human and animal forms in a single figure as a commentary on natural selection
    (B) a commentary on the depiction of females in works of art
    (C) an overreliance on computers and machines rather than direct human contact
    (D) the crisis in global warming and its effect on all of us

Short Essay

This work is *Electronic Superhighway* by Nam June Paik, created in 1995. Paik was fascinated by new media and what it can bring to the artistic expression.

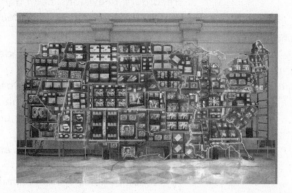

What new media is being explored here?

Using specific evidence, discuss how the new media is being used *and* what commentary it has on the American experience.

Identify another work from the art history curriculum that uses new media *and* discuss how the new media creates a new way to express artistic ideas.

ANSWER KEY

1. **D**   2. **A**   3. **D**   4. **B**   5. **B**

ANSWERS EXPLAINED

Multiple-Choice

1. **(D)** Although Bill Viola's work does need a darkened room to play effectively for an audience, the room can be placed anywhere. It does not have to be in a particular location. The other works were designed for their exact locations.

2. **(A)** Painting with ink is an Asian specialty. Su-nam's work continues that tradition.

3. **(D)** Most art from the Pacific region is traditionally figural. Kngwarreye's work is primarily abstract.

4. **(B)** The Vietnam Veteran's Memorial is about remembering the dead, and so it is appropriate that the viewer descend into a grave-like setting to see the impact of the names as they rise above them.

5. **(B)** Mutu's work *Preying Mantra* references depictions of females in art history from Titian to Manet.

Short-Essay Rubric

Question	Points	Key Points in a Good Response
What new media is being explored here?	1	Closed-circuit video installation, with video recorders, televisions, neon frames, steel compartments, and various electronic components

Using specific evidence, discuss how the new media is being used *and* what commentary it has on the American experience.	2	Answers could include:
		■ Each state has a separate video feed; total of 313 monitors
		■ A camera is turned on the spectator, and its TV feed appears in the monitors for New York State; it turns the spectator into a participant in the artwork.
		■ Paik was intrigued by maps and travel as part of the American experience:
		  – neon outlines symbolize multi-colored maps of each state
		  – fascination with the interstate highway system
		  – neon symbolizes motel and restaurant signs

Identify another work from the art history curriculum that uses new media *and* discuss how the new media creates a new way to express artistic ideas.	2	Answers could include: ■ Bill Viola, *The Crossing* ■ Kara Walker, *Darkytown Rebellion* ■ Mariko Mori, *Pure Land*

PART FOUR
Practice Tests

ANSWER SHEET
Practice Test 1

PRACTICE TEST 1

Section 1

1. Ⓐ Ⓑ Ⓒ Ⓓ
2. Ⓐ Ⓑ Ⓒ Ⓓ
3. Ⓐ Ⓑ Ⓒ Ⓓ
4. Ⓐ Ⓑ Ⓒ Ⓓ
5. Ⓐ Ⓑ Ⓒ Ⓓ
6. Ⓐ Ⓑ Ⓒ Ⓓ
7. Ⓐ Ⓑ Ⓒ Ⓓ
8. Ⓐ Ⓑ Ⓒ Ⓓ
9. Ⓐ Ⓑ Ⓒ Ⓓ
10. Ⓐ Ⓑ Ⓒ Ⓓ
11. Ⓐ Ⓑ Ⓒ Ⓓ
12. Ⓐ Ⓑ Ⓒ Ⓓ
13. Ⓐ Ⓑ Ⓒ Ⓓ
14. Ⓐ Ⓑ Ⓒ Ⓓ
15. Ⓐ Ⓑ Ⓒ Ⓓ
16. Ⓐ Ⓑ Ⓒ Ⓓ
17. Ⓐ Ⓑ Ⓒ Ⓓ
18. Ⓐ Ⓑ Ⓒ Ⓓ
19. Ⓐ Ⓑ Ⓒ Ⓓ
20. Ⓐ Ⓑ Ⓒ Ⓓ

21. Ⓐ Ⓑ Ⓒ Ⓓ
22. Ⓐ Ⓑ Ⓒ Ⓓ
23. Ⓐ Ⓑ Ⓒ Ⓓ
24. Ⓐ Ⓑ Ⓒ Ⓓ
25. Ⓐ Ⓑ Ⓒ Ⓓ
26. Ⓐ Ⓑ Ⓒ Ⓓ
27. Ⓐ Ⓑ Ⓒ Ⓓ
28. Ⓐ Ⓑ Ⓒ Ⓓ
29. Ⓐ Ⓑ Ⓒ Ⓓ
30. Ⓐ Ⓑ Ⓒ Ⓓ
31. Ⓐ Ⓑ Ⓒ Ⓓ
32. Ⓐ Ⓑ Ⓒ Ⓓ
33. Ⓐ Ⓑ Ⓒ Ⓓ
34. Ⓐ Ⓑ Ⓒ Ⓓ
35. Ⓐ Ⓑ Ⓒ Ⓓ
36. Ⓐ Ⓑ Ⓒ Ⓓ
37. Ⓐ Ⓑ Ⓒ Ⓓ
38. Ⓐ Ⓑ Ⓒ Ⓓ
39. Ⓐ Ⓑ Ⓒ Ⓓ
40. Ⓐ Ⓑ Ⓒ Ⓓ

41. Ⓐ Ⓑ Ⓒ Ⓓ
42. Ⓐ Ⓑ Ⓒ Ⓓ
43. Ⓐ Ⓑ Ⓒ Ⓓ
44. Ⓐ Ⓑ Ⓒ Ⓓ
45. Ⓐ Ⓑ Ⓒ Ⓓ
46. Ⓐ Ⓑ Ⓒ Ⓓ
47. Ⓐ Ⓑ Ⓒ Ⓓ
48. Ⓐ Ⓑ Ⓒ Ⓓ
49. Ⓐ Ⓑ Ⓒ Ⓓ
50. Ⓐ Ⓑ Ⓒ Ⓓ
51. Ⓐ Ⓑ Ⓒ Ⓓ
52. Ⓐ Ⓑ Ⓒ Ⓓ
53. Ⓐ Ⓑ Ⓒ Ⓓ
54. Ⓐ Ⓑ Ⓒ Ⓓ
55. Ⓐ Ⓑ Ⓒ Ⓓ
56. Ⓐ Ⓑ Ⓒ Ⓓ
57. Ⓐ Ⓑ Ⓒ Ⓓ
58. Ⓐ Ⓑ Ⓒ Ⓓ
59. Ⓐ Ⓑ Ⓒ Ⓓ
60. Ⓐ Ⓑ Ⓒ Ⓓ

61. Ⓐ Ⓑ Ⓒ Ⓓ
62. Ⓐ Ⓑ Ⓒ Ⓓ
63. Ⓐ Ⓑ Ⓒ Ⓓ
64. Ⓐ Ⓑ Ⓒ Ⓓ
65. Ⓐ Ⓑ Ⓒ Ⓓ
66. Ⓐ Ⓑ Ⓒ Ⓓ
67. Ⓐ Ⓑ Ⓒ Ⓓ
68. Ⓐ Ⓑ Ⓒ Ⓓ
69. Ⓐ Ⓑ Ⓒ Ⓓ
70. Ⓐ Ⓑ Ⓒ Ⓓ
71. Ⓐ Ⓑ Ⓒ Ⓓ
72. Ⓐ Ⓑ Ⓒ Ⓓ
73. Ⓐ Ⓑ Ⓒ Ⓓ
74. Ⓐ Ⓑ Ⓒ Ⓓ
75. Ⓐ Ⓑ Ⓒ Ⓓ
76. Ⓐ Ⓑ Ⓒ Ⓓ
77. Ⓐ Ⓑ Ⓒ Ⓓ
78. Ⓐ Ⓑ Ⓒ Ⓓ
79. Ⓐ Ⓑ Ⓒ Ⓓ
80. Ⓐ Ⓑ Ⓒ Ⓓ

Practice Test 1

SECTION 1

TIME: 60 MINUTES
80 MULTIPLE-CHOICE QUESTIONS

DIRECTIONS: Answer the multiple-choice questions below. Some are based on images. In this book the illustrations are at the top of each set of questions. Select the multiple-choice response that best completes each statement or question, and indicate the correct response on the space provided on your answer sheet. You will have 60 minutes to answer the multiple-choice questions.

Questions 1–6 are based on Figures 1 and 2.

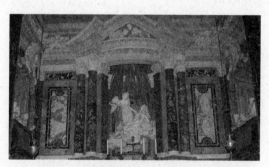

Figure 1

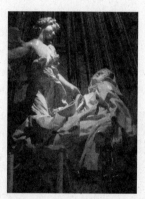

Figure 2

1. Maximum dramatic effect in this work is realized in the

   (A) painted ceiling vault of the chapel
   (B) broken pediment over the sculptural group
   (C) accented difference between the white marble sculpture and the dark framing columns
   (D) interaction between God the Father and the angel

2. Bernini drew inspiration for his work from his experience as a

   (A) writer of religious texts
   (B) friend of St. Teresa
   (C) priest
   (D) stage designer

3. Baroque works such as these have an emotional realism that takes inspiration from

    (A) Hellenistic Greece
    (B) Benin Africa
    (C) Mongol India
    (D) Romanesque Europe

4. This is a multi-media work in that besides marble it includes

    (A) granite, limestone, and porphyry
    (B) glass, painting, and metal
    (C) paper, painting, and fabric
    (D) porcelain, painting, and glass

5. The use of dramatic illusionism seen in this work is similar in effect to the work of

    (A) Bill Viola
    (B) Jaune Quick-to-See-Smith
    (C) Faith Ringgold
    (D) Julie Mehretu

6. The patrons of the work were the Cornaro family of Rome

    (A) who objected to the work and wanted it removed
    (B) whose names are inscribed on the sculpture
    (C) who built the church and the sculptures in it
    (D) whose portraits are visible in the chapel

Questions 7–11 are based on Figures 3 and 4.

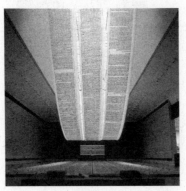

Figure 3

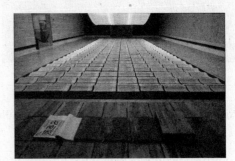

Figure 4

7. This work is inspired by traditional wood-block print technology known in

    (A) India
    (B) Colonial Latin America
    (C) Southeast Asia
    (D) China

8. Many of the characters used in this work

   (A) are the invention of the artist and have no meaning
   (B) are anti-government and a cause for political scandal
   (C) signify progressive attitudes toward family and relationships and therefore caused censure
   (D) are inked upside-down and cause viewer confusion

9. The artist of this work draws upon influence from other cultures like

   (A) New World symbolism and iconography
   (B) French Impressionist painting and printmaking
   (C) African rites and rituals
   (D) contemporary mass production and commercialism

10. This work was created to reflect back upon the

    (A) subversive activities of modern governments
    (B) achievements and disappointments of the twentieth century
    (C) multitude of languages spoken in the modern world
    (D) strides in education in recent years

11. The artist drew criticism for this work because

    (A) the importation of foreign materials into the United States without a permit was against the law
    (B) the Communist government thought it held secret subversive ideas
    (C) the content of the work was viewed as shocking and pornographic
    (D) it became a center of religious worship

Questions 12–16 are based on Figures 5, 6, and 7.

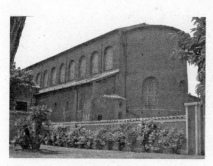

Figure 5

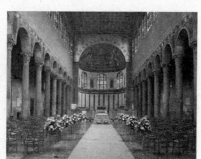

Figure 6

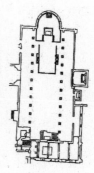

Figure 7

12. This Christian building was probably influenced by buildings such as the

    (A) Catacombs of Priscilla
    (B) Pantheon
    (C) Basilica of Ulpia
    (D) Temple of Amen-Re

13. The building has *spolia*, which are

   (A) the spoils of war
   (B) new types of stained glass having a multi-colored effect
   (C) the reuse of architectural elements from other sites
   (D) permanently placed fountains, impluvia, and other water-based features

14. The ground plan indicates that this building is

   (A) a basilica with a focus on an apse
   (B) a combination of centrally planned and axially planned building formats
   (C) built over a sacred spot
   (D) constructed with a transept for clergy

15. The congregation in this building

   (A) acts independently and prays separately
   (B) worships together as they face the apse
   (C) worships together as they face a holy shrine
   (D) acts independently as they take turns circumambulating the altar

16. The ground plan indicates

   (A) that relatively thick walls support a ceiling that was originally planned to be vaulted
   (B) the shrines added onto the building ultimately obscured movement down the aisle
   (C) that the building is inspired by an ancient Egyptian temple
   (D) the wooden ceiling was built over relatively thin walls

Questions 17–26 are based on Figure 8.

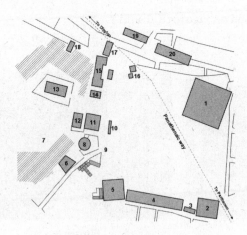

Figure 8

17. The function of the Athenian agora was to

   (A) give athletes space to exercise
   (B) create laws and conduct business
   (C) defend the city against invaders
   (D) hold a council with all the gods

18. Which of the following structures are in the agora?

    (A) A tholos
    (B) The Parthenon
    (C) Temple of Athena Nike
    (D) Altar of Zeus

19. The Panathenaic Way, which runs through the agora, was used for

    (A) the Olympics
    (B) secret diplomatic missions
    (C) sacred processions
    (D) shipping and commerce

20. The best preserved temple from the Classical period is found in the agora. What is it called?

    (A) The Temple of Olympian Zeus
    (B) The Hephaestion
    (C) The Temple of Apollo
    (D) The Parthenon

21. A stoa is a

    (A) circular shrine with surrounding columns
    (B) meeting place set aside for the gods
    (C) prison for traitors to Athens
    (D) place of business and commerce

22. Which of the following is not true about individual buildings in the agora?

    (A) The Metroon housed the city's archives.
    (B) The Bouleuterion is where the city senate met and voted.
    (C) The Tholos is where a subset of senators were on call twenty-four hours a day.
    (D) All of the above are true.

23. The agora was also a place for religious observances and sacrifices, hosting numerous temples. One of these, the Hephaestion, honored which Olympian god or goddess?

    (A) The god of wine and revelry
    (B) The goddess of wisdom and battle
    (C) The god of fire and the forge
    (D) The goddess of hearth and home

24. The Panathenaic Procession processes from the

    (A) Royal Stoa to the Stoa of Attalos
    (B) Parthenon to the Temple of Apollo Eleutherios
    (C) Dipylon Gate to the Parthenon
    (D) Temple of Athena Nike to the Parthenon

25. The Panathenaic Procession is illustrated in a group of sculptures located on the

   (A) agora
   (B) Parthenon
   (C) stoa
   (D) Temple of Athena Nike

26. The Panathenaic Procession is similar to the imagery displayed on

   (A) The Temple of Zeus
   (B) *The Bayeux Tapestry*
   (C) Great Zimbabwe
   (D) Presentation of Fijian mats

Questions 27–30 are based on Figures 9 and 10.

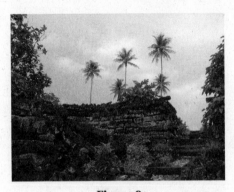

Figure 9

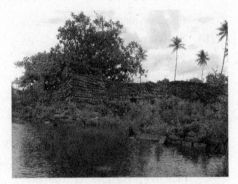

Figure 10

27. The location of Nan Madol is meant to

   (A) have a private enclosure for prayer and worship
   (B) simulate trade and growth among merchants in the kingdom
   (C) ensure prosperity of the country
   (D) bring the nobles to live in one place

28. The exterior walls of the complex serve the practical function of

   (A) allowing ample space for storage
   (B) ensuring a proper fresh water supply
   (C) giving the king a private set of quarters to live in
   (D) being a water break against waves that might strike the complex

29. The complex is similar in layout to

   (A) Ryoan-ji
   (B) Versailles
   (C) the city of Venice
   (D) Great Zimbabwe

30. This complex is unusual in Polynesian societies because it

    (A) is made of stone
    (B) is surrounded by water
    (C) is on a small island
    (D) contains a religious center

Questions 31–35 refer to Figures 11 and 12

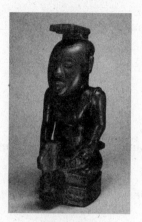

Figure 11

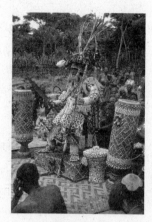

Figure 12

31. Ndop sculptures are

    (A) commemorative portraits of kings
    (B) fetishes
    (C) representations of the ideal spirit of the ancestors
    (D) divinities

32. Ndop sculptures were produced by which of the following peoples?

    (A) Chokwe
    (B) Kongo
    (C) Baule
    (D) Kuba

33. Ndop sculptures are characterized by all of the following EXCEPT

    (A) the face seems uninvolved; above mortal affairs
    (B) a peace knife is held in the left hand
    (C) it is kept in the king's shrine with other works called a set of "royal charms"
    (D) it is presented at performances in which an individual is honored by having ritual dances and tributes performed

34. In Figure 12, the king has

    (A) shown his power by calling upon the spirit of his ancestors
    (B) displayed a costuming that renders him into a holy reliquary
    (C) sought to imitate the sculpture in Figure 11
    (D) come to symbolize his wealth, status, and power

35. Ndop sculptures represent a tradition that

    (A) disappeared with the British occupation
    (B) is still apparent today
    (C) is performed, but has lost its original meaning
    (D) is celebrated throughout Africa, and wherever Africans have traveled

    _____

36. Which of the following is set in a chapel with other paintings based on a similar theme?

    (A) Pontormo, *Entombment of Christ*
    (B) Caravaggio, *Calling of Saint Matthew*
    (C) Leonardo da Vinci, *Last Supper*
    (D) Raphael, *School of Athens*

37. All of the following characteristics are part of the Islamic architectural aesthetic EXCEPT

    (A) a honeycomb-like ceiling of intricate web work
    (B) water passing from room to room and surfacing in low bubbling fountains
    (C) thin columns giving a sense of weightlessness
    (D) interiors with a dominant central focus sweeping the eye to a given point

38. The Hudson River School was

    (A) set up to train New York artists
    (B) a school of arts and crafts
    (C) a group of landscape painters
    (D) closed during World War II by the Nazis

39. The term "pendentive" describes

    (A) a transitional element between a dome and a wall
    (B) a series of arches one atop the other
    (C) an opening in the center of a dome
    (D) a type of capital on an ancient column

40. Many Byzantine icons

    (A) were meant to be touched and handled
    (B) represented the real world and our approach to everyday problems
    (C) were painted by ivory carvers
    (D) were kept in isolation so that few could see them

41. There are several versions of all of the following works of art EXCEPT

    (A) *The Burghers of Calais* by Rodin
    (B) *The Kiss* by Brancusi
    (C) *The Scream* by Munch
    (D) *The Stone Breakers* by Courbet

42. A mudra is

    (A) a sculpture of Buddha
    (B) a gesture in Buddhist art
    (C) a Buddhist temple
    (D) the direction Buddhists face in prayer

43. The Rosetta Stone was important to ancient art because it

    (A) led to the discovery of King Tutankhamun's tomb
    (B) unraveled the mystery of the pyramids
    (C) listed the order of Egyptian pharaohs
    (D) led to the deciphering of hieroglyphics

44. Painters interested in the sublime characteristically

    (A) saluted the achievements of the Industrial Revolution
    (B) were impressed by the opulence of the court of Louis XIV
    (C) reveled in the realm of geometric precision
    (D) had a religious reverence for landscape

45. The tea ceremony is an integral part of the culture of

    (A) Japan
    (B) India
    (C) China
    (D) Indonesia

46. The Pergamon Altar depicts the battle between the gods and the giants, but also symbolically represents the

    (A) building of the Acropolis
    (B) rise of Greek power under Alexander the Great
    (C) Greek defeat of the Persians
    (D) Roman defeat of the Greeks

47. The impluvium is where Romans gathered

    (A) in the Forum to celebrate
    (B) for baths
    (C) to conduct business
    (D) water

48. All of the following artists of the twentieth century sought to create art work that was devoid of historical associations EXCEPT

    (A) Piet Mondrian
    (B) Frank Lloyd Wright
    (C) Diego Rivera
    (D) Helen Frankenthaler

49. The sibyls on the Sistine Ceiling are meant to

  (A) align Christian belief with classical allusions

  (B) increase the monumentality by having figures seem small against large painted architecture

  (C) make the imagery reach across religious boundaries and incorporate all faiths

  (D) show the equality of Old and New Testament themes

Question 50 refers to Figure 13.

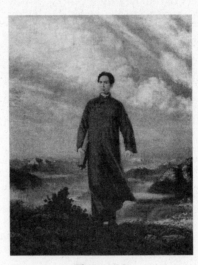

Figure 13

50. The painting in Figure 13 depicts an actual event in Chinese history when Chairman Mao

  (A) lead a miner's strike

  (B) conquered the Nationalist forces and set up his own government

  (C) entered the Forbidden City and created a Communist state

  (D) rallied troops against a Japanese invasion in World War II

---

51. Alfred Stieglitz's photograph, *The Steerage*, shows the impact of

  (A) Surrealism in its grouping of unalike images in one composition

  (B) Cubism in its angles and planes intersecting at odd points

  (C) Dada in its understanding of the foolishness and helplessness of the situation

  (D) Expressionism in its jarring use of brutal forms

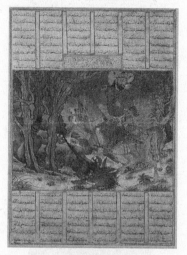

Figure 14

52. This manuscript in Figure 14 draws inspiration from an episode in the history of the

    (A) Sassanians
    (B) Persians
    (C) Assyrians
    (D) Muslims

53. The work in Figure 14 shows the influence of Western art in its use of

    (A) classical contrapposto
    (B) atmospheric perspective
    (C) di sotto in sù
    (D) tenebrism

---

54. The art work of Jeff Koons is dependent upon

    (A) references to objects in popular culture
    (B) multi-media art work
    (C) commentary on contemporary political issues
    (D) the dump-dot technique of paint application

Figure 15

55. The landscapes of Fan Kuan, as seen in Figure 15, depict a

    (A) strong relationship between European and Asian art forms
    (B) complex interweaving of Buddhist and Confucian thought
    (C) reflection of Daoist philosophy and teachings
    (D) connection between Japanese and Chinese painting

56. The painting shown in Figure 15 can best be described as

    (A) an image that depicts the struggle against the forces of nature
    (B) one in a series of works that narrates the story of humanity's civilizing effect on nature
    (C) a work that shows how people can dominate their environment
    (D) people and nature living together in a harmonized universe

_____

57. Brush effects are achieved by using techniques involving

    (A) classical composure
    (B) ink washes for special effects
    (C) tenebroso
    (D) the introduction of tempera paint into China

Questions 58–60 refer to Figures 16 and 17.

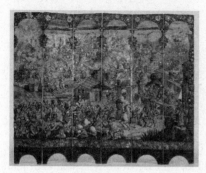

Figure 16

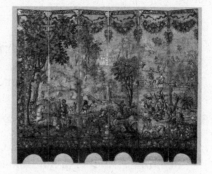

Figure 17

58. This screen has two sides, one showing a war scene and another showing a hunt. The war scene was meant to

    (A) display Habsburg power
    (B) illustrate Mexican military victories
    (C) encourage people to enlist in the army
    (D) offer peace as an alternative to war

59. The hunting scene is meant for

    (A) grand rooms with large receptions
    (B) display of cultural artifacts
    (C) more intimate spaces
    (D) showing trophies of the hunt, like firearms and stuffed animal heads

60. This work contains enconchados which are

    (A) free-standing screens
    (B) paintings that show people of mixed descent
    (C) shell inlay mother-of-pearl fragments
    (D) techniques imported from Europe and given a new expression in Mexico

_____

61. The terra-cotta fragment from the Solomon Islands shows the characteristic use of

    (A) stamped patterns of circles and dots
    (B) cross-hatching to build up forms
    (C) realistic human anatomy
    (D) painted and sculpted figures

62. The work of Jean-Michel Basquiat shows various influences including all of the following EXCEPT

(A) graffiti art
(B) the African-American experience
(C) jazz music
(D) ancient Egyptian body formulas

63. Shirin Neshat's photographs from the Women of Allah series challenge the viewer to

(A) accept the reality that Iranian women will defend their faith
(B) determine whether or not women clothed like this are treated as sexual objects
(C) agree that Iranian women have their rights taken from them by an oppressive male-dominated society
(D) understand women from both the Western and Iranian points of view

64. The Catacombs in Rome were built to

(A) bury the dead in underground tombs because land prices were too high in Rome for above ground burials
(B) hide Christians from Roman persecutions in the second and third centuries
(C) provide space for the burial of Roman emperors during times of crisis
(D) hide the Roman art work from the barbarian invasions

65. In which period did artists consistently paint sculpture?

(A) Renaissance
(B) Mannerism
(C) Neoclassicism
(D) Gothic

66. Kufic script is an Islamic form of writing that is

(A) unusually read from left to right
(B) very angular with the uprights at right angles to the baselines
(C) flowing, having a curved and running look
(D) found only on holy vessels and holy books

67. William Hogarth's works often contain narrative elements

(A) taken from ancient myths and Biblical subjects
(B) which underscore a satire of the King of England
(C) illustrating stories taken from pre-existing plays
(D) which are generally seen in large scale individual portraits done in the Grand Style

68. Monticello is influenced by European models although it

    (A) shows evidence of American Indian motifs
    (B) is made from local materials
    (C) references the African-American experience
    (D) is daring in its use of metal in its substructure

69. Gestures in Caravaggio's *Calling of Saint Matthew* are appropriated from the works of

    (A) Raphael
    (B) Leonardo DaVinci
    (C) Michelangelo
    (D) Pontormo

70. Titian's sensuous color harmonies were especially influential on the works of

    (A) Peter Paul Rubens
    (B) Jacques-Louis David
    (C) Édouard Manet
    (D) Claude Monet

71. The Forbidden City is a highly expanded version of a Chinese architectural format called

    (A) the courtyard style residence
    (B) an axial plan
    (C) a central plan
    (D) a hypostyle hall

72. Dry Japanese gardens

    (A) serve as centers for tea ceremonies
    (B) symbolically represent the formations found in nature
    (C) are modeled on landscape depicted in hanging and hand scrolls
    (D) are built to complement adjacent wet gardens

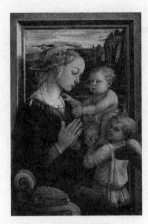

Figure 18

73. Realistic details set this work in

    (A) the home of a Medici prince with a view of his estates
    (B) a Florentine home with a view of the Arno valley
    (C) a monastery with a view of its extensive grounds
    (D) an orphanage with a view of an Alpine landscape

74. This painting is by

    (A) Jan van Eyck
    (B) Raphael
    (C) Leonardo DaVinci
    (D) Fra Filippo Lippi

75. Which of the following statements is NOT true?

    (A) The use of atmospheric perspective gives the effect of deep recession into space.
    (B) The artist sought to humanize the holy figures by giving them earthly personalities.
    (C) The use of shadows creates an impression of the figures in the window frame.
    (D) Symbolic elements dominate the interpretation of the work.

Question 76 refers to Figure 19.

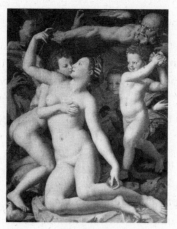

Figure 19

76. This painting can be attributed to a follower of Pontormo based on which characteristic?

    (A) Use of tenebrism
    (B) Elongated figures
    (C) Pyramidal composition
    (D) Stress on great emotions

---

77. Chokwe masks show a matriarchal society in African culture by having

    (A) women wear masks that call upon their status in African culture
    (B) women perform rituals wearing masks that identify their ancestors
    (C) men wear masks and perform dances in which they move like a woman
    (D) women wear male masks that depict male ancestors

78. A basic building technique of African architecture involves using a *toron* which is used in buildings like

    (A) Great Zimbabwe which is constructed of ashlar masonry
    (B) Great Zimbabwe which needs vertical supports to frame the structure during construction
    (C) the Great Mosque at Djenne which is made of adobe
    (D) the Great Mosque at Djenne which needs to support a large community around the structure

79. A traditional symbol of Saint Luke, as seen in the *Lindisfarne Gospels* and elsewhere, is a calf, which symbolizes the

    (A) pastoral nature of Saint Luke's gospel·
    (B) sacrificial nature of Saint Luke's gospel
    (C) powerful and strong message of Saint Luke's gospel
    (D) determination of Saint Luke to write the gospels down as accurately as possible

80. Navigation Charts used in the Marshall Islands were noted for all of the following EXCEPT

    (A) they were not meant to be used at sea
    (B) they used shells to indicate islands
    (C) the diagonal lines represent wind and sea currents
    (D) they were painted to make the formations clearer to read

SECTION II

TIME: 120 MINUTES
6 QUESTIONS

Section II has two parts, each an hour. Part A contains two 30-minute questions. Part B contains four 15-minute questions. Although it is permissible to move freely among all the questions in Section II, it is advisable to stick to the time limits for each question to ensure an adequate response. During the actual exam, proctors will announce when each time period is over, and suggest that you move on to the next question.

Part A

> **DIRECTIONS:** You have 1 hour to answer the two questions in Part A. You are advised to spend 30 minutes on each question. Be sure to respond completely to all sections of every question.

1. Artists often create works of art that are site specific. Removing such a work from its location would impair interpretation. Conversely, knowing the original context of a work of art can often contribute to its meaning. This work is Matthias Grünewald's *Isenheim Altarpiece*, from 1512–1516, oil on panel.

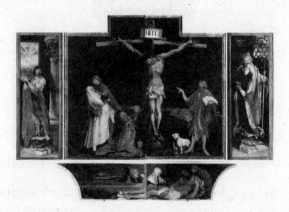

Explain the original location of this work.

Discuss how this work's original location enhances the meaning of the painting.

Select and completely identify another work of art whose original location is known.

Explain the original location of this work.

Discuss how this work's original location enhances its meaning.

You may select from any medium, in any period or culture you find relevant. You may either select a work from the list below or select one of your own choosing. You are not limited to the works in the official image set. (Suggested time: 30 minutes)

Dome of the Rock
Kaaba
Maya Lin, Vietnam Veterans Memorial
Frank Lloyd Wright, Fallingwater

2. Cultures often have burial traditions that are represented in works of art. This work is Tutankhamun's Tomb and innermost coffin from the New Kingdom of ancient Egypt. It is dated from c. 1323 B.C.E., and is made of gold with inlays of enamel and semiprecious stones.

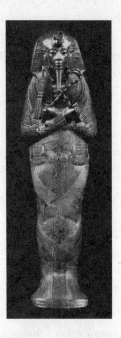

Show how this work represents a burial tradition associated with ancient Egypt.

Discuss specific elements of the work that reflect this burial tradition.

Select and completely identify another work of art that represents a burial tradition.

Show how this second work represents a burial tradition associated with its culture.

Discuss specific elements of the work that reflect this burial tradition.

You may either select a work from the list below or select one of your own choosing. You are not limited to the works in the official image set. (Suggested time: 30 minutes)

Catacomb of Priscilla
Etruscan, Sarcophagus of the Spouses
Stele of Hegeso
Taj Mahal

Part B

DIRECTIONS: You have 1 hour to answer the four questions in Part B. The suggested time for each question is 15 minutes, but you may move freely among the questions. Be sure to respond completely to all sections of every question.

3. The work on the left is the *Anavysos Kouros*, 530 B.C.E., made of marble. Both works are from ancient Greece. The work on the left is older than the work on the right.

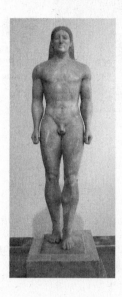 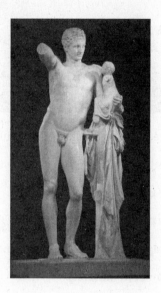

Fully identify the work on the right.

Both works express idealization. Discuss how the concept of the ideal has changed from the work on the left to the work on the right.

Discuss how the concept of the ideal has remained the same from the work on the left to the work on the right.

(Suggested time: 15 minutes)

4. This building is the Hagia Sophia in Istanbul. Over the course of centuries this building has been modified, altered, and reconstructed for various purposes.

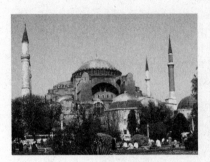 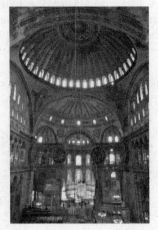 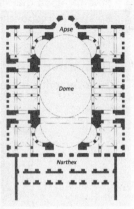

What was the original function of this building?

How has this building's function changed over time?

Discuss why these changes took place.

Discuss how these changes have altered the appearance of the building.

Use photographs of the exterior, interior, and ground plan in your discussion.

(Suggested time: 15 minutes)

5. Identify the period in which this work was done.

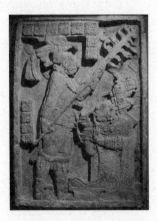

Justify your attribution by comparing it to another work in that period.

Discuss specific formal and/or contextual characteristics in this work that are generally associated with this period.

(Suggested time: 15 minutes)

6. Many artists depict scenes of knowledge and learning, feeling that they represent among the highest of human achievements.

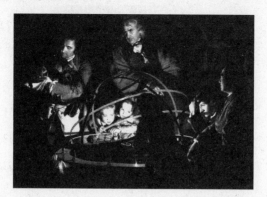

This work is Joseph Wright of Derby's *Philosopher Giving a Lecture on the Orrery* from 1763–1765. It is an oil on canvas.

Identify the subject the philosopher is lecturing on in this painting.

What broader philosophical points is the artist making in this painting?

Analyze the reactions of various participants in this painting, by discussing what those reactions tell us about the attitudes toward knowledge and learning.

(Suggested time: 15 minutes)

Section 1

1. **C**	21. **D**	41. **D**	61. **A**
2. **D**	22. **C**	42. **B**	62. **D**
3. **A**	23. **C**	43. **D**	63. **D**
4. **B**	24. **C**	44. **D**	64. **A**
5. **A**	25. **B**	45. **A**	65. **D**
6. **D**	26. **D**	46. **C**	66. **B**
7. **D**	27. **D**	47. **D**	67. **C**
8. **A**	28. **D**	48. **C**	68. **B**
9. **D**	29. **C**	49. **A**	69. **C**
10. **B**	30. **A**	50. **A**	70. **A**
11. **B**	31. **A**	51. **B**	71. **A**
12. **C**	32. **D**	52. **A**	72. **B**
13. **C**	33. **A**	53. **B**	73. **B**
14. **A**	34. **D**	54. **A**	74. **D**
15. **B**	35. **B**	55. **C**	75. **D**
16. **D**	36. **B**	56. **D**	76. **B**
17. **B**	37. **D**	57. **B**	77. **C**
18. **A**	38. **C**	58. **A**	78. **C**
19. **C**	39. **A**	59. **C**	79. **B**
20. **C**	40. **A**	60. **C**	80. **A**

ANSWERS EXPLAINED

Section I

1. **(C)** The accented difference between the white marble sculpture and the dark framing columns causes the figures to appear as though on a stage with dramatic lighting from above.

2. **(D)** Bernini wrote plays, designed their stage settings, and built the theatres they took place in.

3. **(A)** The emotional realism seen in Bernini's work is inspired by Greek works from the Hellenistic period, such as the *Nike of Samothrace*.

4. **(B)** This work contains glass and metal elements, and the ceilings are painted.

5. **(A)** Bill Viola uses a dramatic sense of illusion, as seen in his work called *The Crossing*. The other artists do not seek to create this kind of illusionistic world.

6. **(D)** There are eight portraits visible on the sides of the main sculptural group. These are portraits of the donors, the Cornaro family.

7. **(D)** Traditional wood-block printing is a Chinese specialty.

8. **(A)** The artist has declared that the characters in his work have no meaning.

9. **(D)** The multiplicity of forms is inspired by mass production.

10. **(B)** The original title of the work was "An Analyzed Reflection of the End of This Century."

11. **(B)** Because the Communist government could not read the meaningless inscriptions in this work, they thought it was subversive.

12. **(C)** The Basilica of Ulpia has the same long nave that leads to a focal point. The other buildings do not.

13. **(C)** Spolia are the reused elements from older architectural monuments.

14. **(A)** The building is a basilica whose focus is on the apse.

15. **(B)** Worshipers in this building are Christians; they pray congregationally, facing a common point where the priest stands.

16. **(D)** This building has a light-weight wooden ceiling, requiring thin walls for support.

17. **(B)** The agora had many functions, among the most prominent of which was to conduct state and financial business.

18. **(A)** A tholos is a round shrine, as seen in #8, Figure 8.

19. **(C)** The Panathenaic Way was used for several occasions, the most important of which were the sacred processions.

20. **(C)** The Temple of Apollo is probably the most intact Greek temple in existence.

21. **(D)** A stoa is a commercial center that conducts business and commerce.

22. **(C)** The tholos is a round temple, therefore not having a governmental function.

23. **(C)** The Hephaestion honors the god of fire and the forge, as well as craftsmen.

24. **(C)** The Panathenaic procession leads from the Dipylon Gate to the Parthenon.

25. **(B)** The Panathenaic procession is depicted on the relief sculptures on the Parthenon.

26. **(D)** Since the Panathenaic procession depicts the movement of presentation goods to a given point, it resembles the Presentation of the Fijian mats, which directs presents to a monarch, in this case Elizabeth II of England.

27. **(D)** Nan Madol was built, in part, to bring together nobles in one place.

28. **(D)** The exterior walls are built out into a lagoon and act as a breakwater for the complex.

29. **(C)** The layout of Nan Madol, a city located on islands, is similar to that of Venice, Italy.

30. **(A)** Not many Polynesian buildings are built of stone. This is unusual.

31. **(A)** Ndop sculptures act as commemorative portraits of kings.

32. **(D)** Ndop sculptures are produced by the Kuba people.

33. **(A)** The king is reserved and free of the cares of this world, as symbolized by the repose on the face of the ndop figures.

34. **(D)** The extravagant costuming symbolizes the king's wealth and power.

35. **(B)** The Ndop sculptures represent an aspect of Kuba culture that is still active today.

36. **(B)** The Caravaggio painting is in a chapel with three works based on the life of Saint Matthew: *The Calling of Saint Matthew, Saint Matthew and the Angel,* and *The Martyrdom of Saint Matthew.*

37. **(D)** Islamic interiors often have a forest of columns; they almost never have an open space that directs the viewer to a focal point.

38. **(C)** The Hudson River School was not really a school in the traditional sense. It was a group of landscape artists who shared the same artistic philosophy.

39. **(A)** As seen in the Hagia Sophia, the pendentive is a triangular element that transitions between a round-based dome and a flat wall.

40. **(A)** Many Byzantine icons have worn away features from so many faithful handling them.

41. **(D)** There was only one version of Courbet's *The Stone Breakers*, destroyed in 1945. There are many versions of *The Burghers of Calais*, four painted versions of *The Scream*, and at least three of *The Kiss*.

42. **(B)** A mudra is a symbolic gesture seen in Buddhist painting and sculpture.

43. **(D)** The Rosetta Stone is important in the history of Egyptian art because it was the tool used to decipher hitherto unreadable hieroglyphics.

44. **(D)** Painters interested in the sublime often had an appreciation for the awesome aspects of nature, as seen in *The Slave Ship* by Turner.

45. **(A)** The tea ceremony is a distinctly Japanese tradition.

46. **(C)** Although the Pergamon Altar depicts the victory of the gods over the giants, it also references the Greeks as the gods and the Persians as the giants.

47. **(D)** An impluvium is a water basin in a Roman home.

48. **(C)** Rivera's work is filled with historical associations, particularly in his *Dream of a Sunday Afternoon in the Alameda Park.*

49. **(A)** The sibyls are Greek classical prophetesses who are aligned with Old Testament prophets on the Sistine Chapel ceiling.

50. **(A)** This work shows a young Mao marching off in support of a miner's strike.

51. **(B)** Stieglitz was heavily influenced by modernist European trends in painting, including the analytical nature of Cubism.

52. **(A)** The Iranian manuscript of *Bahram Gur Fights the Karg* depicts an episode from the history of the ancient Sassanians.

53. **(B)** The background of this painting shows the European technique of atmospheric perspective.

54. **(A)** The work of Jeff Koons is heavily dependent on appropriating works from popular culture.

55. **(C)** Fan Kuan isolated himself away from civilization to be with nature, study nature, and engage in a Daoist philosophy.

56. **(D)** The people in the painting, although tiny, live in harmony with the landscape.

57. **(B)** Fan Kuan was noted for achieving special effects with his delicate ink washes.

58. **(A)** The war scene illustrates the Siege of Belgrade and victory for the Hapsburg troops in eastern Europe.

59. **(C)** The hunting scene is meant to face a more intimate environment.

60. **(C)** Enconchados are shell inlays made of mother-of-pearl.

61. **(A)** The terra-cotta fragment from the Solomon Islands is marked with stamped patterns of circles and dots.

62. **(D)** There is no trace of Egyptian body formulas in the art work of Jean-Michel Basquiat. His work, which resembles graffiti art, is filled with references to the African-American experience, including jazz.

63. **(D)** Many of Neshat's images can be interpreted as having a positive and negative message, depending on the viewer. Her work seeks to present both points of view.

64. **(A)** The catacombs were tombs, not refuges from persecution as tradition alleges. Emperors would not have been buried in such humble locations.

65. **(D)** Almost all Gothic sculpture, including the Royal Portals at Chartres and the *Röttgen Pietà*, were painted.

66. **(B)** Kufic script is noted for its angular forms, with direct uprights and perpendicular baselines.

67. **(C)** *Marriage à la Mode* is derived from a seventeenth-century play by John Dryden.

68. **(B)** Jefferson was strongly influenced by European design principals when he built Monticello, but the building is made from local materials found in the colonies.

69. **(C)** Caravaggio's paintings often reference Michelangelo's Sistine Ceiling, including Jesus' gesture in *The Calling of Saint Matthew*, which comes from *The Creation of Adam*.

70. **(A)** Titian's color harmonies were a direct influence on the art of Peter Paul Rubens. He was less influential on Neoclassical painters like Jacques-Louis David, or Realists and Impressionists like Édouard Manet and Claude Monet.

71. **(A)** The Forbidden City is a large version of a traditional Chinese courtyard style residence.

72. **(B)** Japanese dry gardens use materials such as stone, plants, and sand to symbolically represent formations found in nature.

73. **(B)** Lippi's paintings often take sacred subjects, like this Madonna and Child, and place them in the context of an Italian home with a view of the Arno river valley in the distance.

74. **(D)** This painting is by Fra Filippo Lippi.

75. **(D)** This is not a work that is filled with heavily symbolic elements.

76. **(B)** This painting was done by Bronzino, a follower of Pontormo. Bronzino uses the same kind of elongated figures found in Pontormo's work.

77. **(C)** Men wear Chokwe masks and ceremonially dance in imitation of a woman during rituals.

78. **(C)** Torons are used to hold the adobe walls of buildings like the Great Mosque at Djenne in place.

79. **(B)** Many Christian stories deal with sacrifice. St. Luke's gospel is symbolized by a calf, a sacrificial animal.

80. **(A)** Although they are called navigation charts, they were not actually meant to be used at sea. They were to be memorized beforehand, and not usually used for navigation during a voyage.

Section II

MODEL RESPONSE FOR QUESTION 1

The <u>Isenheim Altarpiece</u> is a sixteenth century painting by Northern Renaissance artist Matthias Grünewald. The piece was specifically made for a monastery in Isenheim, which treated people affected by the gruesome disease of ergotism. This disease caused sores to form on the body and limbs to become gangrenous. Thus, Matthias Grünewald connected patients of the monastery to the painting by displaying the effects of ergotism. He accomplishes this by representing Christ, the main figure in the altarpiece, as a person affected by ergotism.

On the central panel of the altarpiece, a crucified Christ displays signs of ergotism; his limbs are gangrenous, his body is thin and withered, and his skin is discolored. This was to give the patient the impression that he or she was not alone in his or her pain and suffering. Grünewald's use of color is especially important emphasizing disease and suffering in Christ. In addition to these characteristics, Grünewald does not place Christ in the center as most artists traditionally did. Instead he places Christ more to the right, to give the impression of his arm being amputated when the panel was opened. Amputation was often used as a treatment to eliminate gangrenous limbs. Similarly, on the predella of the central panel the corpse of Christ shows signs of ergotism. Grünewald creates the impression of Christ's gangrenous legs being amputated when the predella is opened.

Finally, in the second view of the altarpiece Grünewald presents a scene of the resurrection of Christ. He presents Christ as a glorified and healthy being. This was to symbolically give patients in the monastery hope; they too would escape the pain and suffering of this world after death. Once again Grünewald's use of color emphasizes a theme in the scene. The bright and radiant colors add to the aspect of glorification.

In conclusion, Matthias Grünewald created the <u>Isenheim Altarpiece</u> for a monastery, which treated victims of ergotism. By presenting Christ with signs of ergotism Grünewald successfully connected the painting to the site and patients. This, in turn, enhanced the meaning of the painting by creating hope for patients who saw the altarpiece.

The Kaaba is located in Mecca, Saudi Arabia. It is a granite structure with a silk covering which contains gold and silver thread. It was built in the seventh century.

There are many traditions associated with the Kaaba, including the belief that the stone fell from heaven for Adam and Eve, so that they would have a spot to build an altar upon. Muhammad himself is generally attributed with the setting of the original blackstone in the eastern corner in the wall of the Kaaba. The Kaaba itself was said to have been built by Ibrahim and Ishamel, revered Islamic prophets. Because of its lengthy history involving so many important Islamic figures, the Kaaba has become a focus for Muslems to face in prayer five times a day.

Because of its central position in Islamic thought, the Kaaba has become the endpoint of pilgrimages throughout the Muslem world. These pilgrimages are called the hajj. The faithful come to this spot and circumambulate the Kaaba seven times. Thus the work unites with its location, its tradition, and its design.

Criteria	Student Response	Points Allotted for Task	Points Earned
Task: Explain the original location of this work.			
The essay must state the original location of this work.	"The piece was specifically made for a monastery in Isenheim, which treated people affected by the gruesome disease of ergotism…"	1	1
Task: Discuss how this work's original location enhances its meaning.			
The essay must unite the original placement of the work with its meaning.	"Grünewald does not place Christ in the center as most artists traditionally did. Instead he places Christ more to the right, to give the impression of his arm being amputated when the panel was opened. Amputation was often used as a treatment to eliminate gangrenous limbs…"	0–2	2
Task: Select and completely identify another work of art whose original location is known.			
The essay must fully identify a second work.	"The Kaaba is located in Mecca, Saudi Arabia. It is a granite structure with a silk covering which contains gold and silver thread. It was built in the seventh century."	1	1
Task: Explain the original location of this other work.			
The essay must state the original location of this work.	"Because of its lengthy history involving so many important Islamic figures, the Kaaba has become a focus for Muslims to face in prayer five times a day."	1	1
Task: Explain how this other work's original location enhances its meaning.			
The essay must unite the original placement of the work with its meaning.	"Because of its central position in Islamic thought, the Kaaba has become the endpoint of pilgrimages throughout the Muslim world. These pilgrimages are called the hajj. The faithful come to this spot, and circumambulate the Kaaba seven times…"	0–2	2
		Total Points Possible: 7	This essay earned: 7 This is an exceptional essay.

MODEL RESPONSE FOR QUESTION 2

Responsible for being the creators of the most widely known burial ritual, the ancient Egyptians are noted for their acclaimed ornate and elaborate customs, such as mummification. The prolonged process started with mummification of the body, which was a method of preservation by dehydrating the body. Mummification was necessary in order to live for all eternity and to be presented in front of Osiris. After the mummy was prepared, a priest would ceremoniously utter a spell to ensure the mummy would be animated in his afterlife. At the body's final destination in the mortuary temple, incense was burned, prayers were recited, and more rituals were performed. At last, the King's mummy would be left in the pyramid with copious amounts of jewelry, riches, food, drinks, and other needs of the pharaoh in his afterlife.

The pyramid was then sealed to ensure that no one would enter the pyramid ever again; only the King's soul would be allowed access in and out of the pyramid. The most prominent component of the burial would be the sarcophagus, or the coffin.

The coffins would be decorated all around with symbols, hieroglyphics, and there would often be more than one, known as "false lids" because they would imitate the real coffin. The lids had an outline of the men with their hands clenched. King Tutankhamun's Tomb and innermost coffin evidently display the cultural burial signs of the Ancient Egyptians.

For one, the tomb was filled with over 3,500 items in total fortune, all items prepared for King Tutankhamun's afterlife. In the tomb were a burial chamber, treasury, and annex. The gold inner-most coffin was not uncommon, especially not the figure displayed. The coffin displayed the classic pharaoh, with the snake on his forehead, a nemes-headdress, a staff, and a beard. The staff was one of the ancient symbols of authority. Beards were a sign of divinity; consequently, the pharaohs wore fake beards to explicitly display their divinity.

On top of King Tutankhamen's head is an Uraeus, an Egyptian cobra that represented sovereignty, deity, and authority. When an Uraeus is accompanied by a Nekhbet, a vulture, it represents Lower Egypt while the Nekhbet would represent Upper Egypt. The gold coffins truly depict the level of respect given to the pharaohs, even when passed away. All the riches, authoritative symbols, and the amount of gold help convey the importance of the burial ritual. The Ancient Egyptians took their mummification and burial rituals quite seriously, and it is apparent in the tomb and sarcophagus of King Tutankhamun.

A second work that shows a burial tradition is the Catacomb of Priscilla in Rome, Italy. This huge tomb lies beneath the city of Rome, dug out of tufa rock, and frescoed on the interior. There are many Christian martyrs and popes lying inside the tombs of this catacomb.

Inside the catacombs there are a number of chapels used for administering final prayers over the deceased, as is the Christian tradition. Delicately painted biblical scenes are displayed on the walls. The nature of these paintings makes an appropriate tie-in with the services rendered in the chapels. Many have orants figures, which have their hands extended in prayer, as would the grieving people in the chapels. Some have figures of the Good Shepherd, a Christian symbol from the New Testament. The Good Shepherd is a representation of Christ as someone who leads his sheep (those who believe in him) to a new life.

Parallels are drawn between the burial customs taking place in the tomb, and the Christian symbolism of the wall paintings. For example, Jonah and the Whale, an Old Testament scene, shows a figure symbolically rising from the dead by emerging from a large fish. The people being buried in the catacombs similarly are promised life after death because they believed in Jesus.

Criteria	Student Response	Points Allotted for Task	Points Earned
Task: Show how this work represents a burial tradition associated with ancient Egypt.			
The essay must prove that this burial is typical of customs associated with Egyptian funerary rites.	"...the ancient Egyptians are noted for their acclaimed ornate and elaborate customs, such as mummification..."	1	1
Task: Discuss specific elements of the work that reflect this burial tradition.			
The essay must indicate how particular elements of the work indicate it is part of a burial tradition.	"The gold coffins truly depict the level of respect given to the pharaohs, even when passed away. All the riches, authoritative symbols, and the amount of gold help convey the importance of the burial ritual..."	0–2	2
Task: Select and completely identify another work of art that represents a burial tradition.			
A complete appropriate identification is required.	"A second work that shows a burial tradition is the Catacomb of Priscilla in Rome, Italy. This huge tomb lies beneath the city of Rome, dug out of tufa rock, and frescoed on the interior."	1	1
Task: Show how this second work represents a burial tradition associated with its culture.			
The essay must prove that this burial is typical of customs associated with traditional funerary rites.	"Inside the catacombs there are a number of chapels used for administering final prayers over the deceased, as is the Christian tradition."	1	1
Task: Discuss specific elements of the work that reflect this burial tradition.			
The essay must indicate how particular elements of the work indicate it is part of a burial tradition.	"Parallels are drawn between the burial customs taking place in the tomb, and the Christian symbolism of the wall paintings. For example, Jonah and the Whale, an Old Testament scene, shows a figure symbolically rising from the dead by emerging from a large fish. The people being buried in the catacombs similarly are promised life after death because they believed in Jesus."	0–2	2
		Total Points Possible: 7	This essay earned: 7 This is an insightful essay.

MODEL RESPONSE FOR QUESTION 3

The work on the left, <u>Kouros from Anavysos</u> and the work on the right, the <u>Doryphoros</u> by Polykleitos, are from two very distinct time periods in Greek history, Archaic and Classical. Being that they are from two different time periods under the same civilization, they are bound to have differences and similarities. The first difference between them would be the angle of which they are meant to be looked at. The piece on the left is clearly meant to be looked at exclusively from a frontal view, while the piece on the right can be looked at from several different angles.

Another difference is the use of contrapposto on the work on the right, contrapposto is that relaxed, natural stance that the work on the right is displaying; meanwhile the work on the left looks rather stiff and not natural. The contrapposto gives the work on the right an almost sensual shape.

The poses of these two works give off completely different auras. The aura on the left has an authoritative, stern aura, while the pose of the work on the right gives off a more relaxed aura.

Another difference is the ideal figures for the time: the work on the left is sturdier and beefier, while the work on the right shows a more muscular style. As for similarities, they are both similar in that they both use idealized figures, neither of the figures show age or imperfections. Another similarity is how both works are for the most part, completely cut out. This shows the mastery of sculpting the Greek sculptures had, even in the Archaic times.

Criteria	Student Response	Points Allotted for Task	Points Earned
Task: Fully identify the work on the right.			
The essay must use at least two identifiers for the second work.	"the Doryphoros by Polykleitos"	1	1
Task: Discuss how the concept of the ideal has changed from the work on the left to the work on the right.			
The essay must have two reasons explaining how concept of the ideal has changed over the course of Greek art.	"Another difference is the use of contrapposto on the work on the right, contrapposto is that relaxed, natural stance that the work on the right is displaying; meanwhile the work on the left looks rather stiff and not natural…. The aura on the left has an authoritative, stern aura, while the pose of the work on the right gives off a more relaxed aura."	0–2	2
Task: Discuss how the concept of the ideal has remained the same from the work on the left to the work on the right.			
The essay must have two reasons explaining how concept of the ideal has remained the same over the course of Greek art.	"As for similarities, they are both similar in that they both use idealized figures, neither of the figures show age or imperfections. Another similarity is how both works are…completely cut out."	0–2	1 This would have been more articulate if the student explained the use of negative space instead of only stating "completely cut out."
		Total Points Possible: 5	**This essay earned: 4**

MODEL RESPONSE FOR QUESTION 4

The Hagia Sophia was built in the sixth century in what is now Istanbul, Turkey. When first built, the church combined a central plan and an axial plan. The ground plan of the building shows that the building is almost square, with three aisles separated by columns.

The nave is covered by a large dome which has an arcade of forty windows at the base. These windows act as a halo when they are filled with light.

The Hagia Sophia's original plan could not hold up the concrete dome, and therefore the dome had to be rebuilt. This caused a change in the diameter of the dome, making it slightly more elliptical. The church was also reconstructed a few times after suffering damage from riots and fire.

During the eighth and ninth centuries, there was a period of iconoclasm in the Byzantine Empire. This led to the destruction of many of the mosaics inside of the Hagia Sophia. However, others were added by later emperors.

After the Byzantine Empire collapsed, the Ottomans took over and converted the Hagia Sophia into a mosque. This is why there are now four minarets outside of the church. The purpose of minarets in the Muslim faith is to let people know when to pray. The call to prayer was made five times every day from the minarets. The Ottomans also covered many of the mosaics inside of the church.

Today the Hagia Sophia is neither a church nor a mosque—it is a museum.

Throughout the centuries, the Hagia Sophia has undergone many changes, not only in its structure, but in its purpose. It displays the architecture and art of two very different empires.

Criteria	Student Response	Points Allotted for Task	Points Earned
Task: What was the original function of this building?			
The essay must state that the function was a church.	"The Hagia Sophia was built in the sixth century in what is now Istanbul, Turkey. When first built, the church combined a central plan and an axial plan."	1	1
Task: How has this building's function changed over time?			
The essay must describe the subsequent changes.	"After the Byzantine Empire collapsed, the Ottomans took over and converted the Hagia Sophia into a mosque.... Today the Hagia Sophia is neither a church nor a mosque—it is a museum."	1	1
Task: Discuss why these changes took place.			
The essay must discuss the reason for at least one change in the building.	"During the eighth and ninth centuries, there was a period of iconoclasm in the Byzantine Empire. This led to the destruction of many of the mosaics inside of the Hagia Sophia. However, others were added by later emperors."	1	1
Task: Discuss how these changes have altered the appearance of the building.			
The essay must address at least two ways in which the appearance of the building has changed.	The above quotation, and this quotation: "...converted the Hagia Sophia into a mosque. This is why there are now four minarets outside of the church. The purpose of minarets in the Muslim faith is to let people know when to pray."	0–2	2
		Total Points Possible: 5	**This essay earned: 5**

MODEL RESPONSE FOR QUESTION 5

This piece of work was done during the ancient Mayan time which is about from 300 c.e. and later. By labeling this piece of work as Mayan we can attribute it to this time period. We can tell that it is Mayan for many reasons. One reason is that it appears to be carved from limestone and Mayan relief sculptures were typically carved from stone. Another way that we can tell that this work is Mayan is by the glyph located at the top and side of the sculpture. Mayans usually carved glyphs into their sculptures to tell a story or narrative about what the piece of work means. The glyphs in the piece of work were depicted and tell us that this scene shows royal bloodletting where the queen, the kneeling figure, is pulling a thorny rope through her tongue and letting blood onto a paper in a basket. The King, the standing figure, is holding a torch above her head which he will later use to light the papers on fire. Mayan art usually depicts religious rituals such as this one through relief sculptures. We can relate this relief sculpture with a Mayan sculpture Yaxchilan lintel 25. The Mayan head has a special headdress that is very detailed and we can relate this to the relief sculpture above because the King and Queen are also wearing detailed headdresses. Many figures or people depicted in Mayan art wear costumes and head pieces that have feathers, etc. The crisp lines in the head piece of the Mayan head piece are also found in the details of the relief sculpture. Both of these pieces are also made of stone because Mayans were masters of carving stone and used stone as their medium most of the time.

Criteria	Student Response	Points Allotted for Task	Points Earned
Task: Identify the period in which this work was done.			
The essay must correctly identify the period as Mayan.	"This piece of work was done during the ancient Mayan time which is about from 300 C.E. and later."	1	1
Task: Justify your attribution by comparing it to another work in that period.			
The essay must correctly compare it to another Mayan work.	"We can relate this relief sculpture with a Mayan sculpture Yaxchilan lintel 25."	1	1
Task: Discuss specific formal and/or contextual characteristics in this work that are generally associated with this period.			
The essay must be able to assess at least three characteristics of Mayan art that can be seen in this work.	"One reason is that it appears to be carved from limestone and Mayan relief sculptures were typically carved from stone... Mayans usually carved glyphs into their sculptures to tell a story or narrative about what the piece of work means....Mayan art usually depicts religious rituals such as this one through relief sculptures."	0–3	2 Some of the examples are repetitive, vague, or lack full discussion.
		Total Points Possible: 5	**This essay earned: 4**

MODEL RESPONSE FOR QUESTION 6

The painting shows a meeting of middle class people representing all ages of men and women of the eighteenth century. Some are young, some are old. The young are depicted as frivolous and playful, the young adults are interested in each other, and the older people are serious and thoughtful.

The society in question, the Lunar Society, met only once a month to discuss intellectual ideas of the day, including, in this case, the nature of the solar system. The orrery was an early form of a planetarium, and the lamp in the center (unseen) is in the position of the sun. The children view this device as a toy. The adults see it as an indication of just how small human beings are, and how little their accomplishments will amount to.

The philosopher, who looks somewhat like Isaac Newton, lectures on the orrery to a notetaker who records his comments. He brings to our attention how the orrery functions as a representation of the solar system.

Criteria	Student Response	Points Allotted for Task	Points Earned
Task: Identify the subject the philosopher is lecturing on in this painting.			
The essay must state that the philosopher has a miniature solar system before him.	"The orrery was an early form of a planetarium…"	1	1
Task: What broader philosophical points is the artist making in this painting?			
The essay must express what broad philosophical points the artist is trying to make.	"The adults see it as an indication of just how small human beings are, and how little their accomplishments will amount to."	0–2	1 This is true, but it is incomplete. There should be a fuller discussion of this point.
Task: Analyze the reactions of various participants in this painting, by discussing what those reactions tell us about the attitudes toward knowledge and learning.			
The essay must fully address the people in the painting, all of whom have different reactions to the scene depicted. How do they express their age and sex in their reactions?	"The young are depicted as frivolous and playful, the young adults are interested in each other, and the older people are serious and thoughtful."	0–2	1 Although true, this point needs to be elaborated on, because there are many more people in the painting, all with various reactions.
		Total Points Possible: 5	This essay earned: 3

TEST ANALYSIS

NOTE: Because the AP Art History exam will be new in 2016, there is no way of knowing exactly how the raw scores on the exams will translate into a 1, 2, 3, 4, or 5. The formula provided below is based on past commonly accepted standards for grading the AP Art History exam. Additionally, the score range corresponding to each grade varies from exam to exam, and thus the ranges provided below are approximate.

SECTION I: MULTIPLE-CHOICE (50% OF GRADE)

Number Correct: _____ (out of 80)

Number Correct × 1.25 = _____ (out of 100)
(Multiple-Choice Score)

SECTION II: ESSAYS (50% OF GRADE)

Essay 1: _____
(out of 7)

Essay 2: _____
(out of 7)

Essay 3: _____
(out of 5)

Essay 4: _____
(out of 5)

Essay 5: _____
(out of 5)

Essay 6: _____
(out of 5)

Total: _____ × **2.942** = _____ (out of 100)
(Essay Score)

FINAL SCORE

_____ + _____ = _____ (out of 200)

Multiple-Choice
Score

Essay Score

Final Score
(rounded to the nearest
whole number)

Final Score Range	AP Score
150–200	5
132–149	4
110–131	3
75–109	2
0–74	1

ANSWER SHEET
Practice Test 2

Section 1

1. Ⓐ Ⓑ Ⓒ Ⓓ
2. Ⓐ Ⓑ Ⓒ Ⓓ
3. Ⓐ Ⓑ Ⓒ Ⓓ
4. Ⓐ Ⓑ Ⓒ Ⓓ
5. Ⓐ Ⓑ Ⓒ Ⓓ
6. Ⓐ Ⓑ Ⓒ Ⓓ
7. Ⓐ Ⓑ Ⓒ Ⓓ
8. Ⓐ Ⓑ Ⓒ Ⓓ
9. Ⓐ Ⓑ Ⓒ Ⓓ
10. Ⓐ Ⓑ Ⓒ Ⓓ
11. Ⓐ Ⓑ Ⓒ Ⓓ
12. Ⓐ Ⓑ Ⓒ Ⓓ
13. Ⓐ Ⓑ Ⓒ Ⓓ
14. Ⓐ Ⓑ Ⓒ Ⓓ
15. Ⓐ Ⓑ Ⓒ Ⓓ
16. Ⓐ Ⓑ Ⓒ Ⓓ
17. Ⓐ Ⓑ Ⓒ Ⓓ
18. Ⓐ Ⓑ Ⓒ Ⓓ
19. Ⓐ Ⓑ Ⓒ Ⓓ
20. Ⓐ Ⓑ Ⓒ Ⓓ

21. Ⓐ Ⓑ Ⓒ Ⓓ
22. Ⓐ Ⓑ Ⓒ Ⓓ
23. Ⓐ Ⓑ Ⓒ Ⓓ
24. Ⓐ Ⓑ Ⓒ Ⓓ
25. Ⓐ Ⓑ Ⓒ Ⓓ
26. Ⓐ Ⓑ Ⓒ Ⓓ
27. Ⓐ Ⓑ Ⓒ Ⓓ
28. Ⓐ Ⓑ Ⓒ Ⓓ
29. Ⓐ Ⓑ Ⓒ Ⓓ
30. Ⓐ Ⓑ Ⓒ Ⓓ
31. Ⓐ Ⓑ Ⓒ Ⓓ
32. Ⓐ Ⓑ Ⓒ Ⓓ
33. Ⓐ Ⓑ Ⓒ Ⓓ
34. Ⓐ Ⓑ Ⓒ Ⓓ
35. Ⓐ Ⓑ Ⓒ Ⓓ
36. Ⓐ Ⓑ Ⓒ Ⓓ
37. Ⓐ Ⓑ Ⓒ Ⓓ
38. Ⓐ Ⓑ Ⓒ Ⓓ
39. Ⓐ Ⓑ Ⓒ Ⓓ
40. Ⓐ Ⓑ Ⓒ Ⓓ

41. Ⓐ Ⓑ Ⓒ Ⓓ
42. Ⓐ Ⓑ Ⓒ Ⓓ
43. Ⓐ Ⓑ Ⓒ Ⓓ
44. Ⓐ Ⓑ Ⓒ Ⓓ
45. Ⓐ Ⓑ Ⓒ Ⓓ
46. Ⓐ Ⓑ Ⓒ Ⓓ
47. Ⓐ Ⓑ Ⓒ Ⓓ
48. Ⓐ Ⓑ Ⓒ Ⓓ
49. Ⓐ Ⓑ Ⓒ Ⓓ
50. Ⓐ Ⓑ Ⓒ Ⓓ
51. Ⓐ Ⓑ Ⓒ Ⓓ
52. Ⓐ Ⓑ Ⓒ Ⓓ
53. Ⓐ Ⓑ Ⓒ Ⓓ
54. Ⓐ Ⓑ Ⓒ Ⓓ
55. Ⓐ Ⓑ Ⓒ Ⓓ
56. Ⓐ Ⓑ Ⓒ Ⓓ
57. Ⓐ Ⓑ Ⓒ Ⓓ
58. Ⓐ Ⓑ Ⓒ Ⓓ
59. Ⓐ Ⓑ Ⓒ Ⓓ
60. Ⓐ Ⓑ Ⓒ Ⓓ

61. Ⓐ Ⓑ Ⓒ Ⓓ
62. Ⓐ Ⓑ Ⓒ Ⓓ
63. Ⓐ Ⓑ Ⓒ Ⓓ
64. Ⓐ Ⓑ Ⓒ Ⓓ
65. Ⓐ Ⓑ Ⓒ Ⓓ
66. Ⓐ Ⓑ Ⓒ Ⓓ
67. Ⓐ Ⓑ Ⓒ Ⓓ
68. Ⓐ Ⓑ Ⓒ Ⓓ
69. Ⓐ Ⓑ Ⓒ Ⓓ
70. Ⓐ Ⓑ Ⓒ Ⓓ
71. Ⓐ Ⓑ Ⓒ Ⓓ
72. Ⓐ Ⓑ Ⓒ Ⓓ
73. Ⓐ Ⓑ Ⓒ Ⓓ
74. Ⓐ Ⓑ Ⓒ Ⓓ
75. Ⓐ Ⓑ Ⓒ Ⓓ
76. Ⓐ Ⓑ Ⓒ Ⓓ
77. Ⓐ Ⓑ Ⓒ Ⓓ
78. Ⓐ Ⓑ Ⓒ Ⓓ
79. Ⓐ Ⓑ Ⓒ Ⓓ
80. Ⓐ Ⓑ Ⓒ Ⓓ

Practice Test 2

SECTION 1

TIME: 60 MINUTES
80 MULTIPLE-CHOICE QUESTIONS

> **DIRECTIONS:** Answer the multiple-choice questions below. Some are based on images. In this book the illustrations are at the top of each set of questions. Select the multiple-choice response that best completes each statement or question, and indicate the correct response on the space provided on your answer sheet. You will have 60 minutes to answer the multiple-choice questions.

Questions 1–5 are based on Figure 1.

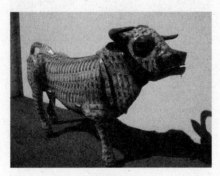

Figure 1

1. Michel Tuffery's reuse of existing materials draws inspiration from recycled materials as seen in

   (A) the Kaaba
   (B) the Golden Stool
   (C) Duchamp's *Fountain*
   (D) the Intihuatana Stone

2. Michel Tuffery's sculpture is made of used cans of corned beef which symbolize

   (A) a rejection of the traditional vegetarian diet
   (B) the reliance on packaged meat rather than traditional food gathering activities
   (C) Polynesian traditional welcoming of new people and products
   (D) an affirmation of a meat-based diet

3. The reuse of the materials in this work is akin to the works of

    (A) Julie Mehretu

    (B) Emily Kame Kngwarreye

    (C) Mariko Mori

    (D) El Anatsui

4. Michel Tuffery's objects become animated

    (A) when used in traditional coming-of-age ceremonies

    (B) when put on wheels and used as part of a multi-media performance art

    (C) when lit up from within and resembling an active bull

    (D) in cartoons and used to entertain children

5. Michel Tuffery's sculpture shows an indictment of

    (A) Polynesian obesity

    (B) the slave trade

    (C) global warming

    (D) the treatment of animals

Questions 6–12 are based on Figure 2.

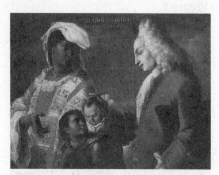

Figure 2

6. Works like this from New Spain betray a knowledge of European artistic traditions during which of the following periods?

    (A) Renaissance

    (B) Baroque

    (C) Gothic

    (D) Neoclassicism

7. This work presents a contrast in cultural identities. The figure on the right represents

   (A) the King of Spain and his generous actions towards his subjects
   (B) a member of the Spanish priesthood blessing a young child
   (C) a member of the Spanish aristocracy who cares for children who are born on his land
   (D) a member of the upper classes who has had a child with a Native American woman

8. The work is called a *casta* painting, a term that implies

   (A) it is meant to show how children of mixed race need adoption
   (B) its purpose is to introduce the notion of mixed races to a European audience
   (C) it is a painting in a series of works that shows different levels of ancestry and hierarchy
   (D) that it was used as a screen to divide rooms from one another

9. The woman on the left represents a Native American

   (A) but she is painted as a European woman with dark colored skin
   (B) who is dressed as a European woman of the eighteenth century would be dressed
   (C) who tries to adopt the culture and conditions of her new home in Spain
   (D) who is eager to give up her children to the European male in the painting

10. When this was painted it was not considered a work of art, but rather

   (A) the work of an illustrator
   (B) a work of anthropology
   (C) because it was a print, it was not considered as fine as a painting
   (D) as a model for a future sculpture

11. The idea of mixed races seen here is also picked up in the work of

   (A) Wilfredo Lam
   (B) Pablo Picasso
   (C) Frida Kahlo
   (D) Wangechi Mutu

12. We know that this work must have been done by an artist trained in Europe because

   (A) it is done in fresco, a time-honored tradition in Europe
   (B) it uses a mixture of experimental painting techniques
   (C) it is life-size
   (D) the artist uses the established oil on canvas technique

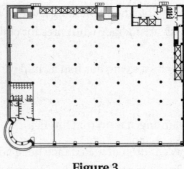

Figure 3

13. By examining this ground plan we can determine that the building represents a

    (A) temple
    (B) cathedral
    (C) department store
    (D) home

14. It was likely this building used which of the following architectural systems?

    (A) Groin vaults
    (B) Skeletal structure
    (C) Cantilevering
    (D) Fan vaults

15. The interior resembles the ground plan of

    (A) the Mosque at Cordoba
    (B) the Parthenon
    (C) the Temple of Minerva
    (D) the Great Stupa

16. When walking into this building the viewer is greeted by

    (A) a central open nave
    (B) flights of stairs
    (C) an atrium surrounded by glass
    (D) a myriad of columns

17. The ground plan indicates that the building

    (A) faced Mecca
    (B) was oriented toward the sun
    (C) has long banks of windows so people can see in
    (D) was aligned for a ceremonial purpose

Questions 18–25 are based on Figures 4 and 5.

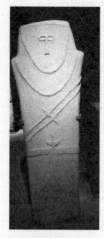

Figure 4

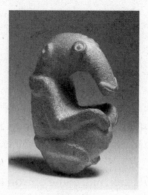

Figure 5

18. The work on the left has been anthropomorphized, meaning that

    (A) it was discovered by anthropologists
    (B) it is a work depicting a woman
    (C) it has characteristics of a human, but is not human itself
    (D) archaeology has yet to determine what this is

19. The work on the right, called the Ambum Stone, was carved in stone by artists who

    (A) used another stone to carve with
    (B) specialized in metalwork
    (C) used the repoussé technique
    (D) used hard-edged ceramics to smooth the stone surface

20. The work on the right has many theories surrounding its use. Among them is the hypothesis that it represents

    (A) a ceremonial animal that humans created in order to sacrifice
    (B) an anteater in a fetal position
    (C) a stylized kangaroo with a pouch ready for a newborn
    (D) a fish used to bait other fish

21. The work on the left was probably carved in what is now called

    (A) Arabia
    (B) Nigeria
    (C) Japan
    (D) Polynesia

22. The work on the right was probably carved in what is now called

   (A) Australia
   (B) New Zealand
   (C) Hawaii
   (D) Papua New Guinea

23. They are both stylized which means they

   (A) are in the contemporary style
   (B) have later been recognized as part of a style
   (C) are schematic and represent the natural world in a non-realistic way
   (D) are done in different parts of the world but are in the same style

24. The work on the left, unlike the one on the right, was done

   (A) by a shaman
   (B) as a stele
   (C) as a part of a rock painting
   (D) in a cave

25. Both works are likely to have had a function that was

   (A) religious and ceremonial
   (B) funerary and burial
   (C) commemorative and memorial
   (D) civic and governmental

Questions 26–30 are based on Figures 6 and 7.

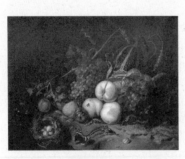

Figure 6

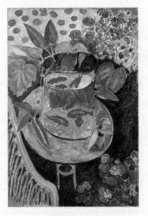

Figure 7

26. Both of these works are examples of

   (A) genre paintings
   (B) still lifes
   (C) frescoes
   (D) di sotto in sù

27. The work on the left was created in the

    (A) sixteenth century
    (B) seventeenth century
    (C) eighteenth century
    (D) nineteenth century

28. The work on the right was created during a period called

    (A) Cubism
    (B) DeStijl
    (C) Expressionism
    (D) Fauvism

29. Unlike the work on the left, the work on the right shows an influence from

    (A) Asian decorative patterns
    (B) African masks
    (C) Renaissance perspective
    (D) color theories based on musical notation

30. The work on the left, unlike the work on the right, is concerned with

    (A) the arrangement of objects in relationship to one another
    (B) the study of botany
    (C) demonstrating the artist's ability to depict objects in a natural environment
    (D) ecology

---

31. Mblo masks are works of art that

    (A) resemble kings and act in their place when the king is absent
    (B) seek to create a connection to fertility gods through ceremonies and rituals
    (C) honor an individual by being presented with an artistic double
    (D) have nails driven into them to prod the spirits into action

32. Mblo masks are characterized by their

    (A) powerful and aggressive nature
    (B) introspective and thoughtful look
    (C) faithful adherence to the likeness of the person or spirit depicted
    (D) feminine qualities

33. *The Lamentation* by Giotto is a work that is set in a context that

    (A) parallels Old and New Testament stories
    (B) emphasizes the punishment of the damned but not the forgiveness of sins
    (C) seeks salvation for those who refuse to repent
    (D) criticizes the Church and wants to reform it

34. Giotto's works most influenced the art of

   (A) Michelangelo
   (B) Rembrandt
   (C) Jan van Eyck
   (D) Lucas Cranach

Questions 35–39 are based on Figure 8.

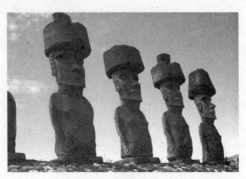

Figure 8

35. These monumental stone sculptures are called

   (A) Tapa
   (B) Maori
   (C) Moai
   (D) Bisj

36. The sculptures are arranged facing

   (A) inland and toward the center of the island signifying protection from the sea
   (B) outward and toward the sea signifying where their creators came from
   (C) the sun signifying their creator's worshipping of solar deities
   (D) many directions signifying the artists' interest in adapting the sculpture to the individual site

37. The images on the sculptures are of

   (A) ancestral chiefs who have been deified after death
   (B) shamans who have led their congregations in worship
   (C) ancestors who have had the ability to contact the spirit world
   (D) Europeans who were considered gods in the eyes of the natives

38. Stone altar platforms on which these works sit are

   (A) common in Pre-Columbian art, where this tradition comes from
   (B) common in Polynesian sacred religious sites
   (C) uncommon in Pacific Island cultures and unique to this grouping
   (D) uncommon in Polynesian art, but common in the rest of the Pacific

39. These sculptures were probably

    (A) clothed during ceremonies
    (B) attacked as enemy spirits
    (C) painted in bright colors
    (D) organized in groupings

Questions 40–42 are based on Figure 9.

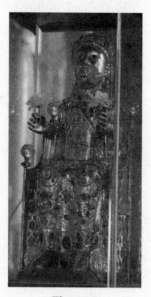

Figure 9

40. This reliquary commemorates

    (A) a king's splendid court
    (B) a martyr's death for her faith
    (C) victory over pagan gods
    (D) episodes from the life of a saint

41. Works like these were under criticism because some contemporaries felt

    (A) people used the objects for satanic rituals
    (B) the objects encouraged idolatry
    (C) the objects were ghoulish and disturbing
    (D) they were pagan and sinful

42. This reliquary

    (A) was encased in a large sarcophagus
    (B) contains elements of pottery and stained glass
    (C) uses medieval coins in its overall decorative patterning
    (D) contains the head of a child

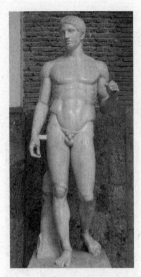

Figure 10

43. This sculpture is an expression of idealization developed in the

    (A) fifth century B.C.E. and called a canon
    (B) fourth century B.C.E. and called contrapposto
    (C) third century B.C.E. and called symmetry
    (D) fifth century B.C.E. and called contrapposto

---

44. The Egyptian *Book of the Dead*

    (A) charts the progress of a soul to the afterlife
    (B) measures the time a soul has on earth and in the afterlife
    (C) shows how to embalm bodies for preparation to the afterlife
    (D) illustrates the funeral processions of the deceased

45. The Egyptian sculpture *The Seated Scribe* is

    (A) depicted as a heroic figure, because the act of writing immortalizes the subject
    (B) shown as tired and weary, because writing is exhausting and draining
    (C) dressed as a member of the upper class, because only aristocrats were taught to read and write
    (D) illustrated as sedentary, because the lifestyle of a writer is one of long hours spent sitting still

46. The *Court of Gayumars* tells the story of

    (A) Sultan Muhammad and his rise to power in Tabriz
    (B) the Persian conquering of the Greeks under the reign of Xerxes
    (C) the legendary reign of the first Shah of the Persians
    (D) *The Arabian Nights* tale of Scheherazade

47. The mood and style of the *Court of Gayumars* can best be described as

   (A) monumental, grand, and awesome
   (B) intricate, decorative, and lively
   (C) serious, somber, and desolate
   (D) humorous, satiric, and farcical

48. Leonardo DaVinci's *The Last Supper* was painted in a location that was meant to make a connection between a Biblical scene of eating and

   (A) pilgrims eating along a pilgrimage journey
   (B) a refectory where religious people ate
   (C) a banqueting hall for a royal court
   (D) a church celebrating the Eucharist

49. Claus Oldenburg's *Lipstick (Ascending) on Caterpillar Tracks* was made as an ironic commentary on

   (A) the Feminist movement
   (B) the art of Andy Warhol
   (C) the Vietnam War
   (D) consumerism and modern culture

Questions 50–53 are based on Figure 11.

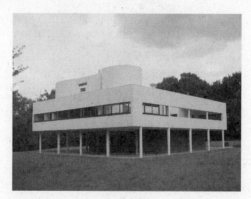

Figure 11

50. This house was designed by

   (A) Le Corbusier
   (B) Frank Lloyd Wright
   (C) Philip Johnson
   (D) Frank Gehry

51. The architect's philosophy of building is expressed by the idea that

   (A) construction should be environmentally friendly
   (B) only the use of natural material would be permitted
   (C) less is more
   (D) a house is a machine for living

52. Some of the functional aspects of the house that were unusual for the time include all of the following EXCEPT the

(A) carport
(B) roof patio
(C) house held up on stilts
(D) use of glass in a home

53. The approximate date for this building is

(A) 1930
(B) 1950
(C) 1970
(D) 1990

Questions 54–56 are based on Figure 12.

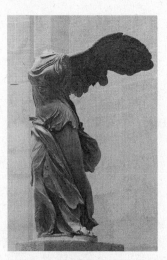

Figure 12

54. This work was originally positioned

(A) on the top of a building
(B) on a mountainside
(C) above a fountain in a town square
(D) in a river

55. The work is a representation of

(A) Nike
(B) the Spear Bearer
(C) Aphrodite
(D) Caryatid

56. The theatrical feeling of the work is enhanced by all of the following EXCEPT the

    (A) twisting movement of the figure
    (B) clinging drapery
    (C) ability to view the figure from many angles
    (D) use of classical composure

Questions 57–58 are based on Figures 13 and 14.

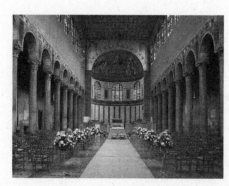

Figure 13

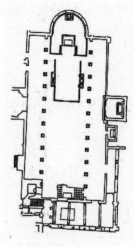

Figure 14

57. The interior columns in Santa Sabina, as seen in Figure 13, were

    (A) created from porphyry columns imported from Egypt
    (B) removed from a Roman temple and reused here
    (C) taken from Jewish temples in Jerusalem, whose significance was held in high regard
    (D) made of transparent gypsum and appear opaque in certain lighting conditions

58. The ground plan in Figure 14 shows a central nave and two side aisles constructed

    (A) so that worship can be done by men in the nave and women in the side aisles
    (B) for the clergy to use the nave as a processional space
    (C) for baptisms in the nave as the congregation watches in the side aisles
    (D) for the use of initiates in the side aisles

59. *The Last Judgment* appears in all of the following contexts EXCEPT

    (A) the Sistine Chapel
    (B) the Arena Chapel
    (C) the Tympanum at Conques
    (D) the Cornaro Chapel

60. Marcel Duchamp's work as an artist prefigures the work of

    (A) Emily Kame Kngwarreye
    (B) Song Su-nam
    (C) Naum June Paik
    (D) Jeff Koons

Questions 61–62 are based on Figure 15.

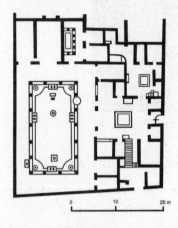

Figure 15

61. This plan is that of a Roman house. It tells us that

    (A) there is limited access to the inside from the outside
    (B) windows are plentiful on the perimeter of the house
    (C) the rooms are large and comfortable
    (D) there is an accent on privacy

62. The large area on the left is probably

    (A) an agora
    (B) an amphiprostyle
    (C) a stoa
    (D) a peristyle

Question 63 is based on Figure 16.

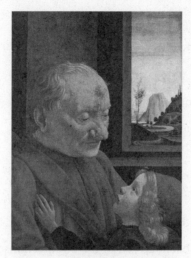

Figure 16

63. This painting by Domenico Ghirlandaio is inspired by works by

    (A) Giotto di Bondone
    (B) Sandro Botticelli
    (C) Fra Filippo Lippi
    (D) Diego Velázquez

---

64. Doris Salcedo's *Shibboleth* relies on the viewer understanding the title which means

    (A) a dangerous procedure that needs proper attention before pursuing
    (B) a crack or a gulf in relationships symbolized by anti-social behavior
    (C) a word or custom that a person not familiar with a language may mispronounce
    (D) a virus that can contaminate a person both physically and morally

65. The strength of the female persona is strongly articulated in the works of

    (A) Kiki Smith
    (B) Mariko Mori
    (C) Julie Mehretu
    (D) Yinka Shonibare

66. Song Su-nam's works express an interest in

    (A) adapting traditional formulas onto contemporary works
    (B) moving people away from purely aesthetic concerns to contemporary issues
    (C) instructing young people in the arts of today
    (D) multi-media presentations of ancient works

67. Sinan, the chief architect for Suleyman the Magnificent, was chiefly influenced by

    (A)   the Parthenon in Athens
    (B)   the Hagia Sophia in Istanbul
    (C)   the Dome of the Rock in Jerusalem
    (D)   the Kaaba in Mecca

68. Aspects of the Enlightenment period in European art can be seen in the works of

    (A)   Jean-Honoré Fragonard
    (B)   Joseph Wright of Derby
    (C)   William Hogarth
    (D)   Peter Paul Rubens

69. The Jowo Rinpoche from the Jokhang Temple is unusual in that

    (A)   it is thought to have been blessed by the Buddha himself
    (B)   it is conceived of as a metal object, but ultimately was crafted in porcelain
    (C)   Buddhists, Hindus, and Muslims all revere the object
    (D)   it is a composite statue made from different parts of other works

70. Regeneration and fertility are often symbols depicted on images found in

    (A)   Islamic manuscripts
    (B)   tapa bark cloths
    (C)   Indian temples
    (D)   American Indian pottery

71. In the tomb named Al-Khazneh, called the "The Treasury" at Petra, Jordan, there is a mixture of traditions that includes all of the following EXCEPT

    (A)   Greek, Egyptian, Assyrian gods on the façade
    (B)   Greek and Roman temple designs
    (C)   rock carving traditions of the Arabian peninsula
    (D)   burial practices gleaned from Egyptian funerary rites

72. Congs were symbolic in Chinese culture because jade

    (A)   is linked with durability, subtlety, and beauty
    (B)   has a soft quality that associates it with female virtues
    (C)   is iridescent and stands for the heavenly realm
    (D)   is found in small quantities and therefore is very expensive and symbolizes wealth

73. Ashlar masonry is used in the construction of

    (A) the Walls at Saqsa Waman in Peru
    (B) the Colosseum in Rome
    (C) the Houses of Parliament in London
    (D) the Alhambra in Granada

74. Symbols that appear on the frontispiece of the Codex Mendoza inspired images that appear on

    (A) the murals of Diego Rivera
    (B) the flag of Mexico
    (C) the Screen with the Siege of Belgrade and Hunting Scenes
    (D) the seal of the Organization of American States

75. Prehistoric art can be found in groupings of objects as well as by themselves. Often groupings indicate that

    (A) they were done by a workshop with a unified artistic vision
    (B) artists traveled from place to place to establish a reputation
    (C) they were done over a vast period of time
    (D) there was commentary made on previous works by other artists

76. Joseph Turner's *The Slave Ship (Slavers Throwing Overboard the Dead and Dying, Typhoon Coming On)* was exhibited

    (A) with a poem composed by the artist
    (B) as part of an anti-slavery exhibition in London
    (C) in a private space so that authorities would not confiscate the work
    (D) in Paris, because it was safer to represent anti-British works abroad

77. An example of a work that is a caprice is

    (A) Jean-Honoré Fragonard's *The Swing*
    (B) Francisco de Goya's *And There's Nothing to Be Done*
    (C) Gustave Courbet's *The Stone Breakers*
    (D) José Maria Velasco's *The Valley of Mexico from the Hillside of Santa Isabel*

78. In Paul Gauguin's *Where Do We Come From? What Are We? Where Are We Going?* the artist has used symbols derived from all of the following sources EXCEPT

    (A) Egyptian figures used for inspiration
    (B) Japanese prints in the solid fields of color and unusual angles
    (C) Tahitian imagery in the Polynesian idol
    (D) French Impressionism in the atmospheric effects

79. Based on the artistic style of his work, which of the following artists was a pupil of Gianlorenzo Bernini?

(A) Johannes Vermeer
(B) Giovanni Battista Gaullì
(C) Caravaggio
(D) Peter Paul Rubens

80. Although an Impressionist, Mary Cassatt often deviated from the works produced by other artists in that

(A) her work shows an affection for landscape
(B) group portraits are the dominant element in Cassatt's oeuvre
(C) still life takes on a greater meaning for Cassatt than for other Impressionists
(D) Cassatt emphasizes the role of women living lives independently from men

SECTION II

TIME: 120 MINUTES
6 QUESTIONS

Section II has two parts, each an hour. Part A contains two 30-minute questions. Part B contains four 15-minute questions. Although it is permissible to move freely among all the questions in Section II, it is advisable to stick to the time limits for each question to ensure an adequate response. During the actual exam, proctors will announce when each time period is over, and suggest that you move on to the next question.

Part A

> **DIRECTIONS:** You have 1 hour to answer the two questions in Part A. You are advised to spend 30 minutes on each question. Be sure to respond completely to all sections of every question.

1. Rulers from around the world often influence the way their residences or official royal buildings are designed. Sometimes these influences dictate the scale, materials, location, and quality of the workmanship.

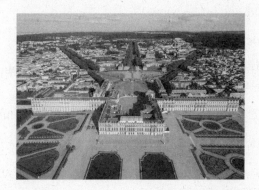

This building is the Palace of Versailles by Jules Hardouin-Mansart and Louis Le Vau from 1669.

Identify the patron of this building.

Discuss the artistic decisions that were made that reflect the interests of the patron.

Choose and completely identify a second building or building complex that was designed for a ruler.

Identify the patron of the second building.

Discuss the artistic decisions that were made that reflect the interests of the patron.

You may either select a work from the list below or select one of your own choosing. You are not limited to the works in the official image set. (Suggested Time: 30 minutes)

Audience Hall of Darius and Xerxes
Chavín de Huántar
Forbidden City
Monticello

2. Sometimes cultures that were once unaware of one another encounter one another through historic events. When these cultures meet, the artistic styles of indigenous people often show a combination of both the native techniques and the newly experienced art forms.

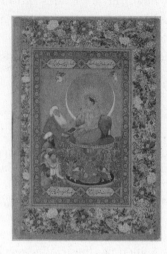

This work is by Bichitr. It is *Jahangir Preferring a Sufi Shaikh to Kings* from c. 1620, done with watercolor, gold, and ink on paper.

Explain what historical event led to the encounter.

Show *how* and *why* traditions of that culture have been both maintained and yet altered by this encounter as seen in this work.

Select and completely identify a second work of art that represents a cultural exchange.

Explain what historical event led to the encounter.

Show how traditions of that culture have been both maintained and yet altered by this encounter as seen in your chosen work.

The choice may be from any medium, in any period or culture you find relevant. You may either select a work from the list below or select one of your own choosing. You are not limited to the works in the official image set. (Suggested Time: 30 minutes)

Attributed to Cotsiogo (Cadzi Cody), Hide Painting of a Sun Dance
Gottfried Lindauer, *Tamati Waka Nene*
Master of Calamarca, *Angel with Arquebus, Asiel Timor Dei*
Lenape (eastern Delaware) tribe, Bandolier bag

Part B

DIRECTIONS: You have 1 hour to answer the four questions in Part B. The suggested time for each question is 15 minutes, but you may move freely among the questions. Be sure to respond completely to all sections of every question.

3. Many works of art require performance in order to complete their meaning. Both of these works are considered performance pieces.

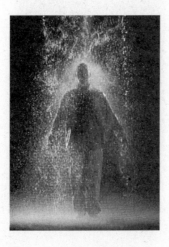 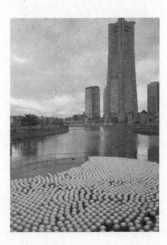

The work on the left is Bill Viola's *The Crossing*, a 1996 sound and video installation.

Fully identify the work on the right.

Analyze how the work on the left uses performance to achieve an artistic result.

Analyze how the work on the right uses performance to achieve an artistic result.

(Suggested Time: 15 minutes)

4. The work on the left is the frontispiece of the Codex Mendoza, c. 1542, pigment on paper. The work on the right is one page from the *Golden Haggadah*, c. 1320, pigment on vellum. Both works show how different cultural traditions can be seen in a single work of art.

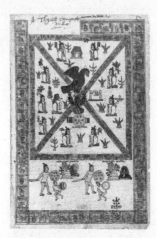 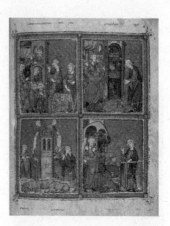

Explain the purpose of both works.

Using specific details, show how the work on the left reflects diverse cultural traditions combined into a unified work of art.

Using specific details, show how the work on the right reflects diverse cultural traditions combined into a unified work of art.

(Suggested Time: 15 minutes)

5. These two panels are by Ogata Korin. They are entitled *White and Red Plum Blossoms* and were painted in 1710–1716, a watercolor on paper.

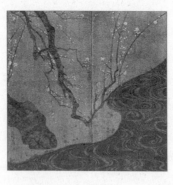 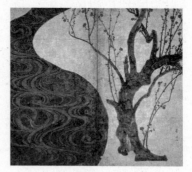

Identify the culture in which this work was done.

Discuss the characteristics this work has that makes it identifiable with its culture.

Contrast these characteristics with those of a western-style landscape.

(Suggested Time: 15 minutes)

6. This is Jeff Koons' *Pink Panther* from 1988, made of glazed porcelain.

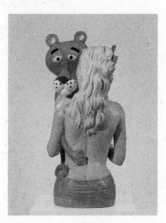

Artists sometimes use popular culture references in their work. What references is Koons using in this work?

How does the artist combine popular culture images to create a sculpture with an artistic message?

What interpretations have been achieved with this new combination of images?

(Suggested Time: 15 minutes)

Section 1

1. **C**	21. **A**	41. **B**	61. **A**
2. **B**	22. **D**	42. **D**	62. **D**
3. **D**	23. **C**	43. **A**	63. **C**
4. **B**	24. **B**	44. **A**	64. **C**
5. **A**	25. **A**	45. **D**	65. **A**
6. **B**	26. **B**	46. **C**	66. **A**
7. **D**	27. **B**	47. **B**	67. **B**
8. **C**	28. **D**	48. **B**	68. **B**
9. **A**	29. **A**	49. **C**	69. **A**
10. **B**	30. **B**	50. **A**	70. **C**
11. **C**	31. **C**	51. **D**	71. **D**
12. **D**	32. **B**	52. **D**	72. **A**
13. **C**	33. **A**	53. **A**	73. **A**
14. **B**	34. **A**	54. **C**	74. **B**
15. **A**	35. **C**	55. **A**	75. **C**
16. **D**	36. **A**	56. **D**	76. **A**
17. **C**	37. **A**	57. **B**	77. **B**
18. **C**	38. **C**	58. **A**	78. **D**
19. **A**	39. **D**	59. **D**	79. **B**
20. **B**	40. **B**	60. **D**	80. **D**

ANSWERS EXPLAINED

Section I

1. **(C)** Marcel Duchamp used a recycled urinal to create his work *Fountain*.

2. **(B)** When Europeans encountered Polynesians they brought with them cans of packaged meat, including corned beef, which led to the abandonment of traditional food gathering activities and a reliance on the convenience of canned meat.

3. **(D)** El Anatsui uses recycled pieces of metal in his sculptures.

4. **(B)** Oftentimes Tuffery's sculptures are enlivened in multi-media performances by being placed on wheels and mounted with motors.

5. **(A)** The use of canned goods of high caloric content has been a contributing factor to widespread obesity in the South Pacific island cultures.

6. **(B)** The drapery found in the costuming of the figures is similar to that used in Baroque Europe.

7. **(D)** The figure on the right is not a specific individual, but rather a symbol of upper class Europeans who have had a child with a Native American.

8. **(C)** Casta or "caste" paintings show the degrees of ancestry and hierarchy in Spanish society in the New World.

9. **(A)** The woman has the skin coloring of a Native American, but otherwise has the features of a European.

10. **(B)** The work has artistic value, but was meant more as a demonstration of the anthropology of the New World.

11. **(C)** Frida Kahlo's work often mixes the European painting technique with symbols of ancient Mexican cultures.

12. **(D)** This work is oil on canvas, a technique unknown in the New World prior to the arrival of the Europeans.

13. **(C)** This building is the Carson, Pirie, Scott Department Store in Chicago. It does not have a central focus the way temples and cathedrals do. It could not be a typical home because of the great number of interior columns.

14. **(B)** This is a skeletal structure, held up by an interior framework rather than by exterior walls.

15. **(A)** The Mosque of Cordoba does not have a single interior focus, but rather is a forest of columns that divide up the space into segments.

16. **(D)** The plan tells us that the entrance is in the lower left hand corner, and the interior is marked by large columns indicated by the evenly placed dots.

17. **(C)** The double sets of lines along the left and bottom sides of the plan indicate rows of windows.

18. **(C)** An anthropomorphized figure is one that has some human characteristics, but essentially is not human.

19. **(A)** Many prehistoric objects are made of stone, and carved using another stone.

20. **(B)** It has been theorized that the Ambum Stone may be an anteater in a fetal position. There have been other theories as well, but none of the other choices fit those theories.

21. **(A)** The work on the left is from ancient Arabia.

22. **(D)** The work on the right is from ancient Papua New Guinea.

23. **(C)** A stylized work does not show a realistic view of someone or something, but rather a schematic rendering.

24. **(B)** This work is a stele, a stone slab used to mark a grave or a site.

25. **(A)** Although the work on the left may have been part of a burial or funerary ritual, the work on the right was probably not. Both works were used for religious or sacred purposes.

26. **(B)** These are two still lifes, that is, paintings of inanimate objects.

27. **(B)** The work on the left, by Rachel Ruysch, is from the seventeenth century.

28. **(D)** The work on the right, by Henri Matisse, is from the Fauvist period in the early twentieth century.

29. **(A)** Matisse is said to have been generally influenced by Asian decorative patterns in many of his still lifes.

30. **(B)** Ruysch's father was a professor of anatomy and botany and influenced his daughter's interest in these fields.

31. **(C)** Mblo masks are artistic doubles of a real person, who is honored by receiving these works.

32. **(B)** Mblo masks are not realistic portraits, but seek instead to characterize the introspective nature of a person.

33. **(A)** Giotto's work is in a setting that parallels stories from the Old and New Testaments side-by-side.

34. **(A)** Giotto's sense of scale and size influenced the art of Michelangelo more forcefully than the other artists listed as choices.

35. **(C)** These famous stone sculptures are called Moai.

36. **(A)** The sculptures are arranged on platforms and face inland toward the center of the island.

37. **(A)** The most prevalent theory is that the sculptures represent ancestral chiefs who have been deified after death.

38. **(C)** Large stone sculptures are extremely uncommon in Pacific art, as are the stone platforms on which they sit.

39. **(D)** There is no evidence that these works were draped, painted, or attacked. They are, however, arranged on platforms in groups.

40. **(B)** This reliquary is of Sainte-Foy, a young woman who was martyred for her faith.

41. **(B)** Works like these were often criticized at the time because the faithful often treated them as idols.

42. **(D)** The relic in this reliquary is the head of a child, said to be that of Sainte-Foy herself.

43. **(A)** The sculptor, Polykleitos, is famous for having written a canon of human proportions, which no longer exists, in the fifth century B.C.E.

44. **(A)** The Egyptian *Book of the Dead* charts the progress of a soul in the afterlife, among other things.

45. **(D)** The Egyptian sculpture of *The Seated Scribe* depicts a figure who has been used to a sedentary lifestyle, unmuscular and a bit flabby.

46. **(C)** This manuscript tells the story of the legendary ruler of early Persia.

47. **(B)** The intricate details, depicted in a decorative and lively fashion, are characteristic of this manuscript and many other manuscripts painted in Persian art.

48. **(B)** Leonardo's painting was painted in a refectory used by monks. The image of a sacred scene of eating complemented the activity in the room.

49. **(C)** Oldenburg's *Lipstick (Ascending) on Caterpillar Tracks* was done during the height of the Vietnam conflict and was an ironic commentary on the war.

50. **(A)** This is the Villa Savoye, designed by Le Corbusier.

51. **(D)** The architect often proclaimed that a house is supposed to be "a machine for living."

52. **(D)** There are many innovative aspects of this home, including the carport, the stilts, and the roof patio. However, glass had been used in homes for centuries before this building was designed.

53. **(A)** The Villa Savoye was constructed about 1930.

54. **(C)** This sculpture was originally designed to be placed above a fountain in a town square to symbolize a naval victory.

55. **(A)** This work is a Nike, a symbol of victory.

56. **(D)** The Hellenistic approach to the design of this work shows a theatrical treatment of the drapery, and a twisting movement that requires the viewer to look at the work from many angles. These is no classical composure in this work.

57. **(B)** The columns in Santa Sabina are spolia, which are taken from a Roman temple and repurposed here.

58. **(A)** In Early Christian churches men worshipped in the main aisle, and the women were separated, worshipping in the side aisles.

59. **(D)** The Cornaro Chapel contains Bernini's famous work *The Ecstasy of Saint Teresa*. It does not have a scene of the Last Judgment.

60. **(D)** The reuse of common objects, as seen in Duchamp's *Fountain*, can be seen in the works of Jeff Koons.

61. **(A)** The ground plan of this Roman house shows few entrances.

62. **(D)** The large area on the left, surrounded by columns, is a peristyle courtyard, open to the sky.

63. **(C)** This painting by Ghirlandaio was done in the late fifteenth century, and has the same characteristics of Fra Filippo Lippi's *Madonna and Child with Two Angels*. The humanized figures are placed before a window frame depicting a landscape that fades atmospherically into the distance.

64. **(C)** A *shibboleth* is a word or a custom that is used to separate or discriminate against people. Hence, this work is a huge split down the center of the floor.

65. **(A)** Kiki Smith uses positive strong images of women in her work.

66. **(A)** Traditional Korean ink painting has been updated in the work of Song Su-nam.

67. **(B)** Sinan was influenced by the Hagia Sophia when he designed the Mosque of Selim II.

68. **(B)** Joseph Wright of Derby's paintings often show activities of intellectual groups who gathered to discuss the latest advances in scientific theories.

69. **(A)** There is a tradition around the Jowo Rinpoche that it was blessed by the original Buddha himself.

70. **(C)** The façade of many Indian Hundu temples often contains scenes of fertility and regeneration. There are no images depicted on tapa cloths. Few images are on American Indian pottery, and those that are usually are extremely stylized. Persian manuscripts have images, but they virtually never show fertility in a direct manner. Other Islamic manuscripts have no images of humans.

71. **(D)** We have no idea what the burial practices at Petra were because no human remains have been found.

72. **(A)** Jade is symbolic of durability, subtlety, and beauty in Chinese culture.

73. **(A)** Ashlar masonry, that is masonry without mortar, is used in the walls as Saqsa Waman in Peru.

74. **(B)** The image of an eagle on a cactus appears both in the Codex Mendoza and on the current Mexican flag.

75. **(C)** Prehistoric works that are found in large quantities were done over an extended period of time generally by different groups of people.

76. **(A)** Turner composed a poem called "The Fallacies of Hope" to accompany his painting.

77. **(B)** Goya's etching *And There's Nothing to Be Done* is a caprice, which is a work with a strong fantasy element.

78. **(D)** There is little influence of French Impressionist atmospheric effects in the mature work of Paul Gauguin.

79. **(B)** Gaulli's dramatic use of color and action in his work stems from his tenure working under Gianlorenzo Bernini.

80. **(D)** Cassatt emphasized in her work how women could lead fulfilling lives independent of men. No other Impressionist took up this theme.

Section II Answers

MODEL RESPONSE FOR QUESTION 1

Throughout the history of art, powerful leaders have impacted the way their buildings and homes appear. Often times, rulers aimed to portray their superiority and wealth by living in extravagant, monumental palaces. One such ruler was Louis XIV of France, also commonly known as the "Sun King." Louis XIV was an absolute ruler who reigned from 1643 to 1715 and was a strict believer in centralizing all state power in his hands. Therefore, he hired Jules Hardouin-Mansart to remodel a hunting lodge into a massive palace in Versailles, famously known as the Palace at Versailles. Louis influenced every aspect of his residence, including the size, architecture, location, and quality; therefore, the palace ultimately became a symbol of his lasting power and influence throughout Europe.

Louis XIV's main concern was dominating every aspect of France and putting the entire country under his control. He feared losing power to nobles who could gain support from the French citizens in the cities. For this reason, Louis purposely wanted his palace distanced from Paris in order to protect himself from civil unrest in the cities and to force the nobles to travel to Versailles. The nobles would reside in the palace for years so Louis could domesticate them, which is why he had hundreds of apartments built specifically for his visitors. The location of the building was also important in that it was lined up directly along the West/East axis so that the sun would rise and set in alignment with the house. In addition, a town complex and streets radiated from the building in all directions, like the rays of the sun. Thus, Louis made certain that he was symbolized as the sun, once again.

Since the building was built during the Baroque era, the entire building, both inside and out, was ornately designed. However, due to Louis' fascination with classical Roman and Greek rulers, the exterior of the building was modeled after classical buildings. For example, the façade was subdued and mostly white with few gold ornaments, Roman arches, and Greek columns and capitals. With this, Louis evidently showed his connection with his intellectual predecessors. In addition, Louis was influenced by other French chateaus, such as the Vaux-le-Vicomte, which was surrounded by vast gardens. To ensure that he was the most prominent king yet, he had elaborately designed gardens with hundreds of fountains and statues. The gardens were supposed to overpower his visitors and radiate out from the house to symbolize the sun's rays. Because Louis admired the classical past, the statues throughout the garden were mostly busts of mythological characters and prominent Roman rulers.

In comparison to the exterior of the building, the interior was much more elaborately decorated in order to further convey Louis' power and wealth. To once again symbolize himself as the "Sun King," his bedroom was the center of the building and all other designs radiated out from here. In this room, two important ceremonies took place each day: the lever, when he awoke, and the "coucher," when he would go to sleep. Another extremely decadent room was the Hall of Mirrors. On one side of the wall are windows looking out to the boundless gardens, while the other side has mirrors with huge panes of glass. Therefore, when the sun rose and set, the light would reflect off the mirrors and illuminate the entire room for Louis' ceremonies. On the ceiling, Louis had painters depict scenes of his civil and military achievements such as when he led his army across the Rhine River. He was often portrayed as a victorious king over foreign powers or as a Roman emperor. In contrast, Louis wanted paintings in the Salon of Peace to show that his reign would bring peace and prosperity to the kingdom. The remainder of the rooms was dedicated to music and the arts since he was an excellent musician and dancer, and he loved to play billiards and cards. Furthermore, since Louis was fascinated with astronomy, he devoted seven rooms in the Grand Apartment for each of the planets. Although there were hundreds of rooms and salons throughout the palace, they were mostly dedicated to Louis' intellectual interests, favorite leisure time activities, and entertainment for his guests.

It is evident that Louis XIV had a significant influence on the design and location of his palace at Versailles. Like many other rulers during his time, Louis wanted to convey that he was a divinely appointed king with supreme power. Through the monumentality, location, and design of the building, Louis succeeded in conveying his political and economic achievements, as well as his military victories.

A second building done with the clear ideas of the patron in mind is Monticello, designed and built by Thomas Jefferson from 1770 to 1806. The purpose of this building was to be the headquarters, so to speak, of Jefferson's plantation.

Jefferson also designed it as the central space in an intellectual household, in which he dominated as a lawyer, and then as president of the United States. As such, the building is built in the European style, that is with a pediment and a set of columns, reflective of the great buildings of Europe. In the center he placed a dome which in most buildings would have been an open space. Here it is an office for his private use.

He was inspired by ideas of the neoclassical era. He investigated Roman temples in the south of France, and then purchased books by the Renaissance architect Palladio. All of this cemented his ideas on what a great home should look like.

Jefferson's study of the intellectual ideas of his time determined the design and the construction of this home. Even the naming of the building as Monticello, or "little mountain" in Italian shows its European roots. Jefferson, however, did not have the marble available to him that European architects did. So although it is done in the European style, the heavy use of brick and stucco facing indicate that it was done in America, where raw materials were more difficult to come by.

Criteria	Student Response	Points Allotted for Task	Points Earned
Task: Identify the patron of this building.			
The essay must be able to identify the patron, if known.	"Louis XIV was an absolute ruler who … hired Jules Hardouin-Mansart to remodel a hunting lodge into a massive palace in Versailles."	1	1
Task: Discuss the artistic decisions that were made that reflect the interests of the patron.			
The essay must examine how the patron directly influenced the construction or decoration of the palace.	"To ensure that he was the most prominent king yet, he had elaborately designed gardens with hundreds of fountains and statues…"	0–2	2 The essay is filled with good examples, this being but one.
Task: Choose and completely identify a second building or building complex that was designed for a ruler.			
The essay must completely identify the second building.	"A second building done with the clear ideas of the patron in mind is Monticello, designed and built by Thomas Jefferson from 1770 to 1806."	1	1
Task: Identify the patron of this building.			
The essay must be able to identify the patron, if known.	"…designed and built by Thomas Jefferson…"	1	1
Task: Discuss the artistic decisions that were made that reflect the interests of the patron.			
The essay must examine how the patron directly influenced the construction or decoration of the palace.	"He was inspired by ideas of the neoclassical era. He investigated Roman temples in the south of France, and then purchased books by the Renaissance architect Palladio."	0–2	2
		Total Points Possible: 7	**This essay earned: 7 This is an exceptional essay.**

MODEL RESPONSE FOR QUESTION 2

<u>Jahangir Preferring a Sufi Shaikh to Kings</u> by Bichitr is one such work which expresses the cultural exchange between two peoples whom were generally unaware of each other up until a certain point. These two peoples are the Mughal Empire and the Europeans.

History tells us that it was the Portuguese naval commander Vasco da Gama who first founded a direct sea route from Europe to India at the close of the fifteenth century. This exploration saw its efforts culminate in what is known as the Portuguese East India Company which began the cultural-crosspollination between the European countries and India.

The Portuguese East India Company may have finally established accessible links and sea trade to the exotic and foreign land of India, but the reason why the Mughals began to adopt European ideology and iconography into their artworks is because of Jesuit missionary work—traveling across the globe spreading the teachings of Christianity. The Jesuits understood the potential art held as a teaching tool.

A few Jesuits found themselves in the Portuguese colony of Goa, India where Jahangir's father, Emperor Akbar, being both curious and interested in who they were and their missionary work, invited them to the Mughal court in 1580. As missionary tools, the Jesuits lavished the emperor with Christian works—notably European engravings—which later proved to be greatly influential on the court painters during his and his son, Jahangir's, reigns. After this introduction of artworks, elements of European realism found new life in Mughal painting. Both Akbar and Jahangir encouraged their artists to specifically imitate or loosely model their works after the European engravings they so much adored. Jahangir especially was a connoisseur of Western Renaissance art, adopting finer brushwork, lighter colors, and liner perspective—contrasting to the flattened perspective of traditional Mughal miniatures—into his royal atelier.

Much like his father, Jahangir respected the holy men of India. Mughal emperors opted to underscore the ascendency of divine authority over temporal authority and thereby extolled Islamic religious doctrine. Emperors hoped to glorify this link between Mughal dynasty and religious doctrine, resulting in court painters creating symbolic works merging the veneration of royal resplendence with the reverence of spiritual authority—particularly through the depiction of sheikhs, the religious title specific to Muslim dignitaries. This depiction of sheikhs expresses the unrivaled spiritual command of the emperor.

Ironically, the link between Islamic orthodoxy and imperial power was further strengthened through the use of European iconography.

Jahangir Preferring a Sufi Shaikh to Kings by Bichitr is one such example of everything mentioned up until this point: the assimilation of European and Christian ideology and iconography into Mughal art; the traditional Mughal theme of expressing imperial authority taking backseat to spiritual authority, while simultaneously heralding the dynastic might Jahangir possesses over all.

Analyzing closely, this allegorical miniature allows us to understand a few things. The scene is obviously fictional, but this does little to take away from the symbolic moment of an emperor choosing a man of God and renouncing the royalty that is beneath him. This hierarchy is traditional to Mughal art; it is an effort by Jahangir to show the level of imperial prowess he possesses. He deems himself more important than the two figures below the sheikh: a Turkish Sultan and King James I of England. In the act of handing over a book to the sheikh, Jahangir is symbolically signifying the superiority of a religious soul over that of other temporal rulers.

Many foreign iconography are abound in this painting. Putti in Western culture are usually an expression of imperial sovereignty while here Bichitr is using them to lampoon temporal authority when in the presence of religious revelations. The putto on the right shields his vision from Jahangir's action, while the putto on the left is waving around a flimsy bow in one hand and a broken arrow in the other. Alternatively, they also function as a celestial canopy for Jahangir. Haloes were introduced to the Mughal court through Western religious engravings and were quickly incorporated into Mughal iconography. It was Jahangir, though, who saw the power behind the halo and he immediately took to using it. By having himself drawn with a halo he was in essence erecting a barrier between him and the other subjects in his paintings, while also making a statement of symbolically elevating the monarchy and his clergy to a semi-divine status. Just as the putti were celestial symbols, the halo Jahangir is seen with is a personification of the title he took on upon his ascension to the throne. Jahangir sits on an hourglass as both his throne and as a medium for alleviating his fears: "O Shah, may the span of your life be a thousand years," is being written at the bottom by two angels.

The royal atelier of Jahangir was revolutionary for its time. Juxtaposing European and Mughal themes within the same works solidified the growing interest the court had in, not only European imagery, but Christian iconography as well. They understood the reinforcement that it added to their culture was beneficial to their imperial propagandistic desires; this gave the Mughal Empire an identity completely its own while expressing sovereign dominance in taking over alien symbolism. <u>Jahangir Preferring a Sufi Shaikh to Kings</u> shows the merging of naturalistic forms and non-representational patterns with Islamic manuscript detailing, particularly in its bordering, and is a fine example of European assimilation into the Mughal culture.

The British exploration of the south Pacific brought with it an encounter of the native peoples of New Zealand, including the Maori who had occupied the land for centuries. Some Maori converted to Western religions rather rapidly, including Chief Tamati Waka Nene, who was a respected leader of his people.

After his death in 1890 his followers sought to commemorate his memory by commissioning an oil on canvas done by a European artist, Gottfried Lindauer. They did not chose a Maori artist, instead they took a photograph—itself a European invention—taken by John Crombie and used that as a basis for a realistic portrait of their leader. Indeed, the choice of oil on canvas is western as well as is the use of shading, atmospheric perspective, and chiaroscuro.

The painting however shows the chief with Maori symbols. We see elegant tattooing showing his distinguished rank, a staff with feathers (also a symbol of rank), and a costume of the Maori people. In some sense, this is almost an anthropological portrait of the leader because it contains all the trappings of Maori leadership preserved for the viewer.

Criteria	Student Response	Points Allotted for Task	Points Earned
Task: Explain what historical event led to the encounter.			
The essay must state the reason that the cultures encountered one another.	"Portuguese naval commander Vasco da Gama who first founded a direct sea route from Europe to India at the close of the fifteenth century. This exploration saw its efforts culminate in what is known as the Portuguese East India Company which began the cultural-crosspollination between the European countries and India."	1	1
Task: Show how traditions of that culture have been both maintained and yet altered by this encounter as seen in this work.			
The essay must point to details in the work that show a combination of cultural traditions.	"Putti in Western culture are usually an expression of imperial sovereignty while here Bichitr is using them to lampoon temporal authority when in the presence of religious revelations....Haloes were introduced to the Mughal court through Western religious engravings and were quickly incorporated into Mughal iconography."	0–2	2 This essay gives many examples; these are just two.
Task: Select and completely identify a second work of art that represents a cultural exchange.			
The essay must completely identify a second work that shows a cultural exchange.	"...Chief Tamati Waka Nene, who was a respected leader of his people....After his death in 1890 his followers sought to commemorate his memory by commissioning an oil on canvas done by a European artist, Gottfried Lindauer."	1	1
Task: Explain what historical event led to the encounter.			
The essay must state the reason that the cultures encountered one another.	"The British exploration of the south Pacific brought with it an encounter of the native peoples of New Zealand, including the Maori..."	1	1
Task: Show how traditions of that culture have been both maintained and yet altered by this encounter as seen in your chosen work.			
The essay must point to details in the work that show a combination of cultural traditions.	"Indeed, the choice of oil on canvas is western, as well as is the use of shading, atmospheric perspective, and chiaroscuro."	0–2	2
		Total Points Possible: 7	This essay earned: 7 This is an exceptional essay.

MODEL RESPONSE FOR QUESTION 3

The work on the right is Yayoi Kusama's <u>Narcissus Garden</u> from 1966. The medium is mirrored balls.

Yayoi Kusama's <u>Narcissus Garden</u> and Bill Viola's <u>The Crossing</u> utilize both the environment and medium to enhance a desired artistic result. The 1500 mirrored balls in Narcissus Garden relates to the ancient myth of Narcissus, where a young man becomes infatuated with his reflection and turns into a flower. The connection to the myth is further supported by the works' installation in water, as the current and wind allow the viewer to see many different reflections in the many mirrored surfaces. The sign above the installation that reads "Your Narcissism for Sale" and the fact that the balls could be bought for a cheap price alludes to the growing commercialism and vanity of the art world.

Bill Viola's <u>The Crossing</u> is a video installation projected on two 12 foot back-to-back screens in a large gallery. Its scale and placement in a large, dark gallery allows the work to appear more imposing, which adds to the spiritual drama of the piece. The repeated actions and the use of fire and water are similar to the purification and destruction cycles common in some religious traditions, including Zen Buddhism and Islamic Sufism.

Criteria	Student Response	Points Allotted for Task	Points Earned
Task: Fully identify the work on the right.			
The essay must fully identify the work.	"The work on the right is Yayoi Kusama's Narcissus Garden from 1966. The medium is mirrored balls."	1	1
Task: Analyze how the work on the left uses performance to achieve an artistic result.			
The essay must explain how the work cannot be understood without performance.	"Its scale and placement in a large, dark gallery allows the work to appear more imposing, which adds to the spiritual drama of the piece."	0–2	1 The essay repeats facts about the work, but does not directly address the question.
Task: Analyze how the work on the right uses performance to achieve an artistic result.			
The essay must explain how the work cannot be understood without performance.	"The sign above the installation that reads "Your Narcissism for Sale" and the fact that the balls could be bought for a cheap price alludes to the growing commercialism and vanity of the art world."	0–2	1 The essay repeats facts about the work, but does not directly address the question.
		Total Points Possible: 5	**This essay earned: 3**

MODEL RESPONSE FOR QUESTION 4

The work on the right shows the story of Moses leading the Jews out of Egypt and how God punished the pharaoh and his people. It also serves as reminder of God's mercy. Since "Haggadah" means "narration", the book is a story. Although the Jews themselves write it in Hebrew, Christians did the illumination work, as it resembles French Gothic manuscripts. It was painted in Barcelona, Spain in 1320 and is titled The Plagues of Egypt.

The work on the left is another narrative. It tells the history of the Aztecs. It was meant to go to Charles V, of the Holy Roman Empire. This work shows daily life in the tribe, even using Aztec pictograms. It shows the conquests of Colhuacan and Tenayucan: temples on fire and warriors carrying clubs and shields. Although the pictograms were Aztec, they were annotated in Spanish, thereby blending the two cultures together. It was created in 1542, 20 years after the Spanish conquest of the Aztecs.

PRACTICE TEST 2

These two works show a combining of two very different traditions and how they came together to become one unified artwork. The work on the right draws on both Jewish and French Gothic tradition to create an illuminated narrative. This piece did not have just one artist, it had two, one to write in Hebrew and one to illuminate. The work on the left draws from Spanish and Aztec traditions to create a narrative of what The Holy Roman empire had gained when they conquered that area. Two artists were involved in creating this work: one from the Aztec empire to draw the pictograms and one from the Holy Roman Empire to annotate them in Spanish. Thus, these two works combined two different traditions to form one amazing piece.

Criteria	Student Response	Points Allotted for Task	Points Earned
Task: Explain the purpose of both works.			
The essay must assess why these books were created.	—	1	0
Task: Using specific details, show how the work on the left reflects diverse cultural traditions combined into a unified work of art.			
The essay must use particular details within the work to prove they were done by different traditions at the same time.	"This work shows daily life in the tribe, even using Aztec pictograms…. Although the pictograms were Aztec, they were annotated in Spanish, thereby blending the two cultures together."	0–2	2
Task: Using specific details, show how the work on the right reflects diverse cultural traditions combined into a unified work of art.			
The essay must use particular details within the work to prove they were done by different traditions at the same time.	"The work on the right draws on both Jewish and French Gothic tradition to create an illuminated narrative."	0–2	2
		Total Points Possible: 5	This essay earned: 4

MODEL RESPONSE FOR QUESTION 5

This work was done in the Japanese culture by Ogata Korin. Korin is known for using twofold screens. This means that he split the work into two halves. Korin usually uses colorful golden screens. In both pieces, the two sides of trees are separated by a stream.

Korin uses a wet-pigment technique called tarashikomi. Korin's style produces a harmonious rhythm which can be seen in both works. A characteristic of the Rimpa School, which Korin was a part of, is to have the imagery look random even though it's not. Rimpa Masters excelled in decorative designs using strong expressive force. The school was known for working in multiple mediums.

The screens usually were asymmetrical with almost abstract patterns. These masters tried to simplify and dramatize the scene. Their pieces would contain a combination of two-dimensional and three-dimensional parts with basic mineral colors.

In contrast, western-styled landscapes concentrate on vistas, panoramas, or wide-scale effects, as in the works of Cole or Velasco. Korin's work is much more intimate in the way it approaches landscape.

Criteria	Student Response	Points Allotted for Task	Points Earned
Task: Identify the culture in which this work was done.			
The essay must say Japanese.	"This work was done in the Japanese culture by Ogata Korin."	1	1
Task: Discuss the characteristics this work has that makes it identifiable with its culture.			
The essay must discuss at least two Japanese characteristics.	"Korin uses a wet-pigment technique called tarashikomi…" "The screens usually were asymmetrical with almost abstract patterns…"	0–2	2
Task: Contrast these characteristics with those of a western-style landscape.			
The contrast must discuss in depth the difference between Japanese and western landscapes.	"In contrast, western-styled landscapes concentrate on vistas, panoramas, or wide-scale effects, as in the works of Cole or Velasco."	0–2	1 This needs more explanation. The statements here are true, but vague.
		Total Points Possible: 5	This essay earned: 4

MODEL RESPONSE FOR QUESTION 6

The Pink Panther is a sculpture that is focused around aspiration and sex. It is a topless woman who is supposed to represent Jayne Mansfield (a 1950s sex symbol). The woman is carrying a Pink Panther that covers one of her breasts and is holding the other one with her hand. She has a "worry free" look on her face, which is showing how everyone in the world should be. The panther is a figure from a series of American movies from the 1960s.

Koons unites two problem areas in American culture into one with the creation of the Pink Panther. It focuses on materialism as well as desire. The panther is created from stainless steel that is supposed to lure the viewer in. The steel is supposed to represent silver that is something that everyone hopes to acquire, thus showing the materialistic view. When people view this sculpture they are supposed to desire the situation of a beautiful woman. The Panther has lost control and does not know what is going to happen next in life.

Koons believes that he should stress many controversial topics in his artwork honestly. He feels that everyone needs some controversy in his or her lives. This is one of the reasons why his art sells so well.

Criteria	Student Response	Points Allotted for Task	Points Earned
Task: Artists sometimes use popular culture references in their work. What references is Koons using in this work?			
The essay must articulate where the two major images in the piece come from.	"It is a topless woman who is supposed to represent Jayne Mansfield (a 1950s sex symbol).... The panther is a figure from a series of American movies from the 1960s."	1	1
Task: How does the artist combine popular culture images to create a sculpture with an artistic message?			
The essay must address how the combination of images creates a new work with a message.	"When people view this sculpture they are supposed to desire the situation of a beautiful woman."	0–2	0 There are several inaccuracies in the essay, including the idea that the viewer is asked to desire the situation of the woman.
Task: What interpretations have been achieved with this new combination of images?			
The essay must focus on how the image has created a new set of interpretations.	"It focuses on materialism as well as desire."	0–2	1 A greater articulation of the materialistic view is needed.
		Total Points Possible: 5	This essay earned: 2

TEST ANALYSIS

NOTE: Because the AP Art History exam will be new in 2016, there is no way of knowing exactly how the raw scores on the exams will translate into a 1, 2, 3, 4, or 5. The formula provided below is based on past commonly accepted standards for grading the AP Art History exam. Additionally, the score range corresponding to each grade varies from exam to exam, and thus the ranges provided below are approximate.

SECTION I: MULTIPLE-CHOICE (50% OF GRADE)

Number Correct: _____ (out of 80)

Number Correct × 1.25 = _____ (out of 100)
(Multiple-Choice Score)

SECTION II: ESSAYS (50% OF GRADE)

Essay 1: _____
(out of 7)

Essay 2: _____
(out of 7)

Essay 3: _____
(out of 5)

Essay 4: _____
(out of 5)

Essay 5: _____
(out of 5)

Essay 6: _____
(out of 5)

Total: _____ × **2.942** = _____ (out of 100)
(Essay Score)

FINAL SCORE

_____ + _____ = _____ (out of 200)

Multiple-Choice Score   Essay Score   Final Score
(rounded to the nearest whole number)

Final Score Range	AP Score
150–200	5
132–149	4
110–131	3
75–109	2
0–74	1

PRACTICE TEST 2

Glossary

Abbey: a monastery for monks, or a convent for nuns, and the church that is connected to it (Figure 11.4a)

Abstract: works of art that may have form, but have little or no attempt at pictorial representation (Figure 22.14)

Academy: an institution whose main objects include training artists in an academic tradition, ennobling the profession, and holding exhibitions

Acropolis: literally, a "high city," a Greek temple complex built on a hill over a city

Action painting: an abstract painting in which the artist drips or splatters paint onto a surface like a canvas in order to create the work (Figure 22.22)

Adobe: a building material made from earth, straw, or clay dried in the sun (Figure 27.2)

Agora: a public plaza in a Greek city where commercial, religious, and societal activities are conducted (Figure 4.15)

'Ahu 'ula: Hawaiian feather cloaks (Figure 28.4)

Aka: an elephant mask of the Bamileke people of Cameroon (Figure 27.12)

Aerial perspective: *see* **Perspective**

Altarpiece: a painted or sculpted panel set atop an altar of a church (Figure 14.1)

Ambulatory: a passageway around the apse or an altar of a church (Figure 11.3)

Amphiprostyle: having four columns in the front and rear of a temple

Amphora: a two-handled ancient Greek storage jar

Anamorphic image: an image that must be viewed by a special means, such as a mirror, in order to be recognized (Figure 19.9)

Andachtsbild: an image used for private contemplation and devotion (Figure 12.7)

Animal style: a medieval art form in which animals are depicted in a stylized and often complicated pattern, usually seen fighting with one another (Figure 11.1)

Ankh: an Egyptian symbol of life

Annunciation: In Christianity, an episode in the Book of Luke 1:26–38 in which Angel Gabriel announces to Mary that she would be the Virgin Mother of Jesus (Figure 14.1)

Anthropomorphic: having characteristics of the human form, although the form itself is not human (Figure 1.2)

Apadana: an audience hall in a Persian palace (Figure 2.16)

Apocalypse: last book of the Christian Bible, sometimes called Revelations, which details God's destruction of evil and consequent rising to heaven of the righteous (Figure 12.9a)

Apotheosis: a type of painting in which the figures are rising heavenward (Figure 21.7)

Apotropaic: having the power to ward off evil or bad luck

Apse: the end point of a church where the altar is

Aquatint: a kind of print that achieves a watercolor effect by using acids that dissolve onto a copper plate (Figure 21.7)

Arabesque: a flowing, intricate, and symmetrical pattern deriving from floral motifs (Figure 9.1)

Arcade: a series of arches supported by columns; when the arches face a wall and are not self-supporting, they are called a **blind arcade**.

Arcadian: a simple rural and rustic setting used especially in Venetian paintings of the High Renaissance; it is named after Arcadia, a district in Greece to which poets and painters have attributed a rural simplicity and an idyllically untroubled world

Archaeology: the scientific study of ancient people and cultures principally revealed through excavation

Architrave: a plain nonornamented lintel on the entablature (Figure 4.14)

Archivolt: a series of concentric moldings around an arch (Figure 11.5)

Ashlar masonry: carefully cut and grooved stones that support a building without the use of concrete or other kinds of masonry (Figure 23.7a)

Assemblage: a three-dimensional work made of various materials such as wood, cloth, paper, and miscellaneous objects (Figure 29.15a)

Athena: Greek goddess of war and wisdom; patron of Athens

Atmospheric perspective: *see* **Perspective**

Atrium (plural: **atria**): a courtyard in a Roman house or before a Christian church (Figure 7.2)

Avant-garde: an innovative group of artists who generally reject traditional approaches in favor of a more experimental technique

Axial plan (Basilican plan, Longitudinal plan): a church with a long nave whose focus is the apse, so-named because it is designed along an axis (Figure 7.2)

Bandolier bag: a large heavily beaded pouch with a slit on top (Figure 26.11)

Baptistery: in medieval architecture, a separate chapel or building in front of a church used for baptisms

Barrel vault: *see* **Vault**

Basilica: in Roman architecture, a large axially planned building with a nave, side aisles, and apses (Figure 6.10a). In Christian architecture, an axially planned church with a long nave, side aisles, and an apse for the altar (Figure 7.2)

Bas-relief: a very shallow relief sculpture (Figure 23.5b)

Bay: a vertical section of a church that is embraced by a set of columns and is usually composed of arches and aligned windows (Figure 11.2)

Bieri: in the art of the Fang people, a reliquary guardian figure (Figure 27.13)

Biombos: folding free-standing screens (Figures 18.3a and 18.3b)

Biomorphism: a movement that stresses organic shapes that hint at natural forms

Bodhisattva: a deity who refrains from entering nirvana to help others (Figure 24.9c)

Bottega: the studio of an Italian artist

Buddha: a fully enlightened being; there are many Buddhas, the most famous of whom is Sakyamuni, also known as Gautama or Siddhartha (Figure 23.5)

Bundu: masks used by the women's Sande society to bring girls into puberty (Figure 27.9)

Bust: a sculpture depicting a head, neck, and upper chest of a figure (Figure 6.14)

Calligraphy: decorative or beautiful handwriting (Figure 9.2)

Calotype: a type of early photograph, developed by William H. F. Talbot, that is characterized by its grainy quality; a calotype is considered the forefather of all photography because it produces both a positive and a negative image

Camera obscura: (Latin, meaning "dark room") a box with a lens which captures light and casts an image on the opposite side (Figure 20.7)

Caprice: usually a work of art that is an architectural fantasy; more broadly any work that has a fantasy element (Figure 20.2)

Cantilever: a projecting beam that is attached to a building at one end and suspended in the air at the other (Figure 22.15)

Canvas: a heavy woven material used as the surface of a painting; first widely used in Venice (Figure 17.11)

Capital: the top element of a column (Figure 3.3)

Caricature: a drawing that uses distortion or exaggeration of someone's physical features or apparel in order to make that person look foolish

Caryatid (male: **atlantid**): a column in a building that is shaped like a female figure

Cassone: (plural: **cassoni**): a trunk intended for storage of clothing for a wife's trousseau (Figure 16.4)

Casta paintings: paintings from New Spain showing people of mixed races (Figure 18.5)

Catacomb: an underground passageway used for burial (Figure 7.1c)

Cathedral: the principal church of a diocese, where a bishop sits (Figure 11.4a)

Cella: the main room of a temple where the god is housed

Central Plan: a building having a circular plan with the altar in the middle (Figure 9.12b)

Chacmool: a Mayan figure that is half-sitting and half-lying on its back

Chalice: a cup containing wine used in a Christian ceremony (Figure 8.6)

Chapter House: a building next to a church used for meetings

Chasing: to ornament metal by indenting into a surface with a hammer (Figure 10.1)

Chevet: the east end of a Gothic church (Figure 12.2)

Chiaroscuro: a gradual transition from light to dark in a painting; forms are not determined by sharp outlines, but by the meeting of lighter and darker areas (Figure 16.4)

Choir: a space in a church between the transept and the apse for a choir or clergymen (Figure 12.2)

Cinquecento: the 1500s, or sixteenth century, in Italian art

Cire perdue: the lost-wax process. A bronze casting method in which a figure is modeled in clay and covered with wax and then recovered with clay. When fired in a kiln, the wax melts away leaving a channel between the two layers of clay that can be used as a mold for liquid metal (Figure 21.15)

Clerestory: the third, or window, story of a church (Figure 12.4d); also, a roof that rises above lower roofs and thus has window space beneath (Figure 3.8b)

Cloissonné: enamelwork in which colored areas are separated by thin bands of metal, usually gold or bronze (Figure 10.1)

Close: an enclosed gardenlike area around a cathedral

Codex (plural: **codices**): a manuscript book (Figure 10.2a)

Coffer: in architecture, a sunken panel in a ceiling (Figure 6.5)

Coiling: a method of creating pottery in which a rope-like strand of clay is wrapped and layered into a shape before being fired in a kiln

Collage: a composition made by pasting together different items onto a flat surface

Colophon: 1) a commentary on the end panel of a Chinese scroll; 2) an inscription at the end of a manuscript containing relevant information on its publication (Figure 24.3a)

Color field: a style of abstract painting characterized by simple shapes and monochromatic color

Composite column: one that contains a combination of volutes from the Ionic order and acanthus leaves from the Corinthian order

Compound pier: a pier that appears to be a group or gathering of smaller piers put together

Confucianism: a philosophical belief begun by Confucius that stresses education, devotion to family, mutual respect, and traditional culture

Cong: a tubular object with a circular hole cut into a square-like cross section (Figure 1.3)

Continuous narrative: a work of art that contains several scenes of the same story painted or sculpted in a single frame (Figure 8.7)

Contrapposto: a graceful arrangement of the body based on tilted shoulders and hips and bent knees (Figure 4.3)

Corbel arch: a vault formed by layers of stone that gradually grow closer together as they rise until they eventually meet (Figure 23.7a)

Corinthian: an order of ancient Greek architecture similar to the Ionic, except that the capitals are carved in tiers of leaves

Coyolxauhqui: an Aztec goddess who dies when she tries to assassinate her mother, Coatli-cue (Figure 30.15)

Cornice: a projecting ledge over a wall (Figure 8.3b)

Cubiculum (plural: **cubicula**): a Roman bedroom flanking an atrium; in Early Christian art, a mortuary chapel in a catacomb (Figure 7.1c)

Cuneiform: a system of writing in which the strokes are formed in a wedge or arrowhead shape

Cupola: a small dome rising over the roof of a building. In architecture, a cupola is achieved by rotating an arch on its axis

Cyclopean masonry: a type of construction that uses rough massive blocks of stone piled one atop the other without mortar. Named for the mythical Cyclops

Daguerreotype: a type of early photograph, developed by Daguerre, which is characterized by a shiny surface, meticulous finish, and clarity of detail. Daguerreotypes are unique photographs; they have no negative (Figure 20.8)

Daoism: a philosophical belief begun by Laozi that stresses individual expression and a striving to find balance in one's life

Darshan: in Hinduism, the ability of a worshipper to see a deity and the deity to see the worshipper

Di sotto in sù: "from the bottom up," a type of ceiling painting in which the figures seem to be hovering above the viewers, often looking down at us (Figure 17.6)

Documentary photography: a type of photography that seeks social and political redress for current issues by using photographs as a way of exposing society's faults (Figure 25.33)

Donor: a patron of a work of art who is often seen in that work

Doric: an order of ancient Greek architecture that features grooved columns with no grooved bases and an upper story with square sculpture called metopes (Figure 4.11)

Drypoint: a printmaking technique in which the artist uses a needle to incise into a metal plate; different from etching in that it does not use acid to create the image

Earthwork: a large outdoor work in which the earth itself is the medium (Figure 22.26)

Embroidery: a woven product in which the design is stitched into a premade fabric (Figure 11.7a)

Encaustic: an ancient method of painting using colored waxes that are burned into a wooden surface

Enconchados: shell-inlay paintings; tiny fragments of mother-of-pearl placed onto a wooden support and canvas and covered with a yellowish tint and thin glazes of paint (Figure 18.4)

Engaged column: a column that is not freestanding but attached to a wall (Figure 3.2)

Engraving: a printmaking process in which a tool called a **burin** is used to carve into a metal plate, causing impressions to be made in the surface. Ink is passed into the crevices of the plate, and paper is applied. The result is a print with remarkable details and finely shaded contours (Figure 14.3)

Entablature: the upper story of a Greek temple (Figure 4.14)

Entombment: a painting or sculpture depicting Jesus Christ's burial after his crucifixion (Figure 16.5)

Escudo: a framed painting worn below the neck in a colonial Spanish painting (Figure 18.6)

Etching: a printmaking process in which a metal plate is covered with a ground made of wax. The artist uses a tool to cut into the wax to leave the plate exposed. The plate is then submerged into an acid bath, which eats away at the exposed portions of the plate. The plate is removed from the acid, cleaned, and ink is filled into the crevices caused by the acid. Paper is applied and an impression is made. Etching produces the finest detail of the three types of early prints (Figure 17.9)

Eucharist: the bread sanctified by the priest at the Christian ceremony commemorating the Last Supper

Exemplum virtutis: a painting that tells a moral tale for the viewer (Figure 19.6)

Façade: the front of a building

Ferroconcrete: steel-reinforced concrete; the two materials act together to resist building stresses

Fête galante: an eighteenth-century French style of painting that depicts the aristocracy walking through a forested landscape

Fetish: an object believed to possess magical powers

Fibula (plural: **fibulae**): a clasp used to fasten garments (Figure 10.1)

Flood Story: as told in Genesis 7 of the Bible, Noah and his family escape rising waters by building an ark and placing two of every animal aboard

Flying buttress: a stone arch and its pier that support a roof from a pillar outside the building. Flying buttresses also stabilize a building and protect it from wind sheer (Figure 12.1)

Foreshortening: a visual effect in which an object is shortened and turned deeper into the picture plane to give the effect of receding in space (Figures 6.12a and 6.12b)

Forum (plural: **fora**): a public square or marketplace in a Roman city (Figure 6.10a)

Fresco: a painting technique that involves applying water-based paint onto a freshly plastered wall. The paint forms a bond with the plaster that is durable and long-lasting (Figure 6.13)

Frieze: a horizontal band of sculpture

Frottage: a composition made by rubbing a crayon or a pencil over paper placed over a surface with a raised design

Genesis: first book of the Bible that details Creation, the Flood, Rebecca at the Well, and Jacob Wrestling the Angel, among other episodes (Figure 8.7)

Genre painting: painting in which scenes of everyday life are depicted (Figure 14.6)

Gigantomachy: a mythical ancient Greek war between the giants and the Olympian gods (Figure 4.9)

Glazes: thin transparent layers put over a painting to alter the color and build up a rich sonorous effect

Gospels: the first four books of the New Testament that chronicle the life of Jesus Christ (Figure 10.2a)

Grand Manner: a style of eighteenth-century painting that features large painting with figures posed as ancient statuary or before classical elements such as columns or arches

Grand Tour: in order to complete their education young Englishmen and Americans in the eighteenth century undertook a journey to Italy to absorb ancient and Renaissance sites

Groin vault: *see* **Vault**

Ground line: a base line upon which figures stand (Figure 2.3)

Ground plan: the map of a floor of a building

Haboku (splashed ink): a monochrome Japanese ink painting done in a free style in which ink seems to be splashed on a surface

Haggadah (plural: **Haggadot**): literally "narration"; specifically, a book containing the Jewish story of Passover and the ritual of the Seder (Figure 12.10)

Hajj: an Islamic pilgrimage to Mecca that is required as one of the five pillars of Islam

Hammerbeam: a type of roof in English Gothic architecture, in which timber braces curve out from walls and meet high over the middle of the floor (Figure 12.5)

Hanja: Chinese characters used in Korean script with a Korean pronunciation

Happening: an act of performance art that is intially planned but involves spontaneity, improvisation, and often audience participation

Harlem Renaissance: a particularly rich artistic period in the 1920s and 1930s that is named after the African-American neighborhood in New York City where it emerged. It is marked by a cultural resurgence by African-Americans in the fields of painting, writing, music, and photography

Henge: a Neolithic monument, characterized by a circular ground plan; used for rituals and marking astronomical events (Figure 1.12b)

Hierarchy of scale: a system of representation that expresses a person's importance by the size of his or her representation in a work of art (Figure 3.4)

Hieroglyphics: Egyptian writing using symbols or pictures as characters (Figure 3.12)

Horror vacui: (Latin, meaning "fear of empty spaces") a type of artwork in which the entire surface is filled with objects, people, designs, and ornaments in a crowded and sometimes congested way (Figure 23.5b)

Huitzilopochtli: an Aztec god of the sun and war; sometimes represented as an eagle or as a hummingbird

Humanism: an intellectual movement in the Renaissance that emphasized the secular alongside the religious. Humanists were greatly attracted to the achievements of the classical past and stressed the study of classical literature, history, philosophy, and art

Hypostyle: a hall in an Egyptian temple that has a roof supported by a dense thicket of columns (Figure 3.8b)

Icon: a devotional panel depicting a sacred image (Figure 8.8)

Iconoclasm: the destruction of religious images that are seen as heresy (Figure 23.3)

Iconostasis: a screen decorated with icons, which separates the apse from the transept of a church

Ignudi: nude corner figures on the Sistine Chapel ceiling

Ikenga: a shrine figure symbolizing traditional male attributes of the Igbo people (Figure 27.10)

Impasto: a thick and very visible application of paint on a painting surface

Impluvium: a rectangular basin in a Roman house that is placed in the open-air atrium in order to collect rainwater (Figure 6.7b)

In situ: a Latin expression that means that something is in its original location

Installation: a temporary work of art made up of assemblages created for a particular space, like an art gallery or a museum (Figure 22.25b)

Ionic: an order of Greek architecture that features columns with scrolled capitals and an upper story with sculptures that are in friezes (Figure 4.11)

Isocephalism: the tradition of depicting heads of figures on the same level (Figure 4.5)

Iwan: a rectangular vaulted space in a Muslim building that is walled on three sides and open on the fourth (Figure 9.13)

Jali: perforated ornamental stone screens in Islamic art

Jamb: the side posts of a medieval portal (Figure 11.5)

Japonisme: an attraction for Japanese art and artifacts that were imported into Europe in the late nineteenth century

Ka: the soul, or spiritual essence, of a human being that either ascends to heaven or can live in an Egyptian statue of itself

Keystone: the center stone of an arch that holds the other stones in place (Figure 11.5)

Kiln: an oven used for making pottery

Kitsch: something of low quality that appeals to popular taste (Figure 29.10)

Kiva: a circular room wholly or partly underground used for religious rites

Kondo: a hall used for Buddhist teachings (Figure 25.1a)

Kouros (female: **kore**)**:** an archaic Greek sculpture of a standing youth (Figures 4.1 and 4.2)

Krater: a large ancient Greek bowl used for mixing water and wine (Figure 4.19)

Kufic: a highly ornamental Islamic script

Lamassu: a colossal winged human-headed bull in Assyrian art (Figure 2.5)

Lamentation: shows scenes of Jesus' followers mourning his death; usually includes Mary, Saint John, and Mary Magdalene (Figure 13.1c)

Lancet: a tall narrow window with a pointed arch, usually filled with stained glass (Figure 12.8)

Last Judgment: in Christianity, the judgment before God at the end of the world (Figure 13.1b)

Last Supper: a meal shared by Jesus Christ with his apostles the night before his death by crucifixion (Figure 16.1)

Linear perspective: *see* **Perspective**

Lintel: a horizontal beam over an opening (Figure 1.12)

Literati: a sophisticated and scholarly group of Chinese artists who painted for themselves rather than for fame and mass acceptance. Their work is highly individualized

Lithography: a printmaking technique that uses a flat stone surface as a base. The artist draws an image with a special crayon that attracts ink. Paper, which absorbs the ink, is applied to the surface and a print emerges (Figure 24.7)

Loculi: openings in the walls of catacombs to receive the dead

Lost Wax Process: see **Cire perdue**

Lukasa: a memory board used by the Luba people of central Africa (Figure 27.11)

Lunette: a crescent-shaped space, sometimes over a doorway, which contains sculpture or painting

Madonna: the Virgin Mary, mother of Jesus Christ (Figure 15.3)

Mandorla (Italian, meaning "almond")**:** a term that describes a large almond-shaped orb around holy figures like Christ and Buddha (Figure 23.2)

Maniera greca: (Italian, meaning "Greek manner") a style of painting based on Byzantine models that was popular in Italy in the twelfth and thirteenth centuries

Martyrium (plural: **martyria):** a shrine built over a place of martyrdom or a grave of a martyred Christian saint (Figure 8.4)

Mastaba: (Arabic, meaning "bench") a low flat-roofed Egyptian tomb with sides sloping down to the ground (Figure 3.1)

Mausoleum: a building, usually large, that contains tombs (Figure 9.17)

Mblo: a commemorative portrait of the Baule people (Figure 27.7)

Mecca, Medina: Islamic holy cities; Mecca is the birthplace of Muhammad and the city all Muslims turn to in prayer; Medina is where Muhammad was first accepted as the Prophet, and where his tomb is located

Megalith: a stone of great size used in the construction of a prehistoric structure

Megaron: a rectangular audience hall in Aegean art that has a two-column porch and four columns around a central air well

Menhir: a large uncut stone erected as a monument in the prehistoric era

Mestizo: someone of mixed European and Native American descent (Figure 18.5)

Metope: a small relief sculpture on the façade of a Greek temple (Figure 4.14)

Mihrab: a central niche in a mosque, which indicates the direction to Mecca (Figure 9.10)

Minaret: a tall slender column used to call people to prayer (Figure 9.13a)

Minbar: a pulpit from which sermons are given

Mithuna: in India, the mating of males and females in a ritualistic, symbolic, or physical sense

Moai: large stone sculptures found on Easter Island (Figure 28.11)

Mobile: a sculpture made of several different items that dangle from a ceiling and can be set into motion by air currents

Modernism: a movement begun in the late nineteenth century in which artists embraced the current at the expense of the traditional in both subject matter and in media; modernist artists often seek to question the very nature of art itself

Moralized Bible: a Bible that pairs Old and New Testament scenes with paintings that explain their moral parallels (Figure 12.8a)

Mortise and tenon: a groove cut into stone or wood called a **mortise** that is shaped to receive a tenon, or projection, of the same dimensions

Mosaic: a decoration using pieces of stone, marble, or colored glass, called **tesserae**, that are cemented to a wall or a floor (Figure 8.5)

Mosque: a Muslim house of worship (Figure 9.14a)

Mudra: a symbolic hand gesture in Hindu and Buddhist art (Figure 23.1)

Muezzin: an Islamic official who calls people to prayer traditionally from a minaret

Muhammad (570?–632): the Prophet whose revelations and teachings form the foundation of Islam

Mullion: a central post or column that is a support element in a window or a door (Figure 15.2)

Muqarnas: a honeycomb-like decoration often applied in Islamic buildings to domes, niches, capitals, or vaults; the surface resembles intricate stalactites (Figure 9.13b)

Narthex: the closest part of the atrium to the basilica, it serves as a vestibule or lobby of a church

Nave: the main aisle of a church (Figure 11.4b)

Ndop: a Kuba commemorative portrait of a king in an ideal state (Figure 27.5a)

Necropolis (plural: necropoli): a large burial area; literally, a "city of the dead"

Negative space: empty space around an object or a person, such as the cut-out areas between a figure's legs or arms in a sculpture

Nike: ancient Greek goddess of victory (Figure 4.8)

Niobe: the model of a grieving mother; after boasting of her twelve children, jealous gods killed them

Nirvana: an afterlife in which reincarnation ends and the soul becomes one with the supreme spirit

Nkisi n'kondi: A Kongo power figure (Figure 27.6)

Oculus: a circular window in a church or a round opening at the top of a dome (Figure 7.15)

Odalisque: a woman slave in a harem (Figure 20.3)

Ogee arch: an arch formed by two S-shaped curves that meet at the top (Figure 13.3)

Oil paint: a paint in which pigments are suspended in an oil-based medium. Oil dries slowly allowing for corrections or additions; also allows for a great range of luster and minute details (Figure 14.2)

Orans figure: a figure with its hands raised in prayer

Orthogonal: lines that appear to recede toward a vanishing point in a painting with linear perspective

Pagoda: a tower built of many stories. Each succeeding story is identical in style to the one beneath it, only smaller. Pagodas typically have dramatically projecting eaves that curl up at the ends

Panathenaic Way: a ceremonial road for a procession built to honor Athena during a festival (Figure 4.15)

Papyrus: a tall aquatic plant used as a writing surface in ancient Egypt (Figure 3.12)

Parchment: a writing surface made from animal skins; particularly fine parchment made of calf skin is called **vellum** (Figure 10.2)

Passover: an eight day Jewish festival that commemorates the exodus of Jews from Egypt under the leadership of Moses. So-called because an avenging angel of the Lord knew to "pass over" the homes of Jews who, in order to distinguish their houses from those of the pagan Egyptians, had sprinkled lamb's blood over their doorways, thus preserving the lives of their first-born sons.

Pastel: a colored chalk that when mixed with other ingredients produces a medium that has a soft and delicate hue

Paten: a plate, dish, or bowl used to hold the Eucharist at a Christian ceremony (Figure 8.5)

Pediment: the triangular top of a temple that contains sculpture (Figure 4.14)

Pendentive: a construction shaped like a triangle that transitions the space between flat walls and the base of a round dome (Figure 9.1)

Peplos: a garment worn by women in ancient Greece, usually full length and tied at the waist (Figure 4.2)

Peristyle: a colonnade surrounding a building or enclosing a courtyard (Figures 4.16b, 6.7a)

Perspective: having to do with depth and recession in a painting or a relief sculpture. Objects shown in **linear perspective** achieve a three-dimensionality in the two-dimensional world of the picture plane. All lines, called **orthogonals**, draw the viewer back in space to a common point called the **vanishing point**. Paintings, however, may have more than one vanishing point, with orthogonals leading the eye to several parts of the work. Landscapes that give the illusion of distance are in **atmospheric** or **aerial perspective**

Pharaoh: a king of ancient Egypt (Figure 3.11)

Photogram: an image made by placing objects on photo-sensitive paper and exposing them to light to produce a silhouette

Pier: a vertical support that holds up an arch or a vault (Figure 11.4b)

Pietà: a painting or sculpture of a crucified Christ lying on the lap of a grieving Mary (Figure 12.6)

Pilaster: a flattened column attached to a wall with a capital, a shaft, and a base (Figure 16.6a)

Pinnacle: a pointed sculpture on piers or flying buttresses (Figure 12.1)

Plein-air: painting in the outdoors to directly capture the effects of light and atmosphere on a given object

Porcelain: a ceramic made from clay that when fired in a kiln produces a product that is hard, white, brittle, and shiny (Figure 24.11)

Portal: a doorway; in medieval art they can be significantly decorated (Figure 11.5)

Portico: an entranceway to a building; it has columns supporting a roof

Potter's wheel: a device that usually has a pedal used to make the flat, circular table spin, so that a potter can create pottery

Positivism: a theory that expresses that all knowledge must come from proven ideas based on science or scientific theory philosophy, promoted by French philosopher Auguste Comte (1798–1857)

Post-and-lintel: a method of construction with two posts supporting a horizontal beam, called a **lintel** (Figure 1.11)

Predella: the base of an altarpiece that is filled with small paintings, often narrative scenes (Figure 14.4a)

Propylaeum (plural: **propylaea**)**:** a gateway leading to a Greek temple

Pueblo: a communal village of flat-roofed structures of many stories that are stacked in terraces. They are made of stone or adobe (Figure 26.3)

Puja: a Hindu prayer ritual

Pwo: a female mask worn by men of the Chokwe people (Figure 27.8)

Pyxis (pronounced "pick-sis"): a small cylinder-shaped container with a detachable lid used to contain cosmetics or jewelry (Figure 9.4)

Pylon: a monumental gateway to an Egyptian temple marked by two flat, sloping walls between which is a smaller entrance

Qiblah: the direction toward Mecca which Muslims face in prayer

Quattrocento: the 1400s, or fifteenth century, in Italian art

Qur'an: the Islamic sacred text, dictated to the Prophet Muhammad by the Angel Gabriel

Ready-made: a commonplace object selected and exhibited as a work of art

Register: a horizontal band, often on top of another, that tells a narrative story (Figure 3.4)

Relief sculpture: sculpture which projects from a flat background. A very shallow relief sculpture is called a **bas-relief** (pronounced: bah-relief) (Figure 3.4)

Reliquary: a vessel for holding a sacred relic. Often reliquaries took the shape of the object they held. Precious metals and stones were the common material (Figure 11.6)

Repoussé: (French, meaning "to push back") a type of metal relief sculpture in which the back side of a plate is hammered to form a raised relief on the front (Figure 26.7)

Reserve column: a column that is cut away from rock but has no support function

Rib vault: a vault in which diagonal arches form rib-like patterns; these arches partially support a roof, in some cases forming a weblike design (Figure 11.1)

Roof comb: a wall rising from the center ridge of a building to give the appearance of greater height (Figure 26.2a)

Rose window: a circular window, filled with stained glass, placed at the end of a transept or on the façade of a church (Figure 12.3b)

Sakyamuni: the historical Buddha, named after the town of Sakya, Buddha's birthplace (Figure 23.3)

Salon: a government-sponsored exhibition of artworks held in Paris

Sarcophagus (plural: **sarcophagi**): a stone coffin

Scarification: scarring of the skin in patterns by cutting with a knife. When the cut heals, a raised pattern is created, which is painted (Figure 27.7)

School: a group of artists sharing the same philosophy who work around the same time, but not necessarily together

Scriptorium (plural: **scriptoria**): a place in a monastery where monks wrote manuscripts

Seder: a ceremonial meal celebrated on the first two nights of Passover that commemorates the Israelites' flight from Egypt as told in the Bible. It is marked by a reading of the Haggadah.

Sfumato: a smoke-light or hazy effect that distances the viewer from the subject of a painting

Shaft: the body of a column (Figure 4.14)

Shamanism: a religion in which good and evil are brought about by spirits which can be influenced by shamans, who have access to these spirits

Shiva: the Hindu god of creation and destruction (Figure 23.6)

Sibyl: a Greco–Roman prophetess whom Christians saw as prefiguring the coming of Jesus Christ (Figure 16.2b)

Silkscreen: a printing technique that passes ink or paint through a stenciled image to make multiple copies (Figure 22.23)

Skeleton: the supporting interior framework of a building

Spandrel: a triangular space enclosed by the curves of arches (Figure 6.4)

Spire or **Steeple:** a tall pointed tower on a church (Figure 12.4b)

Spolia: in art history, the reuse of architectural or sculptural pieces in buildings generally different from their original contexts

Squinch: the polygonal base of a dome that makes a transition from the round dome to a flat wall (Figure 8.2)

Stele (plural: **stelae**): a stone slab used to mark a grave or a site (Figure 4.7)

Still life: a painting of a grouping of inanimate objects, such as flowers or fruit (Figure 17.11)

Stoa: an ancient Greek covered walkway having columns on one side and a wall on the other (Figure 4.15)

Stucco: a fine plaster used for wall decorations or moldings

Stupa: a dome-shaped Buddhist shrine (Figure 23.4a)

Stylized: a schematic, nonrealistic manner of representing the visible world and its contents, abstracted from the way that they appear in nature (Figure 1.2)

The Sublime: any cathartic experience from the catastrophic to the intellectual that causes the viewer to marvel in awe, wonder, and passion (Figure 20.5)

Sunken relief: a carving in which the outlines of figures are deeply carved into a surface so that the figures seem to project forward

Tarashikomi: a Japanese painting technique in which paint is applied to a surface that has not already dried from a previous application

Tapa: a cloth made from bark that is soaked and beaten into a fabric (Figure 28.6)

Tapestry: a woven product in which the design and the backing are produced at the same time on a device called a **loom**

Tempera: a type of paint employing egg yolk as the binding medium that is noted for its quick drying rate and flat opaque colors (Figure 15.3)

Tenebroso/Tenebrism: a dramatic dark-and-light contrast in a painting (Figure 17.5)

Tepee: a portable Indian home made of stretched hides placed over wooden poles

Terra-cotta: a hard ceramic clay used for building or for making pottery (Figure 5.5)

Tessellation: a decoration using polygonal shapes with no gaps (Figure 9.3)

Theotokos: The Virgin Mary in her role as the Mother of God (Figure 8.8)

Throwing: to mold forms on a potter's wheel

Tholos: (1) an ancient Mycenaean circular tomb in a beehive shape; (2) an ancient Greek circular shrine (Figure 4.12)

Tlaloc: ancient American god who was highly revered; associated with rain, agriculture, and war

T'oqapu: small rectangular shapes in an Inkan garment (Figure 26.10)

Torana: a gateway near a stupa that has two upright posts and three horizontal lintels. They are usually elaborately carved (Figure 23.4a)

Torons: wooden beams projecting from walls of adobe buildings (Figure 27.2)

Transept: an aisle in a church perpendicular to the nave (Figure 12.2)

Transformation mask: a mask worn in ceremonies by people of the Pacific Northwest, Canada, or Alaska. The chief feature of the mask is its ability to open and close, going from a bird-like exterior to a human-faced interior (Figures 26.12a and 26.12b)

Transverse arch: an arch that spans an interior space connecting opposite walls by crossing from side to side (Figure 11.4b)

Trecento: the 1300s, or fourteenth century, in Italian art

Triclinium: a dining table in ancient Rome that has a couch on three sides for reclining at meals

Triforium: A narrow passageway with arches opening onto a nave, usually directly below a clerestory (Figure 11.2)

Trigylph: a projecting grooved element alternating with a metope on a Greek temple (Figure 4.14)

Triptych: a three-paneled painting or sculpture (Figure 14.1)

Trompe l'oeil: (French, meaning "fools the eye") a form of painting that attempts to represent an object as existing in three dimensions, and therefore resembles the real thing (Figure 17.6)

Trumeau (plural: **trumeaux**): the central pillar of a medieval portal that stabilizes the structure. It is often elaborately decorated (Figure 11.5)

Tufa: a porous rock similar to limestone

Tuscan order: an order of ancient architecture featuring slender, smooth columns that sit on simple bases; no carvings on the frieze or in the capitals (Figure 5.2)

Tympanum (plural: **tympana**): a rounded sculpture placed over the portal of a medieval church (Figure 11.5)

Ukiyo-e: translated as "pictures of the floating world," a Japanese genre painting popular from the seventeenth to the nineteenth centuries (Figure 25.5)

Urna: a circle of hair on the brows of a deity sometimes represented as the focal point (Figure 23.1)

Ushnisha: a protrusion at the top of the head, or the top knot of a Buddha (Figure 23.1)

Vairocana: the universal Buddha, a source of enlightenment; also known as the Supreme Buddha who represents "emptiness," that is, freedom from earthly matters to help achieve salvation (Figure 23.2a)

Vanitas: a theme in still life painting that stresses the brevity of life and the folly of human vanity

Vault: a roof constructed with arches. When an arch is extended in space, forming a tunnel, it is called a **barrel vault** (Figure 6.1). When two barrel vaults intersect at right angles it is called a **groin vault** (Figure 6.2) *See also* **rib vault**

Venice Biennale: a major show of contemporary art that takes place every other year in various venues throughout the city of Venice; begun in 1895 (Figure 22.25b)

Veristic: sculptures from the Roman Republic characterized by extreme realism of facial features (Figure 6.14)

Vishnu: the Hindu god worshipped as the protector and preserver of the world (Figure 23.8c)

Votive: an object, such as a candle, offered in fulfillment of a vow or a pledge (Figure 2.2)

Voussoir (pronounced "voo-swar")**:** a wedge-shaped stone that forms the curved part of an arch; the central voussoir is called a **keystone** (Figure 9.14d)

Wat: a Buddhist monastery or temple in Cambodia (Figure 23.8a)

Woodcut: a printmaking process by which a wooden tablet is carved into with a tool, leaving the design raised and the background cut away (very much as how a rubber stamp looks); ink is rolled onto the raised portions, and an impression is made when paper is applied to the surface; woodcuts have strong angular surfaces with sharply delineated lines (Figure 14.5)

Yakshi (masculine: **yaksha**)**:** female and male figures of fertility in Buddhist and Hindu art (Figure 23.4c)

Yamato-e: a style of Japanese painting that is characterized by native subject matter, stylized features, and thick bright pigments

Yin and yang: complementary polarities; the yin is a feminine symbol that has dark, soft, moist, and weak characteristics; the yang is the male symbol that has bright, hard, dry, and strong characteristics (Figure 24.3c)

Zen: a metaphysical branch of Buddhism that teaches fulfillment through self-discipline and intuition

Zeus: king of the ancient Greek gods; known as Jupiter to the Romans; god of the sky and weather

Ziggurat: a pyramidlike building made of several stories that indent as the building gets taller; ziggurats have terraces at each level (Figure 2.1a)

Zoomorphic: having elements of animal shapes

Zoopraxiscope: a device that projects sequences of photographs to give the illusion of movement (Figure 21.5)

The author gratefully acknowledges the contributions of many individuals who have given permission to have their work reproduced in this volume. Any inadvertent errors will be corrected in the next edition.

Allan T. Kohl: 4.7, 6.13; **Ali Zingstra:** 27.1a; **Andrea Fisher Fine Pottery:** 26.14; **ArtHistoryReference.com:** 18.5, 21.15; **Art Institute of Chicago:** 27.14; **Auckland War Memorial Museum:** 28.6; **Author:** 2.4a, 4.10, 4.14, 5.1a, 6.10, 6.16, 9.16c, 13.1a, 16.6a, 17.2a, 19.5b, 21.13, 21.14a, 22.18, 26.1a, 26.3, 26.8a, 27.6, 28.9, 29.4b; **The Bridgeman Art Library** 3.11 De Agostini Picture Library/S. Vannini, 5.3 De Agostini Picture Library / G. Nimatallah, **24.7** Private Collection / © The Chambers Gallery, London, 26.7 Werner Forman Archive; **British Museum:** 29.6; **British Library Board:** 10.2b; 12.10a, 12.10b. 12.10c; **Brooklyn Museum:** 18.3a, 18.3b, 21.2, 27.5a, 27.7, 27.20, 27.22, 27.12, 27.13, 28.8; **David Skerrett:** 24.8a; **Carlos Rodriguez:** 1.11, 3.1, 3.2, 3.3, 4.11, 5.2, 6.1, 6.2, 6.3, 6.4, 6.5, 6.12a, 6.12b, 7.2, 8.1, 8.2, 8.3c, 11.1, 11.2, 11.3, 11.5, 12.1, 12.2, 12.3, 22.15, 24.1, 24.3a, 24.3b; **Cleveland Museum of Art:** 26.1d; **Clipart:** 1.12a, 2.1b, 2.2, 3.8c, 3.12, 4.16a, 4.18b, 5.1a, 5.1b, 6.10b, 7.3c, 9.1, 9.2, 9.3, 9.10, 9.15c, 9.15d, 12.7, 14.3, 17.2c, 17.3c, 19.1, 20.7, 20.8, 22.8, 22.14, 22.10. 22.11, 23.1, 23.6, 24.3c, 28.11; **Corbis:** 2.6b © Gérard Degeorge; 9.11a © ALI JAREKJI/Reuters/Corbis; 23.3 © Christophe Boisvieux/Corbis, 26.1c © Charles & Josette Lenars/CORBIS; **Cowan's Auctions, Inc., Cincinnati, Ohio:** 26.13; **Department of Anthropology at the University of Auckland, New Zealand:** 1.6; **Dreamstime:** 2.6a Stefan Baum; 3.6b; 8.3b Valeria Cantone; 8.5 Tomas Marek; 9.16a; 19.5a; 20.1a, 23.4a, 29.1a; **Dylan Rampersaud:** 27.3; **Freestockphotos.com:** 6.11a; **Galen Frysinger:** 24.2c; **Getty Images:** 27.4 © Marc Deville/Gamma-Rapho; **Harvard Art Museums/Arthur M. Sackler Museum, Bequest of Abby Aldrich Rockefeller, 1960.190:** 9.8; **Heritage-Images.com, Werner Forman Archive:** 28.2; **H. Gardner, Art Through the Ages, (New York: Harcourt, Brace, & Co., 1926), p 409, fig. 119:** 23.4d & e; **Istockphotos:** 9.16b, 23.8a, 24.8b, 27.2; **Jonathan Rutchik:** 21.14c, 25.2c; **KufoletoAntonio De Lorenzo and Marina Ventayol:** 4.12; **Library of Congress** 22.16b; **Los Angeles County Museum of Art:** 18.4; **Morguefile:** 1.12b, 16.2e; **National Gallery of Australia—Canberra:** 1.4; **National Gallery of Art, Washington:** 21.7; **National Library of NZ & Alexander Turnbull Library:** 28.10; **National Museum of African Art, Smithsonian Institution:** 27.5b Photograph by Eliot Elisofon, 1971, Eliot Elisofon Photographic Archives; 28.2 Photograph by Franko Khoury; **Photos.com:** 3.9a, 4.16b, 6.11b, 8.3a, 9.12a, 9.12b, 9.14d, 9.17a, 12.4b, 17.7; **Richard Ashworth/Robert Harding World Imagery:** 2.1a; **Richard Nici:** 4.13; **Scala/Art Resource:** 7.1a, 7.1c; **Storebridge:** 22.24; **Universal Color:** 5.5, 21.11, PT1 Figure 20; **Western Pennsylvania Conservancy:** 22.16a ; **Wikimedia Commons:** DT18; Question 4; Question 5 Right; 1.1 Marrovi; 1.2 Wolfgang Sauber; 1.3 Prof. Gary Lee Todd; 1.5 Madman2001; 1.7 Locutus Borg; 1.8; 1.10, 4.3, 4.8, 9.4 Marie-Lan Nguyen; 2.3a and 2.3b BabelStone; 2.4b Mbzt 2011; 2.5 Rmashhadi; 3.4; 3.5 Rama; 3.6a kallerna; 3.7 Jen; 3.8a Steve F-E-Cameron; 3.8b P. Bintor; 3.9b Postdlf; 3.10 Keith Schengili-Roberts; 4.1 Mountain; 4.2 Marsyas; 4.4 Yair-haklai; 4.5 Jastrow; 4.9 Miia Ranta, 4.15 Madmedea; 4.17; 4.18a; 4.19 Bibi Saint-Pol; 4.20; 5.4; 6.6 Ad Meskens; 6.7a M.violante; 6.7b AlMare; 6.8a; 6.8b; 6.9a Bernard Gagnon; 6.9b Markv; 6.9c Berthold Werner; 6.10a Forma mentis; 6.14; 6.17 Caiuscorentin; 7.1b; 7.3a MM, 7.3b Tango 7174; 8.4a DavidConFran; 8.4b Matthias Holländer; 8.4c Vask; 8.6; 8.7a and 8.7b Dsmdgold; 8.8; 9.5 Senemmar, 9.6 Captainm, derivative work by Poke 2001; 9.7a; 9.7b; 9.9; 9.11b Al-Fassam; 9.13a Alex O. Holcombe; 9.13b; 9.13c engraving by Eugene Flandin;

9.14a Toni Castillo Quero; 9.14b Michal Osmenda; 9.14c Jebulon; 9.14e Hameryko; 9.15a Balbo; 9.15b Jim Gordon; 9.17b William Donelson; 10.1 17.4b Sailko; 10.2a Eadfrith; 10.2c; 11.4a Jean-Pol Grandmont; 11.4b PMRMaeyaert; 11.6a Titanet; 11.6b Daniel Villafruela; 11.6c ZiYouXunLu; 11.7a Ealdgyth; 11.7b Myrabella; 12.4a Olvr; 12.4c; 12.4d PMRMaeyaert; 12.5; 12.6 Nina Aldin Thune; 12.8 Eusebius; 12.9a; 12.9b; 13.1b Rastaman 3000; 14.1; 14.2; 14.4a 14.4b; 14.5; 14.6 Google Art Project; 15.1a; 15.1b; 15.2 Sailko, 15.4; 15.5 Patrick A. Rodgers; 16.1; 16.2a Antoine Taveneaux; 16.2b; 16.2c; 16.2d Stinkzwam; 16.3; 16.5; 16.6b Philippos; 17.1 Gaspa; 17.2b Sixtus; 17.3a ToucanWings; 17.3b Jean-Christophe Benoist; 17.3d Myrabella; 17.3e Jorge Eduardo Guimarães, brasileiro; 17.4a Nina Aldin Thune; 17.5; 17.6 Larrambia; 17.9; 17.10; 17.11; 18.1; 18.2; 18.6; 19.2; 19.3; 19.6; 19.7 AlbertHerring; 20.1b Jorge Royan; 20.1c; 20.2; 20.3; 20.4; 20.5; 20.6, 21.3, 21.4, 21.5, 21.6, 21.8, 21.12, 21.14b Beyond MyKen; 22.3; 22.4; 22.16c Arsenalbubs, 22.17 Valueyou; 23.2a and b UNESCO F. Riviere, 23.4b Biswarup Ganguly, 23.4c Raveesh Vyas, 23.5a Tropenmuseum of the Royal Tropical Institute, 23.4b & c Gunawan Kartapranata, 23.7a: Christopher Voitus, 23.7b Arnold Betten, 23.7c Rajenver, 23.7d, 23.8b BluesyPete, 23.8c Markalexander100, 23.8d HansStieglitz, 23.8e Baldin, 23.9, 24.2a Kallgan, 24.2b, 24.2d Tommy Chan, 24.4 Periclesofathens, 24.6, 24.9a Aberlin, 24.9b Headrock, 24.9c Alex Kwok, 24.10 somedragon2000, 24.11, 25.1a Wiiii, 25.1b, c and d sailko, 25.1e Jakubhal, 25.2a Dingy, 25.2b Hiro2006, 25.3a, 25.3b, 24.4a & b Bigjap, 25.5, 26.1b Reto Luescher, 26.2a, 26.2b Simon Burchell, 26.2c Joaquin Bravo Contreras, 26.4 Timothy A. Price and Nichole I., 26.5a Wolfgang Sauber, 26.5b Miguelão, 26.5c Ceridwen, 26.5d Madman, 26.6 Maunus A, 26.8b Hâkan Svensson, 26.8c McKay Savage, 26.9a icelight, 26.9b Colegota, 26.9c Cynthia Motta, 26.10, 26.11 and 26.12a and b Children's Museum of Indianapolis, 27.1b Siyajkak, 27.9 Daniel Schwen, 28.1a & b CT Snow, 28.3 Sterilgutassistentin, 28.4 Luis Garcia, 28.5a Kuki31, 28.5b, 28.7, 29.31 Roy Smith, 29.3b, 29.1b Zarateman, 29.26 Nmnogueira, 29.27Mike Peel (*www. mikepeel.net*) PT1 Question 3 right, PT1 Question 5; **William Storage Photo: 6.15; The Yorck Project: 1.9, 13.1c, 15.3, 16.4, 17.8, 19.4, 21.1, 21.9, 21.10, 24.5**

Modern Art Permissions:

22.1: Photo Courtesy of the Matisse Estate; © 2014 Succession H. Matisse / Artists Rights Society (ARS), New York; 22.2: Universal Color; **© 2014 Artists Rights Society (ARS), New York / ADAGP, Paris; 22.5 Universal Color; © 2014 Estate of Pablo Picasso / Artists Rights Society (ARS), New York; 22.6 © 2014 Artists Rights Society (ARS), New York / ADAGP, Paris; 22.7: © 2014 Artists Rights Society (ARS), New York / ADAGP, Paris, 22.9: Universal Color; © Succession Marcel Duchamp / ADAGP, Paris / Artists Rights Society (ARS), New York 2014, 22.12 © 2014 Artists Rights Society (ARS), New York / ADAGP, Paris; 22.13 Giraudon / Bridgeman Art Library;** Art © Estate of Varvara Fedorovna Stepanova/RAO, Moscow/VAGA, New York, 22.19: © 2014 The Jacob and Gwendolyn Lawrence Foundation, Seattle / Artists Rights Society (ARS), New York. The Phillips Collection, Washington D.C.; 22.20: **© 2014** Banco de México Diego Rivera Frida Kahlo Museums Trust, Mexico, D.F. / Artists Rights Society (ARS), New York; 22.21: © 2014 Artists Rights Society (ARS), New York / ADAGP, Paris; 22.22: © 2014 Helen Frankenthaler Foundation, Inc. / Artists Rights Society (ARS), New York; Bridgeman Images; 22.23: © 2014 The Andy Warhol Foundation for the Visual Arts, Inc. / Artists Rights Society (ARS), New York; Album / Art Resource, NY; **22.25a, 22.25b** Yayoi Kusama; 22.27a, 2.27b The Architectural Archives, University of Pennsylvania, by the gift of Robert Venturi, and Denise Scott Brown, photo by Matt Wargo; 22.26 : Universal Color; Art © Estate of Robert Smithson/Licensed by VAGA, New York, NY; 29.2a: © Hélène Binet, 29.2b © Roland Halbe; 29.4a **© Maya Lin Studio, courtesy Pace Gallery;** 29.5 **© The Estate of Jean-Michel** Basquiat /

Index

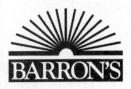
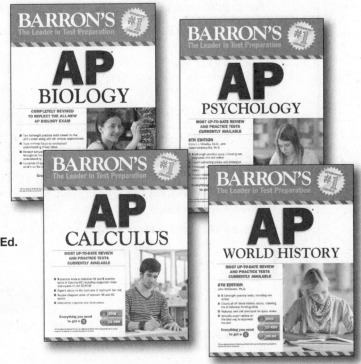

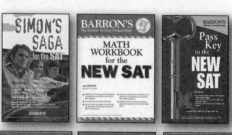
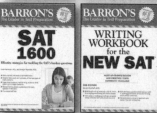
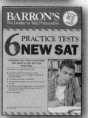
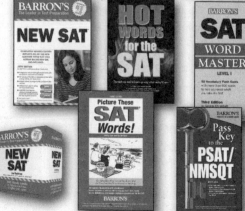
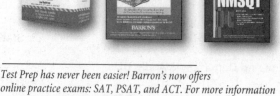

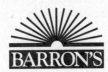

How to Use the CD-ROM

The software is not installed on your computer; it runs directly from the CD-ROM. Barron's CD-ROM includes an "autorun" feature that automatically launches the application when the CD is inserted into the CD-ROM drive. In the unlikely event that the autorun feature is disabled, follow the manual launching instructions below.

Windows®

1. Click on the Start button and choose "My Computer."
2. Double-click on the CD-ROM drive, which will be named **AP_Art_History.exe**.
3. Double-click **AP_Art_History.exe** to launch the program.

MAC®

1. Double-click the CD-ROM icon.
2. Double-click the **AP_Art_History** icon to start the program.

SYSTEM REQUIREMENTS

Microsoft® Windows®
2.33GHz or faster x80-compatible processor,
or Intel Atom™ (1.6GHz or faster processor
for netbook class devices)
Microsoft® Windows® XP, Windows Server 2008,
Windows Vista® Home Premium, Business, Ultimate,
or Enterprise (including 64 bit editions) with
Service Pack 2, Windows 7, or windows 8 Classic
512MB of RAM (1GB recommended)

MAC® OS X
Intel® Core™ Duo 1.83GHz
or faster processor.
Mac OS X v10.6, v10.7, v10.8, or v10.9
512MB of RAM (1GB recommended)